Rockland County Century of History

Edited by

Linda Zimmermann

The Historical Society of Rockland County
20 Zukor Road
New City, N.Y. 10956

Edited and designed by Linda Zimmermann

Printed in Canada

Library of Congress Cataloging-in-Publication Data

Rockland County century of history / edited by Linda Zimmermann.—1st ed.
    p. cm.
    Includes index.
    ISBN 0-911183-48-5 (alk. paper)
     1.Rockland County (N.Y.)—History—20th century. I. Zimmermann, Linda, 1959-II.
    Historical Society of Rockland County.

    F127.R6 R63 2002
    974.7'2804—dc21

                                                                    2001039910
Third printing, November 2003

Front Cover: Oil painting of Davies Farm, by Ruth Ellen Carlsen, c. 1967.
              Aerial view of the Palisades Center in West Nyack, 5/2/98, by Bob Vergara, All Photographic Services,
              courtesy of the Palisades Center.

Back Cover: Fred E. Crum photo of Eleanor and Alva Crum walking to the Brick Church School in Monsey, c. 1907,
             courtesy of Rachel Kaufmann.

Preface

by

C. Scott Vanderhoef
County Executive

The twentieth century was an exciting time of immense change and progress for the County of Rockland. We entered the 1900s as a rural, agrarian county and rounded out the century as a thriving suburban community with one of the most diverse populations in the nation.

The importance of preserving Rockland's beautiful landscape and vistas was recognized early in the 1900s as expansive lands were donated to establish state parks in Rockland, including the Bear Mountain State Park. This tradition of protecting our environment continued throughout the twentieth century as our county park system grew from three acres in 1950 to more than 2,100 acres by the year 2000. Today, more than one-third of our county is forever preserved as parkland.

While some property was preserved in Rockland, other land was quickly developed after the opening of the Tappan Zee Bridge in 1955 and the completion of the Palisades Interstate Parkway and the New York Thruway in that same decade. New transportation routes increased residents' ability to commute to jobs in New York City and attracted many newcomers who were looking for the "American dream" of living in suburbia. Farmland quickly disappeared as new homes were constructed. In 1950, there were 406 farms in Rockland County utilizing more than 17,000 acres. By 2000, just five farms remained. As farmland decreased, local industries grew and prospered. The once popular industries of fishing, brick making and ice cutting faded away as pharmaceutical industries, technological industries and retail industries flourished.

Rockland County's population soared as new arrivals from many different countries made Rockland their home. According to census figures, 38,000 people lived in Rockland in 1900. That figure grew more than sevenfold to 287,000 in 2000. Rockland County has become a microcosm of the American "melting pot" with people of diverse races, ethnic backgrounds and religions living harmoniously.

Rockland County's future is filled with hope and promise. Once again, as so many times before in Rockland's history, the Hudson River is taking center stage. Communities located along the Hudson are working to increase public access to the river, revitalize downtown areas, and entice tourists.

As Rockland looks toward a bright future, we should be vigilant in our efforts to preserve historic buildings and sites which make history come alive for both young and old alike. These remnants of a time gone by are our link to the past and a reminder of what Rockland once was.

Our history is the undeniable preface for the realities of our present and the foundation of our future. Our best days are before us.

Introduction

by

Scott E. Webber

Years ago Barbra Streisand sang the song, "The Way We Were," whose lyrics included the lines:

Memories light the corners of our mind,
Misty water color, memories, of the way we were.
Can it be that it was all so simple then?
Or has time rewritten every line...
If we had the chance to do it all again,
Tell me would we? Could we?

For those of us who lived for most of twentieth century, this is a journey back into the years when things were much different than now, as we enter the twenty-first century. People who lived in 1900 would not recognize Rockland in 2000. It would be like going on a Buck Rogers adventure on another planet.

In 1900, President William McKinley was re-elected for a second term with his new vice president, Theodore Roosevelt, the young governor of New York, just 42 years old and the hero of San Juan Hill. With McKinley's assassination in 1901, young Roosevelt became president and set the pace of America for the next 100 years.

Rockland's twentieth century story mirrors much of the nation's history. In 1900, Rockland's population was just 38,298, with a total U.S. population of 74.8 million. Now ten decades later Rockland's population stands at 286,753, while the U.S. has grown to 281 million.

At the end of the nineteenth century, Rockland had no paved roads, no cars, and few bathrooms (in a time when most people had outhouses, some of them with several seats!). Few had electricity. There were hardly any telephones, no radio, no television, no internet. After long hours of work, most people lived their lives between the church, school and home. Travel was by horseback or carriage; long distance was by trains which in those days operated around the clock.

Nyack Turnpike was the Thruway of earlier days over which horse-drawn carriers transported goods from the western sections of the county to Nyack where the goods were loaded onto barges to be taken down to New York City. Barges were also the way the bricks from the yards in Haverstraw got to the city, as well as ice from Rockland Lake.

The New York State Thruway of today parallels the old dirt Nyack Turnpike. The Thruway opened in December 1955, when the Tappan Zee Bridge was opened, linking Rockland directly to Westchester and causing the demise of the car ferries. The new bridge also would be the catalyst for the demise of the old way of life in Rockland.

World War I took many of Rockland's sons out of this area for the first time in their lives to cross the Atlantic and thrust them into the war in France. It was an experience that bonded them together for the rest of their lives. As a young newspaper reporter, I became friends with John E. Cook of Haverstraw, one of the doughboys from "The Great War," who held annual reunions every May in Suffern in what they called "The Last Man's Club." Their last reunion was in 1971 when about five of the old soldiers showed up.

The Great Depression left many Rocklanders struggling to make ends meet, but the effects of the economic collapse were softened by the self-sustaining lifestyles of the local farmers. Even those who did not have large farms usually had gardens and chickens to help them put food on the table.

December 7, 1941 was a day that changed everyone's life forever in America as the country mobilized for an all-out war. I was nine years old, and with the sounds of bombs exploding in London coming over our radio from England, I expected the same thing would start happening here. I stayed up that night looking out into the darkness from my bedroom window, listening for planes coming.

In Rockland, Maxwell Anderson and Kurt Weill set up a tower overlooking the Hudson at the end of South Mountain Road to search for enemy aircraft. Their log journal is in the Rockland Room at the New City Library, and each shift is recorded in their handwriting.

Rockland's big role in World War II was Camp Shanks, a city capable of accommodating 50,000 troops, built on 2,040 acres in the hamlets of Blauvelt, Orangeburg and Tappan, running along Western Highway and extending over to Rockland State Hospital. About 5,000 area people were employed at Shanks which operated twenty-four hours a day receiving troops from all across the country. The men arrived by train and were processed and made ready to be sent overseas. It was a holding area until space was available on ships down in Jersey City and Manhattan. From there they sailed across the Atlantic, first to North Africa and later to England.

After the war, Camp Shanks became Shanks Village as the 1,500 barracks were made into three small apartment units in each. There some 4,000 veterans studying at metropolitan-area colleges lived with their young families until 1956, when the area was sold to private developers. Shanks Village brought into Rockland thousands of well-educated and talented people from different parts of the country who went into all walks of life. Many liked Rockland so well they decided to live here permanently.

The assassination of President Kennedy in November 1963 triggered a turbulent decade, with rioting, violence and unrest in the civil rights struggle here in America and over the Vietnam issue where American troops went in as "advisors" in trying to repel the invasion of South Vietnam by North Vietnam. The antiwar movement was fodder for news-hungry TV and press, and they played it up big. Like the rest of America, Rockland residents were divided on the war. Attempts to discuss the issue often gave way to shouting matches. The hippy peace, love and drug culture, and the women's liberation movements fuelled the turmoil and it appeared as if nothing in America would ever be the same.

The fifties and sixties were also growing years in Rockland, as more and more houses were built and there was a constant need for more schools as the "Baby Boomer" children were born. It seemed that as soon as one bond issue was passed by the voters, the school board had to start planning another building program and bond issue. It was a heyday for developers.

Public complaints on the quality of home construction multiplied. I recall a group of new homeowners who had just paid $70,000 each for new homes in Orangetown in 1967. They went before the town board wanting to know who approved the construction where houses were being held up by a single 2x4. Floors were sagging.

Control over land and the use of land was the bottom line as new (and old) residents sought to tighten the zoning code to keep out those who were trying to get in. They came to oppose any new housing projects being considered at planning board meetings which often ran to four o'clock in the morning These were NIMBYs—Not In My Back Yard people. As we go into the twenty-first century, the suburban sprawl line is now in neighboring Orange County where the NIMBY element is much in evidence.

One serious effort to slow down growth was in Ramapo where John F. McAlevey, a one-time Shanks Villager and Town Supervisor from 1966-1974, introduced a land bank program limiting growth to areas which had the sewers, water and other necessary facilities for more houses. The State Court of Appeals upheld it and the U.S. Supreme Court refused to hear the case. Developers were unhappy. However, the state's financial crisis of the 1970s precluded the program's implementation.

In Orangetown, the Town Board rushed through a new Office Park zoning provision to accommodate the Uris Buildings Corporation's plans for a four-building office complex that featured a 20-story tower building, the tallest in Rockland County (the present-day Blue Hill complex).

Residents formed a lot of civic associations to battle for controlled growth. One was the Tappan Civic Association with women like Ruth Katzaroff and Barbara Porta who were authorities on the zoning code. The group backed the "Save the Mountain" movement which persuaded the Nature Conservancy to buy a whole chunk of Clausland Mountain in Orangetown for park instead of having it developed for housing by Columbia University. John and Sue Allison were leaders of that effort,

Other groups formed to block the building of the massive Palisades Center mall. However, after years of protests, court battles and numerous accusations of bribery and misconduct, the second largest mall in America nonetheless now stands in West Nyack. While thousands of people flock to the Palisades Center every day, its popularity has had an adverse effect on many small businesses across Rockland. Development gives, and development takes away.

Looking back, life in Rockland in 1900 was primitive compared to 2000. However, what will people who read this book in 2100 think about our life today?

***

For several years, Linda Zimmermann and I talked about producing a twentieth century history. From the outset we received strong encouragement to go ahead with this project from Paul Melone, so instrumental in the publication of that classic local history, *Tappan 300 Years*. John Scott made available both his extensive knowledge and his collection of 7,000 historical photos. Marie Koestler, Chairman of the Publications Committee of the Historical Society of Rockland County, set the wheels in motion and kept them running smoothly. Albon P. Man, who edited my Camp Shanks book in 1991, took up his red pencil and offered his wise counsel as a copy editor. I was able to draw upon my four decades as a local reporter and offer articles and insights that had been long forgotten. And the book's editor, Linda Zimmermann, spent years turning mountains of material into the finished product you now hold in your hands. Thanks to this group of dedicated people, the book finally became a reality.

We who lived most of our lives in the twentieth century are now of the past. We leave with you some of our stories, you who will live most of your lives in the twenty-first century and the centuries to follow. Would we want to do it all over again? No, I don't think so. We went through a lot of pain and misery in our "good old days." We hope that on these pages you may learn from our experiences and in so doing enhance your own lives.

v

Editor's Note

As future generations read this book, I doubt they will stop to think about how it was put together. As an author, I may be a bit biased, but I believe that the people and the process are as important as the finished product. Since three years of my life went into this book, I hope you will indulge me while I spend a few moments discussing some of those people and that process.

It was Scott Webber who tirelessly championed the cause of twentieth century Rockland history. It is thanks to his persistence that this book project was finally begun. Scott is a truly dedicated historian, and committed to telling the facts—even if those facts might ruffle a few feathers. During the course of the research phase of this book project, Scott and I would meet about once a month at a local diner, and speak on the phone at least once a week. While I valued his vast knowledge of local events, I equally appreciated his sense of humor. A project of this magnitude can be rather daunting, and a good laugh was often just what I needed.

One of the greatest benefits I received as a result of this project was getting to know historian John Scott. I spent many happy hours at his home in West Nyack going through his enormous collection of photographs, and listening to his almost encyclopedic knowledge of local people and events. I recall one afternoon when I had gathered a stack of photos that looked interesting, but I was not familiar with the people or scenes. As I held each photo up one at he time, John immediately identified all of the people, the dates and the events depicted. I was nothing short of amazed. If I have gained even a small percentage of his knowledge of Rockland, I consider myself fortunate. Knowing John, he would shy away from such titles, but he is clearly "Mr. Rockland History" in my book.

No team can be successful without a good coach, and our team was lucky to have Marie Koestler at the helm. She was the person "in the trenches" handling meetings, schedules and paperwork. Her infinite patience and skillful management of all the details left me free to do my work, and for that I am very grateful. (And for the freshly baked cookies she made for each meeting, we are all grateful!)

At one of the publications committee's first meetings, Albon Man said that he would be editing and proofreading the final manuscript. His reputation as a grammar and punctuation perfectionist had preceded him, and after shaking off a brief twinge of intimidation, I welcomed his expertise. He did a magnificent job of editing, and if any typos still exist they are the result of my fingers, not his eyes.

Thanks also to Paul Melone, James Boylan, Kenneth Kral, Marjorie Bauer and Craig Long for their expertise and moral support.

I would also like to thank the people of Rockland for their outpouring of support. They enthusiastically contributed their personal memories and helped make this book more than a dry collection of facts and figures. If Abraham Lincoln will pardon me, this is truly a book of the people, by the people and for the people.

On a personal note, I have to say that it would be impossible to accurately convey what life has been like for me the last few years. At first, I was thrilled that I would have the honor of putting this book together. However, as my office began to fill up with tens of thousands of files, photos, letters and newspaper clippings, I couldn't help but ask, "What have I gotten myself into!?" At times it seemed like I would never be able to complete this task—it was both mentally and physically draining. However, hard work, determination and regular visits to my chiropractor (Dr. Charles Holt) got me through.

Many people have asked me why I ever took on this project, and why I didn't give up. The answer is simple—I love Rockland County. I was born and raised in Rockland, and no matter where I may live in the future, Rockland will always be the place I consider to be home. As you read this book, please remember the effort that went into it, but please also appreciate that it was the result of the dedication and love of Rockland's residents.

It has been a long road. Although the journey was often difficult, I met some wonderful people along the way, and the experiences have become a part of me. I am grateful for having been given the opportunity to create this book. It has been a long road, but one I will always be able to say I am proud to have traveled.

Linda Zimmermann
February 7, 2002

Table of Contents

Turn of the Century   1

1900-1909: Life on the Farm   22

1910-1919: Telephones, Automobiles,   46
            Flying Machines and War

1920-1929: A Soft Roar   79

1930-1939: Hard Times   102

1940-1949: America Comes to   Rockland   145

1950-1959: The Bridge and the Boom   177

1960-1969: The Decade of Change   205

1970-1979: A Different Way of Life   239

1980-1989: Real Estate Rises, More Farms Fall   259

1990-1999: In With the New   280

The New Century   305

Our Home Towns   323

Special Acknowledgements   364

Index   365

Notes on the text:

Some of the articles were written during the time of the events described, while others were written decades later. Sources, authors and dates are listed with each piece. Accounts are presented as written to preserve their original styles, including ethnic references.

The Historical Society of Rockland County's publication *South of the Mountains* is abbreviated *SOM*. *Phoenician Tales* by Carl Nordstrom is an unpublished manuscript.

Notes on the photographs:

The majority of the photographs are from the collection of John Scott. Over the decades many of these photographs were obtained from other sources and collections, but for the sake of simplicity, they are attributed with either his name or JSC.

Photographers are credited where known, otherwise the name of the contributor is listed.

Photographs from the Orangetown Museum may also be attributed with the abbreviation OTM.

Photographs by Linda Zimmermann may be abbreviated LZ.

Acknowledgements:

Many thanks to everyone who contributed material and time to this project. Special thanks to Thomas Brizzolara of O&R for his enthusiastic support and for making the company archives available. Thanks to Mindy Scher for her collection of newspaper clippings, and to Barbara Janicki for saving every Rockland section of the paper in the last few years. Thanks are also due to J. Martin Cornell, Esq., of the law firm of Doig, Cornell & Mandel, LLP, New City, N.Y., for preparing legal documents relating to the publication of this book. We also greatly appreciate the help of the WVNJ radio station for the announcements asking listeners to contribute their memories to this book.

As always, thanks to Bob Strong for his steadfast support through all of my endeavors.

TURN
OF THE
CENTURY

It is a modern misconception that during the latter part of the nineteenth century Rockland was strictly an isolated, rural farming community. While it is certainly true that there was abundant farmland and enough property to be as isolated as one chose to be, there was another side to county life that hinted at the changes to come.

Rocklanders commuted to New York City for work, or went in the evenings to see a play. Local industries drew immigrants from many different countries. Although farms still dominated the landscape, they thrived, in part, because of Rockland's proximity to one of the fastest growing urban centers in the world.

In the waning decades of the 1800s, waves of new inventions and other innovations began to sweep away the old ways of life. For the majority of Rocklanders, however, these early tremors of the earthshaking changes to come went unnoticed. Children still gathered in one-room schoolhouses, local doctors rode horses to visit patients, cows and chickens were fed and crops harvested, and the traditions of generations past seemed to be deeply rooted enough to withstand whatever the future would bring.

The generation that witnessed the dawn of the twentieth century had the rare opportunity to see whatever it was they chose to see: life continuing on the family farm as it had for over a hundred years, or a county poised to redefine itself with every passing decade.

Broadway in Nyack in 1872 (above) with an election banner for U.S. Grant.
The Jewett family (right) at the caretaker's cottage on their estate in Upper Nyack, c.1880-5.

The Piermont Empire Engine Company in 1895.

George (l.) and Frank Ofeldt in an 1896 automobile in Nyack.   Photos courtesy of John Scott.

...The first "moving-picture" is shown in New York in 1890...Aspirin is manufactured in 1899...

CIVIL WAR VETERANS AT GETTYSBURG

Civil War veterans from Haverstraw at a reunion at Gettysburg in 1895. Among those present were Napoleon Brooks, William Benson, Alonzo Bedle and Ira Hedges. During the twentieth century, Rockland veteran organizations grew in size and number as local men and women were called into service around the world. JSC

Medal of Honor

Nick Erickson, of Haverstraw, was born July 18, 1870 in Finland. Erickson was awarded the Medal of Honor with the citation:

Onboard the U.S.S. Marblehead during the cutting of the cable from Cienfuegos, Cuba, on May 11, 1898, while facing heavy fire of the enemy, Erickson set an example of extraordinary bravery and coolness throughout the action.

After the war, he and many other Spanish-American War veterans were employed at the ammunition depot on Iona Island.

3

MADE IN ROCKLAND:
The Enterprise of Industry

Remarks on the occasion of the opening of the exhibit at the
Historical Society of Rockland County, February 20, 2000

An old document in the County Clerk's office shows that in 1829 Rockland County was dotted with iron works, tanneries, cotton and woolen factories, grist and sawmills. There were several small iron mines in the northwest end of the county. Quarries operated all along the Hudson, ships were being built in Nyack, and large farms existed in Orangetown and Clarkstown.

By the turn of the nineteenth century many new businesses had sprung up but many of the old ones still existed. The Ramapo Foundry and Wheel Works succeeded the Pierson ironworks which began operation in 1798, the brick industry in North Rockland was begun by James Wood in 1815, and the quarries in Tomkins Cove, then part of the New York Trap Rock Corporation, were opened by Daniel Tomkins in 1838.

One of the great nineteenth century industries that was eliminated by twentieth century progress was the ice industry, which was centered at Rockland Lake. The Knickerbocker Ice Company once employed between 700 and 1000 men and had a capital of forty million dollars in 1901.

The Knickerbocker Ice Company in 1846.
Lithograph by J.W. Hill.   Courtesy of John Scott.

Garnerville was the center of Rockland's textile industry throughout much of the nineteenth century and well into the twentieth century. At one time the Rockland Finishing Company employed over 800 workers. A combination of the effects of the Great Depression and competition for cheap labor in the south resulted in the plant's being sold in 1930 and the machinery moved south.

The plant was turned into the Garnerville Holding Company where space was leased to independent manufacturers, attracted by low rent, reasonable labor

and nearness to New York. This was one of the first industrial cooperatives in the nation.

Nyack for many years was a center for the shoe industry and was once known as "Shoe Town." In the year 1884 almost 700,000 pairs of shoes were manufactured in Nyack. Outside competition and cheap labor brought this industry to a close shortly after the turn of this century.

One of Rockland's many shoe factories. Early factories had only oil lamps for lighting, no central heat, no air conditioning and workers often worked twelve-hour days, six days a week.   Courtesy of John Scott.

Geology laid the groundwork for one of Rockland's great industries, quarrying. As early as 1735 Rockland's red sandstone was used in New York City homes and in our colonial houses, some of which still exist.

Rockland trap rock was used throughout the twentieth century for highway and other types of construction. The New York Trap Rock Corporation, a predecessor of Tilcon Industries, had large plants in Haverstraw and Tomkins Cove.

Haverstraw was at one time one of the great brick-making centers in the East, with an unending succession of brickyards from Haverstraw to Grassy Point. About 1900 over 326 million bricks a year were being manufactured and much of New York City was built with Haverstraw bricks.

The combination of the impact of the Great Depression and competition from concrete and cheaper brick manufacture in other areas brought the industry to an end with the last brickyard closing in the early 1940's.

For nearly half a century the Dunlop Silk Mills at Spring Valley was an important business in the county. Established in 1887 by John Dunlop, they continued in operation until 1935. Dress fabrics were woven at the Spring Valley mills using raw silk. At the height of the business 150 to 200 people were employed. The depression of 1929 together with the demand for cheaper dress fabrics such as rayon brought an end to the business.

At one time if you were suffering from a stomachache anywhere in the world, the chances were that you would have sought relief from a product made in Rockland County. Bell-ans produced billions of these tablets in its plant in Orangeburg.

David McConnell, founder of the California Perfume

The Dunlop Silk Mill in Spring Valley operated from 1887 to 1935. Courtesy of John Scott.

The Dexter Folder Company began in Iowa in 1880. With the increased demand for newspapers, Talbot Dexter invented a machine that folded newspapers. The company moved to Pearl River in 1894. By 1940, 23,000 machines of various types had been manufactured. At one time Dexter machines folded eighty percent of all books printed in the United States and its stitching machines bound most of the national magazines. Throughout its history, 300 to 500 employees were employed by the company. Prior to the demise of the business in the post-World War II period, postcards manufactured by the Dexter Press could be found throughout the United States.

Another industry that lasted well into the twentieth century but now has disappeared was the manufacturing of cigars. Before 1900 there were seventeen tobacco factories in the county producing a million and a half cigars a year. A third of those were made by the W.S. Forshay Company in Viola.

In a similar vein, Briarcraft, Inc. manufacturer of Smokemaster Pipes, continued an industry begun in Spring Valley in the 1880s. Prior to World War II, a million and a half pipes a year were produced and shipped throughout the world.

Local banks played an important role in supporting the expansion of business and industry in the county. The Provident Bank has served its depositors for over a hundred years.

Company, built his first factory in Suffern in 1886. The company, eventually known as Avon, initiated the direct selling system. For much of its history all Avon Products were manufactured in Suffern and sold throughout the world. At its height Avon employed over 600 workers in Suffern.

Lederle Laboratories, founded by Dr. Ernest Lederle in the first decade of the twentieth century, was once the largest biological laboratory in the world. At its plant in Pearl River, life-saving medicines, serums and anti-toxins were developed.

Today with over 3,300 employees, making Lederle, now Wyeth-Ayerst, the largest private-sector employer in the county, it is known throughout the world for the manufacturing of Centrum and Stresstabs.

It is obvious that Rockland has an outstanding business history. In recent years, businesses such as Novartis, Fujitsu Communications, Well-Bred Loaf, Prentice-Hall and Dress Barn have prospered. Much of this growth related directly to the opening of the Tappan Zee Bridge in 1955.

Our County Executive C. Scott Vanderhoef has attributed Rockland's strong business atmosphere to our competitive real estate and utility costs, a qualified workforce, a prime location and an attractive quality of life.

Thomas F. X. Casey

...1896 William Ramsey discovers helium...Puccini's "La Boheme" is performed for the first time...

Postcard (above): The half-mile ice run from Rockland Lake to the Hudson River.

Disguised as a boy named Jo, Josephine Hudson (age 19) was the only woman working at the Knickerbocker Ice Company.

A Rockland Lake ice train (left), circa 1915. William Hartman stands in the center of the photo holding an oil can. Mrs. Johanna Hartman is on the far right.

Felter's ice wagon (bottom left), driven by Philip Westfall Babcock (1879-1960) of Nyack. The horses are Kate, Tom and Dandy.

Ice barges (below) on the Hudson River at Rockland Lake landing, c. 1904. Ice was cut from the lake, sent down the run to the river, and then shipped by barge to New York City.

Photos courtesy of John Scott.

The Men Who Made the Bricks

After the ice age, melting glaciers left huge deposits of blue clay along the Hudson River. In the early 1800s James Wood, a brickmaker, settled in the Haverstraw area and recognize the clay's potential. He perfected the process of mixing ground anthracite coal with the clay, making for a stronger brick.

At the height of the industry in the 1800s the brickyards extended from the Short Clove in the south to the Stony Point Battlefield in the north. In those record years there were 40 brickyards producing 300 million bricks per year. The great majority of the brick was shipped out by river barge, going to New York City where tenements were popping up like mushrooms to house the waves of arriving immigrants. If you grew up in the city, your tenement was probably built of Haverstraw brick.

Around World War I, concrete construction became increasingly popular. This, together with the advent of cinder blocks and competition with European bricks, brought the decline of the local brickmaking. The Great Depression finally gave the death knell to the industry.

Of equal interest to the history of this industry, is a look at the men who worked in the brickyards. The various groups of workers reflected the waves of immigrants to the area. The first workers were men who came in from the nearby farms, but their number was nowhere sufficient for the tremendous demand for brick.

However, a terrible historic event proved to be a boon for the early brickmakers' need for workers. That event was the Great Potato Famine which sent waves of Irish to the New World. This potential pool of workers was quickly recruited to move up the river and work in the brickyards. The Irish provided the bulk of the workers throughout the nineteenth century. After the Civil War, they were augmented by blacks from the South who were transported to the area at the beginning of the season and then returned at the end of the season.

About the turn of the century the new group of workers were men from the Austro-Hungarian Empire, especially Hungarians who settled in Stony Point and Slovaks who settled in Haverstraw. The Slovaks built their own church, St. Mary's, to hold services in their own language. The last group of workers in the brickyards before they closed were the Italians.

What did all these workers do when the yards were closed for the season? Many of them *walked* to Rockland Lake where they cut ice all day, then walked home at the end of the day.

The brickyards are all gone and you have to look pretty hard to find any trace of this once flourishing industry. The workers themselves were absorbed into the community, to become the "old-timers" with memories of a way of life long gone in Rockland.

Robert Burghardt

Aerial view of the Haverstraw brickyards.
JSC

...W. Judson invents the clothing zipper in 1891...Tchaikowsky's "The Nutcracker" debuts in 1892...

Progress is a double-edged sword. While few complain about better transportation, a wider selection of goods and services becoming available, and better employment opportunities, people are rarely willing to sacrifice their accustomed quality of life. A term was coined in the late twentieth century for this mindset: NIMBY, meaning "Not in *my* back yard." While residents may applaud a new road, factory or shopping center in *another* community, those whose lives and property are disrupted generally fight the changes. While the term NIMBY may be relatively new, the situations that prompt such backlashes are not, as the following article demonstrates.

Blasting Upper Nyack

Upper Nyack's Village was incorporated on September 28th, 1872. Its boundary line on the north was eventually extended more than half a mile further to prevent a dynamite factory along the shore at Hook Mountain. This object was successfully accomplished and the dynamite works were established just north of the new boundary.

While the people of Upper Nyack were still congratulating themselves upon their narrow escape from the dynamite works, the Mack Paving Company, in 1889, came to Upper Nyack and purchased the Varker place, under the very shadow of the Hook, to build a crushing plant thereon. The news of this purchase was a surprise to nearly everyone in Upper Nyack when they read it in the local papers, and those living near the mountain, realizing that a large stone crushing plant there, with its heavy blasts every day, would be detrimental to the value of their property, protested earnestly against the "new industry," as it was called. The work went on, however, until it possessed a value, it is said of nearly $300,000.

James P. McQuaide and Arthur C. Tucker, prominent wealthy citizens who lived near the Hook, brought proceedings in the Supreme Court. They succeeded in getting an order from Judge Dickey to restrain the blasting, except when done under strict limitations. The Trap Rock Company went to the Appellate Division of the Supreme Court which reversed Judge Dickey's order.

Blasting was to continue into the twentieth century.

Credits to Arthur L. Tompkins History of 1902 and John Lodico, Sr.

The electrification of America can not be understated in its importance; even the briefest of modern blackouts reminds us of our dependence upon electricity in almost every aspect of our daily lives. Natural gas is also an essential component of homes and businesses and vast networks of gas lines provide us with heat, hot water and a reliable way to cook our food. While bringing electricity and gas to urban areas was a daunting task in itself, relatively rural locations such as Rockland presented special challenges. The process of supplying and maintaining these services, first to distant farms, and then to communities exploding in size, is an amazing story of foresight, determination and dedication. While people grumble when they receive their utility bills, no one appears willing to return to the candle and coal stove days.

O&R: The Origins of Rockland's Power

The origin of the company goes back to 1859 when local individuals organized the Nyack and Warren Gas Light Company. This company manufactured coal gas to supply street lighting in the village on moonless nights. Apparently, if the moon was out, it was brighter than the gas lights.

The electric part of the company also had its beginning in Nyack, when the Nyack Electric Light and Power Company was formed in 1887 by local individuals. This company was formed to supply current for 37 carbon arc street lights, and a few commercial establishments. In 1889, S.R. Bradley organized a corporation called Rockland Light and Power Company. This corporation acquired all the interests of the Nyack Electric Light and Power Company, and the Union Electric Company in Orangeburg (which had been started in 1890 by the Orangeburg Fibre Conduit Company to manufacture and charge storage batteries).

Thus, the actual incorporation of the company was in 1899, although its roots go back to 1859 for gas and 1887 for electric.

Other gas and electric companies were subsequently organized in Haverstraw, Spring Valley, and Suffern. All of these companies were merged into Rockland Light and Power Company at various times.

In 1926, the Tenney Company acquired the Orange County Public Service Company and merged it into a Rockland Light and Power Company, which was divided into the eastern division (Rockland County) and the western division (part of Orange and Sullivan Counties).

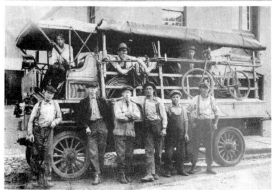

These two divisions were not contiguous, but were separated by a portion of Orange County served by the Orange and Rockland Company of Monroe. (This company served a small portion of the town of Stony Point, which explains the name.)

The Orange and Rockland Electric Company (ORECO) was organized at Monroe in 1905 by Roscoe W. Smith, a former employee of Rockland Light and Power Company in Hillburn. Over the years, Mr. Smith acquired a number of neighboring utilities.

On February 28, 1958, Mr. Smith merged his Orange & Rockland Company into the Rockland Light and Power Company, and the merged company became Orange and Rockland Utilities, Inc. The ORECO portion of the company became known as the central division and now all three divisions were contiguous.

Article and Photos: O&R Archives

This circa 1906 photo (top left) shows a Rockland Power and Light road crew at work. The foreman in the wagon is Bill Campbell. The men on the pole are Everett Ackerly, Roy Kolter and Bill Hegner. In the background is Charlie Haines, Jr. The horses were hired as needed.

A few years later, horses and wooden wagons were replaced by trucks (center). Perhaps these early vehicles were not the most reliable, which may account for the bicycle strapped to the side.

As the century progressed, utility vehicles grew in sophistication as this 1957 photo shows (bottom left). Crews evolved from men with a few simple tools to highly trained men and women with state-of-the-art equipment.

Safety also became a primary concern, as crews often face bad weather and adverse conditions.

Traveling the County by Railroad

Back in the late 1800s and the early 1900s, one could travel from any given hamlet or village in Rockland County to any other in the county by train on the many interlacing lines of track.

On Sundays when a given community's baseball team was playing in another county community, a special train would be hired and almost the entire populace would go to the game. Railway travel was a way of life.

The Hackensack & New York Extension Railroad came into Rockland County from the south in 1872. Its name was eventually changed to the more appropriate one of New Jersey & New York. The tracks of the Erie's Piermont branch were used from Nanuet and Spring Valley and then its own tracks turned north to Stony Point. The terminus was soon moved to Haverstraw. For many years the line depended upon 20 passenger cars and seven locomotives.

They burned anthracite coal and were very good-looking from a railroader's point of view. The cars were painted orange and had a broad, dark red band across the

windows on which the name of the line was painted. Sometimes for a holiday rush, New Jersey and New York would borrow a red Erie car. The railroad was in a receiver's hands at least once, and had threats of strikes, but it survived. Five locomotives and several more cars were added and business increased.

In the beginning a theater train ran from Jersey City to Stony Point on Saturday nights, but was soon discontinued. However, later such a train was scheduled as far as Spring Valley on weekday nights.

The service in 1890 was excellent. One could get a train almost any time of the day or night. The monthly rate for 60 round-trip rides between Pearl River and Jersey City was around $7.50. Single round-trips were $1.10.

The four-mile long Nanuet and New City railroad was the product of the local people. They had no rolling stock and it was soon taken over by the New Jersey and New York. A branch line train met some of the main line trains in Nanuet. Florent Verdin of New

City was president of the branch line. His name is carved on the stone support of a bridge in Nanuet.

Once there were more than 30 trains daily between Jersey City and Spring Valley. Today, many track lines are torn up, others abandoned and the tracks grown over with weeds.

C.B. Comes, *The Journal-News*, 10/24/67

Origins of the County Road System

The vitality of any community often depends upon the ease of flow of its goods, services and citizens. By the turn of the twentieth century, it was clear that Rockland's old country road system needed help. The following are excerpts from the official proceedings that led to the county road system. It may be helpful to use a current map to trace the routes of the roads that were to become the main thoroughfares for generations of Rocklanders.

John Campbell and Ed Seaman grade a local road in preparation for paving in 1916.   JSC

June 19, 1893: Upon the recommendation of Governor Roswell Pettibone Flower, the State Legislature enacted a law authorizing the County Boards of Supervisors "to adopt what is termed the County Road System. The roads so designated shall, so as practicable, be leading market roads" in the county.

It was resolved that the Chairman of the Board would appoint a committee to designate such roads through maps and surveys "that connect the most business portions of the County." Also, the committee would designate which roads were in good condition, as well as those in need of repair and the estimated cost of repair.

October 17, 1893: The Chairman is to employ some qualified person to make a map of the following roads should the Board decide to adopt a County Road System.

"The 1st of which begins on the division line between the Counties of Orange and Rockland and Northerly from the dwelling house and store of George W. Dater at Sloatsburgh in the Town of Ramapo, and running from thence Southerly and Easterly as the public road now runs through Sloatsburgh, Sterling Junction, Ramapo, Suffern, Tallmans, Monsey and Spring Valley to the division line between the Towns of Ramapo and Clarkstown."

"The 2nd begins on the aforesaid road Southerly from the railroad station at Spring Valley, and runs thence Northerly through Spring Valley as the public road now runs, past the English Church to the residence of Harry Gurnee, near Mt. Ivy Station on the New Jersey and New York Railroad, continuing thence in an Easterly direction to the Corporation line of the Village of West Haverstraw, and the residence of the heirs of David Burns."

"The 3rd begins on the last mentioned road at its junction with the first public road leading Easterly, North of the railroad Station at Spring Valley and runs thence Easterly as the public road now runs until it comes to the public road leading Northerly from the railroad station at Nanuet, continuing thence Northerly and Easterly as the public road now runs past New City and Staggs Corner until it comes to the Corporation line of the Village of Haverstraw."

"The 4th begins at DeBevoise's Corner on the last mentioned road and Southerly from New City, and runs thence Southerly to Germonds Corner, thence Easterly to Popp's Corner, thence southerly to Nyack Turnpike and continuing on through Blauveltville and Orangeburgh until it comes to the Corporation line of the Village of Piermont, also beginning at the Corporation line of the Village of Piermont running thence Westerly as the public road now runs to Tappan and continuing through Tappan to the State line by what is known as the new road."

"The 5th begins at the intersection of the roads on Gate Hill near the residence of Moses Babcock and runs thence Easterly as the public road now runs to Willow

Grove Schoolhouse, thence continuing on past the residences formerly of Phineas Hedges, deceased, and Levi Knapp's Corner, until it comes to the Corporation line of the Village of West Haverstraw, West of the Rockland Spring Works."

"The 6th and last begins at the intersection of the last mentioned roads near the residence of Moses Babcock aforesaid, and runs from thence Northeasterly as the public road now runs past the residence of William Benson, deceased, Henry D. Goetschius and Knight's Corner to Grassy Point."

The map should cost an approximate $235, "or so much thereof as may be necessary is hereby appropriated."

November 20, 1893: Mr. John D. Christie, Surveyor-Engineer, hired by Mr. Felter, reported to the Board that the approximate cost to repair the roads for the "County System" would be $6100. Mr. Christie recommended that the "three quarter Tomkins Cove gravel" be used. He further stated that there is "no other material conveniently at hand which can be conveniently transported." The Tomkins Cove gravel is "more economical, more durable than other material at the same expense. It has proved very well where it has been used in Rockland County."

The Board unanimously approved Mr. Christie's Report.

March 26, 1894: The Board unanimously approved a "County Road System."

By 1900, County Engineer James Lee, was able to make the following report on the County System.

	Miles Macadam	Miles Gravel	Miles Dirt	Total Miles
Orangetown	8.26	---	2.0	10.26
Ramapo	3.0	4.0	22.26	29.26
Haverstraw	5.0	---	2.25	7.25
Clarkstown	6.75	---	7.075	13.825
Stony Point	---	8.481	3.5	11.981
Total	23.01	12.481	37.085	72.576

(*Note that 52% of the 72 miles of road were dirt.*)

...Jack the Ripper terrorizes London in 1888...The Eiffel Tower is built in 1889...Surgeons use rubber gloves in 1890...Sir Arthur Conan Doyle publishes The Adventures of Sherlock Holmes in 1891...Monet paints the cathedral at Rouen in 1892...Henry Ford builds his first car in 1893...Gillette invents the safety razor in 1895...Röngten discovers x-rays in 1895...Becquerel discovers radioactivity in 1896...H.G. Wells publishes War of the Worlds in 1898...

Helping others has been a Rockland way of life for generations, as the following few pages illustrate.

The Christian Herald Children's Home

On June 15, 1894, officers of the steamboat *Chrystenah* welcomed on board a set of lively, young and excited passengers. The 30 children crossing the gangplank at the West 10th Street wharf had been rounded up by a dedicated team of Sunday school teachers, street missionaries and public health workers, busy among the dim tenements and dismal alleys of New York City's Lower East Side. Parents of these children had recently passed New York Harbor's Statue of Liberty as immigrant Americans and had been promptly shoveled into one of the world's worst slums.

The voyage up the Hudson River landed the young travelers at the Village of Nyack, beautifully surrounded by fields of wildflowers and rimmed by wooded hills. Horse-drawn wagonettes carried the wide-eyed "tenement waifs" a final two miles to the impressive estate above Upper Nyack, called Mont Lawn. The Reverend A.D. Laurence Jewett, whose first pastorate had been at the First Reformed Church of Piermont in the 1850s, bought the Mont Lawn estate in 1890 and then, after only four years, turned over this hillside property to his friend Louis Klopsch, proprietor of *The Christian Herald* magazine. The estate was presented to Klopsch at a nominal rental, for the enjoyment and enrichment of New York City's poor and deserving boys and girls.

Within a few years of the vacation home's founding in 1894, additional structures were added to the original homestead, barn, small chapel and cottages at Mont Lawn. Soon, each summer, between two and three thousand children were romping on the lawns and climbing the steep hillsides of the estate. The program was incorporated in 1898 as the Christian Herald Children's Home, with financial support from readers of the weekly magazine. On July 4, 1905, the picturesque Children's Temple was dedicated with Jacob Riis as the chief speaker. The structure was claimed to be the only chapel of its kind in America, designed expressly for children's worship.

After Mr. Jewett's death in 1898, his son, Major E.D. Jewett, who was active in the Spanish-American War, continued to offer the property for the benefit not only of the summer children but also as a convalescent home for war veterans. Soon after this, the Christian Herald organization acquired the Mont Lawn estate, while the

11

The Christian Herald Children's Home, Montlawn, Nyack, N.Y.

Christian Herald Children's Home was moved to a new location near Bushkill in eastern Pennsylvania. The original estate was sold, to become Camp Ramah, as it remains today.

Although scattered across the country, an amazing number of former campers communicate with one another as an extended family. A United States Army chaplain remembers how his South Bronx church missionary sent him to camp as a small boy. A former camper, who received a college scholarship, is now a speech pathologist, teaching children with special needs. A school principal recalls the tough, unconditional love of a camp supervisor. An attorney wonders whether troubled defendants might have turned out more positively had they gone to Mont Lawn as he did. A musician, who first sang in public in the camp chapel at the age of nine, reports on his La Scala Opera debut in Milan.

Jewett family continued to reside in nearby Upper Nyack.

In 1925, permanent facilities for the disabled were built and presented by philanthropist Edwin Gould. These buildings were equipped with coal furnaces so that crippled children with crutches, braces and wheelchairs could experience fall and spring outings when the Hudson Valley is at its loveliest. It is important to remember that this was a time when so many children endured dreadful living conditions. A *New York Telegram* cartoonist would note that "one quarter of all the city's children live in tenements where 250,000 rooms have no windows." Clementine Paddleford, a noted columnist, wrote in *The Christian Herald,* "Mont Lawn is like a big window in the world's darkness."

Mont Lawn continued to expand both its facilities and the scope of its programs until 1961, when the

These and countless other community leaders, honest mentors, and positive role models have spread the Mont Lawn spirit to thousands, as spiritual descendants of those "waifs" who first sailed across the Tappan Zee on the brave *Chrystenah,* a hundred years ago.

Eugene Brown
South of the Mountains, April/June 2000

Dominican Congregation of Our Lady of the Rosary

The Dominican Congregation of Our Lady of the Rosary was founded by Alice Mary Thorpe, who was born in London, England, on June 18, 1844. A convert from the Anglican Church, she and her sister Lucy began ministering to the sick poor when they arrived in New York City in 1872.

The seeds of the Congregation took root at St. Joseph Mission Home, New York City, dedicated to providing a refuge for needy women and girls and to serving people in poverty and illness. Under the leadership of Alice Thorpe, now known as Mother Catharine M. Antoninus, the Congregation received approval from Cardinal John McCloskey of New York on May 6, 1876. Soon there developed the necessity of caring for destitute children.

After the death of Mother Antoninus in 1879, Mother Dominic Dowling played the leading role in establishing the Congregation on a firm legal and financial basis. In the spring of 1884, Mother Dominic learned that the Johnson farm in Sparkill was for sale. Immediately after the purchase of the property, the house was remodeled and St. Agnes Home and School for Boys opened on June 19 of that year. By 1889, the institution had grown to eleven buildings to accommodate the growing number of boys. In 1895, the Motherhouse and Novitiate were moved to Sparkill. Holy Rosary Convent continued to serve as a home for girls.

On the night of August 28, 1899, a disastrous fire razed the buildings in Sparkill to the ground. The sisters and children were moved to the former Seminary in

Troy, leaving behind them the destruction of the fruits of fifteen years of labor and sacrifice. Mother Dominic frequently visited the sisters and children to encourage them, and she began at once to organize fund-raising efforts to rebuild St. Agnes. However, her indomitable spirit was crushed and it was at Troy on July 14, 1900 that she died at the age of forty-six years.

In August 1900, Sister Thomas Gargan was appointed her successor and immediately began to follow through on plans for a larger, fireproof building. The new St. Agnes rose on the ruins of the old and on September 24, 1902 the sisters and children returned to a new fireproof building large enough to house 500 boys.

Sacred Heart Chapel was completed in 1914 and St. Agnes School was opened in 1922. A Vocational High School (Bronx Vocational Annex) was opened in 1935 to provide additional training for the older boys. Academic subjects were pursued at Tappan Zee High School.

St. Agnes Memorial Gymnasium was built in 1955. During World War II when Captain James Faulk, the beloved athletic coach for the boys, and Carl Trezini, an alumnus of St. Agnes, met in New Caledonia, they conceived the plan for a gymnasium to be built with money contributed by the members of the alumni in memory of those who had given their lives in the service of their country.

By 1900, the work of the Congregation had expanded to include teaching in elementary and high schools. Eventually, education became the principal ministry of the Congregation. In Rockland County the sisters serve in the parishes of St. Anthony, Nanuet, St. Paul, Congers, St. Gregory Barbarigo, Garnerville, Sacred Heart, Suffern, and St. Catharine, Blauvelt.

St. Thomas Aquinas College addressed higher education when it opened in Sparkill in 1954. A secondary school for girls, Rosary Academy, followed in 1965. When Rosary Academy eventually closed, the building was sold to Camp Venture, Inc., for Venture's Day Treatment Center for the developmentally disabled. The Rockland Campus of Long Island University is also located here. In 1984 property on Kings Highway was sold to Venture to build the John A. Murphy Community Residence.

St. Agnes Home and School closed in 1977, reflecting the trend away from large institutional facilities. The Congregation's efforts shifted to providing housing for senior citizens at Thorpe Village in 1981, and assisted living for senior citizens at Dowling Gardens in 1996.

Dominican Convent, in addition to serving as the Motherhouse of the Dominican Sisters of Sparkill, hosts various programs that serve the neighboring Rockland County community. Dominican Center provides retreat programs, spiritual direction, workshops and lectures. The House of Prayer offers retreats and liturgies as well as opportunities for prayer and reflection. Thorpe Senior Center serves as a nutrition center with a full range of activities and services. A Literacy Program brings sisters and recent immigrants together for English lessons. From 1976 until its closing in 1991, Thorpe Intermedia Gallery presented art exhibits and other cultural programs.

The founding spirit of Mother Antoninus Thorpe continues to inspire the Dominican Sisters of Sparkill although their ministries have expanded since Vatican Council II. Since 1980, Associate members have shared in the mission of the sisters. While continuing their traditional work in the realm of direct care, the sisters have broadened their response to the needs of contemporary society and collaborate with other groups and individuals to bring about a more just and peaceful world. They serve in 18 dioceses in cities, suburbs, and Indian reservations.

Sr. Margaret Harrison

Postcard of St. Dominic's Convent, Blauvelt. JSC

Women in New Roles

In 1890, twice as many girls as boys graduated from high school in the United States. While working women in offices was still generally frowned upon, and typewriters were considered too complex for females to handle, businesses slowly began to realize that women were a valuable untapped resource.

Of course, few employers were willing to compensate women workers fairly. Even though many women were more educated and skilled, men were always paid more for the same job. Today, women still earn less on average.

The Dorcas Society of the Clarkstown Reformed Church (above), circa late 1890s. The society was dedicated to charitable works. Those who have been identified are: front row, third from left, Martha Blauvelt, second from the right, Jane Benson, second row, left to right, Alice Blauvelt, Ettie Blauvelt, Adeline Smith (nicknamed "Linnie").

A menu from one of the society's dinners (left) held on November 16, 1899 at "Dame Van Houten's." Some interesting items are "Potato Salad, Clarkstown Style" and "Biscuits & Butter, N.Y. fashion."   JSC

A late twentieth century view of the Van Houten house on the corner of Demarest and Strawtown Road. Perhaps this was the site of the dinner?   JSC

14

The Beginnings of Rockland's Jewish Communities

The Rockland Jewish community of the twentieth century had its beginnings in the previous century. Contrary to popular belief, these beginnings were not in Spring Valley or Monsey, which are at present the largest Jewish population centers of Rockland, but the river communities of Haverstraw and Nyack.

Jews first came to Rockland County in the 1830s and 1840s traveling from New York City as traders and merchants. They arrived sporadically before the Civil War, some on foot with packs on their backs and others in wagons, and peddled their wares in the most populated areas. The river communities of Haverstraw and Nyack preceded Spring Valley. Gradually several settlers opened businesses including shops and hotels and became permanent residents. Until the turn of the century their numbers remained small.

The Goldsmith family was the first to arrive in Haverstraw, some time in the 1830s. Approximately ten other families followed in the next few decades, including of course the Newmans, as well as the Nadlers and Levys, who opened saloons that catered to the workers in the brickyards.

They worshipped in private homes until 1877, at which time fifteen families met in the Simon Building to eventually organize the Congregation Sons of Jacob. On September 9, 1899, the congregation dedicated its first synagogue on Clove Avenue.

By 1848, Abraham Brown had purchased a farm in Orangeburg, becoming the first recorded Jewish landowner in that section of Rockland. A few years later he and Moses Oppenhimer opened a business in Piermont, and then Nyack, where they became active in the Underground Railroad during the Civil War.

Nyack's Jewish Community grew slowly until, in the spring of 1870, twenty families established the Jewish Society at Abraham Brown's store. Twenty years later, on September 9, 1890, they were incorporated as the Congregation B'nai Israel, and by the turn of the century, were supporting a religious school. In 1907 the congregation moved to the top floor of a building in downtown Nyack, and the Torah had a permanent home.

The earliest known Jewish resident of the Spring Valley area was R. H. Rapinsky, who operated a tailor shop at the corner of Main and Church Streets in the late 1870s. Simon Rackow, an early peddler, arrived in the 1880s, from Poland. First selling his wares door to door, he soon married, settled down and opened a store on Main Street. His business met with success and was handed down to his sons. Others such as the Kaplans, Shapiros, Smiths and Selmans arrived and opened clothing stores on Main Street.

Spring Valley became an important shopping area for a growing rural farm community. Most of the Jewish-owned businesses were located between the Erie Railroad Depot and Maple Avenue and were Mom and Pop shops.

The Jewish community remained very small, however, until Charles Falkenberg purchased land on Pascack Road in 1892 and four years later opened a factory for manufacturing men's shirts. Several Jewish families purchased small plots of land and settled there, establishing one of the first Jewish neighborhoods.

Falkenberg was aided in his enterprise by Jacob Mendelson, a peddler, who carried much of the original machinery to Spring Valley on his wagon. Later, Mendelson traveled regularly to New York's Lower East Side to meet arriving immigrants and brought them directly to Rockland to work in the growing Falkenberg Shirt Factory.

Jacob Mendelson also purchased farmland, about 17 acres, on Pascack Road. Most of it was not cultivated and remained a dairy farm. Rooms in the large farmhouse were rented to supplement the income of Jacob, who was now working at the shirt factory. Later, the rooms and bungalows were rented to a growing summer trade. Mendelson's Lake had become a popular swimming spot.

The first Jewish family settled in Suffern in 1886. Thirty years later there were thirty families living in the community and holding religious services in the clubrooms of the Hebrew Benevolent Society.

In response to the influx of new workers, one of Rockland's first housing developments began on land east of Main Street, purchased by Peter Lespinasse in 1894. Formerly the Greening Farm, the area was soon known as "Jew Hill" and became one of the focal points of Jewish settlement for many years. Another important Jewish neighborhood, known as "Rich Hill," was located south of present-day Route 59, running south to the Old Nyack Turnpike and west to Summit Avenue.

Spring Valley's first synagogue was organized in 1899 as the Farmer's Synagogue. Before long, the name was changed to the Congregation Sons of Israel. In 1922, the members purchased the former Methodist Church building on Metropolitan Avenue (now Memorial Park Drive). The building underwent several changes in the next few decades.

Harold L. Laroff

...April 22, 1895: Burglars broke into the Nyack post office and stole $1,000 in cash and stamps...

William Henry Myers

In March, 1888 Orangetown's Republicans nominated William Henry Myers of Nyack for the office of Constable. At that time, Town Constables were elected, with five to be chosen. In its pre-election editorial, the *Rockland County Journal* described Myers as an "eminently respected citizen," and endorsed his candidacy. But 1888 was a poor year for Republicans, however, and all their Orangetown candidates lost. While the *Journal*, in its review of the election, argued that the Prohibition Party had taken votes from them, its competitor, the Democratic *City and Country*, attributed the GOPs' poor showing to Myers. Even though Myers had garnered 386 out of 1,200 votes cast, the newspaper claimed that many voters who would normally have supported a Republican candidate had not done so in his case.

Myers was an African-American. He was also the only black man ever to stand for office in Rockland during the nineteenth century.

In many ways a remarkable man, William Henry Myers was one of those who, in the tradition of Frederick Douglass, had made himself from slave to man. He was born in bondage in Virginia in 1848. Sold west at the age of 12, he worked on a cotton plantation in Mississippi until he escaped to the Union lines in 1863. In June of that year, he enlisted in the 5th U.S. Colored Troop Regiment. While in service, he was wounded, captured by the Texas Rangers, escaped again, and by the end of the war was First Sergeant of K Company. He was 17 years old.

On his discharge from service, Myers was appointed Justice of the Peace for Tallula, Mississippi. Later, he was elected to the same office. While a Justice, he sought, he writes, to reconcile antagonisms so that "harmony, order, peace and good will might be the result." Unfortunately, things didn't work out as he had hoped, and some time after 1870 he left Mississippi for good. Most likely, there

had been pressure from the Ku Klux Klan.

Many years later, in response to the published comments of a southerner visiting Nyack, Myers gave some hint of what those pressures had been:

Having been a victim of Southern outrage myself, having been driven from the polls with a seven shooter held too close to my head for comfort, for no other offense than giving tickets (ballots) to poor, ignorant negroes and explaining them, I am anxious to testify as to what made me and thousands more lose all interest in politics while in the South...

Why Myers chose to live in Nyack is not known. Both he and his uncle, Charles Mayo, were recorded in the state census of 1875 as residents there, with Myers listed as a servant in a white household and Mayo as a coachman. Undaunted by the loss of the 1888 election, for several decades Myers remained constantly active in politics, the church and veterans' affairs.

The lessons William Henry Myers had tried so conscientiously to teach, both through his own estimable actions and through his own accounts of his experiences in the South, never penetrated. Again and again, Myers and other black leaders had showed a willingness to seek a reasonable accommodation, one that would allow the village black people self-respect and a measure of opportunity. Yet, in the final analysis, the people-to-people approach that President Roosevelt had recommended bore little fruit in Nyack. Restraint and good will were never enough. In terms of respect and of concrete improvements in economic and social status, the results of forty years of accommodation were meager. No matter how correct their behavior, there seemed little local black people could do, objectively, to erase prevailing stereotypes and to temper the deep-seated prejudice that held the surrounding whites in its grip.

Carl Nordstrom, *Phoenician Tales*

The pre-Revolutionary John Sickles house, located on the west side of Sickletown Road. This photo was taken around 1900, when it was known as the Rand Farm. The house was later owned by film star Zita Johann who starred in the 1932 movie, *The Mummy*. Note the simple log bridge.

JSC

The World's Fair That Wasn't

Few realize that quiet, rural Rockland County was to be part of one of the major attractions of the nineteenth century, the Columbian Exposition, and there is no telling how this event would have changed the course of the county's history.

The Columbian Exposition, commemorating the discovery of America by Columbus 400 years earlier, was instead held in the city of Chicago in 1893 (a year late). The New York City area and Rockland were passed over at the last minute in favor of Chicago after Republican President Benjamin Harrison (up for re-election in 1892) figured he might woo some votes away from the likely Democratic candidate, Grover Cleveland, if the fair was held in a city that had leaned toward Cleveland in the previous Presidential election.

As it turned out, changing the site at such short notice delayed the opening of the exposition a full year, and Harrison lost the election to Cleveland anyway. Rockland not only lost its big chance to participate in the fair, the county also suffered a major economic depression in 1893, from which it did not substantially recover until the coming of World War II and the Tappan Zee Bridge half a century later.

For Rockland history buffs rugged enough to go poking around in the woods, however, the ruins of the county's contribution to the planned exposition can still be seen as a reminder of that hopeful, prosperous era long ago.

To go back to the high-flying 1880s in Rockland and the early plans for the Columbian Exposition that included the county, it must be remembered that the various entrepreneurs of the day assumed, rightly, that the fair was going to be held somewhere in the New York City area. While the site had not been officially designated, there was talk of holding the exposition in Central Park or in Harlem (then mostly open fields), or even in lower Westchester County. An odds-on favorite, it was rumored, was Verplanck's Point, an undeveloped cape of land on the east side of the Hudson in Westchester comprising the present day hamlet of Verplanck and village of Buchanan, and facing Dunderberg Mountain in Rockland directly across the river.

Whether Verplanck was ever seriously in the running, three New York City businessmen must have thought so, and in 1889, the trio, James Morgan, Henry Mumford and David Proudfit, conceived of building a combination hotel, restaurant and observatory at the top of Dunderberg, the 1,100-foot summit of the mountain to be reached by an open-air inclined railway that would transport passengers to the top from a point at the base of the mountain near the West Shore Railroad above Tomkins Cove. To get to Tomkins Cove from Verplanck, the businessmen contemplated a ferry service, with the pier at Tomkins made large enough to handle steamboats from the city as well.

From the observatory at the top of Dunderberg, the fair grounds seen below across the Hudson would be one of the most magnificent sites of the age, the businessmen believed. It was also their opinion that long after the fair ended, the summit would continue to provide the "strengthening, invigorating life-saving oxygen of a purer air" to the "toiling millions of people who take an outing once or oftener during the summer."

"Who can doubt that such an enterprise will be profitable to those interested?" the businessmen asked in the prospectus to potential investors in the Dunderberg Spiral Railway, organized in 1889 under the General Railroad Act of the State of New York. Accordingly, the railway corporation, capitalizing at three-quarters of a million dollars, began offering $600,000 worth of first mortgage bonds, each bond to run for 30 years at six percent interest per year. In addition to building the facilities at the summit of Dunderberg, the corporation planned to landscape a 20-acre tract at the base of the railway that would be the site of the "main station," and include the corporation offices, a loading and unloading platform, car houses, repair shops, coal pockets, a freight yard and a second restaurant and hotel. Rolling stock was to consist of one locomotive, 15 open passenger cars, two closed passenger cars, four coal cars, two flat cars and one box car.

While the trip down the mountain was to be a gravity run on a nine-mile spiral railway, two engine houses (one half-way up the mountain and the other at the summit) were to contain boilers capable of producing enough steam to haul people up the inclined railway at the rate of 2,500 an hour.

To boost the feasibility of the project, the prospectus pointed out that Mumford and his brother Thomas had taken over a similar railway at Mauch Chunk, Pennsylvania, and had converted it into a recreational attraction that returned a considerable profit each year to investors. If the new railway carried only 300,000 passengers a season, "our lowest estimate," Mumford and the others said, the profit to investors in Dunderberg would be close to $100,000 a year. Expecting profits far in excess of that, especially with the word of mouth publicity the railway would receive around the world from visitors to the Columbian Exposition, the planners began construction at Dunderberg in the spring of 1890. Road gangs blasted through rock, built dry supporting walls, filled ravines and started tunneling through ridges along the proposed route. By 1891, according to an article in the *Peekskill Evening Star*, $1 million had been spent and 13 miles of railroad bed completed, while, at the same time, public interest in the project remained high.

Then came the fateful decision to move the Columbian Exposition to Chicago, and all work on Dunderberg ceased. For a while, many investors held out hope that construction would eventually resume in spite of there being no fair, but by that time the economic depression had settled into the lower Hudson Valley and Dunderberg mountain was left to return pretty much to its natural state.

Anyone who wishes to climb Dunderberg today can see a little bit of what might have been in Rockland.

Many grades of the spiral railway are still in evidence, and there is a tunnel about 100 feet long that would have covered a section of the spiral railway where it passed under the incline.

At the summit of Dunderberg, climbers may have to close their eyes to imagine the great Columbian Exposition below, for across the river now, in contrast to a world's fair and a celebration of America's past, is the Consolidated Edison atomic power plant at Buchanan, a rather grim indicator, perhaps, of America's future.

John Dalmas

In October of 1898, Teddy Roosevelt made a whistle stop in Suffern (above left). Behind Roosevelt is U.S. Senator C.M. DePew. Many U.S. presidents, and presidential hopefuls, have come to Rockland County to campaign.

The great Blizzard of 1888 (above right) dumped several feet of snow along the East coast. This photo shows the mountains of snow on Broadway in Nyack. Some residents were trapped in their homes for days and were forced to burn furniture for warmth.

Meat hangs above the sidewalk in this 1890 photo of Keesler's Meat Market in Nyack (left).

A train wreck in Blauvelt (below), circa 1890.   JSC

...July 10, 1889, President Grover Cleveland came to Rockland and stayed at the Prospect House in Nyack as a guest of T.J. Porter...January 1893 the Hudson River froze and Van Houten's livery stable burned...

Evolution of Firefighting

Bucket brigades, hand-drawn and hand-pumped fire engines, and local church bells were all integral parts of Rockland's early firefighting efforts.

As Rockland celebrates its bi-centennial in 1998, those early firefighting techniques seem a far cry from today's space-age technology that includes infrared scanners to see through smoke and lightweight air packs that allow firefighters to breathe for up to 30 minutes in fires.

The history of Rockland's all-volunteer fire service is recorded in the anniversary journals of the 44 fire companies that make up the 26 departments serving the county.

The Valley Cottage bucket brigade in 1915, after fighting a brush fire at Casper Hill. Identified are: Mr. Garrabrant (far left), A. Hicks (third from left), William Navin (in overalls, center), Mr. Snapps (behind Navin), H. Hess (far right) and Mr. Foster (second from right). JSC

Orangetown Fire Company 1 opened for business in 1834 in South Nyack, the first fully organized fire department in Rockland. The newest department, the David B. Roche Volunteer Fire Company, was formed in 1960 as the Thiells Fire Department. In between, the other 42 companies were chartered, and the only thing that has changed is the technology available, which the firefighters of the early "iron men and wooden hydrants" era could only dream of.

Orangetown's first piece of apparatus was a small bucket engine operated by crank handles, with leather buckets and copper-riveted leather

hose. It was the only fire engine in Nyack for 18 years and served until 1895. And it was hand-drawn by firefighters who were alerted to fires by fire bells and even church bells.

Piermont followed in 1851 when Empire Hose Company 1 was formed, followed by Mazeppa Fire Engine Company 2, Nyack, in 1852; Rescue Hook and Ladder Company 1, Haverstraw and Gen. Warren Emergency Company 2, Haverstraw, both in 1854. The first inland fire companies were Nanuet Fire Engine Company, founded in 1860, and Columbian Engine Company 1, Spring Valley, in 1861.

A history of the Nyack Fire Department records that the 1861 fire that destroyed the Knickerbocker Ice Co. in Rockland Lake and brought units from both Piermont and Haverstraw, was responsible for the chartering of the aptly named Knickerbocker Engine Company 1 of Rockland Lake in 1862.

Many of today's fire departments were organized for specific reasons, like the 122-year-old S.W. Johnson Steam Fire Engine Company 1, which came into being when William Garner decided to protect his investment, the current Garnerville industrial terminal. Garner named the company for Samuel W. Johnson, his brother-in-law, and equipped it with a then state-of-the-art 1869 Button Steamer, which can still be seen preserved in the Garnerville firehouse.

Nyack got its first motorized fire truck on Sept. 30, 1911, when Jackson Hose Company 3 took delivery of an "auto hose wagon," which was actually a fire engine body "transplanted" on a Steams touring car. This is believed by most county fire service historians to be the first motorized fire apparatus in Rockland.

What many consider one of the most destructive fires in the county's history occurred Jan. 31, 1919. The 9:30

The New City Fire Department (and their Fire Dog), circa 1900. The steam powered water pump was pulled by a team of horses.   JSC

19

a.m. explosion and fire killed two, injured 13, and leveled a block of buildings known as the American Aniline Products factory at Cedar Hill and Railroad Avenues in Nyack. The blast, which rocked buildings on the Tarrytown waterfront, was directly across the street from the Liberty Street School, where 1,200 students were in class. Except for a few minor glass cuts, no other injuries to the children occurred.

Haverstraw put the first hydraulically operated ladder truck in the state into service in 1936. Before that, spring-loaded aerial ladders that reached the then-incredible height of 75 feet were the norm.

Today, firefighters use trucks that can pump more than 2,000 gallons of water per minute and aerial platforms that reach 125 feet in the air. They employ self-contained air masks instead of water-soaked handkerchiefs; wear bunker suits made of fire-resistant Nomex, an outgrowth of NASA research; and carry helmets with infrared viewers that can see through smoke.

Today's firefighters must pass a state-mandated, 13-week Essentials of Firefighting course before they fight a fire. And the 3,000 volunteers have the facilities of the county Fire Training Center, opened in Pomona in 1973, at their disposal to refine their craft.

Firefighting has become a science. Rockland Community College offers an associate's degree in applied fire technology, and bachelor's and master's degrees can be earned at numerous four-year colleges in the New York metropolitan area.

Around the corner for tomorrow's firefighters are computers in firetrucks that can print out floor diagrams and list fire hazards or individual buildings. They are already being used by several county police departments.

John Kryger, *Rockland Journal-News*, 5/16/98

Grand View train station, 1885.   JSC

The dedication of the Nyack Missionary School, April 17, 1897.   JSC

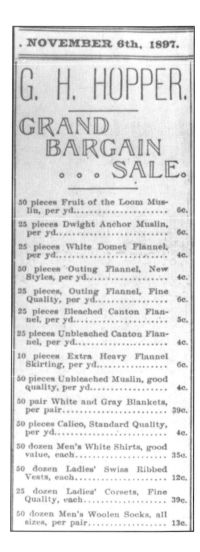

. NOVEMBER 6th, 1897.

G. H. HOPPER.

GRAND BARGAIN ... SALE.

50 pieces Fruit of the Loom Muslin, per yd.....................	6c.
25 pieces Dwight Anchor Muslin, per yd.....................	6c.
25 pieces White Domet Flannel, per yd.....................	4c.
50 pieces Outing Flannel, New Styles, per yd..................	4c.
25 pieces, Outing Flannel, Fine Quality, per yd..............	6c.
25 pieces Bleached Canton Flannel, per yd.....................	5c.
25 pieces Unbleached Canton Flannel, per yd.....................	4c.
10 pieces Extra Heavy Flannel Skirting, per yd..............	6c.
50 pieces Unbleached Muslin, good quality, per yd..............	4c.
50 pair White and Gray Blankets, per pair....................	39c.
50 pieces Calico, Standard Quality, per yd.....................	4c.
50 dozen Men's White Shirts, good value, each....................	35c.
50 dozen Ladies' Swiss Ribbed Vests, each....................	12c.
25 dozen Ladies' Corsets, Fine Quality, each..................	39c.
50 dozen Men's Woolen Socks, all sizes, per pair..................	13c.

20

Anne Raab at the family's Christmas tree in their home in Blauvelt in the late 1890s. (Today, the former Raab house is the Blauvelt Library.) Although the wide-eyed wonder of children on Christmas morning will always be the same, styles, fashions and our way of life would change in the coming century. Little Anne would grow up to see automobiles replace horses, radios bringing the world into your home, flying machines take to the air, and households transformed by electricity and appliances. However, she would also witness the horrors and uncertainties of war. If the county's isolation and innocence was to be shattered in the next generation, here, at least for a moment, we can indulge in the nostalgia of the "good old days."

Courtesy of the Orangetown Museum, donated by Rachel Wade.

1900~1909

Life
On the
Farm

As the new century dawned, a banker was quoted as saying that America was the "envy of the world." Optimism reigned supreme; the American dream was alive and well, and the path of progress and prosperity seemed to be the only course for the country to take.

This optimistic attitude was not confined to the United States. In 1900 in England, Queen Victoria still ruled a vast empire that stretched around the globe. The great Paris Exposition displayed the height of mankind's achievements in the arts and sciences. The second modern Olympic games were held in France and brought many countries together in good-spirited competition. There was some unrest, and a few wars, but nothing the powerful and confident nations of the world felt they could not handle.

However, in 1901, a stock market panic hit America, and once dignified and wealthy investors actually punched and kicked one another in their frenzy to sell. Almost two million children under the age of 16 worked in factories and mines across the country, and it was not uncommon for a 6-year-old to work a 13-hour day. President McKinley was assassinated by an anarchist.

Daily newspapers brought these events to the county's 38,298 residents, but for the average Rocklander the rest of the world was far removed from the gates of their quiet farms and homes. Although town centers such as Suffern, Spring Valley, Haverstraw and Nyack were growing, there were over 800 farms in operation across the county. If you didn't live on a farm, you were probably rarely out of sight of one.

In the years of 1900 to 1909, county fairs brought residents together to celebrate their way of life. Two devastating disasters also brought Rocklanders together. As one Suffern resident said, "In those days, if a neighbor was in trouble, you helped. You didn't even think about it, you simply helped as best you could."

Someone once asked why people reply that they are from Rockland County when asked where they live, instead of naming their town as everybody else does. Perhaps the concept most difficult for outsiders or new residents to comprehend is that feeling of community that once pervaded the county. You were not only part of a family, a neighborhood or a village, you were part of a community that encompassed all of Rockland. Of course, there were still healthy rivalries among towns, but the county was small enough and homogeneous enough to have that sense of unity.

That sense of community would be both strengthened and tested throughout the century, but during the first decade, the county could basically relax and enjoy life on the farm.

The Herbert Farm in Doodletown.   JSC

23

Good Old Days?

People tend to romanticize the past, looking upon the "Good Old Days" as simpler, happier and more relaxing times. However, after examining the daily household chores in a typical home in 1900, the old days don't look so good. The following is from *The Expert Maidservant* by Cristine Terhune Herrick.

Rise at six o'clock and have clothing in readiness, so as to be dressed and downstairs by six-thirty. Strip the bed and open the window before leaving the room. If the care of the furnace is in your hands, open the draughts and put on a little coal. Light the kitchen fire, fill the kettle, put on the breakfast cereal and potatoes, or anything that requires some time to cook.

Open the windows in rooms on first floor, brush up the floor and the halls, and sweep off the front steps. Go over bare floor in the dining-room with a cloth and dust the dining-room. Put more coal in furnace, close draughts, and give a look at the kitchen fire.

Set table for breakfast. If a square of damask or doilies are employed at breakfast, lay them on evenly. Crooked spreading of a table is an abomination.

After a lengthy discourse on the proper way to set a table, the list of the day's chores continues.

While the family is eating the last course of breakfast go to the bedrooms, strip the beds, turn the mattresses, hang the bedclothing over chairs, and leave it to air while going over the floors with a carpet-sweeper.

Go downstairs, clear the table, scrape the dishes. Return to the second floor, make the beds, dust and clean the bathrooms. Return downstairs, wash and put away the dishes, rinse out dish-towels and put them over to boil. Wipe off the shelves of pantries and refrigerator every day. Scald out ice-box three times a week. Clean and fill the lamps.

Go now to any special work, such as sweeping, washing windows, or general cleaning. Stop this in time to prepare luncheon. After luncheon clear table, darken dining-room, and finish any small duties that have been left over from the morning. Plan your work so as to have only light tasks in the afternoon.

The lighter afternoon tasks would include serving tea and preparing for the largest meal of the day, dinner. In addition to all of these tasks, the maid would usually spend Mondays washing the laundry and Tuesdays doing all the ironing.

Of course, most families could not afford servants, so the woman of the house would have to do all of these chores, in addition to caring for all of the children (between five and ten children was not uncommon). Many homes in Rockland had small farms and livestock, which also needed tending.

Children were expected to share in the farming chores and household work. They would also have to walk long distances to poorly heated school houses and risk getting hit by the teacher if they did anything wrong.

Men were no less burdened as they were often the sole providers for their large families. Working twelve-hour days, six days a week in dirty, strenuous jobs was typical.

The modern world may seem too fast-paced and hectic, but it is doubtful that many people would give up their cellular phones, microwave ovens, SUVs, computers and dishwashers to return to those mythical "Good Old Days."

Linda Zimmermann

Mrs. Erastus Johnson (seated) and daughters in their Spring Valley home, c.1900. Standing left to right: Annie, b.1857, Elizabeth, b. 1855 and Ida, b. 1861.

This is a typical Victorian-style home. Note the oil lamp on the wall, which would indicate there wasn't any electricity. While the ornate furnishings and wallpaper, and the somber and conservative clothing would change drastically in the "Roaring Twenties," this generation still firmly represented a nineteenth century way of life.

Rockland County Fairs

Rockland had its first agricultural fair in 1843. The fairs were originally held in Spring Valley and New City, then moved to Orangeburg. They prospered until the 1920s when agriculture began to decline in importance. Haverstraw Village Historian Dan deNoyelles recalls the fair as the highlight of the year for Rockland.

By World War I the Orangeburg Fair every Labor Day was firmly established at a race track on what is now Route 303 near World Wide Volkswagen Corp. Horse shows and horse racing were perennial favorites, and as automobiles became common they also became an entertainment feature.

Louis Hoyt, a nationally known race car driver in the 1920s, lived in Haverstraw. Hoyt had been an auto dealer on Route 9W who kept a tame bear that people could wrestle to win small amounts of money. Hoyt had often raced his cars at the fairs and once offered to race an aviator from the ground around the horse track.

For 97 years the fairs prospered in varying degrees until American involvement in World War II brought them to a halt. After the war they were never successfully revived. Yet contemporary newspaper accounts of the last one in 1940 describe it as drawing a record crowd of 15,000 despite inclement weather. Featured in 1940 were vaudeville acts and other curiosities. "Dr. Bernard's famous troupe of elephants from the Clarkstown Country Club" was there. So were "Captain Jimmy Smith and his All-American Thrill Divers" engaging in "a series of rolling, crashing, smashing duels and combats using both motorcycles and automobiles.

There was a bicycle exhibit showing the evolution of the vehicle from the crude "boneshakers" of yesteryear to the modern, streamlined, gear shifting models of today. Very popular was the "Jaloppy Jalopp," a competitive event to determine the "oldest, and most amusing form of transportation of by-gone days." Among the entries were a one-cylinder 1904 Cadillac, "as well as other

unique specimens propelled by mule, oxen, pony, and foot power."

There were the usual school exhibits, fireworks, contests for children and horse shows and races. A big event in the latter category was the Judge Tompkins Memorial Trot—nine heats of harness racing in honor of one of the county's then recently deceased biggest competitors in the sport.

School children and couples celebrating their Golden Wedding anniversary were admitted free to the fairgrounds. The traditional focus of the fair on agriculture and farm crafts was still there. There were livestock and poultry exhibitions and competitions. Specifically for farmers there was a demonstration of "tomato packing—a group of 10 expert packers and sorters from Florida displayed their skills and professional dexterity in preparing and packing tomatoes."

"Women's exhibits" were a large part of the fair. These included classes for various types of jellies, jams, preserves, pickled and canned fruits and vegetables, condiments, juices, and unfermented wines. The last category covered dandelion, elderberry, rhubarb, red currant, grape, blackberry, raspberry, and cherry wines.

Baked goods were also judged and then later sold "providing an excellent opportunity for the homemaker who doesn't want to bake over the holiday." Classes in baking and needlecrafts were also offered, all under the auspices of the Ladies' Auxiliary of the Rockland County Agricultural and Horticultural Association.

A revival of the old county fairs was held in Rockland in 1983. However, with the county so changed from its early farming days, the fair was more nostalgia than agriculture.

Susan Corica, *Rockland Review*, 2/16/83

Horse racing at the Orangeburg Fair (left), c. 1900-05. Looking for a parking space is clearly not a modern problem as this lineup of horses and carriages illustrate.

The Industrial Fairs held in New City (postcard, below) were also popular events in Rockland.   JSC

THE ROCKLAND CO. INDUSTRIAL FAIR **NEW CITY, N. Y.** Aug 29, 30, 31 ...Sept. 1, 1910...

25

There may not have been roller coasters, but the Orangeburg Fair did provide balloon rides (above left), which in the age before airplanes were the only way to fly. The popularity of the fairs often meant long lines (above right). Note the style of clothing for the children. By the 1920s, balloon rides and horse racing gave way to new thrills—the car and the daredevil. JSC

Rockland's Worst Natural Disaster

The October storm and floods of 1903 were the worst natural disaster ever recorded in Rockland and nearby counties, yet are rarely remembered except by a few old-timers. For almost a century the blizzard of '88 has been cited as the worst storm ever. While it was surely a prodigious blow, halting all transportation for days, there was little lasting damage.

After a lull of 15 years—from '88—the forces of nature were ready for a new onslaught. Starting with a drought in April 1903 was to be a year of severe contrasts in weather. May was the driest month in weather bureau records. Only one-third of an inch of rain had fallen in a 53-day period. The Hackensack tributaries were so low, the water companies asked customers to conserve every drop of water. Forests became dry as tinder from New Jersey to as far north as Maine and Canada. Great tracts of woodland were swept by fire, spreading dense clouds of smoke over the skies of New York City, surrounding counties, and far out to sea. Sail and steam craft approaching New York harbor lost their bearings as if in dense fog and incoming vessels wondered whether the city itself was being consumed by fire.

In June the rains came almost every day for three weeks until 8.6 inches had fallen, the heaviest rainfall ever recorded in that month. Streams and ponds were filled to overflowing. The West Nyack (Greenbush) swamp was flooded as usual, turning the unpaved turnpike into a quagmire.

A huge southern storm with low barometric readings first appeared on the New York Weather Bureau map Thursday, October 8. It was then centered some distance at sea off the North Carolina coast. Its hurricane-force winds up to 90 m.p.h. were already spreading destruction to Virginia beaches. High pressure conditions here accelerated the storm and forced surging shore tides into inlets and rivers of New Jersey, into New York harbor and up the Hudson as far north as the Mohawk River and raised waters to the highest levels ever recorded.

Rains and wind, coming in gusts occasionally accompanied by booming thunder and vivid flashes of lightning, increased in velocity. By the evening of October 9, this large system had established itself over our region, where it was met by another major storm front bursting in from the colder northwest Great Lakes area. As winds shifted around from the northwest, a large-scale dynamic conversion and stalling process occurred—very moist maritime air combining with cooler continental air—causing torrential rains for the next 24 hours.

From the time the storm started Thursday morning until late Friday afternoon, 10.05 inches of rain had fallen with the heaviest precipitation between 9 and 10 o'clock Friday morning, when 2.42 inches fell. The greatest previous rainfall in such a short period was 6.17 inches.

Much of the riverfront in Piermont, Grand View and Nyack was flooded. Logs and debris swept in by the wind and waves caused severe damage to boats and marine installations and obstructed roads. The steamboat *Chrystenah,* bravely attempting to make its daily run from Peekskill to Nyack, turned back at Grassy Point for there were no docks for mooring; the piles were covered with water. Old river men at Nyack said they had never seen anything like it.

The Nyack brook overflowed Felter's ice pond with more than usual force. Willie Atkins, who was 18 at the time, witnessed the village streets awash from Franklin Street to Park, forming a lake to Cedar Street. Waters of the West Nyack (Greenbush) swamp rose to unprecedented heights, flooding the steam fire boxes in the water company's pumping station, which became inoperative for days.

Hilda Smith Campbell, then 10 years old, lived near the railroad in West Nyack. She recalls the excitement of the rapidly rising waters following two days of blinding downpour. Hackensack River currents became so swift that Clarence Campbell (her future father-in-law) feared for the safety of his horses in his barn that stood about where the closed Pathmark parking lot fronts on Route 59 (across from the Palisades Center mall). He and Edwin Smith waded across the turnpike, hitched each horse to a wagon and started over the old turnpike bridge on the Hackensack. Campbell's heavier wagon just made it across but Smith and the lighter rig were swept away in the torrent. The horse swam to safety; Smith was drowned and his body was not recovered until the next day.

Thomas B. Storms of West Nyack was 15 years old at the time and had vivid memories of the flood for the rest of his long life. His family then lived in Bardonia and it was his daily routine to hitch up the horse and buggy and take his two brothers to the West Nyack station to catch the 6:05 train for Weehawken each morning. The first day of the flood they rode down Strawtown Road to the turnpike and found the water in the "little swamp" lapping the front of the Clarksville Inn. The turnpike was impassable except by boat, and the train from Haverstraw that had come through stalled at West Nyack. Until the waters receded, commuters were taken to the station by rowboat.

Berne Sickels recalls his family's account of the flood. His father and two uncles walked down the Erie Railroad tracks to the high viaduct over the Hackensack near Sickeltown road. The water had risen to within three or

Rockland roads became rivers as this 1903 photo of boaters on Nyack Turnpike shows. This view, looking east toward Nyack, was the stretch of road just after the bridge over the Hackensack River. Today, this area is Route 59 in front of the Palisades Center mall, and a century later, it still floods. JSC

four feet of the top of that steep embankment. The enormous force of the river rushing through the narrow opening gouged out a 75-foot deep hole on the other side. This later silted in and became the famous 40-foot hole known to generations of bathers.

One mile to the south, a small community first called Orangeville Mills and later Van Houten Mills in Naurashaun, contained the Van Houten farm and two mills on the Naurashaun creek near its junction with the Hackensack. The Van Houten children often played in their gristmill, a four-storied structure powered by the largest millwheel in New York State. Seventy years later, Mabel Van Houten Clark still remembered feeling the warm flour ground between the huge millstones.

In 1903, she and her younger brother Jim attended Nyack High School. Each day they hitched a horse and buggy and rode to school, a 14-mile round trip. But not during the storm. Most travel ceased when the bridges across the Hackensack were swept away. Mabel and Jim were home when the big upstream dam burst destroying the gristmill and wheel.

Like other riverfront towns, Haverstraw suffered severely, with destruction beyond the memories of its oldest citizens. The rampaging Minisceongo Creek was so inundated that in places its course was changed. Every town bridge was carried away. Garnerville Print Works and other factories were flooded. Water rose so rapidly that people fled for their lives. Some sustained broken bones in the tumult; horses and cattle were drowned. In the brickyards, water flowing over decks and through sheds extinguished fires in burning kilns and boilers in central engine houses. Green seasoning bricks were destroyed; the ruined kilns had to be rebuilt and re-fired to fulfill end-of-the-season business and contracts. Huge financial losses were incurred. Silt and debris in the creek and channel by the brickyards caused future barge shipments to carry loads of 50,000 fewer bricks to enable navigation into the Hudson. Grassy Point, too, was under water. Goetschius' ice pond dam gave way, destroying the bridge below.

Dr. Laird of Haverstraw was called over the mountain to Centenary for an emergency at 3 a.m. during the storm. At 8 a.m., he and his driver started home and attempted to cross the bridge over the Hackensack near Trumper's place. They were swept off the bridge into the swollen stream; the horse's legs became entangled and the animal drowned. Doctor and driver remained stranded mid-stream until 1 p.m. when a boat was brought over from Haverstraw to rescue the exhausted men.

Throughout Rockland County, villages situated on streams or waterfronts suffered destruction. In Ramapo, Pierson's Cranberry Pond dam burst and those surging waters destroyed the Ramapo Lake dam. Almost every bridge on the Ramapo, Mahwah and Pascack Rivers was destroyed and the hamlet of Ramapo was almost obliterated. The valley became a sea inundating and destroying most factories in Sloatsburg, Hillburn and Suffern. Whole sections of main line Erie Railroad tracks were swept away, as were adjoining highways and hundreds of buildings.

One of the many Rockland bridges that was destroyed was this Erie Railroad bridge in Suffern. The sturdy network of supports was swept away and the tracks were left hanging in midair. JSC

In Spring Valley the pipe factory dam gave way destroying and flooding numerous houses and a blacksmith shop.

A bizarre accident, a collision between a locomotive and a boat, took place in South Amboy. High tides were washing across a trestle of the Central Railroad on the Long Branch Line. An engine was cautiously attempting to cross over when a 30-foot sailboat was carried against the trestle and suddenly rose on a high wave smashing into the train and badly injuring the fireman.

An aftermath of the flood and a grave menace was the quantity of dead animals strewn through the valleys for miles around. Few farmers and householders came through the experience without a loss of livestock. The carcasses needed speedy disposal to prevent an epidemic.

All low-lying areas of New York City, Staten Island and Long Island were flooded. By October 11, there was a milk famine in the city and it was October 16 before the first Erie trains were able to run over the main line to Jersey City with milk and farm produce from Rockland and Orange Counties.

The year 1904, though a quieter year, still managed to set a couple of new records:

On January 5, the thermometer at Nyack plunged to 12 below zero and did not get above zero until the following afternoon. The usually colder inland regions recorded 22 below at Spring Valley, 30 below at Nanuet and 40 below at Monsey! All of these were unofficial readings on home thermometers of questionable accuracy; still it must have been a bitterly cold night.

Again there was a quiet spell until the summer of 1904, when nature put on a spectacular show, never seen before or since in Rockland County. Saturday, July 16 was an intensely warm, humid day. Most people were out of doors and saw the phenomenon. Between 2 and 3 p.m., large thunderclouds gathered overhead and around the horizon. A rumble of distant thunder, accompanied by flashes of lightning, was heard. Wind and rain swept down the eastern shore of the river with cyclonic force, while Rockland remained relatively clear with a baseball game in progress at Nyack, attended by a sizeable crowd. The storm over Westchester appeared to split into two sections. One traveled eastward toward Chappaqua as a thick black cloud, assumed the form of an inverted cone, reached toward the ground, and was accompanied by rain and hailstones. This huge funnel-shaped cloud swept over a tract about 150 feet wide, leveling everything it struck and leaving a mass of ruins all the way to White Plains. One elderly woman died in the wreckage of her home and many others sustained injuries.

The other section of the storm (near Ossining) veered westward over the Hudson and formed a huge waterspout about 50 feet in diameter which seemed to gather force as it sped across the river. Hundreds of people on the Nyack hillside observed its progress and were uncertain of what course to pursue. Interest in the ball game was suspended as spectators watched in awe this incredible sight. Some people fled to their houses. Some considered it a religious manifestation.

The wind came up like a hurricane with a tremendous roar. Those near the shoreline said the volume of water and the suction force was so great that it bared the river bottom for a long distance. The waterspout struck the Upper Nyack shore where it tore out trees and destroyed a large dock under construction. Heavy planks and posts were scattered for hundreds of feet.

While the cloud rapidly dissipated near Crumbie's Glen, the greatest number of victims had yet to be discovered. For days thereafter, the river tides carried thousands of dead fish ashore in the Nyacks. Catfish, tomcods, perch, mossbunkers and eels had to be carted away by the wagonload. Local experts concluded these poor fish had been sucked up and killed by the enormous forces of the twister.

John Scott, *SOM*, July/Sept., 1978

A rare sight in this area, a powerful waterspout over the Hudson River photographed from Nyack.

JSC

...In 1903 the Wright brothers made their first flight...In 1901 President McKinley was assassinated and was succeeded by Teddy Roosevelt...Puccini's "Madame Butterfly" debuts...

Dr. Davies

Dr. Lucy Virginia Meriwether Davies, one of Rockland's historic women, was a physician, botanist, civil libertarian, suffragist, philosopher and informed devotee of music and art.

Known to friends, family and patients as Dockie, she was the wife of Arthur B. Davies, the renowned artist. From 1892 until her death on April 21, 1949, she lived on a farm near Rockland Lake, N.Y.

A pioneer woman physician, she made her Rockland rounds in buggies, sleighs and automobiles until three weeks before her death. Healing the sick, comforting the dying, rejoicing with young mothers and their newborn babies, she brought to all not only medical aid, but the wisdom of a richly perceptive and informed mind and heart.

At least twice during her remarkable career she was in serious accidents: once she inadvertently took a wrong turn at Valley Cottage and found herself driving down the railroad track toward an on-coming train; and on

September 30, 1943 her car was rammed by a bus, leaving her with four broken ribs, a broken arm, two fractures of the left leg and a shattered kneecap. She was rushed to the Nyack Hospital after that mishap. Five weeks later, with sling and crutches, she was visiting her own patients in the hospital. She was then 81. A month later she was home—still seeing patients, still wholly involved in the life about her. She delivered her last baby just two months before she died, at age 87.

The 38-acre farm that she and her husband acquired bordered the northerly end of Rockland Lake, with the Hudson hills and Hook Mountain on its southeastern horizons. It was a setting her artist husband would use repeatedly in his most haunting paintings, but in the workaday world in which Dockie functioned, it would create some of the harshest demands on her skills and resources as a physician.

In his book about Arthur B. Davies, *The Artist and the Unicorn,* Brooks Wright tells why: "Half a mile east of

A young Lucy Davies. JSC

the farm was the community of Rockland Lake... Some 2500 men, mostly Polish and Irish immigrants, worked on the lake in winter cutting ice. Great cakes weighing as much as three hundred pounds were cut and hauled by a winch on small carts... then slid down the hill through a sluice to the river edge, a drop of two hundred feet, where large barges carried them to New York. In summer the same men worked in a quarry at the north end of Hook Mountain.

"These laborers were Lucy's first patients ... Once when a severe explosion occurred at the quarry she was the first doctor on the scene and her kitchen table was pressed into service for emergency operations...".

At other times, Dockie was called to treat men who had broken through the ice on the lake or who were suffering from frostbite.

Some of her beliefs, as Brooks Wright points out, were ahead of their time. "She believed that the place for most deliveries was at home. She encouraged mothers to nurse their children. Terminal patients, she felt, belonged at home where they could die with dignity, among familiar surroundings, with their family near...".

That was the way she herself died, in the spring of 1949, in the familiar old farmhouse in which she had lived for more than half a century and which was then occupied by her son Niles (Rab), his wife, Erica Riepe Davies, and their children Niles, Jr., and Sylvia.

Isabelle K. Savell, *SOM*, April/June, 1985

Dockie continued making house calls even into her eighties.   JSC

...In 1902, Rockland Light & Power Co. advertised that it only cost one cent an hour to "operate an electric fan and keep cool"...In the early 1900s, telephone service was $2 a month and coffee was 33 cents per pound...In 1904 the Rolls-Royce Company was founded...

Park or Prison?

In 1908, the New York State Prison Commission decided to move the outdated prison at Sing Sing to a new location at Bear Mountain. Hundreds of convicts were moved to wooden stockades built on the lawn just south of the present Bear Mountain Inn. The prisoners were put to work clearing the timber for sites for permanent prison buildings. As the work on the prison went on, public opinion was growing against this misuse of the glorious scenery of the Hudson Gorge.

West of the site, the family of Edward Harriman, the railroad developer, had accumulated more than 20,000 acres as part of their estate. Consequently, in 1910, Mrs. Mary Harriman, carrying out the wishes of her recently deceased husband, donated 10,000 acres adjoining the prison site and a trust fund of $1 million. Her stipulation was that work on the Bear Mountain prison site be discontinued and the prison be located elsewhere. The deal was made with Gov. Charles Hughes, so today we have Bear Mountain and Harriman State Parks with their natural beauty, lakes and recreational facilities.

Robert Burghardt

Although times were changing, horses still ruled the streets of Rockland in the early 1900s (photo left, JSC). There were faster ways to travel, however, as these messengers on motor bikes demonstrate. This 1905 photo (above, courtesy of the Orangetown Museum) shows two men who delivered messages between Pearl River and New York City.

Orangeburg Pipe

Stephen Rowe Bradley, Sr., established one of the oldest and largest industries in Rockland County. A native of Brattleboro, Vermont, he moved to New York City and became active in the electrical manufacturing business. In 1883 he moved to Nyack and engaged himself in several successful local enterprises that led to his family's becoming one of the largest property owners in Rockland County.

Mr. Bradley was a man of rare judgement and keen executive ability. He was president of the Union Electric Company, established in Brooklyn, which made and charged batteries, and the Nyack Electric Light and Power Company. He founded the Fibre Conduit Company in Orangeburg, which gave birth to the Rockland Light and Power Company. Stephen Bradley was public spirited and was one of Nyack's most prominent citizens. He helped to establish the Nyack Hospital and was president of the hospital and the Nyack Public Library.

In the late nineteenth century, Thomas Edison's electric light had come into use in cities and in many larger towns. Municipalities strung power lines on poles along the streets to carry the necessary current. Bradley foresaw the value of installing these power lines underground, out of sight, and out of danger. A German process had been developed to make a conduit suitable for this purpose. It consisted of a wood fiber tube impregnated with coal-tar pitch. Bradley acquired the know-how for making this conduit. On February 2,

1893, the Fibre Conduit Company was established and manufacturing facilities were soon constructed at Orangeburg.

The company flourished and soon began to expand. A major expansion took place in 1907 and again in the late twenties. Stephen R. Bradley, Sr., died at the age of 75 in February 1910. Stephen Bradley, Jr., filled his father's shoes as president of the Fibre Conduit Company until 1932.

A profitable product sold in these years was underfloor duct, and many miles are in the floors of the Empire State Building and in other skyscrapers in New York and other cities.

I came to work as a young engineer for the company in early 1940. It was a good place to work, where there were capable and helpful people. Hugh J. Robertson, an in-law of the Bradley family, was the progressive president of the company.

During World War II the demand for fiber conduit was overwhelming. The Army and the Navy appropriated millions of feet of electrical conduit for power distribution and lighting of airports. At a time when construction materials were rationed, the company was permitted to add capacity to the plant.

The name of the Fibre Conduit Company was changed to Orangeburg Manufacturing Company in 1948. The post-war building boom had started and with it came a new product. Builders and homeowners then had no good choices of pipe for drains and sewer lines.

The pipe is loaded onto trains, c. 1905-1910.   JSC

Clay pipe was easily broken and poorly joined. Cast iron pipe was heavy and expensive. Some local people, particularly Orangeburg employees, were using fiber electrical conduit for drainage purposes. The successful experience with it stimulated the company to develop a heavy wall product and market it as Orangeburg Pipe. It was light, easily attached, and if properly installed would last indefinitely.

Demand for the new drain pipe as well as perforated pipe could not be satisfied. Major expansions in 1946 and in 1951 tripled production of pipe and conduit. Five hundred tons of pipe and conduit were shipped weekly from the Orangeburg plant during the 1950s and the 1960s.

The Orangeburg Manufacturing Company was sold to the Flintkote Company in 1958, with no change in personnel. In the 1970s, the equally as good plastic pipe was being produced in such large quantities and at such low cost that the Orangeburg plant could not compete. In the fall of 1972, the company announced that the Orangeburg plant would be closed at the end of the year.

In the 80 years of its existence, the Orangeburg plant produced a million tons of pipe and conduit. Today, millions of feet of fiber conduit are encased in concrete under city streets in the United States and in foreign countries. Millions of feet of Orangeburg pipe are serving householders and farmers for land drainage, for leaching fields, for house-to-sewer connections, and for irrigation. The Orangeburg trade name was universal. Some years after the plant closed, I purchased some fiber pipe from a building supply house. It was made by the Kyova Company in remote Ironton, Ohio. The clerk wrote down "Orangeburg pipe."

Harold S. Fredericks, *SOM*, Jan./March, 1994

An arc light (far right) on the corner of North Broadway and Van Houten Street in Upper Nyack, circa 1900 (JSC). Although common today, early streetlights were a tourist attraction.

Credit for the invention of electric lights has gone to Thomas Edison, but there is evidence to support the claim that Pearl River resident Julius Braunsdorf was actually the first to invent an electric light.

Some Pearl River residents, never having seen such a light before, thought that there was magic or the work of the devil behind this mysterious invention. However, science prevailed and Braunsdorf's lights were the first to illuminate the Capitol in Washington, D.C.

...In 1901, the first Nobel prizes were awarded...In 1908 Bakelite was invented...In 1909 Bleriot crossed the English Channel in an airplane and Robert Peary reached the North Pole...The world's largest diamond, (the Cullinan, weighing 3,106 carats), is discovered in 1905...The New York City subway officially opens in 1904...In France in 1907, Paul Cornu flies the first helicopter...A powerful earthquake devastates San Francisco in 1906...

Libraries are indispensable resources for practical information and educational material, as well as a wide range of entertaining novels and children's books. Going well beyond the printed word, modern libraries also offer audio, video, the internet, and lectures and programs for all age groups. While it is hard to imagine a community today without a public library, such facilities were few and far between in the beginning of the twentieth century. Thanks to the efforts of dedicated groups and individuals, libraries began to take root in Rockland, sometimes with the humblest of beginnings in someone's house or garage. The following are just some of the earliest of the local libraries, the rest are featured in other chapters.

Piermont Public Library
153 Hudson Terrace

Since 1896, the Piermont Library (right) has been serving the village of Piermont, having been housed in various rooms around the village. In 1909, an elegant hillside 1880's Greek Revival house overlooking the Hudson River became home to the library. Plans are currently under way to build a new library in downtown Piermont. The library's strengths are in the fields of boating, gardening, and environmental issues.

Nyack Library
59 South Broadway

One of the oldest county libraries, Nyack Library was chartered in 1901. In 1806, twenty village residents had started a collection of books which, after 1835, was housed in a Nyack storefront. The present building, Rockland's only Carnegie library, was constructed in 1903. In 1975, a substantial addition was completed, and in 1992 a major renovation included a mezzanine.

The first librarian was employed from 1890-1957. In 1908 (Memorial Day), a large boulder on the front lawn, inscribed with the Gettysburg Address, was dedicated with several Civil War veterans in attendance. The library has an extensive local history collection.

This photo (above) shows a man on a horse passing a few barns on South Broadway in Nyack. The photo had to have been taken before 1903, because the barns were removed to build the Nyack Library (left).

JSC

Blauvelt Free Library
541 Western Highway

In 1909, the library was chartered in the beautiful colonial building (circa 1752, top right photo) which was the former home of Judge Cornelius Blauvelt. The main sandstone structure was added in 1852. A reference area and workroom were added in 1988, and a major expansion was completed in 1998. The additions to the library were designed in order not to detract from the character and beauty of the original historic structure. The library has the complete Blauvelt family genealogy in its collection.

King's Daughters Public Library: Haverstraw
85 Main Street
Branch: 1 Rosman Road, Garnerville

Chartered in 1895, through efforts of the King's Daughters Society of Haverstraw (a ladies' charitable organization), the library began in borrowed space at Jenkins Hall, then moved to the National Bank Building. With funds donated by brickyard owner Denton Fowler, matched by the King's Daughters, a library building was constructed on the banks of the Hudson. The Fowler Library opened on May 14, 1903. In 1983 the Kay Freeman wing of the Fowler Library was dedicated, and in 1991 the library building was listed on the New York State and National Register of Historic Places.

The Thiells branch was opened in 1978, starting in a store on Route 202, Garnerville, subsequently moving to the basement of the Haverstraw Town Hall in 1981. A new library is under construction on Route 202.

The King's Daughters Public Library in Haverstraw (above). The Thiells branch in Garnerville (left). Library photos and text courtesy of the Library Association of Rockland County, unless otherwise noted.

...Upton Sinclair's The Jungle is published in 1906...Anton Chekhov's "Three Sisters" is published in 1902...Gertrude Stein's Three Lives is published in 1908...

Historians such as William Haeselbarth, Frank Green, the Rev. David Cole, the Rev. Eben Cobb and George Budke preserved Rockland's history through their research and writings. There was also Winthrop Gilman: "A banker by trade, he lived in Palisades around the turn of the century. It is said he was pleased when the family firm failed in the Panic of 1907, for thereafter he could stay home and concentrate on his real interests—the church, the public school, and the library. In the course of his years in Palisades, he designed and built its church, supported its school, and collected and annotated its history. His work, which can be seen at the Palisades Library, can be recommended as a model to follow for anyone who would dig deep in the history of their own back yard." Quote by Carl Nordstrom, *South of the Mountains*, Oct./Dec. 1959

John L. Dodge

John Lanphere Dodge was born in New York City, September 4, 1865. His father served as a surgeon in the Federal Army during the Civil War. At the age of fourteen, he went to work in a drug store, and while in the employ of Kilgour's drug firm he invented several pharmaceutical formulas, one of which he sold to his employer in 1897 for $1000, using the money to enter the drug business for himself.

To manufacture his products he formed the firms of Bell & Co. and Hollings-Smith Co. at Orangeburg. Their most popular product was a stomach medication known as Bell-ans.

During the last thirty years of his life he devoted much time to the breeding, training and racing of trotting horses, and came to be considered the most successful amateur trainer and driver in the world. (Dodge's racetrack in Orangeburg was the site of the annual Rockland County Fair.)

He was a fair-minded and clear-sighted man with a keen sense of humor and noted as a raconteur. After his death in 1940, the companies continued operation under Dodge's son and grandson. In 1971, Bell & Co. went out of business when the formula for Bell-ans was sold, and Hollings-Smith Co. closed its doors in 1977.

Catherine Dodge

Nanuet residents greet Governor Hughes during the campaign of 1908 (top). This Pearl River postcard (above) depicts the post office and general store, circa 1909.   JSC

Health care has been something of a cottage industry in Rockland County in the twentieth century, with many groups leaving New York City to "come up to the country" for better physical and mental health. Two of the county's most successful health care facilities are Nyack Hospital and Good Samaritan Hospital, both of which began at the beginning of the century.

Nyack Hospital

June 17, 1895—Certification for Nyack Hospital is drawn up by Gilbert H. Crawford.

December 1895—The original four acres of land are purchased from Mutual Life Insurance Company for $1,000 cash and a $2,000 mortgage.

Nyack Hospital in 1900 (above, JSC) and how that building looked in 2001 (right, Linda Zimmermann).

Jan. 1, 1900—Nyack Hospital (a two-story house) opens its doors. The facility features nine beds, one private room, a reception area, operating room, nurses' parlor and dining room.

1902—Nyack Hospital undergoes its first expansion, adding 12 beds, another private room and a second operating room.

1926—A three-story, fireproof building raises hospital capacity to 80.

1949—County population growth at the end of World War II prompts an expansion to 104 beds. By 1952, there are 125 beds.

1963—New construction on the south wing brings number of beds to 127 and bassinets to 22.

1971—The $8.2 million Montgomery Maze Pavilion is opened, increasing hospital capacity to 323 beds and 27 bassinets.

1977—Hospital surgeons perform the first organ transplant in the Hudson Valley.

1981—A building program adds a five-story nursing tower, and expands the emergency room, pediatrics,

coronary care and radiology units. By 1985, the Doctors' Pavilion building is completed, and other areas are modernized.

1995—Hospital stays are growing shorter because of new technology and health care costs. In response, the hospital debuts a new ambulatory care unit for same-day surgeries.

1995—The hospital celebrates 100 years in the community. Today the hospital has nine operating rooms, 375 acute care beds, 27 bassinets and more than 350 employees.

Information from the *Rockland Journal-News*.

Physician staff (left), c. 1900 (JSC). One of the modern additions of Nyack Hospital (above, photo by Linda Zimmermann, 2001).

Good Samaritan Hospital

By 1902, the population of Suffern had reached just over 1,800 people. There were four hotels, three churches, one school, a lumberyard, an opera house, and about 40 small stores that comprised the business district. On November 12, 1902, a seven-bed "emergency hospital" joined this growing community. A former mansion in the heart of town had been transformed into the Good Samaritan Hospital. How this small village became home to Rockland County's second hospital was the direct result of one of Suffern's seasonal residents, Mrs. Thomas Fortune Ryan.

Suffern had become an important and busy station on the main line of the Erie Railroad. New Yorkers, in search of a cool, quiet retreat to relieve the stress of their urban lifestyles, filled the passenger trains bound in summer for the surrounding rural regions. Relatively isolated prior to the 1860s, Suffern served as a welcome mat for the upstate Erie traveler. Twenty trains a day, loaded with seasonal tourists, stopped at the impressive Victorian depot. Word soon spread among travelers that "romantic scenery, fascinating beauty and rich land" could be found at the "pleasant summer resort." Suffern played host to the traveling public, whether accepting

the hospitality offered by the resort hotels and boarding houses or just switching trains.

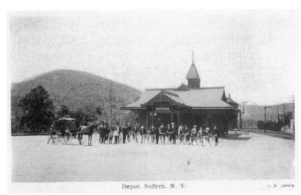

Suffern Depot postcard, c. 1900.   Marjorie Bauer.

The list of guests, visitors and part-time residents who were attracted to Suffern's rural charm included the names of many families from New York's affluent "upper crust." Some came as seasonal vacationers, choosing to rent an estate, while others bought property from the abundant amount of undeveloped land. Picturesque rolling hills and vast wooded lands guarded by the Ramapo Mountains provided a rustic setting for the development of elegant country estates.

One such estate was that of wealthy New York financier Thomas Fortune Ryan. In August 1897, the Ryans purchased the former Groesbeck mansion on the outskirts of town and developed a country estate that they called Montebello. Within three years, they had the elegant frame dwelling torn down and replaced with a large brick and stone mansion at a cost of $600,000. The new summer home contained such amenities as a two-lane bowling alley, an electric elevator, and a private chapel. Aside from a fashionable home on Fifth Avenue, the Ryans maintained homes in Washington, D.C., and a second summer home in Lovingston, Virginia, all reflecting the wealth of one of America's most prosperous and devoutly religious Irish Catholic families.

Postcard of Ryan estate, Montebello.   JSC

Thomas Fortune Ryan's riches were in vast contrast with his humble beginnings in rural Nelson County, Virginia. Orphaned at age nine, Ryan would eventually become the tenth wealthiest man in the nation. After leaving his native state in 1868, he traveled to Baltimore and found a job in the dry goods business of John S. Barry, a highly successful entrepreneur. It was at this time that Ryan met Ida M. Barry, the boss's daughter, whom he later married. Using his wife's wealth as a foundation on which to build his own, Ryan launched his business career. Upon moving to New York, he engaged in the stock market trade and at age 23 became the youngest man ever to purchase a seat on the New York Stock Exchange. From there he amassed millions in urban transit, railroads, tobacco, insurance, banking, rubber, diamonds, and even the Thompson submachine gun.

The Ryans were as generous to philanthropies as they were rich. It has been estimated that Mrs. Ryan gave $20 million dollars to various charities and endowments across the country. Most of these were affiliated with the Roman Catholic Church; however, there were also sizable donations to nonsectarian institutions as well. By 1905 it was reported that Mrs. Ryan's munificence

covered the building of "at least one hundred new chapel schools, churches, hospitals, homes for the Sisters of Charity and homes for the aged and infirmed."

Mrs. Ryan displayed a special fondness for her new neighbors by contributing equipment to the newly formed Suffern Fire Department. She also built a new church and established a girl's school and a seminary in Suffern, among other things. Shortly after the turn of the century, she turned her attention to the health needs of the community.

Prior to the opening of Good Samaritan Hospital, medical care was administered by one of Suffern's three local physicians. For any complicated illness or serious accident a person was required to travel to one of the area's local hospitals: St. Joseph's Hospital in Paterson, N.J., Nyack Hospital, or Middletown Hospital in neighboring Orange County. Such emergencies, however, did not always coincide with the railroad's timetable. Critically ill or injured individuals had to wait at the Suffern station for the next passing train. The alternative was to be transported by horse and wagon over rugged dirt roads. It comes as no surprise, the mortality rate in these cases was consistently high. If the injury didn't kill the patient, the trip usually did.

Just such a case of delayed medical treatment may have been the impetus for the founding of Good Samaritan Hospital. In the account most frequently related, and later recounted in an article that appeared in the *New York Herald,* Mrs. Ryan was at the Erie depot in the winter of 1901 waiting for her private railroad car, the *Pere Marquette.* Lying on a baggage cart, waiting to be put on a train bound for Paterson, was a trainman whose leg had been severed in an accident. Before he could be transported, the man died. Village physicians declared that if Suffern had had a proper medical facility, the man's life might have been saved.

Another event that probably helped motivate Mrs. Ryan occurred when the wife of her coachman suffered a ruptured tubal pregnancy. Dr. Sylvester Demarest of Suffern decided the patient could not be moved. He summoned Dr. John C. McCoy and nurse Frances Osborne of Paterson, and together they performed emergency surgery in the kitchen of the coachman's quarters above the Ryan stables.

Precisely what set of circumstances prompted Mrs. Ryan to underwrite the establishment of Good Samaritan Hospital will never be known for sure. The fact remains that Mrs. Ryan, through her concern and generosity, the trademark of her life, single-handedly spearheaded the hospital's birth.

By July of 1902, Mrs. Ryan had found a location for her hospital at Suffern. The former Maltbie/Messimer mansion, a Civil War era Italianate-style estate located on Orange Avenue and East Park Place (present site of O.T.B.), was purchased by Mrs. Ryan for $7,500. At the time of its acquisition, the mansion was in use by

Dr. William Eckoff, who had been conducting the Herbart Preparatory School. Since Mrs. Ryan negotiated to pay off the lease within five days, Dr. Eckoff was compelled to move at once.

Mrs. Ryan originally intended to call the hospital Good Samaritan Home. She felt that people might avoid a "hospital" due to the prevailing fear that people had of such an institution. But the doctors with whom she had consulted persuaded her to call it Good Samaritan Hospital.

The work of remodeling the mansion into a hospital was placed under the direction of George Sutherland, a carpenter who worked for the Ryans at Montebello. By late fall, the former estate was transformed into a seven-bed emergency hospital complete with a hand-operated elevator and fully equipped kitchen. The front parlor became the reception area and the cupola housed an operating room.

Familiar with St. Vincent's Hospital in New York City, and the Sisters of Charity who founded it, Mrs. Ryan had by this time approached the New Jersey community headquartered in Convent Station to run her fledgling hospital. Without any special ceremony, four sisters arrived on the morning of November 12, 1902, to take charge. Sister Melita was appointed superior, Sister Mary Basil, the cook and laundress, and Sisters Anna de Sales and Margaret Josephine were the nursing staff. They were greeted that day by Dr. Demarest and Mr. Sutherland. It was later recalled that "the carpenters were still working and the whole place had to be cleaned." However, the sisters did find the pantry well supplied and they all sat down to a "delicious" boiled ham dinner.

The medical staff consisted of six doctors, headed by Dr. Demarest of Suffern. He was joined by Drs. M.J. Sanford of Suffern, Frank E. Pagett of Spring Valley, John C. McCoy and Frank R. Sandt, both of whom were surgeons from Paterson, Raymond Kiefer of Ramsey, N.J., and Dr. E.C. Rushmore from Tuxedo was a consultant.

After the opening of the hospital, the pioneering sisters did virtually everything, "the kitchen work, house cleaning, care of the patients, and the operating room work." Good Samaritan Hospital saw its first patients on November 27. The admission book lists "Willie Mann, age 12, Hillburn, N.Y. Fractured Femur. John Rae, age 40 years, Suffern, N.Y. Stab wounds in thigh." Rates were $1 a day for the wards and $10 to $14 a day for a private room. Ten patients received care the following month. Joseph Sidgemore was the first patient to undergo surgery.

By the end of its first complete year, the hospital had to be expanded. Mrs. Ryan paid for the construction of a two-story addition and had a cottage built next to the hospital for a convent. The budget for that year was $4,529.44. The expenditures were as follows:

Provisions	$1,594.75
Wages	319.32
Repairs	193.38
Fuel and light	677.00
Medicines	768.00
Miscellaneous	976.99

In 1904 the New York State Board of Charities in Albany approved the charter for Good Samaritan Hospital. Mrs. Ryan continued to make numerous and sizable donations to the hospital. In 1905 she purchased the former John Young farm on Haverstraw Road and turned it over to the Sisters of Charity. This "fully equipped farm of 19 acres" was to supply food for the staff and patients at the hospital. Several months later she added to that gift the purchase of another property, the "old Jacob Wanamaker Mill," which included 40 acres. Local papers reported that farm produce from the estate would be sent to St. Vincent's Hospital in New York City.

In 1907, Mrs. Ryan, in recognition of her enormous contributions to the church, received from Pope Pius X the rare distinction of being proclaimed Countess of the Holy Roman Empire. Mr. Ryan was bestowed with the title of Marquis of the Papal Court.

In the decade that followed, numerous improvements were made to the institution. Patient care continued to improve as bed space increased to 35 patients. The hospital's medical staff added "3 specialists" and the horse-drawn ambulance was replaced by a new motorized vehicle. It was also during this decade that Good Samaritan Hospital's foundress, Mrs. Ida Ryan, died at the age of 62, October 17, 1917 at Montebello.

As Good Samaritan Hospital celebrated its 90th anniversary, it had become a modern 370-bed facility with a budget that exceeded $100 million and provided a full range of medical, surgical, psychiatric, and social services to the people of Rockland and Orange Counties as well as Bergen County, N.J.

What started out as a small humble seven-bed emergency hospital had burgeoned into a regional medical center. Almost 26 years to the day after Good Samaritan Hospital first opened the doors to the mansion on Orange Avenue, it closed those doors and relocated to its present site on Lafayette Avenue. Ironically, the land that the "new" hospital was built upon was once the property of Mrs. Ryan.

Craig Long, *SOM*, Oct./Dec. 1992

The evolution of Good Samaritan Hospital. The top two postcards (courtesy of Craig Long) depict the Maltbie/Messimer mansion (left) that was converted into the first hospital, and the "modern" brick hospital (right) built in 1938. Good Samaritan Hospital in 2002 (photo above, by Linda Zimmermann) shows the brick building in the center, now surrounded by the many additions.

...in 1903 President Roosevelt sends a message over the new Pacific Cable—the message takes only 9.5 minutes to reach Governor Taft in the Philippines, which is several hours shorter than it would have taken before the cable...The first coast to coast auto race takes 51 days...

Hillburn photo labeled: "Third Annual Clam Bake Blacksmiths and Machinists Aug. 22, 1903"
   Courtesy of Chuck Stead

The Haverstraw Landslide

Monday, January 8, 1906, was a bitterly cold and windy night. Snow from earlier that day lay in a blanket of white on the Village of Haverstraw as it sat majestically on the high bank of the Hudson River. On that fateful night, one of the county's worst disasters would destroy the northeast section of the village.

Since the beginning of time, rich deposits of clay and sand had lined the shore at Haverstraw—the very elements to make bricks. Unforeseen was that this unique and beneficial set of circumstances was both a blessing and a curse for Haverstraw.

As the brick industry thrived, workmen dug the clay back from the river into the high banks of the Hudson below the village. By the late 1890s there was some cause for concern as a series of small landslides occurred. Although they were not close to the business or residential sections, it should have been evident to the brickmakers that the constant clawing of the clay in the direction of the village was a prelude to disaster.

Haverstraw village officials, recognizing a public safety issue, went to court to "fight against ravages of the brickmakers, who threatened the streets of the village by burrowing clay." As litigation dragged on, it appeared that the brickmakers, the area's largest taxpayers, always seemed to find a way around the injunctions and restraining orders. The courts allowed the excavations to continue and the brickmakers dug dangerously close to populated areas.

About 4 p.m. on that cold Monday in 1906, a crack appeared on Rockland Street. That the clay bank was settling and the ground becoming unsteady caused alarm and concern among many. Some people evacuated, others chose to remain. Seven hours later, the cold of the winter encouraged residents to stoke the fire one last time and retire for the evening.

Suddenly, in an instant, the clay bank broke and a section just wide enough to take both sides of Rockland Street began to move. First it was like the movement of a distant earthquake and the buildings began to quiver. In a second the loosened sections of the bank gathered momentum and then, with a terrific roar, it began to move toward the chasm with the rapidity of lightning while the houses with a frightening grinding sound, were crushed like fragile glass vases.

What followed that first jolt was chaos and confusion as hundreds of village residents sprang from their beds and poured into the streets. Some thought Armageddon had come. Approximately 20 minutes later, a more horrific slide let go. The *New York Times* reported that the noise was a "loud rushing sound like the incoming of a huge wave as the soft clay slid out."

These slides took with them a crescent-shaped strip of land extending from Allison Avenue to Jefferson Street, dumping it 150 feet below into the dark clay pits of the Excelsior, Gillies, and Eckerson brickyards. Swallowed up in the cave-in were an entire block of Division Street and two blocks of Rockland Street: 13 houses and stores plunged into darkness.

A wall of flame suddenly enveloped the newly widened clay pit, as stoves in the houses overturned and set fire to them. Flames also shot out of ruptured gas lines.

Local firefighters gallantly battled the blaze, but the weather also played a factor as the *Times* reported that "the whole village might have been burned" had it not been for the blanket of snow. Three Haverstraw fire fighters were killed in the line of duty

Scores of men from the village banded together in "fearless acts of bravery" during the numerous rescue efforts to pull victims from the wreckage. Despite these efforts, the massive clay avalanche entombed at least 19 people.

Despite District Attorney Thomas Gagan's promise to "do my best to sift this disaster to the bottom," no criminal charges were ever filed. In an ironic twist, the brickmakers actually profited from the landslide, as over $200,000 worth of clay had slid down onto their properties.

Photo courtesy of John Scott.
Article by Craig Long, *SOM*, Jan./March 1996

41

Prejudice and racial tension are not limited to the Southern states or large cities. Rockland County has unfortunately been the scene of several incidents where the acts of individuals or small groups led to opinions and reactions against entire sections of the population. Throughout the century, minorities, ethnic groups and members of various religions have tasted the bitterness of prejudice and persecution.

Yellow Journalism on Black and White Issues

It is August 1905. You, an established merchant in Nyack have just settled down in your favorite chair to the paper and your evening cup of coffee. Your paper, the *Star*, is a daily published by the same firm that puts out *City and Country*. On its front page, in scare headlines three columns wide, you read, with horror, "HUNT FOR NEGRO MURDERERS, 1 MAN KILLED, 1 WOUNDED."

Had your paper been the *Evening Journal*—the *Rockland County Journal's* daily counterpart—the headline would have been somewhat more restrained, "POLICE OFFICER SHOT DEAD."

From the stories themselves, you would have discovered that the Chief of Police of Haverstraw, together with two of his officers, had been on patrol Saturday night looking for persons who might be carrying concealed weapons. It was standard procedure. They had stopped at a dance hall in the "Black Belt" where, according to the *Star*, a cakewalk was under way— to the *Journal* it was the "usual negro orgy," to search the patrons. These searches, a common occurrence in the Belt, were greatly resented. During the search, one man, while waiting his turn, suddenly pulled out a revolver and shot point blank at the two officers, killing one outright and wounding the other. Despite return fire by the Chief, he escaped.

On the following day, a suspect was apprehended upriver, in Newburgh. According to the *Journal*, "Word of this arrest soon spread through the village (Haverstraw), and a large body of men, some of whom had ropes with them, went to the station to meet the train." Fortunately, a warning about the lynching party had been telegraphed ahead, and it did not stop at the station that day. In subsequent newspaper accounts, this suspect was not mentioned again. Other than his having been at the dance hall on the fatal night, there was nothing to indicate he had had any role in the shooting.

A follow-up story in September in *City and Country*, reported, under a headline announcing that the priests in Haverstraw planned to carry arms for their personal safety, that:

Conditions in the village are serious and the better class of citizens declare that if the police do not soon act in the matter they will take the law into their own hands and drive the negroes out of the vicinity even though they have to kill a few of them to teach them a lesson. The record of the month of August shows that there have been four murders, one of them of a police officer; several attempted murders, one of the victims also a cop, and innumerable assaults on citizens, all committed by negroes inflamed by cheap liquor. Armed negroes have openly paraded in the streets and insulted men and women and have congregated in the 'black and tan' dives and made nights and Sundays hideous with vile language and actions.

After two additional murders in October, the cry for a lynching was raised again. Of these murders, the *Journal's* reporter wrote, "The two crimes, both the work of the negro element, aroused the townspeople, and all that saved the colored people from a visitation of wrath yesterday was the lack of a leader."

Circumspection prevailed even in the instance of the Haverstraw police murder. Some three years later, the son of one of those shot in 1905 announced that he had proof positive against one "Red Henry," a notorious hood with a long record of violence, and that Henry had been located in a New Jersey jail. Nevertheless, the Sheriff made no move to extradite. The excitement was over, and practical considerations about costs involving incarceration and trial discouraged the passion for revenge.

Most of these lurid stories featuring brawling and murderous assault in 1905 originate in Haverstraw. Nyack, by contrast, comes off in its newspapers as a place of peace and harmony. It was a commonplace for editors of that day, whatever their political stripe, to use Haverstraw, together with Piermont, as convenient foils when reflecting on the glories of the "Gem of the Hudson." An editorial in *City and Country* in April 1905 entitled "Church Influence in Nyack" reflects this indulgence. Describing Nyack as a "village of churches" the editorial adds:

Besides the natural beauty and attractiveness of the place, acknowledged by all who see it, Nyack is one of the most peaceful and law abiding towns of its size on the map of the world. Where can you find less criminals, less crime, or less disorderly drunkenness? Nowhere...

Nevertheless, and before 1905 had ended, the "village of churches," also was to have its own bout with violence. And, as was so often the case with its sister village to the north, that violence highlighted racial prejudice in the community. Late in November that year, a desperate young man named Jones, rebuffed in love, entered a Nyack house and shot the two brothers of the young woman whose affection he sought. He then attempted to set fire to the house. Subsequently, one of the two died; the other was badly hurt. The streets of the village soon filled with people calling for blood. It was said that a lynching was planned should Jones be apprehended, but the opportunity never materialized. The next morning he was found in a nearby churchyard, dead by a bullet wound. He had taken his own life.

Jones was described in a story in the *Nyack Star* as "light complexion" and "apparently Caucasian to the casual observer." Nevertheless, inch-high headlines over the story announced, "EXTRA! NEGRO MANIAC LOVER KILLS." In an editorial referring to the murder and suicide, the *Journal,* for its part, commented, "Jones' nativity is not known, but his claim to be a Cuban is improbable, for while his complexion was light, it is likely he carries a minor strain of negro blood." The newspaper then went on to conjecture that this presumed "minor strain" may have prompted Jones rejection. "Not one member of the distressed family ever in any way gave the slightest encouragement to his advances," the *Journal* added. Summarizing the lessons to be drawn from the unfortunate incident, the paper concluded, "For the sake of this locality it may be said that the individual who wrought this evil was neither native nor a resident of Nyack."

The episodes, themselves, are idiosyncratic, the responses by the general public, while menacing, insubstantial. Normally, it was the perpetrators, themselves, who were most hurt by their own outrageous acts. Ugly but incidental, these occurrences apparently existed, or were offered up by local editors and reporters as existing outside the range of normal interaction. In their opinion, such violence had no object and did not represent responses that made sense to proper Rocklanders.

Poor, unhappy Jones, and Red Henry, with his smoking gun, both represent defiance. They had responded to their plight by striking out directly against whites. In earlier years, the black people of Rockland County, no matter what the indignity, had always sought to keep their troubles to themselves, to maintain a low profile. As for the whites, the recurring invitations to lynching parties were also uncharacteristic. Mostly, cool indifference to what went on with the blacks had been their common pose.

One explanation for these disruptions to the normal order lies, no doubt, in the fact that with the century's turn, the age of yellow journalism had begun. In recent years, the village newspapers had become dailies, and each new day brought hungry space to fill. To slake that voracious appetite, the newspaper people turned private distress into public entertainment.

But technical advances in handling news and the profits to be earned out of public excitement are not the only explanations for the tumult. There actually were an extraordinary number of murders. Forces, which can be blandly described as social and economic, apparently were promoting discord and confusion on a broad scale. And, at their core, was a profound transformation in lifestyles, one that, while long in coming, had reached crescendo proportions by the turn of the century.

Carl Nordstrom, *Phoenician Tales*

The Southern Negroes who come here in the summer months to labor in the various yards are, as a rule, better citizens than the foreigners; they are more thrifty and cause less trouble than any class of brickyard workers…For every colored brickyard laborer that is in the court for drunkenness and disorderly conduct there are at least ten Slavs, Dagos, Greasers, Syrians, and what not…
City and Country, February 10, 1906

The thrill of adventure has led some Rockland residents to exotic and remote locations. One of the most famous of those world travelers is highlighted in the following article.

Leonidas Hubbard
Explorer of Labrador

At the time of his 1903 expedition to Labrador, Leonidas Hubbard was an editor for *Outing,* a popular adventure magazine in New York City, and he was living on 32 Friend Street in Congers with his wife, Mina Benson Hubbard, a native of Canada. He also lived, or had a summer home, in Wurtsboro in Sullivan County, New York. But neither Wurtsboro nor Congers was his native home.

Leonidas Hubbard, Jr., was born on a Michigan farm on July 12, 1872 and came from a family that could trace its Dutch and English roots back to the 17th century. In 1899, with supposedly only $5 in his pocket, he came to New York City and found employment contributing articles to the *Daily News* and the *Saturday Evening Post,* including one noteworthy article on the preservation of Adirondack Park. Around 1900 Hubbard contracted typhoid fever, which forced him to spend a period of time convalescing in Wurtsboro.

After his recovery he took on a position as assistant editor of *Outing* and probably at that time began to live in Congers. It was in the late fall of 1901 while walking in the Shawangunk Mountains near Wurtsboro with his friend and fellow journalist Dillon Wallace that Hubbard first mentioned the idea of going to Labrador. The interior of

Labrador, explained Hubbard to Wallace, was one of the last unexplored regions of North America.

For the next year and a half Hubbard made preparations for the trip with final approval coming from *Outing* magazine in January 1903. A large map of Labrador hung on the wall of his home in Congers, which Hubbard and Wallace, who would accompany him on the trip, studied intensely.

On July 15, 1903, Leonidas Hubbard, accompanied by Dillon Wallace and a half-blooded Cree Indian by the name of George Elson, left the Northwest River Post of the Hudson Bay Company for the George River, 150 miles in the interior. Using what appears now to have been faulty geological survey maps, the party went up the Susan River rather than the Nascaupee River. This mistake would prove costly, taxing their food supply and energy. They were within sight of their goal, Lake Michikamau on September 15, but with a dangerously low food supply, decided to abandon their original plan and go back the way they came.

The trek back to the Hudson Bay Company post became a race for survival. Unable to find much food other than some fish and an occasional bird, their situation became desperate, especially for Hubbard, who was left in a makeshift hut while the other two continued on. Later Wallace was also too weak to go on and had to be left, leaving Elson to get help. Finally Elson managed to reach the post, and a rescue party set out in the snow for Wallace and Hubbard. Wallace was found alive but Hubbard had already died many days before.

Hubbard's body was recovered in the spring and brought back to the U.S. and laid to rest in Haverstraw.

Wallace recorded:

We laid him to rest in a beautiful spot in the little cemetery at Haverstraw, at the very foot of the mountains that he used to roam, and overlooking the grand old Hudson that he loved so well. The mountains will know him no more, and never again will he dip his paddle into the placid waters of the river; but his noble character; his simple faith, a faith that never wavered, but grew the stronger in his hour of trouble, his bravery, his indomitable will—these shall not be forgotten; they shall remain a living example to all who love bravery and self-sacrifice.

(At the time of the expedition, Hubbard was a Sunday school teacher at a church in Congers, and apparently this church used Mount Repose in Haverstraw as a resting place for its members.)

Hubbard looks forward to his trek into the wilds of Labrador.   JSC

During his Labrador expedition, Hubbard kept a diary in which one can find several references to Congers. On October 8 he wrote:

How I wish for that vacation in Michigan or Canada! or a good quiet time at Congers..

Mina Benson Hubbard was determined that her husband's work would not go unfinished. So in a bold decision and accompanied by George Elson and other scouts, she went to Labrador in 1905 in an attempt to complete her husband's work. Her experiences were recorded in her book, *A Woman's Way through Unknown Labrador,* published in 1909.

Mrs. Hubbard was to place three tablets near her husband's grave, honoring his bravery, her adventures and the heroism of George Elson:

1872-1903
To the memory of Leonidas Hubbard,Jr.
Sportsman-Writer-Explorer-Christian
Who died in his tent in Labrador alone-
but in spirit triumphant and free.

To record
Completion in 1905 of his undertaking by Mina Benson Hubbard, his wife, who explored and mapped the Nascaupee and George Rivers, thereby obtaining world recognition of his work and for all time associating his name with Labrador.

To the honor of George Elson
Faithful guide, who recovered Mr. Hubbard's body and his records from the interior of Labrador in the depth of winter and whose devotion made possible Mrs. Hubbard's work 1903-1905.

Anthony X. Sutherland, *SOM*, Oct./Dec. 1993

The Jewish Community
1900-1909

The Congregation Sons of Jacob, in Haverstraw, survived the disastrous landslide of January 8, 1906, but Rabbi Alden lost his life while attempting to aid Harry and Benjamin Nelson, members of the congregation, in their downtown store. Wolf Provitch, Mr. and Mrs. Abraham Silverman, residents of the community also died in the landslide. David Eldenbaum, a door-to-door peddler, from Brooklyn and William Hughes also perished.

The synagogue's cemetery behind Mt. Repose Cemetery on Route 9W was established. The Baum family plot, nearby, was the first Jewish cemetery in the county.

Harold L. Laroff

Rockland County Sports Hall of Fame

In 1974, the Rockland County Sports Hall of Fame was founded by former County Clerk and New York State Senator, Joe Holland. The Hall of Fame's purpose is to honor outstanding athletes and sports figures who either gained prominence while living in Rockland, or who have brought fame and recognition to the county. Each year, five new members are inducted, and individual plaques bearing their names are added to the collection housed in the Allison-Parris County Office Building in New City.

While many inductees had careers spanning more than one decade, they have been listed in the decade most significant to their careers or the decade that began their career.   Hall of Fame information is courtesy of Jamie Kempton.

1900-1909

John Koster (West Nyack, b. Germany) "Long John" Koster is the premier bowler in Rockland County history. First bowler to win four American Bowling Congress titles. Charter member of the ABC Hall of Fame. Had an 819 series and bowled 19 perfect games over his forty-year career.

Victor Shankey (Haverstraw) One of 15 children, Shankey was a baseball player known for his many home runs. Played with Yankee minor league organization. Ended professional career upon entering military service in World War I. Was Town of Haverstraw Supervisor for 36 years.

Pearl River basketball team, the "Uniques," in 1909. There is no question they are unique by today's standards.   OTM

45

1910-1919

Telephones
Automobiles
Flying Machines
and
War

Arguably, no other decade in history witnessed so many dramatic changes. In 1910, telephones and automobiles were limited to very few households. The sight of an airplane in the skies brought people running into the streets. Women's clothing was still elaborate and restrictive (mirroring their places in society), and the idea of the "weaker sex" earning the right to vote was considered laughable by the overwhelming majority of men.

The American male felt confident in his dominant position in his home, in local politics and in his country's place on the world stage. He still thought, acted and dressed much as his father and grandfather had, to the point that the "modern" practice of wearing a watch on one's wrist was considered to be too effeminate. Real gentlemen wore pocket watches, upheld the stuffy conventions of years past, and never dreamed of allowing their wives to work outside the home and earn money.

By 1919, old world customs, manners and morals had been shattered by the First World War. As men left their cities, towns and villages and answered the call of military service, women shed their corsets and pitched in on the home front, or even went to Europe as nurses. A generation of young people suddenly saw that their lives didn't have to follow the same path as their parents. A line from a popular song summed up the changes the war brought about: "How can you keep them down on the farms, after they've seen Paris?"

Even for those who remained at home, shortages touched every household and casualty lists stunned the most complacent individuals. Ten million men died during the war, and at least another twenty million people would perish in the influenza epidemic that spread across the globe through infected soldiers. For perhaps the first time in its history, America realized just how small the world had become. Isolation and innocence were gone, and the new inventions and technologies would greatly accelerate the changes already coming about.

The next decade would find women in Rockland driving cars to work, male politicians trying to win female's votes, once remote farms only a phone call away, and a new generation that didn't look or act anything like the world had ever seen.

A day at the beach at Fort Comfort in Piermont (left). The office of Dr. Pardington (above), 1915. West Nyack butcher making deliveries, c.1915 (bottom left). The first class at the Pigknoll School in Pomona (below), c. 1915.   JSC

Impact of the Car

Main Street in Spring Valley looks dramatically different in the span of less than a decade, from a few carriages and horses (and resulting droppings in the middle of the street), to long lines of new automobiles. The economic and social changes brought on by the car were staggering. Small, isolated communities became accessible to commuters and developers. Suburbia was born, and Rockland, in particular, would experience the associated growing pains throughout the remainder of the century.

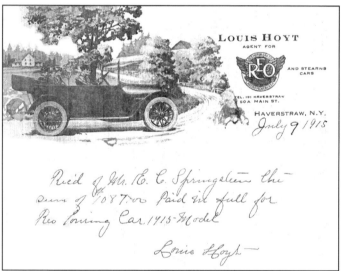

This receipt (left) is for a new Reo Touring Car, dated July 9, 1915. The dealer was Louis Hoyt of Haverstraw, the famous Rockland racecar driver, and the amount paid by Mr. Springsteen of Summit Park for the new automobile was $1,087. (Reo cars were very expensive for the time.)

Mr. Springsteen also received a handwritten guarantee signed by Hoyt. The guarantee assured that any part that broke would be replaced for free, for a period of two years.

As automobiles hit the roads of Rockland, they were bound to start hitting other things. This 1918 photograph (below) of a car accident on Kings Highway in Valley Cottage is the earliest known photo of an accident in Rockland.

Such accidents were bound to happen; in the early days the county's bumpy dirt roads had no traffic lights and no street lighting, and cars had no directional signals. Originally, a driver didn't even need a license. Linda Zimmermann

Hoyt letter courtesy of Rachel Crum Kaufmann, photos courtesy of John Scott.

...China abolishes slavery in 1910...Roald Amundsen reaches the South Pole in 1911...Titanic sinks in 1912...Robert Goddard begins his experiments with rockets in 1914...Einstein presents his General Theory of Relativity in 1915...

A-1586. Old Barker Farm, Near Congers, N. Y.

For the most part, Rockland's roads were dirt, packed down by centuries of wagon wheels. This typical road in Congers (left) passed by the Barker farm.

By the end of the twentieth century, Route 9W would be one of the busiest roads in the county, but in 1915, this section in Upper Nyack (below, left) was hardly ready for the age of the automobile. JSC

Cinder Road

The present Central Highway in Garnerville and Stony Point was originally the roadbed of a branch of the New York and New Jersey Railroad. The railroad came to an end at the present intersection of Central Highway and Route 210 in Stony Point. South of the present intersection of Filor's Lane and Central Highway was the North Haverstraw station with a turntable to turn the coal-powered steam engines. At the end of run, the engineers had to dump the cinders. The owner of the Garner West estate invited the engineers to dump the cinders on the dirt road leading to his mansion,

thereby providing a better base for the road. The local people soon came to call the road "the cinder road." Years later, when Haverstraw and Stony Point took over the road, it was given the official name of Cinder Road.   Robert Burghardt

The First Bridges to Open Rockland

In the early years of the 1900s—especially 1916 to 1922—engineers began to see Rockland County as being more than just agricultural. In 1790 our area was about 90% agricultural, in 1860 about 60%, in 1910 about 30% and by 1987 only 3%. Forward-looking people saw the county as a prize to be opened for new homes and population growth, but the dangerous gorge at the north entrance to the county near Bear Mountain and the chasm where the Sparkill Creek flowed near Rockland's south border were two handicaps to development. Thus, when the Popolopen Creek at the north entrance was spanned in 1916, as was the Sparkill Creek about the same time, the county's future was forever changed.

Other bridges quickly followed to complete Rockland's transition to a residential and commercial status: one over the Beaver Pond Creek at Stony Point

in 1922; the Bear Mountain-Hudson River Bridge on November 26, 1924; the George Washington Bridge on October 25, 1931; and finally the Tappan Zee Bridge on December 15, 1955, which put the finishing touches to our county's private, pastoral existence.

The following is an article that appeared in the *Rockland County Times* of July 20, 1916:

FORMALLY OPEN—NEW BRIDGE
Dangerous "Hell Hole" eliminated... Is higher than the Brooklyn Bridge

"Hell Hole" is no more. It is only a memory. Instead of the rickety old wooden bridge spanning the gorge of Popolopen Creek just below the dam, there stands a magnificent steel and concrete cantilever bridge, 600 feet one inch in length and 153 feet above tide water. The new bridge is higher than the famous Brooklyn Bridge. Instead of the dangerous curves and steep dip down to the old bridge, on one side the sheer mountains, on the other the yawning precipice, guided by only a broken down wooden fence, there is a straightaway boulevard, commanding one of the finest views along the Hudson River.

Daniel deNoyelles, *SOM*, July/Aug. 1987

The construction of the Bear Mountain Bridge (right) in 1923-24 and the opening of the Popolopen Bridge in 1916 (below). JSC

...In 1911, Harriet Quimby is the first woman in the United States to earn a pilot's license...Charles Kettering invents a self-starter for the automobile, which replaces the need to crank the engine manually...Chevrolet Motors is incorporated...In 1913 Grand Central Station opened in NYC...The final section of the Panama Canal is blasted, joining the waters of the Atlantic and Pacific...

Harry Atwood and His Flying Machine

When Harry N. Atwood, one of early aviation's now largely forgotten stars, was forced to land his biplane in an Upper Nyack field on August 24, 1911, during a headline-making flight from St. Louis to New York, it would have been hard to say who were more excited, the scores of local residents who rushed to the site or the editors of Nyack's two daily newspapers, the *Rockland County Journal* and the *Nyack Evening Star*.

Flying machines were still so new...it had been about eight years since Wilbur and Orville Wright had proved such contraptions could be made to fly. Few, if any, Rocklanders had ever been close to a plane. Police had to guard the craft to keep the souvenir-prone from carrying away its moveable parts. "People had to content themselves with writing their names on the canvas,

which was covered already with signatures of persons from places where Atwood had landed," said the *Star*.

As for the editors, their newspapers scooped the New York press.

The Nyack papers had carried occasional reports on Atwood's progress, but it had been "big news" in the city papers ever since he had tuned up the tiny engine on his biplane ten days earlier in the Missouri city and had set out for New York in an effort to capture the world record for man's longest trip by air. The young Boston aviator already had in his pocket the record he sought when a connecting rod on his plane broke as he was rounding Hook Mountain on his way down the Hudson from a stop at Cold Spring. He was compelled to land in a pasture on the W. D. Davies property, just

50

west of the present Nyack Tennis Club courts on North Broadway.

Thanks to the enterprise of George Helmle, publisher of the *Rockland County Journal,* hundreds of local residents were waiting along the river to watch "the daring navigator of the air" pass the Nyacks. Helmle had arranged with the *Newburgh Journal* to wire him the moment Atwood reached Newburgh and to have three blasts blown on the whistle of the Peerless Finishing Company factory at Nyack to alert villagers that the plane would soon be over the Tappan Zee.

Atwood, "600 feet in the air," was rounding Hook Mountain, his plane clearly visible to the waiting spectators, when the plane suddenly veered and disappeared from sight. While people waited for his reappearance, Atwood had come down in the Davies' hayfield and cow pasture. He narrowly missed a hayrick in landing, but he was uninjured and his aircraft undamaged.

One of the few who actually witnessed Atwood's landing was John Logue of Nyack, now 87, then a 14-year-old delivery boy for Sayres' meat market. Logue was pedaling his bicycle north on Broadway, Upper Nyack, with an order for the LeRoy Frost home around 11:30 a.m. When nearly there, he saw "this thing" come flying around Hook Mountain, then "plummet to the ground" in a pasture just over the brow of a nearby hill. Abandoning the order of meat he was supposed to be delivering to the care of a workman nearby, he set off as

fast as he could to investigate. He found that "the thing" he had seen was Atwood's plane. He didn't dare stay long enough to get a really good look at the aircraft, but he remembers that it "was an open plane and that the flier sat out in front." When Logue returned to pick up the order he was supposed to be delivering, he found the meat had been stolen. His employer, he says, gave him the devil and told him never to do that again but did not make him pay for the meat.

Reporters for the two Nyack newspapers lost little time in getting there. If the accident had to happen, as far as they were concerned, it couldn't have happened at a better time. With 1 p.m. deadlines, they still could write their stories for that day's papers and have them in print before the New York papers came out with their editions.

During all this, the calmest of everybody was Atwood himself. Assured that the plane would be unharmed, Atwood walked to the nearby home of Wilson P. Foss and put in a telephone call to Sheepshead Bay to tell the people who were waiting for his arrival there that afternoon what had happened. He also called B. W. Church at the Hudson Yacht and Boat Company (now Petersen's Shipyard) to see what could be done about repairing the connecting rod. It was fixed by machinist Henry Koch, who worked nearly all night on it.

In the meantime, Nyackers enjoyed having a celebrity in their midst. The *Rockland Journal* and the

Atwood and his flying machine in Nyack. JSC

Nyack Star reported Atwood's comings and goings as carefully as today's *Journal-News* would those of the astronauts if they were to land in the county.

The first to offer Atwood hospitality was Foss, who invited him to be his guest for lunch at the Hotel St. George—an offer which the *Star* said he accepted "with alacrity." That evening, the flier was a dinner guest at the Davies' home. The family also invited him to stay overnight, but there were so many telephone calls for him while he was there that, to save the Davies from being annoyed by more, he came back to the St. George.

Early the next morning (August 25), he was back in Upper Nyack. Atwood had hoped to take off for New York, but two things prevented it: an apple tree on the property of Miss Elizabeth Green, directly south of the Davies' field, was in the way of a take-off; and it began to rain.

Miss Green was not at home, but neighbors thought if she were, she would give permission for her tree to be cut down, the *Journal* said. Davies took the responsibility.

Atwood asked for 25 volunteers to help him get the plane to another field. Instead of 25, the *Star* reported, "everyone who could get a hand on the machine did so, some 50 persons all told," moved it to the fence separating the Davies and Green properties. "There were some small trees in the way and someone got permission to cut them down. This done the plane was lifted over two fences and into the open field. From this position there was a fairway to the river." According to the *Journal* it took nearly half an hour to start the motor. In priming it, some gasoline escaped and caught fire. "This was fortunately put out, but it caused a great deal of excitement…After another effort the propeller began to whirl, and, to the cheering of the crowd, the young and fearless aviator was off." He passed over the Nyacks "going at a tremendous speed" (probably no more than 50 miles an hour).

Forty-two minutes after his Upper Nyack take-off, Atwood landed on Governor's Island, having stopped at Yonkers on the way. Atwood received $10,000 in prize money from Victor Evans, a Washington attorney, and a St. Louis newspaper paid the flier $1,500.

Virginia Parkhurst, *SOM*, April/June 1984

Ferry Tales of the Hudson

The ferry experience was once as intrinsic to the Hudson River as the small villages and towering scenery which frame its banks. As a cradle for much of the ferry's evolution from an oar-driven, hollow log to a diesel-powered goliath capable of carrying hundreds of passengers and automobiles, the Hudson was rewarded with a fleet of ferries that traversed its breadth from New York City to Albany. Now the ferry, and its subtle pleasures, are all but lost to the river.

The three principal ferry routes, from Tarrytown to Nyack, from Yonkers to Alpine, N.J., and from Dobbs Ferry to Snedens Landing, supplied the area with more than just transportation in their almost 250 years of service.

The dozens of boats which traversed the Hudson during that era, and the memorable men and women who worked them, imparted to the river color and life and a palpable identity. Eventually, the ferries succumbed one by one to a more hurried pace of life and the bridges that now effortlessly span the Hudson.

But in their era, the ferries dominated the life of the Hudson as the more glamorous, graceful steamers and sailing ships never did. Ferries were accessible; they were the turtle to the steamship's hare, winning river residents' hearts with their reliability and their longevity. Their passing marked the end of a more romantic and less pedestrian era.

One ferry line ended quite abruptly: The sky looked foreboding to Richard Salmon as he got off the train at Dobbs Ferry. It was about noon, on Sept. 21,1938 and he was returning to his home in Sneden's Landing after an abbreviated day of work in New York City. Rain had begun to fall, and the wind whipped up whitecaps on the normally tranquil Hudson. It was with reservations that he boarded the small pedestrian ferry that took him across the river on the last leg of his daily commute. "The wind was going like mad as we crossed the river," he said. "When we got to the dock, I could see we were in for a big blow, and I warned the captain, a fellow by the name of Joe Niero, 'Don't go back for the next train.'" Niero, a stubborn, former bricklayer who had commanded the 20-foot boat, the *Katamah*, for about 10 years, ignored the advice and returned through the choppy water to Dobbs Ferry. There was no one waiting. (Salmon had been the only passenger on the previous crossing.)

While Niero went up to the train station in search of fares, the storm—a nascent hurricane—began pounding the area in its full force. He waited futilely, then in disgust, returned through the driving rain to the dock. The ferry was gone. It had been ripped from its mooring and dragged under water. So ended the reign of one of the longest-lived ferries on the Hudson.

It was begun in 1729 by a descendant of English immigrants, William Dobbs, a 23-year-old who lived with his new bride on the Manor of Phillipsburgh near the river. Dobbs, a farmer, a fisherman and, apparently, an entrepreneur, decided to supplement his income by taking travelers across the river in a hollowed-out, flat-bottomed log, called a periauger, that he had to propel with oars.

When the Dobbs relinquished control of the ferry in 1759, it was taken over by their neighbors across the river, the Snedens. The Snedens retained control of the route until the ferry entered its modern incarnation as a motor boat in the early twentieth century. When it died, there was little call for a revival: Its existence had been rendered a luxury by the bridges which already were beginning to appear over the Hudson, and by the larger and more imposing ferries south at Yonkers, and north at Tarrytown, which had long overwhelmed the diminutive descendants of Dobbs' Ferry with their size, their number, and their impact on the river.

Tarrytown was by the mid-nineteenth century a more logical setting for a river crossing than Dobbs Ferry and its direct juxtaposition across the river with another thriving community, Nyack, created a need for a link between the communities' merchants and farmers. Thus the residents of the two communities chartered a wealthy landowner with large holdings on the waterfront to begin ferry service in 1839, requiring "that at all reasonable times between sunrise and sunset a boat shall be kept in readiness to transport passengers, horses, carriages, cattle, wagons, etc., across the river."

Cars waiting in Nyack to take the ferry
Rockland to Tarrytown, c. 1912-15.   JSC

The popularity of that first ferry across the Tappan Zee led to larger, faster successors. The growth of the line proceeded uninterrupted until the third ferry to ply the waters, the paddle wheeler *Tappan Zee,* caught on fire at its dock in Nyack on a spring night in 1887. A new ferry appeared on the river in 1888. This one was something special. It was large and white and immaculate, a magnificent prototype of the ferry boat of the era.

The *Rockland* was a memorable boat, perhaps the most famous ferry ever to toil on the Hudson, with a personality and a flair that became known to several generations of the area's residents. It was a perfect ferry for the run between Tarrytown and Nyack—large

enough to carry many carriages and later, automobiles, in addition to more than one hundred passengers, but sufficiently small and nimble to avoid the sandbars which plagued navigators of the Tappan Zee. Its captain complemented and augmented the *Rockland's* special status. John Lyon, a 5-foot Scotsman with cotton-white hair and beard, blue eyes, and a red complexion, was a feisty little riverman who piloted his ferry with fierce pride and unmatched skill and "the loudest voice!—you could hear him saying 'All ab-o-a-a-a-r-r-d' all the way up to the Tarrytown railroad station."

The ferry *Rockland,* with its indomitable captain, John Lyon, standing near the wheelhouse.   JSC

One of Lyon's crewmen for many years, John Rice, said Lyon was a complete dictator while aboard his ferry. In a newspaper interview in 1949, Rice (who died in 1955) said Lyon once saw a man "who weighed 250 pounds if he weighed an ounce" sneak on the ferry without paying the 25-cent fare. The 5-foot captain jumped on the man's back with a vengeance and forced him to fork over the quarter.

Still, Lyon could be a merry man, and under his captaincy the *Rockland* was often a floating party. As long as passengers did not disembark, Lyon permitted them to ride as many times as they wanted for a single fare. During the summer, women from as far south as Yonkers would take their sewing and their children and spend the afternoon riding back and forth across the river. (At the time, doctors commonly advised mothers to expose their children to the sun and fresh air as a means of preventing disease.)

While the women talked and sunned themselves on the top deck, Rice often was charged with entertaining the children down in the boiler room. He'd keep them busy by showing them how to operate the ship and by telling them stories, shooing them with mock seriousness when they became too playful. Rice also obliged mothers and nursemaids by tying a string around baby bottles and heating them in the boiler.

A ferry war begun in 1912 ended the relaxed atmosphere aboard the *Rockland*. The North Ferry River Company challenged Lyon's supremacy on the Tappan Zee, leasing his Tarrytown berth out from under him and starting a new ferry, the *Rye Cliff*, on the route. The *Rockland* temporarily had to cease operations before Lyon managed to lease another slip for his ferry. Then the war was on in earnest.

Lyon used his knowledge of the Tappan Zee to embarrass the *Rye Cliff*, steaming past it with his horn sounding as the larger, inexperienced craft piled up on the sandbars and maneuvered laboriously to get into its slip. His competitors quickly shifted to another boat, then another, and finally a fourth before finding a ferry that could keep up with the veteran. The *Rockland* and its challenger, the *Flushing*, would race across the river, cutting each other off, and "actually bumping each other, and stopping halfway across to go back and pick up passengers so as to steal them from each other. People used to go down to the waterfront just to watch the competition."

Lyon maintained the upper hand until the *Flushing's* captain became so frustrated one day he rammed the *Rockland* as the two boats battled for position. Neither ship was badly damaged, but the *Flushing's* captain and pilot had their licenses suspended. Lyon kept his white ferry running until his death in 1923. The *Rockland* continued to run for three years before the North Ferry River Company bought it out, with the *Rockland* winding up as a summer home for a Perth Amboy, N.J. resident. With much of the color and romance gone, and with increased competition from the George Washington to the south, the Nyack-to-Tarrytown ferry began losing business and was discontinued as unprofitable in 1941.

Small pedestrian ferries were operated periodically after that until the construction of the Tappan Zee Bridge in 1954. But the demise of the *Rockland* and then the route it established signalled the imminent death of the Hudson River ferry boat.

Bill Falk, *The Journal-News*, 9/10/78

This original ferry schedule from 1915 (right) had the timetable on one side and a photo of the *Flushing* (left) on the other.

JSC

The Emeline

Emeline Park on the river in the village of Haverstraw is named for a once-famous river boat that used to dock there. The *Emeline* was a high-speed paddle wheel steamer bought in 1885 by Capt. D.C. Woolsy, who lived in a multi-columned Greek revival house on Front Street. The *Emeline* had Haverstraw as its home port and made all the local stops between Haverstraw and Newburgh.

The shopping trip from Haverstraw started with a sail through the Hudson Highlands to Newburgh, a walk up the hill to all the department stores, lunch and more shopping, then a return to the dock for the trip downstream to Haverstraw. This was a means of travel for a more leisurely time!

But "progress" was to overtake the *Emeline* in the guise of the West Shore Railroad and later the first automobiles. Then her end came in 1918. The winter of 1917-18 was one of the coldest in Rockland County with eight straight days below zero, one of them being 16 below zero. People crossed the Hudson to Croton by skates or horse-drawn sleighs.

Unfortunately, the sudden freeze caught the *Emeline* unawares at her dock in Haverstraw and twelve inches of ice crushed her hull causing her to sink in the mud. No attempts were made to raise her and over the years she began to disintegrate and sink further. When interest was finally revived in trying to salvage something, the action of the tides, currents and mud had wiped out all traces of this once proud steamboat.

Robert Burghardt

The Daily Commute?

In 1917, with many Rockland men off to war, Lederle Labs hired women to fill the vacancies. However, getting the women there was a problem, especially in winter, so this sled ran from Nyack to the plant in Pearl River to transport the employees.

(Mr. Palmer is the driver, Margaret Springsteen is fifth from left, second row and Dorothy Haerle, second from right, second row.) JSC

In the time before reliable automobiles and effective snowplows, horse-drawn sleds were the most sensible means of travel in snow.

This photo, taken in 1910, shows Jim Finegan with his brewmaster in a "one-horse open sleigh." The brewery, owned by Thomas Finegan, was on West Broad Street in Haverstraw. JSC

Halloween in Haverstraw

Halloween was a great time in Haverstraw. There wasn't as much vandalism as there is now. There was an occasional gate that disappeared, but there weren't that many gates around our area anyway, and no outhouses to be pushed over. What the kids in our neighborhood would do would be to go to Hall's blacksmith shop, which was next door to Washington Hall on West Street, steal a wagon and haul it through the streets. I think Mr. Hall would purposely leave an old wagon out front which we would take, because most of the others were generally chained.

We didn't have any costumes or masks. Our false faces were usually a black stocking with holes cut out for the eyes, nose and mouth, and another stocking would be filled with flour or dried horse manure, which we got at Hall's also. I never had flour in mine. When we met up with the other gangs in the community, we would smack them across the backside. Of course, those that used flour would leave a white mark.

I recall an incident that occurred one day after Halloween when our principal, Mr. Markham, got up and bawled everybody out for desecrating the soldier's monument on Hudson Avenue. Somebody had placed a potty on the soldier's head. In his criticism, he said he understood it was we boys from the lower end of the village that were the culprits. He said unless we confessed, everybody was going to get an hour's detention, which was to continue until somebody owned up to it. After a few days detention was lifted. Who was the culprit? The son of one of the teachers!

Joseph Komonchak (1904-1975)

Cleary Murder Case

One of the most highly publicized and scandalous court cases in county history incurred in Haverstraw in December 1914. The case involved William V. Cleary, who had been town clerk of the Democratic stronghold for 14 years. He was charged with the cold-blooded murder of Eugene M. Newman on the afternoon of July 23. Cleary shot Newman four times, and the shooting incurred in Cleary's office in the presence of several witnesses, including the Chief of Police Michael Ford, whose own revolver was used in the murder. Despite what seemed to be an open and shut case, Cleary was acquitted.

The sensational details of the murder and trial made daily headlines in the *New York Times*. Locally, there was an enormous amount of coverage in the press, due in part to the fact that Eugene Newman, 18 at the time of his murder, was the son of Fred Newman, owner of the *Rockland County Messenger* newspaper. Eugene had been a childhood sweetheart of Cleary's daughter, Anna, who was a year younger than Eugene. However, Cleary did not approve of the relationship.

In Cleary's own words, he "hated Gene Newman" and did not "consider him fit to associate with my daughter. His mother eloped at 16. His father was at one time insane. One policeman told me that he associated with negresses."

To keep Anna away from Newman, they sent her to New York City to study music. They thought she had no further contact with him, but on the evening of July 22, the family physician told Mr. and Mrs. Cleary that Anna was pregnant, and that Eugene Newman was the father. Cleary, in a state of shock and rage, went on an all-night drinking binge. One man testified that Cleary, "Drank everything on the calendar. He had all of 50 drinks. We couldn't stop him. He was wild."

In this state, Cleary went to his office in the town hall the next day. When the young Eugene Newman went to see Cleary at 2 p.m. on July 24, Cleary shouted at him, "You thought you had the best of me, but I've got you now!" and immediately shot the boy twice in the head, once in the arm and once in the back of the neck. He never gave Newman a chance to speak. If he had, he would have discovered that Newman and his daughter had been secretly married. Cleary had just killed his own son-in-law.

Moments after the shooting, Cleary ran into District Attorney Thomas Gagan's office and announced, "I have shot Gene Newman. I killed him. He ruined my daughter. He seduced her. He broke up my home!"

Remarkably, Cleary was not arrested until the following day. Despite the fact that he was seen numerous times walking along the streets of Haverstraw, police claimed they could not find him. The policemen who had been present at the shooting could also not account for bullets missing from their guns.

Cleary's indictment for murder occurred on October 3 and the trial began on December 18. He pleaded not guilty due to insanity from "drink and shock." In a bizarre twist, the lead prosecutor, District Attorney Gagan, was called as a defense witness, since he had heard the shots and saw Cleary immediately after the murder. Prosecutor Gagan turned out to be one of the defense's most effective witnesses, admitting that Cleary had appeared drunk and incoherent.

Police officers were reluctant to testify and then gave conflicting reports. Fred Comesky, Cleary's lawyer, personally knew most of the jurors. The all-powerful Haverstraw Democratic party seemed to have all the wheels in motion to get Cleary acquitted.

One of the most poignant moments of the trial came on December 19, when a soft-spoken Anna Cleary testified about her pregnancy and secret marriage. As she was leaving, Cleary attempted to hug his daughter, but she pulled away from him. This public rejection of her father brought even more sympathy for Cleary from the all-male jurors.

The following day, the jury returned a verdict of not guilty, on the grounds of Cleary's "twilight state" at the time of the shooting. Presiding Judge Morschauser was stunned, expecting at least a conviction of second-degree murder or manslaughter. He felt there had been a great miscarriage of justice, but there was nothing he could do.

While crowds lined the streets for a victory parade for Cleary, others began drafting complaints that the District Attorney's office had not done its job, that the entire trial had been rigged by the ruling Democrats. Charges were eventually brought against Gagan, himself, and in the "bitterest fight" Haverstraw had ever seen, he was finally exonerated by the governor in 1915. Despite all the verdicts of innocence, the case was not forgotten and ill feelings between rival factions festered for many years.

Justice was once again to receive a slap in the face in the 1920s, when Cleary was charged and convicted of embezzling a fortune in county funds. Though finally behind bars, Cleary was pardoned by Governor Al Smith, and once again set free.

These disgraceful episodes left a black eye on the county's history, and illustrate the dangers of one political party becoming too powerful.

Linda Zimmermann

An Old Feud

There was a feud between Mike McCabe, the publisher of the *Rockland County Times,* and Thomas Gagan, one of the most prominent Rockland County attorneys. As I recall its being told, it stemmed from the time of the Cleary trial when Gagan was District Attorney.

If that was the reason for the feud I don't know, but what I observed many times was Mike McCabe waiting in front of his *Times* office for Tom Gagan to pass. Gagan, if he was not at the courthouse or elsewhere, was a man who punctually left his office at twelve noon to go home to lunch. As Gagan would reach the edge of his sidewalk, McCabe would take his broom and sweep Gagan's footsteps off the sidewalk.

It was a common thing for those of us in the People's Bank, where I worked, to watch for Gagan and McCabe go through this routine. Gagan, with his head held high, would continue walking, paying no attention to McCabe.

Joseph Komonchak

The town where you grew up usually holds a special place in your heart and mind, and sometimes the best history is written by the people who are simply recalling what life was like for them.

My Home Town

It was (so I've been told) a beautiful, sunny day with the temperature about 90 degrees.

That was August 16, 1911, the day that I was born in the family home on Hunt Avenue in Pearl River. I was the second son of Charlotte and Otto Peckman.

To my mind there couldn't have been a more wonderful family—my mother and father, my brother Arthur and myself. Through all my early years I had the wonderful feeling of being secure in this great home in Pearl River. Now, all these years later, I'm proud to say that I still call Pearl River my home.

Let me tell you what it was like during my early childhood in "The Town of Friendly People." Let me explain why I sometimes feel that my life has spanned a time when we lived almost like backwoodsmen compared to the fast-paced, space-age, high-tech, Windows 95 lifestyle that we know today.

Those days we had no electricity, no gas to heat or cook with and no running water.

But we had a sense of community within our own family and in Pearl River—which will always be our Home Town.

And we had a lot of other things—like fresh-baked bread for four cents a loaf, or a gallon of milk or a pound of butter for 34 cents each. In those days the average yearly family income was only $1,213. But the average cost of a new home was only $3,395 and you could buy a brand-new Ford car right off the showroom floor for $780. And we could drive it on gas that only cost ten cents a gallon.

What was going on in the world back around 1911? Well, for one thing, headlines showed William Howard Taft. In sports, Ray Harrison had set a record of 74 mph at the Indy 500. In business, the Dow Jones stood at 82.98 for the day. That same year, gold was selling at $20.67 an ounce and silver at 54 cents while copper was going for 18 cents an ounce.

…There was always so much to do around the house—and the whole family pitched in. We didn't know from Nintendo or Power Rangers or television—we had chores to do.

In the morning before we went to school we used to take all of the small rag rugs from the house, hang them on a line in the back yard and clean them by whacking them with wicker beaters.

After school, in winter, we'd have to take the coals from the previous night's fire in the furnace and sift them in the back yard. That way the chunks of coal that hadn't burned completely didn't sift through the wire mesh and then we could burn them in that night's fire.

Going to school in Pearl River was a lesson in geography itself. There was a shortage of school buildings and I recall going to six or seven different buildings every day. Buildings like the Odd Fellows Hall, the old Bader Building, the top floor of the Hook and Ladder Fire Company, the Unique Hall and over Joe Fisher's Livery Stable. Every day we'd march back and forth, from one class to another.

…For me, "the good old days" in Pearl River were a rich mixture of excitement, fun, good times, and sometimes, tragedy. I remember the dreadful day of the bank robbery. One of the most exciting days from my early youth came with the ending of World War I. And would you believe that it was exciting back then when an airplane would go over?

…Like thousands of other hamlets and towns all over the United States, Pearl River grew to be a virtually self-contained community with its own purveyors of foods, goods and services.

But to me, nowhere else can rival nor touch my heart like my home town.

Herbert Peckman,
excerpts from *Pearl River, Then and Now,* 1998

Then and Now—c.1910 vs. 2001

First row: The northwest corner of Main Street and Central Avenue in Pearl River. Second row: the northwest corner of Railroad Avenue and Central Avenue. Third row: the Odd Fellows Hall on Franklin Avenue.

"Then" photos courtesy of the Orangetown Museum, "Now" by Linda Zimmermann

...In 1910, taxes for a 76-acre piece of property in Rockland totaled $20.93...In 1913, Niels Bohr formulates his theory of atomic structure...In 1915, Margaret Sanger is indicted for distributing birth control information..."Buffalo Bill" Cody dies in 1916...Mata Hari is executed in 1917...The Russian Czar and the royal family are executed in 1918... In 1918 the U.S. Bureau of Education introduces guidelines for new classes called "Kindergarten"...

The Great Suffern Fire

The struggle against fire in Suffern's business district has been a continual drama since the village's incorporation in 1896. A spectacular blaze occurred Wednesday, September 29, 1915. Within 5 1/2 hours, flames leveled a major portion of what was then the principal business section of Suffern, the Comesky Block. There have been several major fires since that date, but this one has retained the title, "The Great Suffern Fire."

Constructed in the shape of an L, the Comesky Block was comprised of 14 structures, the majority two-story wooden frame buildings. Located on Lafayette Avenue and around the corner to Orange Avenue, it was adjacent to the fashionable Hotel Rockland, a saloon and boarding house. The area, with the busy Erie Depot and park across the roadway, was a prime location. The buildings and property were owned by Frank Comesky, a prominent attorney who dealt in real estate and insurance.

The day of the great fire began as a typical autumn morning with a stiff, cool breeze blowing through the streets of the tranquil village. The serenity was abruptly broken at 1:35 a.m., when the sound of the fire alarm and whistles of two steam locomotives in the Erie yard warned of trouble. The commotion awakened sleeping residents, many of whom climbed from their beds to investigate. A bright glow emanated from the rear of the Comesky Block, where fire of unknown origin had started in the livery stable of M.E. Stall. The flames gained considerable headway before being discovered by Joe Vilord, a tenant in one of the Comesky building apartments. By the time the alarm was turned in, the fire had eaten through the stable roof and was a roaring inferno.

Members of the Suffern Fire Department soon realized there was insufficient manpower and fire apparatus available. Alerted telephone operators, with the assistance of James J. Brown, clerk of the Town of Ramapo, began summoning help from neighboring departments. The operators remained at the switchboard, continuing to call as the "heat cracked the windows beside which they worked."

Fire departments from Tuxedo, Hillburn, Tallman, Haverstraw, Spring Valley, Nyack, West Nyack, Allendale, Ramsey and Ridgewood responded to Suffern's plea for help. All arrived in record time.

The first outside department on the scene was Hillburn, responding with automotive apparatus. Within 11 minutes after their alarm sounded, firemen arrived, laid hose and began poring water on the flames. Five other departments responded with automotive apparatus and manpower. Two Nyack Fire Departments soon (Mazeppa Engine Co. and Orangetown Engine Co.) made the emergency run in less than 30 minutes, a cross-country record for those days. The Mazeppa Engine Co. brought ten men and about 2,000 feet of hose in their big Seagraves truck. Orangetown Engine Co. dispatched their big Knox fire truck. Spring Valley sent both their fire companies, Columbian Engine Co. and Spring Valley Hook and Ladder. This combined force included six automobiles equipped for fire service, three hose cars, a large steamer, a pump truck and one chemical automachine. South of the border, help came from Allendale's new Reo fire truck; Ramsey Fire Department loaded all their available hose into automobiles and raced towards Suffern.

Several prominent residents "came in their automobiles" to render assistance to the firefighters. They were Joseph J. Ryan, son of Thomas Fortune Ryan; Otis H. Cutler, president of the American Brake Shoe and Foundry Co.; David H. McConnell, president of the California Perfume Co. (today Avon Products Inc.). Area residents responded by foot, horse and buggy and autocar as word spread of the great fire.

The volunteers faced a seething furnace. The livery stable blaze, fed by the stiff autumn wind, sent sparks and heat upward and outward. Immediately other buildings were aflame. People living in the upper floors of the endangered buildings and guests of the Hotel Rockland fled to the streets. These "scantily clad" individuals assembled on the lawn of the Erie Depot park, "where they were obliged to remain for hours before clothing could be provided."

Heat from the fire forced firemen to work in three-

minute relays. Above the flames' roar was heard the crash of falling buildings as one by one they succumbed to the fire. The wind carried to other sections of the village sparks which ignited smaller fires on "eight or ten other buildings." Men and equipment from the main fire had to be sent to battle the smaller blazes.

The more than ordinary manpower and fire apparatus increased demand for water. Twenty-one fire hoses were pouring a constant stream of water in an attempt to quell the raging fire. The village reservoir was so greatly taxed there were fears the water supply might soon run out. An appeal to the Ramapo Iron Works of Hillburn was made for the use of its pumping plant. The two plants were able to keep water flowing while firemen struggle for nearly 5 1/2 hours until the fire was brought under control shortly after daybreak.

All that remained of the Comesky Block was a smoldering pile of rubble. The buildings of the block were not the only casualties of the fire. There were 25 families left homeless by the blaze. No lives were lost and only two injuries were reported. Joseph Doyle of the Suffern Fire Department suffered a fractured leg when he was caught under a falling brick wall. A truck from Nyack's Orangetown Fire Co. was turned into an ambulance as firemen "placed him in their truck and rushed him to the Suffern Hospital" (Good Samaritan Hospital). The other injury was to a member of the Spring Valley Fire Department who was overcome by smoke. The fire interrupted telephone service in the center of town as wires burned and service was cut off. Erie Railroad property near the scene was severely damaged: Mrs. Thomas F. Ryan's private rail car, the "Pere Marquette" and 19 freight cars on the Piermont branch "narrowly escaped destruction." Early reports of damage placed losses at $65,000; later evaluations brought the total to $150,000. The fire had consumed all buildings on the Comesky Block except for the Hotel Rockland, which remained untouched, and a portion of

the two adjacent buildings, partially saved by the first fire line set up at the outbreak of the fire.

The Great Suffern Fire had "threatened the destruction of the entire town" and the hundred or more firemen, exerting in "every effort and skill known in the fire extinguishing game," had "faced the fight of their lives." Newspapers credited the volunteer firefighters and added that their efforts and skills "saved the remainder of the town from destruction."

On the Sunday following the fire it was reported that "over 5,000 people from all over the country visited Suffern to view the ruins."

One year prior to the great fire (on June 25, 1914) Mr. Comesky had come before the village of Suffern board and "showingly urged that steps be taken toward the consideration of a sewage and disposal plant." He stressed this endeavor would be advantageous to property owners and advised the board that if they would retain the services of an engineer to prepare plans and specifications for such a system, he would "personally pay the cost of such engineer...if there was no money available to the board for the payment."

The board adopted his suggestion and formed a resolution to study the project. If the village built the storage and disposal plant, Comesky agreed to "build a trunk line sewer in front of his property on Lafayette and Orange Avenues," and at the completion of the sewage system "would one year or their about...tear down the old buildings on sight [sic] and build modern buildings to take their place." It appears that the fire was just an unfortunate incident, and that the buildings were destined to come down one way or another.

A year later the finishing touches were placed on the new Comesky Block. After removal of the two partially saved buildings next to the Hotel Rockland, a brick and concrete two-story structure was erected. It covered the entire burned-out section of Lafayette and Orange Avenues. Modern conveniences, such as the latest in lighting and ventilation, were incorporated in the building and the new stores were large and roomy. A newspaper reporter noted, "The careful observer is impressed with the symmetry and correct proportions of the long building as well as by the artistic detail" and the exterior "embodies a color scheme of brown brick and concrete with white stone trimming and a green tile roof which is nicely blended." This building stands today much in the same fashion as when first constructed. Born out of the Comesky Block fire, it has remained while others in Suffern's business district have fallen. The Comesky Block is a fitting symbol of a bygone age.

Article and photos courtesy of Craig Long.

60

The Jewish Community
1910-1919

Not all those who arrived in Spring Valley to work at Falkenberg's were content to stay in the shirt business. Max Averbach came to the factory and worked there on and off until about 1916, when he purchased land on First Avenue and established Averbach Hotel. A neighbor, Murray Rosner, founder of Rosner's Hotel, soon joined him. For a short time the two were partners but they operated their hotels separately. Eventually, both sold their interests to Louis Sauberman, who continued the business until the 1960s.

In time Louis Bader, founder of Bader's Hotel, and Louis Singer of Singer's Lakeside Manor, joined them. These five were among those who established an important resort industry which once flourished in Spring Valley and Monsey. By the 1920s, thousands of New York City Jews began to vacation in Spring Valley. There were dozens of bungalow colonies, boarding houses, and rooms with kitchen privileges known as *kochaleyans*. Many of the rooms were in homes that were used by family members the rest of the year. When the "season" approached children were relegated to attic rooms to make place for the summer residents.

The hotel industry was brisk, often in competition with the famed Catskills. At its peak there were over thirty hotels, many year-round establishments, which were Jewish owned, kosher establishments and many had small shuls (synagogues) on their premises. Some of the other better known were Bauman's on Pascack Road, Spring Valley Gardens on Main Street, the Fairview Hotel south of Route 59, and Weissman's Hotel on the hill.

The Fair Oaks Hotel, Gartner's Inn, Monsey Park Hotel, Raim House, Epstein's and the Pine Tree Villa had their regular cliental. Today all of the hotels are gone, having made way for housing developments and apartment house complexes. Temple Beth El, the county's largest Reform synagogue is located where Epstein's Hotel once stood.

In Suffern, in 1916, Samuel Greenstein urged the formulation of a building fund for the construction of a permanent building to be used as a community synagogue. The following year, on the occasion of the Bar Mitzvah of George Honig, the fund was given great stimulus when pledges were made.

On June 23, 1919 the building fund committee purchased a 50' x 125' lot on Suffern Place for $1,000. The following month the Society's name was changed to the Congregation Sons of Israel. On September 21, the cornerstone for the new synagogue was laid. The building, which cost $25,000, was dedicated for use by the High Holy Days, the following year.

Harold L. Laroff

Camp Bluefields

On land once belonging to the Blauvelt family, a rifle range was built around 1910 for the New York National Guard. Solidly constructed, it was much more than just a series of target walls, for each battalion brought to Blauvelt would camp at the range for several days. Therefore, the complex contained such structures as a mess hall, range office, headquarters building, and storage houses, in addition to high concrete target walls connected by safety tunnels.

When completed, the Blauvelt Rifle Range had cost half a million dollars—no small sum in those days. At that price, it should have been a model of military endeavor, but it wasn't. It just didn't work right.

For some reason—probably because of the height of the land on which it was built—bullets that were supposed to hit the target area often overshot their mark and landed in South Nyack. Plans were immediately made to correct what was then thought to be only a minor problem in logistics. But it wasn't so minor.

Nyack Evening Journal, June 5, 1912: *RIFLE RANGE SHOOTING TERRORIZES SOUTH NYACK...Bullets through the roof and into the kitchen of* *Mrs. Grenville D. Wilson and another in a nearby tree...Superintendent Lamb of the Rifle Range came to Nyack today to obtain evidence of possible danger from flying bullets in this vicinity. He examined Mrs. Wilson's home and saw the leaden missiles...promised to take prompt measures...would have shields placed at the Range to prevent bullets from coming over the hill.*

June 11, 1912: *THIRTEENTH REGIMENT MARKSMEN OFFER CRITICISM...RANGE NOT PROPERLY LAID OUT... "IT SHOULD HAVE BEEN DONE BY ENGINEER OFFICERS," SAYS A HIGH OFFICIAL OF THAT REGIMENT..."It puts us in the position of hitting everything in the country except the targets. "*

Another $73,000 was spent to improve conditions at the rifle range. Large overhead screens were installed near the firing point to keep the bullets in Blauvelt instead of raining down on South Nyack. But the new screens didn't solve the problem, and rumor had it that the rifle range was cursed.

Cursed or just not constructed properly, the range became an embarrassment to the officials in charge, and they were only too glad to hand over their "white elephant" to the Palisades Interstate Park Commission. At that time—1913—the Blauvelt Rifle Range had been in operation less than three years. A mighty costly and short-lived white elephant, to be sure!

During the next five years, from 1913 to 1918, the YWCA (Young Women's Christian Association) rented the land as a summer camp for New York City working girls, who paid $3.50 for a full week's vacation. It was a regimented vacation, however, and followed the military theme of its predecessor. Campers were required to wear uniforms consisting of bloomers and middy blouses. They slept in tents, and their daily activities were signaled by bugle calls.

Then in 1918, the property was turned into a state-run camp for the military training of young men between ages of 16 and 19. ROTC units used the site during and immediately following World War I, after which some members formed a "Comeback Club" and obtained permission to build summer homes at Bluefields. For several summers thereafter, the rifle range was the scene of a gala "Fete Militaire" sponsored by the club, with the 1925 celebration featuring a costume ball in one of the camp buildings.

Such peaceful pursuits all too soon reverted to more serious maneuvers as it became evident that the "War to End All Wars" wasn't. In 1930, the Army sent soldiers to Blauvelt for training (presumably without target-practice, since the problem of errant bullets had never been solved). And when World War II broke out, Blauvelt again became a training ground—this time for soldiers from nearby Camp Shanks—as well as an air raid post. But eventually the war clouds dispersed, the soldiers departed, and the deserted rifle range was subjected to the ravages of nature...and man.

Today, tenacious tree roots have collapsed several sections of the tunnel system, while other natural forces have been at work crumbling the concrete. The ruins of the old rifle range are still fun to explore, though care should be taken especially in the shadowy tunnels.

Patricia Clyne, *SOM*, Oct./Dec. 1985

The Promenade at Rifle Range, Blauvelt, New York

Soldiers standing in front of the mess hall at Camp Bluefields (top) and practicing at the infamous rifle range (above). Remains of one of the tunnels (below) in 1983.

JSC

...Of the 65 million men who fought in World War I, 10 million were killed and 20 million were wounded...

WWI Soldier:
Daniel J. Hannigan

Daniel J. Hannigan was born on December 8, 1896 in Haverstraw. His father, William, was born in Ireland and emigrated with his mother to America when he was three years old. Dan's mother died of childbirth complications and Dan was raised by his father and grandmother at their Stony Point residence on Tomkins Avenue. He attended the local schools and upon graduation obtained a job as a clerk at a Stony Point grocery store.

Dan enlisted in 1917 in the 71st Regiment of the New York National Guard. His unit was called into service by the governor and assigned to guard duty for the utility and transportation systems serving New York City. Dan was assigned to the Haverstraw Railroad Tunnel of the West Shore division of the New York Central Railroad. On July 15, 1917 this regiment was federalized by President Wilson and shipped to Camp Wadsworth, S.C. for additional training and formation into Company F., 105th Infantry of the 27th Division under Maj. Gen. John O. Ryan.

Dan received extensive training in weaponry, machine guns, mortars, and trench and gas warfare. Much of this training was provided by British officers fresh from the trenches in Europe. The 27th Division received training with live artillery cover that greatly helped the soldiers to become accustomed to actual battlefield conditions. In May of 1918, the 27th Division embarked for Europe and landed at Brest, France, on Memorial Day. The unit was detached from U.S. forces and assigned to serve under the 66th British Division of General Sir Douglas Haig.

After two months of additional training with the British units near the front lines, the 27th Division was moved to the front in defense of the East Poperinghe Line, a defensive sector of trenches protecting the British west flank.

On August 6, 1918 Dan's unit went "over the top" in an offensive push. During the course of the battle a German artillery shell burst nearby and Dan and three others were wounded. Dan was able to crawl into a bunker with a sergeant and two officers, but another shell explosion nearby exposed them on the battlefield. The sergeant and lieutenant were killed and Dan lay on the field with head, arm and leg wounds.

The next day he was rescued by his corporal and sent to four dressing stations and then to the hospital for treatment. A letter from Dan to his father describes this action:

Just as we struck the woods, Fritz (the Germans) must have seen us with his light; his artillery opened up on us. It was just as the saying—hell. After a while he let up. We pulled through and got in the line and relieved an English outfit.

Well, Pop, I'll have to make this short; it was hot the whole time we were up till Thursday night at 12:00 when the artillery opened a barrage.

At the same time Fritz opened his barrage on our line and tore everything, leveled the trenches some places and here's where I got mine. Our crew was holding one of the boys with our gun but we were cut off from the rest of the company by the enemy's shells. Everything was blown up from around us, then we realized the trap we were in. Then the corporal said "Stick to it fellows, hold out."

At that moment an artillery shell hit Hannigan's position.

I got a rap in the head and down I went. My head came to whirl and everything went blind for a few seconds. When I kind of come to I could see nothing but shells bursting around me. I laid still for awhile when along came a few of our fellows looking for parts, for there's had been blown up.

I'm not as bad as thought at first. I got hit in the head, both arms and leg, the worst is my head, but I'll be back with my company in little while, I guess they're going down to our own section. I close now hoping everybody is well. I'm feeling good, I can walk and my head is much better. They took a small piece of shrapnel out and one from my arm and my leg is a little stiff so there's nothing to worry about. Such things will happen. I'll be back in the front line soon to get another crack at Fritz.

Upon release from the hospital Pvt. Hannigan was attached to II Corps Replacement Battalion and saw further action in the Ypres-Lys Offensive, Somme Offensive and Defensive Sector action that broke through the Hindenberg Defense Line of the Germans. Offensive action at the Jon du Marc Farm, and La Salle River completed the action service of the 27th Division. On October 23rd, 1918, the unit was entrained to the Corbie Training Area near Amiens where the Armistice was declared on November 11th, 1918.

While awaiting embarkation for the U.S., Dan was able to travel back to some of the battle sites and vividly describes this scarred landscape in letters to his family. On March 19, Dan arrived in New York and was assigned to Camp Upton on Long Island for mustering out. While there, he contracted meningitis and died in the base hospital on May 12, 1919.

Dan was buried in the Hannigan plot at St. Peter's Cemetery, Haverstraw, with full military honors. The Hannigan family was presented with scrolls from the U.S. and French presidents for Dan's heroic service. Dan was also presented with the World War I Victory Medal with three battle clasps.

Two weeks after his burial the New York State branch of the American Legion chartered Post #12 in Tomkins Cove in honor of Pvt. Daniel J. Hannigan. The post would remain active for over 40 years.

On Wednesday July 16, 1919, Welcome Home Day brought out the community of Stony Point to dedicate a monument to the 132 residents who served in the Great War, with special recognition to the families of William Doyle, Thomas Duggan and Daniel Hannigan, who made the supreme sacrifice.

Upon the death of Dan's sister in 1989, the family came upon a box of letters Dan had sent his father and grandmother. Dan's nephew, Dan Hamilton, sought his military records and was able to obtain a Purple Heart posthumously on Dec. 8, 1999 (Dan's 103rd birthday, 80 years after his death). Subsequent research was able to ascertain his additional military decorations due: a second Victory Medal from the Army and a Conspicuous Service Cross and a New York Medal of Honor from the New York State Division of Military Naval Affairs.

These decorations, and the last U.S. flag to fly over the Hannigan Post American Legion, are valued memorabilia that the Hannigan family will preserve for Stony Point and Rockland communities.

Edward Hamilton

WWI Soldier:
Captain B. Eberlin

Captain B. Eberlin was with the Army's 311th Infantry during WWI. He often wrote to his friend (possibly sweetheart?), Bessie Edwards who lived at 19 First Avenue in Nyack. As the tragedies of the war years reached out beyond the battlefields, no one could ever be certain what fate might bring.

The following excerpts are from one of Captain Eberlin's letters and a postcard. While he vividly describes the horrors of trench warfare he is enduring, he still voices his concern as to why he has not heard from Bessie.

October 27, 1918, Somewhere in France:

Dear Bess, A few lines in haste to inquire as to your health and welfare and to let you know that I am still very much alive and in excellent health and spirits. Hope you are likewise.

Sent you a field postal about a week ago, which you have probably received by this time. I am not writing this in reply to any letter of yours for I haven't heard from you in a few weeks...

My promotion to Captain came through on October 15th. It took over 10 weeks to come, but is finally here, so you will now kindly address my mail as Captain B. Eberlin. Am still on the Staff, but hope and expect soon to have a line company to command. Have been in the line for some time now, and am now fighting on the most stubborn front in France. Our boys sure are doing credit to their country, and the Boche (Germans) knows it, too. Word reached us yesterday that Austria-Hungary is willing to surrender practically unconditionally, but with all these peace notes fluttering back and forth, our work goes on with as much determination as ever, but there is no doubt but that this is almost the approach of a successful termination of war.

How are you these days? Your mother and father?

Have probably told you that my only brother was wounded and is now recuperating at an army hospital in Lakewood. His arm will be some time before it gets back to normal, but I do hope he will suffer no ill effects from it later on.

I am writing this in a hole about 8x8x5, with a few pieces of German corrugated iron for a roof, and a few pieces of rough board for a floor. Two boxes constitute my furniture. One is my chair, the other my desk, table, etc... On the table is the field telephone and some maps and orders. Two candles constitute illumination in this palace. It is now 2AM, and it is pitch black and very cold outside. Cold and damp inside. Some people call this hole a dugout, but I have lived in better dugouts than this. You see we don't stop anywhere long enough to build ourselves a good dugout, but when we occupied the ones used by the Boche, they were very palatial. Outside shells of all sizes are flying through the air, and machine guns are getting exercised a bit, too. So as far as we are concerned here, the war is not over yet by any means. We are constantly pushing on and driving the Boche back to their pig pens where they belong, that is only those we don't kill and capture.

I wish you would write to me after regardless of my writing to you. I do write as often as I can, but it is hard for me to write often. We sometimes sit down long enough to eat and perhaps snatch a few hours sleep, but oh, what wouldn't I do for a good, full night's sleep in a real, clean bed with sheets-and-no phone to wake you every two minutes.

Be good and take care of yourself. Eat some turkey and pumpkin pie for me on Thanksgiving Day, won't you? Regards to your folks.

Heartiest wishes to you at all times. Write.

World War I ended when the Armistice was signed on November 18, 1918. Captain Eberlin was expecting to go back to Nyack and to Bessie, but in this November 27 postcard, it is clear that he was worried about his friend.

Dear Bess, How are you? Haven't heard from you for some time. Hope you are well.

This is where I am now (Flavigny), *taking a little rest. Am in excellent health. Let me hear from you, please.*

What Captain Eberlin might have feared, but didn't know, was that Bessie Edwards had died in the great influenza epidemic, on October 13, 1918. And he would never know her fate, because despite his good health in November, he soon also caught the flu and died.   Linda Zimmermann

(This material was contributed by Cynthia Sheridan, a descendant of the Edwards family. Cynthia also relayed the story of the discovery of Bessie's diary several years ago. It was found in the walls of her home when a new owner was renovating. Realizing its sentimental, as well as historic value, the man returned the diary to the Edwards family.)

Spanish Influenza

The Spanish Influenza of 1918, with complications of pneumonia, by mid-October had reached epidemic proportions in every state in the nation.

Flu cases in the Nyacks totaled 800 according to the *Nyack Evening Journal.* Suffern and Spring Valley closed all schools, churches, movie theaters and public meeting halls. Various public buildings throughout the county shut down. According to the *New York Times*, the Spanish Flu outbreak was the most devastating epidemic in history. During the single month of October, influenza killed 196,000 people in the United States.

In many communities, there weren't enough caskets available, nor were there enough cemetery employees to dig the graves to bury the dead. Records were sometimes scattered and lost.

"One day, four women in a bridge group were playing cards until 11 o'clock in the evening. By that morning, three of them were dead." The *New York Times* noted that after 1919 the epidemic had infected almost half the world's population and resulted in 20 to 30 million deaths.

This writer's family was broken up suddenly by the flu in 1918. My father died in October, my one-year-old brother died the following day, and I, two years old, was stricken on the third day. A doctor came to the house but said he couldn't help me. My mother, hysterically crying, picked me up and flung me against her shoulder and somehow the lung and flu congestion flew out of my mouth and I was saved. We both lived or are living to a ripe old age.   John Scott

> The flu deaths in Rockland were responsible for the only decline in population ever recorded in the county.

Medal of Honor

Michael A. Donaldson, Haverstraw- Donaldson was a Sergeant in the U.S. Army with Company I, 165th Infantry, 42nd Division and was awarded the Medal of Honor for actions: At St. Georges Road, France, October 14, 1918. "Donaldson advanced to the crest of a hill, which men had been trying to take, under his own volition in broad daylight to rescue a wounded comrade. He went up that same hill five more times for other wounded men. During his six trips he was severely wounded and gassed."
Dan deNoyelles

WORLD WAR I
In Memoriam

BAUMAN, EUGENE
BLAUVELT, CHARLES R.
BLAUVELT, RAYMOND O.
BOWLES, FRED L.
BROPHY, RICHARD
CAMPBELL, FLORENCE WILDA
CLARK, GEORGE W.
CONWAY, MICHAEL
COOK, ADOLPHUS
COOPER, HIDLEY T.
CRAWFORD, CONRAD
CRAVEN, JOSEPH A.
DEBAUN, HENRY
DEDERER, ELLSWORTH H.
DEGRAW, JOHN HENRY
D'LOUGHY, CHARLES
DOYLE, ABRAM
DOYLE, WILLIAM
DUGAN, THOMAS
DUVALL, HAROLD L.
EICKOFF, RAYMOND
ENGLE, ARCHIBALD J.
FERGUSON, HAROLD
FLETCHER, LEE CHASE
FORMATO, CARMINE
FROHLING, FREDERICK W.
FROMM, JOHN PAUL
GARDNER, WILLIAM HENRY
GORDON, JOHN G.
GREEN, DAVID
HAMILTON, JAMES
HANNIGAN, DANIEL J.
HART, MAURICE
HENION, WILLIAM H.
HINCHELWOOD, JAMES
HOLT, HAROLD B.
HYMEN, SAMUEL
INGALLS, JOHN
JACARUSO, JOHN J.
JAUSS, RAYMOND BOYD
KERR, ALBERT W.
KING, LOUIS W.

KLINE, HARRY L.
KREBS, CHARLES W.
LADERS, LEO B.
LAKE, ALPHEUS GEORGE
LEGGETT, PAUL
LICHENSTEIN, GEORGE J.
LOGATTO, BENJAMIN
LYNCH, THOMAS F.
McELREE, REUBEN
McGUIRE, MICHAEL J.
MAXWELL, WILLIAM H.
MOSCARELLA, ANTHONY
MOSER, DAVID
MURRAY, JOHN L.
O'DOWD, DENNIS H.
OLDFIELD, JOHN CASHMAN
PERRY, JOHN MARDER
RUPPEL, ADAM A.
SCHAPER, HENRY M.
SCHEU, PHILIP
SCHREIBER, LUDWIG T.
SCHROEDER, GOODSON
SHUREMAN, OLIVE
SECOR, JOHN
SEYMOUR, HARRY P.
SHERIDAN, OWEN
SMITH, HALLIDAY SPENCER
SMITH, HILTON H.
STAGEN, CHARLOTTE S.
STAUBITZ, PHILIP
TIFFANY, JAMES GOELET DUBOIS
TOMOVCIK, MICHAEL J.
TOPPING, HUGH
TROINA, CALOGERO
VANDERBEEK, GEORGE R.
VAN DUNK, JOHN
VAN DUNK, WILLIAM H.
VITALE, SALVATORE
VOORHIS, MILTON
WANAMAKER, HARRY S.
WHELEN, WILLIAM
ZELENKA, WILLIAM G.

66

Armistice Parade in Nyack (above, courtesy of the Orangetown Museum). Hillburn children show their patriotism (left, courtesy of Chuck Stead).

Soon after the U.S. declared war in 1917, prominent businessmen and local organizations began holding various events to raise money for the war effort. Over half a million dollars was raised in Nyack alone.

Women rolled bandages and prepared special packages for the troops. As local men went into the armed services, their wives, mothers and girlfriends filled their roles in the factories and on the farms. Volunteers added their names to lists of those willing to help in any way needed.

In many ways, preparations and practices of World War I gave residents the experience they would need to call upon when an even greater crisis was to arise a generation later.

Ponies, Spies and Generals:
Vignettes of World War I in Haverstraw Village

Bill and Brose, my brothers, accompanied me in the trap when we joined the impromptu parade on that glorious day of the false armistice in November 1918. We were very happy following the crowd. Apparently the news that it was a false alarm failed to reach us, ensconced as we were in our fancy wagon.

Darling, our pony, was hitched to the trap, a very elegant two-seated wagon made of wood and basketry. The seats were covered with beige-colored woolen material and the steel back of the front seat could be folded down. This very impressive contraption was reserved for state occasions, such as parades; the run-about, a one-seater, was every-day fare.

We followed a small contingent of hearty souls who continued to celebrate. Leading this group was a handsome man, resplendent in a derby, Herman Purdy. One of the town's leading citizens, for many years he served as county clerk.

First, we paraded a short distance up Broadway. Then the men all went into a store. We waited patiently for the parade to continue. Eventually the men came out and we followed them down Broadway to the bank corner, turned left and down Main Street to approximately where the O. N. Rosenberg and Son store now stands. Again, they disappeared while we poor kids waited for the parade. After the third of these trips between the two stores, discouragement set in and I headed Darling home.

How were we, at the ripe ages of six, nine and eleven and brought up on the edge of the village, to know that stores with green curtains inside the windows were saloons? The Broadway "store" was and still is Adler's. I'm sure if its walls could talk there would be some mighty interesting tales, for it has served several generations.

The night of the real armistice there was an organized parade. This time we did very well in the line of march from downtown up Broadway until we reached the corner of West Side Avenue and Spring Street. As parades do, there we stopped. Suddenly a band blared out, frightening Darling. She reared so high that when she came down her forequarters were outside the right shaft while her hindquarters remained inside. I called, "Some man, some man." Several came to the rescue, released the traces, put Darling back between the shafts and fastened the traces. Miraculously, the harness hadn't broken. When the parade turned at Hudson Avenue to go back downtown, I scooted up West Side Avenue to home and safety.

Peg, Brose, Bill and Frank McCabe in their pony cart at the Elks Parade in Haverstraw in 1914.

During the war years rumors of lights flashed by German spies on High Tor proved false, but we at the north end of the village had a genuine spy captured right under our noses.

Lenore Troup, from the house on the corner, the Feeneys from up the hill, Lu and Bill Post from Conger Avenue and we were allowed to indulge in "Kick the Wicket" and "Run Sheep Run" under the corner street light until eight o'clock. One night our play was disturbed by a very silent man who stood leaning on the telephone post by Troup's home. His hat was pulled down, almost covering his eyes; his coat collar covered his chin; his arms were folded. We ran up to him and spoke, but he uttered not a sound. Scared, we went to Mrs. Troup for aid. With us, she walked the Feeney kids up the hill. As we returned to her home, she walked so close to the man that she practically brushed against him. Again, not a sound nor a move.

Mr. Troup took up the vigil from a bedroom in their home. The next day he reported the man had stood there until eleven o'clock, when a big black car came down the state road and stopped. The man got into the car without speaking.

Just a few weeks later, Mrs. Denton DeBaun, who lived on the same side of West Side Avenue as we and whose house was the second below the tracks, answered the bell at her front door. The two or three men standing there presented their governmental credentials and inquired if a certain person was employed by the DeBauns. Mrs. DeBaun said this woman was their cook. The agents explained their purpose and asked to speak to the woman. Mrs. DeBaun then showed them to the kitchen, where they pulled the wig off the cook and then ripped her apron and skirt off exposing the woman-cook who was wearing trousers and was really a man!

The contents of his/her room disclosed a great many sketches of the West Shore R.R. tunnel between Haverstraw and Congers, then guarded by soldiers. The U.S. Government agents took this spy into custody and off they went. When we heard about this, we kids all knew the silent man who had scared us was the DeBaun's cook.

Mrs. DeBaun must have had a frightful shock. She was extremely active in the Haverstraw chapter of the American Red Cross. She enjoined other women to work with her rolling bandages at meetings in the Presbyterian Church. Many of them knitted helmets, scarves, wristlets and sweaters for our boys in service.

The school affair that stays with me most clearly was on the day that L. O. Markham, superintendent of schools, marched the entire school body up to the West Shore Railroad Station to see Marshal Joffre, leader of the French forces, who was en route to visit West Point.

Unfortunately, the engineer of the private train hadn't been informed that the Haverstraw school children would be out to welcome the famous visitor and didn't slow the train. When he spied the crowd, he tried to slacken speed and the train did slow a bit as it reached the freight station. Several officers on the observation platform of the last car waved to us. Of course we all said we saw Marshal Joffre. Did we?

Margaret McCabe, *SOM*, Oct./Dec. 1976

...In 1919 the first commercial flight from Paris to London took three hours and thirty minutes...

Caroline Lexow Babcock
and the
Fight for the Women's Right to Vote

Caroline Lexow Babcock served in executive posts in half a dozen suffrage organizations fighting to enfranchise women. Then, after an interval devoted to raising her family, she returned to the fray on behalf of the Equal Rights Amendment. Her home during most of that period was South Nyack, but her territory was the county, the state and the nation.

Women suffrage and the full equality of the sexes before the law which its proponents envisioned, were always installed with other controversial issues, and not always inadvertently. It was a primary way by which opponents could and did paralyze action. Nationally and typically suffragists were accused of advocating free love, easy divorce, birth control, racism, prohibition, radicalism, polygamy, and even disloyalty and treason.

As in the rest of the country, profound social problems—among them slavery, trade unionism, recurrent money panics, the "Demon Rum" and what the local press called "the woman question"—demanded attention in nineteenth-century Rockland County. All of the strains of agony issuing from these problems deeply involved women, but with no voice in their government, they suffered twice over: once at the injustices, and once at their inability to do anything effective about it.

The social ferment was intense. From a largely wilderness and agricultural area in the early 1800s, Rockland moved steadily into the industrial age as the century progressed. Haverstraw had its brickyards. Piermont had its railroad terminus. Sloatsburg had its cotton mills, Ramapo its iron works, Garnerville its print works. Nyack was a shoe factory town. Immigrants poured into the county to find jobs, many with limited skills and some illiterate. They lived in a world of hope and fear, on the narrow edge of poverty. Life was harsh and frustrating. In mid-century, men shoe workers were paid $8 a week, women, $3.50. If the breadwinner stopped off at the corner saloon after a 12-hour day of grinding work, it often meant no bread on the table at home. With a population under 5,000 in 1884, Nyack had thirty-one saloons.

Slowly in Rockland as elsewhere, the ferment polarized around women and saloons. Susan B. Anthony campaigned for temperance before she took up the suffrage cause and not infrequently she combined her efforts. When she came to Haverstraw in March 1894, she spoke one day at the Opera House on votes for women and lectured the next day on the evils of drink. Early on, Mrs. Stanton joined her in the crusade against liquor with the rallying cry, "Divorce for Drunkenness." It shocked some sectors of the press and public to near-apoplexy, leading one newspaper to assert that she was "reviling Christianity in thinking of such a thing."

Not all temperance advocates were women, but virtually all saloon advocates were men. When in 1883 the issue reached the ballot box in Haverstraw and it appeared that an anti-saloon faction might control appointment of the excise commissioners, the ballot boxes were overturned and election headquarters set afire and wrecked, so the completion of the canvass was impossible.

By and large, the same people, men and women, who were for suffrage were against saloons, and in Rockland especially the two became effectively identified in the public mind. As Daniel deNoyelles wrote, when the two Haverstraw newspapers carried front page columns on the suffrage issue, they always added as a banner, "Will the county go dry?" And when, in 1915, the suffrage issue was placed before the county electorate (all men, of course), it shared the ballot with the proposition to permit closing every Rockland saloon through local option. Both issues went down to defeat.

Meanwhile, however, there had been a slow but steady increase in the county in support of women suffrage. It began at the close of the Civil War with enactment of the constitutional amendments extending citizenship to freed slaves. Many constitutional lawyers felt that the language of the 14th Amendment was broad enough to enable women to vote, and following its approval by the states in 1868, Rockland County women tried to do so.

A group of Nyack women led by Mr. L. Delos Mansfield, head of the Nyack Female Institute, marched to the polls on November 7, 1871, requesting the right to vote. According to the *Rockland County Journal* of November 11, "about 50 or 60 embarrassed citizens were considerably taken aback when Mr. Mansfield escorted four ladies to the ballot boxes who then and there offered their votes to the inspectors. Mr. George Dickey, one of the inspectors, politely received the ballots, but having doubts as to the legality of the transaction, placed them in a hat and clerks recorded the names of Mrs. Mansfield, Mrs. Merrill, Miss Pettis and Miss Hendricksen, two of whom, as Mr. Mansfield explained, representing Republican principles and two Democratic.

"The utmost stillness and decorum prevailed while the ladies were present," said the *Journal*, "and we think that everyone present was gratified that such a test had been made."

The record is silent as to whether the votes were counted. Almost certainly they were not, for if they had been, the news would have run from one end of the country to the other. But the women had made their point.

It was heady stuff, and it whetted the ladies' determination to claim and exercise the right of franchise. The Female Institute became a focal point of insurrection. The following Election Day, another group of women gathered at the Female Institute and marched to the polls. This time they were rebuffed. That same year in Rochester, Susan B. Anthony was arrested for trying to vote.

Born in 1882, Caroline Lexow Babcock became acquainted early with public affairs and political issues. Her mother, Katherine Morton Ferris, was an energetic woman with a questing mind and sharp sense of justice who regularly challenged the serenity of local women's clubs with discussions of independence for women as envisioned by Charlotte Perkins Gilman, or civil disobedience as practiced by Mahatma Gandhi. Clarence Lexow, Caroline's father, was a New York attorney who served as a state senator from 1894 to 1898 and became chairman of the Tammany-smashing Lexow Commission.

When the effects of the 1893 panic struck Rockland—banks failing, shoe factories and other industries closing down—Caroline, even though very young, witnessed the resultant suffering, anguish and dismay. "Mother always wanted to help people," she said, "but she always wanted people to try also to help themselves." Many days there were people at our house needing food and clothing, and we fed them before sending them to work at the laundry or wood yard. But of course it didn't solve the basic problems, all of which had political aspects that could only be solved by political action. Mother could have used the vote.

"It struck me, very young, that it was extraordinary that my father could vote and my mother could not. I thought it was an indignity. I couldn't endure the thought that she was denied so basic a right of citizenship."

After attending private schools in South Nyack and New York, and studying Greek with a woman tutor (a graduate of Columbia University who had been allowed to attend classes and receive her bachelor's degree— behind a screen—in the all-male bastion), Caroline entered Barnard College in 1900. There she found many young women questioning the justice and legality of franchising men only.

"We had one professor of economics who talked down to us in the most patronizing way, assuming that, as women, we would always be superficial, not contributing members of society," she recalled. "He made us furious."

Following graduation from Barnard in 1904, Caroline organized and became president of the Collegiate Equal Suffrage League of New York State. Handwritten by Caroline, the roster of its members, generally with college affiliation degrees, reads today like a *Who's Who* of leaders of that period and the years to come. Caroline traveled throughout New York State, speaking at suffrage conventions, teas, clubs, wherever she could find an audience, enlisting supporters. In 1908 she was invited to become executive secretary of the National College Equal Suffrage League. In that post she traveled across the country enlisting men and women from colleges and universities in the fight for votes for women.

She later became field secretary for the Women's Political Union, and in 1912 a branch of the W.P.U. was organized in Rockland through the joint effort of Caroline and her mother. Mrs. Conklin of Valley Cottage headed the Rockland branch with Miss Mary Davidson of Hillburn, Mrs. Leber of Blauvelt, Mrs. Fink of Spring Valley and Mrs. Polhemus of Nyack. Other members included Mrs. Lee in Stony Point, Miss Irene Hedges in Haverstraw, Mrs. Conklin in Tallman, Mrs. Hough in Congers, Miss Elsie Suffern in Hillburn, Mrs. Manchester in New City, Mrs. Moffat in Sloatsburg, Mrs. Van Ingen in Spring Valley, and Miss Grace Sitler in Suffern.

For most of these women, work for suffrage was vastly more than tea parties, although there were plenty of those chiefly for money-raising purposes. It meant assignment to election districts where they would ring doorbells, distribute flyers, arrange meetings, and keeping an everlasting check on the men who were for or against, and getting the "pros" out to vote on Election Day.

A surviving record of 1915 compiled by one such worker shows: New City, enrolled voters, 263, those for suffrage, 92, votes against suffrage, 171; Blauvelt and Orangeburg: enrolled voters, 183, votes for suffrage, 70, votes against suffrage, 105.

Slowly but steadily during these years, the number of men voters who could be counted on for support was increasing, and some worked actively. They helped financially, they joined in pressuring legislators, they talked to doubtful voters, and when Election Day came, they went to the polls and voted for women suffrage. Among them were Morris Crawford, who became one of the suffragists' best speakers, the Rev. James MacMurray of St. Paul's Methodist Church in South Nyack, C. Arthur Coan, Thomas Gagan, Robert E. Leber, John Sickels, the Rev. J. McCarrel Leiper, Archibald MacKellar, John W. Sherwood, Thomas H. Lee, and the Rev. A. H. Fish.

The virulence of the campaign in Rockland is illustrated by a flyer circulated by the "antis," which stated, "Destroyers of Home and Country, The Greatest Peril to Civilization and this Government, Woman Suffragettes have cast aside the Ten Commandments." The flyer went on to describe how all governments have been ruined when women usurp the rights of men. Despite such attacks, Caroline Lexow and the suffragists were undaunted. Through speeches, rallies, parades, and constant pressure on politicians, the tide began to turn.

Meanwhile the suffragists had drawn the children into the campaign with the contest on "What is the best reason why your mother should vote?" The prize: $2. Jared Osborne, aged 8, won the boys' prize. "The reason why my mother should vote is as follows: because those who obey the laws should help to choose those who make the laws." Natalie Young, the girls' winner,

Caroline Lexow speaking in Buffalo, c. 1914.
Photo courtesy of her descendant, Katharine Fulmor.

wrote: "The reason that women wishes to vote is that they pay part of the taxes and know more about caring for children, they also stay at home and work for nothing."

Hopes were high for the election of 1915, but the bad news came to Rockland headquarters in the early morning hours of November 3. In Rockland the suffragists had lost by about 400 votes, but, to Caroline's satisfaction, the South Nyack pole carried for suffrage. Statewide, the issue was overwhelmed by 194,984 votes. But the women remained grimly optimistic.

In January, 1915, Caroline was married to Philip Westerly Babcock, and with a home and family to care for, she slowed her suffrage activities to some degree, although her interest remained intense. The women in Rockland and the state, meanwhile, gathered their forces for one more try at amending the New York State Constitution. Mrs. Leber headed the county forces, later turning over those responsibilities to Mrs. William A. Serven of Pearl River, whose husband was elected Rockland's assemblyman in 1915.

As emotions intensified and banners became more inflammatory, suffragists in Washington, D.C. were often assaulted and beaten. Their attackers were never restrained. All told, 287 of the women were arrested and 97 went to prison for periods ranging from a few days to

six months. The only charge ever lodged against them was obstructing the sidewalk traffic.

Finally in 1917, the long years of hard work paid off: the vote for suffrage in Rockland County was 4238 for, 3735 against, a margin of 503 votes. Since it had lost by more than 400 votes in 1915, it meant that in the intervening years almost 1,000 votes had been "turned around." Statewide, New York delivered to the suffragists the majority of 88,000 votes. Suffrage in New York was won.

The story of the final triumph of suffrage in Washington has been fully told elsewhere and need not be repeated here. It is not one of the nobler chapters of our history. It involved courage, tenacity, and sacrifice as well as pettiness and injustice. On June 4, 1919, Congress finally approved the 19th Amendment and sent it to the states for ratification. Only one woman, Charlotte Woodward, who had attended the first Woman's Right Convention in 1848, lived to see the amendment enacted and ratified by the states, and she voted for president in 1920.

Caroline Lexow Babcock remained active in the struggle for equal rights for every person. While in her 90s, she reflected back upon her decades of work and said, "I think we've accomplished more than people realize. I'd do it all again if I had to."

Excerpted from
Ladies' Lib: How Rockland Women Got the Vote,
Isabelle K. Savell, 1979

Women Get Franchise Right on October 12th

New Voters Will See Election Machinery For First Time in Rockland County
Only Questions Demanded by Law Will be Asked by Election Inspectors

Miss and Mrs. Voter will be given her first opportunity to take the preliminary step toward exercising her right of franchise in Rockland County October 12. That is the first of the two registration days. In several congressional districts, however, women have had the opportunity to declare their right to vote, and thousands of them exercised that privilege last spring. In some parts of the state the first registration day is October 7.

No politician underestimates the importance of the woman vote. Both parties are making a bid for the support of the new voters. They are bending their every energy to get the woman voter out to register. They are now wondering whether she will do as man has done in the past—keep the political leaders on edge by refusing to register until the last minute.

Whether or not the women will consider it worth while to take advantage of their right of franchise after they see the trouble a man has to go to in order to register is something the politicians are debating. Some men fear that some of the women may consider the poll clerks impertinent in the queries and refuse to finish their registration. However, the clerk will ask only the questions demanded by law.

However, the male framers of the election laws have made one concession to the women that they have not granted to the male elector. A man must tell his correct age. A woman does not have to tell how old she is if she is more than thirty. For months the political leaders were worried about the age question. They appreciated the sensitiveness of some women who had passed the thirty mark, and who still clung tenderly to the birthday that had passed years and years ago when they were asked how old they were. They also wished to save a good many from perjury. So the election officials decided that it would be sufficient for women who had passed the first score and ten of her life to say that she was more than thirty. This leaves the matter of her correct age in doubt, and election officials are not, however, to say "Well, you don't look it."

Although a woman is the equal of man as far as voting goes, she is not in the matter of citizenship. Whereas a woman takes the same citizenship as her husband, a husband cannot take the citizenship of his wife. Consequently an American woman who is married to an unnaturalized alien takes her husband's citizenship and cannot vote until he becomes a citizen. Her rights as to citizenship are restored if she is divorced. An unmarried woman born in another country can be naturalized if she has lived in this country five years.

Rockland County Times, October 1, 1918

Michael McCabe

The *Rockland County Times,* established in 1889 by Thomas Heatley, was taken over in 1893 by Michael McCabe. McCabe was fearless in fighting for better educational facilities for all children, proper fire fighting equipment, better public utilities, and whatever else his strong convictions told him would better the community.

In the words of his daughter, Anne: In the parlance of electronic communications, my father would be known as a personality; but in his day, he was known as a character. It was always his ambition and his endeavor to make Haverstraw a better place for the people who lived here and he gave unstintingly of his talents and his energies to that cause. He was not always right but he fought tirelessly and courageously for what he thought was right. Many a single-handed battle he fought for what he thought was the good of the community.

McCabe also served as town clerk at the age of 21 and was a staunch supporter of the Democratic Party. What is more, he rode in the first automobile to touch the Haverstraw ground. He was also chief of the Haverstraw Fire Department.

William McCabe was publisher and editor of the *Times* from 1940 until his untimely death in 1973.

From *McCabe Family Reunion* and Haverstraw s *America s Bicentennial*

Parade at Haverstraw railroad crossing in 1913.   JSC

Champion Walkers

Thirty-seven years after Nick Murphy of Haverstraw was named world champion walker at the finish of a six-day contest at Madison Square Garden, New York City, in October of 1879, another great athletic event for Haverstraw and Rockland County came when the walking championship of the Hudson River Valley was at stake in the spring of 1916.

Proposed was a contest for four teams of five walkers, each in a series of ten-mile treks in four locations along the river. Three teams were made up from, and sponsored by, the Newburgh *Journal*, the Poughkeepsie *Star* and the Kingston *Leader*. The sponsors combed the rest of the valley for a fourth team, but no one seemed anxious to challenge the "Big Three." Finally, the *Rockland County Messenger* of Haverstraw, published by the Freyfogle family, accepted late in the season— near the starting date, April 27. It was Wednesday the 24th when some of the boys were asked, "Do you want to race ten miles on Saturday?"

Five Haverstraw youths accepted: William Lane, William Flynn, Lee Mackey, Foster Schreeder and Ed Freyfogel. Charles Bacon was press representative and George Melvin agreed to coach. Thus teams of five walkers selected by the newspapers contested the championship of the Valley for Rockland, Orange, Duchess and Ulster counties. In the first race, Clary of Poughkeepsie was the winner, but considering they started the ten mile grind practically unprepared, all the Haverstraw entrants did remarkably well, finishing 7th, 11th, 12th, 13th and 15th. This gave Haverstraw third-place in the teams' scores. The race drew immense crowds who braved the damp, cold day and waited more than an hour to see the race. The walkers in their stretch over the principal streets of Newburgh were viewed by nearly the whole population of that up-river city and its nearby villages.

In the second part of the race (part of the greatest walking match ever staged in the Hudson Valley) on April 29, 1916, the Haverstraw team proved it had overcome inexperience and lack of formal training to forge its way into the winner's circle. The newly found speed of the Haverstraw boys was little short of miraculous. Their showing at Poughkeepsie proved the local boys could "step some." Lane and Flynn took first and second in the event.

This great showing by the two Haverstraw boys caused a great amount of rivalry between handlers and friends of the other teams. When Lane and Flynn had threatened Clary's lead, one of the Poughkeepsie enthusiasts jumped from his car and proceeded to walk ahead to pace Clary. This was protested at once and started violent arguments. The Poughkeepsians, who by the way were not members of the Board of Judges, then tried to worry Lane and Flynn by yelling that they were running and they would have them disqualified. This launched another argument, finally settled in a hastily arranged truce to let the walkers alone. All hard feelings were forgotten after the race and the Poughkeepsians were loud in their praises of Flynn and Lane.

This four-race challenge of endurance for Hudson Valley supremacy was growing in popularity and enthusiasm. Not only were the contestants whooping it up, but the public was getting more and more aroused by the inner-city rivalry. The newspapers were telling their readers of the spirit which this wholesome sport was developing. On the side, somebody also remarked that their circulations were going up, too.

The third race was held in Kingston on May 6. Lane and Flynn finished second and fifth. Only five walkers were able to complete the marked course because nine other competitors lost their way through Kingston's streets and wound up at the finish line about ten minutes ahead of the leaders.

The Haverstraw team had made the trip in automobiles furnished by George Melvin and Dr. Matthew Sullivan. The Sullivan car ran into all kinds of trouble on the way home and at midnight limped into Newburgh on a flat tire. More trouble developed and they did not arrive home until daybreak the next morning.

The fourth race was scheduled for May in Haverstraw, with the route chosen to start at the *Messenger* office. It was a warm afternoon as the race began at 3:45 p.m., when Police Chief "Kig" Ford fired the starting pistol. Special prizes were donated by County Treasurer Walter Hamilton, coroner Arthur Dutcher, Alfred Miller's drugstore, David Pressler's clothing emporium, Laird Pharmacy, E.P. Vandenburgh's jewelry store, John Zorn hardware, Charles Benson's poolroom, Baum Brothers department store and Clarence Smith's sports store.

The grueling course took its toll on the walkers in the form of cramps and injuries and several had to drop out. The streets this hot spring day were so crowded with local fans and those from the competing cities that automobiles had to force passageways for the walkers. During the last mile, the leaders Flynn and Lane were cheered by the partisan crowds, and William Jenkins, owner of a stationery store, handed Lane a big American flag which he carried to the finish at the People's Bank. Lane won. Flynn was second. Newspaper headlines the following week read, *THE TWO BILLS WIN! Haverstraw boys carry off the honors in Saturday's championship walking match. Match followed with enthusiasm—Hundreds out to see the walkers start at Messenger office-A course lined with interested citizens-*

73

Something new for the village, which now demands more of such sport!

While most Americans were deeply concerned with the tragic events in Europe and with the U.S. punitive raid into Mexico with some of the local boys at the border, our Hudson River Valley newspapers saw this grand race as an outlet for pent-up feelings. And what excitement the contest caused for years to come! Charges continued to shoot back and forth: walking had become

running when the judges were out of sight; some walkers, jostled by the uproarious crowds, lost stride and pace, etc.

The race took place in an era when people were very much impressed by walking and athletic excellence. It was a time that showed Haverstraw youths at their best and demonstrated the grit and courage of Rockland County's athletic prowess.

Dan deNoyelles

Rockland County Sports Hall of Fame
1910-1919

Augusta Bradley Chapman (Nyack) One of the finest women's tennis players nationally of her era, winning over 60 local, regional and national championships during her 30-plus-year career.

Richard "Gus" Shankey (Haverstraw) Pro and semipro baseball player. Also starred in football, basketball and track in high school and college. Coached Haverstraw football, with the team when it won the 1930 county championship.

Donald "Pop" Sherwood (Spring Valley) Official and sportswriter for over fifty years. Played baseball and basketball in high school. Then became one of the county's finest basketball referees and baseball umpires.

Covered sports for thirty years in the local newspaper, *Rockland Leader.*

Howard Parker Talman (Spring Valley) Rockland's first professional athlete. Only person to ever be named to Walter Camp's All-America three years in a row in three different positions. At 6-foot-4, 200 pounds, he was described by his coach at Rutgers as "the fastest big man I ever saw." Also played and held records in baseball, basketball and track. During pro football career played with Knute Rockne. Later became successful coach, wrote three books of poetry, bred champion poultry, was a sportswriter, prospected for gold, silver and oil, worked as a private eye and helped build railroads in Alaska.

The 100-yard dash at a track meet in Orangeburg in 1915. Ed Lovett won the race.

Despite sensational headlines about racial tensions, note that this race was not segregated.   JSC

74

Ice boat racing on the frozen Hudson River, Nyack, 1912. JSC

Columbus Day 1912   Nyack, N.Y.

Reality vs. Fantasy

Lights fill Main Street in Nyack for the Columbus Day celebration of 1912 (left), during a time when many locations had no electricity.

An optimistic postcard from the era (below) is labeled "Nyack, N.Y. in the Future." Note the elevated trolley, as well as the one in the middle of Main Street. A dirigible also flies across the sky.

Photo and postcard courtesy of John Scott.

Along Party Lines

The future did come to Rockland in the form of telephones, but it came with a price. A telephone contract dated 1911 for the town of Ramapo indicated a typical party line (where several people shared the same line, making eavesdropping a local sport) was $24 per year—an amount that was more than the cost of an ounce of gold. Party lines were still common in the county into the 1960s.

Linda Zimmermann

Nyack, N.Y. in the Future.

West Nyack

The Brookside Ice Cream Parlor in West Nyack (left).

In addition to ice cream, the signs advertise "Hot Beef Tea or Clam Broth" for 10 cents, a "Ham & Cheese Combination" for 10 cents and "Coffee, Tea or Chocolate" for 5 cents.

A far cry from the Palisades Center mall, shopping in West Nyack used to take place at Smith's Store (below, left) at the Four Corners. The store also contained the post office.

Behind Smith's store was a blacksmith (below).

This 1915 photo depicts (from l. to r.) Charles Smith, Charles Blauvelt and Ben Smith. The horse is about to be shoed by Blauvelt. John Scott Collection

Haddock's Hall: Piermont

Haddock's Hall was designed and built 1875-1876 for Roger Haddock by his brother-in-law, William H. Hand, for $15,000. The imposing brick building served as a general store and the upper level as a public hall and Piermont's library. In 1900 the Hasbrouck Motor Works manufactured marine motors in the building before it was converted into a silk mill, producing ribbons until 1975. Among the mill's products were to be military ribbons and parachute ripcords during World War II. In 1914 World Pictures of Fort Lee, N.J., used the site for a Venetian palatial scene in its movie *The Hungry Heart,* based on the popular French play *Frou-Frou.*

Maureen and Roger Pellegrini (Orangetown supervisor, 1990-1993) acquired the silk mill in 1976 and spent 13 years restoring it and creating apartments. In 1991 Haddock's Hall was placed on the National Register of Historic Places.

Marianne B. Leese. Photo by John Scott, 1990.

Growing up in Changing Times
Memories of Elizabeth Knapp Anderson

My ancestors, for the most part farmers, established large homesteads—and families—in Sparkill and Thiell's Corners. My father was the estate manager for a well-known lawyer in New York City and commuted to New York on the West Shore division of the New York Central Railroad. He left 7:00 in the morning and returned about 12 hours later.

My two sisters and I spent pleasant days in the spacious backyard, where there was a sandbox, a "four-seater" swing and lots of toys. We also made mud pies and sometimes ate them! Due to a financial crisis in the winter of 1913-1914, we moved into my grandmother's house on Hudson Avenue in Haverstraw. I shared a bed with my older sister Emily, and one night I rolled over Emily in my sleep and dropped to the floor, hitting my shoulder on the rocker of the chair. I cried in pain, and my father appeared in his nightshirt. When I asked where Mother was, he said she was *very* tired and we must not bother her. He tied up my arm in some sort of sling and said that he would have to get the doctor to come as soon as it was daylight.

Early the next morning, Dr. Eugene Laird drove up in his horse and buggy and hurried into the house with his little black bag. He set my fractured clavicle and placed my arm in a sling. The next day he returned to see my mother and it was whispered that a new baby would soon be here. Toward supper time, Dr. Laird announced, "Guess what? You have a brand-new, healthy baby brother!" We just couldn't *believe* it. After all, we girls had been waiting only one afternoon for a baby brother, but Papa had been waiting for years for a baby son!

I remember that there was often so much snow in winter that the mode of transportation was horse and sleigh or sled or on foot, clad in heavy woolen clothes and "arctics" (galoshes with hook fasteners). It was a fairyland and the lovely silence was broken only by chirping birds, sleigh bells tingling, and the calls of children walking in the "tunnels" of snow that lined the sidewalks.

We moved to a new house in 1914 and we had a telephone installed. Our number was 56, which meant that 55 other households enjoyed telephone service before we did, and when we cranked the bell on the side of the box, the operator said, "Number please?" Papa warned us not to talk about "family business" over the phone because he was sure the operator listened in. Of course, if one had a party line, several people could eavesdrop!

Mother could order provisions over the telephone, so life was a little easier for her. Milk was delivered every day, and ice as often as needed. Regular visitors to Hudson Avenue in the summertime were the "umbrella man" and a man who sharpened scissors and knives. We were so happy when the organ grinder made his rounds playing such beautiful music! We loved his monkey, who quickly and gracefully passed his little hat to collect our pennies. There was also a small merry-go-round on a truck bed that came by once or twice during the summer, and we rode to the tunes of "Sweet Rosie O'Grady," "On the Sidewalks of New York," etc. Once during the summer, the circus came to town and the calliope drove through the streets. What excitement!

In 1918 we all had the influenza, and it was a serious strain that carried off a great many people during that year. Mother managed to escape it, but we children all suffered with it. The only "cure" prescribed by the doctor was "milk medicine" (milk laced with whiskey), which we all *hated.*

During the war years, Mother and I kitted furiously for the Armed Forces. I preferred to knit sweaters for the sailors, because the gray wool was so soft; the khaki wool used by the soldiers was scratchy and I felt sorry for the soldiers who had to wear those helmets, mittens and sweaters. I always had my knitting with me, and even took it along when we went to the Saturday matinees (5 cents plus one cent war tax), because I could watch the movie and "knit one row, purl one row" at the same time.

After the war was over and the armistice signed in November 1918, life gradually returned to normal. Foods and other products that had been scarce were again available, and life became more relaxed and pleasant than it had been for the "the duration." Of course, life would never be the same for the families who lost their menfolk, and it was very hard for them when "the boys came marching home."

By 1920 the prosperity that was just around the corner had arrived, and Papa's income had increased so that we could afford to lease a large house on the waterfront. The house, said to have been built in 1792, was known as the Van Houten Tavern for years before it was renovated after the war. It provided a great deal more space than we had ever enjoyed, and a wonderful place to spend our adolescent years.

Women's styles changed drastically. One's hair was "bobbed." The cloche (hat) was in style. My mother didn't adopt this extreme style, her hemline was below the knee. Her hairstyle changed, but she did not have a "flapper cut."

We and all our friends were very active. We roller stated, ice skated, danced and played softball. On cool afternoons after a game we would have a bonfire, "borrowing" potatoes for my mother's pantry for "roast mickies." As I look back on this era, I realize that there was a great deal of variety to our activities as we matured. With the Hudson River at our doorstep and High Tor behind us, there was always swimming and mountain climbing in addition to the regular activities related to church and school.

Mother was paid for playing the organ and training the senior and junior choirs at the church, but she donated all her other skills towards the betterment of the community. My father didn't object to her various community activities, but he didn't like the fact that she was paid as an organist. He was "of the old school" and didn't want her to have money of her own.

In 1920, the 19th amendment gave women to right to vote, and there was a great deal of discussion as to whether or not this was a wise move on the part of Congress. Most men believed the amendment was a big mistake, and in those days of the double standard, most of the wives agreed, to keep peace in the family. Only some of the strong-minded single ladies who were earning their own living had the courage to express their approval of the amendment. I believe the first time mother exercised her right to vote was in 1928, when Papa *instructed* her to vote for Herbert Hoover.

One summer evening my uncle, Irving Brown, presented a Model T to Mother. Mother had given my uncle money to help him start his career, and the Model T was the first of many gifts he gave her in appreciation. After experimenting with her driving for a few days, Mother thought she was ready to take the family for a spin.

After dinner one evening, the whole family got into the car and chugged along Front Street toward Main Street, a few blocks away. As we approached Main Street, Mother suddenly put on the brake and said that she had thought she had forgotten to turn off the gas under the water heater. She turned the steering wheel to the left and then reversed the car to turn around. We went backwards over the curb, across the sidewalk and onto a lawn before Mother put on the brake. Beyond this lawn there was a sheer drop, unprotected by a fence. My father got out of the car and told the children to get out and walk home with him. "Your

mother will kill you all!" he said.

In the summertime, we drove in the Model T to a camp in the Ramapo Mountains and swam in a lake. Mother usually invited some of our playmates to come along, and we often had seven or eight children in the car. On the way to camp there was a long, steep grade called Gate Hill by some, Goat Hill by others. It was said that the reason why it was called Goat Hill was that only a goat could traverse it! Sometimes the car would not make it to the top, and Mother would tell everyone else to get out of the car. Then she would slowly back down, turn around at the bottom and back up. Since cars in those days were gravity fed, this was the only way to keep the engine from stalling on the steep incline. All the children would then climb back into the car at the top of the hill, Mother would turn the car around and we would be on our way.

Getting down Goat Hill was a different proposition. Mother had always told us that she did not want anyone to tell her how to drive because it would just make her nervous. One day when we started down, the car accelerated at a great rate because the brakes failed. Fortunately, her steering ability could not be surpassed, and we eventually came to stop a few miles beyond the bottom of the hill.

"Mother, why didn't you step on the reverse pedal?" I asked. (In the Model T, stepping on the reverse pedal had the same effect as stepping on the brake pedal.)

She replied, "Why didn't you say that at the top of the hill?"

"You said we shouldn't talk to you when you were driving."

After a minute or two mother laughed and said, "Well, all's well that ends well. *Don't tell your father!"*

Postcard of Broadway in Haverstraw, with High Tor in the background, circa 1910.

JSC

78

1920–1929

A SOFT ROAR

It may have seemed as if the post-war party was over when Prohibition began in the first month of the new decade, but the real party was only beginning. The Roaring Twenties was an age of optimism and exuberance—an age of flappers, jazz, glamorous movie stars, flamboyant gangsters, speakeasies and growing prosperity. Duke Ellington was playing in the Cotton Club, Babe Ruth was playing for the Yankees and everyone seemed to be trying to break a record as the fastest, longest or most expensive. Charles Lindbergh captivated the country in 1927 when he flew solo across the Atlantic, bolstering the feeling that Americans could succeed at any venture to which they set their minds.

In 1928, presidential candidate Herbert Hoover promised "A chicken in every pot, and a car in every garage." He declared that poverty was about to become a thing of the past. A year later, the country was on the verge of experiencing the greatest depths of poverty the nation has ever seen.

In Rockland County there was optimism, but not too over-inflated. There were flappers doing the Charleston and parties with bootleg liquor, but nothing as wild as in the cities. To be sure, the 1920s was the first decade to solidly have both feet in the modern world, but the roar was a little softer here. This turned out to be a good thing, because when boom turned to bust, the majority of Rocklanders still had a leg to stand on.

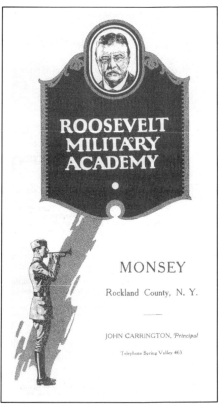

1920s sheet music (above, Marianne Leese), advertisements in the 1927 *Red Book* (above right and below) and August Dumkin's "Blacksmith Tea Shop" in Palisades (right, OTM).

Prohibition: Rockland's Longest Dry Spell

In January of 1920, the 18th Amendment, prohibiting the manufacture, sale or transportation of liquor, went into effect across the nation. Prohibition in Rockland, like the rest of the country, was to last almost 14 years.

However, a mere constitutional change did not stop several enterprising Rocklanders from going into business for themselves. While there were no doubt many small stills throughout the county, one of the largest illegal liquor making operations was discovered in July of 1931 in the barn of the Blauvelt farm behind the Blauvelt railroad station. Built at an estimated cost of $75,000, the huge stills were producing over 100 gallons a day of potent 195 proof liquor.

Rockland County Sheriff Thomas Farley and federal agents raided the barn and destroyed the operation. However, in alleged retaliation for the tip that led to the raid, arsonists set fire to the barns of local farmers John and Philip Klee. Over $40,000 in livestock and property was lost, and thousands of people flocked to see the devastating blazes.

Several days later, another raid took place on the property of Dominick Filleggi in Stony Point. A careful investigation led to the discovery of a large still twenty feet underground. A third still was destroyed on the grounds of the Shankey Pill Company in Stony Point. It had a capacity of 3,000 gallons. Among those arrested for this operation was Richard Shankey, brother of Board of Supervisor Victor Shankey.

While the liquor from these stills was shipped to New York City, Rockland had a steady supply of its own. It was rumored that every town had at least one secret speakeasy where thirsty patrons could go for some bootleg liquor. It was reported that Suffern had as many as five speakeasies, with one of its most popular ones being located in the back room of a soda shop.

Bootlegging was serious, and often deadly, business. Rival gangs across the country fought for control of the trade and incidents such as the St. Valentine's Day Massacre in Chicago in 1929 were stark reminders of the true price of illegal liquor.

John Stead of Hillburn, who ran one of the first pump gas stations, saved a Canadian bootlegger who had been left for dead on the railroad tracks (his fellow gang members did not appreciate the fact that he had gone into business for himself). Risking his own safety, Stead carried the man, whose arms and legs were all broken, to his home where he nursed him back to health in secret.

Once Prohibition was repealed, local restaurants and liquor stores raced to get licenses to serve and sell the first legal liquor in over a decade. However, since officials were concerned about opening the alcoholic floodgates, they initially approved only nine requests from liquor stores throughout the entire county. They wouldn't even consider an application from a store if it was less than 700 feet from another liquor store.

Within days of the store approvals, nine restaurants in Nyack, Suffern, Spring Valley, New City and Orangeburg also received liquor licenses. Remarkably, despite the frantic scrambling to get a license in many parts of the county, not a single request was received from anyone in Haverstraw, Pearl River, Sloatsburg, Hillburn, Piermont or Sparkill. Apparently, residents there had not become as thirsty from the 14-year dry spell as other county residents.

That situation, of course, was not to last too long.

Linda Zimmermann

Eight million women had jobs by 1921—50% were teachers and 37% were secretaries. Relatively few women were professionals such as lawyers and doctors, which was not surprising considering the fact that 92% of America's hospitals refused to allow women to be interns. Regardless of the jobs women held, however, their salaries were considerably less than their male counterparts.

Children were also still being exploited. Although the number of children in the workforce between the ages of 10 and 14 was only half of that in the previous decade, the number still stood at 8.5%.

Schoolmarm Recalls Rural Teaching Days

At 85, Katherine Gibbons Hedges already has outlived most of the 36 children she taught at the Willow Grove Road School in Stony Point in 1920-21. She taught there for only one year but her vivid recollections of the year could have been those of any teacher working in a small, rural school of the time.

Although the world was on the brink of the Roaring Twenties, Mrs. Hedges recalled the social restrictions of the time. It was after World War I, and many young women were bobbing their hair and smoking cigarettes. But if you weren t 21, you couldn t do anything, she said. Women teachers, especially, couldn t be married and couldn t have bobbed hair!

The day after Labor Day in 1920, she stepped through the door of the schoolroom for the first time, and met the 36 children in the first through seventh grades she would teach that year. Among them were Conklins, Babcocks, and Roses, from farm families in the area and families of the Garnerville factory workers.

Mrs. Hedges said the subjects taught were very fundamental basically the 3 R s. The books included readers, spellers, history, geography, and arithmetic, and health and health problems were discussed in the classroom. The program gave one a chance to be innovative. But it was harder for a rural school teacher who had to teach all subjects and all levels.

Mrs. Hedges said the school had no running water, but the janitor provided water in a bucket. Behind the school was a woodshed that doubled as a privy. The woodshed was stocked with coal for the school, and the school was heated by a pot-bellied stove. I remember I used to make cocoa for the youngsters on that stove, she said.

School days, which ran from 9 a.m. to 3 p.m., started out with the Lord's Prayer, followed by a reading from the Bible, the salute to the flag, and calisthenics. There was a 20-minute mid-morning recess, and everybody brought their own lunch. "In the winter, there were men with shovels, but there were no snow plows at the time," she said. No matter how deep the snow, teacher and students made it to school on foot.

"Corporal punishment was permitted in those days," she continued. "And student teachers had been told to hang a paddle on the wall the first day of school. Later, I was told that a razor strop would be better. So the first day of school, in I marched with my book bag, lunch, attendance forms, and razor strop." Mrs. Hedges said she only had to use the strop once during the year, when she escorted the offending student outside. "He wasn't hurt or humiliated, but it broke my heart," she said.

For two years after she left Willow Grove, Mrs. Hedges went on to teach fourth grade boys and kindergarten girls at the nearby Letchworth Village school, but finally quit to marry and raise a family. "I was the next to last teacher ever to teach at Willow Grove," she added. "The following year, the rural schools were discontinued, and the kids took the first school buses in the area to the Garnerville school.

Nancy Cacioppo, *The Journal-News*, 2/8/85

Freshmen Hazing

High school back in the late 20s was something like college. It meant, in those days at the Liberty Street School in Nyack, coming up to the third floor to live in an entirely new world. It also meant you were "freshies" and subject to hazing.

Liberty Street School postcard. JSC

Hazing could happen before school, at lunch and after school, if the upperclassmen caught you. Each "freshie" had to carve out a nice, large wooden paddle for the benefit of his upperclassmen benefactor, who then proceeded to use it on your posterior.

The question was, how to avoid getting paddled, still get to school on time, "spout" the speeches they gave you to say about how "lowly" and "dumb" you were and keep out of trouble. My trick was to always stay away from the school until the last bell rang and then run like the devil up the three floors to my seat in the "freshie" homeroom. Luck was with me just about all the time, except for the first day.

Actually, freshman hazing only lasted a few weeks but it seemed some upperclassmen weren't satisfied. One day about 12 upperclassmen came barging into our homeroom, went directly after two freshman they'd picked out in advance, paid no attention to our homeroom teacher, dragged the two out of the class, paddled them in the hall and then sat them on the water fountain, with the water on while doing it.

Kenneth F. Harniman

Boy Scouts

The pioneers of scouting in the county were a group of public-spirited men who wanted to accept the challenge on behalf of the boys of the community. Throughout the spring and summer of 1924, they worked on programs and personnel and finally they met in the Reformed Church in Spring Valley with more than 100 men present and a budget of $5,600 a year. The group met with great success even in its first year and new troops were organized in Nanuet, Suffern, Pearl River and other communities.

An early recipient of the certificate of heroism was scout Francis A. Goetschius of Suffern, for saving the life of a small boy playing on the tracks of the Erie Railroad.

Daniel Carter Beard (Uncle Dan), National Commissioner of the Boy Scouts of America, came to Rockland because he vowed that when the subway came to Flushing he was going to pick up stakes. So in 1929 he moved to Montebello Road in Suffern. Beard wrote and illustrated articles for *Boys Life* and *Boy Scout Magazine*. He was 90 when he died and is buried in the Brick Church Cemetery in Monsey.

Miriam Chason, *Rockland Review*, 8/2/84

Rockland's First Fast Food?

"Fast food" restaurants were an invention of the twentieth century—a convenience created to meet the demands of the modern world. This hot dog stand at the Four Corners in West Nyack may be the county's first fast food establishment.

The two women on the right in this 1920s photo have been identified as members of the Haerle family.

Photo courtesy of John Scott.

The Movies in Rockland County:
Adolph Zukor and the Silent Era

Paramount president Adolph Zukor's impact on Rockland County was by far the largest of any of the early silent movie personalities, especially in rural New City, which at the time of his arrival in 1918 had a permanent population of about 600, but he was certainly not the first to set foot in the area. Others had already used Rockland County for location shooting, fanning out as they did from points south in New York City and Fort Lee.

The production records of the Biograph Company first mention Rockland County in 1903, with a travelog entitled *From Haverstraw to Newberg*, probably filmed from the deck of a steamer as it traveled up the Hudson. It wasn't until 1911 that Rockland was the single site of a Biograph production when D. W. Griffith and his cameraman, Billy Bitzer, shot *Love in the Hills* on Spook Rock Road in Suffern. It starred Blanche Sweet as an innocent young girl with three suitors vying for her favors in "a tale of the Tennessee Mountains where strangers are unwelcome." Pondering the difficult choice between two country boys and a city slicker on a hunting trip, she had about twelve minutes to make up her mind.

In 1912, a more ambitious project began in Rockland when the Helen Gardner Picture Players established a studio in Tappan for the production of feature films. Her first release, a five-reel production of *Cleopatra,* opened in New York in December 1912, within a month or so of the premiere of Adolph Zukor's first Famous Players film. Helen Gardner was in the feature picture business as early as Zukor, and *Cleopatra* was therefore one of the first films of its type to be made in the United States.

The Helen Gardner Picture Players was the only company that operated a studio in Rockland County and in the next two years, she made seven more movies in Tappan, ranging in length from a seven-reel extravaganza called *A Princess of Bagdad* to several shorter subjects.

Parts of many other movies have been made in the area, from the earliest days up to and including the present. There was 1917 *The Hungry Heart* and the 1922 production of *The Legend of Sleepy Hollow.* In 1924, John Ford was in Nyack filming *The Iron Horse* and, at about the same time, Babe Ruth made a movie in Haverstraw.

The list could be continued through the century, with Woody Allen's use of Piermont for *The Purple Rose of Cairo* and Nyack for a street scene for *Manhattan.* Haverstraw was the site of the firehouse segment of Paramount's, *Ragtime.*

One spot that was conspicuous for an absence of movie making was, surprisingly enough, the Zukor Mountain View Farm estate in New City. Stories continue to circulate about the many pictures that were made on the grounds, but, in fact, none of those who lived and worked there can recall even a single instance of filming. Neither were there any wild parties or late night debauches of the type that have come to be identified with the movie business. Certainly, most of Paramount's major stars were weekend guests at one time or another, and some are remembered for isolated outrageous incidents, but in no way was life at Mountain View Farm a subject for the scandal sheets. Rather, it was a family affair, a quiet orderly place where Adolph Zukor could indulge his inclinations toward empire-building and rule as a patriarch.

When he bought the first 300 acres in 1918 from Lawrence Abraham, a young heir to the Abraham and Strauss Department Store fortune, Zukor acquired property that already included a large house, pool, and nine-hole golf course. He later bought another 500 acres

Adolph Zukor (right) with S.R. Kent on Zukor's estate. JSC

of farmland and unimproved woodlot, and then started building a number of new structures, as well as an additional nine holes for the golf course. He was also apparently striving for a good measure of self-sufficiency, because he spent considerable energy developing a dairy herd, poultry house, vegetable garden, and several acres of feed crops for the livestock. By the mid-twenties, his estate resembled a European manor as much as an executive retreat.

Though he was never overly ostentatious, he was extravagant, spending large sums to import European trees and build a huge swimming pool lined with Italian tile. He also maintained a palm house complete with an alligator pool; a large resident staff that included a propertyman, gardeners, greenskeepers, maids, a chauffeur, and a golf pro; a fleet of automobiles; and, last but not least, a huge yacht that he used to commute from Haverstraw to Manhattan.

By the early thirties the entire movie industry was different as the talkies totally dominated the screen. Adolph Zukor's position changed, too, as after 1935 he was Chairman of the Board rather than President. He continued to be a powerful force at Paramount for decades, however, and though his role was gradually reduced to that of an advisor, he went to work regularly until he was well into his eighties. He died in 1976 at the age of 103.

His life in New City changed, too, and when he became unable to maintain the property as a private estate, he began to open it up for membership as a golf club. The operation ran fairly well, all things considered, but it was not like the old days, and the Zukors gradually faded from sight. By the late thirties, they hardly ever came to Rockland. Finally the property was sold in 1948, and Mountain View Farm became the Dellwood Country Club on Zukor Road in New City.

The silent era has long since passed away, and with it a multitude of screen stars and a mountain of celluloid have become images only imperfectly remembered. It was the beginning, though, and as such set the pace for all that followed. Adolph Zukor and his contemporaries not only laid the foundation, but also directed the growth of the modern film industry.

Excerpts from Ralph Session's book
*The Movies in Rockland County:
Adolph Zukor and the Silent Era,* 1982

Babe Ruth

In 1920, Babe Ruth hit 54 home runs in his first year with the Yankees. Though only 26, he was well on his way to becoming a legend.

However, one of his not-so-legendary accomplishments was a movie he filmed in August of that year in Haverstraw, *Headin' Home*, a flimsy vehicle made purely to exploit the Babe's popularity.

According to journalist Grant Jobson, *Headin' Home* had Babe "lugging ice to carry out the story of the hard-working, small-town boy who won the big game and his sweetheart with a mighty home run."

The great "Sultan of Swat" would drive up to Rockland after a day game at the Polo Grounds to shoot scenes at Eckerson's Field in Haverstraw. The final location shots were filmed on a Sunday when the Babe had a day off, since playing baseball games on a Sunday was prohibited in New York State. While *Headin' Home* did not prove to be a financial success for Ruth, it did help to promote his growing national image.

Unfortunately, an incident during filming caused him to be sidelined for several games in early September. During a night scene shot in Valley Cottage, one of the thousands of bugs drawn by the bright movie lights dared to bite the home run king on the right arm. The bite later became infected and had to be lanced.

Hopefully, Babe Ruth left Rockland with fonder memories than of his bug bite. To the countless local fans who came to see their baseball hero, he left more than autographed baseballs and bats. He left memories that lasted a lifetime.   Linda Zimmermann

The Local Headless Horseman

The first Sleepy Hollow movie based upon Washington Irving's famous story was a silent film, made in 1922, called *Headless Horseman.* It starred Will Rogers as Ichabod Crane, the new schoolteacher in town. Will Rogers (1879-1935), a star of the stage and screen, was generally recognized as the foremost American comedian of his day. He was also a political commentator and satirist.

One of the principle settings of *Headless Horseman* was the Van Houten sandstone house in Nauraushaun, about a mile east of Pearl River. My father, Morris Van Houten, rented the outside of his home to the film company. The movie's leading lady insisted on having a room in the house to change costumes and freshen up and the Van Houtens agreed to that use. I think Will Rogers changed in the barn. The movie company also used my father's horses and other local items. The house was chosen because it looked like a typical Hudson Valley Dutch house that could have been used as a tavern. Many of the scenes in the 50-minute movie took place on the lawn.

The only tangible souvenir of the making of the movie is a pewter reproduction mug given to my parents, but my father had fond memories of Will Rogers. He told about the actor appearing on the stage that summer in New York City in the Ziegfeld Follies and of Rogers, practicing for this show by the outside hand pump at the back of the house, twirling his lariat and roping the family dog that kept getting into the movie scenes.

Wallace C. Van Houten, *South of the Mountains,*
April/June 2000

Nyack Hailstorm

Back in the 1920s, I used to go to the movies for ten cents at the Broadway Theater on South Broadway, across from the Nyack YMCA. (There was also the Lyceum on Main Street.) They had vaudeville back then, plus an orchestra. One act that played there one time was Fred Waring's Pennsylvanians, then fresh out of college and just starting the climb to stardom.

On Saturdays, we watched Our Gang comedies, and Fatty Arbuckle and Jackie Coogan. Then there was "Hoot" Gibson and Tom Mix. That's when westerns were really westerns---and the "good guys" always won.

One day in the midst of a gripping Western, a terrific, continuous pounding sounded on the tin roof, something like someone throwing rocks on it, an awful lot of rocks. It sounded like continuous thunder on that ample tin roof. Finally, the usher opened one of the side doors, looked out and quickly closed it again. "Hailstones as big as baseballs" was the word passed around. They announced that everybody was to "stay inside until you're told to go out."

From that point on, little attention got paid to the picture being shown—kids wanted to look out and see for themselves. When we did, we found out it was hailstones, and they "were as big as baseballs," lying all over the street.

Cars back then had canvas roofs, most of which were ripped to shreds from the power of those ice bricks. However, the hardest hit of all were the greenhouses of the florists, especially Pye's on Third Avenue and Gomersall's in Grand View. Those big hailstones demolished their glass-pane roofs and ruined floors as well as flowers.

However, there was a brotherliness and camaraderie back then that's questionable if it would be around today. The other florists around the county got together, came over to Nyack and helped repair all those panes—all within a few days.

Kenneth F. Harniman

The Rose House

This house on Thiells Road in Stony Point was built in 1819 by William Henry Rose. The photo was taken shortly after Stephen Anderson (who married Sadie Rose) bought the house in 1920. Anderson was often asked to sell the windows, but repeatedly refused as they held the original glass. Despite making many improvements, original elements such as the wide plank floors were carefully maintained.

The house was sold again in 1955, several years after the death of Mr. and Mrs. Anderson. Future owners allowed the house to fall into disrepair, the brook on the property was rerouted to underground pipes and time and neglect threatened to eliminate another local treasure.

This picture and information was submitted by Marjorie Anderson Fioriti (seated on her mother's lap on the steps in this photo), who at the age of 81, bought a computer and began gathering and recording her family's long history in Rockland, thereby preserving it for future generations. The new owners of this property have asked Marjorie for her photographs and memories, as they have plans to restore the house, in order to preserve it for future generations, as well.

Linda Zimmermann

Recollections of a Valley Cottage Old-Timer

After Edward Lock (owner of Lock's Hardware and Mower Service in Valley Cottage) and the 11 other children who attended the Valley Cottage school in the 1920s, finished their school day, they would cross the dirt street to watch the blacksmith make spokes for wagon wheels and shoe horses.

"Valley Cottage was like a town in the wild west," said Lock, who was born in the hamlet in Clarkstown in 1919. "The railroad depot on Kings Highway was always bustling with commuters going to New York City or Newburgh, which was then a thriving river town. We had double rails running through Valley Cottage at that time."

There were horse-drawn carriages, dusty roads and "everybody knew everybody because there weren't a whole lot of people living here," said Lock, whose father was a carpenter. But there was the old post office near the railroad station and the saloon with a hitching post.

During Prohibition, when the Valley Cottage folks wanted to kick back, they could draw a little white lightning from one of the several local stills. "I never tried it, because I was too young, but I smelled it though," said Lock, who opened the hardware store 10 years (1972) ago after working 38 years for Lederle in Pearl River.

"Valley Cottage slowly began to change as the years went by and then it just started to boom with the rest of Rockland when the Tappan Zee Bridge was built," he said.

But he still hears the ring of the hammer on the anvil and he can still smell the dust kicked up by the high-stepping horses.

Rockland Review, 2/24/82

Campbell's blacksmith shop in 1890, once located to the left of the Valley Cottage post office. Pictured are: W.N. Campbell, H. Campbell, and Harry, Lilly, Edna and Walter Hick.   JSC

Public Enemy Kills Two in Pearl River During Bungled Bank Heist

The year was 1921, just four days after Christmas, and Pearl River was covered with a fresh blanket of snow. Nobody imagined that the serenity would soon be shattered by one of Rockland's most outrageous crimes of the century.

It happened shortly after noon, when a diminutive man wearing a black derby strolled into the First National Bank of Pearl River and announced a stickup. By the time he fled through the bank's rear window, two young tellers lay dead of gunshot wounds. A passer-by who tried to intervene was critically wounded.

The bungled robbery left Pearl River numb and sent police officers on a bizarre manhunt that lasted nearly a decade. They wouldn't learn until years later that their suspect was a nationally-wanted "public enemy" of the 1920s.

A real estate office now occupies the old bank site near the corner of Central and Railroad Avenues. Only a simple bronze plaque on a flagpole in a park nearby remains as a tribute to the slain tellers. "In Memoriam. James B. Moore and Siegfried W. Butz who lost their lives in defense of the First National Bank of Pearl River December 29, 1921," the plaque reads. But old-timers say they never will forget the gruesome events of that bone-chilling day.

Warren Harding was in the White House, Prohibition was a year old, silk stockings were on sale for $1.95 a pair and teenagers were dancing the foxtrot to tunes with lyrics like "five foot two, eyes of blue." In Pearl River, Moore and Butz were minding the bank while the rest of their colleagues were out to lunch. Then, a well-dressed gentleman who had rented a safe deposit box nearly two months earlier entered the bank and asked for his key.

Before the employees had a chance to respond, the customer pulled out a pistol and demanded money. It is believed that the bandit was after the $8,000 payroll of the Dexter company, which was delivered to the bank three hours earlier by two armed guards.

"They (Moore and Butz) used their guns, but the bandits overpowered them and both were shot through the heart," said a story in the December 29, 1921 edition of the *Nyack Evening Journal*. Early newspaper accounts reported that as many as four robbers were involved in the holdup. But only one man was ever caught and later accounts indicate that the culprit was a lone gunman.

Adolph Miller, a watchman at a railroad crossing near the intersection of Central Avenue, was standing at his post when he heard shots inside the nearby bank. "Miller dashed to the front door to see Moore grappling with a man in the doorway. Butz was lying near the two men. As Miller entered the bandit fired four shots at both men,

Miller sank to the floor," according to *The Nyack Evening Journal*. Moore was 35 years old, Butz was 19.

The suspect then escaped through a rear window and fled in a new Ford touring car that was parked behind a nearby lumberyard. He took no money. At the same time, in their home a few blocks away, the Butz family was sitting down to the traditional afternoon dinner. "We heard the fire whistles and my mother and I ran to the window," recalled Butz's sister, Louise Butz Secor.

The 73-year-old Spring Valley resident remembers it clearly. It wasn't until after the dinner dishes were cleared and her mother picked up the telephone to make a call that Mrs. Secor, then 11 years old, learned her brother had been slain.

"We had a four-party line," she said. "My mother picked up the phone to make a call and she heard that Siegfried Butz was killed."

The brutal slayings forced cancellation of the annual Pearl River New Year's Eve ball. "Out of respect for the dead men," said an account in *Journal*, "no demonstration for greeting the new year was held in Pearl River."

Clues and dead-end leads sent police "and posses of men" searching across the country. Finally, the manhunt led to a lamp and electrical supply shop in nearby Westwood, N.J., owned by a man called Henry Darsche. The mild-mannered electrical contractor, it turned out, was actually Henry Fernekes, better known as the "Midget Bandit," one of the country's most daring and cold-blooded criminals of the 1920s.

As the story goes, it was largely the amateur detective work of Augustus M. Geiger, a one-time noted stage artist known as "Vail the Magician," that traced the crime to Fernekes. By the time his identity was uncovered, Fernekes had disappeared. The case ground to a frustrating halt until several years later, when the infamous "Midget Bandit" was jailed in Chicago for the murder of a bank employee there. But after only a few months in jail, the shrewd gangster escaped, walking out of the prison in a suit of clothes that had been smuggled in to him. Fernekes next surfaced when Chicago police caught him years later in a plot to kidnap the son of the owner of the giant Marshall Fields department store empire, according to Ralph Braden, Orangetown's town historian.

By that time, the "Midget Bandit" had become a ringleader of one of Chicago's South Side organized crime syndicates that flourished during the turbulent 1930s. In 1935, faced with the prospect of life behind bars, Fernekes took his own life after the failure of a plot by members of his gang to break him out of jail.

Hilary Waldman, *The Journal-News*, 1/1/84

Ku Klux Klan

An organization engendering considerable public interest made the newspapers in 1923—the Ku Klux Klan. In August, a huge fiery cross was set to burning near a saloon in Nyack. It was said at the time it could not have been the work of the Klan, as there was no such thing in Rockland County. Later the same month, though, the Presbyterian Church in Palisades was treated to a "donation visit" by a platoon of the hooded knights. They entered as a group, incognito in their awesome robes, and sat, impassively, while the pastor lauded them for their noble intentions. They aspired, he said, to help the needy. During the offertory, the Kluxers contributed generously to the collection plate, and then, following the benediction, drove off in their automobiles, leaving as mysteriously as they had come. Reports suggested they were from New Jersey.

In September of the same year a bomb exploded on a mountain above Suffern. In May the following year, a second cross was burned at the same saloon in Nyack that had been a target before, and note was made in the newspaper of the owner's being under indictment for the sale of intoxicants. Similar incidents continued in Rockland intermittently throughout the twenties.

Standard practice was for the Ku Klux Klan to mix piety with intimidation. From time to time, groups such as the one that had come to Palisades, would visit Protestant churches in a show of support for the congregation and for Christian principles. Their other prime activities were to post handbills and to burn crosses, the object being to frighten those they deemed in need of a lesson about the true meaning of the American way. They also held rallies at which the automobile helped considerably to create the illusion of a mass organization. By the middle of the decade there was no doubt in anyone's mind that there was a large and active Klan in Rockland County. But, it is interesting to note, names were never published.

During the twenties, blacks, to all appearances, were relatively free of harassment by the Klan in the county. In one instance, though, at Upper Nyack, a speaker—most likely, an outsider from the national office—rapped inter-racial marriage, and urged a ban against admitting 'mongrel races' to the United States. Otherwise, little or nothing was reported about the Klan's racial attitudes. Instead, the local hooded knights concentrated on those they deemed alien, with Italians, Catholics, Jews, and even Masons the special targets of their animus.

Carl Nordstrom, *Phoenician Tales*

Personal Experiences with the Klan

We moved from Brooklyn to West Nyack when I was 15, in 1923 or early 1924. West Nyack was a snobby neighborhood. A neighbor told us, "You come from the wrong side of the tracks. You have to be careful talking to these people, because they're all interrelated. You criticize one of them and it'll get back to them."

In fact, when we moved to the farm, the Ku Klux Klan burned a cross up on a little knoll. My mother said, "Look, they think they're going to frighten us away, but they're not going to; they have another thing coming."

It was because we were Catholic and it was a Dutch Reformed sort of neighborhood. Later we found out who two of them in the white sheets were: one later became the police chief and the other one, the head of the roads and highways for many years. But at the time they did that they were only about 17 or 18 years old, smart guys, you know.

I also met with prejudice against Catholics when I applied for a teaching job in West Nyack. I had been told the job was practically mine, and when I didn't get it a man told me it was because, "you bless yourself with the wrong hand."

Hazel Meehan Komonchak

Gypsies in Rockland County

From the 1880s to the early 1900s, European and Russian Gypsies were being forced out of their countries and many of them chose North and South America for exploration.

Numerous groups entered New Jersey, the New York City area and Rockland County, then encamped in the summer in their own special kind of large wagons pulled by teams of horses, close enough to villages to find enough work. During the winter period they established large family groups in isolated forests.

Many of the townspeople were not certain whether they wanted to let them stay. Usually, a spot was selected where they were allowed to make camp. Generally, a sharp eye was kept on them. Chickens were stolen and Gypsies were known to have difficulty understanding things should be paid for before being carted off to their campsite.

However, the bright, many-colored petticoats the women wore and the way they bound their long braids made them a picture to watch as they walked into town seeking to make money telling fortunes. Although the children were tagging along at their mother's skirts, bright eyed and already wearing swirling skirts like their mothers, the village children watched but at a distance. Too many times had parents warned the children, "Be careful, or the Gypsies will take you away."

Gypsy Camp

North of Kings Highway (South Greenbush Road) and the old Nyack Turnpike heading east toward Central Nyack, the first road on the right has been known for many years as Gypsy Camp Hill Road, now Laurel Road. The large field on the right of this intersection was a favorite gathering place and camping ground for itinerant bands of Gypsies. These colorful people, ever on the wander, would come in the night, stay a while to make some money on odd jobs and various crafts they excelled in, and when they got restless again they packed their wagons, hitched up their ponies and wandered off to return another year. The last encampment there was some time in the late 1920s.

In other seasons traveling carnivals and small circuses used the camp field. It was also a favorite baseball field. Each local community had its own ball team and there was fierce rivalry among the teams and their local supporters who followed them.

The migrating Gypsies arrived each spring in their family horse-drawn wagons and encamped along the Haverstraw brickyards. They brought additional young horses to trade with the yard owners who had need for the heavy towing of bricks and loaded wagons. The Gypsy men sold and refinished pots and pans and other utensils and did chores about the farms, the women did fortune telling in towns.

The men were excellent horsemen and trading with the farmers and sportsmen was an annual business until the early automobiles became popular for towing the large family wagons.

In the Depression years of the late 1920s and 30s, horses were no longer necessary for travel or trading. Automobiles were plentiful and Gypsies flocked to larger cities where various relief and welfare programs became available if they remained there. Abandoned buildings and empty stores were used for living, trading, fortune telling, etc.

The Gypsies' large family groups are led by a "Big Man," the leader and contact man, when dealing with the police and problem family members. He is assisted by a Council of Elders when necessary.   John Scott

The Gypsy Queen

Each spring during the 1900s, and I dare say before then, the Gypsies would pass through the county on their way to the fairs—such as the Danbury Fair in Connecticut and our own Orangeburg Fair.

They would camp for the night, or longer, on land between Monsey and Spring Valley, before crossing on the Nyack Ferry. Some years they would camp on Levison's Hill, at the corner of Greenbush Road and Nyack Turnpike.

It was about the early 20s when their queen was brought to Nyack Hospital, dying of pneumonia. It was

A Gypsy camp on the Short Clove in Haverstraw, c 1905-10.   JSC

my honor to be with her and my good luck to have witnessed the following crowning of the new queen.

We knew the queen was dying and her attendants were called to be with her. Reverence and sorrow were expressed by each and every one of them, but no tears.

As the end was near, they asked if they might place her gold-rimmed purple velvet robe about her and place her mace at her side. It was granted.

The queen was dead!

Reverently at her bedside, her robe and crown were transferred to the new queen with only a low chant and prayers by all in the room.

We moved the group to a room by themselves until the necessary procedures were taken for the queen's removal with them.

I assure you we watched that proud little band go on their way and it was our turn to be reverent, and I am not ashamed to say I shed a few tears.

Caroline Venturini, *SOM*, Jan./March 1972

The Gypsy King

Bill Meyer told an amusing story about his father's first experience with the local Gypsies. Needing a horse for his Haverstraw grocery business, he went to the Gypsy camp to purchase one. Unfortunately, he was young and inexperienced in the subtle art of horse trading, and his purchase was wheezing and out of breath before he even made it back home.

Annoyed at having been duped, the naïve Meyer immediately returned to the Gypsy's camp and demanded to see their king. The Gypsy king did consent to see him, and instantly realized that the youth was something less than a savvy businessman.

The king graciously offered to give Meyer his money back or have his pick of any other horse. However, the king also made it clear that this was a one-time offer, and that if Meyer intended to do business with them again, he had better be well prepared the next time.

Thus the age-old saying of "Buyer Beware" was a lesson taught and learned that day, thanks to the King of the Gypsies.

Linda Zimmermann

The Nyack YMCA

Ceremony for the laying of the cornerstone (above, JSC) for the Nyack YMCA on Broadway on September 18, 1927, and the building in 2001 (right, LZ).

For those who grew up in Rockland, buildings and places hold very personal memories that no one else can quite understand. The following is an example:

The YMCA in Nyack has been the site of countless meetings and events over the decades, but one incident always comes to mind every time I walk by, even though it took place years before I was born. My father, Walter, was a boxer in his youth, in both school and the Marines. One day, the "Champ" came to town and my father decided to spar a few rounds with him. It didn't last that long.

The Champ connected with a powerful punch that sent my father over the ropes, through the front doors and out onto the sidewalk, where he woke up a few minutes later. Despite the outcome, he was always able to laugh about it.

To this day, I can't look at the Y building or walk over that section of sidewalk without picturing my Dad lying there, shaking his head and wondering what had happened.

Linda Zimmermann

St. Anthony's Church

St. Anthony's Church was once a major shrine in the New York area and helped put Nanuet on the map. In 1920, the German families of the area started building their church using the local fieldstone. The building was completed and dedicated in June 1923. Father Nicholas Hans dedicated a shrine to St. Anthony and began spreading the idea of pilgrimages on Pilgrim Sunday, the Sunday closest to the Saint's feast day, June 13.

Hundreds came in the beginning; by the late 1930s when the shrine reached its peak, fifty to sixty buses came, plus hundreds of cars. In the tradition going back to medieval days, Pilgrim Sunday was a blending of religious exercises and family recreation. The recreation, picnics and entertainment were held in the grove west of the shrine church. However, times change and with it a change in taste and religious fervor, so that the Pilgrim Sunday eventually faded from the Rockland scene.   Article by Robert Burghardt, postcard courtesy of Ken Kral.

The Magic of the Automobile

Through the magic of the automobile, it was possible for a person to work at one corner of the triangular county, shop at a second, and live in the third. It was no longer obligatory for stores and factories to be built in close proximity. Consequently, the villages, which originally had emerged in response to unique, nineteenth century transport imperatives, had, in measure, become superfluous.

The village of Nyack was also superfluous in another way. As the twenties wore on, exciting talk about a bridge to span the Hudson developed. The river, originally the reason for the village's existence, had, by 1925, become an obstacle to be conquered, one that was to be overcome when, in 1931, the George Washington Bridge, connecting Manhattan with New Jersey, had been completed. A direct trip to the city by auto had become possible.

Carl Nordstrom, *Phoenician Tales*

The Jewish Community: 1920-1929

In Spring Valley, Jewish life centered on the home and the family-owned businesses. Many children worked with their families. Main Street was their front yard. The synagogue was also an important entity in Jewish life.

The Jewish Community Center of Spring Valley, an outgrowth of the Congregation Sons of Israel, was organized in the home of Harry Herzog in 1923. The congregation met in storefronts and private homes until they purchased a large home on North Main Street, which was dedicated on January 15, 1928.

In 1924, the Congregation Sons of Israel in Suffern purchased the adjourning 50' x 125' lot for $850 for expansion of their growing congregation.

In 1926, the Congregational Sons of Israel (Nyack), as they were then named, dedicated their first synagogue on the corner of South Broadway and Hudson Street, on property acquired six years before. Growth continued over the next number of decades and in 1955 the members voted to affiliate themselves with the Union of American Hebrew Congregations (the Reform movement). Nine years later, they purchased a three and a half acre site in Upper Nyack, and the following year reestablished their affiliation with the United Synagogue of America (the Conservative movement).

Kehilath Israel, on Old Nyack Turnpike, is an Orthodox Congregation. Established in 1930 to serve the south end of the Spring Valley it was known as the "little shul" and was the first to offer a release time program for religious instruction of public school children.

Harold L. Laroff

91

Celery Farms

The celery farms of Don L. Bates, Inc., half a mile north of Congers, between the State road and the West Shore Railroad, occupy 68 acres, 40 of which are under intense, scientific cultivation, largely in celery.

Six years ago a worthless swamp, the area is now (thanks to engineering skill and considerable expense documented by the fact that 3 1/4 miles of ditches were dug) perhaps the most productive of any in Rockland County. There are grown annually 10,000 crates of celery and many car loads of other vegetables, much of which is shipped to Philadelphia.

Besides the usual farm buildings, the box factory and office and the manager's residence, there is one of the best looking lunch and refreshment halls and complete auto service stations along the roads of the County.

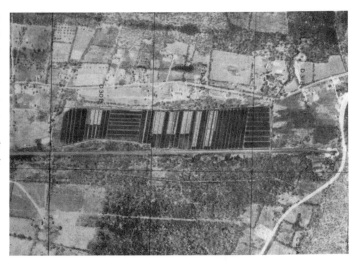

Rockland County Red Book, 1927   Aerial view of the celery farm.   Courtesy of John Scott.

Conger Property Sold

Lamborn Interests Acquire Great Farm Track Running From Lake Road to Top of Long Clove to Make Big Development

With the employment of lawyer Fred Penny to make an exhaustive search in order to clear the title because of the extensive litigations and previous transfers, the possession of the once princely estate possessed by Abram B. Conger when that gentleman in his activities, practically owned all the land from Rockland Lake to Main Street, Haverstraw, and from the Congers-Haverstraw Road to the river (with the exception of small acreage farms owned by members of the Snedeker family, the Gurnee place and the Nash property), the property is to pass into strange hands.

Fifty to sixty years ago, this farm was rated as one of the great stock breeding establishments in the State of New York. There are many families like the Allisons, Tierney, Anderson, Nelson and others who were foremen, superintendents and men in charge of the great Congers enterprises.

After the death of Mr. Conger, there was much litigation and the property went into the possession of Catherine M. Hedges, a relative. From time to time, parcels of this property had been sold. The Palisades Interstate Park acquired by condemnation all the property along the river, taking from the estate the biggest part of its income which was received as royalty from the sale of crushed stone. The subdivision of all the Conger property in Haverstraw and its sale by parcels, lots and sections to individuals has been told from time to time, the big swamp lying between the Congers Long Clove road and the West Shore Railroad was the last big parcel sold a few years ago to the present operator of the truck farm.

The present transaction, therefore, if we are correctly informed, includes all the balance of the Conger's farm, perhaps from seven to eight hundred acres. This is a family real estate enterprise and has been purchased for the purpose of real estate development.

Newspaper article, August, 1924

The Organ Factory

Robert Clark, the son of a furniture craftsman and organ builder, began his own business on Brookside Avenue in South Nyack in 1921. Composed of many exotic materials and requiring extensive calculations and planning, each organ took an average of one and a half years to build and install. He also serviced and tuned several of the local church organs. Clark sold the business in 1964.   Linda Zimmermann

... In 1925 a Tennessee law is signed making it a crime to teach the theory of evolution in public schools...A major show in Paris highlights the new "art deco" style...Adolf Hitler publishes *Mein Kampf*...Charlie Chaplin stars in "The Gold Rush"...40,000 Klansmen parade through Washington, D.C....

Rockland County Sports Hall of Fame: 1920-1929

Henry (Peck) Artopee (Nyack)

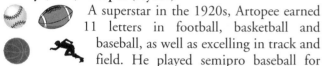

A superstar in the 1920s, Artopee earned 11 letters in football, basketball and baseball, as well as excelling in track and field. He played semipro baseball for several teams.

Bob Bacheller (Congers)

Although earning 16 letters in high school in baseball, basketball, track and tennis, Bacheller is best known for his achievements on the tennis court. For over thirty years, he won tournaments throughout Rockland and surrounding areas. Bacheller was a tireless ambassador for tennis, helping to form the Nyack Field Club and lobbied successfully for the construction of tennis courts in Clarkstown.

Johnny Burns (b. Long Island)

Moving to Rockland in 1925, Burns became a trailblazer in the development of sports programs for persons with disabilities, a precursor to the Special Olympics. He was recreation director at Letchworth, a boxing referee for many televised fights and promoter of offbeat but popular events such as the swim across the Hudson. A selfless humanitarian, after retiring Burns moved to Jamaica and worked in an orphanage.

Billy Hogan (Piermont)

The "Pride of Piermont," Hogan was Rockland's first boxing great, beginning his career at age 13. As an amateur, this lightweight had a 29-match winning streak and was 78-6. Turning pro, he fought 51 bouts in four years, with an impressive record of 32 wins, 12 losses and 7 draws. Hogan was never knocked out, and lost by a TKO only once. Many Rocklanders will remember him in later years as the owner of Hogan's Diner on Route 303 in Orangeburg.

Jerry Hollahan (Pearl River)

Earned 9 varsity letters in football, basketball and baseball. Was offered football scholarship to Georgetown, but declined in order to help his family during the Depression. Played semipro football and baseball. After moving upstate, Hollahan became a champion golfer.

Art Hopper (Pearl River)

Helped found Pearl River Little League, Rockland Sports Hall of Fame and the Pearl River Soap Box Derby. In school, he was a star in baseball, tennis and other sports despite having a withered arm from polio. A reporter for the *Journal-News* for 14 years, and a great advocate for many civic causes.

Edward J. Maurer

"E.J." was a giant in Rockland bowling, and organized and was president of the RC Bowling Assoc. Averaged over 200, when 200 scores were not common. Wrote for the *Journal-News*, including his popular column, "Down the Alley." Is remembered by the annual E.J. Maurer Golden Pins tourney. Also semipro baseball umpire and coach for several sports.

Ira Shuttleworth (Pearl River)

Outstanding Pearl River High School coach and athletic director from 1927 to 1960, affectionately known as "Coach" and "Uncle Ira." During his tenure, his teams won or shared 23 championships in football, basketball and baseball, with an aggregate record of 380-273-11. Shuttleworth was a model of composure and decorum who earned universal respect.

...The "Charleston" dance is first seen in New York and the "flapper" dress is in style in 1925...Television is demonstrated in 1926...The American Association of Professors declares that college football promotes drinking and dishonesty and students should be limited to playing for only one year so they do not neglect their studies...Bennett and Byrd fly over the North Pole...American golfer Bobby Jones wins British Open...A government committee hears testimony that Prohibition has caused an increase in alcoholism, crime and insanity...Gene Tunney beats Jack Dempsey to win the heavy-weight boxing title...Harry Houdini dies...

Threefold Community

...It is fitting that there has come among us the experimental group in Spring Valley who demonstrate the latest findings of Swiss science in soils and plant secrets, stemming from Goethe by way of Rudolph Steiner.

Excerpt from Mary Mowbray-Clarke's address, "Rockland County People," read at the New York World's Fair on June 29, 1939

The original farm house.   Courtesy of the Threefold Community.

That "experimental group" first arrived in Rockland County in 1926, seeking farmland and a retreat from its center in New York City. Since that time, it has grown into a virtual small village, occupying a space of approximately 250 acres in Chestnut Ridge (formerly South Spring Valley).

It includes a number of institutions involved in education, the arts, medicine, agriculture and economics, all based on the insights of Austrian philosopher, scientist, and spiritualist Rudolf Steiner (1861-1925). It is the Threefold Community, a place where philosophy and practical work join, creating a unique environment that is immediately apparent when one turns onto Hungry Hollow Road from Route 45.

The original core of the Threefold property on Hungry Hollow Road contained a farm house, a "cow byre" and various outbuildings, all surrounded by farms and forest. By 1928 the farm house had become a guest house and restaurant and 1933 saw the transformed barn as a lecture center for the first international conference "for the study of Anthroposophical theories and practice..." Also established in the 1930s was the Threefold Community Store (now the Hungry Hollow Co-Op) and the Weleda Apothecary.

By 1948 the architecturally unique Threefold Auditorium was completed, and has been widely used by a multitude of performing artists and groups from that time to the present. Expansion continued through legacies and purchases. In 1956, Green Meadow Waldorf School was born from the seeds of an earlier kindergarten group, which continued on through high school in 1974.

Other expressions of Steiner's philosophy that have grown and developed here are the Fellowship Community (1966), an inter-generational, work-based, long-term care residence; the Eurythmy School (1972) for study of this art of dance/movement; the Waldorf Institute (in 1985 relocated here from Detroit), renamed Sunbridge College and state certified, offering teacher training and adult education courses; and the Pfeiffer Center for Biodynamics (1996), where farming and beekeeping are fruitful and buzzing endeavors.

I myself am one of thousands who have migrated to Rockland County since 1926 to participate in the Threefold Community. Recently, a visit there began with coffee and fresh-baked dessert at the Fellowship Community's friendly Hand & Hoe cafe, where I also shopped for biodynamic farm products and a hand-woven, plant-dyed scarf. A stop at the Sunbridge College Book Store and the Hungry Hollow Co-Op completed my shopping agenda. Throughout the visit I noted postings for myriad upcoming events, which it was hard to imagine having enough time to attend!

Ironically, while the Threefold Community draws visitors and students from every continent, some of its immediate neighbors scarcely know of its existence. Public recognition was earned in 1999 when the Rudolf Steiner Fellowship Foundation received the County Executive's Historic Preservation Merit Award for having purchased the adjacent 33-acre Duryea Farm. A farm it will remain, as it is converted from conventional to biodynamic. Indeed "...It is fitting that there has come among us the experimental group in Spring Valley..."

Aleksandra (Alice) Becnel

...In 1926 Herbert Hoover declares that prosperity is at an all-time high, unemployment is almost non-existent, the stock market is booming and Americans are enjoying their highest standard of living in history...

Maxwell Anderson and South Mountain Road

James Maxwell Anderson's world began in a tiny, farmland community in Atlantic, Pennsylvania—difficult to find on the map. By the time he was 19, his father had moved the family 11 times to other little farming communities of Pennsylvania, Ohio, Iowa and North Dakota, to a new town, a new house, a new school and new friends every year or, at most, every two years.

There was a reason for William Lincoln Anderson to suffer his family this nomadic life. When Maxwell was three years old and they were living in Andover, Pennsylvania, his father was offered a Baptist ministry and promptly took it, happy to quit working on the railroad. He was hale, hearty, bluff, good-natured, and bombast came easily to him.

Maxwell, the eldest son, inherited his mother's personality and none of his father's. He was quiet, reserved and thoughtful. His mother managed to supply her children with books to read, and Max, as he was nicknamed, developed a voracious appetite for reading. He devoured the English poets and the plays and poems of Shakespeare and began to write poetry, a pursuit he hid from everyone but his sisters for a time. Writing poems was not considered acceptable activity for a healthy young male in the Middle West farm communities.

After graduating from the University of North Dakota, Max married his classmate, Margaret Haskett, a tiny Irish beauty, bright and independent, who loved words as much as he, and by late 1918, they moved to New York City.

Dad was hired first by the *New Republic* magazine and then as an editorial writer for the *New York World*. Frank Hill, who had been a classmate and was now on the paper with him, told Dad about Rockland County and we all settled in a little house in Grand View-on-Hudson for one year. The nomadic life had not ended. Next was Glen Cove, Long Island, then back to a bigger house in Grand View for another year and finally, in 1922, to South Mountain Road in New City.

The Move to Rockland

There were three or four farm families who owned large stretches of South Mountain Road. Among them were George and Peter Jersey. Peter Jersey had over a hundred acres for sale with three houses. Dad and two friends, Frank Hill and Rollo Peters, an actor, decided to buy the land and the houses together. That done, the next problem was to decide who would get which house. Two of them were built in the 1700s and were far more attractive and valuable than the third, which was built about 1880 or 1890 and was quite undistinguished. The property on which this third one stood did, however, have one very distinctive feature: a wide, deep ravine

lined with eaves with a magnificent waterfall over which a large brook splashed and roared impressively.

Dad simplified the choice for the other two by announcing that he had decided on the humblest house of the three. Frank chose the one right across from Dad because it had flat land on which he could build a tennis court. Rollo was happy with the third, which he called Brook House for the very good reason that it was snugged between "The Road," as South Mountain Road was often referred to, and a fast-running trout stream, the same stream that created Dad's waterfall.

Maxwell Anderson's house on South Mountain Road (top) and the cabin (above) on the property in which he wrote many of his plays.   JSC

Coming to Rockland was to begin the most creative period of my father's life. Once *White Desert* was produced on Broadway in 1923, he was determined that the theater would be his career. The next year when he read the rave reviews of *What Price Glory*, he phoned his boss at the *World* and said, "I'm not coming in. I've quit," and hung up. Teaching and newspaper work were behind him forever. For the first time, the nomadic pattern was broken.

Dad's life was to center on South Mountain Road for the next 30 years, during which he wrote an astounding 39 plays, 28 of which were produced on Broadway. Of the remaining 11 full-length plays, several were produced in regional or university theaters. In addition to this massive productivity, he wrote several radio plays, which were broadcast during and after World War II, a volume of poetry, which was published in 1925, and the novel about his childhood, published in 1952.

Remodeling and a New Pool

In 1924, with the success of *What Price Glory*, Dad set about improving our lives in various ways. He began by enlarging and improving our house, putting in a huge fireplace, more bedrooms and more space in every direction. The design and supervision of the remodeling was done by a friend who lived just below us. He was Carroll French, an artist and wood carver

With money coming in from Dad's success in the theater, his next project was to have a dam built to create a large swimming pond to replace the modest little pool we had created with rocks, sticks and mud. Again, he turned to a neighbor for the job. Mary Mowbray-Clarke, who lived in a lovely old Revolutionary house on The Road, had a son we called Bumper. His real name was Bothwell, but I never heard it used. When Dad discovered that Bumper wanted to be a contractor and had a Chevrolet dump truck for the purpose, he asked Bumper to build the dam. Almost instantly, the pond became very popular in the neighborhood and all summer long our friends and neighbors and their children could be found at "The Andersons' Pond."

20th-Century Encroachment

Dad developed a very deep affection for South Mountain Road and Rockland County as it was in the years after World War I. And although it changed, the change was gradual at first. The dirt road was paved, electricity and telephones were installed, the taxes went up and everyone started to buy cars.

The Rockland Light and Power Company planned to build a huge high-tension power line north and south across Dad's waterfall and house. Captain Ed Jones, a sea captain who had become the chief pilot for the Panama Canal, lived next door to us and the line also went through his property.

Every time the power company finished surveying their proposed power line, Dad and Ed went out in the middle

Bothwell "Bumper" and Mary Mowbray-Clarke. JSC

of the night and removed every one of their surveying stakes and markers. They went to court, wrote letters, got community support and kept pulling up the stakes. Eventually, the power company gave in and moved the line eastward so that it crossed the brook at a part where it ran quietly through a field.

The Rockland Light and Power Company had gained a nickname in those days, given it by one of our neighbors: Rotten Loot and Plunder. Like all utilities, it was always struggling to improve its image. And in the South Mountain Road community, among the artists and writers and individualists of every sort, image was not easy to come by. It took a high degree of honesty.

In the 1930s, Dad and his neighbors were faced with another enemy of their tranquil valley and the mountain for which the road was named. The New York Trap Rock Company had purchased large sections of South Mountain, including the ridges near High Tor, the highest peak. Their objective was to break up the igneous rock and crush it into various sizes for use in building the thousands of miles of roads that everyone was clamoring for to smooth the way for the country's newest love object, the automobile.

Dad became a leading voice in the opposition to the traprock company when it attempted to buy High Tor from the owner, Elmer Van Orden. Dad wrote a play, *High Tor,* about the philosophical question involved in fighting to hold onto a piece of the earth.

The Neighboring Craftsmen

Our neighbors were mostly artists, writers, musicians, actors, weavers and other crafts people. Dad attracted some of his theater associates from Broadway to The Road, or nearby. Burgess Meredith starred in *Winterset, High Tor* and *The Star Wagon* and after the first play, promptly bought a house in Pomona so that he and his wife could be near Dad. Kurt Weill bought Brook House from Rollo Peters, and he and his wife, Lotte Lenya, spent the rest of their lives there. Kurt and Lotte became close friends of Dad and of my stepmother. Marion Hargrove bought Marjorie Content's and Harold Loeb's house. Loeb had been a central figure in Ernest Hemingway's life and therefore in *The Sun Also Rises*.

Helen Hayes, Charles MacArthur, Ben Hecht and his wife, Katharine Cornell, and Guthrie McClintic had all lived in Rockland for many years. Helen and Kit Cornell both starred in Dad's plays; Guthrie directed five of them, including *Winterset* and *High Tor.*

Kurt Weill and Dad wrote two musicals together, *Knickerbocker Holi*day and *Lost in the Stars,* and began a third which was cut short by Kurt's death. Lotte Lenya played major roles in two of Dad's plays, *Candle in the Wind* and *Barefoot in Athens.*

Kurt's death was a very serious blow to Dad from which he never fully recovered. Their collaboration was vitally important to Dad because he was comfortable working with Kurt. They felt the same about the world, and writing lyrics became an outlet for Dad's love of poetry that gave him a new impetus in the theater.

Barefoot in Athens was the last play Maxwell Anderson wrote while he lived in Rockland County. It was a play about Socrates, a challenge he had wanted to fulfill for many years. He felt some kinship with the Athenian's lack of respect for the pompous, the pretentious and the dishonest, but it was difficult to find a flaw in Socrates that would make him the subject for tragedy.

With the death of his second wife, Dad had to abandon South Mountain Road in 1952 and start a new life with his third wife. He sold his house on The Road and bought one in Stamford, Connecticut, about 50 feet from the sound of the waves rolling in on the beach.

Alan H. Anderson, *SOM,* July/Sept. 1988

Residents of the Road

Other South Mountain residents included artist and architect Henry Varnum Poor, sculptor and painter Hugo Robus, theater and film director John Houseman, textile designer Ruth Reeves, artist Martha Ryther, illustrators Milton Caniff and Bill Maudlin and author Marion Hargrove.

Nancy Cacioppo, *The Journal News,* 3/12/2000

Poverty: South Mountain Road Style

Street School, today Clarkstown's Street Community Center, stands at 31 Zukor Road north of downtown New City and not far south of South Mountain Road. Parents of Street School students were at one time very privileged; the parents included stars of Broadway and the intellectual world, to the extent that some of the teachers felt the students did not get a realistic picture of ordinary life.

In an attempt to foster a greater understanding of those less fortunate, one teacher gave a homework assignment of writing a story about "A Poor Family." One student is said to have submitted the following:

"Once upon a time there was a family that was very poor. The father was poor. The mother was poor. The children were poor. The butler was poor. The cook was poor. The chauffeur was poor. The maids were poor…".

Jim Shields

Rockland Lake Goes Up in Smoke

In Rockland Lake on April 20, 1926, workmen were using dynamite to bring down the old, abandoned structures of the once thriving Knickerbocker Ice Company. Unfortunately, they overlooked the fact that the buildings were still packed with the sawdust that used to insulate the ice, and that it was also an extremely windy day. What began as a simple demolition turned into one of the worst fires in the county's history, destroying not only the Ice Company buildings, but nine homes and acres of woods, as well. It took fourteen county departments to fight the blaze, resulting in eight injured firefighters.

"Barns, chicken-coops, garages, houses, woods, everything in sight seemed to be on fire and the smoke was stifling," the *Nyack Evening Journal* reported. It was feared that the wind-driven fire would burn its way to Nyack and continue its devastating work. Eyewitnesses were both amazed and traumatized by the blaze.

"I recall that day and believe me, I'll never forget it," said Andrew Van Cura, who was an 11-year-old student at the time. The schoolchildren were evacuated to a brick church, and Van Cura was unable to make it home because of the fire. "Tremendous wind was blowing that day. Every place you looked was burning and woods were burning. I never got over my fear of fires until the war in Europe, when I saw real horror."

At least one eyewitness, however, "was thrilled by the fire and the brave firemen." This excited onlooker was the vacationing Countess Watari who tried to do her part by supplying the firefighters with bananas.

Rockland Lake was never the same, and the formation of Rockland Lake State Park sealed the fate of this lost community.

Linda Zimmermann

…In 1926 Laurel and Hardy become a team…In 1927 Al Jolson stars in the first "talkie," *The Jazz Singer*…Will Rodgers stars in a radio broadcast to all 48 states in 1928…Mickey Mouse is born…

Lost Treasures

The Treason House

This was the home of loyalist Joshua Hett Smith and on September 22, 1780, it was the scene of an important event in United States history. American General Benedict Arnold met British Major John André here, and Arnold gave André vital information on the fortifications at West Point. This information could have led to the British capturing this strategic point, possibly leading to the ultimate defeat of the American forces.

However, the British plot failed; Major André was captured and eventually tried and executed in Tappan, while Benedict Arnold fled to England and his name became synonymous with the word traitor.

Despite this amazing history, the Treason House was demolished in 1929. An historic marker on Route 9W in front of Helen Hayes Hospital is all that remains to identify the location of this infamous event.

The Lederle Farmhouse

Unusual to the Rockland landscape, this Greek Revival style farmhouse was built in the 1790s. It was purchased by Dr. Ernest Lederle in 1904, and at that time the farming property had just ten small buildings. The house was used as a residence by the Lederle plant superintendent until 1942.

Unfortunately, there was to be no fanfare for the historic farmhouse's bicentennial anniversary. In the late 1990s the house was dismantled, although plant officials claim that it will be reconstructed some day.

This Lederle postcard depicts the house, surrounded by various plant buildings and has the somewhat ironic caption "He who loves an old house…"

"He who loves an old house.."

Linda Zimmermann, photos courtesy of John Scott

Memories of Pearl River

I lived in Pearl River from 1923 to 1986 and I have many wonderful memories of that time of my life. We lived on 42 Ridge Street across from the old library and in back of Ablondi's Bar. First, a few family memories: My father, John Cucchiara (who later anglicized his name to Spooner), was a chemical dyer and owned his own dye house in New York City. There he dyed feathers and material for the "Follies Girls" and he held the patent for "Navy Blue" dye. When the dye house burned down, we came to Pearl River.

Here, Dad became known as "John Spooner, the Green Grocer," from 1927 to 1941. Every morning, Dad would drive to the market in Paterson, N.J.; upon his return he would make his deliveries of fresh produce, street by street throughout the town from his open truck.

My brother, Pete Spooner Cucchiara was born with spina bifida. While he was still very young he went through an operation in which, by mistake, the doctors cut the cords of his legs, which left him without any use of them. Later he had polio. One day while he was in high school, Governor Franklin D. Roosevelt came to Pearl River. He somehow learned of Pete's problems, came to the school and took Pete with him to see his (Roosevelt's) own doctor in order to have Pete fitted with braces like those the Governor wore. Pete became a sports writer at the *Journal-News* and when he died at the age of twenty-two, even *The New York Times* had a story about him.

My brother Dominick (Tom) was captain of his basketball and football teams; he was a one-mile runner and was "All County." Since retiring from Lederle Laboratories and the Carpenter's Union, he has been refereeing baseball and football games.

My grandfather, Dominick Bonomolo, was a banker in New York City and he helped lay the corner stone at the then National Bank in Pearl River. At times he was in the chorus at the Metropolitan Opera and at other times he was hired by the Metropolitan as a "clapper," whose job it was to keep the applause going for the opera stars like Enrico Caruso. His daughter, Angelina married Angelo Mendolia. Every morning Angelina would drive her father and my mother, Mary Cucchiara, in her horse and buggy to the train station so they could catch the train to New York.

As for the people and places in Pearl River, Joseph A. Fisher had a livery stable at Central Avenue and Pearl Street. There was a social center on the top floor that was rented out for dances and parties. The Dexter Folding Company was on the south side of the Erie Railroad tracks. This was formerly the site of Julius Braunsdorf's Aetna Sewing Machine Company and presently the OTB is located on the property.

Hadeler's Hardware Store is located by the corner of North Main and Central Avenue. Prior to 1905, it was McKniffs General Store, at that time it was purchased by George W. Hadeler. The store is now operated by the third generation of Hadelers, George and Harry.

The Serven Coal and Lumber Supply Company became the Comfort Coal Company about 1913; it was destroyed by fire in June of 1944. Other shops along Central Avenue were the Pearl Shop next to Field's Jewelry Store. The Five & Ten Cent Store was across

the street. Baren's Bakery Shop was on the corner across from the movie house; then there was Edsall & Bargmann's Butcher Shop which was previously the shop of Charlie Kandler. There were Umbland's Soda Shop, the Marine Midland Bank, and Charlie Braunfield's Newspaper Store.

Schumacher & Timmerman's Grocery Store was located next door to Ratgen's Eyeglass and Jewelry Store. A drug store and Paolle's shoe store, on the corner of Central and Main, were across the street from the then National Bank and Sanford's Drug Store. Ed Bouton had a newspaper store. As a young man he worked for Rudy's Newspaper Store on Franklin Avenue. There were a real estate business, the Pearl River Savings & Loan, and a movie house run by Johnny Panteleom. The shop next door was to become a barbershop.

Victor Prezioso's Barber Shop was across from Dexter's. Victor, Jr., and Kirk Gebnor, son of the owner of Gebnor's Printing Shop on Williams Street, were both prisoners of war during WW II. Pete Rizzo's Sanitary Barber Shop, later owned by Angelo Mendolia, was on Main Street. At a later date, Mendolia moved the shop to the corner of Central Avenue and Williams Street.

View of Pearl River in 1907 from the western part of town.   JSC

Kenny Pilgrim operated Pilgrim's Market on Franklin Avenue in a building owned by George Retz. There was a fabric store, Andy's Men's Store, Mel's Men's Shop (now Mel's Army and Navy Store), and Gavel's Dry Goods Store where linens and clothing could be purchased. Les Bowers had another dry goods store, and there was Model's Grocery Store—both were across from the Park on Main Street.

A few itinerant tradesmen were: the "Fish Man" who came by train from the Fulton Fish Market in New York City. He would collect his bicycle that he stored at the railroad station, load his fish basket on it and peddle off to make his deliveries to local families and businesses (1928 to 1950). Ken the "Scissor Sharpener" also plied his trade from 1928 to 1950; and there was the man who sold "Geval" bleach (now sold under the trade name of Clorox). His customers would bring their own jugs to him to be filled. These tradesmen were welcome visitors as they brought bits of gossip for the ladies to pass the time of day.

The Prudential and the Metropolitan Life Insurance Company representatives came to their customers each week to collect their payments of 5, 10 or 25 cents for insurance coverage.

The medical profession was represented, among others, by Dr. Cameron Carpenter, a dentist whose office was above Sanford's Drug Store; Dr. Hoffman, a chiropractor; Robert Felter, M.D.; Dr. Fred Schroeder, Sr. (Dr. Fred Schroeder, Jr., retired in the year 2000). Two other names that I recall are Dr. Ed Parizot and Dr. Steven Monteith.

Dr. Felter used to make house calls. Each time he came to our house, we kids would have a good laugh because he always made a mistake and walked into the bathroom instead of into the hallway.

Pete Fato's Barber Shop and Oakley's Taxi Stand were on Williams Street, next to Gebner's Print Shop (1935-1950). On Central Avenue, across the street from Andy's Men's Store was the Pearl River Hook and Ladder Company. In a large brown building on a lot in front of the firehouse, on the corner of Williams Street, there was a dress factory from 1935 to 1950. Across from the Hook and Ladder, Sam Rizzo, Jr., opened Rizzo's Italian Delicatessen in memory of Sam Rizzo, Sr., his father. Sam, Sr., was a fireman (1967-1983) from the age of 16. Sam always wanted to have a deli of his own. What better location for his son to have a deli than opposite the fire house that his father had devoted so much time to, and where he enjoyed cooking for the firemen on so many occasions.

The Orangetown Police Department was not officially established until 1934. Fred Kennedy was a constable in 1924 and he became Chief of Police with the establishment of the four-man department. Fred retired in 1955 and Edmond Nelke took over as Chief of Police.

Grace Marie Spooner-Cucchiara Molloy Campbell

A Day in the Park

With the automobile came freedom—freedom to hit the open road. For many city residents, as well as locals, that meant spending the day at one of Rockland's parks, where it soon became apparent that picnic lunches weren't the only things that were packed.

Swimmers at Fort Comfort in Piermont.   JSC

"Scenic Mountain Trips Conducted by the Palisades Interstate Park."

JSC

100

Top photo: Cars lined up at Hook Mountain. Above: The parking area at Bear Mountain in 1924. JSC

The Roaring 20s came to a crashing halt in the final months of 1929. On October 23, a day that would become known as "Black Thursday," the stock market plummeted resulting in the loss of billions of dollars. The economic euphoria that had swept the nation only a few years earlier became a distant memory—personal fortunes would vanish, businesses would close, unemployment would skyrocket and the country would spiral downward into the Great Depression.

1930-1939

Hard Times

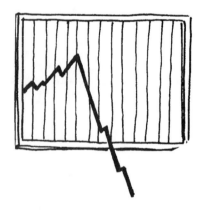

Although Prohibition was repealed in the early 1930s, there wasn't much to celebrate. The Great Depression had a stranglehold on the economy as jobs and human dignity were stripped down to levels never seen before. Fortunes were lost in the blink of an eye, businesses went broke and even mighty banks were forced to close.

If the Depression hit you, it hit hard, but some county residents were barely touched. These fortunate people were basically self-sufficient; they grew their own food, kept livestock and knew how to live with the simple necessities. The land supported these people in a manner that the future suburban landscape never could.

Of course, not everyone was destitute, and those that had a few extra cents in their pockets wanted to be entertained, to forget about the hard times, if only for a few hours. This was the era of Garbo, Flynn and Cagney. While Fred Astaire and Ginger Rogers danced across the screen in a fantasy of tuxedos and evening gowns, the Marx Brothers starred in a series of zany comedies. *Gone With the Wind* would go on to become part of American culture. The glamour of Hollywood was completely unrealistic, and just what a downtrodden public needed.

Radios helped spread the swing craze, and Rocklanders grabbed their instruments, hoping to be the next Benny Goodman or Glenn Miller. Sports also offered a great escape—whether it was from baseball or boxing matches on the radio, or from the Clarkstown County Club, and a host of local teams.

However, as America struggled out of the Depression, it became dangerously self-absorbed. Few recognized that the light at the end of the tunnel also held the flames of war. The popular opinion was that Japan was an Asian problem, and Hitler was a European problem—nothing that concerned us. In fact, pro-Nazi groups were active across the country, including in Rockland County.

The short-sightedness of the 1930s would cost us dearly—and a single day in December of 1941 would change the county and the country more than any other day in the twentieth century.

1937—History in the Making—Typical Rockland County Women's Jury

A local publication shows how progressive Rockland is by allowing women to be jurors (above).

The Clarkstown Country Club provided entertainment in many forms (above right, JSC), while the Ramapo Polo Club shows no signs of depression during this game on Cherry Lane in Tallman (right, courtesy of Rachel Kaufmann).

103

Recalling the Great Depression

Gertrude Wanamaker was on the Atlantic Ocean when the word came. It was October 30, 1929, and her uncle, Suffern butcher Herman Imwolde, was handed a telegram from the ship's communications room. The New York stock market had crashed, his partner, Dave Christie, had wired.

"They were in the stock market and Mr. Christie telegrammed him about this terrible crash—they had bought stock on margin and he was asking what to do. And my uncle just said, 'Dave, forget about it. I'm on vacation. There's nothing we can do about it,'" Wanamaker, now 90, said.

There was nothing anyone could do about what many people remember as the Great Depression. From the stock market crash of 1929 until about the mid-1930s, the country suffered from one of the most massive slumps in business activity ever to hit the United States.

The small, mostly rural Village of Suffern was not immune from the joblessness and lack of money affecting the rest of the country. Two large manufacturing businesses operated in town, American Brake Shoe and California Perfume Co., later renamed Avon. Neither closed, but many workers who did not have jobs at either of the factories found themselves in desperate straits.

Large gardens dotted the countryside and many people kept chickens. There was no television and no radio in most homes. Children got up early to help in the garden or do odd jobs to earn money and then went to bed at 7 p.m. Families struggled and laughed and provided aid to neighbors who were worse off than themselves.

Wanamaker, who returned to Suffern in 1930 after three months visiting relatives in Germany, said her family was luckier than most during those years. "We weren't really affected that much by it; we were already a self-sufficient family, and we weren't hurting," she said. "I always considered (my family) as poor, but we had plenty to eat."

Most Suffern residents got by with their home gardens and the help of neighbors, she said—a statement echoed by Nona Prall, also 90, and Estelle Maxwell, 96. Prall, a Sloatsburg native, was living in Suffern at the time. Maxwell's family owned a farm in Suffern.

"When the 1929 crash came, we ate beans and were very glad to get them," Maxwell said. "You didn't have much. It was terrible."

"I had two children and we didn't have any money," Prall said. "It was a bad time. My husband was a lather—wood and metal lathes—he put up the ceiling at the Suffern Theater—and sometimes we would burn coal and if we didn't have it, we would burn wood to keep warm."

"One thing I remember was my father (William Haring) worked for American Brake Shoe," Wanamaker said. "Back then, you would buy a big bag of potatoes and save the burlap bag. The trains would come by with big coal cars and my father bought a great big sled and some of these men (his co-workers), when it was night time and dark, would shovel the coal off (the train) and put it in the bags and pile it on the sled. We'd give it to our friends and neighbors who needed coal to keep warm," she said.

Merchants were generous with credit, Maxwell said. Many families purchased food from the stores with the understanding that the payment would be made when money was available. The town supervisor, whose name was Shuart, would hire residents to shovel snow in the winter and do other work for the government in the warm months. That helped Prall and her family get by.

"It was a different time then, a smaller community," Wanamaker said. "Everybody helped one another. People went to church and knew each other. There were people who were hungry, but we were more aware of it and did something."

Randi Weiner, *Rockland Journal-News*, 5/20/97

Hit by the Crash

Charles R. Carroll of Grand View was a junior executive with General Motors and riding high on the stock market when the crash hit. "It's too painful for me to go over but I was cleaned out," said Carroll, who was in Washington, D.C., the day of the crash and telephoned his broker only to find out he had lost everything.

"In 1929 I was in a fair way to becoming a very wealthy S.O.B. I just missed it, but by only that much," recalled Carroll, who "smartened up" after that, he said, and stayed away from the market for a long time. "I had a lot of friends who were wise enough to pull out of the market ahead of the crash, but who were persuaded to come back in again in 1931. The next year, as you know, was the real valley of the Depression."

Though Carroll recalls no one in Rockland County jumping out of a window, he said a number of people in the Nyacks were never the same again. "It ruined a lot of them mentally. If it has never happened to you, you just don't know what it is to be stripped clean."

Daniel deNoyelles, who once owned one of the largest brickyards in Haverstraw, said that even before the market crash, construction was down, mainly because the banks were more interested in lending money to stock speculators than to home builders. This, in turn, was partly responsible for the slump in the brick industry.

"Another was the importation of cheap foreign bricks, plus the changeover in construction from brick to poured concrete," deNoyelles said. He remembers the general optimism that prevailed in his industry even after the crash. "A lot of us didn't believe it then, but we should have seen it coming because construction started to decline after 1926. You couldn't get mortgage money."

DeNoyelles said the year before the crash he spent considerable money transforming his yard from an "open yard" to an indoor operation where bricks could be made all year round. "We also bought more improved machinery. "After all, bricks were still one of the important parts of the building industry, even though it was going down each year. The main trouble was in the cities where the new skyscrapers had to be built with lighter materials. But it was a great era. All of us were sitting on the edge of a precipice and didn't know it."

Like many another businessman of that era, deNoyelles could not resist the temptation to speculate on the stock market, where for 10 percent down (or what was called "on margin") anyone could purchase as many shares of stock as a bank or broker would approve. "I ran up $5,000 to $30,000 in two years, from 1927 to 1929, but I never bought any on margin. Of course, a lot of my friends did. They were wiped out when the brokers wanted their 'call money' (the rest of the money)."

The former brickyard owner said he also invested heavily in the local bank, then called the National Bank of Haverstraw, one of three banks in Rockland that failed during the Depression (the others were the Ramapo Trust Company and the First National Bank of Spring Valley).

"The stock was selling at $400 a share before it went under. I lost all my shares plus most of what I had in deposits. When the bank reorganized (it is now part of Empire National Bank and occupies the same building at 2 Main St.) I got only so many cents back on the dollar. I don't remember how much, but it wasn't much."

One wealthy family in South Nyack that managed to save their mansion were the Hands of Hand Manor, one of the few elegant estates in the village that survived the Depression. "We were fortunate in that we happened to own a sizeable number of shares of North River Insurance stock, a company that did well in those years, and because of the dividends we were able to pay the taxes," said Dorothy Hand Crawford, present owner of the manor.

With 10 percent margins no longer available, it would be difficult for history to repeat itself, although it is still possible to go broke, Carroll said, who came out of the Depression in good shape because he had a steady job.

"If it was not for my job I might not have made it, but most of all my philosophy of living was never based on material things principally. I think that's the big difference. For all those who went under after '29, wealth was everything, and when the money went there was nothing left."

John Dalmas, *The Journal-News,* 10/29/79

Log cabins still existed in Rockland and the families who lived there were often self-sufficient, so they were not as hard hit by the Depression. Julian Salomon stands in front of the Hogenkamp log cabin, built in 1932 (above left). Located on Sky Meadow Road in Suffern, it is one of two known structures of its kind still standing in Rockland. Maggie and Gilbert Pitt, Ramapo mountaineers, sit outside their cabin (above right), circa 1930. JSC

The Depression and Political Realignment

Oddly, it is difficult to find comprehensive evidence in Nyack village newspapers of the time of the Depression's catastrophic impact and, in that sense, it remains an enigma. Apparently, the gloom it generated was too pervasive to be readily reduced to the chitchat and recapitulation that was the stock in trade of the *Journal*. A powerful force governing events and their outcomes, it was, as recorded, incorporeal and elusive. Periodically, there would be mention of empty downtown stores, of the staggering cost of relief and of the record numbers of the unemployed; nevertheless, no coherent picture emerges of the hardship it engendered. Most telling of all were stories describing the straits to which people were reduced to survive.

During the summer of 1934, in Haverstraw, several families were reported to be eking out a living scavenging in the village dump and selling what they found back to their more prosperous neighbors. Along with the usual run of crime stories that year, there were numerous accounts of coal and chicken stealing. From time to time, there would be reports of attempts by relief recipients to alter township food orders.

As has been noted, local governments soon exhausted their resources in their attempts to fight the Depression. The state then stepped in, but even it was not up to the task and, after Roosevelt's election in 1932, everyone turned to the federal government for help. Relief, however, was not recovery and, as the years of misery wore on, there emerged in the minds of the unemployed the possibility that their predicament might be permanent. As a practical matter, they had also become dependents of the relief agencies and, in a larger sense, of the federal government. For them, local governments had to a large extent become irrelevant.

The various projects—CWA, PWA, TERA, etc.—were administered by professionals who often had no roots in the region to which they had been assigned. Their constituency was the unfortunates who came to them for help. Early on, the notion that federal monies were supposed to be distributed in an even-handed way, regardless of race, color, or creed, had gained acceptance. The administrators were responsible for maintaining fair standards in regard to that distribution, as well as for ascertaining that those who received grants qualified as needy. For that reason, relief provided a mechanism through which people, normally silent, had an opportunity to speak to someone in a position of authority, something that had been denied by coalition government.

There was always a political element in relief distributions. With the shift from local to federal jurisdiction, the focus of patronage also shifted, from the villages and towns where Republicans were entrenched, to the county, where the Democrats were strong. Through Jim Farley, local Democrats had, in addition, a special connection to the national party. To the degree any local politician had influence with the relief administrators, the advantage clearly lay with Democrats identified with the New Deal.

Work relief projects brought the poor and dispossessed together. As a result, cooperation was promoted both within ethnic blocs and among them. There was also competition. As identities hardened, leaders emerged who established their own initiatives.

The guiding principle of anti-discrimination in federal disbursements provided a stable ideological foundation on which to build such initiatives, and the proximity the projects enforced provided fertile seed beds for deliberation. Agitation about rights to be sought and wrongs suffered flourished in this stimulating environment. It was not difficult, in the context of those fecund times, to translate such agitation into political power, and ethnic blocs the Republicans had always taken for granted joined the Democrats. Prominent in that last group were the African-Americans.

On the other hand, old line Democrats, whose orientation was parochial—that is, on towns and villages rather than on national issues— were likely to be ignored by the New Deal Democrats. Snubbed, they often took common cause with the Republicans and, as a result, a fairly comprehensive political realignment was engineered with the poor and dispossessed identified with the Democrats, and the old, village-centered establishments with the Republicans.

Carl Nordstrom, *Phoenician Tales*

...In 1930, Grant Wood paints "American Gothic"...In 1931, over four million workers are unemployed...Bela Lugosi stars in "Dracula"...The world's tallest building, the Empire State building, officially opens...Auguste Piccard reaches a record height of 52,462 feet in a balloon...

James A. Farley (1888-1976)

One of Rockland's most prominent citizens was Jim "Big Stretch" Farley, who was born in the Grassy Point hamlet of Stony Point on May 30, 1888. He attended the two-room Grassy Point School and went to the Stony Point High School on West Main Street until 1905, when he was elected Stony Point town clerk.

Farley remained in that position until 1914, when he was elected town supervisor. During his eight years as supervisor, the concrete road was built between Tomkins Cove and West Haverstraw. In 1923, he served in the State Assembly.

During these years, he served as town and county Democratic Chairman. He joined the staff of Franklin D. Roosevelt in 1928 and helped elect him as governor. After that, Farley became State Democratic Chairman and set out to round up convention delegates for FDR's nomination for the presidency in 1932. Years later, FDR credited Farley and Louis Howe as being the two who more than anyone else got him elected president of the United States.

Farley became postmaster general in the Roosevelt cabinet in 1933 and as the person who gave out patronage jobs he became the most powerful man in America, second only to FDR himself.

While postmaster general, Farley oversaw the building of five post offices in Rockland County: Suffern, Spring Valley, Pearl River, Nyack and Haverstraw. He was also responsible for getting many contracts by New Deal agencies to help build Rockland County.

Farley broke away from FDR in 1940 over the third term and Senator Carter Glass put his name in nomination for president at the party convention. He then moved to the Waldorf-Astoria Towers Apartments and served as chairman of the Coca-Cola Export

Jim Farley at Grassy Point. Photo courtesy of Scott Webber

Corporation until his death in 1976.

Even though he personally knew five presidents, popes and world leaders, Jim Farley never forgot his roots. He once played first base on the Stony Point baseball team, earning himself the name of "Big Stretch Farley," and tended his family's bar business, although he never drank or smoked. He lived in Stony Point until 1929, when he moved to New York City with his wife,

Jim "Big Stretch" Farley (second from left, top row) when he played first base for the Stony Point team.　JSC

the former Elizabeth Finnegan and their children.

Every election night, including 1932 and 1936 when FDR was running, he stopped off at the polling place in Grassy Point to see how the vote went before going on to Hyde Park and informing FDR how Stony Point had voted. He was then Democratic National Chairman.

On his birthday every year, he rented a limousine and drove to St. Peter's Cemetery in Haverstraw, to visit the grave of his parents and then called on old friends. Once a year he sent the limousine up to Stony Point to round up his old ball team player friends and treated them to a day at Yankee Stadium in Coca-Cola's first base box where they were introduced to all the Yankee greats like Babe Ruth and Lou Gehrig.

I had many lenthy conversations with Jim Farley about his life. Looking at me, late one afternoon, he recalled that if it had not been for a group of staunch Republicans in Stony Point who had been willing to elect an Irish Catholic Democrat as town clerk, he would not have ever left Rockland County and gone where he did in life. He never forgot them or ever stopped appreciating them.

He laid down to take nap before dinner on June 9, 1976. He never woke up. Two weeks earlier, he had made his last visit to Rockland on his 88th birthday and left some books at the Farley Middle School in Stony Point. He loved God and his Catholic church, his family, his country, and his Democratic Party. He was a real friend to all who knew him. I was lucky enough to be one of them.

　　　　　　　　　　　　　　　　Scott Webber

Grassy Point Immortalized on Stamp

Thanks to the efforts of Jim Farley, this 1939 stamp commemorating the hundredth anniversary of baseball depicts the old baseball diamond in Grassy Point. In the background: St. Joseph's Church and the Grassy Point School, which Farley had attended as a boy. The school, the last of Rockland's one-room schools, did not close until 1963, when its eight pupils and one teacher were transferred to Stony Point Elementary School.

Hillburn Fire Department baseball team in the 1930s
Left to right, front row: unknown, Walt Stead, Mr. Lemond, unknown, Bob Steel, Dutch Stead.
Left to right, back row: Mike Sovak, Walt Flannery, Ed Green, Mr. Winter, Mal Stead, Walt Halbone and "Red."
Photo courtesy of Chuck Stead.

...In 1930, Babe Ruth is earning $80,000 a year...In 1939, a new car costs $680 and a three-bedroom house costs $3,850...In 1932, Linbergh's baby is kidnapped...Amelia Earhart becomes the first woman to fly solo across the Atlantic...Over eleven million workers are unemployed...

Rockland County Sports Hall of Fame: 1930-1939

Warren Austin (Congers) At the 1939 Dexter Press Field Day, Congers entered only a 2-man team. Austin won the 100- and 220-yard dash and the broad jump, was second in the 440, third in the pole vault, shot put and discus and Congers took the team title. Austin later became involved in youth bowling organizations.

Ralph Cordisco (Haverstraw) Excelled in football, basketball, baseball and track. Became very successful coach for North Rockland teams.

Jerry D'Auria (Nyack) Excelled in basketball and baseball. Played pro baseball before and after serving with distinction in WWII.

Pat D'Auria (Nyack) Football, baseball and boxing standout. During WWII won USO softball championship in the Far East.

Pete D'Auria (Nyack) Outstanding all-round athlete. Went on to play with the Detroit Clowns, the baseball equivalent of the Harlem Globetrotters.

Harold "Hale" Dechelfin (Haverstraw) Excelled in baseball, football, softball, bowling, basketball, tennis, track and billiards. Known for fast, aggressive style. Played semipro baseball, had 190 lifetime bowling average over 45 years.

Jim Faulk (b. Alabama) Moving to Rockland in 1933, Faulk became "Mr. Everything" for St. Agnes School in Sparkill, developing many successful sports programs. He turned down a lucrative coaching offer at Villanova to remain with the St. Agnes boys. His motto: "It is better to build boys than mend men."

Dan Fortmann (Pearl River) First Rocklander to be enshrined in a professional Hall of Fame (Pro Football, 1966). Six-time all-pro in 8 years with Chicago Bears. High School valedictorian, Phi Beta Kappa in pre-med at Colgate, played pro football to finance education, becoming an accomplished surgeon.

Nick Gamboli (Haverstraw) Eldest of 12 sons, Gamboli was a nationally recognized boxing official for 44 years. Also, Rockland baseball umpire and organizer. The six-brother Gamboli bowling team competed in National Championships.

Ed Greene (Suffern) Excelled in football, baseball, basketball and track. Successful coach and first athletic director of RCC, set up scholarship fund.

Harry Jackson (Spring Valley) Great mile champion, once finishing second to world record holder. Missed qualifying for Olympics by 2 seconds. Won 250 of 680 races.

Lester Lepori (Spring Valley) "Leck" earned 16 letters in baseball, basketball, football and track. Baseball was his favorite sport—he batted close to .400 and struck out 17 in several games. Mayor of Hillburn for 16 years.

Ervan Levine (Suffern) Blessed with incredible speed, he was undefeated for three years in the 100- and 220-yard dash. Using his speed as a running back, "Swervin" Ervan left defenders in his wake.

Brit Patterson (Pearl River) Earned 15 varsity letters in four sports. All-County 7 times. He was later a manager and coach for several sports.

Bill Perry (Nyack) Outstanding athlete in many sports who especially excelled in basketball. Standout playmaker and scorer. Physical training supervisor for Liberty Street School.

Jim Schnaars (Congers) Renowned amateur and pro tennis player, winning many regional and national titles. Competed against players like Pancho Gonzales and Rod Laver.

Walt Sickles (Pearl River) Outstanding baseball and football player in high school and college. Pitched in International League. Professional athletic career ended when he was wounded in action in WWII.

Bob Tierney (Pearl River) While excelling in football, baseball and basketball, he had his greatest moments as captain and offensive tackle at Princeton.

Horace Tyrus (Nyack) All-County quarterback and an almost unbeatable pitching star. In high school he was 19-2 with a 1.69 ERA, and was undefeated when he pitched for the Rockland County All-Stars.

Emil Willis (Spring Valley) "The Devastating Duke" was a record-setting football player and track runner. Premier punter, receiver and defensive end. County champion in track.

Bill Yuda (Pearl River) Powerfully built fullback who earned a football scholarship, then played professionally for the Philadelphia Eagles. Spent 38 years as gridiron official.

Alex "Zilch" Zilko (Pearl River) Excelled in every sport. Only injury kept him from pro baseball career. During WWII he flew 20 combat missions and was awarded the Bronze Star.

…Jesse Owens infuriates Hitler by winning four gold medals in the 1936 Berlin Olympics…

Clarkstown Country Club

Her name was Mom, and when she died, they hauled her to the Nyack dump and put her 9,100 pounds to rest in swamp land now part of what is the Palisades Center mall. She was 93, which was a ripe old age for an elephant. And during her last few years, she was one of the biggest attractions of the Clarkstown Country Club's circus and zoo.

Mom hauls away rocks, preparing land for the sports center, c. 1933.   JSC

The Clarkstown Country Club once stood high on Nyack's South Mountain overlooking the Hackensack Valley. It was encompassed by Tweed Boulevard, South Highland Avenue, Highland Avenue, Castle Heights Avenue, Broadway and Birchwood Avenue at the Hudson River. It spanned 160 acres and 34 buildings and was begun in 1918. Part of its operation lasted until the 1950s, although the zoo that housed the elephants was nearly gone by 1940, said long-time Central Nyack resident Frank M. Fassler.

The CCC was more of a commune than what people today consider a country club. The buildings included guesthouses, artists and writers studios, concert rooms, exercise rooms, salons and the theater. Outdoors there were a stadium, dog-racing track, stables, farmlands, trails, outdoor fire pits and extensive formal gardens. It had no golf course.

It also boasted what was billed as "the finest collection of Sanskrit lore in the United States (original texts, manuscripts and translations)," some 7,000 volumes belonging to the man who ran everything, Pierre Arnold Bernard.

Bernard's interest in Eastern thought permeated the programs, workshops and entertainments offered at the club. Yoga sessions were a big draw and people from all over the state would gather at the club to discuss and practice Eastern philosophies.

Bernard married a practicality with his philosophic bent. His "sanctum sanctorum" main office, as pictured in a 1935 club booklet, is the office of a successful businessman. Pictures taken in the early 1930s show him not only studying Sanskrit, but training the elephants to plow the club's farmland.

But it wasn't just for plowing that the CCC had elephants. The elephants were a major attraction at the club's circus. And what a circus it was.

The 1935 club booklet bills the circus as "closely imitating the great American tent show, except that instead of the talent being imported, it is the audience that is brought from far and near. For the club crowd puts on the performance.

"The parade, the elephants and other animals, the side shows and concessions—all are there. There is also a program of tumbling, balancing, juggling, clowning and wire-walking, with the diversity of other feats on ground and aerial apparatus. The show concludes with the traditional 'grand concert and afterpiece' put on by the Inner Circle Theater," the club's amateur theatrical group.

The Swedish actor and producer Ernst Rolf dropped by the circus in the early 1930s, and rhapsodized about its appointments in several thousand words, all reproduced in the booklet. The gist of his comments was

Clarkstown County Club circus sign, c. 1930s.   JSC

that "I was ready for nice, polite little entertainment—of society circus. In my whole life I have never been more astonished. ...Artists of the very first-class—phenomenal." And chief among the attractions were four elephants, led by Mom. Mom had two calves born in captivity, at least one of them in Clarkstown, if you can believe the pictures of the booklet. The other elephants were named Babe (or Baby), Bood and Juno, and all were "raised and trained at the club."

All of them were elephants trained to perform: walking over a prone woman without touching a feather on her costume, standing on hind legs and taking the trainer's head in their mouths. In addition, the elephants were used for heavy hauling at the club, plowing the land and moving rocks to build walls and the arena.

More than two books and 50 articles about Mom and the CCC elephant troop were written by author Courtney Ryley Cooper. A *New York Herald-Tribune* story on November 26, 1933, called "Old Mom" the queen and dowager among elephants.

Pathe, Fox Movietone and Paramount each made a nationwide film release of their act, which also included the four animals playing selections on chimes, Juno dressed as the clown while boxing and riding a tricycle around the platform and Bood's elevated tightrope act—walking forward and backward and balancing cross-wise in the center on an elevated steel reinforced plank four inches wide and twenty feet long.

Mom was often seen in local parades, carrying Republicans.

She fell ill in November 1933 and died within 10 days of "senility." Her autopsy, which took six men six hours to complete, said her "kidneys were atrophied, her liver degenerated and her heart muscle flaccid and without tone." Her obituary said she lived "in elephantine luxury" while in Bernard's care, and that her heart weighed 27 pounds and her brain 13 pounds.

Fassler, who was born in 1933, the year Mom died, said he remembered seeing one of the other elephants at the club when he was six or seven years old, but by that time the zoo and circus were just memories to people.

"People used to talk about it," Fassler said. "Back in those days, Bernard was a big thing. He gave a lot of employment to the people in the area. He brought a lot of money into the county."

Not to mention inspiring the exotic and romantic notions of the decade's worth of young children.

Randi Weiner, *Rockland Journal-News*, 12/16/97

Dr. Pierre Bernard

Dr. Pierre Bernard was many things, although being an actual doctor was not one of them. While he was an expert in Hindu scripture, he never even attended high school and his three degrees were only honorary. However, he would have been the last person to discourage anyone from referring to him as "Dr." Bernard.

Nicknamed "Oom the Omnipotent," Bernard's involvement in the spiritual teachings of the East did not seem to dull his appetite for wealthy widows, and unsubstantiated rumors of his "love cult" circulated among the tabloids. Notwithstanding the rumors and the realities, his Clarkstown Country Club with its blending of yoga, philosophy, dance and theater was not only unique in the county, but it was the first of its kind in the entire country, as well.

Beginning in Nyack in 1920, with the financial help of Cornelius Vanderbilt's widowed daughter-in-law, the club was both an entertaining resort and a serious place of meditation. For many, it was simply a circus, literally, boasting spectacular performances from both the human and animal participants.

Bernard's Clarkstown Country Club continued to amuse and amaze visitors and locals into the 1940s. Bernard died in 1955 and his wife, Blanche DeVries (who had abandoned the idea of a singing career to teach yoga with Bernard by 1918), died in 1984. Many of the club's buildings are now part of Nyack College, and Bernard's papers have been divided between the Historical Society of Rockland County and the Nyack Library.

Win Perry, president of the Historical Society of the Nyacks, summed up the man and his life: "The man we know as Dr. Pierre Bernard was a dreamer, philosopher, yoga teacher, entertainer of wealthy women, entrepreneur, impresario—and perhaps a total charlatan. He made exciting things happen in the Nyacks that dazzled the imagination."

Linda Zimmermann

The Start of County Tennis

Back in the mid-30s Nyack High School tennis courts opened up to the public during the summer I had been placed in charge. Working as a physical instructor under the W.P.A., I ran the tennis courts during the spring, summer and fall. During the winter I was assigned to the YMCA as an assistant physical instructor and to the high school as an

assistant coach.

Involved in the W.P.A. deal was an agreement for the YMCA to have season tennis memberships at $5.00 per person and the right to run tennis matches on Saturday afternoons. Public play charges--and this was during Depression days—was 10¢ per person per hour.

It was during the early spring of 1936 that Phil Lenhart, a former Ivy League tennis star, approached me and Bob Nelson, a Y physical instructor. Phil wanted to see us get involved in running a Rockland County Men's Singles Tournament. These were the days when Don Budge and Baron Van Cramm were the world's best and getting all the headlines. Phil thought the "time was ripe" to get tennis into the mainstream of county sports.

We hashed it over and rehashed it, wondering if there were enough players around the county to make a tournament worthwhile. As time went on we brought in Al Schnaars and Bob Bacheller from Congers, Gardner Watts and Wes Bogle of Suffern, Guelich from the Valley Cottage area and McDonald Deming of New City, plus Orville Lewis from Haverstraw and Nikola in Spring Valley. To our surprise, we picked up well over 50 players that first year and knew "we had something going." Phil had been right, the time was ripe.

Even more to our surprise, we received entries from Charles MacArthur, Ben Hecht and Charles Lederer. These three gave their address as Helen Hayes home on North Broadway, she being the wife of MacArthur. Let it be said that Charlie MacArthur and Ben Hecht always "went first class." About an hour before the time to play, on this perfect summer's day, the three arrived with their wives, picnic basket, drinks and all.

They proceeded to sit down and enjoy themselves thoroughly as the matches progressed. When their three stalwarts took the courts, Helen Hayes led the cheering for them. Unfortunately, each was soundly thrashed in that opening round, putting a slight damper on their picnic fun.

Phil Lenhart managed to be present throughout the days of the tournament and was there for the finale. The first Rockland County champion turned out to be MacDonald Deming of New City, former Dartmouth University star, as I recall.

The next year, and for two years in a row, Parke Smith took the title and Bob Bacheller took it in 1939. Later on it was to go to Jimmie Schnaars, New York State Junior Davis Cup champion, and then World War II came along.

Coming back after the war, the Nyack tennis courts now being defunct, I was instrumental in working with the Pearl River Tennis Club in reorganizing this county tennis tourney once more, this time on the Merritt tennis courts.

We named it after Ed Amory, a sergeant and tail gunner on a B-17 in the Eighth Air Force, a casualty over Holland on July 28, 1943. He had entered the war from Pearl River.

Working out the tournament restart with me were Blackie Langer, Leo Vassilakos, Ray Partridge, and Jack Bratton. Jimmie Schnaars, coming back that year, rewon the title and then donated the trophy back to the tournament for a continuous year-by-year use.

Nyack had run a mixed doubles tournament back in the 30s but it hadn't gone over too well. After WW II we got it started again. Men's doubles started in Suffern and, as I recall, were picked up again, after the war, by the Nyack Field Club. It was then that this tourney was named after Phil Lenhart and rightly so.

The women's singles tournament was started by the Rockland County Tennis Association, reorganized after World War II in 1947. The 1947 winner was Mrs. Hildegarde Byrnes, followed by Mrs. Marion Jewett and then Mrs. Elaine Bacheller.

Kenneth F. Harniman

Boxing

Boxing was also popular in Rockland, in part because of Gus Wilson's training camp in Orangeburg. In the photo on the left, boxer Jack Sharkey spars with child film star Jackie Cooper at Gus Wilson's camp. Sharkey defeated Germany's Max Schmeling for the heavyweight title in 1932.

In the photo in the far left, massive 263-pound heavyweight boxer Primo Carnera stands next to local fighter Hugo Kolb of Upper Nyack, c.1931-32. In 1933, Carnera defeated Sharkey to become the first Italian heavyweight champ.

Nyack Sea Scouts

For those who had been Boy Scouts and were looking for something different, there was the Sea Scouts. I joined the scouting navy when I was about 14 or 15 years of age.

The Nyack Sea Scout Troop had a 26-foot cutter called the *Half Moon*, which they had received from the U.S. Navy. At this particular point of time, the early 30s, Sam Handley was the skipper. He's the same Handley that built the "Star" racing boats that were showing their heels to all opposition in that class in the East.

One weekend, we started late Saturday afternoon heading upstream, and had just run under the Bear Mountain Bridge when the motor conked out. This was not too unusual for the *Half Moon*, but usually our teenage mechanics could locate the problem in a hurry. In the dark, we used our flashlights to check the engine inch by inch, but nothing was found. Then came trouble!

Bearing down on us out of the night, all lit up like a Christmas tree, was the Bear Mountain night liner cutting a pretty fast swath, and we were right in its path in the middle of the channel.

There we were—powerless, no sails up, no motor, no nothing but a small dinghy. Harold Atterbury, about 20 and one of our huskiest, got into the dinghy and, rowing like mad, pulled us out of the ship's path, but that didn't end our woes.

They extended right through the next day. Do you know what it's like to "sweat out" a whole, becalmed, hot day on the Hudson, too proud to let other boats know you're in trouble?

Eventually, Atterbury took the dinghy and rowed towards Hook Mountain to seek help from Sam Handley, or some other Hudson Riverite connected with the Sea Scouts. By dusk we had drifted in near the Croton shore, and those that had to go to work Monday morning swam to shore, packing their duds in 18-inch high biscuit tins. They walked the tracks to the railroad station and then took the train to Tarrytown, arriving just in time to miss the last ferry boat to Nyack, ending up sleeping on the landing overnight.

Early the next morning, a small boat came chugging up the river and it turned out to be Sam Handley. It took Sam less than five minutes to locate the trouble and we were soon heading back toward Nyack, finally arriving there a short hour later, but about 36 hours late.

Kenneth F. Harniman

Skiing Down Fifth Avenue

When we were kids we used to go skiing in our own yard, also in the circus field, now a part of the New York State Thruway, or at the Oratamin, over in Blauvelt, a large field that dropped steeply from Bradley Parkway down practically to Greenbush Road. The terrain was like a washboard with natural jumps that only the best of us went all the way down without a flop.

There was also Bear Mountain where the great Tokle was setting long-distance jumping records. Every weekend this resort was loaded with skiers and viewers. One of the prime sports for family fun was the tobogganing. One year they had a chuted run that went all the way down to Hessian Lake.

We went skiing and sleighing wherever the mood moved us, whether in the Oak Hill Cemetery, down on Hudson Avenue, Nyack, or over at the Blue Hill Golf Club. Back in those days Fifth Avenue, Nyack, was shut off for sleigh riding and skiing from about even with the old high school all the way down to Broadway. At the bottom there were ashes and dirt to slow the speed of the sleighs. Skiers usually angled off to the side before they got there.

At Franklin Street, Fifth Avenue gave you a sort of leveling-off, dipsy-doodle bumping as you crossed that interrupted your zooming downhill drop. It was just before this spot that a jump was made for those skiers having the intestinal fortitude to try it. Few did after seeing how steep it was.

I did try, but I was the only one with a toe strap, although no skiing harness. Luckily, I made the jump and went all the way down, and that once was enough. Brad Brush, with a harness, came down behind me, fell hard as he landed, and ended up in the Nyack Hospital with a broken leg. That ended the jumping for good.

Kenneth F. Harniman

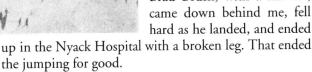
The Bear Mountain ski jump in the 1930s. JSC

Christie's Airport

The droning buzz of early airplane engines has long-since vanished from a sleepy cow pasture in northern New City. And barnstorming pilots no longer drop daredevil parachutists out of the skies or take tourists on sight-seeing flights. Today, neat rows of suburban houses stand where early Cessna 150s and classic Ford tri-motors used to take off and land.

But the sights and sounds of 40 years of early aviation history are still fresh in the mind of 83-year-old James Christie of New City who, along with his father, William, and younger brothers, John and Bill, founded and operated Christie Airport—the first commercial air field in Rockland County—from 1929 to 1969.

Christie's book, *Early Aviation in Rockland County, New York*, recounts the airstrip's turbulent rural years—how the airport provided the county's first airmail delivery in the 1930s, and was the frequent stopping-off point for military personnel and flight school for several celebrities—before finally surrendering to the pressures of modern suburban development.

In 1916, the Christies left Scotland and settled in Nyack where Christie's father, a plumber by trade, found work and Christie—just before his 16th birthday—got a job with the Wilcox and Gibbs sewing machine company. But the desire to have a family business was strong. In 1922, the Christies bought a sandstone farmhouse (circa 1800) and 55 acres of land in northern New City that had once been run as a boys camp by William Randolph Hearst. "We first tried to have fruit orchards, but the frost killed the peaches, and that was the end of that," said Christie.

The family's next endeavor was dairy farming. But the romance and adventure of airplanes were in their father's blood, and in 1929, the senior Christie left the dairy business to pioneer in aviation in the county. It was just two years after Charles Lindbergh's historic solo nonstop flight across the Atlantic.

The Christies carved a 1,600-foot airstrip out of their cow pasture. But along with the airport, they decided to open an automobile repair and service station "when gas was cheap, and each check-up was accompanied by the latest gossip," noted Christie in his memoirs.

As told in his Scottish brogue, Christie is full of interesting anecdotes about the airport and some of the well-known people the family dealt with over the years—among them Paramount Pictures president Adolph Zukor, actor Burgess Meredith, and cartoonist Milton Caniff. He related how Ernest Gann, author of *The High and the Mighty* and other aviation novels, learned to fly at Christie Airport in 1936, and later described the airport in his book *Hostage to Fortune*.

Christie's brother, Bill, who had served in the air corps in two wars and had earned a Bronze Star for aviation, moved out West with his family after World War II when he felt the airport would never achieve the expansion necessary to compete with others that had sprung up in the county. After their father's death in 1952, Christie's other brother, John, managed the airport until its closing in 1969. "John didn't want to sell the airport, because aviation was his life," said Christie. But eventually spiraling operating costs convinced him to sell when real estate developer Bernard Nemeroff offered more than $300,000 for the land. Christie said his brother continued to work as an independent flight instructor out of Ramapo Airport in Spring Valley until his death in 1978.

Christie said the airport was never a money-making operation. But there was the family's satisfaction at having promoted aviation in the early years of this century. Nancy Cacioppo, *The Journal-News*, 3/31/85

Other Airports

Rockland had many airports in the 20th century, including Miller's in West Nyack (right, JSC). The airport was by Routes 59 and 303 on the present site of the Palisades Center mall. (Mont Moor Cemetery is in the center of the photo at the edge of the woods.)

Other airports included a Civil Defense airport in Pearl River, which is now the site of the reservoir. The Ramapo Airport in Spring Valley (where the Marketplace now stands) was the largest. There was also an airstrip at the site of the abandoned drive-in in Monsey.

Unfortunately, the aviation craze of the 1920s was never to be seen again, and the high price of real estate doomed the local airports.

The Youngest Aviator

Joseph Sheehan, Jr. (left), was the son of a cashier at the National Bank & Trust in Suffern. On his twelfth birthday, as a student of Suffern Grammar School, he accomplished a feat that even caught the attention of Charles Lindbergh.

On January 17, 1931, young Joe climbed into the cockpit of a plane—needing a soap box and two cushions to be able to see out. Alone, he taxied his plane down the runway at Roosevelt Field in Long Island, lifted off and became the youngest boy to make a solo flight.

By age 19, he was already a seasoned pilot, and in 1938 he made the first Rockland airmail flight from Kakiat Field in Suffern to Floyd Bennett Air Field in Brooklyn. The photo (below) shows Sheehan (center, in flying gear) shaking hands with Postmaster Anthony Kennedy.

Also identified in the photo are Police Officer William Whalen (far left) and band members (l. to r.) John Greco, Frank Greene, Henry Cutler and Gordon Personeus. The group behind Sheehan includes Mr. Motta, Mr. Osborne, William Maxfield, Eddie Hartwell, Mrs. Cecile Taylor, Babe Byard, Mr. Beard, Jim Mulligan, Carmen Maurello and Tony Collins.

Photos courtesy of Craig Long.

Gloria Hollister

Gloria Hollister (right) was two years old in 1903 when her father, Dr. Frank Hollister, purchased the Lloyd residence on Haverstraw Road on the outskirts of the village of Suffern (which today is in Montebello).

She obtained her Master's degree in zoology at Columbia University. Later, she became acquainted with Dr. William Beebe, one of the men who developed the bathysphere—the deep-sea exploration sphere. Hollister became Beebe's chief technical associate and accompanied him on many research trips.

On August 15, 1936, off the coast of Hamilton, Bermuda, Hollister climbed into the bathysphere and descended 1,208 feet, an event which "marked the first time a woman ever had descended to such a depth."

The *New York Times* reported that Hollister "became a celebrity in the 1930s, a time when only a handful of women earned headlines for their feats in a man's world of discovery." Hollister continued exploring on land and sea, and is credited with numerous discoveries.

Sadly, when she died in 1988, few remembered the accomplishments of this Montebello explorer, scientist and conservationist. Craig Long

Grand Opera in Stony Point

After the Russian Revolution, many exiles settled in Stony Point. This was in part because of the plans of Max Rabinoff to create a 4,200-acre center for the arts in Stony Point.

The American Institute of Operatic Art was an ambitious concept that was to utilize the numerous talents of his fellow Russian transplants and establish a self-contained musical village. There would be a large theater, a decorative arts studio, a library, dormitories, offices and storage buildings. Productions would not only be created and performed at the center; the grand opera company would tour the nation, and perhaps the world.

Stony Point could have become known as one the great cultural centers of the world, had it not been for the crushing effects of the Great Depression.

Linda Zimmermann

The Decorative Arts building (left) of the American Institute of Operatic Arts was completed in 1925. When the Institute failed as a result of the Depression, the abandoned buildings fell into ruin (right) as this photo from the 1980s of the former Decorative Arts building shows.

JSC

The Best Laid Plans

The following is from the 1932 study, "Rockland County and the Regional Plan," which cost taxpayers $1.25 million dollars, and was obsolete and ineffective by the end of the decade:

Every Resident of Rockland County
Is Vitally Concerned
with the future development of this area, which was the scene of many historic struggles during the American Revolution and has lately come to be both an important playground for metropolitan residents and a suburban residential area of increasing importance.

Rising abruptly from the Hudson River along a great part of its eastern border, the major part of the triangular shaped county is gently rolling in character, offering large areas suitable for agriculture and forestry. Much of it is heavily wooded. The entire northwestern part of the county lies within the Bear Mountain Reservation of the Palisades Interstate Park Commission which also has extensive parks along the eastern section, so that one-sixth of the total area of the county is park property. With better communication to the south by rail and highway, Rockland County should gain rapidly as a recreational center for the Region and an important outer suburban area with local industrial centers along certain parts of its Hudson River waterfront.

The county has experienced a fairly steady growth ever since Revolutionary times but this showed a decided jump during the decade ending with 1930 when the county population increased from 45,548 to 59,599. It is estimated that by 1940 the population will reach 63,500 and that by 1965 Rockland County will be the home of about 76,000 people.

(*Editor's Note: The population in Rockland was already 74,000 by 1940, and by the end of the 1960s, it had exploded to almost 230,000. The million-dollar regional plan was grossly myopic.*)

But to accommodate this increasing population, make more attractive the undeveloped residential and recreational areas and encourage a proper expansion of its industrial districts there must be prompt and intelligent planning. Parkway routes for passenger vehicles should be established to preserve and protect its stream valleys and accommodate through traffic without detriment to its residential areas; local parks are needed in addition to natural extensions of the large regional parks; local transportation should be improved; the natural water supply must be controlled; and proper guidance must be given to the planning of undeveloped areas, the zoning of both developed and undeveloped areas, the regulation of housing and the location and architecture of public buildings. Much must be done, and how it is done will be a matter of deep interest to every taxpayer and resident of the county.

Population Patterns
Rockland County and its Major Villages: 1900 to 1940

	1900	1910	1920	1930	1940
County Population	38,297	46,843	45,548	59,599	74,261
The Three Nyacks	6,329	7,278	6,781	8,446	8,223
Nyack Village	4,274	4,619	4,444	5,352	5,206
The Two Haverstraws	8,014	8,038	7,244	8,455	8,442
Haverstraw Village	5,935	5,669	5,226	5,621	5,909
Suffern	1,619	2,663	3,154	3,757	3,768
Spring Valley	1,530	2,353	3,818	3,948	4,308
Piermont	1,153	1,380	1,600	1,765	1,876

Percentages of County Total

	1900	1910	1920	1930	1940
The Three Nyacks	16.7	15.5	14.9	14.2	11.1
Nyack Village	11.2	9.9	9.8	9.0	7.0
The Two Haverstraws	20.9	17.2	15.9	14.2	11.4
Haverstraw Village	15.5	12.1	11.5	9.4	8.0
Suffern	4.2	5.7	6.9	6.3	5.1
Spring Valley	4.0	5.0	8.4	6.6	5.8
Piermont	3.0	3.0	3.5	3.0	2.5
Total, 8 Villages	48.4	46.4	49.6	44.3	35.9
Rest of County	51.2	53.6	50.4	55.7	64.1

Carl Nordstrom, Source: Rockland County Population R. C. Planning Board, 1968

Census Figures
From the 1934 *Rockland County Almanac and Year Book*

	1910	1920	1930
Indians	0	2	7
Chinese	10	3	22
Japanese	5	15	5
Mexicans	0	0	4

...In 1937 Du Pont patents a new plastic called nylon...21,000 frenzied fans dance in the aisles of The Paramount Theater in NYC listening to the "King of Swing," Benny Goodman, and his band...Disney releases "Snow White and the Seven Dwarfs"... In 1938 Adolf Hitler takes Austria...President Roosevelt signs an act setting the minimum wage at 40 cents an hour...British Prime Minister Chamberlain meets with Hitler and agrees to the annexation of the Sudetenland in order to secure "peace in our time"...

117

Events of 1933
From the 1934 *Rockland County Almanac and Year Book*

March 4—Gov. Lehman issues closing order to all banks. Beginning of long "bank holiday." *(Note: There were numerous bank closings due to the Depression.)*

March 15—Eight of Rockland's eleven banks reopen for business as usual.

April 7—Sale of beer becomes legal in the county.

May 11—Federal agents raid still on Tower estate, Spring Valley, and dump 2,000 gallons of alcohol.

May 23—Rockland County votes 10 to 1 for repeal of 18th Amendment.

June 22—Dr. Pierre Bernard, of Clarkstown Country Club, opens his new $100,000 Rockland Sports Center in Central Nyack, with 1,500 present to witness program of events, including performance by four elephants and a night baseball game under powerful lights.

July 11—John D. Rockefeller, Jr., makes $5,000,000 real estate gift for parkway along top of Palisades north of George Washington Bridge.

July 29—Baum Brothers Department Store, Haverstraw, closes after 75 years.

August 1—Rockland County pledges cooperation to President's N.R.A. (National Recovery Administration) program.

August 20—More than 800 attend the Democratic Clambake at the German Masonic Home, Tappan.

September 1—Orangeburg Fair opens for its ninetieth year.

October 1—15,000 people visit annual Traubenfest at German Masonic Home, Tappan.

October 3—One of the largest liquor coups in history of U.S. Customs Dept. made in Hudson River off Haverstraw. $1,000,000 worth of liquor confiscated.

October 4—Two Nyack girls killed by fall in auto from top of plateau at Hook Mountain.

October 20—William Hoke, President of National Bank of Haverstraw, commits suicide at home in Tomkins Cove.

October 31—Rockland County NRA parade climaxed celebration with 3,000 autos covering entire county. Thousands in every section watch spectacle.

November 4—National Bank of Haverstraw and Trust Company reopened for unrestricted banking ending "holiday" begun March 4. All Rockland County banks are now in full swing.

November 9—Mom the Elephant, 92, dies.

December 4—State grants village of Spring Valley $17,000 for employees' wages on five local CWA projects.

December 5—First "legal liquor" sold in county at retail store in Suffern.

December 5—8,900 unemployed men from NYC, Yonkers and Rockland go to work on CWA projects at Bear Mountain.

Necrology 1933
From the 1934 *Rockland County Almanac and Year Book*

March 24—J. Orville Demarest, 92, died at Nyack home. Voted for Lincoln. Was 42 years with railroad before retiring in 1927.

April 13—Milton Sayres, for fifty years well-known Nyack market man.

April 25—Michael Ford, 61, for 22 years chief and 28 years member Haverstraw police force.

April 29—Frank Comesky, 73, dean of Rockland County bar and president of Nyack National Bank. *(Note: Comesky was the defense lawyer in the Cleary murder trial in 1914, and the shooting was committed with Ford's gun.)*

May 18—Francis Colsey, 90, oldest volunteer fireman in Rockland. Fireman for 76 years.

May 29—Ernest Reissmann, 72, old Piermont baker.

June 12—Walter Dahl, Spring Valley, undertaker, died suddenly.

June 19—Robert McKean Jones, Stony Point, inventor of Chinese typewriter.

July 8—Albert Brien, ex-postmaster of Tomkins Cove, drowned in Cove Lake.

July 12—Edwin Gould, 67, patron of needy children, founder of model institution in Rockland.

July 15—Valentine Mott, 72, for 30 years chairman of N.Y. Consolidated Stock Exchange, died at South Nyack home.

August 1—Richard Stalter, 82, of Tomkins Cove. One of the best-known citizens of northern part of county.

August 31—Elsie Bang, 18, Sloatsburg's prettiest girl, killed by auto.

September 22—George Glassing, 66, famous band master, died at home in Havertsraw.

October 23—Samuel DeChelfin, 70, Haverstraw jeweler for over 40 years.

November 10—Thomas Donaldson, Haverstraw world war hero, brother of Sgt. "Mike" Donaldson.

December 7—Mrs. Lavinia Meyers Purdy, 95, former Rockland social leader.

December 23—Fred Fortmeyer, 79, Stony Point native, widely known boating and yachting referee.

New City in the 30s: A Doctor's View

For a long time, New City had no practicing physician. Many people in town stated that New City did not need a doctor and travelled to nearby towns for medical treatment. The following describes some of the personal experiences of one doctor practicing medicine in New City from 1935-39.

After graduating from medical school at University College, Dublin, Ireland, in 1933, I completed an internship in communicable diseases at Kingston Avenue Hospital in Brooklyn. I rounded out my medical training with a rotating internship at Nyack Hospital in 1934. During this period as part of my training, I rode the ambulance on emergency calls and had the opportunity to survey and acquaint myself with various localities in Rockland suitable for practice.

With the Depression raging primarily in the big cities, I entertained the idea of being a country doctor and chose to start in New City. This quiet community, population then about 1,200, nestled between the Ramapo Mountains and the Hudson River, seemed an idyllic setting for my new venture.

On a clear summer day in 1935, my wife Essie, a native of Spring Valley, and I took the plunge. We moved into a 5-room apartment on the second floor of the Fajen building on Main Street, with a two-room office directly across the corridor. This red brick building, with one exit and entrance, on the site of the old New City Hotel, was constructed by John Fajen and his son Henry in 1931.

Other tenants were Clarence Baracks, an attorney, and the Alcohol Control Board, managed by Ken Rose and Charlie Fales, who occupied offices on the same floor, while the Helmke Meat Market and the Fajen Confectionery and Luncheonette were below.

In the early days, I spent much idle time in the offices of Clarence Baracks and the Alcohol Control Board, learning about the town. These bull sessions gave me in insight into social, economic and political life of the people I would need to meet, in order to build practice.

My office was virtually empty. No patients filled the waiting room, and no nurse or receptionist assisted me or answered the phone. I realized that in a small community like New City, practice would often have to be a major task of improvisation, an adjustment to many personal situations. I would need all the resources I could muster to reach the people. However, I hoped that in time my practice would develop.

The Elms Hotel, with its popular bar, hosted by "Doc" Wilson, situated next to the Fajen building on

Hotels Elms (left) and Bardin in New City.   JSC

Main Street, was a landmark in New City, dating back to the Revolutionary War. It was there that I met lawyers, shopkeepers, employees of the courthouse and others, some of who ultimately became my patients.

Jerry's Tavern, owned and operated by Betty and Jerry Carnegie, and well-known for its apple jack during the Prohibition years, was another meeting place where I met similar groups.

Viola Doellner, the town's female mechanic, who owned the garage that serviced my car and supplied me with oil and gasoline, was also my patient. She carefully sized me up before trusting herself to my care.

The town was unique in that one family seemed to dominate, the Eberlings. Henry and Barbara Eberling were brought from Germany to this country by Gen. Louis Blenker, a Prussian Army officer, as caretakers of his large estate near New City Park. It is stated that in 1912, 83 descendants of the Eberling family were in attendance at the celebration of their golden anniversary.

The Eberling shoe factory on New Hempstead Road in New City, c.1910, where many of the workers were children. The building was later reduced to one level and turned into a garage.   JSC

Pauline de Noyelles sent farm, road and other outdoor workers to my office for treatment of poison ivy, skin rashes, cuts, bruises and other accidents. Many of these patients required injections and minor surgery. I appreciated these referrals, since they were supportive in my developing practice.

Judge Samuel Garrison succeeded in obtaining for me a small per diem position as school physician in the two-story frame schoolhouse on Old Congers Road. I often worried that this building was a fire trap, since it had but one entrance and exit.

After climbing up a flight of stairs, I encountered about 10 to 12 children of elementary school age in an unattractive and generally inadequately heated school room. My examination was perfunctory, since I was not allowed to do complete physical examinations or administer immunizations. The prevailing custom was to refer any ill children to their private physicians.

The old schoolhouse in New City (above) and the children and teachers (below), c.1910. JSC

Through the continued good offices of Judge Garrison, George Dorsey, the district attorney of Rockland, assigned me to examine prisoners in the local jail after police interrogations. This was to certify that no bodily injury had been inflicted by the police.

What was so remarkable about a country doctor in the 1930s was how little he had to offer. In his bag, he carried aspirin, phenobarbital, morphine, syrup of Ipecac, Band-aids and a prayer.

At times, with death staring him in the face, he assumed the role of priest, minister or father confessor, and he used every device known to calm a distraught or bereaved family. Nobody would consider this time wasted. The bedside manner was, and is, important.

What kind of practice did I have? The climate of the world was not favorable; in fact, it was dim for me in the development of a substantial practice. Hitler was on the march in Europe. It was rumored that the Ku Klux Klan was burning crosses at one end of New City while the German-American Bund was parading at Camp Gen. Louis Blenker. This Camp, established by the Prussian general, was a riding school for the training of military officers. Religious and political issues were sensitive matters at this time, because of the turbulent conditions of the world.

Most of the cases were routine: colds, sore throats, diarrhea, pneumonia, and the childhood diseases of measles, mumps, chicken pox, scarlet fever. To my surprise, I occasionally encountered more serious cases, such as hepatitis, poliomyelitis, measles, encephalitis, bloody diarrhea and others. Diagnosis and sound judgment were essential, since modern modalities were lacking. All this, in a community that supposedly needed no doctor.

A great deal of social life of the town was centered around the firehouse on Maple Avenue. New City Fire Engine Co. No. 1, strictly volunteer, was organized in 1887, but did not have complete automobility until 1925. During the Depression, card playing in the firehouse was considered an inexpensive form of recreation. When I arrived in 1935, the firehouse raised funds from dances and dinners.

Of course, in a small town, socialization with the people was essential. Thus, my wife and I attended these functions as often as possible. The uninhibited response of the people was indeed refreshing. It was difficult for me to "let my hair down," as I felt my position needed to be upheld: "medical snobbery." The music was always good, and the homemade food delicious. If, after the function, illness followed, I was there to help.

Surprisingly, one day I was called to the home of Maxwell Anderson on South Mountain Road. Anderson, the famous playwright, was suffering from an ongoing complaint. His illness required further investigation and treatment. He was receptive to my opinion and advice.

Late one evening, a beautiful middle-aged actress accompanied by an actor friend from South Mountain Road arrived at my office in excruciating abdominal pain. On examination, I found that she had multiple post-operative abdominal incisions with marked distention. My diagnosis of obstructed bowel urgently required immediate surgery. She elected to be hospitalized in New York City at a later date, thereby resulting in her demise. Unfortunately, the opinion of a country doctor was not accepted.

I had rising expectations that the agony of the Second World War would eventually turn around in favor of the saner world. To foster this hope, playwright Anderson allowed a pluralistic group to hold a "bash" on his estate in order to raise funds for Charles DeGaulle and the Free French cause. I was impressed with his easy intermingling of so many political factions. In an area restricted normally to the wealthy and famous, hundreds of local citizens from all over Rockland attended. It was indeed a great spectacle, all for a good purpose. Some of these people were my patients and sympathetic to the same cause, I felt a sense of camaraderie.

My farewell to New City came with the realization that a population of about 1,200 could not sustain my aspirations. I had anticipated some support from Bardonia and Germonds, but this did not materialize. My experience as a country doctor was of incalculable value to the development of my career. Like a premature infant, New City helped me grow into maturity and develop the wisdom so important in the healing art. The town was a microcosm of a big city. It had all the friendliness, and its share of gossip and human frailties.

In the late fall of 1947, I opened an office limited to the practice of pediatrics in the southeast Bronx, New York City.

George Bialkin, M.D., *The Journal News*, 7/10/00

...In 1939, over 22,000 members of the pro-Nazi German-American Bund hold a rally in Madison Square Garden...Rockland has its own Bund members...The patriotic group the Daughters of the American Revolution refuse to allow singer Marian Anderson to perform in Washington, D.C., because Miss Anderson is black...Eleanor Roosevelt resigns from the D.A.R. in protest...

Prisoner of Love

In a soap opera-style courtroom drama in 1932, a woman accused her riding instructor of "seduction under the promise of marriage." While breaking such a promise today would hardly merit a story in the newspaper, this New City trial made front page headlines in the *Journal-News*. Even more remarkable, the riding instructor was found guilty and sentenced to three years in Sing Sing prison!

After the trial, which was extensively covered with the most minute and lurid details, one headline read, "Jury Which Convicted Him Believed Girl Was Chaste and That Man Is Aggressor In Love." The paper also reported that before the instructor was sent up the river to prison, he was allowed to say goodbye to his two favorite horses.

Linda Zimmermann

In 1936, Viola Doellner took over her brother's business, the Superior Garage in New City. Rolling up her sleeves and putting on a pair of pants (which was not considered lady-like at the time), she fixed cars with an uncanny skill. Viola was to go on to become the first uniformed female postman, and although she did the work of two people, she was only paid less than two-thirds the salary of the men.

Snakes

In 1934, a large party of CWA workers who were engaged in cutting down a cliff at Cedar Flats near Stony Point for fill on a new road, uncovered one the largest snake dens on record. In one week, about 75 rattlesnakes and copperheads were found as an entrance hole to the den was uncovered. The digger's found the ground around the den's entrance worn smooth, as if by many generations of snakes.

Snakes are said to head instinctively to one habitat in early fall and hibernate through the winter some distance below the frost line. It is thought that in dry summers they come down from the hills in search of water.

Experts from the American Museum of Natural History came to observe the find. The digging never did prove the truth of a tradition that had been common in the Pine Mountain and Cedar Flats area since 1916. "Credible residents of Stony Point" were reported on rare occasions to have seen the granddaddy of all snakes in this region—a monster six inches in diameter and 16 to 18 feet long. Whether it was a rattler or copperhead these "credible residents" apparently never stopped to discover. When it wasn't found in the uncovering of the Cedar Flats digging the story gradually was forgotten.

Rockland County Leader, 7/25/65

Beavers and the Hurricane of '38

On September 21, 1938, one of the worst hurricanes of the century hit Rockland County. Winds approaching 90 m.p.h buffeted the area while unprepared residents watched helplessly as trees and telephone poles were toppled. Entire neighborhoods were flooded and sewer systems overflowed.

The result of these few terrifying hours was almost half a million dollars in damage. Electricity was out for days, transportation was interrupted and local farmers estimated that they lost 50 percent of their fruit crop. Fortunately, there were only half a dozen injuries, and the one fatality occurred when a man fell off his roof attempting to remove a tree. As bad as things were, however, they could have been much worse if not for the aid of some furry friends.

Apparently, the county was spared even greater flood damage thanks to a group of industrious beavers. As a result of their Herculean efforts the night of the storm, they not only chewed down enough trees to protect their dens; they also created dams along local waterways which significantly stemmed the destructive power of the runoff.

Linda Zimmermann

A familiar scene throughout the century—flooding on Route 59 in West Nyack during the 1930s.   JSC

Muddy Creek Pearls

There was a small community in the south end of Rockland County known as Muddy Creek. It was so named because of the sluggish, muddy creek that flowed through it. The creek itself joined the Pascack Brook which emptied into the Hackensack River and eventually into Newark Bay.

In the early 1870s, the New York and New Jersey Railroad was built up through the area and it was decided to build a station for the community. However, the name Muddy Creek wouldn't do! The name was changed to Pearl River because of small pearls found in mollusks in the creek bottom. (Although only an optimist could call the creek a river.)

Catholics in the area founded a parish under the patronage of St. Agnes. Mass was first celebrated in the Samuelsons' home on South Main Street in 1893. A permanent home for St. Agnes was built in 1900 on the hill west of town. By this time, the name Pearl River had been established. The congregation, therefore, decided to dedicate the new church to St. Margaret, since the name Margaret means "pearl."

The present brick church was built in 1931, after a fire destroyed the original structure. However, to maintain the link with the past, the rose window over the church entrance depicts St. Agnes.

Robert Burghardt

To Deliver, Or Not To Deliver:
The Pearl River Postal Question

In Pearl River in 1933, there was a great controversy over the mail. Up to that point, residents had to go to the old post office to pick up their mail. On February 9, 1933, a committee of taxpayers voted to request free door-to-door mail delivery.

This brought a swift and negative reaction from storeowners. They argued that they would lose money, because if people did not have to come into town every day to get their mail, they wouldn't shop in their stores.

Others argued that mail carrier delivery would cost the town as much as $450 per year, not to mention the loss of $2,000 in revenue generated from residents renting the 800 mailboxes at the post office.

Despite these objections, progress won out. Not only did residents begin receiving mail at their doorsteps, but much to the old-timers' dismay, a new, modern post office was also constructed.

Linda Zimmermann

Rockland Psychiatric Center: 1931-2000

January 21, 1931 marked the official opening of Rockland State Hospital (RSH), later to be called Rockland Psychiatric Center (RPC). The new state hospital was built on the site of the former 600-acre Broadacres Farm. Under the direction of the New York State Office of Mental Health, RSH was part of a network of public institutions located throughout the state that provided a haven to children and adults with mental illness, as well as the destitute, homeless and the indigent. Removal of mentally ill people from society, far from its conscience and consciousness, was the prevailing philosophy.

Until the late 1960s, RSH thrived as a self-contained community with patients and staff growing, harvesting, manufacturing and building virtually all items needed for their existence. Rockland, like most other state hospitals, grew most of its own vegetables on farms worked by the patients with staff supervision. The farms operated from 1931 to 1960, with 40 to 125 acres under cultivation at any one time.

RSH, which had its own nursing school and medical hospital, as well as a research unit, became a testing ground for new treatment modalities as they became available. Until the advent of antipsychotic drugs, treatments were mostly limited to recreational therapy, occupational therapy, physical labor, continuous flow tub therapy, insulin coma therapy, electric shock therapy and lobotomy. Innovative programs such as the child guidance clinics, treatment for alcoholism, care of those retarded persons who also suffered from mental illness, and psycho-educational programs flourished at RSH.

During World War II, a portion of RSH was used by the U.S. Army's Camp Shanks as a field hospital. Some 1260 patients were relocated to other hospitals to make room for soldiers recovering from their wounds.

From 1931 to the mid 1950s, the census continued to climb, reaching an all-time high of 9600 patients in

1953. With the introduction of antipsychotic medications in the mid 1950s, some of which were pioneered in the research unit, and the passage of community mental health legislation in the early 1960s, many patients were discharged into the community. Deinstitutionalization had begun, accompanied by a changing mental health care philosophy. The focus gradually shifted from inpatient care to outpatient services with its network of mental health clinics, community mental health centers and community residences. However, in many communities, homelessness among mentally ill people became a growing issue as more and more people were discharged to their home communities. Fortunately, Rockland County, with its community mental health center and network of mental health services, worked in tandem with RSH to provide mental health services to Rockland County residents.

By 1970, when children's services became a separate entity with the creation of Rockland Children's Psychiatric Center, the census had declined to about 2,700 men and women. In the meantime, the number of patients receiving outpatient services in Rockland,

Rockland State Hospital in the 1930s. Courtesy of RSH.

123

Westchester and NYC swelled to over 2,500.

Innovative programs such as the creation of a unit for deaf people with mental illness and the concept of centralized treatment malls took root at RPC, as well as the development of community residences by the Rockland Hospital Guild at RPC. These were the first residences of their kind to be established by a nonprofit agency on a state campus. RPC also nurtured the family and consumer empowerment movement with its innovative patient and peer advocacy programs and family support services.

During the next decade, a steady downsizing of inpatient services, including a reduction in the number of staff, led to the closing of many of the campus' 100 antiquated buildings. Subsequently, a sizable portion of the campus became surplus property and in the year 2000 it was in the process of being sold. RPC continues to share the campus with a number of service and community agencies including Kids' Corner day care center, the Gaelic Athletic League, Rockland Children's Psychiatric Center and the Nathan Kline Institute for Psychiatric Research with which it actively participates in joint research.

Both the Nathan Kline Institute and RPC embarked on major renovation projects during the 1990s. For RPC, the renovations resulted in the consolidation of all inpatient and administrative services in the renovated mid-rise complex. Housed in a contemporary, therapeutic environment, Rockland Psychiatric Center's 400-bed inpatient units specialize in the treatment, rehabilitation and support of people with severe and complex mental illness from Rockland, Westchester and New York City.

Heidi Kistler, Volunteer Services, RPC

Justin DuPratt White
(1867-1939)

J. DuPratt White was a resident of Upper Nyack for over 50 years. He graduated from Nyack High School in 1885, from Cornell University in 1890 and was admitted to the bar in 1892.

White was appointed to the Palisades Interstate Park Commission in 1900 by the then governor of New York, Theodore Roosevelt. He was the first secretary of this commission and then became its second president. He served this commission for nearly forty years. White worked to develop the project into a great recreational center for the residents of both New York and New Jersey. He was responsible for the inclusion of the Hook Mountain and Tallman Mountain sections into this vast interstate park system.

Professionally, the law firm that White established in 1901 called White & Case at 14 Wall St., New York, developed into one of the most important law firms in the country and is still in existence today. J. DuPratt White served as counsel to the French High Commission during World War I and was recognized by the French government in 1919 when it made him a Chevalier of the French Legion of Honor.

White also served on the Board of Trustees of Upper Nyack. He was chairman of the committee that collaborated with the Board of Supervisors in the building of a new county courthouse in New City in the late 1920s. In addition, he was a member of both the New York and Rockland County Bar Associations. White also served as president of the Rockland Country Club.

Throughout his life, White was deeply involved with his alma mater. As an illustrious alumnus of Cornell University, White became a member of the Board of Trustees in 1913. In 1919, he was chairman of the university's endowment fund and raised $6,000,000 for the university.

His funeral in Nyack on July 17, 1939 was attended by representatives of the Palisades Park Commission, Cornell University and prominent lawyers and bankers. Seventy members of the Palisades Park Police formed a guard of honor. Ezra Cornell, grandson of the founder of Cornell University, was one of the ushers. J. DuPratt White was buried in Oak Hill Cemetery, Nyack.

Genevieve Stolldorf

Volunteer Ambulance Service

The Pearl River Alumni Ambulance Corps was founded in 1936, the first in New York State. The ambulance service was founded following a terrible automobile accident, which claimed the lives of several Pearl River youths.

Recognizing the need for fast, reliable emergency transportation, several graduates went door to door and business to business and raised the money to buy and equip an ambulance. (Thus the official name Pearl River *Alumni* Ambulance.) Volunteers staffed the ambulance.

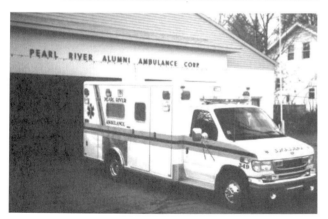

This beginning led to two traditions that continue to today:

➤ Pearl River's Ambulance is supported by contributions from the community and takes no tax money.
➤ Pearl River Ambulance is a volunteer organization. Both drivers and EMTs donate their time and skills in service to the community.

By the year 2000, Pearl River Ambulance had over 30 active members and two rigs. In 1999, Pearl River answered over 1,200 emergency calls.

I think it's a tribute to the spirit of Pearl River in particular and Rockland County in general that in the year 2000 we have an excellent Emergency Medical Service based on the efforts of skilled and caring volunteers.

Other ambulance corps serving Rockland are: Congers-Valley Cottage, Nanuet, Nyack, Sloatsburg, Hatzolah, Ramapo Valley, New City, Piermont, South Orangetown, Haverstraw, Spring Hill, Stony Point, Tuxedo, and William P. Faist.

Jack Flynn, Training Officer, PREMS

Top: 1936 Charter Members in front of their first ambulance.

Center: A Cadillac ambulance leaving quarters, ready to "scoop and run" (scoop up the patient and run 'em to the hospital)—circa 1950.

Bottom: An "ER on Wheels," this 2000 ambulance allows paramedics and EMT's to begin patient care on the way to the hospital.

Grand View resident Radcliffe Hall (1915-1997) was an NBC radio and television announcer from 1935 to 1976. Hall's career spanned the "Golden Ages" of television and radio and over the decades he interviewed many of the twentieth century's most important figures. He was the first to break the news to America that "Germany has invaded Poland," at 2 a.m. on September 1, 1939. He was also an announcer for the first commercially broadcast major league baseball game in 1939. Hall shared the master of ceremonies honors with Helen Hayes at the opening of the Tappan Zee Bridge. When asked to look back on his career, Hall replied, "I've had a full and rich career, seen it all, did a good job. I had standards and I maintained them. The industry standards changed, and I wasn't about to change mine."

The Yellow Jail and the New School

Due to the flourishing brick industry, Haverstraw had an ever-increasing population of school-aged children. In 1884, a larger Haverstraw school was opened on the corner of Fairmont Street and Hudson Avenue. The school continued to expand over the years, with the largest addition coming in 1908 so the school could accommodate all grades K-12.

To make the entire structure look uniform, it was painted yellow. It wasn't long before the high school students began calling it *The Yellow Jail*. The Yellow Jail served the community well until 1936 when it was destroyed in a spectacular fire. The rumor around town was that the son of a prominent family put a torch to the school, but the story was never substantiated. For two years, children were scattered to makeshift classrooms all over the village until the new Haverstraw school was completed in 1938.

The plot of land where the old school had stood was too small for the new larger structure. The only suitable space available in the village was a marshy field bounded by Grant Street and Conklin Avenue. This field was long used as a ballpark by the many amateur and semi-pro teams in the area. It was also the spot where the carnival and circus pitched their tents when they came to town.

In order to build the new school it was first necessary to drive piles through the marsh and clay to bedrock. On these piles was built a truly fine school constructed to last for generations.

Shortly after the school opened, the art teacher, Florence Daly, painted on canvas a mural to cover one wall of the Home Economics room. The mural, completed in 1941, depicted all phases of the brick manufacturing industry in Haverstraw. After 1969 when the new North Rockland High School was opened it was decided to renovate the Grant Street school. This renovation was to include nailing wood paneling over the mural. Joe Corrado, then president of the school board, was alerted to the impending "desecration" and put a halt to it. An artist was commissioned to remove the canvas from the wall, clean the painting and mount it on a stretch frame. The fine mural was then hung in the middle school.

Robert Burghardt

The Lost Towns

There were at least eleven Rockland hamlets that are now extinct. Many of them owe their destruction to the creation of the Palisades/Harriman Parks. They were Sandyfields (aka Beaver Pond), Johnsontown, Pitt Town (aka Pittsboro and Shirley Hollow), Baileytown, Queensboro, Pine Meadow, Doodletown, Rockland Lake, Bulsontown, Jones Point, and Carr Pond Mountain. Carr Pond Mountain was discovered only in the late 1990s by a descendant of its settlers. There may yet be more waiting to be discovered.

Not much has been documented about the lost towns until recent years. The reasons for this are basically threefold: it was very hard for the families to lose their ancestral homes so they didn't like discussing it. Secondly, the authorities didn't want it to be discussed because of the heavy-handed way in which they conducted the takeovers, essentially duplicating scenes right out of *The Grapes of Wrath*. Finally, some did discuss it with various reporters and folklorists, but the information they gave in innocent good faith was often twisted and reported with prejudice so that it made the mountain folk appear in a very negative light. Naturally, after having been burned, they turned inward and refused to discuss their experiences with "outsiders."

Which of the towns was the first to disappear is difficult to define. Queensboro was totally gone by WWII. Pine Meadow's last resident, Ramsey Conklin, left in 1935 when the lake's waters almost reached his doorstep and he realized that he was beaten. Baileytown wasn't far behind as its last resident died just before Pearl Harbor. Pitt Town seems to have had residents into the 1950s. Sandyfields and Johnsontown lasted through the war to some degree with Johnsontown's last resident (Muzz Jones, the Park ranger) finally leaving in 1951. We do know that Rockland Lake was demolished in 1964 and Doodletown's last resident (Clarence June, Jr.) left in January 1965.

The founders of most of the towns were reflective of the founders of the nation in terms of their origins. They were Dutch, English, Scotch-Irish, and some German and French Huguenots. Later on there seems to have been some Scandinavian influence in Sandyfields. Rockland Lake is an exception as it was geographically separated from the others by distance and had numerous Italian and Polish residents.

What attracted people to these places is basically work and lifestyle. The mining industry brought people to places like Baileytown and Doodletown. The lumber industry brought people to Johnsontown, as its founders were in the timber and shipbuilding business. This also had some influence on Pine Meadow, as the Woodtown Road, which was a thoroughfare to and from it, was maintained by the Christie family, who had an extensive lumber business along its route (hence its name). At one time there was a mill along the Christie Brook. Nearby was also the Christie Mine (iron), which fed the file factory with the material for its business (it, too, stood in close proximity).

During the nineteenth century, Doodletowners worked at Beveridge Island (now Iona Island), as Dr. Beveridge maintained an estate and experimental farm there where he dabbled in cultivating apple trees and grape vines. Once it became a Naval Ammunition Depot (from the Spanish American War through the 1950s), many residents worked there, as did some at the post WWII "Mothball" or "Reserve Fleet" at Jones Point. Many others from the villages worked at West Point, Bear Mountain Park, Letchworth Village, Arden Farms, Avon and so forth.

However, during their heyday, life in the villages was built around subsistence farming. It has been said by many from the hamlets that they weren't affected by the Great Depression. They heard of the problems of others, but they themselves were doing fine, as a bad economy doesn't affect cows giving milk or crops growing in the fields. One old timer, Norman Conklin from Pitt Town, said after I asked what they grew in their gardens, "Didn't need a garden. There was plenty just growing around wild on its own."

Andrew J. Smith

The church that once stood in Doodletown.
JSC

Blacker Farm

Meyer Blacker came to Rockland in 1920. His farm consisted of a house, a barn, chicken coops and acres of vegetables and fruit trees. The house had no indoor  plumbing, and the only sources of heat were a furnace in the basement that sent warm air up through a grating in the living room floor, and the coal stove in the kitchen.

According to family history, Meyer Blacker was a well-liked and respected member of the Nanuet community. At a town meeting, members of the Ku Klux Klan actually told him which judge to see to help him obtain his citizenship papers. It's doubtful that present-day Klan members would be so helpful to a Jew.

Blacker fell ill in the 1940s, and he and his wife, Lena, were unable to maintain the farm. In the 1960s, the Blacker farm became the site of the E.J. Korvettes shopping center on Route 59. Today, the shopping center contains many stores, including the Pathmark supermarket and The Wiz electronics store.

Information and photo (left) provided by Robin Lefkowitz,
Meyer Blacker's great-great granddaughter

The shopping center on the site of the Blacker farm in 2001. LZ

127

Virginia Parkhurst Remembers *The Journal-News* in the 30s

There's an old saying that has become so trite that any writer should cringe at its utterance. It's the one that describes the employees of a particular firm as "members of one, big, happy family." Yet this was largely true of *The Journal-News* staff of the 1930s. There was a camaraderie among those who worked in the composing and mechanical departments, which as the newspaper grew larger, could never occur again.

Editorial, advertising and circulation departments were all housed in the large front office of the newspaper's headquarters at 53 Hudson Avenue, in Nyack, with the offices of F.R. Miller, business manager, and Emma Burnett Conace, the bookkeeper, in glass cubicles at the side. The composing and mechanical departments were at the rear of the one-story building. The press was in the basement.

Reporters felt free—after their copy was in—to wander into the composing room and watch as linotypists Eddie Maurer, Jack Joyce and Don Maher turned their stories into imperishable lead, then lean against the "stone" or makeup bank where the foreman, Lewis Stockmeyer, was making up the pages, putting lead together in a "chase" or form. Sometimes Lew even permitted them to pick up some of the type and arrange it in the form themselves. It was a pleasure, which reporters in today's age of electronic journalism will never experience.

If later one should get a smudge of ink on his sleeve as he grabbed a wet copy of the day's paper as it came off the press, it didn't matter much—it was all part of being a newspaper person.

The composing room crew felt equally free to wander into the front office and exchange yarns with reporters Charlie Wilson and Vince Martire.

When reporter Robert F. Deed married Miss Louise Salla, the backroom crew and reporters joined to put out a "special edition" with a banner headline announcing the wedding, which they hawked to passersby outside the Nyack Presbyterian Church on Broadway, where the ceremony had just been concluded.

Nights after reporters' stories had been written and younger members of the mechanical department had finished an overtime stint, the strains of "Abdul, the Bulbul Ameer" and other barbershop quartet favorites could often be heard drifting from the *Journal-News* building.

There was a *Journal-News* softball team, which played in the county leagues. A picnic for employees and their families was held each summer at Hook Mountain in Upper Nyack. There were mountains of shrimp, which Belle Maurer, Eddie's wife, had cooked the night before; and corn, which Norman Baker, the sports editor, had allowed to stay in the huge pot of water he

had boiling over a charcoal fire just long enough to retain its sweetness. There were hot dogs for the children and quantities of pies and cakes, which the wives of members of the backroom crew had baked.

Employees left the paper usually for only one or two reasons: World War II was looming and they went into the service, or as was true with all country papers—as the *Journal-News* was then—the pay they received was not that great.

Following World War II the camaraderie among all departments, which was so much a part of *Journal-News* life in the 1930s, did not return. Indeed, it would never have been possible if the staff had not been so small.

The roster of employees included besides those already mentioned: G. Wilson Bartine, J. Fred Geist and myself in the editorial department; proofreader Marian Deed; Helen Phillips, Mary Conace, Kenneth Marshall, Leon Cobbett and Dan Nemeth of the classified and display advertising departments; Martin Magai, George Mueller and Bill Muise of circulation; and Steve Danko, Bob Scharpf, George Begbie, Bill Hoehn, George Thiesen and Joe and Tony Costino of the composing and mechanical departments.

The staff also included a very special person, Philip Lenhart. Then, as now, the most popular features in the paper were the columns authored by staff members. Phil's was captioned "Wheelin' Around." The heading told much of Phil's story. Shortly after his graduation from Harvard University, he had been paralyzed in an automobile accident and was never to leave a wheelchair. Phil wrote about books and plays. Like Mariruth Campbell, a *Journal-News* theater critic of a later day. Phil did not hesitate to call the shots as he saw them. Producers were not always pleased with his reviews.

Perhaps even better liked by the average *Journal-News* reader than Phil's reviews were Bob Deed's "The Traffic Booth" and Wilson Bartine's "Heard and Seen," which he wrote under the pseudonym of Frank Ernest. Both columns were filled with gently humorous anecdotes about people who lived in their territories as reporters—Bob's in Nyack and Bart's in North Rockland. Both were friends of policemen, politicians and judges, and most of all, the man in the street.

In this they were like Walter Williams, who had lived in the county since the early days of the century and had a list of acquaintances as long as a telephone directory. He loved politics and his huge store of information of county and town governments in Rockland made him knowledgeable as the paper's editor. Walter's own writing was straightforward and incisive and he had little tolerance for a reporter's sloppy copy, particularly if it was filled with mistakes in grammar. His comments could be cutting, but the targets of his remarks usually forgave him because they realized he never was without pain from neuritis, a degenerative disease of the nerves.

Young newspaper people, just starting out, found him kind, and he could be sentimental about old cronies and old times. He died in 1940 and was succeeded by Norman Baker, an able writer, as knowledgeable of the county and its institutions as Williams.

Norman had once been the Ramapo reporter. He was followed in that post by J. Fred Geist. Nothing on that beat ever escaped Freddie. During a disagreement with Chief Abe Stern, Freddie told Stern that he would get Ramapo police news from outside sources rather than the regular police channels, and he did. Freddie would call up Stern each morning and innocently ask if there was any news. When Stern said "no," Freddie, who had already found out to the last detail what had happened overnight in the chief's bailwick, would write the story. This went on for weeks. Freddie and Stern became good friends again, but the story of how he succeeded in getting the news in that period is one of the paper's legends.

That the *Journal-News* prospered in the 1930s, when many other county institutions were on shaky ground, was due to the business acumen of Rudy Miller. Rudy was Nyack born. He could remember when schooners laden with stone docked at the Main Street pier and when the freighter, *Raleigh*, traveled the Hudson River between New York and Nyack. He had been a printer's devil at the old *Nyack Star* and had done everything from sweeping the floor to setting type. Even though he was the *Journal-News'* business manager, he was never above lending a hand in the composing or press rooms when help was short.

Bob Deed, who came to the paper straight from Nyack High School, was chief copy editor for "Business Week" when he retired from that nationally known publication. Charlie Wilson left newspaper work, but was to write four lively historical novels for young people. Lew Stockmeyer became Rockland's most widely known photographer and is particularly remembered for his aerial shots of the building of the Tappan Zee Bridge.

Nothing, of course, ever remains the same, but it was a great game working for the *Journal-News* in the 1930s.

Virginia Parkhurst, *Journal-News*, 7/5/82

A word about our Virginia

You have only to say "Virginia" in Nyack and just about everyone will know who you are talking about: Virginia Parkhurst, reporter.

For 40 years, from 1934 until she retired in 1974 at the age of 71, Miss Parkhurst was a dedicated journalist, covering society news at first and then the Nyack and

Orangetown beats. She never left a meeting early, no matter how long it went on, and she always got both sides of the story. Her legend at the *Journal-News* is such that even some of today's reporters and editors who never met Virginia know of her work and respect her as one of those who set the standards of journalism.

Journal-News, 7/5/82

Virginia Parkhurst served with the WACS for 27 months during WWII. She is pictured here working on aerial photographs in the Philippines. (US Army photo)

Ritt and Bottsy

I don't think there's a Nyack High School graduate from 1932 to 1952 that didn't love and respect the school's principal, A. W. Rittershausen, whom all called "Ritt" for short.

However, it wasn't always Ritt. Initially he earned the nickname "Pussyfoot" and it took him years to live it down. That was because he used to prowl the halls between classes, shoo you off to your next class and raise the dickens about the noise you made.

One such noisemaker was John Bott, whom we all called "Bottsy." John had one of those voices that just naturally carried and reverberated throughout the hallways, even if he was talking in a low voice. He could be two corridors away and you'd know it was Bottsy making all the noise. He gave Ritt fits and would always be apologizing. Bottsy later became an editor on the *New York Post*. I can just imagine seeing everyone jump when he'd yell out "Copy!"

Kenneth F. Harniman

Experimental Living

Ralph Borsodi began his new style of country living, later labeled as "agrarianism for commuters," in 1919. He, his wife Myrtle Mae Simpson and two small sons moved from New York City and rented a small, unimproved farmhouse on seven acres near Suffern. While Borsodi commuted to work in the city, they began their initial family experiments.

With little capital and a small income, they remodeled their first tiny building, learning the use of necessary tools, and began growing fruits and vegetables. Acquiring a goat, cow and chickens, they tested their theories and dreams of self-subsistence and economic freedom while enjoying the beauty of nature.

In 1924, they selected a larger 18-acre site off the present DeBaun Avenue in Airmont to design and build the homestead they really wanted. Combining their own amateur labor with the skilled labor of local workmen, they cleared the land, gathered native fieldstone and built the west wing of the house to live in while completing the rest. Construction was based on Ernest Flagg's experiments in building attractive, economical, sturdy houses made with a concrete slab and available fieldstones for walls.

In a period of 10 years, they constructed an enclave of five buildings, including a barn and their own homestead, "Dogwoods," (below, JSC) which contained a workshop for weaving, a laundry, billiard room, printing plant and an outdoor swimming pool. Here they first experimented with a theory called the School of Living that would later lead to classes in self-sufficiency.

Borsodi had written several books on economics, but *This Ugly Civilization,* published in 1929, brought

him national attention. In it he deplored the smokestack industries and factories that he viewed as dominating civilization, contributing to the noise, congestion and filth in towns and cities and reducing the workers to servitude and mere cogs in the throbbing factory machinery. At the same time, the collapse of the stock market and the beginning of the Great Depression caused widespread unemployment and financial insecurity for millions of Americans. Borsodi offered a better way of life and was proving it in rural Rockland County.

His best-selling book, *Flight From the* City, appeared in 1933 when the country was mired in the depths of the Depression. Firing the imagination of struggling families, many with low-paying inner-city employment and an aimless future, the book described a way to seek out a good agrarian lifestyle and graphically detailed his family's experiences and accomplishments at homesteading in Suffern.

Borsodi's lecture tours and writings describing the decentralization movement and his family's experiments in self-sufficiency received support nationally; his theories gained the endorsement of leading educators, sociologists, economists and numerous organizations. The news media gave wide attention to his activities, which often appeared in featured articles. Mrs. Eleanor Roosevelt's interest in social engineering projects brought her to "Dogwoods" to observe the Borsodi methods.

Bayard Lane

In 1935, Borsodi launched Bayard Lane, a small experimental cooperative community off Route 202, Suffern, consisting of a group of 17 houses built of native fieldstone by the Flagg method. Housed in a separate building, the School of Living was organized in 1936 to handle research and promotion of the movement, and the Independence Foundation to finance it. Most of the funds were derived from his associate, Chauncey D. Stillman, a financier who had an absorbing interest in the decentralist movement.

The school taught the essentials of do-it-yourself agrarianism, including canning, poultry raising, animal husbandry, masonry, carpentry, use of tools and household equipment. A guild plan was formulated as a business relationship between owners and builders. Homes

could be constructed by various building craft guilds under a special arrangement with the Independence Foundation. A professional staff would provide architects, estimates, record keeping and construction. The guild wages were low but the workmen eagerly accepted them since they were guaranteed year-round employment. There was almost no other construction work in the county in those lean years. The benefits to the homeowners were considerable as they could do as much of the work as desirable, calling in help when needed.

The initial success of the Bayard Lane experiment in homesteading, coupled with his own family experiences, convinced Borsodi that larger, better-organized groups could be developed. Van Houten Fields offered the opportunity he needed for the large-scale venture he envisioned would attract national attention and forever change the American life-style.

A Bayard Lane home and the historical marker commemorating the community. JSC

In November 1937, the *New York Times* ran a feature article that caught the attention of many families, especially New York City dwellers looking for a new and more satisfying life, some of whom would be the pioneer settlers, "city farmers," in Van Houten Fields:

Old Farm in West Nyack Will Be Site for New Cooperative Homestead Project

A new cooperative community to be made up of homesteads which will be at least partially self-sustaining and which will be modeled after Ralph Borsodi's School of Living Colony at Suffern, N. Y., will be started next week at West Nyack. The second project provides for more *than*

fifty homes, making it more than three times the size of the original [at Bayard Lane]... .

The site of the new development will be the old Van Houten farm on the Sickletown Road overlooking the upper Hackensack Valley... .

An ad in 1939 asked, "*Do You Earn About $3,000 a Year and Wished You Lived in the Country?*" The enticements of such advertising and the publicity were many and varied: the pleasures of homestead and country living for city dwellers, the agrarian lifestyle, the low-cost acreage and the economy of do-it-yourself construction when desirable, all with almost unbelievably small monthly payments. For those families struggling through the Depression years of the 1930s, Borsodi's utopian offer was almost too good to be true.

The homebuilder would pay for the leased land in monthly installments ranging from $4.65 to $7.68 per acre, including taxes, road costs and community improvement. Title was to remain with the Independence Foundation as trustee.

From the beginning, the Van Houten Fields development attracted numerous artists, writers, actors, musicians and craftsmen. Among the early settlers were: Fred Rockwell, garden editor of the *New York Times,* and his wife Esther, who collaborated with him on many horticultural books; Thomas Wilfred, famed lutenist and singer of Elizabethan ballads and creator of Lumia, a visual art that uses moving light as a medium of expression; Hal Borland, nature writer for the *Times* and author of numerous books; Richard Lyman, *Herald Tribune* writer; and Fred Gruin, *Times* U.N. correspondent. Over the years others in the arts continued to arrive as well as educators, doctors, business and professional people, all contributing a varied mixture of personalities, adding to the social life of the Fields.

The pioneers, or first settlers, at the Van Houten Fields development were generally considered to be those who arrived, cleared the land and commenced building between 1938 and 1941. During the war years, as materials gradually became unavailable, most construction ceased.

Murmurings of discontent began spreading throughout the two Rockland settlements. Although an effective theorist of homesteading and agrarianism, Borsodi was not a good organizer. Some complained that he insisted on overseeing every detail of construction; others, that the promises made to them of various kinds of assistance were never fulfilled, that the School of Living occupied most of his time. There was increasing dissatisfaction with the terms of the land indenture that prevented their owning the land in their lifetime. An elitist, Borsodi had an attitude of superiority that disturbed some who considered him, at times, openly arrogant. Patience was noticeably not one of his virtues.

A combination of events befell the Borsodi activities in Rockland and in other communities, some still in the planning stages. The war in Europe and our military build-up to supply support for the Allies heated up the stagnant economy and created new, better-paying employment. The continuing controversy over land-tenure agreements and shortages in building materials, which curtailed new construction and furthered more discontent among the guilds, made it obvious that some new arrangements had to be made.

Chauncey Stillman, the financial angel, was going into active military duty. Expressing a desire to consolidate his financial holdings, he agreed to renegotiate the earlier contracts to the satisfaction of the homesteaders.

A long, page-one feature article in the *New York Times,* May 5, 1940 fully aired the problem. Among the hopeful solutions: Borsodi's resignation.

Three years after the project started, Borsodi stepped down and the Van Houten Fields settlers severed their connection with the Independence Foundation, forming their own association. Working together under new bylaws, the Van Houten Fields association continued into the new century.

The original families at Van Houten Fields had not been out to revolutionize the world; they were mostly survivors of the worst Depression America had ever known, existing on a tiny income and desperately seeking a better way of life for themselves and their children. While it may not have became the functional agrarian cooperative Borsodi envisioned, it is one the most attractive places to live in Rockland County, and it did prove his theory that there was great joy and satisfaction in owning your own home.

Still passionate about his theories, Borsodi continued to write and lecture, and his travels took him around the world. His best seller, *Flight from the City,* had a resurgence of sales in 1961, and 1972 paperback editions where discovered by the hippy generation interested in communal living. In 1973, Borsodi revisited Rockland, meeting with old acquaintances at Bayard Lane and Van Houten Fields. He was 90 years of age when he died, as the result of an accident, in New Hampshire in 1977.

John Scott

...In 1937 the Japanese commit atrocities in the Chinese city of Nanking, executing as many as 340,000 people and raping 80,000 women; Japanese newspapers print photos and report the totals as if they were sports scores...In 1939 the New York World's Fair opens with its distinctive symbols of the Perisphere and Trylon and present an idealized view of "The World of Tomorrow" ..."The Wizard of Oz" starring Judy Garland premieres...Germany and Italy create an alliance by signing the "Pact of Steel"...The Spanish Civil War ends with victory of Franco's Nationalists...

Meyer's Grocery Market

In 1989, Bill Meyer chuckled at a local supermarket's offer of overnight home delivery of groceries for a $9.95 fee. Meyer remembered that he and his father, William H. Meyer, Sr., used to provide free delivery and credit—without finance charges—to customers of Meyer's Grocery Market, which served Haverstraw and other Rockland communities for more than 60 years.

"Supermarkets did not exist locally until 1940," Meyer said. "Prior to that, grocery stores had long counters. And behind those counters clerks—about 20 of them at Meyer's—assembled the needs of the shopper. Most of the orders were delivered to the lady's home free of charge, and without cost for the privilege of credit."

Meyer said his father, who died in 1973, liked to describe the honesty of people to whom credit was extended. Families working in Haverstraw's brickyards often ran up tabs during the winter months when they were without work, and were careful to pay when work resumed in the summer.

"Everything was done on a handshake," Meyer said. "No interest charges, and no written contracts."

Meyer said he continued the home delivery practice for many years when he took over operation of the store in 1935. Meyer described how horse-drawn wagons made deliveries. "The wagons were heavily loaded because there was no pre-packaging in those days, and flour, sugar and potatoes were usually sold in one hundred-pound barrels. In fact, it took four horses to pull the wagon through the Short Clove rock cut to get to New City."

Later, the horses and wagons were replaced by motor trucks. One delivery truck was the Stewart, an open-canopy vehicle with racks built into the running boards to hold five-gallon cans of kerosene. The fuel was delivered to customers in rural Rockland, who used it for cooking, heating and illumination long before public utilities were widely available.

Meyer's market later converted to self-service, and Meyer bought what he calls the first supermarket carts from the Wire Form Co. of New Jersey. The carts, several of which Meyer still has, featured removable upper and lower wire baskets, and folded for ease of storage.

Meyer's father opened his store, "Wm. H. Meyer, Fine Teas and Coffees," on Haverstraw's "Bank Corner" in 1910. The corner, the intersection of Broadway and Main Street, was named for the People's Bank and the National Bank, which opened on opposite sides of the intersection in the 1890s.

The elder Meyer was 20 when he bought the store from his uncle, who was part-owner of the Rickborn and Meyer chain of 34 grocery stores. The uncle had taken the elder Meyer in when he was eight years old, after the boy's parents died during a typhoid epidemic.

The child was taught simple arithmetic, and without the benefit of further education, he was put to work in the company's stores. He managed the chain's interests on both sides of the Hudson before buying the Haverstraw store.

Years later, when Bill Meyer graduated from Columbia University in 1935, his father offered to take him on at the store for $25 per week. "This was when the Great Depression had influenced the economy," Meyer recalls. "It was common for Ivy League grads to wait as long as six months to get a position paying $19 per week. So $25 per week was a tremendous opportunity."

Meyer operated the store until he retired in 1977, but grew restless soon after selling his business. He took a part-time job as an assistant manager at the Orchards of Concklin in Pomona, where he still works, using one of his old shopping carts to stock shelves. He said Orchards customers know him as "the man in the blue store coat," and seek him out for advice on purchases.

Besides his business experience, Meyer has participated in his local fire department and Rotary Club for the past fifty years. "I've made friends with so many people from both ends of the county, I should run for public office," he joked.

Meyer has a collection of items spanning the store's history, including a painting of the corner grocery by Nyack artist William Bruckner. An opening-day advertisement for 1910 featured, among other things, 5 pounds of coffee for 95 cents. An old contract with Rockland Light and Power Company, provided power for the store for $1.10 a month.

Gary Pallassino, *The Journal-News*, 5/28/89

Robert Gair Company, Piermont

July 1939: Several hundred people turned out in Piermont last Friday morning for a parade and commemorative ceremonies at the Robert Gair Company, Inc., plant on the 75th anniversary of the company's founding in New York City in the 1860s.

A group of forty employees with service records from 20 to 42 years and a total aggregate service of over 1,100 years participated in the ceremonies. In an opening speech, Harry Van Decker, manager of the plant, paid tribute to the late Robert Gair, who, fresh from the battlefields of the Civil War, founded the business of the company in a small loft on Reade Street, New York City, and developed the company to a leading position in its industry, and which at the present time, has 22 plants in the United States and Canada, for the manufacture of boxboard, folding cartons and corrugated shipping containers.

Mr. Van Decker also stated that 75% of the 835 employees at his plant had service records of ten years or more.

Other speakers were John Pabst, thirty-eight years with the company; Elmer H. Curtiss, Dennis Hogan, mayor of Piermont, who, in a short speech congratulated the company on its anniversary, and Edward Stebbins, Piermont police commissioner.

Mr. Van Decker's speech was as follows: "Mr. Mayor, distinguished guests, friends and fellow workers:

"We are assembled here this morning to commemorate, in a simple ceremony, the 75th anniversary of our company.

"To remain in business for 75 years, through depressions, panic and turbulent times, is a record to be proud of—to continue a leader in an industry is an even greater accomplishment.

"Seventy-five years ago, on July 7, 1864, less than sixty days after he was mustered out of the Union Army, Robert Gair started this business in a small loft in Reade Street, New York. Through his inventive genius and business ability, his project grew, until today there stands a monument to his ability 22 plants in the United States and Canada. He devised the modern method of mass production of folding cartons and was one of the two pioneers in the manufacture of corrugated board.

"This Piermont plant was started in 1900 on the historic banks of the Tappan Zee...

"To my mind, the strength of this so-called 'Gair Spirit' which keeps us here and binds us together as friends, is its simplicity—justice—democracy—and high ideals in business and elsewhere. Mr. Gair was a do-er—not a talker—his example in business and social circles of practical business-like and courageous Americanism is an inspiration which will not fade.

"In summation; let us look forward to July 7, 1964—25 years from now—when we can again assemble and rededicate these same principles on the occasion of our 100th anniversary."

Orangetown newspaper article, July, 1939

Note: Gair merged with Continental Can in 1956.

The Piermont Flywheel (above) was installed in 1902 as part of the Piermont Paper Company's steam-driven electrical generator. This massive piece of machinery continued to see service for the Robert Gair Company, Continental Can Company and Federal Paperboard/Clevepak until 1983. Several attempts to demolish it with explosives failed, and in 1991, plans were developed to restore the damaged and deteriorating flywheel. The five-month project, headed by chief restorer Irene Blanchard, turned the antique machinery into a sculpture that is now the centerpiece of Flywheel Park.

Photo by Linda Zimmermann

Fred Crum: Photographer

Fred E. Crum ran a photography business in Spring Valley for most of the first half of the twentieth century. He was a self-taught artist with a great love for his native Rockland County. He took many pictures of village doings—weddings, graduations, parades, school class days—as well as photographs for the coroner and police and of accidents for insurance purposes. He was probably best known, however, for his portraits of babies, families and prominent people in the county.

My father, Fred Crum, was born in 1882 in the large house on Mountain View Farm on Grandview Avenue in Viola (now Wesley Hills). The farm belonged to his maternal grandmother, "Ma Gilbert," Fidelia Forshay Coe Gilbert, whose brother, William Forshay, operated the nearby Forshay Cigar Factory.

When my father was a young man and recovering from a serious operation, he was given a box camera to occupy his time while he recuperated. He began taking photographs of his family— often timing the pictures so that he could jump into them himself—animals and local scenes. He went on to study photography magazines in order to learn how to develop negatives and make prints. He began selling his photographic postcards; one outlet was a shop for summer vacationers at Greenwood Lake in Orange County.

In 1910, Fred Crum bought a studio upstairs at 6 South Main Street in Spring Valley. At the street entrance he set up two enclosed cases, displaying local scenes and portraits, which people always stopped to look at. My father maintained his photographic business

134

at this site, where the Union State Bank now stands, until his death in 1949.

My father enjoyed the personal contact with his customers and his time spent outside the studio on a great variety of assignments that his skills made possible. He did all the work for the New York Telephone Company and was employed by Lederle Laboratories, as well. I also remember once during prohibition he was called away to photograph an illegal still found in the woods in the Monsey area and that he was spooked by a stranger trailing his car back to his home.

Rachel Kaufmann,
South of the Mountains, April/June 2001

A young Fred Crum with a box camera.
Photo courtesy of Rachel Kaufmann.

...In 1938 NBC is reprimanded for airing a radio program starring Mae West that was deemed to be lewd and "offensive to the great mass of right-thinking, clean-minded American citizens"...In 1939 Germany and Russia sign a non-aggression treaty and a week later Germany invades Poland...France and Great Britain declare war on Germany and WWII begins...

Oil Tanks

In the 1920s, Standard Oil built rows of oil storage tanks on property just north of Palisades on land that is now part of Tallman Park.

Complaints of this blight on the landscape reached the ears of John D. Rockefeller, who was previously unaware of the tanks. Rockefeller ignored such suggestions as painting the tanks green so they would blend in with the scenery, and ordered the site to be abandoned and destroyed.

In 1932 the tanks and other buildings were blown up and the ruins quickly became overgrown.

Aerial view of the Standard Oil tanks.   Photo courtesy of the Orangetown Museum.

...Oct. 7, 1932, the so-called "Cain and Abel" slaying occurs in Upper Nyack when a 17-year-old boy kills his 26-year-old brother with a single rifle shot to the heart. Headlines declare that as "Abel is buried, Cain's Life is Searched". A grand jury decides not to seek the death penalty...

Edward Ernest Sauter
1914-1981

Edward ("Eddie") Sauter spent most of his life in Rockland County near Nyack, where many of his innovative compositions and arrangements were created. The unique point of view which he brought to music was deeply influenced by his love of the natural beauty and rich history of the county as expressed in the compositions "Doodletown Fifers" and "High Tor," which conveyed his sure sense of history as did his arrangements for the hit musical "1776."

Always ready for a stroll along the street in his neighborhood or a hike in the woods, his favorite relaxation, he participated in research tracing the old colonial Kings Highway by walking its entire length from New Jersey to Orange County.

While still in Nyack High School (in the 1920s) Mr. Sauter was foremost among the young people in Rockland County who were experimenting in the exciting new big-band jazz sound emerging throughout the land. Playing drums and trumpet, and writing for small groups wasn't enough of a challenge for his imaginative mind, so he started his own dance band, which performed at proms and club dates.

He attended Columbia University and studied musical theory at the Julliard School of Music while supporting himself with trumpet stints in Archie Bleyer's orchestra during 1932-33 and with Charlie Barnett in 1934. Red Norvo, Barnett's piano player, split off to form his own band with singer-wife Mildred Bailey, and Sauter joined him—playing trumpet and arranging in the subtle swing style that soon brought him into national prominence. John Hammond, then scouting for Benny Goodman, recruited him for that band, where his distinctive swing arrangements and original compositions such as "Superman," "Benny Rides Again," and "Clarinet a la King" helped lead the band to its commanding position in the late 1930s and early 1940s.

Mr. Sauter's career included writing for Ray McKinley, Artie Shaw, Tommy Dorsey, Woody Herman, Bob Crosby and numerous other big bands. His original pieces for Ray McKinley, which included "Tumblebug," "Hangover Square," "Sandstorm" and "Borderline," are considered landmarks in the evolution of the so-called "Jazz" compositions.

In 1952, he joined with arranger Bill Finegan to form the Sauter-Finegan orchestra, the most original concept of concert jazz music of the post-war era. While this was a most satisfying period of Mr. Sauter's career in allowing his versatility full range, the economics of supporting such a large orchestra forced it to disband after five years.

Following a two-year sojourn (1957-59) as staff musical director at Sudwestfunk Radio, Baden Baden, Germany, his later years were devoted to his increasing interest in and study of classical music while, at the same time, earning a livelihood orchestrating Broadway musicals, films and television shows.

Among his original compositions of this period was an album entitled, "Focus," which combined a string orchestra with Stan Getz as tenor saxophone soloist—a widely acclaimed suite approaching new frontiers in the history of jazz. His "Tanglewood Concerto," also featuring Stan Getz on tenor sax, was performed by the Boston Pops Orchestra at Tanglewood. His orchestral arrangements of Christmas carols for another album, "The Joy of Christmas," brought together the Mormon Tabernacle Choir and the New York Philharmonic Orchestra under the direction of Leonard Bernstein.

Always known as "a musician's musician," and "ten years ahead of his time," Mr. Sauter was highly regarded throughout the musical world, having occupied a unique place in the fifty-year golden age of jazz and big band music.   Article and photo courtesy of John Scott

SOM, July/Sept. 1981

Ray Bergman (1891-1967) was born in Nyack and like most boys, loved to fish Rockland's waters with his father. Bergman turned his passion to a career by traveling the country and writing numerous articles and four books, including *Just Fishing*, published in 1932, and *Fresh Water Bass* in 1942. His most popular book, *Trout*, was first published in 1938 and is considered to be an unsurpassed angling classic that continues to be reprinted to the present day.

136

The Beginnings of Hispanic/Latino Communities

"If you thought the Depression here was bad, imagine what it was like in Puerto Rico."

Ronaldo L. Figueroa leaned forward in his chair to lay out the picture—a worldwide Depression that meant joblessness, hunger and homelessness for millions in the United States. And in Puerto Rico, a commonwealth of this country, the suffering was magnified because the country itself had fewer resources.

It was then, in the 1930s that the first Hispanic/Latino men and women left Puerto Rico and the Caribbean and South American countries for the promised riches—even in the Depression—of the giant to their north.

Some settled in New York City. Others wanted a place less populated. Many chose Haverstraw, beginning a community of Spanish-speaking people that still sees northern Rockland as the hub in a larger radius.

"They weren't urbanized people, but people from the country," Figueroa said of the earliest Hispanic/Latino settlers. "There was an industrial terminus in Garnerville—there were jobs for unskilled laborers within a five-mile radius: factories, Hornick's, dye houses, jobs in the fabric industries. It was really a working class of folks coming here for the opportunity. There was also migrant work here with the farming."

After World War II, the influx increased as soldiers who had seen the world moved here from their home countries on the recommendation of friends and magazine advertisements. Long-time Rocklander Bolivar Marchand remembers his father moving to the area around 1945.

"There were a few Puerto Ricans and a couple of Dominicans and three or four Cubans living in Garnerville" at the time, he said. "In the 50s, my parents moved to Main Street (in Haverstraw). Then the other people followed, mostly Puerto Ricans. I think the Dominicans actually started to move in in big groups about the 1960s. People came to this country looking for the jobs to make enough money to meet their needs, just like today."

Figueroa's family members came in the 1950s and were also among those who came looking for employment and enough money to support the people "back home." A former president of the Hispanic Coalition, the county's Hispanic/Latino advocacy group, Figueroa has spent years studying the history of the Hispanic/Latino communities in Rockland.

"When I was growing up, the Latino community was concentrated in a very small area of the village of Haverstraw, downtown and all the little streets that came off it," the 43-year-old Rocklander said. "It was mainly people from the Caribbean. I remember meeting a Mexican person or a Colombian—they were exotic. It was mostly Puerto Rico and Dominican Republic."

Many of the early settlers came from small villages in the mountains—Ciales in Puerto Rico and Tamboril in the Dominican Republic. They moved to New York City and settled in the Bronx or Harlem. Those who made a good living moved out into the "country"—Rockland.

There is one place in particular on 9W, he remembers, which caused gasps from his relatives as they drove up from New York City. You turn a corner, he said, and see Haverstraw nestled between High Tor and the Hudson River, with views of the Ramapo Mountains, Dunderberg and Bear Mountain in the background. "People were literally gasping, just looking at the village," he said. "Almost everybody came from a place like that. The location seemed like an emotional nurturance—having that body of water—and in the summer, it felt tropical. I don't think you can overestimate the power of that."

"The country people brought their culture, and the cuisine, music, arts, religious practices were not urban. They were really folk traditions," he said.

Marchand remembers the factories in the area "like a little city," with Spanish-speaking workers making chenille bedspreads or coats. "In those days, the biggest job was the dye house. Most of them worked there," Marchand said, "There was this cafeteria owned by three Greek gentlemen. This little city of factories worked 24 hours a day and the cafeteria was always open."

For entertainment there were the family celebrations of birthdays, weddings and anniversaries. In the late 1950s, taverns like the Landslide Bar and clubs like the local American Legion would rent out large rooms for dances. Those Hispanic/Latino residents who were politically inclined jumped on various Democratic bandwagons and passed out fliers to get people registered to vote.

Many of north Rockland's Hispanic/Latino residents are third-generation Rocklanders, Figueroa said.

"I grew up at a time where at least I felt connected to the traditions. Now I see youngsters struggling with that," Figueroa said, "Not all, of course, I have met many wonderful young people who have a respect for things that are part of the culture, who ask questions. But I try to inspire them with history, from Cortez in the 1400s and now to Haverstraw here and now."

Randi Weiner, *Rockland Journal-News*, 6/17/97

...In 1934 commercial flights from New York to California took 18 hours, which was only half the time it had taken just a few years earlier...Bank robbers Bonnie and Clyde are killed...

The Dutch Garden

On the south side of Rockland County Courthouse there was a pleasant, almost hidden spot, the Dutch Garden (below, JSC). At one time, it was considered one of the finest in the country. The Dutch Garden was the creation of Mary Mowbray-Clarke, a landscape architect, who saw the empty lot and envisioned a formal garden in the Dutch style. The garden was to be a WPA project in the Depression year of 1934.

What she needed was a master craftsmen to do the brick work to execute the bold concepts she had in mind. She found that man in Biagio Gugliuzzo of Garnerville. He was one of the many unemployed masons at that time, but he came with the skill that the others did not possess. In addition to the Tea House pavilion, he built brick walls with the bricks at an angle of 45 degrees with open spaces to give a lattice effect. Many other masons said that the walls would not have sufficient strength and scoffed at Gugliuzzo's plan. But he staked his reputation on the design and Mrs. Mowbray-Clarke supported him. The brick walls were constructed and they stood firm. Later, the New York Brick Manufacturers Association was to write that, "Some of the brick work appears to be that of an artist rather than a mason."

Ironically, as years passed, it was these beautiful latticed walls, marvels of bricklaying, that were to became the favorite target of vandals. Unfortunately, most of the walls were destroyed, although one section was restored in the 1990s. The Tea House was restored in 1998. As for the garden itself, as the turn of the century approached, the New City Garden Club made valiant efforts to care for what little was left.

In its day, the Dutch Garden caught everyone's fancy. In addition to quiet enjoyment it was used for many events. The Garden even won the 1934 Garden of the Year Award sponsored by *Better Homes and Gardens Magazine*.

Robert Burghardt

Editor's Note: The garden was in the process of being restored in 2001.

Jewish Luck of the Irish

The Korn family has had its share of luck, just like most families. But, as Samuel Korn puts it, "It's what you do with the luck that counts."

It was Korn's grandfather, Louis Korn, a long-time Haverstraw resident, who had the incredible luck. In 1938, he bought a ticket for the Irish Sweepstakes, won part of the jackpot, and used some of his winnings to bring family members and a friend who survived the Nazi death camps to Rockland County. Samuel Korn has spent years researching his grandfather's luck and the impact it had on the family.

"He was a kibbitzer," Samuel Korn said of his grandfather. "I would go with my father on Friday nights and just sit out in front of his butcher shop and listen. All I heard about was the horse, and I got tired of hearing about the horse. I wanted to find out about that horse."

Louis Korn was born in Poland in 1892. His father, Max, immigrated to Haverstraw in 1904 and when Louis was about 17, he followed.

Haverstraw around the turn of the century contained the largest Jewish community in Rockland. Max opened a kosher butcher shop in 1910 and expected his children—sons Morris, Louis, Aaron, Jacob (Jack), Paul and a daughter, Fannie—to continue the legacy.

Morris eventually took over the kosher butcher shop. Aaron and Louis opened a non-kosher meat market on Main Street for several years, until Louis opened the Premier Market at 10 Broadway on his own.

The Depression hit the family hard. Louis was barely making a living when a customer, Mrs. James A. Brophy, walked into his shop and offered to sell him a ticket for the Irish Sweepstakes. He bought one because he didn't want to lose the customer.

The ticket entitled Louis Korn to become one of millions of ticket-holders eligible for a bet on the Grand National horse race in England slated for March 26, 1938. His ticket was put into a huge drum along with hundreds of thousands of other tickets. A ticket was drawn from the drum and a horse assigned to the person whose name was listed.

Louis Korn's luck was working full time. His ticket was one of 36 chosen for the 36-horse race and assigned to a 40-1 underdog of an American horse named Battleship. Lloyds of London offered to pay Louis Korn $10,000 for his ticket. Korn refused. He did, however, sell a half-interest in the ticket to Lloyds for $3,000.

When Battleship won the race, Louis Korn and Lloyds collected $150,000.

What Lloyds of London did with its $75,000 share is anyone's guess. Louis Korn's success on the race was toasted in a huge town-wide party.

"The police put up barricades and the beer was free," said J. Victor Timoner of Bardonia, whose wife, Harriet, was Louis Korn's niece and remembers the party she attended as a child of about nine.

Everyone knew the Korns of Haverstraw and everyone celebrated along with them, Timoner said They were active in the synagogue and were volunteer firefighters. Everyone knew Paul Korn, who was a police officer in the village. The bill came to $600. Louis Korn paid for it without comment.

Louis Korn did nothing spectacular with his winnings. He returned to work as a butcher at Premier Meats, and he ran a butcher shop in the area until 1970, when he retired. But he always had available cash for family members in need.

In 1945, none needed his protection more than cousins Stanley Appel and Murray Goldfinger and their friend, Henry Koblick. The three lived in Polish towns just south of Kracow and when the Germans invaded in 1939, they were sent to different internment camps, eventually ending up in Auschwitz and then Glewitz. Their executions were halted by Patton's forces in 1945, and the three were sent to Switzerland where they were asked if they had any relatives.

"One of them remembered when he was a kid his mother used to get packages from Max Korn," Timoner said. "He sent a letter to Louis Korn, Broadway, Haverstraw, N.Y. They delivered it. When Louis Korn found out the three boys survived the war, he made arrangements to have them come over."

The stories of the Korn family still fascinate Samuel Korn, who continues to research the past.

"You have to know where you were in the past to get an understanding of where you are in the present and where you will go in the future," he said. "You find things that show you there's a reason. You understand that luck is there. But what you do with the luck is what's important."

Randi Weiner, *Rockland Journal-News*, 3/11/97

Growing Up in Rockland Lake

The town of Rockland Lake where I was born is no more. The house where I was born was torn down in the 1960s to become part of Rockland Lake State Park.

In the late 1920s and 1930s, Main Street was the original Route 9W and on many a Sunday the heavy traffic was at a standstill due to cars overheating. (9W was the main artery to Albany and upstate New York at that time.)

The town in those days was a summer resort for people from New York City who rented the many bungalows for weekends and summer vacations. On the north end of the lake was Eppie's Grove, owned by the Epstein family, and it consisted of a hotel, bungalows and a swimming area. On the south end of the lake was Quaspeck Casino consisting of a pavilion, a swimming area and picnic area.

Through the town and down the hill to the Hudson River was Hook Mountain State Park. On summer weekends as many as 20,000 people would visit this park each day. Most people came up on the Hudson River dayliners. Sometimes as many as eight or nine dayliners would come up from the city in a single day.

In the park was a roller skating rink, a dance hall, bumping cars, swings, merry-go-round, tennis courts, baseball diamonds and picnic grounds. The police force consisted of 26 men to help control the crowds. Wednesdays was a special day for black people only.

We raised all of our own vegetables in our garden and my mother canned tomatoes and beans and preserved dill pickles. We raised our own chickens for eggs and Sunday dinners. We also raised rabbits for food.

On the property were five Oxhart cherry trees, peach trees and grape arbors. There were wild strawberries as well as cultured ones. We also had white strawberries—when they ripened they would turn pink and cream-colored and were very sweet. In back of our house on the mountain we would pick huckleberries which my mother canned and made into pies along with the cherries.

I attended Rockland Lake School, a three-room schoolhouse for eight grades. We had three teachers, one being the principal. There were about 20 to 25 students total per year. We walked to school year round. In the winter, we walked in car tracks through the snow as the traffic was very light, about two cars per hour. There was no such thing as school closing because of snow.

Rockland Lake school (date unknown). JSC

Living near the lake I learned to fish at an early age. One of first times I ever fished was with my uncle. I was using a small bamboo pole and hooked a rather large pickerel. Somehow I wrapped the line around my uncle's neck, who happened to be between me and my hooked fish, but we did manage to land the fish.

Our house had no plumbing, so we had our own well and had to use an outhouse. The kitchen had a wood stove in which we could also burn coal. The kitchen was the only heated room in the house. We slept under featherbeds (comforters filled with down feathers). We bathed in a metal tub in the kitchen. The water was heated on the wood stove.

I saw many a mink and muskrat when I fished on the lake. One fall I witnessed the Atlantic flight of ducks and geese on Rockland Lake. The flight covered the lake completely and I would estimate there were probably over a million birds as the lake was black with them. The lake is approximately one mile long and a mile wide and it was nearly solid with the ducks and geese. They stayed about a week and then flew south.

Our house was built into the side of a mountain. My grandparents lived on the first level, our family lived on the second level and the third level was used for visitors. We had a root cellar where we kept our preserved vegetables and root crops as well as wine which we made

from the grapes and dandelions on the property. We also stored our pickles there.

In front of the house we had a hand-dug well from which we got our water for the house. We would find an occasional snake, frog or salamander in the pail from the well.

My grandparents came from Czechoslovakia in 1875 at the age of 15. They eventually settled in Rockland and my grandfather got a job working in the rock quarries along the Hudson. Over the years working in the quarry he lost an eye to a chip of stone, a finger which was crushed and suffered a broken hip.

My dad was born in Rockland Lake. He worked for the New York Central Railroad as an engineer on the tugboats. He served as a volunteer fireman with the Knickerbocker Fire Engine Company. When a fire siren went off he would back his car up to a turn on the road in front of our house and wait for the truck to go by. Almost every time they would lose a roll of hose off the truck. He would pick it up and follow the truck to the fire.

My mother was born in Switzerland where she worked in a chocolate factory. She wanted to make a change in her life, which she did by accepting an offer of passage to the United States if she worked off her fare as a domestic. Her family was against this and never forgave her for it.

Her mother (my grandmother) died during World War II. A letter from the Red Cross was sent to her but it took three months before she received it. The German government censored the letter and the envelope was covered with swastikas.

Our family doctor was a woman, Dr. Davies, a general practitioner. She used old-fashioned remedies from plants and herbs that she gathered in the woods. Dr. Davies was the attending physician when we were born at home in Rockland Lake.

We shopped at Banases Butcher Shop in town for meat and butter sold by the chunk from wooden tubs. We shopped at Lappets General Store where flour and sugar was sold by the pound from large sacks and we bought canned goods such as sardines and salmon and canned meats.

We also shopped in Bamburger's grocery in Nyack. We bought our newspapers at Addie's store which was across the street from the school. The store sold candy, ice cream, magazines and school supplies such as pencils, erasers and paper.

It is hard to believe the price of houses and taxes today as compared to the $650 my grandparents paid for a three-story house on one acre of ground. Taxes for the property were about $1.00 a year and the tax collector received three cents for each taxed property. When the school was built a special tax of $1.25 was levied, which was enough to build the brick school.

Transportation was mostly walking. Two buses ran from Nyack to Haverstraw, passing through Rockland Lake, and the fare was usually 5 cents. On Saturdays we would go to the movies in Nyack or Haverstraw. The movies cost 11 cents at that time during the 1930s and 1940s. We would get a comic book and see two main features, cartoon and the Movietone news.

Postcard of the town of Rockland Lake, c. 1919. JSC

Going to Nyack we always passed Helen Hayes' house. She would watch for us and give us candy. We usually went down by the Hudson River and walked the road to Nyack or Haverstraw. Since my father worked for the railroad, we had a pass for the family so we went to New York City by train where we attended Radio City Music Hall, or to the Laugh Movie showing nothing but cartoons, the Three Stooges, Leon Errol,

Laurel and Hardy and Our Gang movies, which ran continuously all day.

We never realized there was a Depression due to the fact we had our own vegetable garden, caught fish out of the lake, had our own chickens, and raised rabbits and that my Dad worked.

During the 1930s, hobos used to come around asking for a meal. Some of them would work doing odd chores such as cutting wood or cutting grass. They rode the freight trains from New York and other parts of the U.S. Most were looking for work as work was very scarce. The hobos or tramps had little camps (old shacks) along the railroads where they would hop on freights and travel the country.

Men with horses and wagons equipped with cowbells came around asking for old rags, newspapers, iron and junk. The junk dealers came around once a month and would pay a few cents for your items.

About eight years after the big ice house fire, I was walking in one of the foundations when the ground gave way under my one foot and I burned my heel in the sawdust that was still smoldering underground. That sawdust burned underground for many years.

After our house became part of the property for the Rockland Lake State Park, it was torn down. We moved to Congers in the late 1930s. I lived there until 1957 when I got married. I now live in Garnerville.

Edward Jansky

Call Hollow

Call Hollow Road branches northward from Route 202. The name comes from a region inhabited by members of the Call family. Originally mountain people or residents of small towns, the Calls were displaced from their homes in forested or cropland tracts early in the twentieth century, about the time the Palisades Park system was organized.

Jim Shields

Camp Hill Memories

Burgess Meredith, the actor, lived across the road from our place. He was married to Paulette Goddard when he bought his large estate on Camp Hill Road. He attended the Ladentown Methodist Episcopal Church. In 1938 he hosted an Easter egg hunt. All the children in our area were invited to the party. He had the perfect place for hiding the eggs in stone walls, etc. I had the honor of attending and collecting the most eggs for both contests. My prizes were enormous stuffed rabbits from Schraft's in NYC, decorated with chocolate galore. In

the winter he had a sleigh drawn by a horse and we would see him on the roads.

From 1931-37, I attended a two-room schoolhouse right next door to our place, three grades in each room. Isabelle Concklin, daughter of Irving Concklin, a farmer, taught the first three grades. Helen Lindner, who boarded with Pincus Margulies in Ladentown, was the teacher of the next three grades. We received a one-on-one education and were more advanced in our studies than the students in South Main St. School.

The 4-H Club was very popular in the country. I joined when I was old enough and Caroline Anthony was the leader. She taught us to sew, cook, and how to help our family. I attended the Club Congress in 1941 at Cornell University. I was awarded a cookbook from the *New York Herald Tribune* called *America's Cook Book* for the greatest contribution to my home thru 4-H for 1941-42. I had to prepare a report to qualify. That summer I had canned 600 quarts of vegetables and fruit from our garden.

My mother worked full time and I had the dinner prepared every evening for my family. I had two older sisters and a younger sister. I also did the laundry and housework to help my mother.

Church was very important in those early days of my life. We were Methodists and attended church every Sunday regardless of the weather. We had to walk over a mile to get there. Church suppers were *the* thing, delicious food served by the ladies of the church.

Mabel Monks

Burgess Meredith

Although later generations may only know him as the Penguin from the Batman television series, or Rocky's crusty trainer, former Rockland resident Burgess Meredith's career began on the stage in the 1930s. His work in radio, on Broadway and in Hollywood earned him such praise as being regarded the best American actor.

Meredith, who was married four times, was known for his lavish parties at his High Tor estate, which were attended by both unusual show business people from Manhattan and more conservative locals. Although he moved to California in the 1980s, he always loved Rockland and was proud to have a park in Pomona dedicated to him.

He died in 1997 at the age of 89.

Linda Zimmermann

40 Foot Swimming Hole

An old stone bridge, a shady pool, shouts and laughing, splashing children, hot summer days of our youth…but not unless you were one of the lucky ones who lived in Blauvelt in the 20s or 30s when it was a rural community.

Years ago in flood seasons, the normally lazy creek became a powerful torrent at that deep hole just as it escaped the frustration of the bridge in its path. Thus was born a Forty Foot Hole that became a favorite haunt for the local youth all summer. Perhaps its depth was measured once or only guessed, but for us it had no bottom. I envied the daring boys who nailed boards to a convenient tree making a ladder reaching very high above the water. They dared each other to dive, but most of the time it was exciting enough to hold your nose and jump. That was scary enough.

I finally decided to follow their example but in a greatly modified way. I wavered on the bridge wall at its highest point, gathering courage, staring into the black water below until with the tight grip on my nose, I launched into space. I hit the water with a shock and plunged down, down, down...I never reached the bottom and remember struggling wildly toward the greenish ceiling where the sun shone through far, far above me.

Forty feet or not, I can testify that it is deep!

Eventually, the surrounding land was bought by the Hackensack Water Company and *No Trespassing* signs went up. The beautiful old bridge was replaced by a new, and no doubt safer, one. Today's teenagers have pools in backyards and cars instead of bikes to take them to more glamorous places, but there are those of us who drive along Fifth Avenue and remember the Forty Foot fondly.

Alice Huested Church
Born Sept. 11, 1913, descended from Dutch settlers.

40 Foot Hole in the 1930s. Note the boy jumping from the "diving tree" on the left. JSC

The Unpopular FDR

Rockland County gave Franklin D. Roosevelt a majority in the presidential elections only once, in 1936, when he won by 253 votes over Alfred M. Landon. In 1932, President Hoover won Rockland by 539 votes, while in 1940 FDR lost by 5,143 votes, an anti-third term protest. In 1944, Gov. Thomas E. Dewey trounced him by 6,509 votes.

Franklin D. Roosevelt (far left) at the Bear Mountain dock in 1921. Roosevelt may have contracted polio from the Boy Scouts he met on this trip, which was his last public appearance before falling ill. This is the last known photo of FDR walking.

Photo courtesy of Scott Webber.

Rockland's Only U.S. Senator

Royal S. Copeland, M.D., holds the distinction of being the only United States Senator ever to have lived in Rockland County. Born in Michigan in 1868, he became an opthalmologist and popular author of health books, and didn't enter politics until the age of 33. He moved to the present day village of Montebello in 1916, and made a successful run for the senate in 1922. He easily won reelection in 1928 and 1934. In 1938, he collapsed and died of a serious illness which he had kept secret. Below is the newspaper article about his funeral, a campaign button and senate pass with his signature.   Courtesy of Craig Long.

A general view of the open-air funeral services held on lawn of the 165-acre Copeland estate in the foothills of the Ramapo Mountains, near Suffern, N. Y. Seated at the left are the son, Royal, Jr., and widow of the late Senator Copeland. Many of the nation's notables, as well as the Senator's farmer neighbors, paid their respects at the rites. Burial followed in Mahwah Dutch Reformed Cemetery in New Jersey.
(Story and Other Photo on Page 4)

The Nazi Party in Rockland

Pro-Hitler groups held numerous gatherings in Rockland County in the 1930s. In 1933, a large group rented the Arthur Johnson farm in the Viola section of Suffern. Local residents complained about the prominent displays of swastikas and the noise from the men marching "up and down the roads singing German songs."

The following headline and article appeared in *Ramapo Valley Leader* on July 28, 1939.

Newspaper articles courtesy of Craig Long.

NAZI BUND SEEKS MEMBERS IN SUFFERN, IMMEDIATE VICINITY

Handbills Begin to Pour Into Community; Contain Wordy Attack on Jews

LOCAL REACTION

One Recipient Denounces Author of Handbill as "Juggler of Facts"

Handbills, presumably being distributed by individuals associated with Nazi organizations, are reportedly making their appearance on porches and doorsteps of homes throughout this locality. The handbills stress the need for unity in fighting Un-Americanism and upholding constitutional government and maintaining patriots in public office.

Titled "Which Way America?", the papers present a "comparison" of Aryan American Nationalism and Jewish-Marxist Internationalism. The former, according to the handbill, is an organization "fighting for a free U.S.A."; the latter, "leading to a U.S.S.R. of America."

The way of the Jewish-Marxist, the paper states, is the way of the "God-hating, international parasite."

The summary of the two "ways" for America is followed by a large-type two-line streamer urging recipients of the handbills to "Join the German American Bund or another courageous American fighting organization."

Reaction in the Suffern community was reflected this week in a statement by a local recipient of the handbills, who declared that, "We have no room in this community for such pernicious propaganda as is pictured in this handbill. It is falsely represented as being patriotic and humane and was quite evidently prepared by an astute juggler of facts."

1940-1949

america
comes
to rockland

World War I was supposed to be "The War to End All Wars," and President Woodrow Wilson had stated that we fought to make "the world safe for democracy." Only twenty years later, European nations began falling like dominoes beneath Adolf Hitler's blitzkrieg, and the Japanese were already creating their brutal Asian empire. While the world teetered on the edge of a dark precipice, America was determined to keep its soldiers out of these foreign wars.

Everything changed in the early morning hours of Sunday, December 7, 1941. The Japanese attack on Pearl Harbor did indeed awaken a sleeping giant, and Americans finally opened their eyes to the realities of World War II. The country focused all its resources, energy and manpower to the war effort. Over 16 million American soldiers were called to duty. Many never returned—over 290,000 Americans were killed in Europe and the Pacific. Estimates place the total human death toll at 61 million.

For those on the home front, rationing became a way of life. Women once again rolled up their sleeves and went to work in factories. And every day, every family with someone in the service dreaded the news of the casualty statistics, and prayed that they wouldn't receive a telegram with the bad news.

When the war finally ended and the men came home, everyone was anxious to take advantage of the new prosperity, and the new American dream—a house in the suburbs, a car in the garage, and a yard for the kids. For many people, including some of the soldiers who passed through Camp Shanks during the war, Rockland looked like the ideal spot. A stream of young couples and families began moving to the county, and the only thing preventing that stream from becoming a flood was a bridge across the river and a few major highways…

Camp Shanks soldiers on the Piermont pier (left, OTM) and a plaque on the pier dedicated to those men in 1985 (below left, JSC).

A local air raid shelter sign (above, LZ), and a young family enjoying the post-war years in Shanks Village (below, OTM).

Cost of Living: 1941

 Average Income
$1,777 per year

 New House
$4,075

Gallon of Gas
12¢

New Car
$850

 **Loaf of Bread** 8¢

Gallon of Milk 54¢

Gold per ounce $35
Silver per ounce 71¢
Dow Jones Average: 121

...In 1940 Churchill becomes Prime Minister of Britain...The Allies are evacuated from Dunkirk...The Nazis take Belgium and Holland in May, and enter Paris in June...The Soviet Union occupies Lithuania, Latvia and Estonia, and Finland surrenders...FDR accuses Italy of "a stab in the back" after Mussolini announces his decision to join forces with the Nazis...Londoners sleep in the subways every night as the "Battle of Britain" rages in the skies above...Japan joins Germany and Italy to create the Axis pact and claims the right to create "a new order in Eastern Asia"...FDR is reelected for a third term and states that America is "the arsenal of democracy," and will continue to supply planes, ships and weapons, but America will stay out of the war...

Farley and Pearl Harbor

In the 1970s, there were three topics former Postmaster General Jim Farley refused to discuss during our more than five hours of conversation on his life going back to his election as Stony Point town clerk in 1905.

One was the Cleary murder case in Haverstraw in 1914. The second was the Kennedys, whom he felt used the Democratic Party to get Jack elected in 1960. To Farley, the party was always more important than any individual.

The third was Pearl Harbor. When this came up, his face darkened and there was anger in his voice. "That was a disgrace. It never should have happened." That was all he wished to say.

Years later in the 1990s, journalists began reporting that a number of both American and British intelligence people all spoke of having intercepted Japanese coded messages back in November 1941 which related that the Japanese fleet was sailing for Hawaii, with an air attack scheduled for Sunday, December 7, 1941.

The intercepts were all sent on to both Washington and London. They said that the matter was brought up in cabinet meetings. One of those in on the secret was Secretary of State Cordell Hull of Tennessee, a close friend of Farley. It was said that Hull was fuming and frustrated that the Roosevelt administration was going to allow this to happen, thereby sacrificing the lives of thousands of American sailors. However, it was necessary to get Congress to agree to go into war against Japan and Germany, otherwise the Allies would lose.

If Hull had to share this with someone, his friend Farley would have been the logical choice. Had I known in the early 1970s what I knew 20 years later, I might have pressed the subject further.

Winston Churchill said he went to bed the night of December 7 relieved; America was now in the war with them against the Axis powers. We would win. December 7 was the date that changed all our lives forever. The day before Congress wouldn't have had a majority to declare war—after Pearl Harbor they rammed the declaration through by voice vote, with only one dissenting, in just two hours. America now mobilized for total war.

The battleships sunk and damaged at Pear Harbor were obsolete World War I ships. New Iowa class ships were under construction in American shipyards at that time, the *Iowa*, *Wisconsin*, *New Jersey* and *Missouri*, among them. However, it wasn't the ships, but the loss of more than 2,300 young boys' lives that is shocking.

Scott Webber

William Hand and the Pearl Harbor Controversy

William Hand of Franklin Street, South Nyack, was the millionaire inventor of the storage battery, who at one time had been an assistant to Thomas Edison. Before and during WWII, Hand was also an aide to Secretary of the Navy Knox. I interviewed him many years later, when he was almost 80, and he had some remarkable things to say regarding Pearl Harbor.

Hand stated that in 1941, numerous cablegrams from Stalin informed President Roosevelt that Japan was going to bomb Pearl Harbor. In fact, Roosevelt knew of the Japanese plans at least six months in advance. Hand even provided the Navy numbers of these "hush, hush" cables and said where they could be found.

The night of December 6, 1941, Hand said he delivered another cablegram from Stalin, informing Roosevelt that Japan would hit Pearl Harbor early the following morning. FDR said, with Harry Hopkins also present, "Thank you very much for delivering this cablegram. You must be tired. Why don't you go to bed early tonight?"

Hand said that the only thing that had been done was to move the *Enterprise* out to sea, knowing that it would have to be used later on. He also stated, "General Marshall got a cablegram also, and he also did nothing!"

Ken Harniman

Regardless of whether our government knew about Pearl Harbor, the fact remained that America was at war. As men and women left Rockland to join the armed forces and aid in the war effort, the U.S. Army had its eye on this strategically located county.

Camp Shanks and Shanks Village

In the autumn of 1942, Western Highway in Orangeburg looked as it had for many years past. With aging farmhouses few and far between, the old road made its way through corn and tomato fields. At night, people whose families had lived there for generations were lulled to sleep by the incessant chirping of crickets. Only the radio and newspapers gave evidence of world-wide war.

Then one day in September, a U.S. Army trailer pulled up near the Orangeburg Post Office. Major Drew Eberson of the Army Corps of Engineers had arrived, and surveys began. Eberson liked what he saw: mostly all farmland, Route 303 connecting easily with Route 9W, quick access to the Hudson River by the Piermont Pier, and most importantly, two railroads serving the area. It was only 15 miles to the shipping docks at Hoboken. This was perfect.

On September 25, Eberson summoned over 100 property owners from Blauvelt Road to Washington Street, to 2.5 miles south in Tappan, to tell them they had two weeks to get out. The Army was seizing their land under the War Powers Act. They would be paid for their property with first option to buy it back after the war. The 2,040 acres would be made into a U.S. Army New York Port of Embarkation center through which ready-trained troops would be processed to North Africa and later England. The camp would be named after Major General David Shanks, commander of the New York Port of Embarkation during World War I.

By mid-October, the land was a major construction site. Some 17,000 workers hired by the Army from the nearby metropolitan area were converting the old farmlands into a city for 50,000 people. Work went on nonstop as bulldozers cleared the land, sewers were installed and roads were built through the muddy fields. Over 1,500 barracks were constructed as well as mess halls, theaters, service clubs, central latrines, gymnasiums and office buildings. Some of the old, smaller houses were left standing to serve as officer quarters.

Camp Shanks officially opened on January 4, 1943. Troops from across the nation began arriving by train around the clock to be processed onto ships that would carry them across the Atlantic to fighting fronts. A permanent staff of 5,000 officers, men and women (400 members of the Women's Army Corps, or WACS) was needed to operate the post 24 hours a day, supported by 1,500 civilians who worked a 48-hour, 6-day week for an average monthly wage of $250.

Camp Shanks, along with Camp Kilmer in New Jersey (which opened in 1942), was the largest Army port of embarkation on the East Coast and became known as the *Last Stop USA*. Together, they sent over three million troops overseas. Shanks alone handled more than 1.3 million from 1943 into the spring of 1945. The camp's busiest month came in October of 1944, when 27,626 troops (roughly two divisions) were processed in one 19-hour period.

Combat ready soldiers were brought to the camp on long trains pulled by steam locomotives on the Erie and New York Central Railroads. They were assigned to barracks, and their equipment checked and their medical and personnel records examined and put in order. Once through the paperwork, they were on

Judy Garland treated them to "Over the Rainbow"; other stars who came to Shanks were Pearl Bailey, Jack Benny, Jimmy Durante, Betty Grable, Myrna Loy, Mickey Rooney, Frank Sinatra, and Shirley Temple. Ethel Merman remembered performing for the troops as they sat with their weapons and duffle bags, ready to board the trains.

USO dances were held in the auditorium of the Rockland Psychiatric Center (then Rockland State Hospital). Girls from Rockland, Bergen and Westchester Counties and thousands of GIs danced to the live music of Harry James, Benny Goodman and Lionel Hampton.

Beginning in January 1945, when the Tower Buildings at Rockland State were converted into

The Camp Shanks version of "Hurry up and wait," an all-too-common scene in the military (above), as long lines of soldiers await processing.

Last Stop USA: Shanks soldiers climb the gangway to board a ship to cross the Atlantic to one of the war fronts (right).

standby until space became available on ships anywhere in the New York area.

When they got the word, they were taken by train or ferry to ports at Hoboken or on Manhattan's west side; later in the war, they would board ships directly at Piermont Pier. Some were fortunate enough to travel on either the *Queen Mary* or the *Queen Elizabeth*. Too fast for German U-boats, these ocean liners crossed the ocean without escort.

Years later, one former WAC remembered shivering in her overcoat and pajamas as she stood by her barracks in the cold night and watched a company of troops marching to the loading area on the east side of Western Highway. They were singing "I'll be Home for Christmas" as they headed for the train and the European battlefront. Many would never come home again.

During their stay at Shanks—an average of three to four days—there was no training; there was no reveille or taps. While they waited, they were entertained by some of America's top talent from Broadway and Hollywood in the camp amphitheater, which was situated at the southeast corner of Orangeburg and Dutch Hill Roads, now the location of a shopping center.

medical wards, the camp served as a receiving center for the wounded from the Battle of the Bulge. The New York Telephone Company assigned 50 specially trained operators to help the men make their first phone call to the folks at home.

After V-E Day in May 1945, Shanks was inundated by joyful returning troops who were eager to get home before they faced the possibility of being sent to the Pacific theater. Fortunately for them, the atomic bomb canceled the invasion of Japan that was scheduled for November.

At the same time, some 290,000 German and Italian prisoners—many of them members of Rommel's Afrika Korps—arrived at Shanks from across the nation for processing back to Europe on the same ships that were bringing our troops home. This phase of camp activity continued until the summer of 1946, when the last German soldiers were put aboard a ship off Piermont.

What would happen to the camp? Some people in Washington proposed that the Shanks land be made

As America's soldiers came to Camp Shanks, so did stars of Broadway and Hollywood. Among the stars who volunteered their talents to the war effort were Helen Hayes (above left, in front passenger seat of jeep) and Judy Garland (above right).

into a national cemetery, like the one in Arlington. But Columbia University officials had other ideas.

They went to the nation's capital and convinced the government to convert the camp into a huge veterans' low-cost housing complex where former GIs could afford to live and attend classes at Columbia under the newly established GI Bill of Rights.

In September 1946, the first renovated barracks were opened, each made into three small apartments that could be rented from the Public Housing Authority for $32 a month. They were painted various colors, furnished, and outfitted with an oil heater. Linen went for an extra $1 a month. The place became known as Shanks Village.

In the months that followed, nearly all of 1,500 barracks became available and soon about 4,000 former GIs, their young wives and babies were living there. Most of them were undergraduate or graduate students at Columbia (others were military officials and Rockland County veterans) earning the Village the nicknames the *Ph.D. Pad* and the *Baby Factory.*

For the residents, Shanks Village was a twentieth century pioneer experience. With little or no money and few possessions, they had none of the modern day appliances to simplify life. In the non-insulated barracks-apartments, the oil heaters warmed only the space above them; there was no air conditioning during the hot summers; refrigerators were merely iceboxes using blocks of ice; the electrical system was easily overloaded. Families learned to grow their own tomatoes and other vegetables to help stretch the budget.

Most of the Villagers were young couples in their 20s or early 30s struggling to make a life for themselves, and

this Spartan existence strained relationships. Many marriages ended in divorce.

It seemed so much was against them; at times even nature. The famous Blizzard of 1947 dumped more than 28 inches of snow on the area the day after Christmas. Huge drifts built up around the drafty homes and clogged roads, causing nearby stores to run out of food and supplies. Families huddled around their stoves to wait out the storm.

But despite the many hardships, the Village endured and grew into a spirited community. Residents set up an elected-council form of government, published their own weekly offset newspaper, organized a theater group, athletic teams, food co-op store and whatever else they

The Spartan conditions of Shanks Village life are evident in this LIFE magazine photo of the inside of a converted barracks apartment.   OTM

Numerous "products" of the "Baby Factory" at play (left) and enjoying cupcakes with Eisenhower (above). LIFE photos, OTM.

needed to survive. They learned to tackle and overcome adversity by relying on themselves and pulling together.

In one instance, the town of Orangetown—fearing young Villagers had radicals political ideas and might upset the balance of power in local elections—tried to bar them from voting on the grounds that they were transient students and should vote where they formerly resided. Student lawyers, who honed their talent before the Village council, fought the town all the way to the New York State Court of Appeals and won the right of Village residents to vote.

When the local bus company raised the fare to Manhattan to $1 each way, Villagers organized carpools between Orangeburg and Columbia University, charging 50 cents for a round-trip. Students were often seen collecting soda bottles to earn transportation money.

Musical and choreographic talents were combined to produce a full-length, Broadway-type show that spoofed life in Shanks Village. It played to packed houses in the fall of 1949. Unfortunately, a complete score of the production did not survive, and only fragments of the lyrics to the songs are recalled today.

Villagers went into many fields. They became politicians, judges, lawyers, doctors, college presidents, university deans, professors, writers and artists.

Numerous famous people visited Shanks Village, including Margaret Mead and General Dwight D. Eisenhower (then president of Columbia University), who came one fall afternoon in October 1948. After touring the apartments, the nursery and the general store, he stood on the steps of the Community Center and addressed some 1,000 residents. He declared that, "Shanks Village is the best damned place to live in this world."

Indeed, many of the Villagers liked the area so well they decided to stay for the rest of their lives. One group got together and collectively bought 30 acres in Tappan, subdivided it, and hired a contractor to lay the foundations for each house to become what is still known as Hickory Hill.

As the Village moved into the 1950s, those original residents who left to make their way in the outside world were replaced by non-students, including welfare residents. Eventually, the property was sold to housing developers in 1956.

To be sure, Shanks Village left an indelible mark on the area. And no matter where they are today, many former residents would undoubtedly agree with General Eisenhower's prediction that someday they would look back on the time they spent there "as the best of their lives."

Scott Webber

The Camp Shanks P.O.W.

During World War II, my dad was too old to take part (he was 51 in 1941). He worked at Camp Shanks, however, building wooden cases and packing boxes for war materials being shipped to Europe. One fall day, probably in 1944, I went to work with him at the camp. It was one day I would never forget.

As anyone watching old movies on TV knows today, almost all my trips to the Skouras Theater in Nyack involved some actor, like John Wayne, convincing me how horrid the war was. Even a six-year-old could understand that the faceless enemies across the battle lines were hateful people.

I rode with Dad to work at the camp just once. Just how I was introduced to a camp guarded with military security shall remain a forgotten mystery. But the chill gray morning found Dad parking our 1940 Studebaker Commander outside one of the long, long warehouse buildings that occupied the camp. When I went inside, Dad at first entertained me with his new alphabet-reciter, a machine used to cut stencils for the labeling of packing crates.

For my young mind, such a machine was grand fun. I could spin a wheel to bring a letter or a digit to a particular spot, and then I could smack a lever to put that character in the cardboard of the stencil. That game kept me occupied for a time. Then, there were moments when one of Dad's coworkers had to really punch a stencil. And perhaps I got in the way.

"Come here, Jack!" Dad probably told me. "I want you to meet this fellow Gino, he's an Italian prisoner of war."

Sure enough, I later discovered, the heavily accented foreigner had the letters "P. O. W." stenciled across the back of his military jacket. And this John-Wayne-influenced six-year-old looked up at the grinning, amused *Italiano* with considerable fear. The man in front of me, after all, was one of those horrid men in horrid helmets that tossed grenades toward the cameras on the studio back lots.

But the man in front of me was pleased to hold out his hand to me.

"Go ahead, Jack, shake," Dad said. Then, "With your right hand." Dad laughed.

And the man who I am calling Gino (because I can't remember his name) took my hand lightly in his own, and shook it happily. With heavily accented now-forgotten jokes he brought a smile to my face.

I don't recall his name, or where he was from. Nor do I know whether the military had flown him to the U. S. from the hell of war in the Libyan Desert or the Italian peninsula. But I did learn that day to conquer one's fears of aliens. In hindsight, I'm also impressed with the good fortune Gino had in going from the heat of some battle to the quiet surroundings of Orangeburg, Rockland County.

Dad trusted Gino enough to send me off with him. It must be said that Gino knew exactly how to entertain this six-year-old. He took me by the hand, led me to a gas-powered railroad cart and the two of us buzzed rapidly about the camp. I remember little more than having a grand time with him until, I suppose, we got back to Dad's building to have LUNCH!   Phil Klein

The Palisades was a newspaper for the soldiers at Camp Shanks. On February 18, 1944, the front page featured this photo of actress Ida Lupino, who would be appearing in the movie *In Our Time* which would be shown in the Post Theater that night. The caption for the photo read, "Miss Lupino is known for her fine dramatic portrayals."

This edition also had an article stating that since the attack on Pearl Harbor, over 2,500,000 service men had gotten married. In some locations, the number of GI marriage applications outnumbered the local citizen population.

The Camp Shanks War Bond drive goal of $300,000 was met, and exceeded, with soldiers and local civilians bringing in a total of $350,000.

The issue also reported sports scores of the camp's teams, featured a couple of cartoons and "GI Gags," and profiled several "Camp Personalities." Perhaps the most important section was the praise given to T/Sgt. Dixson and Lt. Clyde Lee for making it a "pleasure to go to the Mess Hall to eat sunny fried eggs, bacon and toast." After all, despite Miss Lupino's dramatic portrayals, an army does march on its stomach.   Linda Zimmermann

Courtesy of Phil Klein.

152

The Spy Was From Pearl River

While little girls like to pretend to be princesses, few ever dreamed of a life of international intrigue and espionage, especially growing up in the sleepy little town of Pearl River. Even when war began in Europe and then the Pacific, Pearl River seemed about as far away from danger and adventure as you could get.

For Aline Griffith, however, the secure world of her Pearl River home and modeling job in Manhattan seemed hollow. While one of her brothers was a fighter pilot based in England and the other on a submarine in the South Pacific, she spent her days modeling party dresses. That all changed one day with a chance meeting with someone from the War Department.

After expressing her desire to help the war effort, her beauty, natural energy and knowledge of foreign languages plunged her into a whirlwind of events that brought her to Spain as an agent for the OSS (Office of Strategic Services, the precursor to the CIA). Codenamed "Tiger," the 21-year-old Griffith began the dangerous game of spying on the Nazis, a game in which she almost lost her life on several occasions.

After the war, she married a Spanish aristocrat and became Aline, Countess de Romanones, one of the most watched and admired women in international high society. In 1987, she wrote about her WWII adventures in the book *The Spy Wore Red,* and its success led to several other books.

While the term "castles in Spain" often refers to unrealistic goals, in the case of one girl from Pearl River, her Spanish castles became reality, and her life of adventure and intrigue made her one of Rockland's most fascinating women.

Linda Zimmermann

The Greatest Generation: Rockland's WWII Heroes

It is impossible to tell all of the stories of the brave men and women who served their country during WWII. The following is just a small sample of those who have been called America's Greatest Generation.

Purple Heart Is Received for Stony Point Man

Mrs. Irene A. Miller of Reservoir Road, Stony Point, has received the Military Order of the Purple Heart decoration awarded posthumously to her son, CWT Clarence Irving Miller, U.S.N., who was k'lled in action off Formosa on Oct. 16, 1944, when the cruiser on which he was a crew member was bombed. The cruiser is now undergoing repairs at an East Coast Navy Yard.

CWT Miller, who would have been in the Navy ten years on May 20, this year, was made a chief petty officer on Oct. 1, 1944, 15 days before he was killed.

He was at Pearl Harbor on Dec. 7, 1941, when the Japs made their sneak attack on the Navy base there and told his family that his life probably was saved by the fact that he was off duty at the time. He was on the U.S.S. Helena when the cruiser was sunk by the Japanese off Guadalcanal and was one of the few members of the crew who were saved.

Photo and article submitted by Mabel Monks, Clarence Miller's cousin.

Wounded In Action

Sgt. Robert W. Nugent of Suffern, the son of the Republican County Chairman, was seriously wounded in action in Germany. As part of Patton's forces, Nugent's tank suffered a direct hit from a German tank. The shell exploded inside of his tank, killing everyone except Nugent. However, his wounds were so severe that both of his legs had to be amputated.

Photo courtesy of Craig Long

Robert Hoey (1920-1995) was born in Garnerville and served with the 501st Parachute Infantry and 101st Airborne Division. He participated in the parachute drops into Normandy on D-Day and the Battle of the Bulge, and was wounded in Holland during the famous battle for the bridge across the Rhine at Arnhem (the Allies suffered almost twice as many casualties as on D-Day), popularized in the book *A Bridge Too Far.*

William Dolan (1901-1994) of Pearl River joined the Army Air Corps during WWII at the age of 41, embarking for England from Camp Shanks. He flew 35 missions over Germany as a crew chief and top turret gunner on a B-17 bomber. Dolan shot down nine German planes and was awarded the Bronze Air Medal and Distinguished Flying Cross.

Regina Connolly (1913-1997) of Nanuet was one of the first WAVES (Women Appointed for Volunteer Emergency Service) during WWII, and helped develop the LORAN navigation system for the Navy. She was one of the first women to make a solo flight from Christie Airport in 1946.

Donald Ackerson (1921-1996) was with the 8th Bomber Squadron during World War II. He flew 27 combat missions as a bombardier in a B-17 and was shot down over Nazi Germany in 1944. He spent 13 months as a prisoner of war in Stalag Luft No.1. Upon returning home, he was a resident of Shanks Village, became a ceramics artist, was very active in community affairs and served as State Senator from 1970-72.

Russell McCandless (above left) and his brother, Lt. George "Buddy" McCandless, Jr. (in uniform), in Nyack in 1942. Buddy was killed in action on August 1, 1943 when his B-24 Liberator was shot down in Romania on a raid on the Ploesti oil refineries. He was 23 years old.

Lt. McCandless was awarded, posthumously, the Distinguished Flying Cross, the Silver Star, the Air Medal and the Purple Heart. Photo courtesy of Russell McCandless

A young but determined Walter J. Zimmermann (right) of Upper Nyack enlisted with the Marine Corps as soon as he was old enough. In the Pacific, he was to see action at such places as Iwo Jima and Okinawa.

Suffering a serious head wound from the wing of a kamikaze, Zimmermann was scheduled to be shipped back home. However, regaining consciousness after several days, he shoved his helmet on over his bandages and rejoined his unit, remaining until the end of the war.

He was later called back into the Marines for the Korean War.

The Bomb

In 1944 while I was a senior in Congers High School, I decided to enlist in the Navy. I was 17 and my father had to sign the papers when I enlisted. At that time the Navy told me to finish my schooling. In early June 1945 I was called to active duty, missing my graduation ceremony. In late August after boot camp I was shipped to San Francisco, California where I boarded a troop ship with 5,000 troops aboard.

The ship went up through the Aleutian Islands and down to Kwajalein and Eniwetok Islands in the Pacific where 850 Seabees were left to rebuild the damage from a typhoon. The rest of us went on to Hawaii where I was transferred to LST 388—US *Vandenburg.*

We sailed from Hawaii for occupation duty in Japan. The ship stopped off at Iwo Jima and I was shocked how small and barren the island was. There was no vegetation on the island. We continued on, stopping at several ports in Japan: Sasebo, Hirawan, Matasuyama and finally Kure Harbor where we supplied mine sweepers for clearing mines from the harbor. Kure was a major Japanese naval base, and it also was the port entrance to Hiroshima. Many Japanese naval vessels were sunk in the bay.

After the mines were cleared we were given an opportunity to travel where the atomic bomb was dropped. We drove around in a truck for about an hour. About five square miles of flat land of rubble was all that was left of the city. The figures of people were burned into the roadway, the color of their clothing was visible in it. We were told that a stream in the city boiled from the heat, people jumped into the stream to get away from the heat and boiled to death. Because of radiation we were limited where we could go.

I talked to a young girl who was injured on her face from the bomb. She was having plastic surgery to hide the scars. Back in 1946 women were not allowed to marry if their faces was scarred.

The Japanese people did not blame the military for the bombing—they blamed our leaders and their leaders. Between 80,000 and 100,000 people died from the bomb and more have died since then.

After several months at Kure Harbor we were ordered back to Hawaii for Rest & Relaxation. Our ship was ordered to Bikini Island for an atomic bomb test. Shortly after arriving at Bikini Island I contracted a bone infection in a finger and needed an operation.

I was flown back to California and listened to the test on the radio. Later I learned that my ship, the US *Vandenburg*, was sunk in the test. Edward Jansky

Hitler Saved by Lederle Labs

Because of World War II, much of the food was being rationed, and people would often try to steal our chickens. Someone had given us a Great Dane dog and we named him Hitler. One night, someone tried to take some chickens and the dog started to bark and chase the person or persons. One of them had a gun and shot the dog. The next day there were big headlines on the front page of the *Rockland County Leader* that read, "Hitler Was Shot."

My father called the local veterinarian, but at this time only sulfa drugs were available. Lederle Labs was working on a new wonder drug, penicillin. The vet was able to get some penicillin for our dog and he survived.

Franklin Hoffman

USO

Entertaining the troops was important both abroad and at home. The Manse barn in Tappan (left) was one of the Rockland sites of the USO, from 1943-1946.

Many local women volunteered their time as dancing partners, in addition to serving coffee, sandwiches and donuts.

It was inevitable that when so many single young women were thrown together with so many single young men, nature would take its course.

While no statistics exist, many Rockland marriages began with a meeting at a USO.

WORLD WAR II
In Memoriam

ABRAMS, ROBERT L.
ALLEN, EDWARD
ALLISON, WALTER H.
AMORY, EDWARD
ANDREWS, JOHN R.
ARRANCE, EDWIN S.
ATTENA, LOUIS F.
AVERY, WILLIAM H.
BACKELIN, WALTER
BALLAR, CHARLES
BARNES, JOHN W.
BARRETT, CHARLES W.
BATES, ROBERT T.
BAUMEISTER, RAYMOND
BEEDON, JOHN W.
BOLFORD, CHARLES
BOLLINGER, J. NEWTON
BOORMAN, STANLEY H.
BOYAJY, HENRY
BRADNER, VINCENT J.
BREMS, JAMES F.
BRENTNALL, LAWRENCE
BRONICO, ANTHONY J.
BROWN, JAMES
BROWN, SYLVESTER O. (JR)
BUNTING, WILLMAR C.
BURLEIGH, PHILIP T.
BURLEIGH, RICHARD C. (JR)
BYRNE, JOHN B.
CAMERON, ALEXANDER
CARDILLO, JOSEPH P.
CARNOCHAN, GOVERNEUR M.
CARNOCHAN, GOVERNEUR M. (JR)
CHRISTIAN, CLAUDE
CLARK, GEORGE W.
CLARK, JOHN H.
COE, ROBERT W.
COLLINS, JOHN H.
COLLINS, RICHARD R.
CONKLIN, ROBERT C.
CONLON, WILLIAM H.
COVATI, JOSEPH F.
COX, HOWARD L. (JR)
COYNE, WILLIAM M.
CRANDALL, WILLIAM C.
DANIELS, JOSEPH D.
DE BEVOISE, WILLIAM E.
DEC, ALEXANDER
DELLORO, JOSEPH A.
DE LONGIS, VINCENT
DEL REGNO, VICTOR R.
DE PATTO, LOUIS A.
DICK, FREDERICK W.
DINGMAN, BENNY L.
DOANE, PAUL
DORNBURGH, EDMUND
DOWD, ROBERT J.
DRAB, ALEXANDER

DRAKE, JAMES E.
DUCEY, JOHN J.
DUNN, HERBERT B.
EAKINS, ARCHIE
EARL, WILLIAM S.
EASTON, JOHN J.
EDWARDS, DONALD
EDWARDS, WALTER
ELENEL, AMSY
ELLIS, MELVIN T.
ELMENDORF, FRED
FAIRBAIRN, SETON H.
FERRACANE, ANTHONY
FOURNIER, RICHARD E.
FROST, GERARD W.
GALGANO, JOHN J.
GALOWSKI, EDWARD J. (JR)
GASSNER, HUGH J. (JR)
GDULA, ANDREW
GERE, EDWIN E.
GOEHRING, VALENTINE J. (JR)
GOSWICK, JESSE O.
GOTCHER, HAROLD C.
GRANT, WALLACE E.
GREEN, RALPH
GREENE, FRANK A. (JR)
GRIFFIN, DANIEL
GROSULAK, PETER
HADDEN, HAROLD B.
HAGUE, RAYMOND F.X.
HALGREN, ALEX J.
HANDELMAN, IRWIN
HARING, BERNARD F.
HARRIGAN, GERARD J.
HARTY, WILLARD
HECHT, FREDERICK
HECK, CHARLES
HERDMAN, WALTER L.
HIGINSON, VAUGHN L.D.
HIRSCH, DAVID J.
HOFFMAN, JOHN R.
HOGAN, DENNIS (JR)
HOKE, WILLIAM B.
HORN, ROBERT
HUOTT, WILLIAM D.
HURD, DONALD W.
INGRAM, EDWARD L.
JASINSKI, VINCENT
JOHNSON, CLAYTON L.
JOHNSON, KENNETH E.
JOHNSON, KENNETH R.
JONES, JAMES
JONES, LOUIS E.
JORDAN, EDWARD H.
KEARSING, DONALD R.
KEENAN, RICHARD J.
KELEHER, CLARENCE
KELLEY, JOHN J.

KELLEY, LEO E.
KELLY, EDWARD L.
KERCHMAN, THEODORE
KINSMAN, WILLIAM P.
KLEIBER, ALFRED G.
KLEIN, JOHN R.
KNIGHT, HOWARD M.
KWIECINSKI, JOHN W.
LA FRANCE, T.R. (JR)
LAGOIS, FRED G.
LANG, JAMES W.
LANGER, PETER
LA POLLA, MARK O.
LAWLESS, VINCENT G.
LAWRENCE, GEORGE H.
LE CLAIR, ALFRED J.
LEE, FRANCIS X.J.
LEE, IVAN R.
LENTZ, ROBERT J.
LEWIS, CHARLES R.
LINGUANTI, VINCENT S.
LIPMAN, WALTER
LOVETT, WENDELL H.
MACKEY, JOSEPH F. (JR)
MALONE, CHARLES M.
MANGHU, DWIGHT
MARESCA, GEORGE M.
MARSICO, ANTHONY T.
McCANDLESS, GEORGE (JR)
McCULLOUGH, JACK R.
McDERMOTT, W.R. (JR)
McGUIRE, RUSSELL E.
McHUGH, RUSSELL
MEAD, GEORGE J.
MELNICK, JOHN
MERRICK, WILLIAM E.
MEYER, WILLIAM A.
MILKS, DONALD
MILLER, CLARENCE I.
MILLER , ROBERT S.
MISCH, ANTHONY
MITCHELL, HERBERT
MORAN, JAMES T.
MORGAN, NORMAN R.
MORRIS, CHARLES B.
MULLER, CHARLES G.
MULRAIN, HARRY
NAGLE, EUGENE J.
NAPPO, ANTHONY J.
NEWELL, ROGER V.
NEWMAN, CHARLES J.
OLOFSON, GUSTAV
OLSON, ERIC T.
ORTIZ, ROBERT I.
OSBORNE, JAMES
OWEN, ARTHUR J.
PAUL, HENRY C. (JR)
PICARIELLO, R.P. (JR)
PILGRIM, HOWARD D.
PINTO, GEORGE J.
POLHEMUS, WILLIS

PRATO, LEO J.
PYTLIK, KARLO P.
RETZ, GEORGE J.
RITCHINGO, JAMES W.
ROACH, BILLY JOE
ROBBINS, HARRY E. (JR)
ROSE, GEORGE E.
ROSS, CHARLES (SR)
ROSS, DEANE L.
ROTUNDO, LOUIS J.
ROWAN, OGDEN W.
RUSSO, WILLIAM
RYDER, DONALD J.
SAMSON, HARRY
SCHNELL, HAROLD
SCHWARTZ, ISRAEL
SCOLARO, PETER F.
SEYLLER, GUY L.
SHANKEY, JOSEPH I.
SHEA, MORTIMER G.
SHUART, PERCY W.
SILBERSTEIN, HENRY A. (DR)
SIMENOVSKY, SOL
SKERRY, WILLIAM H.
SLATER, CLIFFORD F.
SMITH, ALEXANDER
SMITH, MARVIN
SNEDEN, ARTHUR P.
SPORDONE, G.
STECZ, JOSEPH M.
STEINER, EMANUEL F.
STEINER, JOSEPH
STEVENS, TIMOTHY D.
STOUGHTON, HOMER R.
SUTHERLAND, THOMAS A.
SWINTEK, WALTER J.
TASMAN, DONALD R.
TAYLOR, FRED M. (JR)
THOMPSON, GEORGE C.
TRAVITZ, HARRY
TUCKER, ARTHUR B.
VAN COTT, PETER
VAN HOUTEN, HOMER H.
VELIE, JACK W.
VORONIESK, ALEXIS
VRANISKY, JOSEPH P.
WARNER, CHARLES H.
WEIGAND, ROBERT
WENZEL, CHARLES W.
WHEELER, CRAWFORD (JR)
WIEBICKE, HUGO P.
WILDING, GEORGE H. (II)
WILLIAMS, ROBERT E. (JR)
WILSON, RUSSELL A.
WISNER, EMANUEL
WONZEL, CHARLES W.
WOOD, ANDREW
WYSOCKI, JOSEPH B.
ZELLER, ROBERT F.
ZOMEROWITZ, LOUIS

The Wartime Farmhand in Rockland History

In a burst of patriotic fervor I went from New York City to work on a farm. This experience occurred in 1943, the summer between my junior and senior years of high school. With so many of the able-bodied men away at war the farmers were desperate for help of any kind. Consequently, the government, through the state, was recruiting anyone over the age of 17 to work on upstate farms.

I was sent to an upstate dairy farm for six weeks. After that stint I was sent closer to home, to Rockland County for the tomato harvest. I found my way to the Herriman Farm School on Route 306, north of Monsey, where I was to bunk with boys of my age in a dorm at this school, run by the Brooklyn Children's Aid Society.

Each morning after breakfast, we would walk out to the highway where the farmers would pick us up for the day. Then it was off to pick tomatoes for the day. By the end of two weeks I never wanted to see a tomato again. Unfortunately, I didn't take note as to where this farm was located since I hardly considered that to be important. I wish I had, because many years later when I moved to Rockland County I drove around with my family trying to locate the farm. In the intervening years almost all of the farmland in the county has given way to housing and commercial use, and the Herriman site is now the Blueberry Hill Apartments.

Each evening, after a day of working on various farms, we were brought back to the school, would go for a swim in the pond on the grounds, shower and get ready for supper. More than once we walked into Spring Valley after a full day of picking and working. Especially noteworthy is the realization of how rural the area then was. In Monsey there were the bungalow colonies frequented by the Jewish people from the city. After that there was practically nothing, Route 59 was a dark two-lane road on which we passed an occasional farm house, until we arrived at Spring Valley.

Saturday night in Spring Valley was the busy time with the fathers up from the city and the families out for a night on the town.

At the end of my summer as a farm hand I was ready to go back to school. All my romantic ideas about farming had been changed by good doses of reality. Thinking back to that summer I realize how independent I was and unafraid to go off and try something different.

Robert Burghardt

Truman—1948 Spring Valley

In the summer and fall of 1948, President Harry S. Truman toured the country in the last whistle-stop campaign by train in presidential political history. A national network of rails was still a viable form of travel, connecting small communities here in Rockland and throughout the nation.

There was an announcement that Truman would appear in Spring Valley that fall of '48. My wife Julia and I joined a respectable gathering at the Erie Railroad depot plaza to hear the President. We were not part of a great county event as no one thought Truman, trailing badly in the polls, had a chance against the popular Republican challenger, New York State Governor Thomas E. Dewey. I doubt that there is any record of what was said that day, and a scanning of the microfilms on all available county daily and weekly newspapers of the period produced no record of President Truman's visit. Fortunately, I had taken my new 35mm camera and snapped a picture of President Truman standing with William Averell Harriman, Secretary of Commerce and future governor of the State of New York.

John Scott

County Sheriff Arrested

April 26, 1942: The news "broke like thunderclaps" over Rockland that day, wrote one *Journal-News* reporter later, when Edward C. Dormann, the county sheriff, was arrested in Nyack on gambling charges. The sheriff's arrest dominated the news for three months, including disclosures that Gov. Herbert Lehman had ordered the investigation into Dormann's association with New York City gambling operations. A Republican, Dormann served five years in prison.

But that was just one of a series of political trials which rocked the county before and during WWII. Assemblyman Lawrence J. Murray, Jr., was sentenced to jail after being charged with grand larceny for allegedly rifling the estate of a law client.

And just a month earlier, Rockland Sheriff John E. Cook, and his deputy, Frank Manion, were among 44 persons accused of bilking the government of $1 million in taxes through illegal stills in Rockland and Orange Counties. Cook was cleared but Manion was convicted that year in a case involving $200.

The Journal-News, 7/15/82

Finding Sinners

Reverend Walter Hoffman was a familiar site around the village (Haverstraw). He was a frequenter of Adler's bar, where he rubbed elbows with the villagers. I remember he was a character witness for Sheriff "Bus" Dormann, and as he was being cross-examined by Irving Kennedy about his presence in a bar, being asked if he thought it was a good thing for a minister to frequent bars, I remember his answer so vividly: "You meet more sinners at a bar than you do in church!"

Joseph Komonchak

...In 1946 the United Nations holds its first General Assembly...Emperor Hirohito shocks Japan by announcing that the firmly-held belief in his divinity is a "false conception"...IBM announces an electronic calculator called the ENIAC—it contains 18,000 vacuum tubes...Mother Frances Cabrini is canonized to become America's first saint...Uprising in Vietnam sets off war with the French...

From the Center of the Earth to Rockland: Arlene Dahl

While many Rocklanders have traveled extensively, only one can claim to have been to the center of the earth. For glamorous actress Arlene Dahl, her role in the movie *Journey to the Center of the Earth* (1959) was just another step in her fascinating journey from childhood in Minneapolis, to a brilliant career in Hollywood and Broadway, to a beautiful home in Sparkill.

Beginning her career at the tender age of eight, Miss Dahl dreamed of one day being a musical comedy star. While her hourglass figure and stunning looks may have been what initially attracted attention, her talent was what kept her on the stage and screen for several decades. Though such accomplishments would seem to be more than enough for one person, she can also add to her list of credits being a columnist, having her own line of beauty products and perfume, and winning awards for advertising.

In 1981, Miss Dahl and her sixth husband, Marc Rosen, (Fernando Lamas was the first, and Lorenzo Lamas is their son) bought an 1859 Victorian house in Sparkill. The magnificently restored mansion, called "Treetops," sits on 12 secluded acres. While Miss Dahl still resides in a Manhattan apartment for much of the year, Treetops has become a peaceful haven for the woman who has lived a life that others only dream about, and plans to continue living every day to the fullest.

Linda Zimmermann

Arlene Dahl in *Three Little Words*, 1950.
Courtesy of Arlene Dahl Rosen.

159

Bill "Showboat" Smith

When I was a kid in high school there was one colored youth that was a terrific singer. His deep bass voice would make the walls rock around the auditorium when he sang. His name was Bill Smith. Bill and I were friends in high school and afterwards. I was one of the three white pallbearers at his funeral and had tears streaming down my face every step of the way.

There was no question among us that Bill was "going places" and he did, starting with the Eva Jesse Choir when it reaped fame as the background chorus for the "Ford Motor Hour," when radio was king.

A Hampton College graduate, Bill starred in *Porgy and Bess* when it was an initial top hit, starred in Kurt Weill's and Maxwell Anderson's Broadway hit, *Lost in the Stars*, and then took over the part of Joe in *Showboat* in 1946. Bill went on to play the role of Joe and sing "Old Man River" more than any other bass in the history of this musical, some 2,600 times.

When you stop and think about it, 2,600 times is a lot of times to be singing "Old Man River", so one day I asked Bill if he still got a kick out of singing it.

"Yes, I still do," was his reply, "because every time we do *Showboat* there is something different about the audience reaction. You sense it, feel it, and it is up to you to create 'Joe' into a real-life character that is authentic, believable and have him accepted as the lovable character that he is.

"You know, there's something of a philosopher in Joe. You'll find it in his lines at the end of the show: 'New things come and old things go, but all things look the same to Joe. Wars go on and some folks die, the rest forget the reasons why.'

"That's *Showboat* and that's also life," said Bill.

Kenneth F. Harniman

Drumming Through the Century

Buddy Christian, from South Nyack, is a jazz drummer who played with the Big Bands. Fascinated with drums as a toddler, he gave his first performance at age eight and played with Eddie Sauter's dance band when he was only sixteen. He went on to make four recordings that were named jazz recordings of the year, was the first drummer to play on television and toured across the United States and nineteen other countries, often playing before royalty and heads of state.

Once quoted as saying, "Almost every musician I know plays until he dies," Christian is a living example of how doing what you love keeps you young and active. As of 2001, at the age of 83, he is still performing.

Linda Zimmermann

Buddy Christian in 1940 (above), and still going strong in 1995 (right). Photos courtesy of Mrs. Norma Christian.

160

The Brook School: The Battle Over Segregation

Even as late as 1941, a district in Rockland County continued to operate a segregated school, and it had done so despite a state law of 1938 in which authority to maintain separate schools for Negroes and whites had been repealed. This same school was the only school in Rockland County, as well as one of only three in upstate New York at that date (1938) that employed black persons as teachers.

The school, known as the Brook School, was located in Hillburn. It had originally been built in 1889 for Negro children. As early as 1930, its continued use had been questioned by black people in the district. At a special school meeting in August that year, Edward Morgan ran for school board trustee and lost 34-15. The vote was taken at a meeting of the citizens and, according to the *Journal* reporter, there were 15 colored people in attendance and 34 whites.

One Negro, speaking at the meeting, complained, "We wouldn't even want a trustee on the board if ...(it) would only give us what we have a right to have." The story then continued:

The colored folks point out that their four room school building seats over 125 pupils, two of them often being forced to occupy the same seat, ... They claimed that the old frame building is a veritable fire trap, with inadequate exit facilities. In addition, they point to the fact that the colored children must use outdoor toilets and that they have little or no yard in which to play.

The negroes also state that they have complained on many occasions to both the village and the school authorities, but that their complaints have gone unanswered. They promise definite action, however, possibly by reporting the conditions to the State, in hope of receiving aid from that quarter.

In 1935, in anticipation of school centralization in Rockland, the U.S. Office of Education sponsored a study seeking to determine how best to effect that desired end. The study recommended closing down 25 schools in the county, one of which was Brook School. At the time, there was another school in Hillburn, the Main School, which had eight rooms and better facilities. It was exclusively for whites.

Clearly, there were substantial reasons for abandoning Brook School. Separate schools had long vexed the black parents. Brook School, itself, was obsolete and in poor condition. The integration of student bodies was the law of the state and a desired objective of the consolidation program. Nevertheless, as late as 1943, nothing had been done to achieve integration. In that year, there were 70 white students attending the Main School, and 92 blacks at the Brook School.

In September 1943, the black parents of Hillburn went on strike. Stating they were fed up with the years of procrastination, they refused to send their children to the Brook School. When school opened that year, only six of the 92 black children enrolled there were in attendance. At the same time as they struck, the parents, acting with the support of the National Association for the Advancement of Colored People, and the advice of its special counsel, Thurgood Marshall (Marshall was later appointed Associate Justice of the Supreme Court of the United States), appraised the New York State Commissioner of Education, Dr. George Stoddard, of the situation in Hillburn. Subsequently, the Commissioner's office notified the county superintendent of schools and the school board of the necessity of ending segregation in the district. The parents then formed a chapter of the NAACP and deputized a committee to meet with the school board and demand that Negro children be admitted to the Main School.

Responding, the school board mandated new boundary lines for assigning pupils to the two schools. The result was 33 black children transferred to the Main School. The remainder of the black children were to attend Brook School, which was to continue to be entirely black. The board also announced that children absent from school after September 13 would be considered truants.

The parents of the children assigned to Brook School then countered with the charge that the division line "continued the violation in spirit." They also added that the school was a fire hazard and said they intended to stand fast against the board. To provide education for their children, a temporary school was established in a neighboring church chapel.

Complaints of truancy were then filed against 22 persons, the parents of the 53 black children who were not attending class. These cases were tried in children's court before County Judge John McKenna. In accordance with the confidentiality presumably required in such cases, Judge McKenna refused to make his decision public. However, attorney Marshall, who had been present during the trials, together with one of the parents, revealed to a reporter of the New York City newspaper *PM* what had happened in court.

The parents had been fined $10 each, with the sentence to be suspended provided they returned their children forthwith to an accredited school. Their answer was to attempt to enroll their children in the Main School. On discovering that the secrecy of his court had been violated, Judge McKenna was outraged. Claiming that "there can be but one purpose behind a publication of this kind, and that is to arouse certain elements of our citizenship to a disunity that cannot be tolerated in times of war," he called the revelation a violation of the penal

The Brook School   JSC

law of the state, and threatened grand jury action against Marshall, *PM*, and Gilbert Avery, the parent in question. Marshall then countered by carrying the school case to the Appellate Division of the state.

At this juncture, Commissioner Stoddard sent investigators to Hillburn and summoned the school board to appear before him. Following that hearing, he announced that a local board, in zoning, may not set up a line to maintain school segregation. He then ordered the Brook School closed, and its children and teachers transferred to the Main School. The school board complied. The white parents of students previously at the Main School then responded by withdrawing their children from school and arranged for their transfer to private and parochial schools nearby. Subsequently, contention diminished. State intervention had decided

the issue and the local people were left with the job of picking up the pieces.

With World War II on, and with the nation's leaders calling for unity, the Brook School controversy posed a true moral dilemma, one that had to be faced. Evidence of discriminatory attitudes in oneself and one's neighbors would not be very pleasant to find. No one, it seemed, wanted to acknowledge that the community's controlling tradition had countenanced the kind of discrimination that was currently anathema. Thus, the preferred approach was to wish the school segregation issue into oblivion, and that was what the newspaper, together with many white people, apparently, wanted to do.

In this context, the issue of segregation at Brook School was especially tormenting and required a strong effort at collective superego suppression. Someone was needed on whom to fasten blame. And the way that worked was for that someone to be anyone who had moved for the end of discrimination at the school. In retrospect, the newspaper and, to the degree it represented established opinion in the county, Rockland's people, came out looking rather foolish. The facts were decidedly against them. Official excuses were very lame. Their main hope seemed to be that if putative outsiders could be snarled down, the issue would die a natural death. Given that stance, it seems likely, as it had earlier with slavery and with the vote for black men, that had there been no state intervention, there would not have been integration at Hillburn. As has been the case so many times before, local option had again proved to be a weak instrument for social change.

Carl Nordstrom, *Phoenician Tales*

The Jewish Community
1940-1949

By the early 1940s, Monsey was a popular summer resort where people came to enjoy tranquility of the country. Several hotels that later played an important role in the development of the Orthodox community were later converted to synagogues and yeshivas after closing their doors to summer visitors.

In many ways the founding of the yeshivas marks the beginning of Monsey's Orthodox community. Rabbi Sharga Feival Mendlowitz was dean of a Brooklyn yeshiva before relocating in Monsey and founded Bais Medrish Elyon.

As commuting to New York City became easier with the opening of the Palisades Interstate Parkway, the NYS Thruway and the Tappan Zee Bridge, the community started to grow. Before long Bais Shraga, a high school, joined the elementary and postgraduate schools, making Jewish education in Monsey complete.

Congregation Bais Yisroel, one of earliest Orthodox congregations in Monsey, began in one of Bais Medrish Elyon's buildings and moved several times, finally to the former Monsey Garden Hotel on Main Street and Maple Avenue.

The Yeshiva of Spring Valley began in 1942. Hershel Halberg, the original prime mover with several other area families, saw the need to establish a Torah school, a yeshiva, and established one.

Temple Beth El is the county's largest Reform synagogue. Founded in 1947, it held its first congregational meeting at the Finkelstein Memorial Library, with about seventy-five people. David Sutter, chairman of the steering committee, announced that fifty families had indicated an interest in joining the new synagogue. Sutter stated, "Our congregation will interpret Judaism in the language of America. We shall

162

maintain the essential beliefs of ancient Israel but will we will present it in a language that is inspiring and understandable to the youth of our day.

"In worship our congregation will fuse old traditions and modern thought so that the Jewish religion, its philosophy and customs, history and thought will cater to develop good men and good women and upright citizens."

Rosh Hashanah, 1941, was the first time Jews in the Nanuet area gathered to worship together in an apartment joining the garage on the Stark property. In 1947, in response to the growth of the Nanuet and Pearl River Jewish community, the Center looked to the future and its own building. Construction on the Center (on Middletown Road opposite the entrance to the Nanuet Mall) was completed in June of 1948 at a cost of $30,000 and stood for almost four decades.

Founded in 1948, the Young Israel of Spring Valley met at several locations, including a converted building on Columbus Avenue, before moving to its present location on Union Road in 1960.

The West Clarkstown Jewish Center established in the late 1940s as Congregation Chevra Argudas Achim meets in the former casino of the Sunrise Bungalow Colony, on West Clarkstown Road.

Harold L. Laroff

When Rockland was a Splendid Summer Getaway

Franklin Hoffman of Nanuet was a teen when his family owned and operated a bungalow colony, a hotel and a kosher meat market in the Spring Valley area. Now 64, he looks back on those days longingly. It was a simpler and safer time, a time when everyone got along, when everyone worked and played together, he said.

It was just before World War II when his father, Milton, brought his family to live in Spring Valley. There were many farms still in the area, and they came here to live on one of them, stretching along Rose Avenue, in what was then Clarkstown, from Ewing Avenue to what is now called Fred Hecht Drive. In what is now a largely residential neighborhood, the Hoffmans ran their working farm. "We had cows and goats and chickens," Hoffman recalled.

Back then, Hoffman said, the Clarkstown end of Rose Avenue wasn't even paved, and it wasn't until the 1960s that the area was annexed and became part of the village.

Before too long, the elder Hoffman opened a kosher meat market and sold the farm's chickens to the hotels and bungalow colonies all along Pascack Road and West Clarkstown Road. The cows produced milk, which he also sold to the local resorts and vacationers, along with cheese made from both cow and goat milk.

Throughout the 1940s, Milton Hoffman saw more and more New York City residents coming to Spring Valley in the summer months to escape the heat and grind of city life. "Families would come up and the mothers and children would stay all week, or all summer, and the fathers would go back and forth" to work after visiting for the week and weekends.

By the end of the decade, he had built 20 bungalows on his farm and began renting them to summer residents. Back then, people were coming to Rockland from the city by bus up Route 9W, by ferry from Tarrytown to Nyack, or by train, with a terminus in Piermont. "There was so much then, in terms of transportation," Hoffman said, "and that's all disappeared," replaced with dependency on the automobile.

Hyenga Lake in Spring Valley in 1953. JSC

When the Rockland resorts were booming, the old Tappan Zee Playhouse, too, had its heyday, drawing Broadway stars to perform in shows there during what was known as the Summer Stock season.

But the Tappan Zee Playhouse wasn't the only diversion for vacationers. Traveling theater companies also would bring shows to the family's Spring Valley Gardens Hotel and others like Orner's Hotel, Zelanka's Hotel, the White House on the Lake and the Rosner Auerbach Hotel. Among them were Yiddish theater groups that spoke to the Jewish vacationers, many of them immigrants, in their own language.

But just as the TZ Bridge and new roads brought new residents to Rockland, they carried vacationers right past, Hoffman said. "It started with the Palisades Parkway, but the Thruway really killed the bungalow business in Rockland. People could get to the resorts in the Catskills faster than they could get to Spring Valley."

Sensing that the county was going to be going through another transition, Milton Hoffman tried to adjust again. "He saw more people moving to Rockland and saw the county growing, so he converted some of the bungalows for year-round use, installing insulation and heating. He was trying to look ahead."

But within two or three years of the Tappan Zee Bridge's opening in 1955, the bungalow business in the county was on its last legs. Many of the old hotels and bungalow colonies gave way to homes, businesses or as parkland. Other colonies were converted to year-round residences, and the remnants of some still stand today. The Hoffman family eventually sold the old farm and private homes cover most of the property today.

"Back in the days of the resorts, there was a closeness. Everyone worked together, no matter who you were or what you were. There was no crime, and no one ever locked their doors."

Merchants delivered then, he recalled, and did so whether you were home or not. "The milk man or butcher would walk right in and deliver your order to the refrigerator if no one was home."

Bob Baird, *The Journal News* 7/27/00

The Big Bad Wolf?

My husband and I and our two and a half-year-old son moved to Rockland County in 1947. We lived on Union and Eckerson Roads in Spring Valley.

When my son was three, I would walk with him to Main Street to do some shopping. While I liked living in the "country," one day when we were walking an animal came out of the woods. To me, it looked like a wolf. I picked up a heavy stick and said to my son, "Run home, and tell Mr. Cohen that Mommy needs help!" He turned and ran as I faced the "wolf" with the stick.

I was scared. We stood and faced each other for about a minute, while I was shaking and trembling. Suddenly, the "wolf" turned and went back into the woods. After I regained my composure, I ran back looking for my child. He and Mr. Cohen and another man were on their way to come to my assistance.

After I told him my story, he had a good laugh. He told me that the "wolf" was just a dog who lived there. I tried to laugh, too, but I didn't find it funny. I walked those roads for many more years, but never saw that "wolf" again.

Lynne Levy

Memories

I was born in Monsey (1930) and my husband (1931) in Spring Valley. We graduated from Spring Valley High School in 1949. We were married in Spring Valley in 1954, and moved to Monsey in 1966 and Florida in 1980. My husband was a volunteer fireman in Spring Valley from 1949 through 1979 (Columbian Engine Co. #1).

My family left Monsey for Thiells-Mt. Ivy Road early in the thirties. There were not many houses on the road back then; we loved sleigh riding in the winter. I recall many sleds tied together while our family, along with aunts and uncles, rode down the steep hill gleefully—no automobiles to worry about. My grandparents' home on Thiells-Mt. Ivy Road was so serene and lavishly built of stone by my granddad.

My older brother and I attended Camp Hill Road school—it held classes from grade one through eight. Our walk to school was about two and a half miles.

My grandparents came to the U.S. from Italy with two small children and settled in Pomona, where they eventually built their home and raised seven children, one of whom was my Dad, Anthony Linguanti. Concetto Linguanti was a stone mason and did most of the stone work at Letchworth Village and had large vegetable gardens and raised the greatest grapes. My grandmother had the most beautiful gardens. Their home stood where the shopping plaza stands on Thiells-Mt Ivy Road alongside the Hillcrest Fire Station.

My Dad became a very prominent building contractor in the county, building many schools, homes and industrial buildings. His brother, Charles, also became a contractor and later opened a luncheonette on Rt. 202 called "Dar-Jeans." Vincent lost his life during WWII, for which the "Vincent Linguanti Lodge" was named. One daughter was Jean Coatti, and her husband owned the Coatti Service Station across the street from

Lederle Labs, which was later operated by their son, Aldino.

The highlights of WWII were the blackouts. When the whistle blew for an air raid all black shades were drawn so no light could be seen from the street. Air raid drills were held in schools where we got beneath our desks for cover. We used to love to hear a train coming along Dutch Lane tracks and would always run through the woods and wave to the troop trains. It was such an exciting time to show support to our troops.

I recall on VJ day we carried a dump truck load of people with pots and pans or anything you could bang on to make noise and drove around—we were all so overjoyed. I recall an oriental lady running and crying and she screamed with glee along Central Ave.

Spring Valley was a beautiful old town in the country. Saturdays we spent in the movie theatre where everyone who attended received a dish for ten cents admission (a lot of families sent their children to obtain a set of dishes). Sundays was mass at St. Joseph's and when we got older, we always went to Heald's drug store for hot chocolate in the winter. In our teens we would cater to Brown's Ice Cream Parlor, Arvanites luncheonette and stationery store, and Ziegler's stationary store. During the summer there was a lot of traffic, but, after the summer months were over and visitors went home we had our town back where everyone knew everyone.

During high school days there was a "Youth Center" over the store on Church St. which was overseen by teachers of the high school. We danced to a jukebox, drank Cokes and had good clean fun. Later, the high school shop students built a center in the park.

Our school proms were always in our gymnasium, decorated by students and staff.

Hyenga Lake was a favorite winter spot as we teenagers spent many hours ice skating. Many a hockey game was held there. Requa Lake in Monsey was the summer spot for families for swimming and picnics.

Jean Linguanti Conklin and Raymond I. Conklin

Bill Sutherland and the Minisceongo Yacht Club

By the late 1930s, the Haverstraw Bay shoreline, once the center of the thriving brick industry, was left with abandoned buildings and deep clay excavations, which soon filled with rain and groundwater. Eventually, the river worked its way into these ponds and the tidal flows began to carve and maintain channels connecting them to the river itself. Three examples of this are: the Minisceongo basin (the former Reilley yard), Haverstraw Marina (previously Ghurran's pond and Morrisey brickyard), and the Bowline Pond (a former Excelsior Brick Co. excavation). Even better known is the sight of the great Haverstraw landslide in 1906.

Sometime in the year 1936, Bill Sutherland (below), a boat builder and master mechanic, built a workshop approximately where "Dougie's building" now stands, just beyond the finger 1 parking lot. Like any talented person, Bill attracted a group of volunteer helpers who formed the nucleus of what was to become the Minisceongo Yacht Club. They planned the building of five 19-foot Lightning Class sailboats (right) with the intention of starting a club. At a keel laying party on January 18, 1941, Lightning Fleet No. 41 and Minisceongo Yacht Club were officially organized with Bill as commodore, a post that he held until 1946.

This became a pivotal year for the club. The membership had grown to 55 members who purchased our clubhouse, improved the gap, built docks, and finally met the person who actually owned the land they were "squatting" on—Gus Miller. Gus turned out to be supportive of Bill and the club, further motivating the membership to quickly fill the many projects at hand. Times were much different, and Gus would give his approval without the encumbrances of legal liabilities and waterfront commissions. Eventually, Gus Miller's property, along with neighboring parcels, were purchased

by the club, making up the 20 acres we have here today.

Bill Sutherland was a man who knew no limits. It was just as natural for him to move a 20-ton cruiser using nothing more than planks, pipe rollers and a cable

165

attached to the bumper of his '49 Plymouth, as it was for him to create the stained glass skylight that adorned his workshop. Bill was a collector of construction artifacts and materials and he had an extensive exotic wood collection. As a boy, I had the fortune to visit the shop and remember a magnificent lamp he had made out of 52 different species of wood. He also used his talent to create the spectacular Sutherland Trophy for the races of Lightning Class sailboats he sponsored. By the early '50s, his dream of making boating available to the average man had unfolded. Bill Sutherland is proof that one man can make a difference.

Bill's contributions have been chronicled numerous times throughout the years, and he has been credited with nothing less than "the renaissance of sailing on the Hudson." In retrospect, I think it's fair to say that Bill Sutherland was much more than the founder of our club. His boundless energy and enthusiasm for boating extended far beyond our basin and became a catalyst for much of the boating activity on the Hudson, both then and now.

Our clubhouse (above) was built by the Shankey family on Lake Popolo in 1936, as a summer vacation home. When West Point took over this property in 1942 and after subsequent condemnation proceedings in 1946, it was offered for sale on bids. MYC's winning bid of $333 secured the chestnut log building with yellow pine flooring, which was then numbered, disassembled, transported to its present site, reassembled on a new foundation, and completed in 1948. This type of log building is quite common, but isolated to this area of the Hudson Valley (the Bear Mountain Inn and most of the buildings there are similar examples). They were built prior to World War II when chestnut trees were plentiful and plywood was not.

George Basley, Club Historian, 2000

Rockland Center for the Arts

In 1946, the Rockland Foundation, precursor of the Rockland Center for the Arts, Inc., was founded. It all began at the Market Fair, then on South Broadway, Nyack, a tiny book shop that became a gift and art supply store run by Virginia (Ginny) Johnston and Florence (Curly) Mason. The Market Fair became a crossroads for artists of all kinds, and with that ambience, they began to dream of an art center.

Ginny first expressed the idea for an organization of and for people in the arts in Rockland County. She, Curly, Gordon Dean Smith and his wife Doris Smith discussed it over coffee in the shop on several occasions, and the subject was broached to customers and friends who wandered in. After about ten meetings and discussions, the foundation came into being and claimed such notables as Helen Hayes, Henry Varnum Poor, Kurt Weill, Lotte Lenya, Maxwell Anderson and Maurice Heaton. It became a haven and focal point for a select group of artists and their families. Originally located in the old Knights of Pythias on North Broadway in Nyack, the Foundation encouraged and hosted exhibitions by local artists and concerts by important musicians. Writers were frequent visitors.

In 1960, Mrs. Maryann Emerson, a generous benefactor, made her home on Greenbush Road in West Nyack, its outbuildings and 10 acres of land available as the Foundation's permanent home. The name was changed to "Center for the Arts" in 1972, three years after a new studio building was opened. Since that time, the center has become a full-blown, community-based organization dedicated to education and every aspect of art and culture.

What began with a modest offering of courses and a showcase for local artists has blossomed into a major arts organization, offering courses and programs to all segments of the community. By the time of their fortieth anniversary, the school offered over 100 courses, including introductory courses, intensive advanced programs and special workshops for everyone from pre-schoolers to senior citizens and were taught by experienced professionals, all doing creative work in their fields.

SOM, Oct./Dec. 1987

...In 1948, the 200-inch Hale telescope is dedicated at Mount Palomar in California...The House Un-American Activities Committee creates national paranoia in its hunt for Communists...A new Cadillac costs $2,833...T.S. Eliot wins the Nobel Prize for literature...

The Blizzard of '47

During and after the big snowstorm of 1993, TV and radio announcers kept saying that it was the worst ever. That's because most of them weren't around for the blizzard that hit Rockland County on December 26, 1947, the day after Christmas.

Living in Tomkins Cove, I decided to take the 11 o'clock bus to Haverstraw to exchange a Christmas present. The storm was just starting and I thought I had plenty of time to get down and back. I never got home till noon the next day! I decided to skip the 12:30 p.m. bus home and take the 1 p.m. bus, but by 1 p.m. the buses had stopped running.

The wind was terrific and it was snowing heavily and drifting. Any travel by automobile became impossible by mid-afternoon. I spent my time in stores and toward evening visited a friend on Fairmont Avenue. About 8 p.m., I decided to spend the night at Brown's Diner, an all-night place. Old-time Haverstraw people will remember it well, located at the intersection of New Main Street and West Street.

As I left my friend's house I slipped on the bottom step of the porch and fell into a drift nearly waist deep. On the way to the diner, which was about 500 feet, the wind was so strong that I sat down in the middle of West Street and put my head down on my bent knees and covered it with my arms to get my breath. Usually this was a busy street, but nothing was moving in the whole village. As I reached the diner, I turned before going in and looked up "station hill," where only the roofs of abandoned cars parked this way and that way were visible.

I remember saying to myself at the time, "take a good look because you'll never see it again in your lifetime," and I never have. Inside the diner people slept everywhere, ate and told wild tales of their experiences in the storm. Many spent the night unable to proceed any further.

By morning, 25 inches of snow had fallen in New York City. How much fell here, I no longer remember. Tales of peoples' experiences in the storm were told for months. West Broad Street looked like "the old Oregon Trail" for days, with one-way traffic and people traveling in deep ruts.

Some local people had snow in their yards till May and some people in the Catskills had snow from the storm until Decoration Day.

So when someone tells you that a recent storm was the worst of all, ask them if they remember December 26, 1947.

Pat Ferguson, *Rockland Journal-News*, 4/6/93

Rockland County in the Forties: Seen from Bear Mountain

Because there aren't that many of us who lived here so long ago and are still breathing and moderately coherent, I want to tell the story of Rockland in the war and post-war era with Bear Mountain at its center.

In the autumn of '41, my father, John Martin, who had impressed Robert Moses with his handling of park concessions in the city, was brought here to run the Bear Mountain Inn. Moving from a row house in Brooklyn, with aunts and uncles on every surrounding block, to the deep country with no neighbors wasn't easy for an eight-year-old. Suffice to say I did not feel fortunate. But I was. Incredibly so.

We had barely unpacked when Pearl Harbor plunged the nation into World War II and rationing of gas and meat put a country inn into a pickle. People were not going to use up a precious gasoline allowance for a ride in the country to get to a vegetarian restaurant. So my Dad had to be inventive.

The Bear Mountain Inn, postcard circa 1910s. JSC

The federal government was putting up Camp Shanks down in Orangetown and Dad saw an opportunity to feed those round-the-clock workers. So he secured the concession and then went to the Rationing Board to convince them that these guys needed meat in their sandwiches and sugar in their coffee and any skimping

167

would sabotage the entire war effort.

Then he heard that the major league baseball teams would not be able to go south for spring training because of travel restrictions. So he went to Branch Rickey of the Brooklyn Dodgers to sell him on coming north for spring training, but Rickey was hesitant because the weather would make the Bear Mountain field impossible for practice at least 50% of the time. So Dad went to the West Point Commandant and convinced him that he needed some positive press...that cadets were being perceived as "draft dodgers" and what better way to garner good press than offer their huge indoor Field House to some legitimate Dodgers. It worked. The Dodgers trained at Bear Mountain until the war ended in '45. And since they had a very special place in the morale of our region, they also got meat and sugar.

After the Dodgers came the football Dodgers (does anyone remember them?) and the football Giants, the Knicks, the Golden Glovers and almost every team that came to play against Army. Every Rocklander from those days has happy memories of going to Bear Mountain to watch these teams practice.

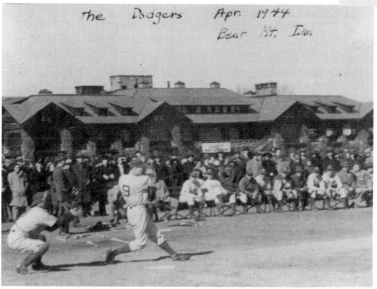

The Brooklyn Dodgers at Bear Mountain in April of 1944. JSC

But the Inn was more than just a sports center. Iona Island just to the south was a thriving naval station during the war and West Point was the center for Army leadership. Every five-star general spent time there. When Madame Chiang Kai-shek came to this country to garner aide for her general husband, she stayed at Bear Mountain (in our own house actually) for a month, with President Roosevelt's personal limousine sitting in the driveway. Out of sheer boredom the Secret Servicemen used to drive my brothers and me to Sacred Heart School in Highland Falls where we became even more envied than we'd been before (as the only kids with meat sandwiches).

Realize that the Bear Mountain Inn was the largest venue in the county; the place where every big affair was held, where anyone who was anyone had weddings and political dinners. My mother's guest book was signed by four future or past Presidents and every major sports figure of the time, as well as everyone from Danny Kaye to a high school football coach named Vince Lombardi who went on to become rather a legend in his own right.

Servicemen skating at Bear Mtn. during the 1940s.
Courtesy of Rachel Kaufmann

My Dad ran the Inn until 1965 and it continued to be an important piece of the county. But the county had changed. When I first moved here there were only two-lane roads and a traffic jam was more than one car at a stop sign. There were only a few traffic lights in the county and none at all in most villages. But with the Thruway and the PIP, Route 9W was no longer the only road to the city. New hotels offered better accommodations than the Inn and the Rockland County where you knew almost everyone in the obituary columns became a sea of strangers

But, to our credit, we welcomed those strangers. We enjoyed seeing young families settling here, valuing what we cherished, discovering our river and mountains. It used to bother me, but now it amuses me (old age does mellow one) that the residents most committed to seeing that no one else moves here ever again only got here yesterday themselves. And they fight affordable housing in their communities—communities carved out of farmland where the only reason anybody moved into them in the first place was because they couldn't afford Westchester and Long Island.

Rockland County is not like it once was. Nothing is. But it's still the most beautiful part of the Hudson Valley (a riverbank with no railroad tracks) and the most accessible because of the Tappan Zee Bridge. And in my twilight years it has provided the most precious gift of all—happy memories.   Terry Martin Hekker
Author and former Mayor of Nyack

Rockland County Sports Hall of Fame: 1940-1949

Bruno Ablondi (Pearl River) One of the finest all-round athletes, excelling in football, basketball and baseball. Ablondi was killed in 1951 in the Korean War at the age of 23.

Chuck Aleno (Pearl River) Had a 20-year professional baseball career including four years with the Cinncinati Reds.

Wil Arietta (Nyack) All-county in football, baseball and basketball. Had greatest success in bowling including a 792 series in 1949, which was the fifth highest in the country.

Ron Becraft (Suffern) Oustanding basketball player who held several records in college and in amateur leagues. He once scored 56 points.

Josh Bolack (Haverstraw) Excelled in all sports, especially baseball, playing for military and minor league teams. Very active in local sports.

Ralph "Blacky" Consiglio (Suffern) Excelled in many sports, went on to successful coaching career.

Harry "Dee" Dembnicki (Suffern) Professional golfer with a long career in tournaments. Was also considered one of the nation's top instructors, and was vice president of the PGA.

Frank DePatto (Suffern) All-County in football, basketball and baseball. After serving with the Army in WWII, he starred in local semi-pro teams.

Ethel Doller (Nyack) Major force in the development of bowling in Rockland. Was president of the RCWBA for 22 years and won numerous awards.

Bill Drescher (Congers) Outstanding multi-sport local athlete and major league baseball player with the New York Yankees.

James "Sham" Feeney (Haverstraw) Record-setting basketball player for Haverstraw High, who also starred in football, baseball and track.

George Garrecht (Haverstraw) Basketball and baseball player for Haverstraw High, and later a softball, sailing, bowling and golf standout, winning several championships.

Fred Hahn (Nyack) Professional baseball pitcher who made it to the majors for a one-game stint with the St. Louis Cardinals. Played with many different organizations across the country.

Martin "Hawk" Jacobs (Haverstraw) Outstanding local basketball star who also played semipro with the Detroit Clowns, as well as semipro football.

Howard Johnson (Suffern) Salutatorian of his class who excelled in football, basketball, baseball and track, helping his teams to many county titles.

Gloria Callen Jones (Nyack) National swimming champion, perhaps the best female athlete in county history. Won many national championships and was favored to win a gold medal in the 1940 Olympics, but the games were cancelled due to WWII.

Jim Kane (Nyack) If a sport is played in Rockland County, he has probably officiated it or assigned an official to it. It is estimated that he handled 10,000 assignments a year from 1969 to 1989 and he never had a game cancelled due to lack of officials.

Joe Klopchin (Congers) Excellent baseball player and an almost "unstoppable" record-breaking soccer player. Played amateur and semipro baseball.

Rocco Marano (Haverstraw) Starred on many football and basketball teams leading the way to county and local semipro championships.

Nick Mottola (Tappan Zee/Suffern) Coached many Tappan Zee teams to championships and as Suffern's athletic director also guided their teams to numerous titles.

Jeffrey Munson (Tappan Zee) Munson accomplished more athletically by age 16 than most people do in a lifetime. Was a champion trapshooter, winning his first title at age 10 in 1949, and "retired" in 1954.

Murray Olderman (Spring Valley) Renowned sportswriter, author and cartoonist. After a start in Rockland papers, his work was eventually distributed in over 800 daily newspapers.

Abe Schuster (Spring Valley) Pillar of wrestling community in Rockland for five decades. Two-time county champion, going undefeated both years. Went on to act as coach, official and administrator.

Joe St. Lawrence (Suffern) Innovative athletic director and coach, leading the Mounties to many titles. Helped introduce lacrosse in the county.

Max Talaska (Pearl River) Teacher, coach and athletic administrator in Pearl River School District from 1947 to 1982. Was a forerunner in establishing competition by school size, led expansion of girl's sports and set standards for fitness in New York.

Paul Urban (Haverstraw) Excelled in 5 sports and was captain of the football, baseball and basketball teams. Signed a major league baseball contract with the Chicago White Sox while still in high school, but the commissioner nullified it.

Bob Wolff (South Nyack resident) National sports broadcaster who called the play-by-play for the World Series, Stanley Cup, Super Bowl and NBA playoffs. Also broadcast Don Larsen's perfect game in the '56 World Series and was inducted into the Major League Hall of Fame.

Local Libraries

Finkelstein Library
24 Chestnut St. and Route 59, Spring Valley

The library began in 1917 as the Spring Valley Free Library in a room in a women's hat shop on Main Street. The family of Joseph N. Finkelstein donated the land and funds for the construction of a permanent building. Dedication of the new facility was held in 1941, at which the name was officially changed to Finkelstein Memorial Library. A children's room was added in 1960. A major expansion in 1969 was followed in 1987 with a new main wing named after Board President Robert H. Finkelstein. This is the county's largest public library, serving over 80,000 residents.

Rose Memorial Library
79 East Main Street, Stony Point

Ezekiel O. Rose, a prominent Stony Point businessman, bequeathed a sum of money and land upon his death in 1928 for the building of the Rose Memorial Library. Subsequently built in 1948-49, it was chartered in 1955. The original brick structure of 950 square feet was extended another 2,500 square feet in 1967. Its collection includes a strong section on local history.

Suffern Free Library
210 Lafayette Ave.

The Suffern Women's Club originally established the library in 1926 in a room in its clubhouse. The library's first building was dedicated on Pearl Harbor day, Dec. 7, 1941. Subsequent additions in 1968 and 1980 enlarged the structure. In April 2000, the library moved to a 37,000 square-foot new building on Route 59 (Lafayette Ave.). The library features a drive-up window, café-art gallery, and large community room. It also has three large stained-glass windows in the local history room that were donated from a post-Civil War mansion across the street.

The original Suffern library building in 2002.
Photo by Linda Zimmermann.

The Best of Times: Growing Up in Nyack

I was born in Nyack Hospital in 1927. I have lived on High Avenue ever since and I have attended the same church (St. Paul's United Methodist Church in South Nyack). I went to Liberty Street Elementary and Nyack Junior-Senior High on Midland Avenue.

Going and coming to Liberty Street proved to be a new experience every day. If I had pennies, I'd buy candy at Strapone's. At Franklin Street and DePew Avenue, the train locomotive came to a turntable where we boys could help the engineer turn the locomotive around. What an important thing for us youngsters—making us feel strong and needed.

The Erie turntable in Nyack in the 1940s.   JSC

Bellows Feed Store was a favorite hideout and carried many different odors and things to see. It became the place I stayed when I decided to play hookey.

George Donzella had a bakery on Main Street. Their specialty was Italian and French breads. There were also Dick Yerg's Buick, the Auto-Electric filling station and the Reliable Meat Market. There was a clock on the corner of Broadway and Main that protruded at an angle so you could see it from either direction. The building was a bank before it became Kerchman's Dress Store and then law and dental offices.

Other Main Street buildings and businesses remembered: Burnweit Garage, Koehler's Meat Market, Star Market, Paone's Pizza, a bowling alley, Lucky's Men's Store, Wagschal's Stationery, Mae Moon, Herbet's Shoes, Spectors, Burns Hardware, Brown's Furniture, Tromm's Deli, Leulick Bakery, Holiday Jewelers, Bluebird Dress Shop, Vander Waldes Department Store, Newberry 5&10, Woolworth 5&10, Worsfold-Havermale Hardware and Grand Union—all of which are gone. Remaining are: Koblin's Drugstore, McManus Drugstore, Lydecker's Insurance, and Travis Monument.

Urban renewal wiped out Main Street south to DePew. Before that, part of South Nyack was eliminated when the New York State Thruway came in. There was a chapel in South Nyack on Clinton and Highland Avenues that was destroyed. The Westminster clock and chimes ended up in the Episcopal Church.

The ice pond was another favorite place. It was located where the Best Western Motel and car wash are now located. It was a haven for the youth of Nyack, especially in the winter for ice skating. Bonfires were a must! In the summer, the pond provided fishing, turtles, tadpoles, frogs, wading, bathing and row boating.

Other hangouts for young people were Smith's, a soda fountain/stationery store, and Eagle Confectionary,

which was a Greek soda fountain, known for its candy. Schmidt's/Blumaneur was an ice cream store. Shea's had a soda fountain where I worked as a soda jerk, and I remember serving Louis Sherry ice cream which was delivered by railway express, packed in dry ice.

We fished off the main street dock. Crabs, eels, white perch and catfish were the main things we caught. At the car ferry from Nyack to Tarrytown, a man with an accordian would entertain, hoping to get a few pennies.

As ice and coal were necessary, there were at least two companies in Nyack—Sherman & White Coal Company and the Nyack Ice and Coal Company. Coal was delivered to homes and then into the basement by chute. People would place a sign in their window when they needed ice. The ice sign indicated the size wanted: 25, 50, 75 or 100.

There were bread men who delivered door-to-door from Widmann's bakery, at twelve cents a loaf.

I found it hard to concentrate on schoolwork in high school because of the view of the Hudson River. Mary MacArthur (Helen Hayes' daughter) sat at my table in study hall. We were not allowed to talk.

The Nyack Beach at the Hook was a wonderful place to be, and still is. There was a pier there until it was struck by lightning and burned.

I belonged to the Highland Hose Fire Company—known as the Buttermilk Boys since drinking was frowned upon.

As a youngster on High Avenue I played baseball in the street. We broke a few windows, but not a word was said about not playing ball. Mrs. Whipfall, an elegant lady, lived across the street and she used to call me over to give me cookies. Her son, Bill Whipfall, told of his flying days with Eddie Rickenbacker in WWI. Mrs. Wanamaker, another neighbor, treated us to warm freshly made bread. What a heavenly smell!

Living close to 9W, I remember watching the Coast Guard convoy of trucks transporting shipments of gold to West Point. The tanks going to West Point were noisy and the ground shook, but what a thrill!

During WWII, I was a plane spotter at an observation tower on South Boulevard. Our code name was Chestnut 2-0. When I spotted a plane, I would call in the kind of plane and its direction. (These were the days before radar.)

We had chickens and turkeys, and grew a victory garden, so we could make our ration stamps go further.

I could go on and on about the people and experiences in Nyack. I can't help but believe I grew up in the best time and in the best place. I'm proud to be a part of Rockland history.

Russell McCandless

171

Nanuet or "Frohlington"

There was a time when Nanuet seemed misnamed. Reading Helen Frohling's obituary in 1998 recalled a kindlier, gentler day, a lasting memory of family life courtesy of Mrs. Frohling, and a time when the crossroads of Rockland probably should have been called "Frohlington."

Well, there was Frank Frohling and his wife, who lived over on Grace Street, another Frohling lived somewhere near the junk yard on then Route 59 (known more recently as West Nyack Road), and on Smith Street there were more Frohlings than people.

When my father moved us from Nyack to Smith Street in 1943, I'm sure someone must have confronted him or my mother about how we were related to the Frohlings, because it seemed you had to be a Frohling, married to one, or somehow related to one, if you expected to take up residency on "Apple Pie Alley," as the locals called that brief stretch of street that ran from then Route 59 and Fred Bremer's prize dahlias, south to the Kadushen property, where the school and library complex now stand.

Through the cobwebs and crags of memory comes one framing recollection in the very old days that I still carry, courtesy of the recently deceased Helen Frohling and her husband, Phil, Jr. (the sign maker). During World War II, Phil, Jr., along with several other Smith Streeters, was off to the wars. Several years before being drafted and domestic car production ceased, Phil, Jr. must have taken delivery of a 1939 Chevrolet two-door sedan, black as I recall, for it was the newest car on Smith Street. And during the War, Mrs. Frohling would tool around town to the extent that errands required and gas rationing permitted.

As the war was winding down, the word in Nanuet, and all the rest of the country, was of course, when would the boys be coming home? On Smith Street, more precisely, the concern was about Phil, Jr.

What follows is what I remember and probably is more fiction than fact, but it remains vivid nonetheless. For it was a bright, sunny day and from our front porch, I saw a car pulling up to the Frohling driveway, because we noticed cars on the street in those days. After the morning and evening rush of Lederle traffic, there was virtually no traffic on Smith Street or Church Street or College Avenue. So I noticed the car, but I'm not sure if it was one of LuRoy Rhodes' cabs or what (yes, we did have taxi service, we even had competing cab companies, in the old days).

A figure climbed from the car, hefted a bag, probably a duffle bag, to his shoulder and started up the driveway when another figure, in a housecoat of some sort, came flying down the driveway to embrace the man with a shriek that all Smith Street could hear, as Mrs. Frohling told us that her husband, Phil, Jr., was home from the wars. There was joy on Smith Street that day and for many days to follow. More than a half-century later, I still see Mrs. Frohling flying down the driveway.

Phil, Jr. subsequently resumed his sign-making business with the famous motto: "Tell the world with a Frohling Sign." Now, with the passing of Helen Frohling at age 81, the resident population of Frohlington has dropped significantly.

R. Clinton Taplin, *Rockland Journal News*, 2/8/98

James Cropsey's Memories of a Life in New City

All the children in our part of southern New City attended Chestnut Grove Elementary School at the bend in Old Middletown Road in the twenties through the forties. I don't think there were any buses, we all walked—from as far as West Clarkstown Road on the west, Route 304 on the east, the Oakbrook (Smith Hill Road) area to the south, and New City Park area and Vanderbilt Road to the north (a dirt road just north of Collyer Avenue which eventually became part of Little Tor Road South).

Each teacher had two grades—first and second, third and fourth, etc. The principal was Mrs. Stegmeyer. The kids living close enough walked home for lunch and back again during the one-hour lunchtime. At recess we made up our own games. The only recognizable "sport" was pickup baseball.

I think our graduating class was about 12 to 15 kids. After eighth grade, most of us were bused to Spring Valley High School on South Route 45. One bus was enough for all, but for any of us who competed in the school's sports programs, getting home at the end of the day after practice was not easy. I believe the Spring Valley graduating class of 1946 was about 105. A lot of the older boys left early and joined one of the military services as the war was still winding down.

We (Spring Valley) were co-champs with Haverstraw in football in the fall of 1945. Someone thought it would be great to put on a high school football game for the troops returning to the USA through Camp Shanks, so Spring Valley and Nyack High played in the winter (long after the season) on a bare dirt (and rocks) lot at Camp Shanks. It was cold and raw and I don't think the troops were very happy being there to watch, and we weren't thrilled to play on a frozen raw dirt field.

The schools that fielded football teams then were Spring Valley, Pearl River, Nyack, Suffern and

Haverstraw. (Congers, the predecessor of the Clarkstown schools, did not have a big enough enrollment for a football team, so they concentrated on soccer and were the perennial soccer champs in the county.) These five schools, plus Congers, had most of the other sports—basketball, baseball, soccer and track—for boys, but not much if anything for girls.

The Congers' basketball team played on the assembly room stage (still there at Congers Elementary) and players had to be careful not to run off the stage. Pearl River had such a low ceiling that the visiting teams invariably bounced some of their shots off the ceiling or ran into the walls.

At the southwest corner of what is now the intersection of Collyer Avenue and Little Tor Road South was a clay tennis court and open playing field where we all met for games of slug ball, basketball and football. Everybody played (boys and girls) because you needed everybody to have enough for teams.

During grammar school, most of the boys were amateur trappers in the winter and a good number got sent home because they and a skunk got too close. Hiking through the woods and walking up the brook on the frozen ice were great pastimes, and hockey on New City Park lake were also girl and boy after-school sports.

New City social life centered round the New City Fire Company and firehouse where the men endlessly played cards. The carnival was always a sellout with wheels-of-chance, baseball pitch and lots of food—really a community event.

There was a railroad spur that ended at Vanderbilt Lumber Company. It followed along Route 304 into Nanuet where it joined the main line into New York City. My mother, being a transplanted city girl, loved to take the train from Durant Station (Laurel Road) into the city to shop.

Until the PIP, Thruway, and the TZ Bridge opened up Rockland, it was still rural enough that productive farms numbered in the hundreds. Apples and vegetables were the main crops, but dairies and greenhouses were abundant. Our own farm produced tomatoes, beans, cabbage, sweet corn, summer squash and fall turnips—all for the New York City markets. It was not unusual for Dad to ship three to four truckloads a night to the Bronx Terminal Market, which was where some of the overflow parking for Yankee Stadium is now.

The farmers themselves were the main salesmen at the market, depending on someone at home to supervise the help who would be harvesting and packaging the next day's shipment while the farmer was at the market trying to sell the produce of the previous day's harvest. There were no supermarkets. All sales were to small storeowners, pushcart, and horse-drawn wagon vendors on a one-to-one personalized sales basis.

The farmers left for New York City in the early afternoon (as soon as the first load was ready) so as to be at their stall in the market by 4 or 5 p.m. . It was about a two-hour trip—at first across the Hudson by ferry, and eventually over the George Washington Bridge. They sold off the back of their trucks into the evening as long as buyers kept coming, sometimes until 8 or 9 p.m., then went up to a little restaurant for a late supper and upstairs to bed where the New City farmers shared a couple of rooms with beds—four or five to a room. Then up again, and down in the market by 5a.m. to catch the morning sales, then stayed until they sold out or had to leave to go home by 10:30 to 11:00 a.m., in order to get back home to bring the next load into market that afternoon. They did this six days a week. It was a killer of a schedule.

My Dad loved baseball, so on Sundays he and his fellow farmer baseball fan friends went in even earlier so they could go to the Polo Grounds and catch at least a few innings of baseball before they felt they had to get over to the market to start selling their loads of produce.

The rapid decline of the farms in Rockland started early in the second World War when the federal government took many of the prosperous farms along Western Highway and Route 303 for the construction of Camp Shanks. Urban pressure took the remainder after the end of World War II.

As a kid, I had the luxury of swimming either at the New City Park lake or at Davies Lake—both old mill ponds on the Demarest Kill stream. Immediately to the north and bordering our farm was the New City Park area built by Norwegians as summer homes during the late twenties and early thirties. To swim at their lake, you needed a button and as an outsider I depended on my friends for a button, as did my friends Dick Baker (son of *Journal-News* editor Norman Baker), and Henny Cyler (Mrs. Joseph Schuck of Tall Oaks Lane).

Davies Lake was a commercial venture that catered to sports clubs from New Jersey and the city, so that on a nice day the picnickers arrived by the busload in high old spirits and often had to be poured back on the buses at night because by then they were loaded with spirits. Both swimming areas had high diving boards, and at Davies Lake, late in the day, it seemed to be the right time to go off the high dive with all your street clothes on before being escorted onto the bus for the trip back home. Where the Little Tor Shopping Center is now was the open field where 30 to 40 buses were regularly parked.

Across the road, where the Union State Bank now stands, was an uphill swamp. Eventually, this road was widened from New Hempstead Road south to Route 59, and all the beautiful majestic trees were taken down, the stone walls disappeared, the road was straightened so that Chestnut Grove Elementary School now sits on a little by-pass known as Old Middletown Road.

After my father's death in 1943, the fields were farmed first by George M. Smith & Sons farm, then the

Katt farm until early in the 1950s. I came home from the service at the end of 1953, and I started farming the fields in 1954 in a small way, and finally full time about 1955. The last year we actually farmed the fields was in 1999, but we are still growing plants in our greenhouses in 2001.

James Cropsey

The History of Cropsey Farm, New City

Our farmhouse and its twin (to the south on Middletown Road) were built of native red sandstone about 1769 by the Blauvelt brothers. The one that owned our house wanted to prove he was richer, so he added the wraparound porch. The red anglicized Dutch barn made with gigantic hand-hewn beams and wooden dowels is one of a few left in the county. (Note: The barn was recently torn down.)

May 3, 1893 was the day that Andrew G. Cropsey's wife, Lizzie, became the owner of the 50 acres of land which is now known as Cropsey Farm. He was a gentleman farmer and a lawyer in New York City who commuted every day after they finally moved here full time, in 1897, from Cropsey Avenue, New Utrecht (Brooklyn, N.Y.). Where Vanderbilt's store is now, is what used to be the Erie Railroad ticket office and the post office. When the commuters got off the train they were "taxied home" by a fine stage and team of horses.

When the family first visited the area in 1891, if they saw two horses and a buggy going by on Sunday afternoon, it was a big day! The house had no running water, so they had to use the outhouse which still stands in the back yard—it's a two-seater!

Andrew died in 1911 and left the family with enormous debts from all the real estate he had purchased as far away as North Carolina. At that time, his son Wallace began farming the land as a business with the help of his sister, Carrie, who were both in their early twenties. The produce was trucked over the mountain to Haverstraw and shipped down to New York City by boat. Eventually, they trucked it down directly over Route 9W. This was many years before there were any big highways so it was a laborious trip. Carrie would stay at home and make sure the men did the harvesting, packing and loading so when Wallace returned there was another load waiting for him to take down to the city to sell.

Wallace married Winifred Berry in 1928 and Jim was born in 1929. When Lizzie died in 1937, the farm passed to Wallace and Carrie. The farming continued until 1943 when Wallace died, leaving the two women with Jim, who was just 14 years old. Winifred, who had been a law secretary, went back to work at the Health Department as a secretary. In the meantime, the farmland was rented to local farmers for many years—until Jim graduated from Cornell School of Agriculture in 1950 and served in the United States Air Force for two years. After working for a few years in the field of agriculture and working with farmers doing what he wanted to be doing, he finally decided to return to the family farm as a livelihood in 1955.

Without the financial help of his mother, he would never have been able to even get started. They struggled for many years trying to get by with the barest essentials of equipment. His aunt would be the sales lady for the strawberries right in our dining room. Eventually they graduated to a table at the end of the driveway, manned by Walt Steinhoff. Jim was also selling and delivering his produce to supermarkets, and that is where he met Vince Trojan, who was the Produce Manager for the Safeway Supermarket in Pearl River. Jim spoke to Vince about building a small store and Vince thought it sounded like a good idea. During the daytime hours, Edna Roper worked the store which, at that time was about the size of a two-bay garage. Then Vince came every evening after work and kept the store open until 9 p.m. and all day during the weekend with the help of young people from the neighborhood. In the early years, the store was just open starting in June with strawberries and closed for the season after Christmas.

In 1963, when Jim married Pat Deacon from Oradell, New Jersey, the first peach orchard was planted, the produce building was doubled in size and Jim began building more greenhouses to spread out the season to make it a year-round business. We found it difficult to hire good people and then tell them there was no work in the winter. By 1970, it was evident the make-shift greenhouse attached to the produce store was inadequate, so we built a free-standing building across the driveway. Then, by 1973, we decided we needed a larger produce store which is the one you see today. At first, our customers were upset with us because they liked the store the "old way" but eventually, they grew to accept it.

By 1985, it was obvious the Garden Center needed a permanent building which is where you now visit Gary Schwarz and all his helpers.

In these past 41 years, we have had the help of many of the neighborhood adults and young folks, employing as many as five children from the same family. Now, we are working on the second generation—and we actually have started on the third generation. So, happily, we appear to be headed in the right direction for the future.

Pat Cropsey

The Reserve Fleet

The Hudson River National Defense Fleet established by an act of Congress in 1946, was first located off Tarrytown, one of eight anchorages in the United States to provide a sizable group of merchant ships to support the military effort at the outset of any war. On April 30, 1946, the Hudson River fleet was moved further north to Jones Point (at one time known as Caldwell's Landing) at the foot of Dunderberg Mountain. Here the anchorage remained until the last two ships were towed away on July 8, 1971, to be sold for scrap to Spain. These two ships, both World War II Liberty ships, were the *Edwin M. Stanton* and the *Earl A. Bloomquist*.

The fleet was at its peak with 189 ships in July of 1965. Anchored in ten rows, it extended from the fleet office at the Jones Point dock several miles to the south—to the Lovett Orange & Rockland Power Plant and the Boulderberg House at Tomkins Cove. Several viewing points were established along Route 9W for the hundreds of motorists who stopped daily to look at the ships.

During the Korean War, a total of 130 ships were taken from the Hudson River fleet leaving only 39 remaining. During the Suez crises in 1956, 35 ships were put back into service when British and French ships were diverted from trade routes to supply their nations' armed forces. The Vietnam War required more than 40 ships.

In 1953, when the U.S. Department of Agriculture needed storage space for large volumes of government-owned wheat, it turned to the Hudson River Reserve fleet. During the following ten years as many as 53,563,948 bushels of wheat were loaded into 231 ships. Approximately 255,000 bushels of wheat were stored in each ship with the number of ships carrying wheat at any given time ranging from 70 to 90. The last ship was unloaded in 1963. Ships that had stored wheat afterwards rose about twelve feet higher above the water surface and exposed a bright orange band of rust.

A ventilation system had been installed in the ships, making it possible to maintain the quality of the wheat for long periods of storage. This saved the U.S. government some five million dollars on commercial storage. None of the grain, sold to foreign countries in the 1960s, was found to be spoiled when unloaded.

In an interesting turn of events, the fleet was subject to litigation filed in federal court by Mrs. Theresa Scozzafava, owner of Barney's Restaurant at Jones Point for many years. She claimed the ships were anchored on what she called her "front lawn" because she owned up to 250 feet out into the river. She also claimed the ships obstructed her view of the river itself.

In her action against the U.S. Maritime Commission, which operated the fleet, Mrs. Scozzafava asked $10,000 in rental fees for using her lawn. The case was discontinued because she did not have sufficient funds to pursue it, but the fleet was actually moved a short distance further south. Mrs. Scozzafava died August 11, 1971, at the age of 87 years.

The ships were kept in condition on a year-round basis by a crew of 86 men under the supervision of Charles R. Gindroz of Pearl River, fleet superintendent, and one-time chief engineer on the *George Washington*, the ship that years before had carried President Woodrow Wilson to France and in 1950 burned at Baltimore.

The reserve fleet ships, valued at over $255 million, had their machinery turned over periodically and their internal surfaces sprayed with a coat of preservative oil on a regular basis. Electrical equipment, such as generators and motor wiring, were cleaned and coated with a fungus-retarding varnish. The entire outside of the ships was sprayed with a gray-tinted preservative oil. This was done at least once a year on each ship. The underwater portion of the hull was protected by means of an electric current, a method known as cathodic protection, in which the hull is made passive, preventing corrosion from taking place.

A young boy looks at the Reserve Fleet in 1968. JSC

In the mid-1960s, the U.S. government was spending $735,280 each year for the preservation and maintenance of the Hudson River fleet. This included salaries of workers, who lived locally, and around-the-clock patrol of the fleet to guard against unauthorized persons entering the ships. The patrol was done by tugboats which also used to ferry workers to and from the ships each day.

Although the last two ships were not taken away until July 8, 1971, the Hudson River site was officially closed April 30, 1971.

Scott Webber

This haunting Warren Inglese photograph of the Reserve Fleet captures the end of an era.

1950-1959

The Bridge
and the Boom

The most important event in Rockland in the 1950s can be summed up in two words—the bridge. The semi-rural life before the Tappan Zee Bridge was swept away by booming suburban development. This development was also accelerated by new highways—the New York State Thruway and the Palisades Interstate Parkway. While some viewed these changes as certain doom, the flood of newcomers saw the county as the ideal place to pursue the American dream.

That dream in 1950s America was, on the surface, one of conservative, wholesome family values. Despite the threat of communism around the world, and the racism and social injustices at home, mainstream America hoped that life in the land of rock 'n' roll, modern kitchen appliances and seemingly limitless acreage in the suburbs, would go on quietly and securely.

The following decade would prove that it had all just been a pleasant dream.

The Tappan Zee Bridge. Photo by Warren Inglese.

An event to celebrate: In 1957 the first drive-in bank in the county opened in Haverstraw on the corner of Main and Broadway. Joining in the festivities were (l. to r.) Anne Gagan McCabe, Rosie McCabe and Joan McCabe.   Photo courtesy of Rosie McCabe.

Drive-in movie theaters were very popular across the country in the 1950s. The 303 Drive-in theater in Orangeburg was one of three in Rockland, and all three theaters closed by the end of the century. This photo was taken in 2002 and shows all that is left of a once-thriving business.   Photo by Linda Zimmermann.

Cost of Living: 1950

 Average Income $3,216 per year

 New House $9,000

 **Gallon of Gas 19¢**

 New Car $1,520

Loaf of Bread 14¢

Gallon of Milk 82¢

Dow Jones Average: 235.42

The Tappan Zee Bridge:
Spanning 70 Years of Controversy

In the year 2000, there has been much discussion about what to do about the Tappan Zee Bridge, apparently in such poor condition that it needs to be replaced by a second bridge or a tunnel, connecting Rockland with Westchester County. This controversy is not new and brings to mind the debates many decades ago prior to the completion of the Tappan Zee Bridge on December 15, 1955. Although the bridge is part of the super highway, the New York Thruway, the bridge itself was proposed as early as 1930.

In February of that year, the first mention of a bridge appeared in the press. In the weeks, months, and years to follow there was a great deal of discussion on the matter. Committees, both pro and con, were established. The New York State Legislature created special commissions and authorities that investigated the feasibility of a bridge connecting the two counties.

The bridge would be the only structure between the new Bear Mountain Bridge to the north, and the George Washington Bridge, yet unnamed and still under construction, to the south. Looking back at microfilm copies of the *New York Times,* I came across dozens of articles on the subject, as the proposed bridge was the topic of discussion up and down the Hudson River Valley. As early as February 1930, Rocklanders were appealing to the New York State Legislature to end their winter isolation when ice kept the Nyack-Tarrytown Ferry locked in its slip.

Judge Arthur S. Tompkins proposed a bridge to connect Rockland and Westchester, so that residents would have a swifter alternative to the slow ferry and rail service. Tompkins had key support in his appeal for a bridge. Rockland Assemblyman Fred Horn filed a bill in

Albany, and several local leaders also took an interest. Supporting the bipartisan effort were George Link, Jr., the Clarkstown Republican leader, and State Democratic Chairman, James A. Farley.

Shortly after the Horn bill was filed, a movement began in Dobbs Ferry, in Westchester County, to link with Rockland at that point. Edwin Storms of that Westchester village began the movement, which gained the support of several village and city mayors on the east side of the river. Storms was quoted as saying the bridge would be a boon to Rockland real estate, a rather insightful remark for the time. The western terminus of Storms' bridge would have been in the Orangetown hamlet of Palisades.

New committees were being formed to push for the bridge. One, with its base of operations in Rockland, was a part of a greater Rockland-Lower Hudson-Westchester Bridge Society, and Judge Tompkins was chosen as its honorary president. By the following year, the Legislature provided for a study of the proposed bridge. By August, State Senator Seabury C. Mastick of Pleasantville wrote a bill that created a Rockland-Westchester Bridge and Tunnel Authority. When it finally passed both houses of the Legislature a real study was conducted and plans to build a bridge between Nyack and Tarrytown went before the Federal government. Shipping interests objected to the structure and the Federal government ditched the plans.

Early in February 1936, the Legislature saw still another plan. This bridge would connect Hastings-on-Hudson with a spot in Rockland County just north of the state line. Mass meetings were held in support of the bridge at the new location. Proponents said this would

179

be a better location because the causeway would be shorter, as the river there is only a mile wide. The river at Nyack-Tarrytown spot is over three miles wide.

Things being as they are (or were), plans for the bridge were dropped and the older plans for a Nyack-Tarrytown link were again brought out. The War Department was approached to approve specific plans for a bridge after the Rockland-Westchester Authority decided it would be more feasible than a tunnel at the same location. In August, the bridge was finally approved. Engineers and others said shipping would not be hampered, nor would the harbor facilities at Tarrytown.

This is when massive objections began to flood in. Letters against the bridge appeared in the *New York Times*. Demonstrations took place in Rockland villages and meetings were held mid-river.

In August 1936, Rockland author Elmer S. Hadar wrote in the *New York Times* that the bridge was unnecessary. Hadar said, "'The bridge is not needed... Taxpayers' money should not go for such an unnecessary project." His letter went on to say traffic would not support a bridge at that point. He recalled the closing of the ferry at Piermont a few miles to the south, "Because there wasn't enough traffic to warrant its operation."

In Hadar's letter he stated the traffic on River Road, which parallels the river, would be too great a burden. He made no reference to his property in Grand View that would be affected by the bridge. He called for construction of the bridge, if there must be a bridge, at Piermont.

The letter had no effect on the state or the crossing authority. On September 12, state surveyors began to work in Grand View-on-Hudson. They began their chores on Hadar's property.

According to articles published in the *New York Times* on that date, a protest occurred in Grand View. "Led by Mrs. Elmer S. Hadar, wife of an author, illustrator, women of this community (Grand View) banded themselves together this afternoon and with the help of local police routed a group of surveyors who had invaded the village to survey the western anchorage for the proposed Nyack-Tarrytown Bridge."

The sortie was a success in one respect—it banded the village together. The *New York Times* article points out the surveyors were working on the Hadar property. Following the protests, the village gave its police chief permission to increase the police force and keep the surveyors away.

Protestors, at another meeting at Nyack, condemned the bridge. Ironically leading the discussion was former Supreme Court Judge Tompkins, who originally brought up the issue. Now the Judge had gone on record as being against the span at Nyack.

The dispute grew. Published sources referred to it as the Bridge War in the Hudson Valley. The newly formed Hudson River Society entered the picture opposing the desecration of the beauty spots in the river valley. As the protestors in Grand View doubled their police force, the State surveyors conducted their operations along 9W, just north of the Grand View line. The people of the village kept a watchful eye, making sure the invaders would not enter the village again.

Leaves were turning autumnal colors in the Hudson River Valley as Rocklanders kept telegraph lines between Grand View and Albany busy. Over 400 residents of the area sent a telegram to Governor Lehman. Articles in the *Times* showed that Hadar had led the telegram protests. The message called for an inquiry into the bridge issue. Hadar said he was confident because of the signatures of prominent figures. Actresses Katharine Cornell of Palisades and Helen Hayes of Upper Nyack were among the signers. Thomas W. Lamont, a large estate owner in Palisades, and Mrs. Mary Mowbray-Clarke, landscape consultant and founder of the New City artists' community, joined them, as well as denizens of the South Mountain Road colony.

By month's end, Governor Lehman told residents that the plan for the bridge was only tentative and the site had not been chosen. Lehman made his comments following the dedication of the State Rehabilitation Hospital buildings in West Haverstraw. That same afternoon, the Governor also received petitions with 5,000 names, favoring the span across the river.

Still another protest followed. This one took place mid-river. Irate residents of both Rockland and Orange counties, with some residents from the river valley, using

This *Journal-News* headline on November 19, 1936 announces the (temporary) end to bridge plans.
Courtesy of Craig Long.

the facilities of the North River Ferry Company, joined at mid-river to continue their protests.

The fight continued. After a six-year battle by those against the bridge, plans were scrapped in 1936, but only for a while. In 1950, the bridge fight was renewed.

Late in 1950, Rockland residents were still critical of the idea of a span across the Hudson. Some opponents said it would cost much more than the State's estimated $65,000,000. Opponents were still highly critical of the location: the widest spot on the river. These critics still called for construction of the bridge three miles to the south at Piermont, where the river is only one mile wide.

Legally, however, the bridge could not be built at the southernmost proposed spot because agreements with the Port Authority of New York would prohibit it. These agreements, written to protect toll interests on Port Authority-owned bridges in and around New York City, were introduced after the controversy of the 1930s.

A prophetic promotion for the bridge in the *Journal-News* on January 3, 1954. Note the arching center span that was the original design plan for the bridge. Courtesy of Craig Long.

In early December 1950, the exact location of the bridge had not been made public. It was almost a sure thing it would be built at a point between the Orangetown villages of South Nyack and Grand View. The speculation as to this fact was proven to be true when final plans were revealed later in the month.

Fear was growing in the Nyack area that more than 250 buildings would have to be razed in the construction of the span. Not only would the span cause the demolition of so many buildings, but the several approach roads would also take more houses as well. At a December 17 meeting, residents of the area again

expressed their opposition to the bridge. New opponents entered the field with more reasons for being against the bridge. Some residents of South Nyack feared the bridge would be a target for atomic attack!

Late in the year, Bertram D. Tallamy, chairman of the New York Thruway Authority, spoke in defense of the bridge. He stated that a maximum of 147 buildings in the Nyack area would be in the path of the new road and bridge. He stated most of these buildings would be relocated on other sites that were available.

Before Tallamy's statements, residents calling themselves the Tappan Zee Civic Association appealed in Westchester County for support against the bridge. Not much support was gained in that camp. The fight against the bridge was now a losing battle.

One last attempt in 1950 to stop the bridge took place at a meeting of the Rockland County Board of Supervisors. According to the *New York Times,* Orangetown Supervisor Harold A. Williams told the board he learned from "competent authorities" the proposed Thruway bridge would cause ice jams which would threaten fuel and oil shipments north of Nyack.

Williams and Clarkstown Supervisor Irvin F. Dillon were appointed to state this fact to the War Department the following month at a special hearing, which they did, according to the published reports. Three months prior to Williams' icy statement the board went on record against the entire Thruway-in-Rockland project and the Hudson span. How's that for progress?

The bridge was built. Now, 45 years after its completion, some people still complain. Some think the bridge is ugly. Some say the opposite. The biggest concern is that the Tappan Zee Bridge is in disrepair and can no longer accommodate the traffic.

For those people with a technical mind: The bridge, over 15,000 feet long, is 90 feet wide. It took 153,900 cubic yards of concrete and 14,160 tons of reinforced steel, not to mention 1,602,200 feet of timber. By the way, that's 303 miles of timber. (Michael Blake, former news director for WLNA Radio in Peekskill dug up these figures.) Mike also stated that one side of the causeway is lighted by Orange and Rockland Utilities, while the opposite side is powered by Con Edison. Months after the bridge was completed it was named after the portion of the river it crosses, The Tappan Zee.

Harold L. Laroff, 2000

181

LOOKING TOWARD NYACK. Ramp nearly completed, center piers under construction.

FABRICATING road bed sections at Grassy Point.

FLOATING a road bed section into place.

CENTER PIER superstructure under construction after all road bed sections are in place.

Different stages of the construction of the Tappan Zee Bridge. Top left: looking toward Nyack and nearly completed ramp. Above right: Fabricating road bed section at Grassy Point. Bottom left: Floating a bed section into place. Bottom right: Construction of the center pier superstructure.

Photos courtesy of Orange & Rockland Archives.

Cutting the ribbon on the opening day of the Tappan Zee Bridge on December 15, 1955. From left to right: Helen Hayes (with flowers), Assemblyman Robert Wamsley, Mrs. Harriman (cutting the ribbon), Governor Harriman and Chairman Tallamy of the Thruway Authority.

Local schoolchildren held parades and marched across the new span. Tolls were free the first day, so one resident drove back and forth for hours, knowing he would be paying and paying for years to come!

Photo courtesy of O&R Archives.

Palisades Interstate Parkway

Stretching for a distance of 43 miles and traversing New Jersey and New York areas west of the Hudson River, the Palisades Interstate Parkway, now under construction, will form an integral part of the comprehensive system of arterial highways and parkways in the New York metropolitan region.

Long advocated by the Palisades Interstate Park Commission for the relief of traffic congestion west of the Hudson, this interstate project will start at the New Jersey end of the George Washington Bridge, extend 12 miles along the top of the Palisades cliffs to the NY-NJ state line, and continue through the Hudson highlands in Rockland and Orange counties for a distance of 31 miles, to the vast 40,000-acre Bear Mountain-Harriman State Parks.

The northerly terminus in New York will tie in with major arterial routes leading to the north, east and west, including the proposed New York State Thruway to Buffalo. The Palisades Interstate Parkway not only will visit the State parks under the jurisdiction of the commission, but will also serve millions of motorists on cross country trips. Like all other parkways in this area, it will be restricted to pleasure cars only.

Continuous traffic movement at reasonable speed, consistent with safety, has been the controlling objective in the design of the parkway. Many unique and modern features have been incorporated into the new parkway such as landscaped center malls, mountable curbs with light-reflecting qualities, accelerating lanes, take-offs ahead of grade separation structures, darkened concrete to prevent glare, and traffic interchanges have been provided at 20 main intersections.

Watt's 'N Therms, April, 1953 (O&R Archives)

The intersection on the Palisades Parkway and NYS Thruway. Note how undeveloped the area was in the mid-1950s. Photo courtesy of O&R Archives.

Make Way for the Thruway

In the fall of 1945 word came from Albany that the decision had been made to construct a great superhighway, called the "Thruway," as a major post-war project. Gov. Thomas E. Dewey had urged the legislature to authorize the Department of Public Works to establish the route for a $202,000,000 six-lane express highway. It was hailed as the "most important single engineering project" in the state since the digging of the Erie Canal, more than a century before.

The Thruway was to span the state from Buffalo to Albany and south to the New York/New Jersey border, terminating at Suffern. This small Rockland County village would serve as the gateway to "New York's Main Street," as the proposed roadway had been dubbed. It was at this point traffic from New York City using the George Washington Bridge would cross over into New Jersey, whose arterial Routes 4 and 2 (later renamed Route 17) would bring the motoring public to the grand highway.

When the project was initially proposed in the mid-1940s, area residents of western Rockland heralded the news. The main streets and side roads of the villages of Suffern, Hillburn and Sloatsburg located at the mouth of the Ramapo Pass, had for years become a favorite route of car and truck traffic, seeking a path to upstate New York, the Catskill regions and beyond. Traffic had become increasingly unbearable, especially on weekends. On Friday nights, a solid line of traffic, bumper to bumper, stretched northbound from Ramsey, New Jersey, north to Sloatsburg. By Sunday, the reverse occurred. Residents complained about being "house-bound" as they watched a steady stream of cars and trucks creep along their main streets.

Official traffic counts conducted in the 1930s showed 2,395 cars an hour passed through the region. By the 1940s, 30,000 cars a day traveled through this narrow gap. The data collected showed what residents knew all too well—traffic had a stranglehold on this narrow valley. The two older highways, Routes 17 and 59, funneled the congestion through this major transportation corridor already crowded by the Ramapo River and the mainline of the Erie Railroad. The historic

Ramapo Pass had become impassable. Recognizing that relief was several years away, however, a 1948 local newspaper editorial lamented, "We can only hope we won't have to wait too long."

In the intervening years, prior to the first shovel of dirt moved in Suffern, plans were on the drawing board in Albany that would change the course of the mighty roadway and forever alter the face of Rockland County's landscape.

In the spring of 1950, two barges floated off the South Nyack and Grand View shore. Engineers on board were taking test borings for a span to cross the Hudson River. This had been done before in 1936. At that time, the idea was to see if a bridge, linking Rockland and Westchester would be feasible—just a bridge, no major highway planned to connect with it. The idea was scrapped.

This time, fourteen years later, they had a roadway—the Thruway at the western end of the county. If engineers could design a bridge to cross the Hudson on the east side of Rockland County, why not connect the two?

Bertram D. Tallamy, chairman of the New York State Thruway Authority, responded to local opposition to the plans with the following statement. "Since the Thruway is an enterprise of the broadest possible scope, the location of any particular portion must be determined in relation to the project as a whole. Local considerations cannot be accepted as governing in the choice of the Thruway route!" He then proceeded to authorize the plans to build the highway across Rockland County.

The first drawings showed the roadway running from the shore of the Hudson at the Nyacks, westward, passing to the north of Spring Valley through Hillcrest and swinging down through the northern part of Suffern, and then into Hillburn and Sloatsburg. When released to the public, the maps produced fierce opposition on both sides of the county.

After studying the issues raised by the public, the Thruway Authority announced a revised alignment in January 1952. This proposed new route passed south of Spring Valley and swept south of Suffern along the New York/New Jersey border. To the delight of the Authority, the new design would save them $1.2 million.

Area residents were outraged as more than 230 homes countywide would be lost. Considerable opposition forced the Thruway to reexamine their plans. By April, they unveiled their third and final plan. The major change involved shifting the road north of Suffern, crossing over Lake Antrim, saving 60 homes and protecting Suffern's well fields located in the west section of the village. The Thruway reported the revisions would add $3 million to the cost of the project. However, it was of a more direct route and a more ideal

alignment. On the eastern shore, more than 140 houses in Nyack and South Nyack stood in the path of the new highway's approach to the bridge.

The New York State Thruway engineers found Rockland's section of roadway more challenging, more intricate, and more expensive. When the highway opened in 1955, the 19 miles of concrete in Rockland resulted in a $41,000,000 tab, excluding the value of properties bought for the right of way. The final tally represented a cost 60% higher than any other portion of the Thruway. The 427 miles between New York City and Buffalo averaged $1,340,000 per mile. In Rockland, the average mile cost $2,138,000.

Rockland's "rocky" geography and existing roadways added to the expense. Blasting and rock cuts were numerous, and needed to maintain the superhighway's standard 3% grade. The county was "crisscrossed by some of the busiest highways in the country" at the time. In order to carry the highway across the county, overpasses, underpasses and other bridges had to be built—an average of two per mile. The six interchanges and two toll barriers (Suffern and Spring Valley) were three times the average for access and control points anywhere along the entire length of the Thruway.

The interchange at Suffern (which was really located in Hillburn), was billed as the "most complex and one of the busiest anywhere on the Thruway." The greatest

Clearing a path to begin blasting the rock cut for the Thruway in West Nyack (looking west) in the 1950s (photo by John Scott), and that same area in the year 2001 (photo by Linda Zimmermann).

184

radial curve on the route was at Suffern, where an elevated road turned to enter the Ramapo Pass. This bridge of "unusual design," had a price tag of $2.5 million and was an all-welded structure 800 feet in length, which carried six lanes of traffic over Route 59 and the Erie Railroad.

What the Erie Railroad had done to awaken a sleepy Rockland County of the 1850s, occurred in a similar fashion a century later with the Thruway. Making way for the New York State Thruway left an indelible mark on our county's history.

Craig Long

The Thruway interchange (left) in Suffern made the cover of Rockland Light and Power Company's (the precursor of O&R) annual report in 1956. The company was accurately predicting the impending demand for gas and electric service in the county in the post-Tappan Zee Bridge, Palisades Interstate Parkway and Thruway era. Photo courtesy of O&R Archives.

The Thruway originally also had a tollbooth in Suffern (above). Postcard courtesy of Kenneth Kral.

Memories of Moving to Rockland

One Sunday morning in early September 1959 at our Cliffside Park, New Jersey apartment, we came across a real estate ad in the Sunday paper that stated "WELCOME TO THE SIXTH BOROUGH," in Orangeburg, New York. The house was a colonial (which was what we always wanted) and the price was a hefty $18,900. We say hefty, because we could only afford at most $15,000 with the salary my husband was making, and I being a full time at-home mom. I was 25 years of age at the time and my husband was 29. This would be our first home. We had a two and a half-year old girl, and one more on the way, and my sick mother would then be able to come live with us so that I could care for her.

Our venture to see this model home happened when my mother was visiting us from New York, and she said, "Why don't you take a drive while I am here to babysit?" My mother then packed us a lunch and drinks, and we headed out to explore this colonial house.

Much to our surprise, we arrived at exit 6 on the Palisades Parkway in Rockland County in about 15 minutes. We had no idea it was so close to Cliffside

Park. We took a tour of the model houses, and just fell in love with the colonial model. Our drawback was still the price of $18,900. We drove back to our apartment in Cliffside, and my mother was surprised to see us back so soon. We told her all about the experience, the price, and her reaction was that she wanted to see the house that we were interested in. Because it was so close, and we still had our lunch in the car that she had packed earlier, we packed diapers and took our daughter and headed out once again to this sixth borough.

My mother's first reaction was the same as ours. She fell in love with the same model as we had. We then sat down with the salesman and went over all the financing. With all the extras that we wanted, totaling $20,500, the salesman convinced us we could afford the house. We went back to our apartment with a full head.

That night we could not sleep, and just talked about should we, or shouldn't we? Could we, or couldn't we? My mother must have had a sleepless night also, because came morning she said we should buy the house. Her statement to us was, "If you cannot carry it, what is the worst thing that could happen, you sell and go back to an apartment." It sounded so simple coming from her. She had more courage than we had, and reassured us we could make it.

After that conversation with her, we then started the procedure to purchase the house of our dreams at $20,500—I at the age of 25, thinking I would never own a house, signing all the required papers as I visualized myself in a striped suit going to prison if I could not make the payments. (Vivid imagination, but true). We now reconciled ourselves to a move to Orangeburg, on December 12, 1959. It was a cold, dreary day, raining, and I was 4 months pregnant—moving from a lovely large apartment near friends I loved, to the unknown. It was a very traumatic day in our lives. (My advice is never to move while pregnant!)

We Orangeburg housewives did not have any means of transportation. We shopped for groceries once a week when my husband was home with the car at the only food store—Grandway on Route 59 in Nanuet. We had a pharmacy and general store here in Orangeburg by the railroad tracks on Western Highway, named Sid's. He literally sold everything you could imagine from drugs to jeans. The Taystee Bread deliveryman would come to the door with a basket full of breads, pies, cookies and doughnuts. We had door-to-door delivery of these items, plus milk, laundry services and dry cleaning services.

In our forty years as residents here in Orangeburg, we have seen our children grow up, going to school at Orangeburg Elementary, St. Catherine School of Religion, then to the Blauvelt Middle School, and then to Tappan Zee High School. We have seen the development of the Betsy Rose Estates, homes go up on Lester Drive, Sid's department store torn down making way for Prell Garden apartments. The local shopping center with food stores as Waldbaum's, then A & P, and now C-town, along with other convenient stores such as dry cleaners, card shop, the bank and post office.

We were growing at such speed that even we, as people moving from a congested area to the country, were beginning to feel crowded in with too much building going on. All the politicians chalked it up to progress. I feel that we are killing ourselves with our chopping down trees to make room for more houses, or industry welcomed to the county polluting our waters and air. We feel there should be a limit, and let suburbia stay what we all had in mind when we all moved to this area. Our children had to move up further north in order for them to afford houses because of the desirability of this area. I wish they could move down the block as we all did growing up in New York City, with families being closer in mileage, and in unity.

Mrs. Patricia Sidoti, 2000

Building a Home

Joseph and Diane Michalak were planning to get married in May of 1959. In the fall of 1958, they crossed the Tappan Zee Bridge from Westchester for the first time since the bridge had opened, and soon found themselves on Ludvigh Road in Nanuet. The following is their story of moving to Rockland.

We spotted a model Cape Cod home in a development known as Sunrise Estates. They were advertising the homes on lots for $16,300, or $17,050 with two roof dormers.

Well, we looked, saw what lot we liked and put down a $10 deposit to hold it. A few weeks later we made our $1,300 down payment. We were told our taxes would be $380 a year.

In January of 1959 we found out that our house would not be ready for May, so we postponed our wedding. They promised to complete the house by the first of September. We were married on September 12, but the house was not ready until October so we had to live with my parents.

When we moved in there was still no driveway, no walks, no landscaping (just mounds of dirt), and wooden planks ran from the street to our steps. We were the first to move into the development and the first night was scary. It was pitch black—no streetlights or

neighbors' lights. When Halloween came, we were ready for the trick or treaters, but nobody showed up.

Now after forty years we are still here. We raised three children who all married and left the nest. So much has changed in that time—it was hard to find a pizza parlor other than the Nanuet Hotel, there was a big swamp where the Nanuet Mall now stands, there was no mail delivery, and few stores in the area.

Now, forty years later, we still love Rockland County as much as we did when we first took that ride across the Tappan Zee Bridge that beautiful fall afternoon.

Joseph W. Michalak

In this series of photos (continued from previous page): Diane Michalak stands on the mounds of dirt on their home site. The Cape Cod house begins to take shape, and the house is finally completed.

Photos courtesy of Diane and Joseph Michalak.

An Insider's View: Shanks Village

The twenty-two months we lived in Shanks Village could be considered some of our finest as well as our most trying times, and definitely our growing up years.

Russ and I met at a teacher's college in Illinois in September 1949. We were married in June 1950 and our first son was born in 1951. In June 1951, we were living in a two-bedroom apartment in Shanks Village. We slept on cots, the bathroom had a shower, but no tub, and the apartment was heated by only a space heater in the living room. The rent was $35 a month and we had to pay an extra dollar monthly because we had an electric refrigerator.

The wives were wary of one of our neighbors, as she was quite a looker—with no husband around. She was always in need of "small repairs," which required a man to "fix or repair." Another family across from us had several children and everybody always yelled.

We were not too happy when our nextdoor neighbor moved. The new tenants caused us great concern—too many comings and

goings, which made us wonder if drugs were being sold, but we never did know. Emmet Maines, Chief of Police, recommended we look for other housing.

Once the government was anxious to close down the Village, we decided to move out. But even though almost fifty years have passed, we still keep in touch with our closest neighbors with whom we shared so many wonderful memories.

Mary McCandless

The McCandless' registration certificate from June 21, 1951.

...In 1950 North Korea invades South Korea...The population of the U.S. is 150 million...The number of drive-in theaters doubles to 2,200...In 1951 the Rosenbergs are found guilty of giving atomic bomb secrets to Soviets...The U.S. tests the first hydrogen bomb...Tibet falls to China...

187

Images of Korea

Charles Miller and his wife, Winnie, lived in Pearl River for 38 years. He enjoyed a very successful career with IBM, retiring in 1987. In 1997, he and his wife moved to Ormond Beach, Florida.

While visiting family and friends in June of 2001, we met to discuss his experiences in the Korean War. He brought along a photo album that documented his time there. (His girlfriend at the time had put together the album. He would mail her the film. She developed it and sent the pictures back to him in Korea. He labeled them and sent them back to her to mount in an album—and amazingly none were lost!) Although the events he discussed occurred fifty years earlier, the recollections were as vivid as if they had happened yesterday.

When Charles Miller was graduating high school in 1950, the situation was heating up in Korea and military recruiters were trying to persuade the members of his class to enlist. Two of his friends did enlist, and Miller was also willing (his two older brothers had served in WWII), but his father, who had been in WWI, insisted that he should stay home and learn a trade. However by April of 1951, Miller realized the plumbing supply business was not for him, and he enlisted in the U.S Marine Corps.

Miller became a radio specialist and arrived in Korea with the 2nd Amphibian Tractor Battalion in February of 1952. He soon learned that his two high school friends who had enlisted earlier had been in the hellish battles at the Chosin Reservoir.

Death was a constant reality in Korea, especially on their river patrols on the Han and Imjim rivers where bloated bodies regularly were pulled from the water. "You get used to it," Miller stated plainly, although emotion played in his eyes.

His unit was also subjected to artillery barrages that lasted for days. North Korean infiltrators were constantly trying to penetrate their positions, including young boys who would detonate grenades—while holding them.

Upon returning home in March of 1953, there were no parades or celebrations awaiting him. No one thanked Miller and the other soldiers for risking their lives. Korea is often called the "Forgotten War," but for soldiers like Charles Miller who experienced so much, and for the families of those killed, wounded, or missing in action, the memories will live on.

Linda Zimmermann

Miller in camp (left) in Korea. He labeled "My Tent" in this photo (above) taken from a hilltop overlooking the Marine's camp near the Han River. Miller and Buddy Harp (below left) return enemy fire with a 50-caliber machine gun.

Photos courtesy of Charles Miller.

Charles Miller in 2001. Note the license plate—once a Marine, always a Marine.
Semper Fi.
Photo by Linda Zimmermann.

188

...On July 27, 1953, an armistice was signed in Panmunjom ending the Korean War, on terms that had roughly been agreed upon two years earlier. The final toll was over one million South Koreans killed, over one million Communists killed, over 100,000 Americans wounded and 25,000 killed. America's first experience with "limited war" would be repeated with even more devastating results just a decade later in Vietnam...

KOREAN WAR
In Memoriam

ABLONDI, BRUNO
AUGENBLICK, IRA
BAKER, PHILIP T.
BROWN, ROBERT A.
CAPUTO, LOUIS
CERVENE, SAM J.
COOK, HENRY M. (JR)
DE FREESE, SAMUEL W.
DE GROAT, ROLAND
DIEDERICH, HAROLD M.
DUHAIME, LOUIS S.
FREYTAG, PETER D.
FLOTARD, RAYMOND
HERRING, WILLIAM

HIRSCHBERGER, ALEX
HORN, CHARLES
KEENAN, GREGORY
LAYDON, ROBERT
LUCAS, WILLIAM H.
MACKEY, JOHN R.
McDADE, WILLIAM
McGRATH, EDMUND
NORTH, NORMAN P.
OSBORNE, JAMES
SMITH, JAMES N.
TYRELL, STANLEY
VAN DUNK, WILLIAM

Missile Air Defense System

During the 1950s, most residents were concerned about over-development, schools, sewage systems and taxes. There was also something else to worry about—something that if it occurred would make everything else meaningless.

The threat of nuclear warfare hung over the heads of all Americans, and especially for Rocklanders who quite literally dealt with nuclear weapons above their heads every day.

Jokingly referred to as the big "golfball" on the hill in Orangeburg, the grim reality was no joke—the "golfball" was a radar installation that was part of a missile defense system with both high explosive and nuclear capabilities. The launcher and control areas were in operation from 1955 to 1974, and held Nike Ajax and Nike Hercules missiles.

According to Rockland resident Paul Suchanyc, a retired General in the Army Reserve, who was stationed at the Nike base, the idea of a nuclear missile defense system was simple, yet deadly. If an aircraft was approaching the New York area carrying nuclear weapons, conventional explosives alone would not be effective. The aircraft and nuclear weapons onboard would need to be vaporized, and that's where the missiles with nuclear warheads would do their job.

Fortunately, the missiles never needed to be launched, and with the end of the Cold War, there seemed to no longer be any need for local missile defense systems, and the installation was eventually dismantled.

However, after the terrorist attacks of September 11, 2001, missile defense once again became a hotly debated issue. Had modern missile batteries been in place in the area, perhaps the hijacked jets would never have struck the World Trade Center towers. But that debate will have to enter the annals of history's "what ifs."

Linda Zimmermann

Previous page: A guard stands by the HIPAR radar dome in Orangeburg. Left: The launcher site in Orangeburg. Below: Two Hercules missiles on the launch pads at the site.

Photos courtesy of Paul Suchanyc.

During the Cold War, the Army deployed 145 Nike Hercules batteries. Four were in the New York area.

The Mighty Midget

On March 25, 1954, the Valley Cottage Civic Association hosted a lecture entitled, "Transistor, the Mighty Midget." Mr. W.H. Britnell, engineer for N.Y. Telephone Co., demonstrated this new "marvelous invention" that would "streamline our homes, our industries, our military concepts, revolutionize our communications and affect our everyday life."

These were no exaggerations. The tiny transistor did indeed bring about revolutionary advances from bulky vacuum tubes, and made all kinds of electronic gadgets available to the consumer, such as handheld transistor radios. A second electronic revolution would occur with microchips in the 1970s, paving the way for personal computers.

Fortunately, more than electronics would change in the decades following the 1950s, as the transistor lecture announcement had stressed that the material would be simplified and presented in a manner that could be "clearly understood by women and men alike."

Linda Zimmermann,
from material contributed by Phil Klein

Attracting Teenagers: Appliances or Rock 'n' Roll?

A teenagers' Rock 'n' Roll party in our Nyack appliance store—future customers learn about electric table cookery.

The Company received national publicity in an electrical merchandising journal with a report of a "teenage cook show" in September that attracted 450 youngsters. A rock 'n' roll party took place in the main floor showroom (Nyack), and cooking demonstrations were held in the auditorium. The purpose of the show was to encourage the teenagers to prepare party foods with electric appliances.

O&R Annual Report, 1957

Caption reads: A teenagers' Rock 'n' Roll party in our Nyack appliance store—future customers learn about electric table cookery.

190

Simpler Dining Recalls a Simpler Way of Life

The restaurants of my youth, though fewer in number in a much smaller Rockland, were as notable then as they are now in memory.

As a Spring Valleyite, I must note Cullen's well-presented hotel/restaurant off North Madison Avenue; the Villa Lafayette on Route 45, where service clubs met for years; and Perruna's on Main Street, mecca for many Rockland and Bergen County youngsters on weekends. I'll also include Nanuet Restaurant, the king of all pizza places, in a hamlet so vital to adjacent Spring Valley, that in the forties and fifties it could have been a geographic extension.

In the 1940s and 1950s Rockland restaurants were well known for their ambience (they all had a special, though simple character), food and the people you were bound to run into. Most families could not afford much eating out, nor would most mothers acquiesce to other than their home-cooked meals. But there were always special occasions, like birthdays or weekend evenings when a trip to a Rockland restaurant or one in Bergen (Rocklanders' second home) was in order.

The mood of the diners determined whether it would be, say, Cullen's or, on special occasions, John Martin's Bear Mountain Inn, which he managed from 1941 to 1965. Many a Rockland youngster got his first taste of the woodsy elegance at Bear Mountain, either at dinner with his parents, or in my case, after a junior prom at Spring Valley High. I can still recall the grown-up atmosphere of the Inn, with its huge, wagon wheel-type lighting, massive tree-trunk supports and the Big Band music that got me on the floor with the basic box step. The Bear Mountain Inn so captivated me that I would return there often in later years until about the time John Martin left and many things changed.

Those were the times, too, the 1940s and 1950s, when pizza had not yet come to Rockland via the downtown and shopping strip parlors. You bought tavern pie from certain restaurants, and their slower ovens made for a 20-minute wait, but produced pies with a different flavor, distinctive to the restaurant's old recipes.

When Martio's pizza of Spring Valley appeared, now in downtown Nanuet, the modern-day tradition of the 10-minute pizza came to Rockland. There was a somewhat smaller pizza operation in Nyack, but Martio's became THE Rockland pizza parlor. The taste of Martio's original pizza still lingers, as does the memory of the 15-cent slice, just right for young person's budget.

When I was about 19 or 20, I happened upon the Cedar Restaurant in Tomkins Cove, off Route 9W, where what had to be my mother's double (in cooking abilities, that is) offered up the best roast beef platter available, with thinly sliced meat; mashed potatoes minus lumps; fresh snappy green beans; and with gravy that wasn't greasy, all served leisurely but efficiently for about four dollars. Given the right company, it was elegance of its own sort.

It's difficult to find simple roast beef platters anymore. And the cost is much higher.

Simpler times. Simpler palates. But for young people in Rockland then, even the limited restaurants, with their unique menus and welcoming hosts and waiters, opened the door far and wide to an occasional treat.

Arthur H. Gunther, *The Journal News*, 1/00

Henry Kulle's School of Life in the Valley

History and heritage, are passed along as much by mouth as by the written word. It was in the former manner that many young people learned from Henry Kulle about Spring Valley's past. This man of Rockland automobile tire fame actually got his start in harnesses and saddles, in his father's shop that began in the village in 1885. The horseless carriage literally drove Henry to change.

I make note of him because the family business is now 100-plus-years-old. When it began, Spring Valley was a crossroads for travelers and freight haulers on the Old Nyack Turnpike from Nyack to Suffern, and for people heading into and out of New Jersey. Good place for a harness and saddle shop.

By the time I first visited Kulle's, about 1959, Henry was purely into the tire and battery business. If you were a young driver in the Spring Valley of my day, two things happened when you turned 16: you got your junior license and you went to Kulle's for your first set of tires on your first jalopy.

You quickly learned that there was no waiting room at Kulle's, just a line that sometimes stretched down Lawrence Street and into Kulle's alley, where Henry, speaking quietly but *always* speaking and hopping around (he never sat down), eventually came to your car, helped you decide on tires and then took hand tools to break the bead on the rims and to mount the new tires.

You were expected to help dismount the tires from the car, to hustle as much as Kulle did for all the days of his life (until he died at 84 in 1987). You were thus introduced into grown-up society, where ordinary folk, as well as rich and famous ones, chewed the fat, made jokes and welcomed the new kids on the block to the world of cars and tires and batteries, a few curse words and other "adult" talk. So it was with your father, your grandfather, and then perhaps your own offspring.

At Kulle's you also learned about Spring Valley's history, things such as its last "president" (Charles Heitman) and his organizational changes that pushed the Valley into the modern age. It was like going to a meeting of the Spring Valley Historical Society, with Henry as the sole director, board of trustees and resident historian.

Kulle's has served more than generations, more than businesses (he once got the battery concession for the large Widmann Bakery Co. truck line in the 1930s when he guaranteed all of the trucks would start for each morning's delivery). He and Edward Ball (his nephew) and now Ball's sons Thomas and James, offered and continue to offer tires with civility, camaraderie and conversation. You get all that in an alley "waiting room," and the wait is worth the effort.

Young people are still joining the "club" and it looks as if Kulle's is ready to mount another 100 years on our rim of history.

Arthur H. Gunther, *Rockland Journal-News*, 2/13/96

The Drive-In

America's love affair with the automobile in the 1950s spurred a new industry. There were restaurants, like the A&W on Route 303 in West Nyack, where waitresses would serve you in your car. In 1957, the first bank with a drive-up window opened in Haverstraw. Drive-in movie theaters became wildly popular for families, groups of teenagers, and couples looking for a little romance. It appeared as if people wanted to do everything in their cars.

Rockland had three drive-in movies. Route 303 had two of them, one in Orangeburg and one in West Nyack. The third was the Rockland Drive-in on Route 59 in Monsey, which opened in 1955 with capacity for 1,800 cars.

Each drive-in had a substantial snack bar that would be bustling with activity during the intermissions between movies (there was always a first-run movie, followed by a second-run movie, with the first often repeated again for those who really didn't want to go home). And who can forget those ten-minute intermission films of dancing hot dogs, piping hot pizzas and buttery popcorn, with reminders every minute as to the time remaining to the next movie?

As a child, I particularly loved going to the Rockland Drive-in, because they not only had a wooden-horse carousel, but a small train that would take its tiny passengers through a tunnel under the movie screen! So much excitement—it's no wonder I could never stay awake through the second feature.

When I reached my teens in the 1970s, the drive-in continued to be a popular destination, albeit for somewhat different reasons. Sometimes we even watched the movies.

Unfortunately by the 1980s, escalating operating costs and high taxes, coupled with cable television and video rentals, spelled doom for all of Rockland's drive-in theaters. The speakers that used to hang on your car window are now collectibles being sold on eBay, weeds have overtaken the parking lots and the massive outdoor screens are slowly crumbling from neglect.

Of course, it wasn't always smooth sailing at the drive-in—there were the mosquitoes, and the smells from the sewage plant in Orangeburg, and sometimes it would be too hot, or too cold, or it would rain—but there was something unique about the drive-in, something for young and old alike.

Watching a movie under the stars with some first-rate junk food and your family, friends or a date, was a wonderful part of American culture that is now all but lost. For the DVD and microwave popcorn generations of Rocklanders who will never know the experience of the drive-in, I feel sorry.

Linda Zimmermann

1950s Memories

- From 1950 to 1960, Clarkstown's population increased from 15,674 to 33,196, an increase of 112%.
- In 1956, the Nanuet Bowling center boasted new "automatic electrical pin spotters."
- In 1957, there were record sales of air conditioners, fans, refrigerators and freezers.

- In the business area in Nyack, there were three great places for ice cream:
  1. McDermott's on Route 59
  2. Eagle on Main Street
  3. Jerry D'Auria's on Main Street

- The best pizza, and teen hangout, was Paone's. Cy and Terri were the owners and took us all under their wings.
- The building of the NYS Thruway was a big event for me and the other kids in our South Nyack neighborhood. At noon every summer day, we would run home to get our bagged lunch and sit under a tree with two workers, whose names were George and Peck.

Shortly before the TZ Bridge was opened to traffic, we were able to walk the length of the bridge.
- While skating on the Hudson River, a boy named Tommy Steen drowned. Nyack then opened the skating rink at Memorial Park to allow a safe place for local children to skate.

Maureen Clune

The Ice Storm of 1953

The middle of January 1953, will be remembered for a long time by most Rockland Light employees as the time of The Ice Storm. It all began quietly enough with a gentle fall of snow during the early morning of Thursday, January 8. This changed to rain during the day and by night things began to get icy.

By Friday morning, ice had built up on trees and wires and failures occurred faster and faster. By afternoon, it was a losing battle in spite of the best efforts of every lineman and troubleman, plus extra contract crews. By evening, it was estimated that 28,000 of the 42,000 customers in Rockland and Bergen Counties were without service. Branches and trees, even wires, gave way under the tremendous weight of ice. Not less than a thousand service lines had been pulled away from houses. Travel became dangerous and repair work extremely so. The cracking and crash of ice-laden branches was continuous throughout the night.

Saturday morning presented a picture of wreckage never before seen in this section. Branches, trees and wires were all over, tangled in a hopeless looking mess, the whole covered with a thick coating of ice, and it was still raining from time to time. The ice did not begin to melt until Saturday afternoon, and in some sections still clung to the trees as late as Monday.

Help was called from as many sources as possible, with some crews coming from as far as Elmira and Binghamton. Sleeping accommodations taxed the hotels

of Rockland County almost to their limit. Employees familiar with our territory and lines had to be assigned as guides and others as messengers to maintain contact with trucks not radio equipped. Despite the dangerous and back-breaking work, service throughout the county was eventually restored—without any injuries to the crews.

Photo and article from O&R Archives

The Train Wreck They Knew Was Going To Happen

The early morning of Monday, August 11, 1958 was like any other commuter day on the Erie Railroad as workers made their way into the city. However, shortly before 7 a.m., railroad officials discovered that a terrible accident was about to take place. Police, fire and ambulances were alerted to the fact that two trains were on a collision course, and there wasn't anything anyone could do to stop them.

The fateful mistake occurred when Frederick Roth in the control tower at Suffern was distracted by other business and forgot to lock in a switch, a switch that would have prevented a passenger-freight train from

leaving the Suffern station. The train was supposed to be held until an eastbound commuter train from Port Jervis had passed through.

Roth, realizing the westbound train had left prematurely, frantically attempted to radio the two trains that were due to impact head-on within five minutes. Due to "dead spots" in the mountainous terrain, the radio messages never got through. Fortunately, Roth had the presence of mind to contact all the appropriate authorities to tell them that a horrible tragedy was only minutes away. It would be the longest five minutes those involved would ever experience.

At 6:55 a.m., the engineers of the two trains spotted one another and threw their massive locomotives into full reverse. It was too late. The enormous impact jammed cars together like an accordion. Dozens of people were trapped in the twisted wreckage. The engineer of the eastbound was killed instantly, and the final toll amounted to 5 dead and 34 injured.

The death toll might have been higher, had it not been for the fact that emergency services were on their way before the crash even occurred. The injured were all taken to Good Samaritan Hospital, where by "the providence of God" (according to Sister Miriam) there were beds that had just been cleared that weekend, and the timing was such that both night and day shifts were available to help. The hospital's Dr. Petrone also felt that some of the staff's wartime medical experiences greatly enhanced the rapid, calm and efficient response to the flood of victims.

Later that same day, the county coroner, Dr. Max Moses, and Rockland County District Attorney John Skahen conducted an inquest. They cleared towerman Roth of any "culpable negligence," concluding that what happened was simply a "lapse of memory." The scene of the wreck quickly became somewhat of a tourist attraction and heavy traffic clogged Route 17 for several days after, as curious onlookers stopped to see the results of the fatal train wreck.

Scott Webber

The point of impact: the wreckage of the two engines.   Photo courtesy of Craig Long.

The Historical Hikers

The Suffern Historical Hikers were founded by Gardner and Josephine Watts in 1956. As the 1990s began, the organization had reached its 35th year of introducing thousands of men and women, young and old, to the Ramapo Mountains.

The HH developed out of an active Suffern High School hiking club called "The Explorers" started by the writer in 1952. After a lecture on local history to the faculty in the Ramapo School District, there was a request that a course "Historical Hiking in the Ramapo Mountains" be offered. Eventually, this course was sponsored by ten public school systems of Rockland

and Bergen Counties through their adult education programs.

Healthy exercise, increased knowledge of local history, appreciation of the beauty of the streams, lakes and hills of the Ramapos, and the development of many friendships have been a common denominator over the years. Hikers with special backgrounds have always shared their knowledge of botany, geology and trail lore with newer members.

The hikers have visited many Indian shelters and rockhouses, and tramped over mountain trails and sites of the American Revolution. Visits to the numerous iron mines and furnaces of the Ramapos have been a major and rewarding activity. Evidence showing the disappearance of the old mountain farms and settlements has always intrigued the hikers.

Activities other than the scheduled twenty Sunday afternoon hikes each year have been numerous. They include winter outings for experienced members, indoor programs on both travel and local history, and participation in Revolutionary Bicentennial activities. For five years there was a popular offshoot: The Historical Hikers Singles.

Sections of the Suffern-Midvale and Suffern Bear Mt trails were marked and maintained by the HH under the sponsorship of the NY-NJ Trail Conference. Members have done research on sites visited in the Ramapos and presented papers on these themes at later outings. A major forest fire was extinguished. Several marriages are the result of growing companionship along the trails.

Of the several hundred hikes over the past 34 years, the following are recalled as being among the most memorable or exciting:

➢ The André-Arnold meeting site with seldom-seen rock inscription on the Hudson shore south of Haverstraw.
➢ Remote High Mountain near Hillburn with its long-abandoned granite quarry near the summit.
➢ Ramapo Torne with Revolutionary War outlook on its summit, and Indian shelters beneath its cliffs.
➢ Doodletown Brook and Doodletown itself with old building foundations. Side path to Indian rockhouse.

Gardner Watts

The Jewish Community
1950-1959

June 14, 1951 was the day that Temple Beth El dedicated their new shul. Past presidents Irving Siegel and Percy Auerbach led the Torah processional to the new sanctuary. Nathan Robbins kindled the new Eternal Light for the first time. Rabbi Louis Frishman arrived shortly after the dedication and was with the congregation into the 1990s. In response to immediate growth, Beth El purchased the former Epstein Hotel on Viola Road and constructed their present synagogue, which was dedicated in 1965.

Monsey has the most diverse Jewish population in the county and so supports more synagogues and yeshivas (Jewish Day Schools) than any other community. Many of the shuls are Orthodox, ultra Orthodox or Hasidic. Some are found in private homes and others in larger buildings constructed for that purpose. Communities of Orthodox Jews continued to develop over the years, supporting over 60 synagogues and about two dozen yeshivas in Monsey by the year 2000.

The numbers of yeshivas have also increased dramatically as several thousand children attend their private schools. One of the oldest and largest is the Adolph H. Schreiber Hebrew Academy of Rockland, also known as ASHAR. Established in 1952 when it was known as the Hebrew Institute of Rockland County (HIRC), two classes were opened the following year at its

first home in the Community Synagogue of Monsey on Maple Avenue.

By the time Rabbi Nachum Mushel joined the staff in 1955, plans for their own building were under way. The Meislin Bungalow Colony on Highview Avenue had been subdivided and a portion of the land sold to HIRC, "at a good price." A small building was constructed the following year. At the same time other land had been subdivided making way for new, affordable homes in Monsey. The post war boom saw a large influx of Jewish families from New York City. The school grew by geometric proportions, which made it necessary to expand three times over the next several decades.

According to a recent publication "the life oriented programs emphasize human value, love of Torah and Zion and American citizenship." In addition to secular studies outlined by the State of New York, the curriculum offers various courses of Jewish studies including Bible, Talmud, Jewish customs, laws, history and the Hebrew language.

Growth and development of the Jewish community in the southern part of the county resulted in the founding of the Orangetown Jewish Center in the late 1950s. The synagogue is located on Independence Avenue, Orangeburg, near the former Camp Shanks.

Harold L. Laroff

...In 1953 Jacqueline Bouvier married John F. Kennedy...*Ozzie and Harriet* is one of America's favorite television shows...In 1954 Joe DiMaggio marries Marilyn Monroe...The U.S. launches its first atomic submarine, the *Nautilus*...The sale of frozen foods reaches the $1billion mark—75% of American households buy frozen food...14 tobacco companies form a committee to prove that cigarettes don't cause lung cancer...The first color TVs sell for $1,295—they have 12.5" screens...

Marian Shrine

In 1945, the Salesians of Don Bosco purchased the Grey Ridge Farm in West Haverstraw, to build there a high school to train young men interested in becoming Salesians. Youngsters already in training moved to the new property, and additional recruits joined them.

The young men's parents and friends, as well as many people who visited the property, were impressed by the natural beauty of the grounds. In the early 1950s, the flourishing community, under the leadership of Fr. Ernest Giovannini, Provincial, undertook the development of a Rosary Way, which was completed in 1954. Life-size statues of the mysteries of the Rosary were placed along a pathway running through a beautiful wooded area. The Rosary Way attracted many visitors, and served as a source of inspiration and contemplation for them. In 1961, a Director of Pilgrimages was appointed, and the work of promoting a pilgrimage center in honor of Mary Help of Christians began in earnest.

prayerful meditation. The bronze statue stands 48 feet high and was designed by Martin Lumen Winter of New Rochelle, New York, and the model was blessed by Pope John XXIII at the Vatican. Processions in honor of our Blessed Mother either begin or end at this statue.

Grottoes depicting the apparitions at Fatima and Lourdes are tucked away in wooded areas and beckon one to pray and meditate. A memorial to the Unborn, sponsored by the Knights of Columbus of Rockland County, was erected in 1997 and has become the focal point of the popular July 4th Pro-Life celebration.

The Becchi House is another attraction at the Marian Shrine. It is a replica of the house in which young John Bosco grew up under the gentle guidance of his saintly mother, Mamma Margaret. The replica at the Marian Shrine was built by Brother Andrew LaCombe, a Salesian architect, who spent time in Don Bosco's hamlet, studying the original and gathering materials for the construction of the replica.

Statues along the Rosary Way.   Photo by John Scott.

For years Fathers John Lomagno, Peter Lappin, and August Bosio labored with energy and devotion to spread devotion to Mary Help of Christians in the tri-state area. Assisted by Salesian Brothers and lay volunteers, they promoted visits to the shrine, organized liturgical celebrations, led pilgrims along the Rosary Way and were available for the spiritual needs of visitors.

The number of pilgrims and visiting groups began to increase, and additional buildings and statues were added. The giant statue of the Rosary Madonna dominates the grounds and invites many pilgrims to

The shrine attracts countless individuals, and among the large groups that hold their celebrations are the Salesian Family, Cursillistas and Charismatics from the tri-state area, Pro-Life groups, participants in Jornadas de Vida Cristiana and Pascua Juvenil, the Friends of Maria Goretti, and devotees of the Divine Mercy. Family days are enjoyed by Polish, Italian, Latino, Filipino, Korean, Slovak and Vietnamese organizations. John Cardinal O'Connor designated Marian Shrine a pilgrimage site for the Jubilee Year of 2000.

Article provided by the Marian Shrine.

⚜ St Thomas Aquinas College

In the late 1940s, the Dominican Sisters of Sparkill, nearly 1,000 strong, were notified by the New York State Education Department that although they did have undergraduate degrees in a specified subject area, they would be required to have teacher certification to teach at the elementary or secondary level. The Sisters took it upon themselves to seek out options for their congregation. With little accessibility to metropolitan area colleges and universities, the Sisters decided to start their own college—in 1952 they completed their quest and opened St. Thomas Aquinas College in Sparkill. Spellman Hall housed the first college classrooms and the first class graduated in 1958.

In the mid-1960s, the Dominican Sisters recognized the College's growth potential and turned it over to an independent board of trustees with mostly lay board members and representation from the congregation. By the early 1970s the doors were opened to men and the first lay president, Dr. Donald T. McNelis, began his 21-year tenure as president. In 1995, Dr. Margaret M. Fitzpatrick, S.C., took the helm as the College's eighth president and led the College into the twenty-first century by forging alliances with regional colleges and universities that could offer more options to students without overburdening St. Thomas Aquinas College.

In 1958, the College graduated its first class into the ranks of the alumni—30 strong! In 1960, the College was empowered to grant the degrees of Bachelor of Arts, Bachelor of Science and Bachelor of Science in Education as well as to admit other religious women and lay-women. In 1967, the College was granted the charter amendment to open its doors as a coeducational institution.

In 1981, the College was granted a charter amendment to offer the associate in arts and associate in science degrees at the United States Military Academy at West Point. The program was designed and implemented at the Army's request for enlisted military personnel, officers, spouses and dependents and civilian employees at the military base at West Point and the Stewart Army Subpost.

In 1985, the New York State Education Department authorized St. Thomas Aquinas College to confer the Master of Science in Education on duly qualified students and, simultaneously, approved the first graduate program in special education. Additional programs, in elementary education, in secondary education and in reading were authorized in May 1992.

In 1994, the NYS Ed. Dept. authorized STAC to confer the Masters of Business Administration with concentrations in finance, marketing or management.

Vincent Crapanzano, STAC

Marian Hall at St. Thomas Aquinas College.   Photo courtesy of STAC.

Rockland Community College

It came down to one vote.

The date was April 28, 1959. For the previous three and a half years, a group of business, civic, and education leaders had worked assiduously to prove that Rockland County was ready for a community college.

Now it was crunch time. The fate of a community college in Rockland rested in the hands of the Board of Supervisors, the five town chiefs who ran the county in the days before the Legislature was created in 1970. Last-minute presentations were delivered by Dr. Lester Rounds, the superintendent of Ramapo Central School

District No. 1 (Suffern), whose doctoral dissertation at Columbia University had provided a blueprint for the establishment of the college; Frank Manley of Nyack, president of Orange and Rockland Utilities and chairman of the steering committee to create the college; and Dan Brucker of Valley Cottage, a prominent lawyer in Nyack and vice chairman of the committee.

Two supervisors, Democrats Victor Shankey of Haverstraw and Edwin Wallace of Ramapo, wanted to put the issue to a public referendum, despite the fact that no community college in the state—there were

197

seventeen at the time—had resorted to such a measure. All had been approved by vote of the local governmental sponsor. The amendment to referendum was defeated, 3 to 2. The vote was now squarely in the hands of the supervisors. John Coyle of Clarkstown and Arthur Jobson of Stony Point, both Republicans, were known to be in favor of the college. Clarence Noyes of Orangetown, the board chairman and also a Republican, had been noncommittal in previous public meetings. It was to him that Brucker and Manley directed their most fervent entreaties.

Harold Laskey, a book publishing consultant from New City and key steering committee member, was too nervous to witness the taut proceedings, held in a basement meeting room of the county courthouse in New City. Instead, he stood outside the door and listened.

"I could hear Dan Brucker inside begin to wind down his last plea urging them to finally take action," Laskey remembered. "I heard one of the supervisors, Victor Shankey I think it was, say something like: 'Why do we need a half-baked college school here anyway? Our kids can go to school anywhere.' The tireless efforts of so many good-hearted, dedicated people, the work of those who had prepared the presentations, the work of all of us for all of those years, stood riding on one vote."

Supervisor Coyle introduced a resolution that the college be approved. Jobson seconded the resolution. Shankey and Wallace voted against it. That left it up to Chairman Noyes. One month before, in the steering committee's final appearance before the board, Brucker and Manley had ratcheted up the pressure on the supervisors, mindful that Noyes had not yet tipped his hand.

"This time we threatened them; 1959 was an election year, and they all were running," Brucker recalled. "We said that if they didn't pass the vote, we'd have a representative at every meeting they attended, someone who would ask them over and over again what their position was on the community college. By October or November, they'd be so damned sick of hearing about it that they'd wish they had passed it in the spring."

The full-court press apparently worked. Noyes voted yes. The college had been approved, 3 votes to 2.

Fashioning a Campus

The transformation from Poor Farm property to community college campus proceeded right through the first year. From a place housing the dying, the impoverished, the infirm, this tranquil 26.5-acre plot evolved into a vibrant epicenter of intellectual vigor. Nestled on the crest of a sloping rise in a former farm community known as Mechanicsville, renamed Viola when a post office was established in 1882, the property included a barn, a cabbage field, a "potter's field"

The Alms House, Viola.
Where the County's dependent poor find a comfortable home.

The county alms house property that was transformed into the campus of Rockland Community College. JSC

cemetery, a small square building with barred windows that served as an early Rockland County jail, a root cellar and other dilapidated buildings. The centerpiece of the complex was the brick, three-story Almshouse, which was to serve as the main academic and administrative building.

A Spectrum of Students

On the first day of registration in late September, 1959, Trustee Harold Laskey remembered driving to the college, mindful of the vicissitudes of the five previous years. "As I turned into the campus from old Almshouse Road," he said, "I saw the parking lot filled with cars. The people in this community really wanted this college, and they were showing it. It was, I might say, the most exciting day of my life."

There were 139 students that first year: 87 men and 52 women.

The first graduating class, June 11, 1961. Of the original 139 students, 39 (22 men and 17 women) graduated.

198

The Twenty-First Century

Thanks to a handful of devoted teachers and administrators, the dream of a community college grew into a highly successful reality. By the year 2000, enrollment stood at over 6,000 students, including over 180 foreign students representing over 50 countries. The faculty included 124 full-time faculty members, and approximately 235 part-time faculty members.

The campus grew to 175 acres and included:

Eugene Levy Fieldhouse: A two-acre, multi-use facility, the largest of its type in the northeast, serving as a center for public and commercial events and for the College's physical education program.

Cultural Arts Center: Housing a professional quality 500-seat theater, extensive fine art and performance studios, Culture Cafe and glass atrium dining area.

Library Media Arts Center: Containing over 125,935 volumes, subscriptions to over 450 periodicals, journals, newspapers and computerized databases.

Jamie Kempton

The first modern building: Academic I opened in the fall of 1964, beginning a new era at RCC.

...In 1954, Roger Bannister becomes the first man to break the 4-minute mile...Rosa Parks is arrested in Montgomery, Alabama for sitting in the "Whites-Only" section of a bus...In 1955 Disneyland opens in California...In 1956 the Prince of Monaco marries Grace Kelly...Elvis Presley appears on the Ed Sullivan television show...In 1957 the Soviet Union shocks the world by launching Sputnik, the first manmade satellite to orbit the earth...In 1959 the Dalai Lama leaves Tibet to escape arrest from Chinese occupying forces...Hawaii becomes the 50th state...

Polio Vaccine

This sign welcoming people to Pearl River at the border with Montvale, N.J., may not have the catchiest slogan, but the importance of its message can not be underestimated.

Polio had been killing and crippling children around the world for generations until Jonas Salk developed the first vaccine in 1952. In the following years, scientists at Lederle Laboratories in Pearl River helped develop an oral vaccine that would ultimately be given to millions of children across the globe.

Linda Zimmermann
Photo by John Scott.

Monkey Chase

A fish net wielded by Hugo Kolb ended seven glorious days of freedom yesterday for the second monkey which escaped on July 30 from Hunt's Circus when it played in Central Nyack. The monkey did not submit to capture, however, without a chase. The monkey, which had been living in the treetops along DePew Avenue back of Kolb's Garage and McDermott's Milk Bar, was lured into the garage by Mr. Kolb, who had left bananas for it in the boiler room and in his office.

The Journal-News, 8/10/51

New City, N. Y.

Modern Shopping

The shopping center was still a new concept in suburbia in the 1950s.

This shopping center on Main Street in New City was obviously considered worthy of being the subject of this postcard.

The center still exists in the twenty-first century, although it has undergone numerous changes in tenants.

Postcard courtesy of Rose McCabe Lebreton.

Lost Treasures

This 1917 photo (above, JSC) was of the oldest house in Nyack, built about 1738, and known as the Cornelison or Salisbury House. In the 1950s, a developer wanted to tear down the historic structure to build an apartment complex.

There were protests, but the climate of the 1950s was clearly "progress" over preservation. After standing for over 200 years, Salisbury House was demolished. The present Salisbury Point apartments (above, right, LZ) now stand in its place. If any good was to come of the destruction of this historical and architectural gem, it was the recognition that organizations needed to be formed to protect, preserve and restore Rockland's treasures. The forming of the Historical Society of Rockland County was one of the results of that mission.

Linda Zimmermann

...In 1957 the European Common Market is formed...The *Nautilus* submarine sails under the ice pack at the North Pole...In 1958 the morning sickness drug thalidomide causes over 7,000 birth defects...In 1959 Fidel Castro's forces take over Cuba...The whaling industry has reduced the Blue Whale population to near extinction...Home fallout shelters are being marketed for $1,195...

Palisades Free Library
19 Closter Road

The library was founded as a reading room by Mrs. Lydia Lawrence in the old Watson House in 1891. For its first six decades, the library occupied three different sites. In 1953, the Jordan House, a Victorian farmhouse dating back to 1865, was purchased, becoming the library's permanent home (right). In 1964, a 560-square foot addition was added to the south of the building, and in 1996, a new expansion was completed, doubling the size of the library. The library is notable for its indexed local history collection.

West Nyack Free Library
65 Strawtown Road

Located on Strawtown Road, the library was chartered in 1959. It occupies a brick building (left) constructed in 1922 as an addition to the West Nyack Elementary School. It is situated in a neighborhood of important historical buildings, some dating to pre-Revolutionary War days. Extensive renovations and an addition were completed in 1998. Among the library's treasures is a painting of a Clarkstown saw mill by 19th century landscape artist John William Hill. An archive of rare historic photographs is on permanent exhibition in the Community Room.

Tomkins Cove Public Library
419 Liberty Drive North (Route 9W)

Calvin Tomkins, operator of the Tomkins Cove Lime Co., presented to the people of his namesake community, a six-room poured concrete schoolhouse in 1874, known as the Union Free School (right). The building's design is probably from a pattern book of school buildings prevalent in the late nineteenth century. It is a massive asymmetrical structure, with entrance doors eight feet high, and the original windows are 9 over 9 sash, and nine feet high. A large cupola still holding the original school bell, rests on top of the roof.

With the advent of school centralization in the 1950s, the building was no longer needed as a school, and again through a gift of the Tomkins family, the building became the Tomkins Cove Public Library. In 1962, it became a school district library. The interior doors are more than eight feet high, the ceilings are of tin, and some interior walls are concrete sixteen inches thick. The library is housed on the main floor, and upstairs is the local history room with photographs and other items of Tomkins Cove history. The library is a recipient of a 2000 Historic Preservation Merit Award from the Historical Society of Rockland County.

Sloatsburg Public Library
1 Liberty Rock Road

The library was established in 1959, receiving its permanent charter in 1986. Since 1975, it has been housed in the old St. Francis Episcopal Church, and now occupies over 5,500 square feet. A new children's wing was added in 1997, and the library houses over 25,000 volumes. Sloatsburg was one of the first county libraries to offer computer access to the public. There is a Sloatsburg local history collection in the library.

Valley Cottage Library
110 Route 303

Established in 1957, the library was chartered in 1959. It had originally been located in a former storefront on Lake Road, subsequently moving to its present site on Route 303. The library is noted for the open architectural design of its building, its landscaping and garden. The library regularly hosts a wide variety of programs for children and adults. It has been a two-time winner of the County Executive's Arts Award for Arts Organizations. The library has an extensive historical photo collection of Valley Cottage.

Motel on the Mountain

To capitalize on the new highways, a new motel opened in the summer of 1955—150 feet above the village of Hillburn. Motel on the Mountain was a unique engineering and architectural achievement for Rockland, and its sweeping views attracted locals and travelers alike. The motel drew great praise, and was hailed as the "most exciting motel in the eastern United States."

However, the beautiful and tranquil Motel on the Mountain was to become a flashpoint for bigotry and intolerance when it was transformed into a gay resort and disco in 1977. Dozens of protestors marched in front of the entrance on opening night. One protestor, Hillburn resident Ron DeGroat, was quoted as saying, "They'll take over the whole town. Property values will go down and I won't be able to give my house away, except to a fag." Ellyn Olsen of New City declared, "God destroyed Sodom because he was a homosexual. If the county and the people here allow homosexuality, it is a horrible sin. Judgment will come to Rockland."

Despite the hysteria and inaccurate Biblical references, financial considerations, not fire and brimstone, saw the closing of Motel on the Mountain. After years of neglect, major renovations transformed the aging motel into an oriental showpiece, Mt. Fuji restaurant, which opened in 1985. Both materials and skilled craftsmen were brought from Japan to create the authentic-looking structure.

Linda Zimmermann

Postcard courtesy of Craig Long.

Rockland County Sports Hall of Fame:
1950-1959

Harry Babcock (Pearl River) First player chosen in the 1953 NFL draft. Played with the San Francisco 49ers until he was injured in 1956.

Jay Bohnel (Pearl River) Broke records and earned 13 varsity letters in football, baseball, basketball, track and volleyball. Very active in local sports leagues for kids.

Jerry Bonomolo (Pearl River/Nanuet) All-County in football, baseball and basketball. Went on to coach for 20 years at Nanuet High School.

Marvin Branche (Spring Valley) Called by the *Journal-News* the "greatest all-round trackman in two decades." Held records in the discus, shotput and javelin, and once won 6 events in one day.

Jim Brown (Nyack) All-County in football, baseball and basketball, and for more than 25 years was one of the foremost recreational softball players in the county.

Lew Brundage (Pearl River) The "go-to" man for the Pirate football team. Very active in Alumni and Midget teams.

Frank Cosentino (Tappan Zee H.S.) Captained the football, baseball, basketball and golf teams. Went on to play golf with Princeton's 1956 championship team, and also was quarterback for their football team. Drafted by the Green Bay Packers in 1956 but decided against a pro career.

Frank Dawson (Pearl River) Excelling in football, baseball and basketball, his record-setting punting earned him an invitation to Baltimore Colts' camp, but chose a coaching career instead.

Joe D'Auria (Tappan Zee H.S.) Magnificent all-round athlete, earning a total of 17 varsity letters in baseball, football, basketball, golf, bowling and track.

Gene Erickson (Spring Valley) Outstanding hockey goalie, he was part of the 1956 Olympic team. Won numerous medals in international competitions playing and coaching.

Dominic "Babe" Gamboli (Haverstraw) "Mr. Little League," involved in Rockland Little League Baseball for over 40 years. As an athlete he excelled in football, baseball, basketball and bowling.

Tony Gamboli, Jr. (Spring Valley) Only pitcher in Rockland scholastic history to pitch back-to-back no-hitters. Set numerous Rockland and New Paltz Teacher's College records. Was signed by the New York Yankees in 1961, but a baseball to the head ended his pro career.

Tony Gemma (Clarkstown and Clarkstown North) Baseball coach named Coach of the Year 5 times. As an athlete he excelled in many sports and briefly played pro baseball for the New York Giant's organization.

Frank Horan (Haverstraw) Five-sport athlete whose best was baseball. Was offered pro contracts, but instead chose to coach local sports.

Hank Kapusinsky (Haverstraw) Swift and powerful running back who set records for points scored and career touchdowns.

Lou Kliewe (Pearl River resident) Winningest coach in Rockland scholastic boys' basketball history with 447 victories, amassed over a 35-year career with Albertus Magnus and Spring Valley.

Vincent "Dugan" Kovalsky (Haverstraw) One of the best basketball players to come out of Haverstraw, and was their leading scorer 3 straight years. Played both semi-pro basketball and football.

Walter "Red" Levy (Spring Valley) A stellar multi-sport athlete who earned 11 varsity letters in 5 sports. Later was very active in local youth sports.

Joe McDowell (Nyack) McDowell built a legacy as a successful and well-respected track and cross country coach, as well as being a beloved art teacher, an outstanding sportsman and a humanitarian.

Ed McGrath (Clarkstown) Very successful high school basketball coach for 20 seasons, from 1957-76, winning numerous championships.

Hubert Nealy (Tappan Zee) Deaf since childhood, it did not prevent him from being an outstanding multi-sport athlete. Went on to play a season of minor league baseball.

Frank Nelson (Nyack) Beginning in 1950, Nelson enjoyed a 28-year soccer coaching career with 260 wins, second winningest record in the county.

Art Orlando (Clarkstown) All-County in soccer, basketball and baseball. Became a coach at Clarkstown right out of college.

Walter Ostrom (Orangeburg) Marksman who became an expert trapshooter, winning the Amateur Championship of North America 4 times.

Joseph "Biscuit" Picarello (Haverstraw) Baseball, football and basketball standout at Haverstraw, was also a top bowler and golfer, and golf for Little League.

Howie Pierson (Tappan Zee) One of the most accomplished athletes in county history. Multi-talented scholastic athlete, college baseball star, pro baseball player, amateur golf champ and outstanding coach.

Jim Ridlon (Nyack) Had an 8-year career as a defensive back in the NFL with the 49ers and Cowboys. He led the NFL in interceptions in 1964.

Chuck Scarpulla (Pearl River) Feared linebacker and hard-hitting centerfielder, who went on to be a college football star and then a coach at Ramapo H.S.

Robert "Red" Schassler (Haverstraw) Top-notch all-round athlete who went on to play pro baseball. An injury ended his pro career, but he continued playing semi-pro.

Al "Snookie" Simonds (Nyack) Fine 3-sport athlete who earned 9 varsity letters in basketball, football and baseball. Went on to be a sportswriter for the *Journal-News*.

Jim Stamos (Spring Valley) Earned 10 varsity letters in 3 sports. Gained All-American honors in college.

Bob Strack (Haverstraw) Premier running back, earning the title of Rockland Player of the Year in his junior and senior years.

Ron Tellefsen (Congers) Umpire and organizer who rose to become president and chief executive officer of the Babe Ruth League youth baseball organization.

1960-1969

The Decade of Change

Tensions ran high in the early years of the decade. Communism and the bomb were on everyone's mind. The civil rights movement stirred the South. The idealistic view of "Camelot" was shattered on November 22, 1963, when President Kennedy was assassinated.

As the decade progressed, hair grew longer as skirts grew shorter. The clean-cut conservatism and innocence of the Fifties gave way to the psychedelic hippy, free love and drugs. There was suddenly a "generation gap," and a "gender gap." We became aware of how we were polluting our environment.

One warm summer night in July of 1969, young and old alike were glued to their televisions to watch man walk upon the Moon. Some local residents claim an even greater miracle occurred that year; the Amazin' Mets won the World Series.

While some locals experimented with communes and spoke about Flower Power and "doing your own thing," others answered the call of their country. Once again, young men raised in the safety and tranquility of Rockland were sent to war, this time to fight and die in the jungles of Vietnam.

New housing developments sprang up as some older neighborhoods began to deteriorate. Crime was on the increase. Residents who had moved to the county only ten years earlier complained bitterly about all the "newcomers."

The 1960s was a tumultuous and pivotal time for Rockland. The county would have to redefine itself in many ways, and either become stronger in the changes, or be torn apart by them.

Stephen and Nancy Webber display their Halloween masks of John and Jackie Kennedy on the steps of their home in Stony Point on October 16, 1963. President Kennedy would be assassinated the following month, and much of the innocence this picture evokes would be lost in the ensuing years of the 1960s. Photo by Scott Webber.

The housing developments that sprang up in the 1950s were the first phase in the building boom. The growing population demanded bigger and better places to shop. For those who were not in Rockland during the building of the Nanuet Mall, it would be hard to describe the combination of excitement and consternation it provoked. To many, it was as if civilization was finally coming to Rockland. To others, it seemed to be the death sentence to the old way of life. While the building of the Palisades Center in the 1990s would stir up considerable opposition, it was ultimately a fight over "another mall," and did not have the same widespread psychological impact as the original Nanuet Mall.

Commercial Boom

The favorable commercial climate during 1967 resulted in plans for or construction of many diversified projects.

Throughout the territory, many new attractive office buildings, shopping complexes, banks, motels, restaurants and churches were erected. Shopping center activity highlighted the commercial field with the start of site preparation on the huge 750,000 square foot complex in Nanuet for Sears Roebuck and Bamberger's (a subsidiary of Macy's), scheduled for completion before the end of 1968.

Twenty-six additional shopping centers were in the planning stage or under way in the area at year end. Construction of or additions to 20 banking facilities in 17 communities is a further indicator of the healthy economic condition of the area. Hotel and motel construction progressed at an accelerated pace to accommodate the increasing number of visitors and business travelers in the area.

Uris Rockland Corporation has acquired land in Orangetown, N.Y. for the proposed construction of a 20-story skyscraper office building as part of a $100 million project in which 10,000 people eventually will be employed. The project embraces 3,000,000 square feet with initial occupancy planned for 1970. The giant complex, which includes a proposed shopping center to serve people who work there, is expected to be a stimulus for further commercial expansion.

Commercial expansion is continuing at a healthy rate during the winter months and the present outlook indicates favorable growth in the future. Uppermost in importance is the fact that the economy in the territory of O&R is maintaining a good balance among commercial, industrial, residential and community activities.

O&R Annual Report, 1967

Postcard of the original Nanuet Mall. Bamberger's is on the left, the individual stores are in the center section, and Sears is on the right.
Courtesy of Marjorie Bauer.

207

The School Boom

In the 1960s, an unprecedented public, parochial and private school building program was under way to meet the educational needs of expanding families. (From the O&R Archives.)

During 1965, the following new schools or additions to schools were completed:

Birchwood Elementary
Clarkstown JH
Dogwood Elem.
Haverstraw High
Hillcrest Elem.
Link School Elem.
North Garnerville Elem.
Nyack Boys' School
Nyack Missionary College
Pomona Elem.
St. Anthony's Parochial
St. Thomas Aquinas College
South Orangetown Elem.

Under construction at year-end:

BOCES No.2
Blauvelt JH
Gilbert Ave. MS
New Square High
Pearl River Elem.
Viola Elem.

Planned and approved but not yet under construction:

Blauvelt Elem.
Grandview Elem.
Kakiat JH
Letchworth Village
Northeast Spring Valley Elem.
Northwest Spring Valley Elem.
Orangeburg Public School
Piermont Elem.
Pomona Elem.
Pomona JH
Ramapo SH
Spring Valley SH
Summit Park Elem.

County Business Panel Sees Shortage of Trained Workers

Business and industrial leaders from Rockland County warned that there will not be enough trained personal to fill an anticipated 97,850 jobs in the area in 1985.

Charles Caldwell, president of the Rockland County Regional Growth Committee and Vice-President of Orange & Rockland Utilities, Inc., asserted that about 58,000 new jobs will be in existence 24 years from now over an estimated 29,000 listed in 1956.

Fred Emerson, guidance counselor in the Nyack schools, noted that part of the future labor force is already in school in Grades 7-12, totaling 11,000 in number. Of these, about half will go to college, leaving the other half to enter the labor force.

However, this remaining number must be cut further to allow for girls who marry soon after leaving high school, Emerson continued.

Fred Palmer, president of the Tappan Zee National Bank, described the financial situation, noting that in 1954 there were twelve banks. While that number has declined to seven at this time, there are now 18 branch banks in the county.

The big problem was attracting deposits in competition with large New York City banks that can offer higher interest rates. The trouble is that while people chose to bank in the city, they want to borrow in Rockland. Unless the county's banking system receives more deposits, it cannot keep up with the demands for credit, he said.

Fred Rella, employment manager at Lederle Laboratories, Pearl River, pointed out the need for closer co-operation between industry and school teachers in understanding what the aims and goals of future business will be in order that the proper training might be given in the classroom. Rella predicted that under today's vocational instruction, students would not be prepared for the type of specialized jobs that will be available in the future.

Scott Webber, *The Record*, 10/31/61

Book Exposes School System

Spring Valley author Benjamin Siegel wrote several novels, including *Doctors and Wives*, *The Sword and the Promise*, and *The Principal*, which detailed what was going on in the Ramapo 2, East Ramapo-Spring Valley Schools in the early 1960s. Everything in the novel is true, only the names were changed. The setting is Spring Valley, complete with the Plaza Restaurant run by the Gene Levy family across from the train station.

The Superintendent of Schools was Dr. Merrill L. Colton and the old principal was Leland Meyer. The new principal who came from Long Island was Dr. Alan Sugarman. The school board president was Joseph

Fishkin. The lady board member was Charlotte Tallman. All the events portrayed really happened.

An interesting note was that Brook Siegel, Benjamin's wife, was private secretary to Dr. Colton, thus an insider's position to know all.

When I asked Dr. Colton about the book, he said he had considered getting an attorney. He was very angry over it. Even his idiosyncrasies are given to the novel's superintendent; he pronounced some words the same way Dr. Colton did. In later years, Dr. Colton declined to write of his years in Spring Valley. He retired to Toms River, N.J., where he became borough councilman.

The years portrayed in *The Principal* were ones of exploding population growth, bond issues to build new schools and growing racial tensions in Spring Valley.

Sugarman's comment on the book: "Very interesting." That's all he would say. Then he just smiled.

Scott Webber

Miracle in Pearl River

The Town That Knocked Out Delinquency

"Pearl River has absolutely licked the juvenile-delinquency problem. No ifs, ands or buts."

So began an article written by Arlene and Howard Eisenberg, published in *This Week Magazine* on November 12, 1961. The article went on to describe in detail how community involvement had given Pearl River a delinquency rate only *one fiftieth* that of the national average. According to high school principal Walter Reiner, a key ingredient in this success was the fact that, "We care about our children, and we let them know it."

However, it wasn't just that simple. "The other part of the explanation is an interesting, old-fashioned, key ingredient: *work*." Thanks to the Youth Activities Committee, chaired by local businessman Ed Bouton, hundreds of jobs were found or created for the young people of Pearl River. Jobs ranged from babysitting, to construction, to hospital assistants. Other organizations and individual volunteers hosted dances, baseball games and other activities, all within the budget of $1 per year per member. Local churches also participated in the programs.

The results of these programs brought more than just keeping kids out of trouble. "Work in Pearl River is more than a summer job. So satisfactory were almost all summer workers that requests for after-school and week-end workers have continued heavily into the school year. Many have begun savings accounts—for college, a senior class trip to Washington, a bike-hostel trip through Europe. All, having earned money, learned its value as well."

"Do students appreciate the community's efforts on their behalf? The best answer to that is to visit Pearl River on Community Service Day. This five-year-old tradition is totally voluntary. It is, says James Van Houten, 'the students' way of saying thanks.' A small army of 200 to 250 teenagers assembles on a Saturday morning with rakes, paintbrushes, brooms and enthusiasm. Peeling off in cheerful squads, to the blare of portable radio pop music, they polish Pearl River till it glistens."

Perhaps Rockland's modern-day communities should re-examine Pearl River's old-fashioned, small town ways.

Linda Zimmermann

WHISTLE WHILE YOU WORK: Pearl River's teen-agers turn out for Community Day, to paint, rake, repair, clean. It's their way of saying thanks to the town

Go to Class or Stay Away?
It's Up to Students at Barker

Whoever heard of a school where children were told they didn't have to go to class unless they wanted to?

Forty years ago in England, a man named Neill threw the education world into an uproar by starting just such a school, a place called Summerhill. Sure enough, the students didn't go to class and that was fine with Neill.

A frankly radical way of doing things, Summerhill was full of strange notions. The students weren't asked to respect their elders. On equal footing with their teachers, they called them by their first names, cursed them sometimes. The children and staff together made the school's rules. On their own time, they did as they pleased.

What happened to them? Did the children grow up to be arch criminals? Did the school go up in flames? Was Neill carted off to the loony bin? No.

What happened was that the thing worked. Summerhill became known all over the world for its principles of freedom and nonrepression. Educators from other countries visited there, saw children who were friendly and self-disciplined, and who considered being kept from class a punishment.

Today, there are five schools in the United States based in part on this approach. One of them is the Barker School in Stony Point, attended by 50 children from the county.

In existence for only two and a half years, it is a small school for children from kindergarten age through early teens. There are three buildings set back from the road and surrounded by trees, a big rambling house (the former Sengstacken residence) for the younger grades, a converted barn for the older ones and a small house where one of the teachers lives.

The school is not quiet. It is not neat. More than one parent toying with idea of enrolling a child there left with eyebrows raised because it's like no school they've ever seen. "How can children learn anything sitting on the floor, drinking ginger ale and chewing licorice all through class? So messy. Heavens!"

Neat or not, the attendance rate at the Barker School is phenomenal. Children love to go there so much that parents have a hard time keeping them home when they're sick. It's almost the same for the faculty, who believe in what they're doing and enjoy it. Frankly admitting the frustration of not being able to teach enough, they keep to the goal of the child being primary, the lesson secondary.

What happens after a child becomes used to freedom in the school situation? The teachers say they are "more self-confident. They're not ashamed, partly because what they say is uncensored. They're not trying to act one way while feeling another way. They are sympathetic and they're tolerant of other views—even adults."

Jay Rae Offen, *Rockland Independent*, 2/20/64

Who Wears the Pants?

In 1968, I was in the fourth grade at Evans Park Elementary School in Pearl River. One frigid winter day, my mother sent me to school in pants so I wouldn't be cold. Although this was a public school, the principal wanted to send me home because I was not wearing a skirt. As ridiculous as it seems, as late as 1968, little girls were supposed to dress like girls, or else be banned from attending school!

A prolonged battle ensued—my mother against school officials (they had no idea who they were up against!). All the while, I continued wearing pants, rather outlandish ones at that, given the styles and bright colors of the 60s. Even at age 9, I was fully aware that my denim jeans were ruffling old conservative feathers, which given my rebel-tomboy nature suited me just fine.

Not surprisingly, the school finally gave into my mother's demands and girls were officially granted the privilege to be comfortable and keep warm.

Linda Zimmermann

...In 1961 Yuri Gagarin becomes the first man in space...The "Bay of Pigs" fiasco fails to oust Castro from power in Cuba...The Berlin Wall is erected...Chubby Checker does "The Twist"...In 1962 there is rioting on the campus of the University of Louisiana because an African-American is enrolled...The Cuban missile crisis brings the world to the brink of nuclear war...

Allen Dykstra (1930-1997) was a Korean War veteran who founded one of Rockland's most popular florist shops in 1960. Dykstra was also very active in community affairs, and among his favorite causes were the Arts Council of Rockland, the American Cancer Society, the Rockland Center for Holocaust Studies and the Chestnut Ridge Little League, receiving dozens of citations for his many years of service.

Rockland County
Home of the Month

Realities of Real Estate

To the twenty-first century reader, this ad in *The New Magazine*, from April 1964, presents the absurd price of only $55,000 for this beautiful, large home on two acres with a Hudson River view.

Of course, it must be kept in mind that the average price for a new home just twenty years earlier was about $4,000. During the 1950s, the difference of a few hundred dollars decided whether or not a potential buyer could afford a house.

By the year 2000, a home that cost $15,000 in the 1960s, could easily command $300,000.

As decades pass and prices rise, it is important to remember that everything is relative. Few would agree to return to prices of the past, if it also meant returning to salaries of the past.

Linda Zimmermann

Recalling the Stars of the Tappan Zee Playhouse

Back in the 1920s and 1930s there were three theaters in Nyack. One was the Broadway, across from the YMCA. The Lyceum was next to Havermale's, west of Franklin fronting Main Street. The Rockland was on upper Broadway, about three blocks up from Main Street on the west side.

The Broadway Theater was the first. It had vaudeville there and its own band. I remember Elmer Henderson played the drums and "Dominick," who later ran the Venice Restaurant on Route 9W, Upper Nyack, also played there. One of the attractions that came back in the 20s was "The Pennsylvanians," with its members just out of college and led by the famous Fred Waring (who also invented the kitchen blender we all use).

Later, in the 60s, the Broadway reopened and became the Tappan Zee Playhouse. Playing there during those brief few years were Caesar Romero, Jack Benny, Barbara Bell Geddes, Helen Hayes, James Daly, Walter Pigeon, Elliot Gould, Liza Minelli and Joel Gray. As theater editor for *The Journal-News*, I would interview each star on Monday and print the story on Wednesday.

Walter Pigeon was a lot of fun. I didn't know it, but he collected "cute but dirty limericks." His friends sent

Postcard of The Tappan Zee Playhouse, circa 1950s.
Helen Hayes is on the marquee. JSC

them to him from all over the world. This star told me limericks for better than a half hour. When I asked him, after all the movies he played in which would he say was his best, he didn't hesitate. "Why, 'Mrs. Miniver,' of course." I sent him a copy of my article in *The Journal News* to his hotel room. His reply came back "Dear Ken, loved your article; too bad you couldn't print the limericks."

Jack Benny, with his Stradivarius violin, at the Tappan Zee Playhouse for "An Hour Plus 60 Minutes with Jack Benny" on June 30, 1965.

Photo by Scott Webber.

Caesar Romero was terrific to interview. He answered every question but one. That was when I asked him: "Of all your leading ladies, Caesar, which one is outstanding in your mind?" He just looked at me and said, "What, are you crazy? If I answered that one, none of the other girls would look at me or talk to me again."

Elliot Gould (who was married to Barbra Streisand at the time) and Liza Minelli appeared in "Fiddlesticks" together. When I first saw them, they had just come from the luncheonette up the street from the Y, and they were taking turns kicking a can down the gutter of the street. Both were licking on ice cream cones. Gould saw a mangy, old dog in front of the theater and came over to pet it, bringing the dog inside to rehearsal. Seeing that the dog was hungry and his ice cream cone gone, he took Liza's, and gave it to the dog.

James Daly lived in Suffern (Tyne Daly is his daughter). Jim was doing a play out on Long Island that was supposed to eventually air on television. We had set Thursday for the interview. What I didn't know when I went to his house was that this play had bombed out Wednesday night and the whole cast had been dismissed.

Upon knocking on his door, I was aghast to find him in his pajamas and bathrobe, half asleep. His greeting was, "What the hell do you want?" I reminded him that he'd set the interview. He backed off and invited me out on his porch for coffee. There he unwound and I had a great interview. I even learned that he had been an Army Air Corps cadet, like me.

Ah, the memories.

Kenneth P. Harniman, *The Journal News*, 6/18/99

Changes in South Nyack

I was born in 1956. I grew up in South Nyack in a middle-income family, with both parents, two sisters and a brother. Our address was 117 South Broadway.

Many of our neighbors, soon to be friends, were large families. I would pick that as the most significant difference in the changing atmosphere of the Nyack area over the years: large families interacting with each other in the neighborhoods, replaced by one child families or no child couples living in more isolated seclusion.

Most of the larger and poorer families have moved away. Money came with the yuppies and housing prices increased, hindering many of us from staying. It started with the influx of antique shops in the late 60s early 70s. My mother was one of the original group of folks who had fun going to the auctions and accumulating the treasures of those who were making room for the next generation. She and her intimate group of shopkeepers turned South Broadway into a bustling center of commerce.

In the early 60s there were as many storefronts empty as there were full. And many of those that were occupied were dusty old places of business from long ago that seemed not to have many customers. Over the years, antique and junk dealers congregated in the area and it developed into an attraction for city people to come for a day in the country. Street fairs were an ingenious plan to promote the idea. They have turned into very popular semi-annual events.

As kids we played in the street, moving for only an occasional car. We walked alone to the store for bread or butter. Sending a child to the store alone today could bring criminal charges of neglect. This is not a quiet little country county anymore.

At one time it seemed as if everyone in town knew each other. Credit at the store was a given. People were involved in local politics out of concern and desire, rather than fear for the encroaching horizon of progress and expansion. We never locked our car doors or the front door of the house.

Times have changed. Yes, but so have I. I don't long for those days. These days have a flavor all their own. It's not better or worse—it's just different.

David Rolls

...In 1964 the Beatles come to America...Ford introduces the Mustang with a price of $2,368...

O&R Saves the Day During the Night the Lights Went Out

The great Blackout of 1965 was one of those events where just about everyone remembers exactly where they were when it occurred. (My brother, Jim, and I had just spilled a large container of marbles on the living room floor!) New York, New Hampshire, Vermont, Massachusetts, Connecticut, Rhode Island and parts of Pennsylvania were plunged into darkness during the evening rush hour of Tuesday, November 9. New York City was in chaos with no streetlights, no runway lights at the airports, and thousands of people were trapped overnight in elevators, high-rise office buildings and subway cars.

While Rocklanders groped for candles and flashlights and listened to blackout news on transistor radios, many were surprised to see the lights come back on within an hour of the 5:16 p.m. event.

Due to alert action by James E. James, a Lovett Plant shift foreman, and his crew, a complete service interruption was avoided. As the drop in frequency and voltage occurred which jeopardized the entire electrical system, James quickly cleared the high voltage at Lovett Plant to save it from a total shutdown. Working on the shift with James were Robert Gilbert, Martin Knapp, Clarence Lent, Jr., Walton Buck, George Sibley, Raymond Heim, Francis Hoey and Fred Wright.

Courtesy of O&R Archives.

First restoration of service was on the circuit between Lovett and West Nyack substations at 5:21 p.m., and only an hour later, 50% of the system had been restored. The rest of Rockland's residents had their lights on by 8:51 p.m. (By which time, Jim and I had fortunately retrieved all of our marbles by flashlight.)

Rockland County gained some fame when newspapers reported that it was "one of the few areas in the Northeast where power service to customers never failed completely." O&R was recognized for its swift, power-saving actions, and was even called upon to "jumpstart" Con Edison generators in New York to restore power to the city.

While life quickly returned to normal, the effects of the massive power outage were actually still being felt nine months later, as the Northeast delivered its crop of "blackout babies."   Linda Zimmermann

JOB WELL DONE, SAYS UTILITY OFFICIAL TO FOREMAN
Charles L. Huiswit, O&R president, congratulating James

Power Crew Forestalled A Blackout

The Development of Medical Practice in Rockland County

Medical practice in Rockland County has undergone great change over the years. There was a time when a handful of doctors, traveling on horseback or by buggy, ministered to the needs of the sparse population. The bag a doctor carried and the skill of his hands were all that stood between the patient and his affliction.

The doctors of today (1961) in Rockland County use an array of scientific equipment that would astound the practitioner of a few generations ago. They have behind them the resources of a vast pharmaceutical industry. Volunteer ambulance corps are on call around the clock to speed patients to our hospitals for emergency treatment. The hospitals of the county provide services and facilities undreamt of in an earlier

day, when the patient had no choice but to struggle through a serious illness in his own bed.

The beginnings of medical practice in the county are obscure. The first doctor of whom I find a record is a Dr. Osborn. He was an Englishman who settled in 1730 in what is now the Town of Stony Point. His patients included the Indians who inhabited the area. Dr. Osborn made many tedious journeys through the wilderness to reach the persons he served. He was followed in his practice by his son, Dr. Richard Osborn, who during the Revolution, records tell us, "was active in the service of Washington." A contemporary of Dr. Richard Osborn was a Dr. Thomas Outwater who practiced in Tappan. An army hospital was located in

Tappan during the Revolution. One of its surgeons, Dr. Van der Weyde, escaped capture after the fall of Fort Clinton by swimming across the Hudson River.

The first Medical Society in the county was organized in 1829, but its meetings were discontinued, perhaps because it was too difficult for members to attend. We must remember that in those days there were but few roads, and travel from one locale to another in the county was not an easy matter. For the most part, the network of roads we now have came only with the automobile. In 1850, the County Medical Society was reorganized with twelve members. In 1906, the present Medical Society of the County of Rockland was formed by the union of two existing societies. It then had 27 members; it now has over 200.

In the two year span of 1957 and 1958 alone, 37 new members joined the Society. Our present dean of Rockland County medical practitioners, Dr. John C. Dingman, started his practice here in 1904, and it is to him I am indebted for much of this material. His father was a physician who came to Spring Valley in 1876. Dr. Dingman recalls that an important part of his father's medical equipment was a pill-rolling machine, in which quinine—the remedy for the then prevalent malaria—was dipped in gelatin. Seventy-five cents was the charge for a house call, and a doctor was expected to continue daily visits until the patient was well. Some of the more frugal patients, feeling that the calls had gone on long enough and wishing to spare themselves further expense, would hurriedly dress when seeing the doctor approach on horseback, and would be found leaning on a broom or hoe when the doctor arrived, apparently restored to good health.

Dr. John C. Dingman's own practice began in the horse and buggy days (above, JSC). Long hours on the road visiting his patients in their homes left little time for regular office hours. An office practice, as we now know it, did not exist in those days. There were few telephones and the customary way of summoning the doctor was to rap on his door.

Dr. Dingman was often so summoned. On such occasions, he would harness a horse and travel five or ten miles to visit the patient. On returning home, he would unharness, blanket and stable the horse. Many of these journeys were made at night and in severe weather. The rough winters sometimes turned a "horseback" doctor into a "snowshoe" doctor. I am sure that many longtime residents of the county can recall examples of the strenuous life of their family doctor of that period. Many of these doctors are remembered with great affection.

The importance of the hospital in medical practice has grown increasingly through the years. Not until just before the present century did the people of Rockland County have a hospital. At that time, Nyack Hospital opened its doors. Its original complement was nine beds; this was later increased to about twenty. Good Samaritan Hospital was founded in 1902 with about twenty-six beds. These hospitals were staffed with local physicians, two or three of whom did most of the surgery in addition to their general practice.

In this period obstetrics was not a hospital procedure. It was done almost entirely in the home and every physician practiced it. In 1924, the first new wing of the Nyack Hospital was opened, and for the first time a delivery room separate from the operating room was available. Most "minor" surgery, including the removal of tonsils, was done in the home or in the doctor's office. Doctors frequently had to use great powers of persuasion to convince a patient of the wisdom of entering a hospital. Many construed hospital admission as a death sentence.

The current problem is to find hospital space for patients, notwithstanding that the first two hospitals have been expanded and that other hospitals have been established in Pearl River and Spring Valley. Local hospitals have even had to resort to placing beds in their corridors.

Many of the diagnostic and treatment facilities now available in the hospitals of the county did not exist in earlier days. At one time the hospitals did not have laboratories or X-ray machines. The doctors did blood counts and urine analyses themselves, but the State Department of Health did throat cultures, a very necessary laboratory aid when diphtheria was a frequent diagnosis.

When I started practice in Rockland County in 1925, some doctors did not send bills for their services, but relied on the patient's gratitude to establish the fee. At that time, fully half of a doctor's practice might be done without remuneration, either because the patient could not afford to pay, or because he was not inclined to pay. Today, our people have freer access to medical services and medical and hospitalization insurance are important factors in meeting the resulting cost.

These backward glances show some of the ways in which the field of medical practice has developed in the county. We can be sure, based on the experience of the past, that medical practice will undergo equally profound changes in the years ahead.

Marjorie Hopper, M.D., *SOM*, July/Sept. 1961

Doctor Chosen By Coin Toss

The Clarkstown Central School Board last night flipped for a doctor.

The Board had bogged down in choosing a doctor for its school district. Some Board members wanted Dr. James A. Dingman of Congers Road; others favored Dr. Fred F. Graziano of College Avenue, Nanuet. Advocates of both doctors pointed out their services in the past to the schools when they were needed.

Board President Dean B. Seifried reached into his pocket and pulled out a coin.

Trustee Mrs. Margaret Van Ness called "heads." Heads it was, Dr. Dingman will be asked if he wishes to assume the post.

"We don't make all our decisions this way," Seifried explained to the press.

Scott Webber, *The Record*, 9/14/61

Peace Corps Duties Outlined by Speaker

Dr. Robert Van Duyn, who is deputy for program development and operations for the Peace Corps in Washington, told the members of the Rockland County Extension Services Association that the group's main concern was that the Peace Corps members represent the best of American ideals to the peoples of other lands. Otherwise, he said, the worker will be valueless. He spoke at the annual meeting of the association at the English Church Hall on New Hempstead Road. (In attendance was the President-elect Niles M. Davies, Jr., Naomi Butler, Secretary and Thomas Coryat, vice-chairman of the 4-H Club Dept. Exec. Com.)

The Peace Corps program hopes to accomplish several purposes, Van Duyn said. One purpose is to help other countries to fill urgent needs for skilled manpower until native workers can be trained. It is hoped the corps will give its workers an understanding of other cultures. These workers belong to the future generations that will be the leaders of our country. A third objective is an effort to reshape the foreigner's concept of the American image.

The revolutionary idea that man can better himself and improve his standard of living was American in origin, he said. However, the Communists have become more identified with this idea than the United States in other countries.

Van Duyn said he was also disturbed by the failure of American business to enter foreign markets. Even though Red China is still 6 years behind the point where Japan was in World War II in production, it will be a key competitor because it will sell its goods at low prices, he noted.

"The revolution revealing that man can live better and better himself is largely our own doing," declared Van Duyn. "But the paradox is that while we are ignoring this revolution, the Communists are becoming more identified with it than we are," he added. Young persons in other parts of the world are sitting on the fence, wanting what others have and wondering why they haven't got it themselves. The danger is that they are thinking of trying the Communist program to achieve these desires, he warned. "We will never see the triumph of freedom over tyranny unless we go where the battle is hot," he emphasized.

To do this, the corps now has 114,000 volunteers who are being screened for acceptance into the Service. Of these, 750 are already in training or overseas.

Scott Webber, *The Record*, 12/1/61

As Un-American as Mothers and Apple Pie?

Politics in Rockland tended to be quietly local. In 1960, however, the New City Library came into the center of a quarrel with the American Legion Post. At the time, the library occupied a building converted from a single-car private garage and was staffed by volunteers. The problem arose when the Post Commander denounced the library for having "Un-American" books on its shelves. The furor quickly escalated into accusations of "book-burning fascist militarists" and "big-city commie corrupters of youth."

Fortunately, the tempest blew away as quickly as it had come, especially when it turned out that the alleged "communist literature" was a Russian children's book titled (in English) "My Mother is the Most Beautiful Woman in the World," and its message was simply that all children naturally love their mothers.   Jim Shields

---

...In 1964 Communist China explodes its first atomic bomb...In 1965 President Johnson authorizes the first use of U.S. combat troops in Vietnam...Winston Churchill dies...The Watts section of Los Angeles is rocked by five days of race riots...Ferdinand Marcos becomes president of the Philippines...In 1966 Indonesia continues purging the country of communists, at least 100,000 are killed...Mao Tse-Tung launches China's "Great Proletarian Cultural Revolution"...

215

Physicist Warns of Nuclear Fire

Tells County PTA Blasts Effects May Turn Shelters Into Ovens

A Tappan physics professor warned members of the Rockland County PTA last night that certain types of nuclear bombs might fatally burn occupants of school fall-out shelters.

Speaking from the audience, Snowden Taylor of Western Highway, Tappan, said that if nuclear bombs were exploded in the air it would start mass fires that would turn underground shelters into ovens. The associate professor of physics at the Stevens Institute spoke during a panel workshop on the need for fall-out shelters in schools.

Dr. Willard Jones, State Coordinator of Civil Defense for schools, warned that with a 30-minute headway between the blasts and the start of fall-out, shelters would be needed with 16 to 18 inches of concrete capable of protecting children and citizens from 99% of deadly gamma rays. With the time limit down from 60 to 30 minutes, there is little chance of sending children home, Jones pointed out. He called for cooperation by all community units in building shelters in schools for use of all residents.

John F. Hopf, Jr., County Superintendent of Schools and coordinator of Rockland County Civil Defense, said that efforts were being made to find the safest places in schools where students and teachers would be free from falling walls and shattering glass. There is one possible fall-out shelter in the county school system: an old school that has an underground potato shed in the backyard. The shed would have to be stocked with blankets, food and water.

Taylor told the panel that fall-out shelters would be effective only when a nuclear bomb exploded on the ground which would stir up dirt and debris which would carry the radioactive fall-out.

Dr. Edmund Gordon of Pomona said the plan to build shelters was immoral and a deception to children, and added that American resources were being used to dig holes. Dr. Gordon said that the important thing was that a move be made in the world today for peace, even with the disbanding of the army if necessary.

Others in the audience contended that the public was being prepared for acceptance of permanent war. They wanted to know how it was possible to prepare for peace by preparing for war.

Scott Webber, *The Record*, 1/4/62

Nuclear Bomb Drills

In addition to fire drills, it was common in Rockland County schools during the Cold War to practice what to do in the event of a nuclear bomb blast. Students were instructed to get under their desks as soon as they saw the bright flash of light of the initial explosion. During one such drill in elementary school, I can remember crouching on the floor, thinking that if a nuclear bomb actually did explode nearby, it wouldn't make any difference if I was under my little wooden desk.

We were also shown films on how to survive after a nuclear attack. One scene left a vivid impression: a housewife was in her kitchen, about to prepare a meal, but everything was covered in radioactive fallout. As she casually brushed the fallout off of the plastic wrapper of a loaf of bread, the narrator reminded us to make sure to remove any radioactive debris from our food before we ate it.

We can only hope that the fear, paranoia and absurdity of those years will never again be experienced by future generations.　　　　Linda Zimmermann

Despite the pensive look, nuclear bombs are the last thing on the mind of kindergarten graduate Bobby Webber in 1969.　　Photo by Scott Webber.

...In 1967 the first heart transplant is performed...The microwave oven is introduced...In 1968 the Apollo 8 astronauts orbit the moon...Author John Steinbeck dies...

The Vietnam War: Two Men, Two Paths

April 30, 2000:

Today, the world is commemorating the 25th anniversary of the end of the Vietnam War. But for 22-year-old platoon sergeant Jerry Donnellan, the war was over in 1969.

Donnellan, who was leading search-and-destroy missions for the U.S. Army's Americale Division on Oct. 24 of that year, lost a leg to a grenade when the North Vietnamese Army engaged his platoon in a firefight in War Zone I in the Central Highlands. Seven of his platoon members would die in the attack.

Four months earlier, in June 1969, Donnellan arrived in Vietnam for assignment with his unit. Fifteen miles away, a 24-year-old conscientious objector named Doug Hostetter was completing three years of alternative service with the Mennonite Central Committee in Quang Tin province.

The war would eventually define the direction both Nyack men would take in their life's work. Today, Hostetter is international interfaith secretary for the Fellowship of Reconciliation, a peace organization. Donnellan is director of the Rockland County Veterans Service Agency.

Hostetter, the son of a Mennonite minister, was born in Pennsylvania and like his Swiss Mennonite ancestors was unwilling to kill for his country. He volunteered for three years of alternative service with the Mennonite relief organization in the middle of the war zone.

"Previously," Hostetter said, "I had wanted to be a missionary doctor, until I realized that souls and bodies both get destroyed by war."

Donnellan, a Rockland native whose father had served in World War II and whose brothers also served in the military, was majoring in English at Texas A&M University when he realized he had to make his own decision about military service. The road of self-sacrifice was the goal of many who emerged from the Kennedy years to join the military, Donnellan said.

"Within the vets community, war was not what it seemed at first," he said. "The mind-set was that democratic liberties were at stake in Vietnam. But as the war dragged on and infantry soldiers were doing the dying, that attitude changed."

Those who fought in Vietnam and those who were active in the peace movement represented many layers of opinions, Donnellan said. Some veterans returned to form Vietnam Veterans Against the War, which eventually became the Vietnam Veterans of America.

Hostetter agreed that the veterans peace movement helped people realize that "veterans were also victims." Hostetter noted Donnellan's work with the Rockland Veterans Shelter as "very important in trying to heal the wounds of Americans who were also victims."

In Vietnam, Hostetter, too, suffered losses when three fellow pacifists were killed. After the war, he experienced post-traumatic stress disorder from seeing his Vietnamese friends killed. But that did not prevent him from returning to Vietnam in 1980 as part of a humanitarian effort to deliver medicine.

Although some veterans have returned to Vietnam to make peace with the past, Donnellan worked through his bouts of post-traumatic stress disorder stateside.

"You can't take anyone out of society, teach them to kill and return them to that society without any psychological baggage," Donnellan said.

Nancy Cacioppo, *The Journal News*

Jerry Donnellan

Jerry Donnellan, who was shot twice before the grenade took his leg, spent over a year recovering in hospitals.

He returned to Rockland and became the stage manager for RCC, the Nanuet Theater Go Round and the Westchester Premier Theater, before taking on the role of Frank Sinatra's stage manager for eleven years.

He decided to help fellow veterans in 1988, after reading the startling statistic that more Vietnam vets have died by their own hands since the war ended than were killed in action.

Donnellan also has the distinction of being the easternmost county resident, living in a houseboat in the Hudson off Nyack.

Rocklanders in Vietnam

There were 46 Rockland residents killed in Vietnam. In the year 2000, there were over 24,000 Vietnam veterans living in the county, with 2,600 of them having been in combat. Among the veterans are judges, politicians, police chiefs and successful businessmen.

> The Vietnam War officially lasted from 1954 through 1975, although there was conflict in the region since the end of World War II. While the average infantryman in the Pacific in World War II engaged in combat about 40 days over 4 years of service, the average infantryman in Vietnam saw about 240 days of combat in a single year, due in part to the mobility afforded by the helicopter. Over 58,000 Americans were killed in the war.

VIETNAM WAR
In Memoriam

AHLMEYER, HEINZ (JR)
ANDREW, WALTER E. (JR)
BATES, ROBERT M.
BAUER, ROBERT E.
BERNTSEN, ROBERT
BROOKS, ANDRE M.
BROQUIST, STEPHEN A.
BROWN, RICHARD C.
BRUSH, RICHARD B.
BURRIS, FREDERICK,
CONKLIN, BERNARD
CONKLIN, JOSEPH P.
CONLIN, PETER E.
DANIEL, ANDREW J.
DEMEOLA, RAYMOND W.
DORSEY, WILLIAM T.
FALDERMEYER, HAROLD
GARRISON, WILLIAM L.
GILLIES, JAMES F.
HAGAN, ROBERT
HARTZ, JOSEPH E.
HORTON, JOHN M. (JR)
JACARUSO, FRANK

KAUFMAN, HAROLD J.
KEITH, KENNETH A.
KERNAN, MICHAEL R.
KILE, JOHN T.
KRASHES, HAROLD D.
LIFRIERI, PAUL J.
MAGRO, JAMES A.
McGOVERN, MICHAEL E.
MORINA, ANTHONY J.
MUNTZ, GIRAUD D.
NATALE, PATRICK H.
PAQUIN, PAUL E. (JR)
PARKER, JAMES E.
RAKENTINE, KENNETH C.
ROSE, LAWRENCE O.
SCHETTIG, ROBERT S.
SHELLITO, WALTER C.
SPRUILL, JAMES P.
STONEHOUSE, ALFRED L.
TROJAHN, DARRELL C.
TURNER, WILLIAM R. (JR)
WITZEL, ROBERT C.
WOODRUM, JOHN J.

Kathleen Lukens, A Life for Others

Kathleen's life work came out of a mother's determination that her fourth child, David, born autistic, would live a life of love and promise that seemed open to her normal children. No such prospect for handicapped children and adults existed here or elsewhere, for that matter, in the early 1960s. Her efforts brought about a social revolution in our midst.

Rockland was a place of massive, impersonal public institutions that by the 1960s and 1970s were so overcrowded and understaffed that the resultant neglect became the stuff of media exposes. The public that decried the shame of neglect was not ready to accept the responsibility for reform. This took years of effort and a powerful and eloquent voice. Kathleen Lukens offered both.

Kathleen Lukens was a child of the Great Depression, which for most people was a time to forget. For young Kathy, however, it was a period of excitement and formation. Her Irish immigrant father was a labor organizer who moved from place to place wherever the movement called. The series of family apartments were filled with people and conversations about the plight of workers and the search for justice. Kathy reveled in all of it and came to nurture the sense that the world could be made better. She carried that sense through her school years and into Barnard College, where she distinguished herself as a leader and activist. She developed a powerful style of writing and following college, pursued a career in journalism.

From the time Kathy moved to Rockland, she felt a special affinity for this beautiful community. It was for her, a place for roots. She resumed her writing career as a part-time feature writer for a local weekly and from her kitchen, chronicled the events of the 1960s and early 1970s on both the local and national scene. The demands of her growing family forced her into late night note taking and thinking. Soon, her notes focused on the problems of David. These notes were the basis of her first book, *Thursday's Child Has Far to Go*.

Kathy's social life centered on her overweening interest in the social and educational exclusion of her son and his handicapped peers. She was elected the head

218

of the Exceptional Child PTA, a newly founded pressure group of parents seeking education for their excluded children. From this group sprang Camp Venture—a unique summer camp opened to any handicapped child regardless of diagnosis or ability to pay. Camp Venture became more than a camp, it became a movement. It still is.

At the invitation of Olegh Wolansky, the director of Letchworth Village, Kathleen toured that overcrowded institution. As part of this crusade, Kathleen confronted Governor Nelson Rockefeller at a press conference and embarrassed him into forwarding state funds to relieve the staff shortages. With her Venture following and with the help of her newly converted partner in work, Rockland County Legislator John Murphy, Kathleen set out to develop Venture Inn, a community residence for retarded adults. It was the first of its kind, and partial insurance that, at least for some, institutionalization was not inevitable.

Kathleen persisted in expanding the reach of care and enriching her programs. A workshop was built thanks to the help of Senator Eugene Levy, Kathy's other partner in the good work. The Dolly Downs project, a doll specially designed both to teach inclusion and give satisfying work to the clients of the workshop, gained nationwide attention in newspaper and television features. Then came the annexation of the former Rosary Academy in Sparkill, where a day treatment program was established. Fundraising events spearheaded by another mother, Barbara Reece, enabled Kathleen to purchase vacation homes for her people at the seashore and in the mountains. A therapeutic pool was built; and she presided over the integration of the camp, taking great satisfaction that a waiting list developed for normal children whose parents wished them to share a camping experience with their handicapped peers.

As Kathleen became a full time director of the Venture programs, she enlarged her mission by serving on the New York State Child Advocacy Commission and the Rockland County Community Services Board. She was honored by governors, recognized by the Congress of the United States, commended by state and local governments, honored by civic organizations and granted honorary degrees by three of our local colleges. Two of her last efforts were the development of The Pond of the 200,000, a memorial to the euthanized handicapped of the Nazi era, and an independent living center at the Venture Center in Sparkill that was named for her. The late Cardinal John O'Connor helped dedicate The Pond in 1997, and the former First Lady of New York State, Matilda Cuomo, gave Kathy her last public recognition at the dedication of The Kathleen Lukens Independent Living Center in 1998.

Her flame is now gone, yet the special glow that was Kathleen continues. It is a light transforming Rockland County, the scene of her work, as the people there now expect that the poor will be cared for, the broken will be made whole, the disabled will be valued, and the children shall have their time and place for laughter.

Jack Lukens

St. Gregory's

Rockland's population boom of the 1950s not only stretched the limits of local housing and community services. Churches, too, felt the effects of overcrowding. As Garnerville's population swelled with young Irish and Italian Catholic couples moving from New York City and New Jersey, St. Peter's parish realized that the church needed to expand to keep up with the spiritual needs of all the growing families.

In response, the new parish of St. Gregory's was founded in the spring of 1961 with the Rev. Thomas J. Darby. Thanks to his efforts and those of the members of the parish, St. Gregory's church and school grew and thrived.

After 25 years, it claimed a membership of 3000 families, with 317 children in its school for grades 1 through 8 and 700 public school children in its School of Religion. In addition to the 25th Anniversary festivities in 1986, a book was published in 1987 to commemorate the people and the events that helped make St. Gregory's an important part of the lives of so many families.

Linda Zimmermann

New Square

Along Route 45, just past a shopping center there is a highway sign that says NEW SQUARE. A right turn at this point plunges the traveler back 200 years to a Polish *shtetl* closer in spirit to *Fiddler on the Roof* than to the supermarkets down the road. New Square is a community whose outlook would have been familiar to the Old Testament prophets.

At this time of year chartered buses and private cars carrying more than a thousand pilgrims, all of them Hasidic Jews, converge on the tiny village—normal population around 700—to observe the ten High Holy days. There is no hotel or restaurant in New Square and its synagogue burned down several months ago. The pilgrims are bedded down all over the village, many at the boys' school where all the Hasidim—residents and pilgrims alike—gather to worship.

New Square has turned away from modern life with the scornful ferocity of Jeremiah longing for the wilderness. All its present residents are Hasidic Jews, descendants of an eighteenth century Polish sect who are now the strictest guardians of Jewish orthodoxy. Having survived or fled from Hitler's concentration camps, these people came to America—specifically to the Williamsburg and the Crown Heights sections of Brooklyn—just after the war. Ten years later, they fled once again—not from persecution this time, but from almost its opposite: the temptations and tolerance of American life, which they were sure could asphyxiate orthodoxy just as effectively as the gas chambers.

A band of a few hundred made the original hegira from the city's lures. They named the new community New Skver, in honor of their Grand Rabbi's birthplace in the Ukraine. A clerk in the Rockland County courthouse recorded New Square, giving it an American flavor appropriate to its ranch houses and Cape Cod cottages.

No one in New Square drops out of high school. But neither does anyone try to write a novel. No one owns a television set, and few own radios. No one reads English-language newspapers.

Yet, to date, nobody has moved away from New Square. The attitude of the villages is like that of a famous rabbi who was reproached for loudly offering thanks for his blessings although he clearly lacked everything that a man needs. "What I need most is probably poverty," he replied, "and that is what I have been given."

Joan Gould, *Life*, 9/23/66

The Jewish Community
1960-1969

Located on Chestnut Ridge Road, Congregation Shaarey Tifloh, a Conservative synagogue, began in 1962. Initially, thirteen families were the nucleus of the new congregation and services were held on the back porch of Helen and Stanley Burda's home, on Midway Avenue. In 1963, builder Jake Landa sold them his model home, on Route 45. The house and adjacent land for future expansion cost Shaarey Tfiloh $31,500, and many of the original congregants signed the first mortgage papers. After years of building and expansion, October 15, 1971 saw the dedication of the completed edifice.

In 1962, the Yeshiva of Spring Valley's new building on Route 306 and Maple Avenue was completed. At the time the boys were on the Route 306 side, the girls on the Maple Avenue side. In 1973 the building was not adequate and construction began on their new facility. Continued growth saw the need for an addition, completed in 1991.

B'nai Israel established on the property of Letchworth Village in 1965, first held High Holy Day and weekly prayer service in the institution's gymnasium. To many residents the gym did not seem a proper place to worship. "For many of the residents," congregation director Paul Reibstein said, "a gymnasium was not a true home of their faith and even if they are retarded they could sense it." Six years later plans were developed for a permanent building on Willow Grove Road, which was dedicated in 1973. "As Jews, we have a natural pride in this small accomplishment," Reibstein said. "However, the greatest reward," he added, "is in knowing we are helping the retardates to share in the world as a dignified human being."

Established in 1965, the Monsey Jewish Center on Route 306 first met in a school building on the old Herriman Farm, where Blueberry Apartments are located today. In June of the following year ground was broken for their permanent synagogue across the street. The Rockland County Hebrew Day School, now known as the Yeshiva of Rockland County, was established there in 1976.

In 1965, thirteen families left the Congregation Sons of Israel of Nyack to establish Temple Beth Torah on Route 9W. Its synagogue was dedicated in 1965 with their first addition completed in 1982. Ground was broken in Pearl River for Beth Am Temple in December 15, 1967, on Madison Avenue, four years after the congregation was formed in September 1963. When the congregation was formed, Rev. Daniel offered the facilities of his church until Beth Am had a home of its own. He said, "The problem of the temple gives the church the chance to practice the brotherhood it preaches." For four years the two faiths co-operated closely with joint services on Thanksgiving.

A charter membership of twenty-three families established the Pomona Jewish Center as a Conservative congregation in April 1967. A farmhouse served as synagogue, meeting rooms, school and parsonage until a new synagogue was completed the following year. On Simchat Torah, (the fall) of 1988, the congregation moved into its new home. Because of its unusual shape the sanctuary is known as the synagogue in the round.

Harold L. Laroff

Stony Point Centennial

In the spring of 1965, the Town of Stony Point celebrated the centennial of its separation from Haverstraw. A two-month celebration was held during which time many men grew beards, a period fashion show was held at the Wayside Inn (now an office building) and a centennial queen was chosen. Some citizens found to be out of step with the event were put in stocks and pies were thrown in their faces. (*Photo below right demonstrates that Mr. Webber was obviously out of step! Ed.*) Another victim was supervisor Robert P. Slocum (below left) who was made to wear a bonnet by order of the nightly kangaroo court. There was a big parade down Route 9W (below center), ending in a costume ball which was held at the Bear Mountain Inn. Stony Point's most famous citizen, Jim Farley, gave an address.

Article and photos by Scott Webber

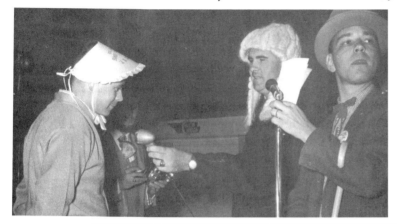 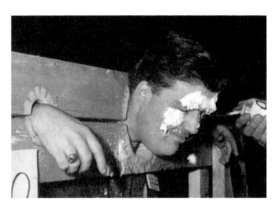

Stony Point Centennial Queen Judy McElroy. Middle row: Barbara and Janet Kornbekke.
Front row: Vicki Shankey, Jane Erickson, Sondra Shankey.

Memories of Garnerville

I was four years old when my family moved from the Bronx to Garnerville in 1960. My father was a NYC fireman and commuted to the city like so many other people, and he also took a second job in Rockland as a bus driver. The neighborhood in Garnerville where we spent the decade of the 1960s was off Main Street on Captain Shankey Drive and Barnes Drive. There were plenty of kids my age in the neighborhood so it made

for a wonderful place to grow up. There were woods and apple orchards to explore and build forts in, have wars or just lose yourself. There was a reservoir to swim in and ice skate on and in back of Barnes Drive was a summer bungalow colony called the Birchwoods, where we could play baseball and football on a large field.

During summer, the Birchwoods became occupied and busy with campers that would come up from the city to spend a summer in the country. Naturally, we felt that the Birchwoods was our domain so we resented the campers coming up and stealing *our* baseball field. There were some great challenge games between us and the campers over the years, but I can remember being thrilled beyond words one summer night when our dads got to talking and decided they were going to band together and challenge the camp counselors who were darn good city ball players bursting with young energy.

I had never seen my father or any other fathers actually play baseball in a competitive setting like this and I was so proud of my dad, but also scared to death he might look bad by striking out or committing some other unheroic sin. Lo and behold, Dad made a fabulous running catch, running up an incline in deep center field, catching the ball as it glanced off the tree, so the "old men" (about 42 years old) did us proud.

Another interesting and legendary part of growing up was "Shotgun Annie" (pronounced Shot-gu-nanny). This was a fierce old woman who owned a large and stately home facing Route 202, with a huge sloping field for a backyard that backed all the way down to Barnes Drive circle in our neighborhood. A trail from our neighborhood to Red's Candy Store (which had packs of baseball cards for 5 cents and 10-cent ice cream cones) passed through Shotgun Annie's property. Stories passed down from the older generation (the 12-year-olds), spoke of a rifle toting old lady who would shoot you with rock salt to keep you off her property. There was nothing more chilling to young hearts than the experience of clambering into the field and beginning to journey down the path and seeing Shotgun Annie in all her majestic and satanic fury emerge from that haunted house on the hill, and bellow, "Get out of my field, go back to your family!" The voice positively rang through the field. I must admit I never saw her famed rifle, but it worked there in our own minds if not in her skirts.

Driving up Route 202 today, one sees the stately old house, now hemmed in by other houses, having yielded its fields to high ranch development, and one wonders what became of Shotgun Annie. For that matter, what became of the neighborhood where parents left their doors open and let their kids roam freely, and where kids organized their own games and grew up without Nintendo, but with each other.

Ken Murphy

The Story of Samsondale

Massachusetts born Elisha Peck went to England to expand his tinplate trade. He returned in 1830 on the ship *Samson*, settled in the West Haverstraw area and built a rolling mill along the Minisceongo Creek at the present location of the Hi Tor Bowling Alley. When the mill prospered, he built a magnificent mansion on the hill overlooking the mill and named his estate *Samsondale*, after the ship that returned him home.

The entrance to the mansion was on the south side of Railroad Avenue adjacent to the present small cemetery on the top of Calico Hill. The three-story Greek revival style mansion was the largest in Rockland County. With its columns and front balcony, it had the appearance of the southern plantation manor.

With the death of the last direct descendant of Elisha Peck, the property was put up for sale. Local citizens attempted to have the village of West Haverstraw purchase it as a municipal building. This didn't materialize and in 1962 the mansion was demolished and the hill upon which it stood was itself leveled. All traces of the estate have vanished into what are now the Samsondale houses and shopping plaza.

The only reminder of the once important Peck family is Peck Lane, a small street in West Haverstraw.

Robert Burghardt

The final moments of the Samsondale house in 1962 (above right). Note the crane on the right side of the photo. The great house falls (right).   Photos by Scott Webber.

Mansions Fall

The Samsondale Plaza shopping center in 2001 (left). The historic Samsondale mansion stood on this site until it was demolished in 1962.

Nearby, the stately Henry Garner mansion once stood on the northwest side of the corner of Railroad Avenue and Route 9W. Built in the 1830s, the house was still occupied in the 1970s by Mrs. Marguerite Hornbaker, a granddaughter of Henry Garner.

After her death, the mansion was torn down and a housing development was built on the site.

...In 1969 test pilots take the Concorde on its maiden flight...CBS cancels the Smothers Brothers show because of its "anti-establishment" humor...400,000 attend Woodstock...Charles Manson's followers murder five...Hundreds of thousands of anti-war protestors march across the U.S. ...

Fake Farms and Milk Trucks

I was born in 1958 at Nyack Hospital, so my childhood memories are from the 1960s. My parents used to take us to the many local farms for fresh produce and I have many fond memories of going to Tices for apple cider straight from the spigot, fresh donuts in the fall and picking strawberries at Duryea's in the summer.

I married a man from rural Ohio and when I told him that when we were kids, we would go to the farms on the weekends, he would refer to them as "fake farms," i.e., the commercial ones like Tices and DiPieros in Bergen County.

However, I also told him that when I was a little girl, Pete the milkman would come by delivering the milk.

All of us neighborhood kids would run to Pete, because he would let us ride in the back of the ice truck and would chip off pieces of ice for us to suck on those hot summer days. My husband just would not believe that we had our milk delivered, or that the truck wasn't refrigerated.

Then one day, I stopped at "Jerry's" in Nyack, only to see Pete sitting at the counter (his brother was "Jerry"). Not only did he remember me, he asked me if I remembered riding on the milk truck. I ran out and got my husband to come in just to prove that Nyack was once a very small town!

Debbi Bailey-Graff

Elizabeth Taylor in Rome, and There's No Place Like Home

On a day in 1960, I was on leave in Rome, taking time off from my work as a seaman aboard the USS *Saratoga* CVA-60. Three of us sailors, all friends, spent the day walking through the Vatican Museum, past art I had studied in college. And that evening, we chose to go out to a movie, in Rome.

The chosen movie was *Butterfield-8* starring Elizabeth Taylor, who played a woman who climbed behind the wheel of a Volkswagen Karman-Ghia with suicidal intent. I sat between my two buddies as absorbed with the story as they were, when I watched Taylor's car make a left turn, off of Route 303 in West Nyack, to get on the Thruway, northbound. I recognized the scene as one that had to have been shot during the construction of the Thruway.

It was one of those artificial shots where the scenery moves and Taylor turned her wheel, but you wonder if it is all real. Taylor may never have set foot on Rockland County soil, or perhaps she did. I don't know. But there I was, in that Roman theater, and my elbows whammed my two buddies' ribs quite smartly. "That's HOME, guys! THAT'S HOME!" I told them.

They got the full explanation at the end of the show.

Should anyone care to see snatches of Rockland County in a movie dating to 1956, all they have to do is rent a copy of *Butterfield-8* and watch for the appearance of the Karman-Ghia. The house behind her in the turn has since been replaced by a gas station. The Palisades Center stands near the site now.

Phil Klein

Bobby Kennedy at the Stony Point Battlefield on May 2, 1965.
Photo by Scott Webber.

The Nyack Riots

On a hot summer's evening in July 1967 a group of youths ran riot in Nyack. The next day it was reported they had broken windows and bottles throughout the downtown section of the village. According to a report in the *New York Times* the next day, the village police, convinced they would be unable to contain the rioters with the forces available, called for reinforcements. The Nyack police, assisted by a score of officers from nearby communities plus the Sheriff's posse, broke up the disturbance. The outburst had lasted approximately an hour and a half. Nearly a score of young men and women had been arrested. All were described in the press as Negroes.

Informants, described in a New York City newspaper as Negroes, offered a different version of the incident. They maintained that it had hardly warranted the attention given it. As extensive rioting was underway in Newark, Plainfield and other New Jersey places, the street speculations had it that the Nyack police had been encouraged to take firm action by what they were seeing on television. In the opinion of these informants the whole effort at enforcement had been intentional—to let the Negro youths know who was boss.

While it is difficult thirty years later to ascertain the truth of this allegation, there is reason to believe that the village police were edgy. Two nights earlier, they had been called out to break up a street fight, and the previous evening three false fire alarms had been turned in, all from the same neighborhood in which the Tuesday disturbance had occurred. Those events, plus apprehensions heightened by events in Newark, probably helped considerably to unsettle the authorities.

During the day following the disturbance, the residents set about assessing the damage. No one had been hurt, physically, that is. No fires had been set and destruction to property was minor. But several windows had been broken and a number of young people arrested. They eventually were to stand trial. By comparison with events in other places, "the disturbance was no more than a fire cracker going off," or, at least, that was how the *New York Times* summed up the episode.

Nevertheless, confidence had been shaken and a certain foreboding had settled in. The day after, residents not quite so comfortable as they had been before.

Early in September, a new disturbance featuring numerous fires and false alarms made the newspapers. In its wake, a petition was circulated by a group purporting to represent the village firemen. It called for strong measures. The fire companies, of which there were eight in the Nyacks, are volunteer and were, in 1967, exclusively white. The petition, which purportedly had been drawn up "with the sympathy of much of the police department," read, in part: "We know that there is a small group allowed to roam through the village streets threatening, abusing, and persecuting policemen and civilians alike. This group causes great embarrassment to both Negroes and whites who have seen our town in the past with no racial disturbances of any kind. We admit that some of these group members are not from the Village of Nyack; some are. It appears to us that this group is bent on one desire; i.e. to disturb, destroy, and perform vandalous acts."

In October, trouble broke out again downtown. The day, Wednesday, the 4th, dawned hot and muggy. Weather people on the New York radio stations were predicting temperatures in the mid-eighties and noted a smog alert was being considered. As the day wore on, the forecast proved altogether too accurate. By evening, the atmosphere was stifling and tensions prompted by the unseasonable heat had begun to grate.

Sometime around 9:30 p.m., it was reported that an "unruly crowd of about 15 Negro youths" had gathered at one of the downtown street corners. A police car was dispatched to investigate. According to subsequent newspaper reports, it was met on its arrival at the scene by a hail of rocks. Reinforcements were called for and several policemen came to its aid. A general melee ensued. During it three of the officers, including the Chief, were hurt. An alarm was sounded and, shortly, police from neighboring villages and towns responded. The Sheriff's posse was again called into action.

Eventually, the crowd dispersed and the streets were cleared. Later, however, windows were broken in a nearby liquor store and three fires were discovered. The captain of the high school football team, three reporters, and an ex-paratrooper, who had seen action quelling the Detroit riots earlier that summer, were among the nine persons apprehended.

Apprehension was widespread throughout the downtown area following that incident. The streets, while quiet, had an ominous cast about them. For several nights, the Sheriff's mounted posse continued to patrol the village streets and the eerie clop-clop of horse hoofs added considerably to the prevailing sense of unreality. When the local branch of the NAACP held a meeting at the high school, it was reported that, "those present were convinced that the scraping and low buzzing coming through the public-address system was (caused by) the police 'listening in' from a nearby office." The subject of the meeting was "Religion and Black Power." And, at dinner parties that weekend, people one met from the surrounding suburbia asked whether it was safe to visit the village. Undoubtedly, many disquieting stories were being circulated.

In response to this crisis in confidence, the mayor and his fellow trustees issued a statement proclaiming that they had "not in the past, do not presently, and shall not in the future tolerate civil disorders and continuous breaches of the peace." According to the summary of the statement published in the local newspaper, persons who failed to show respect for law and order would be "dealt with and punished, by whatever means are allowed by law," and further, that "It is regrettable that a relatively small number of our citizens, provoked and misled by strangers in our community, have seen fit to resort to violence and disorder."

Objectively, nothing much had really happened during the incidents that jarred Nyack in 1967. Several policemen had been wounded—as much in their dignity as in their body—and a number of youths and reporters were jailed. While there was violence, it was tame when compared with what was going on elsewhere in the nation. Nevertheless, something had ripped, something that normally held together.

Carl Nordstrom, *Phoenician Tales*

Civil Rights

Clergymen of all denominations were among the first to put themselves out on the firing line for civil rights. Especially active was the (Roman) Catholic Interracial Council shepherded by Monsignor James Cox, chaplain at Rockland State Hospital. In Pearl River, the Reverend Wilbur Daniel of the Nauraushaun Presbyterian Church stepped forward to challenge the conscience of his neighbors, and at Spring Valley, Seymour Friedman, a leader of the Jewish Community Center there, saluted Negro protest in a message from Birmingham, Alabama. In January 1964, the Nyack Clergy Association topped the cake with a comprehensive resolution against bigotry which included the following statement, "If a Negro wants to worship in our church or synagogue, then we are obligated to see to it that he is not only accepted but welcomed into our full life."

At an earlier meeting sponsored by the Catholic Interracial Council in Sloatsburg, John F. Sullivan, curate at Tomkins Cove, called for an attack on housing and job discrimination, and for an extra effort to encourage students to complete their schooling. "A Christian cannot," he said, "in conscience prevent a man from buying or renting property or from securing employment merely on the basis of race." He then added that it was not sufficient to admit to these principles just in theory, "We must put them into practical application in our own neighborhood and community."

There was also pressure for action from other power centers. Early in July, Governor Nelson Rockefeller wrote to the county Board of Supervisors and recommended it form a Commission on Human Relations. To that request, Victor Shankey of Haverstraw responded that "his town had never had any trouble along this vein and demanded the governor leave this town alone because it is getting along fine." Still wary about what was going on, the four remaining Supervisors kept their mouths shut.

Two days later, the Orangetown township board, confronted by 40 indignant residents charging discrimination in Rockland private swim clubs, put itself on record as being against segregation. It responded in the form of a resolution: Be it resolved that this official body affirm(s) that segregation and discrimination (are) incompatible with the maintenance of a healthy community, that within the functions of the government of the Town of Orangetown it will not be tolerated or permitted and further that private enterprise will be urged to refrain from such practices and assist in the effort to stamp them out.

On July 17, 1963, twelve days after they had sat so mum in the face of Governor Rockefeller's letter, the five members of the Rockland County Board of Supervisors voted approval for the formation of a Human Rights Commission. Using the same resolution Orangetown had offered as their theme, they also declared their unanimous opposition to racial discrimination in the county. In September they appointed Alvin Goldstein of Monsey Chairman of the Commission.

By late 1963, civil rights had become so fashionable that even the *Journal-News* was prepared to join the crowd. But in doing so, it joined in a manner designed to promote reservations. After applauding the appointment of Goldstein, and giving credit to the Board of Supervisors and to Governor Nelson Rockefeller on its editorial page, the *Journal* went on to insist, "Only those who will not see can deny that racial discrimination is a problem in Rockland County, and only the hopelessly optimistic can believe that the county commission will eliminate it."

In a sense, the *Journal* was correct in raising doubts. While support for a strong stand for human rights in Rockland had become substantial, it was not universal. There were people with reservations about the direction public opinion was apparently taking, and shortly they began to give voice to those reservations. Banded together, they called themselves Conservatives. Their opposition first took concrete form when the members of the relatively new Conservative Party in Orangetown charged the township board with "bowing to mob rule." Up until then, the Conservatives had not run candidates for county offices.

The Conservatives argued that an individual owning and running a business such as a swim club must make his own decisions as to how the business should be operated. "In the final analysis, the market place is the determining factor. If a business is not being run properly the people will not patronize it. If, on the other hand, he is making a profit, one can only assume that the public approves of his operation." Following up on their threat of running candidates, they concluded by insisting they would put forward one who would espouse "American principles so vital to our way of life."

In December 1963, at a meeting sponsored by the Catholic Interracial Council at which Assemblyman Bertram Baker of Brooklyn, co-author of the Metcalf-Baker bill proscribing discrimination in housing, was the main speaker, John Lodico of New City took issue. After listing his favorable experiences with Negroes, Lodico then added that, "When legislation is forced upon people it creates more discontent than when not legislated, and tends to stir up hate." Baker responded that, as he saw it, Lodico was operating on the assumption that people have a right to hate.

With the turn to the new year, 1964, the rights controversy reached a boil. There were charges, counter charges, and rebuttals—with all sides represented. The first steps were organizational. Right after New Year's Day, Bill Scott, together with attorney Conrad Lynn, announced the formation of a new political party— Freedom Now. The leadership was to be Negro, but membership was not to be limited to them. Later in January, a CORE chapter was established in Nyack, with black dentist, Dr. Charles James, designated as Chairman. In New City, at a Knights of Columbus meeting, state Conservative Vice-chairman Rice again returned to lecture on conservative principles, Negro rights, and to belabor school busing. While all that was happening, Nauraushaun's Pastor Daniel, who had gone south to work for voter registration, was arrested while demonstrating. It was during this same period that the resolution against bigotry by Nyack's clergymen was issued, and the charge that Nyack's urban renewal program was forcing Negro removal to Spring Valley was raised.

During February 1964, there was evidence of real progress in race relations on many fronts in Rockland. During that month, Leonard Cooke received the Civic Association's "Citizen of the Year" award. Vicki Brooks

226

of Nyack, in a letter to the *Journal*, called on the county Board of Realtors to announce publicly that they were prepared to support the state's anti-discrimination laws. In a breakthrough decision that had taken two years to promote, a Spring Valley black plumber, Harold Mitchell, won seniority rights in his union.

On hearing of Mitchell's success, the county Conservatives called for legislation to curb the power of the New York State Commission on Human Rights. The degree to which black people were being taken seriously was again underscored when, at Temple Beth El in Spring Valley, a panel composed of the Reverend Petty McKinney of St. Philips A.M.E. Zion in Nyack, social worker Mrs. Emory Ellington, and composer Arthur Cunningham (the son of Piermont's Rachel Cunningham) were the speakers. The session was energetic and forthright, with the three speakers demanding total commitment to the rights movement while members of the audience expressed reservations about going too far, too fast.

Two years later, in 1966, the newspaper reported there were only two Negro firemen in all of Rockland County, one in Haverstraw and a second in the outlying hamlet of Thiells. In Central Nyack, three Negroes had applied for membership in its fire company. All were ex-servicemen, and two of the applicants owned homes. Their applications were rejected unanimously.

Despite their efforts to reconcile conflicts, blacks had never been accepted wholeheartedly as citizens. Instead, they lived set off in a tight enclave of houses that were the poorest in town. Coalition government for both the school board and the village board had been contrived to minimize their influence. The carefully devised technique used by the fire companies to exclude them from membership was not only effective in keeping them out of the club, but it also promoted the impression that they could not be trusted. Nor had they ever, to any great degree, succeeded in moving upward in the economic structure.

Faced with that calculated rejection of many years standing, it took a great deal of personal courage for the black people in Rockland to step forward and seek the rights they presumably had been guaranteed with the end of slavery. The battle for those rights had been under way for many years. But it never had been entirely won, and in the sixties of the twentieth century it had broken out again and with new intensity in Rockland.

The long history of indifference and immobility on the local racial front testified to the need for bold approaches. Bill Scott did what he had to do with dash and derring-do; Leonard Cooke, for his part, with cool calculation. But confrontation is never an orderly process, and there were frequent snags. While, at times, they did come into conflict with established authorities as well as with each other, their useful contribution lay in the way they nudged the greater community into action through maintaining a pressure that was both creative and unrelenting

During the period they and their associates were active in promoting social change in Rockland and in Nyack there were many notable advances in black status. By its end, just about every school in the county had one or more black teachers. A major step toward integration had been taken in the building trades and, in many other occupations; affirmative action was underway.

Jobs were better and, relatively speaking, incomes were up. More black students were graduating from high school, and many of those youths were going on to college. In Nyack, a slum had been demolished and adequate substitute housing had been built in its place. A headstart program was also under way. There were political gains recorded, particularly, with Hezekiah Easter's election to Nyack's Board of Trustees and Leonard Cooke's appointment as Chairman of the Water Board. For the moment, at least, blacks, there, were no longer being taken for granted.

Carl Nordstrom, *Phoenician Tales*

Across the country, once flourishing downtown areas suffered a decline as suburbia acquired good roads and automobiles. In Rockland, the problem reached the point where villages that a few decades earlier had been attractive and prosperous, were now being referred to as slums. Those who could afford to, moved out and into one of the numerous new housing developments. New shopping centers also sprang up, further damaging the economies of the town centers. Crime rates were on the rise. Poverty and decay wore heavily on the formerly grand features of places like Nyack, Spring Valley, Suffern and Haverstraw. Something needed to be done, but as always, progress had to run the gamut of local factions and special interest groups.

Linda Zimmermann

Urban Renewal

By 1960, urban renewal had acquired an image problem in Rockland County. Both Suffern and Sloatsburg were considering programs, and in both, vigorous and outspoken opposition had emerged. In Suffern public housing was the main canker. The

problem, as seen in public comments, was that such housing, by law, would have to be racially integrated. At the time, there were no blacks living in the village. As one commentator there phrased it, "...if the village has to house families with immoral character, frequent drunkenness, and other public nuisances, then I don't want it." On the other hand, the same man pointed out that suggestions that merchants and property owners undertake renewal on their own were frivolous. "In 50 years what has been done?" he asked. In Sloatsburg, by contrast, the objectors were traditionalists who stood fast against promised improvements promoted by recent settlers who had moved there from New York City.

At Nyack, promoters encountered frustrations, snags, clever ploys, and seedy little scandals, but nothing so compelling as to sink the program. The village was probably fortunate in its long history of sweeping trouble under the rug, that is, if renewal represented good fortune.

For long periods, it would seem as if there was no progress at all. Then, there would be an announcement of some kind of grant approval at some level that was somehow significant for some purpose. To the casual observer, it looked as if renewal planning would last forever and as if there would never be anything to show for it.

Still, it did keep a number of people employed.

Carl Nordstrom, *Phoenician Tales*

Segregation Threatens Midget Football Game

Spring Valley, December 8, 1961: Last night, the Village Youth Activities Commission voted against sending the Pony Express Police Athletic League Midget Football team to St. Petersburg, Florida, after it was learned that two Negro boys could not play due to the social practices of that state.

December 11: The Governor of Florida has lifted a segregation ban to allow two Negro members of the Pony Express Midget Football team to play in St. Petersburg on December 20.

December 21: The Spring Valley Pony Express team beat the St. Petersburg Gators 20 to 14 before 12,000 spectators. Manager Peter Paddock credited the victory to teamwork.

Scott Webber, excerpts from *The Record*

A Personal View of Racism

Racism is more than just blatant acts of bigotry and discrimination. It is also the subtle, day-to-day occurrences that often pass beyond the comprehension of many people. The following are some examples from Frances E. Pratt, President of the NAACP.

I live today because the segregated South taught me how to survive. The consequences were such that "If I did not understand racism, everything else I did would not make sense."

I learned from my high school textbook, entitled *Adventures in Literature*, how Anglo-Saxons from their inception conditioned themselves not to go against each other. Similarly, the courts in the southern states upheld that an African-American person (called Negroes at that time) had no rights that a white man should respect.

My first encounter of a white person defending an African-American person's rights, where a white person was concerned, was in 1968. I was a nurse's aide at Nyack Hospital. A white physician discovered a wet, bloody gauze on the ground at the entrance to the Emergency Room. He stormed in the Emergency Room, passed all the workers who were white, came up to me and ordered me to go outside and dispose of the gauze. To add insult to injury, it was pouring rain and the night was cold. The charge nurse, hearing what he said, came to my defense. She said, "How dare you make such a request of Frances. She is not your maid. If you want that gauze removed, go pick it up yourself."

This experience taught me that though racism prevailed, there were some well-meaning white people in spite of the privilege they earned due to the color of their skin.

Racism in Rockland does exist. Although Jim Crow Senior might be dead, African-Americans must never forget that Jim Crow, Jr., is alive and well.

Another example is that many people don't give credit to the African-Americans' intellect. The epitome of their thinking is illustrated in what a white nurse friend of mine said to me. She said, "Dr. Johnson is not Black. He can't be. He is the most skilled physician I know." Such an analysis too often has become a rule rather than a fallacy.

During my tenure as Head Nurse, Manager of the Emergency Room at Nyack Hospital, Dr. Martha MacGuffie invited me to her home. Her daughter, Martha, was getting married. I presented myself well dressed. I was wearing an off-white lace dress purchased at Lord & Taylor's, with matching attire from head to toe. I was wearing a wide-brimmed Victorian style hat. I took a seat with the other guests. Within moments, an elderly white woman came over to me and said, "You must be Martha's maid." I said no, "I am Martha's boss. I am the Head Nurse Manager at Nyack Hospital Emergency Room. I am the one that contacts her to come to the Emergency Room when plastic surgical cases need to be taken care of when she is on call." I was not surprised by what she said, but I find it interesting how I was singled out over all the others there.

This brings to mind how I was treated in a convenience store in West Nyack. A white female entered the store ahead of me, a white man was behind me coming through the door. Two clerks were standing behind the counter in the store. The white lady walked up to the clerk on the right side. I went up to the clerk on the left. The white man stood directly behind me. The clerk in front of me motioned to the white man to come forward and proceeded to wait on him. I confronted the clerk about his action, left the store and filed a complaint with the local Human Rights Commissioner.

At the County Clerk's Office in New City I was applying for my passport. I was amazed at the room filled with white employees. I referred to the attendant taking care of me about the number of white employees. He said these jobs are for people who can pass the civil service exam.

The family of Frances E. Pratt, standing l-r: grandchildren Gerald Parker, Patricia Paul, Germaine Parker, seated l-r: daughter Carol Parker, Frances Pratt, husband Marshall Pratt.

The Women's Movement: Betty Friedan in Grand View

The inspiration for the feminist movement in the United States came from the pen of a Grand View housewife in 1963. In that year, Betty Friedan came out with her controversial book, *The Feminine Mystique*, in which she debunked the myth of the post-war woman, that docile soul who tended home and hearth while happily forgoing her own ambitions and interests. It sold more than three million copies. (When *The Feminine Mystique* first came out the publisher was sure her husband was buying up all her books.)

Friedan, who became the founding president of NOW, the National Organization for Women, and a co-founder of the National Women's Political Caucus, always split from the more radical members of the woman's movement in her insistence that women not isolate themselves from men, that women's liberation and men's liberation were intertwined.

At the start of 2000, Friedan was a visiting distinguished professor at Cornell University where at age 79 she was conducting a three-year study on women, men, work, family and public policy, financed by a $1 million Ford Foundation grant. She was living in Washington, D.C.

Of her study for Cornell she said, "We need a values revolution in this culture. We need quality of life to be more important than the bottom line. We need a new

definition of the bottom line, a purpose larger than the self.

"For me, the woman's movement provided such a purpose. To realize you were making a difference, changing history. It was exciting. Fun."

Born Betty Goldstein in Peoria, Illinois in 1921, she was the oldest of three children. She went to Smith College and the University of California at Berkeley for graduate work in psychology, which she abandoned in favor of moving to New York City to become a reporter for labor news agencies and where she married Carl Friedan. She took up freelance writing to stay home with their three children and began researching what would become her *Feminine Mystique* book. She got started on this when she did a questionnaire for a Smith reunion and discovered she was not the only one who "was not having orgasms waxing the family room floor."

Looking back she says, "The hardest thing I ever did was to get divorced. It was much harder than starting the woman's movement. I was terrified of being alone. Families are so important, keeping them intact. I don't think I had any choice by the time I did it. Now, it's not a fate worse than death if a woman makes more money than the man."

Scott Webber—Condensed from an article in the *The New York Times*, May 11, 2000

229

Pressure Dealers in Smut: Silberman Counsels Parents

Rockland County District Attorney Morton Silberman last night advised individual parents to put pressure on county news dealers to remove obscene literature from the magazine racks.

"In the absence of prosecution, if you feel that your children are affected by these publications you should make your feelings known to the dealer," Silberman said. "If you don't get results, take your business elsewhere."

He compared the stationery store to the food stores where customers expect cleanliness in the preparation and sale of food.

Silberman emphasized that he was talking only about protecting children under 18 years of age from obscene literature. He said that what an adult read was his own business. He said he had read *Tropic of Cancer* which was banned in several places in New Jersey.

He found it full of four-letter words but written in a good literary style.

"But I wouldn't want my children to read it," Silberman declared.

Scott Webber, *The Record*, 11/22/61

Miss Rockland 1969

Contestants for the 1969 "Miss Rockland County Scholarship Pageant" in the bathing suit lineup (below left). The winner is crowned (below right): Barbara Baugh (left), Miss Wisconsin of 1968, crowns the new Miss Rockland 1969 (center), Jean Kulhan of Blauvelt, as the first runner-up, Anita Quiros, looks on.   Photos by Art Gunther.

Recalling the Grand Days of the Soap Box Derby in Pearl River

Rockland's once famous Soap Box Derby, held in Pearl River, started out with a bang in 1949 as a roller car derby. Spearheaded by Horace Hunderfund, Joe Zenovic, Sr. and Melvin Pitts, it ended up a full-fledged soap box derby in 1964. It all ended in 1969, though there were talks about reviving the derby in 2000.

Along the way, the derby took on sponsors that included the *Journal News*, the Pearl River Board of Trade, the John H. Secor American Legion Post and the Schmidt, Manly and Driscoll Chevrolet agencies. Its

winner went directly to Akron to compete in the Chevrolet "All-American" finals.

Fred Hartel won it one year, with a peach basket as the hood. Sandra Konagewski won with a painted white sheet attached to the flimsy hood of her car.

Maximum weight for the soap box derby car was 250 pounds, including the driver. The wheels were ball bearing, and the sponsor bought the kit that included wheels, cables and steering gear, for $25. The sponsor got his name painted on both sides of the car.

The winner of Pearl River's first County Derby in 1964 was Tom Zenovic. Subsequent winners included Carl Phelps, Jeffrey Ferrel, Kevin Dillon and Chris von Hemilnijck.

From 1964 and thereafter, the Pearl River Derby group put on a real big show to go along with the derby. Mitch Miller of Suffern and TV fame was the first guest star, followed by Dave Herman, offensive guard of the New York Jets. Pat Hingle, a character actor living on Viola Road, brought his son, daughter and wife with him. That Derby, held on Flag Day with the help of the West Nyack Rotary Club, saw American flags held by marchers blanketing Central Avenue from Main Street to John Street.

A big feature of the Derby was the parade preceding the event. Not only were all entrants participants, but also over the years they included the Hudson View Shamrock Band, the American Legion Band of Pearl River, Troop 363 Bagpipe Band, the 40 & 8 Locomotive, Rockland County's Civil Air Patrol and VFW and Legion color guards.

County beauty queens were also part of it and included "Miss Nanuet Ambulance Corps," "Miss Rockland County Posture Queen" and "Miss Rockland County C.Y.O."

Additionally, all entries were taken to visit the Chevrolet plant in North Tarrytown before the derby and given a banquet the night of the derby. At the banquet, awards were presented and then a few days later all were taken to Palisades Amusement Park.

The awards included a $500 bond to the winner, plus a free trip for him and his parents to Akron. The winning car was always taken to Akron by Joseph Zenovic, Jr., the 1958 winner in Mount Vernon, who also conducted the "show how" clinics for Pearl River's derby.

Other awards were given for "best designed car," "best brakes," "best upholstered," "best looking," "best constructed" and the special award for "best sportsmanship."

Prior to the regular derby, a special "Oil Can Derby" was run. A few of these entries were then Orangetown Supervisor Jack Lovett, Peter Okkense and Clarkstown Town Justice William Vines.

Included on the soap box committee were Horace Hunderfund, Mr. and Mrs. Melvin Pitts, Mr. and Mrs. Kevin Day, George Phelps, Elton Clausen, Don Schmidt, Bill Cadig, Ken Harniman, Art Hopper and Mr. and Mrs. Joseph Zenovic, Sr. (Zenovic also built the ramps that automatically gave an even start to the two cars.)

Why did the derby break up in 1969? Manly and Driscoll Chevrolet pulled out in 1967 as sponsors, leaving Schmidt Chevrolet to cover the cost, which Don Schmidt did for one year. That left the *Journal News*, the Pearl River Board of Trade and the Rockland Jaycees. Not only did that leave a shortage of money, but there was also a shortage of manpower. It took about 50 volunteers to keep the derby under control.

Add to that the police force needed, government clearance for use of Central Avenue, securing of bales of hay to put across Central Avenue to stop cars if their brakes didn't and the use of local radio stations to broadcast the event. Put simply, the coaster car derby ran out of gas.

Kenneth F. Harniman

Ski Stony Point

This 1967 photo by Scott Webber shows a skiing demonstration at the Ski Stony Point facility.
The area now contains a housing development.

231

Rockland County Sports Hall of Fame: 1960-1969

Jim Ashcroft (Spring Valley) "Jimmy the Jet" used his speed to set records in track, as well as for basketball and football. Named Spring Valley Athlete of the Year in 1964.

Roger Brown (Nyack) 300-pound defensive tackle in the NFL for 10 years. Named NFL Lineman of the Year in 1962, All-Pro 4 years, went to Pro Bowl 6 times.

Tom Canty (Suffern) Wrestling coach for Ramapo and Pearl River who led his teams to dozens of county and state titles.

Don Clancy (Nyack) "Dashin Don" was one of the top sprinters in county history.

Tom Collins (Albertus Magnus) Outstanding multi-sport athlete coach for Albertus Magnus H.S.

Steve Drummond (Clarkstown) Excelled in baseball, football, basketball and bowling, as well as being a baseball and softball umpire. Was a sportswriter for the *Journal News* for 1967-1993.

Ron Edwards (Nyack) Earned titles and set numerous records in track, basketball and football. One of Nyack's finest all-around athletes.

Bob Grossman (Upper Grand View) Greatest race car driver in Rockland history. Three-time national champion, won the Grand Touring Class at LeMans twice, won National Grand Prix at Daytona, and had many other significant victories.

Guy Guccione (Suffern) In his 8 years as Suffern High School's wrestling coach, the Mounties won 6 county championships.

Bryan Hassett (Clarkstown) Exceptional three-sport athlete, winning titles and championships in baseball, soccer and basketball. Clarkstown's Most Valuable Athlete in 1966, and three-time "best hitter" in the Deer Head Tournament (softball).

Charles Holbrook (Clarkstown) Excelled in soccer, basketball and baseball, earning 8 varsity letters. Outstanding kicker for Wesleyan University. Taught and coached in Clarkstown, then became Town Supervisor.

George Jakowenko (Nyack) All-County in football and soccer. Played for 6 different NFL teams as a soccer-style place-kicker.

John Jenison (Nyack/Congers) One of the most dominant softball pitchers in county history. In his 20-year career, he amassed the amazing record of 2,146 wins against only 145 losses, with 54 no-hitters and 7 perfect games.

Gerald Kapusinsky (Haverstraw) Four-sport athlete, who went on to numerous coaching and officiating positions across the county.

Harold Lederman (Orangeburg) Highly respected boxing judge, who at the time of his induction in 1986 had judged 49 world-championship fights around the world. Judged bouts with many of the greats including Ali, Norton, Holmes, Foreman and Sugar Ray Leonard.

Jo Jo Mackey (Haverstraw) One of the true superstars in Rockland athletic history, leading Haverstraw to 8 consecutive major sports championships from 1960-62. Outstanding in basketball, football and baseball, and played in the minor league with the Yankees, winning 7 Golden Gloves.

Tom Mounkhall (Albertus Magnus H.S.) All-star basketball player and later a highly successful tennis coach for Spring Valley H.S. Also ran track and played baseball, hitting one of the longest home runs in county school history (well beyond 400 feet).

John Orlando (Suffern) Set the standard for coaching—second-winningest lacrosse coach and winningest ice hockey coach in county school history. In 1975 his lacrosse team was 25-0 and was ranked No. 1 in the state.

Jeanette Paddock (Spring Valley) Named Outstanding Senior Girl Athlete. Scored 50 points in a basketball game, made the boys' baseball team, but as a female was ineligible to play. Played 9 sports with Penn State. While living in Colorado she won many tennis tournaments.

Dennis Pozsar (Clarkstown) Excelled in soccer, basketball and baseball. Coached many teams for Clarkstown, and became the winningest soccer coach in Rockland school history with 275 victories.

Nick Ryder (Haverstraw) All-Conference and All-County fullback who went on to play in the NFL with the Detroit Lions in 1963-64. Later coached at Ramapo H.S.

Marty Springstead (Garnerville) Major League Baseball umpire for 20 years. Umpired 3 World Series and 3 All-Star games. Lectured and taught umpiring around the world.

William Gibson "Gibby" Sweet (Pearl River) Outstanding wrestler and track star in high school and college, later becoming a successful coach.

Paul Toscano (Clarkstown) Superb all-round athlete who made his greatest scholastic impact in basketball, but really shone as a football quarterback in college at the University of Wyoming.

Mickey Wittman (Nanuet) Three-sport athlete, but at 6-foot-7 excelled in basketball. All-County, All-American, invited to Olympic trials but a broken arm prevented his participation.

Burgess Meredith to the Rescue

After the death of Burgess Meredith in September of 1997, Pomona's first mayor, Jan Van den Hende, wrote the following piece for the *Journal-News*:

Burgess lived on Camp Hill and Quaker Roads, just outside what is now the Village of Pomona. He was not an outgoing person, yet he shared his blessings and talents with many. Even though he lived adjacent to Pomona, Burgess was a staunch supporter of our efforts to incorporate the area.

How many people in Rockland still remember the Pomona Horse Show of 1967? When the village had become a reality, and the committee, through the legal maneuvering of the local politicians, found itself deeply in debt, Burgess suggested we have a horse show on his property to recover our costs.

Never having been to a horse show, I had lots of doubts. But it turned out to be a smash. Not just because all of us worked our tails off, but because he finagled to fill in for Hugh Downs on the "Today Show" on NBC during the two weeks before the horse show. He would not shut up talking about "his" horse show on national TV every day.

The USHSA (Horse Show Association) refused to sanction the show, but, nonetheless, and through his connections, the entire U.S. Olympic Team came to participate. Bill Steinkraus, who won the gold in 1968 in Mexico a year later, came in second in Pomona. Burgess, dressed in his Penguin suit, rode around among the crowd to everyone's delight. Batman did not make it, but Robin did. Lauren Bacall made a glorious entry.

It turned out to be a great happening. We had printed just 3,000 tickets, figuring that if that many people would be coming we would be in the black. More than 15,000 attended. The New York TV channels covered it, the *New York Times* devoted space to the show, and last but not least, the USHSA asked if we would please have a repeat performance so that they could make amends.

I believe that the other members of our committee, no matter how large their contribution was, will agree with me that Burgess's largess was mainly responsible for the incredible success. I feel greatly indebted to Burgess, who, though mainly known as an actor, was also an immensely socially involved person who contributed in many ways to furthering the quality of life in Rockland.

I am so pleased that the village has dedicated a park in his name.

Burgess Meredith with his wife, Kaja, and daughter, Tala, at their 50-acre home in Pomona in December 1964.   Photo by Scott Webber.

...In 1961 Disney releases the movie "101 Dalmatians"...Actor Gary Cooper, artist Grandma Moses, writer Ernest Hemingway and baseball great Ty Cobb die...In 1962 the Mariner 2 spacecraft takes the first close-up photos of Venus...In 1966 the miniskirt is all the rage...

Rotella

In 1997, Haverstraw Supervisor Philip J. Rotella stepped down after 34 years in the job he had held since the first election in November 1963, when he defeated the 36-year veteran Victor J. Shankey in a hard fought contest. Between the two of them, they held the office for 70 years in the Democratic-controlled town. In announcing his retirement, Rotella told the town board meeting in April of that year he had accomplished most of his goals, including the opening of a new municipal golf course, a new town hall, police station, two new parks and the Haverstraw Marina. He died soon after leaving office in the following year at the age of 87.

Scott Webber

TV Repair

In 1964, a service call from Rockland Television was $1.75 plus parts. New picture tubes were $18.95.

233

Edward Hopper

Edward Hopper, one of America's most famous artists, was a native of Rockland County. He was born in Nyack in 1882 in the small white house that still bears his name on Nyack's North Broadway. The Hopper family came from Amsterdam, Holland, and the name was originally spelled Hoppen; the fourth generation of Hoppens in America changed the spelling for easier pronunciation.

Hopper went to the local Nyack schools and after studying at the New York School of Art, went to Paris in 1906 to continue his painting. His return to America began his career as a successful artist. Most of his more famous works are of city scenes, although some of them are of county scenes. The most famous local one is entitled, "House by the Railroad," a large Victorian house with the track in the foreground. The model for this painting is still to be seen on Route 9W in Haverstraw. At the time of the painting, the mansion was owned by Thomas Gagan, a prominent Haverstraw lawyer and politician.

Hopper died in 1967 and is buried in Oak Hill Cemetery in Nyack. The Hopper house fell into disrepair and faced demolition in 1970, at which time a group organized to preserve the building.   Robert Burghardt

Edward Hopper, age ten, with his sister Marion, eight. The Hopper House in the 1990s. JSC

Pearl River Library
80 Franklin Avenue

The library (right) was originally a reading association that met in a house in 1895. It moved to a downtown bank building, and later to a garage on Ridge Street in the mid-1930s. In 1963, it moved to its present site as a school district library. The library tripled its size in 1991, with a wraparound addition. The library features frequently-changing exhibits, and its three community rooms are actively used.

Orangeburg Library
20 Old Greenbush Road

In the early 1960s the library (right) was established in a store in Prel Plaza. But it endured a stormy political history in the late 1960s and early 1970s during which time the library relinquished its charter to the newly formed Orangetown Public Library, and was forced from its headquarters for non-payment of rent.

However, by 1973 the reconstituted Orangeburg Library moved into a portion of the old Greenbush

234

School. The library's half of the building, shared with Town offices, was completely renovated and modernized in 1998. The renovation sparked an interest in and increased usage of the library's collection.

Tappan Library
93 Main Street

Housed in an authentic Colonial two-story clapboard building (right), a plaque on the building reads "William DeVoe c.1750." The library is listed on the State and National Registers of Historic Places. The library had its beginnings in Shanks Village, which had a core collection of 2500 books in shelves made out of gun cases. A group of Tappan citizens raised funds to buy the collection, which was subsequently housed in the garage belonging to the present library building. The library first opened in Sept. 1956, moving into its present building in Jan. 1964. The library underwent expansion through the years, with a major one in 1994. Special collections focus on local history, and Major André.

Nanuet Public Library
149 Church Street

Beginning in one room of the Nanuet Elementary School, the library was chartered in 1894. It moved to a Main Street storefront, and in 1968 to a new building at its present site next to the Nanuet Middle and High Schools.

In June 1990, a building expansion was completed, featuring the renovation of the old building, and the construction of a new addition. Major features of the expansion include a storytelling-crafts room, enclosed garden, and a large community room. In its collection, the library exhibits a painting of Nanawitt, a local Indian sachem after whom the hamlet of Nanuet is named.

Japanese Pearl Harbor Ace Gets Lost in Nanuet

March 13, 1967: The man who led the attack on Pearl Harbor got lost in Nanuet last night.

Captain Mitsuo Fuchida, who more than 25 years ago led a flight of Japanese aircraft on the Sunday morning assault on the U.S. Fleet in Hawaii, had as his target last night the Grace Baptist Church where he was to speak.

The 64-year old Japanese air ace arrived 45 minutes late, but still in time to tell his personal story of the day of infamy and subsequent events of his life.

Captain Mitsuo Fuchida (center) with Donald Munkelt of Nanuet (left), who was at Pearl Harbor during the attack, and Richard Cornish of Pearl River (right), who was bombed by Fuchida at Leyte Gulf.

"Today I am very sorry for all the things I did before, but you will have to forgive me for I never had heard of Jesus Christ at the time," Fuchida implored, after describing how he had converted to Christianity after the war. At the conclusion of his talk, Fuchida was mobbed with handshakes, many of them from World War II veterans. Many requested autographs, and for each person he wrote, "Captain Mitsuo Fuchida, Luke 23:34, Father, forgive them for they know not what they do."

Scott Webber, *The Journal-News*

McAlevey and the Ramapo 15 Points

Note: John F. McAlevey was born in Brooklyn in 1923, enlisted in the U.S. Army Air Corps in 1942 and served as a fighter pilot with the 8th Air Force in England, lived in Shanks Village while attending Columbia Law School 1947-1950, served as Mayor of Sloatsburg 1959-1963, served four terms as Supervisor of the Town of Ramapo 1966-1974, served on the Metro. Trans. Authority 1979-1988 and served as chairman of the Metro-North Committee. He still maintains a private law practice in Tallman and lives in Manhattan as the century ends.

In 1987, Mr. McAlevey sat down with Grace Gordon, an interviewer with the Valley Cottage Library, as one of several people selected to be part of *An Oral History of Key Political Figures in the Growth of Rockland County*. The following information is taken from that interview, which is in the Valley Cottage Library collection.

Ramapo's population was just under 8,500 in 1950. In 1960, it had jumped to over 20,400 and in 1966 when McAlevey took office as supervisor it had soared to over 36,400. It comes as no surprise that he found that the town was builder-oriented.

Ramapo, like so many other towns, had what was called Euclidian Zoning, which was based upon a map that set forth what was compatible to be built next to each other and provided set-backs. It also set forth what could and could not be built in an area, but said nothing about what the rate of development should be.

"What we did was inject the element of time in the zoning code," McAlevey said. "Without this element, it leaves the development of the community to the whim of private market forces which had no regard for rational growth."

Before he took office, Mr. McAlevey notes that Ramapo had used some federal grant monies to develop a master plan. What needed to be done now was to draw up a meaningful zoning code, which meant declaring a building moratorium on fifty percent of the vacant land to head off builders rushing in to get permits under the old code. This became known as the Interim or Blue Law, referring to those lands that were shaded blue on the map.

During this period, school costs were known to send taxes up as much as twenty-four percent a year because of uncontrolled growth. One of the first steps was to set

John McAlevey in 1985.
Photo courtesy of John McAlevey.

up a Development Easement Acquisition Commission (DEACOM) that allowed farmers to deed over to the town their rights to sell their land to developers in return for a depreciation of assessed valuation. The town accepted such deeds from farmers from five to ten years. Farmland was zoned for residential. For a five-year deed, the assessment was reduced by fifty percent, for ten years, ninety percent.

When large landowners didn't respond to DEACOM's offer, it was discovered that even though there had been a recent reassessment in the town, many of the big landowners were paying little taxes. Mr. McAlevey called them "fat cats" and ordered a new reassessment.

Calling it "the keystone in the arch of controlled growth," Mr. McAlevey and the town attorney, Robert Freilich, developed a program that would limit construction to keep pace with the town's capital improvement development in six-year plans. The 15-Point Program, as it became known, went into effect in 1969.

Before any project was approved, a developer had to prove that it conformed to the master plan and would not overload municipal services, including sewers, roads, parks and playgrounds. To get a building permit, a developer had to qualify on enough requirements to get fifteen points. If not, then he had to wait or else install the services himself at his own cost.

The builders sent up a storm of protests and went to court, but to no avail. The program was backed all the way up to the New York State Court of Appeals, which ruled against a property owner named Golden who had a contract with a developer for his large tract on Viola Road. The U.S. Supreme Court refused to hear the case.

"It was the ultimate land use control and this is the thing that still is the outer limits of what one can do in land use control in the United States today," Mr. McAlevey said.

The goal was to slow down the town's growth and with it the development of more schools and staggering tax increases, something the town could not directly do anything about. The McAlevey administration also introduced federally subsidized low cost housing, which except for Nyack, was a first in Rockland County. The controlled growth program in Ramapo received national recognition and has afforded the author numerous speaking engagements all the way to Hawaii.

Scott Webber

236

The Battle of Blue Hill

The Blue Hill office complex in Pearl River underwent a storm of controversy before it was built. The following are some examples of the furor the project provoked.

County Getting $75 Million Hub:
Uris To Build Complex On Maze Land
Ania Bojcun, *The Record*, 2/16/67

A $75-million office and research complex, the single largest project ever contemplated for Rockland County, is to be built here on the 370-acre estate of the late H. Montgomery Maze. The complex is expected to yield $1.5 million in taxes annually to the Town of Orangetown. The disclosure came with the announcement yesterday of the purchase of the estate by the Uris Building Corporation, owner and builder of six office skyscrapers in Manhattan.

Although company officials were hesitant to provide details about the complex since they said it is still in the designing stage, a participant in the sale negotiations said plans call for construction of between 2.5 and 3 million square feet of office space at a cost of $50 to $75 million.

The complex would occupy about 230 acres, while the 123-acre Blue Hill Golf Club, situated in the western part of the estate, and approximately 20 more acres would be acquired by the Town of Orangetown for public use. The Town has wanted to buy the 18-hole golf course for more than a year, but the Irving Trust Company, administrator of the estate, refused to sell the land piecemeal.

Construction of the complex is expected to begin within 9 months, with July set as the target date. As many as 15,000 persons would be employed at the complex, to be built over a 5-year period just west of Rockland State Hospital on Orangeburg Road.

The new complex will be in step with the growing trend toward suburban relocation of New York businesses. Uris officials would not reveal the purchase price, but it was learned reliably that it was $2.8 million.

Acquisition of the huge ratable was regarded as a spectacular coup for Orangetown Supervisor John Lovett's administration, which has, as had the preceding one, been markedly successful in attracting light industry to Orangetown, especially along Route 303.

Blue Hill Office Complex Unveiled
to Town Officials
Scott Webber, *The Journal-News*, 5/2/67

Plans for a 12-building office complex in Orangetown were revealed last night, to be built by the Uris Building Corp. in the Blue Hill area. The proposed project will cost between $75 and $100 million and be built over a period of three to five years.

"Oldtimers" still refer to it as the Uris Building, but more recent residents know it as Blue Hill.
Photo by Linda Zimmermann.

Civic Group Opposes Blue Hill Office Units
The Journal-News, 5/5/67

The Independent Homeowners of Orangetown oppose plans for a $100 million office in Blue Hill that will give the town $25 million in ratables.

"While our opposition is not irrevocable, there are certain factors inherent in the plan which we feel are not consistent with the interests and wishes of the people," Herbert Wolfson, the president of the civic group explained last night.

Noting that the 12-building office complex will probably employ 8,000 people and have space for 8,300 cars, Wolfson said this "means an unwanted change in character of our town and the present physical surroundings, a city within a community."

Wolfson's statement was the first to be voiced in opposition to the Uris plans.

Uris Would Cut Taxes in Half
Scott Webber, *The Journal-News*, 6/9/67

The president of the Pearl River School Board of Education last night declared that school taxes would have been cut in half if the $75 million Uris complex was on the tax rolls for the coming year.

Dr. Lee Starker, the president, said that Uris would yield $2,280,000 in taxes for the school district, which would lose $1,140,000 in state aid. This would leave a net gain of $1,140,000.

Supervisor Lovett and Uris officials led the discussion in favor of the office complex, while a majority of those in the audience echoed opposition to the proposal.

"The Long Island Expressway is going to be sissy stuff compared with Orangeburg Road," said Ned Benson, president of the Homeowners Association.

However, one lady said it would be good because jobs would be available in Orangetown rather than New York City.

"Harpies Hampering Progress in Orangetown"
Helen Giordano, *The Journal-News*, 6/22/67

"Semi-professional hecklers and pseudo-intelligentsia who harp on the theme of slowing down all progress are endangering local responsible local government and the most desirable proposition that has come to any area of Rockland County," said Orangetown Councilman Dr. Albert Munson at yesterday's South Rockland Women's Republican Club luncheon at the Silver Pheasant.

"The complex, which will take ten years to complete, will be second to nothing in the United States," according to Munson.

"If this opportunity is allowed to slip through our fingers," said Fred Bonniwell, a member of the Citizens Advisory Council, "the people of Orangetown are extremely foolish and will regret the decision in only a few, short years."

Pearl River Boycott?
Scott Webber, *The Journal-News*, 6/24/67

An economic boycott of Pearl River, a 500-car motorcade through Orangetown and closing the state border were among some of the measures proposed last night by 350 angry River Vale, N.J., residents opposed to the Uris complex, planned to be built in the adjacent New York town.

River Vale Lawsuit
9/18/67

A lawsuit filed by the River Vale Homeowners Association will be brought before the U.S. Appeals Court in an attempt to reverse a lower court's decision which upheld the zoning changes allowing the construction of the Uris Complex. The town of River Vale contends the office and research complex will reduce the value of its land and create traffic hazards and unnecessary expenses, all without sufficient notice of the proposed rezoning, which they claim is against the 14th Amendment to the Constitution.

No Exchange
4/68

Journal-News staff reporter Scott Webber broke the news that the New York Stock Exchange was being offered a deal to move from Wall Street to the Uris complex. Revealing the secret negotiations upset local and exchange officials. New York City Mayor Lindsay made the exchange a better offer and it remained on Wall Street.

As lawsuits and controversy eventually died down, the construction of the Uris complex continued. However, the proposed twelve buildings was scaled down to only two, much of the complex remained vacant for many years, and Orangeburg Road never did become another Long Island Expressway. Of course, had the original plans been realized, with the New York Stock Exchange heading the list of a dozen buildings full of businesses, Pearl River, and all of the surrounding areas, would be a very different place.

In 2000, the tallest building at Blue Hill Plaza is a landmark for local residents, a kind of compass marker to help get your bearings straight while navigating the county's back roads. Offices are now filled to capacity with tenants who enjoy the spectacular views from the upper floors, and the convenience of a large office complex in a quiet setting.

Linda Zimmermann

Instead of the proposed twelve buildings, only these two were built.
Photo by Linda Zimmermann.

1970-79

A Different Way of Life

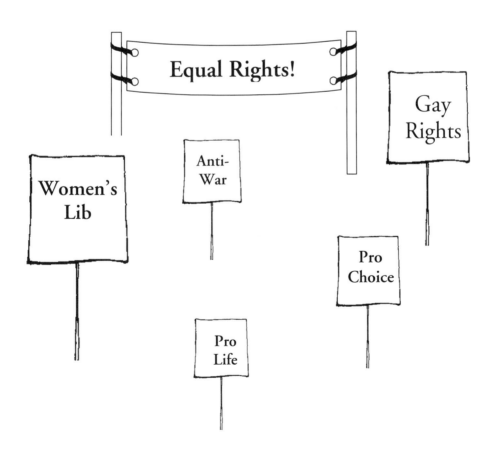

As the 1970s began, it seemed as if everyone was protesting something. There were anti-war protests, women's rights and civil rights and gay rights protests. Many of the movements for change that had exploded on the scene in the 1960s were becoming more organized and successful in the 1970s, and in some cases, more acceptable to the general public.

The end of the Vietnam War in 1975 was a pivotal time, and many people who had been anti-establishment realized that "flower power" would not pay the bills, and they quietly began melting back into the mainstream. Decades of wars and social strife finally appeared to be coming to an end, and peace and prosperity actually looked to be attainable. By the end of the decade, the overtones of pressing social issues started to take a back seat to a more relaxed (and arguably more self-indulgent) leisure suit and disco mentality. For the younger generation, dancing the night away was now preferable to marching in protest.

Rockland County also experienced this shift as it was simultaneously experiencing continued rapid growth. As the 1980s dawned, it was clear it was a different way of life. Cultural diversity, equality and tolerance, in an increasingly high-tech world, would define the county's future.

Yet another flood on Route 59 in West Nyack in the 1970s, looking west. Many of these buildings no longer exist, and the Palisades Center is now located on the right.

Photo by John Scott.

Dummies in the classroom? Although this is a photo that invites many captions, the truth behind it is simple—teacher Gladys Webber's students in Congers made these dummies to represent themselves in 1978.   Photo by Scott Webber.

Launched in 1969, the sloop *Clearwater* sails the Hudson helping to make the public aware of environmental concerns.   JSC

240

Consciousness Raising:
The Cornerstone of Women's Liberation

The cornerstone of Rockland County's Women's Liberation Movement is groups of six to ten women meeting in private to raise questions about themselves, men and society. Each group is engaged in what the Movement calls "consciousness raising."

Mrs. Ruth Kaplan, a leader in the County Movement, adds that Rockland women have different problems than those in the city. She has prepared a separate list of questions designed to raise the consciousness of suburban women as opposed to those in New York City. Her list is available to any woman who wants to start a group.

"A woman gives up everything for the American dream when she leaves the city for the suburbs," she explains, only to find that she is no longer herself but is known "simply as someone's mother and wife."

In the city, a woman had others to join with her in her fight for equality on the job, Mrs. Kaplan noted. Here she is isolated, taking care of children and unable to find work that is suitable to her education and talents. She is unable or unwilling to commute to the city to find the type of work that will satisfy her.

"The process of consciousness raising," Mrs. Kaplan said, "is the only process the Women's Liberation Movement has yet developed which enables women to develop a political consciousness of their oppression, which breaks down carefully imposed cultural barriers to building understanding and love of each other and oneself, and which offers collective experience—communal development of trust, growth, political analysis and action."

Scott Webber, *Clarkstown Courier*, 11/27/72

First Policewoman

There is one policewoman in Rockland County, and Clarkstown's got her. She's Janice Rogan, and she has been working for Clarkstown's finest since January 15, 1967. Her rank is Policewoman, which is the female equivalent of Patrolman, and in May of last year she took and passed the examination to qualify for promotion to Sergeant.

Her work now consists mostly of working with female prisoners of various sorts, mostly, she reports, shoplifters. She also takes a turn as matron at the Clarkstown jail, makes female arrests on warrants, and takes charge of women who have been arrested for various reasons.

Rogan manages to hold her job, keep up with the children, and take courses in Police Science at Rockland Community College. As a woman who has made it in man's profession, how does Mrs. Rogan feel about Woman's Lib?

"I'm not for it. Same pay for same work, definitely. But they've gone to extremes. I don't want to go to a man's bar; men should be able to sit around by themselves if they want to."

Bunny Crumpacker, *Clarkstown Courier*, 10/9/72

Right to Life Protests

Right to Life made its debut in Rockland County last November when more than 2,500 women marched through New City streets in protest against the state's liberalized abortion law. They were heard from when William Baird spoke at Rockland Community College in July at a heated meeting sponsored by the Women's Liberation in favor of abortion. They stormed the county legislature in August to protest the use of tax funds for the college which allowed speakers that attacked the Catholic Church because of its opposition to birth control.

"But we must go much further than that," says Margaret Fitton, chairman of the Rockland County unit. "We believe we have a commitment to the unborn, the handicapped and the aged. We want to point out the dignity of life for all. It was this apathy towards life that led to the mass extermination of the Jews and the handicapped as well as abortion in Nazi Germany in the 1930s."

"I'll tell you one thing," Mrs. Fitton concluded, "We are writing history in New York State. Governor Rockefeller may well go down with King Herod in history."

Clarkstown Courier, 10/2/73

...In 1970 four students are killed during anti-war protests at Kent State University..."Gay Pride" demonstrations take place in an attempt to change discriminatory laws against homosexuals...In 1972 President Nixon visits China and meets with Mao Tse-tung...Airline pilots go on strike to protest the rising number of hijackings...Arab terrorists kill eleven Israeli Olympians in Munich...

Rockland Equals Revolution

I was born in the Bronx in the nineteen thirties. No place was more unlike Rockland County in those days, before the Palisades Interstate Parkway and Tappan Zee Bridge, then the Bronx, not Bronx County thank you, the Bronx.

The Bronx was distinguished by apartment houses occupied by manufacturing or service employees, children of the immigrants from the three I's: Ireland, Israel and Italy. Of course, Israel was just a vision, a hope, in the days before the horrific Holocaust. Most of the Jewish people in the Bronx came from Eastern Europe, as the Italians came from Southern Europe.

Rockland was distinguished by private homes occupied by farmers descendent from earlier settlers of Northern and Western Europe. The only time any of them ever met each other was in the summer when the Bronx residents, mostly Jewish, came to the Rockland bungalow colonies and boarding houses for their vacation. The Bronx Irish went to Rockaway or the Catskills. The Italians mostly stayed home. As a typical Bronxite, a child of an immigrant father from Ireland and an immigrant mother from Italy (they did a lot of that in those days), I went everywhere, but never to Rockland. My people never heard of it.

Twenty, thirty years pass. The Bronx changes and so does Rockland. How and why? The children of the above mentioned Bronxites move to Rockland. I am one of them.

We are mostly veterans now working for the NYC school system or the NYC utilities or municipal services such as the fire, police and transportation departments. We wanted our own new home, not just a rented apartment, with a yard and lawn, within commuting distance of our new jobs. We thought we found a quiet heaven on earth with only crabgrass to fight.

We did not know of Rockland's historical legacy of a strong predilection for revolutionary causes. Who knew about the significant role of Rockland in our nation's Revolutionary War against England? Do you think we ever heard about the "Orangetown Resolutions," which were written in the hamlet of Tappan as the precursor to the sacred Declaration of Independence? Who knew that it was off the shore of Piermont that America was officially recognized as a free and independent nation for the first time by England?

Who knew of Rockland's role in the Civil War, as personified by a Village of Grand View General who convinced Abraham Lincoln to use former slaves as soldiers, or Rockland's stations on the pre-Civil War Underground Railroad?

Who ever heard of Conrad Lynn, the brilliant and brave African-American attorney of Pomona, who was a leader in our Nation's civil rights revolution?

Who knew that a major Suffragette, Caroline Lexow Babcock, a pioneer for Women's rights had lived in South Nyack, or that the book (*Feminine Mystique*) that would trigger the Feminist Movement was written in the Village of Grand View (by Betty Friedan).

Who knew that one of the great environmental struggles of the century would take place in Rockland, a battle royal against the quarry industry to save the great palisades of the river and the county's geological legacy from the ice age?

It was a battle that resulted in one of the most glorious park systems in the world, the Palisades Interstate Park System. Historical giants such as Theodore Roosevelt, J.P. Morgan, the Rockefellers, the Vanderbilts, and the Harrimans all played leading roles right here in little ole Rockland, the second smallest county in the state, which is now one-third parkland. The battle started ironically enough at the turn of the century, in 1900, and is still going on in 2000.

Who knew that the 1960s-70s revolution for deinstitutionalization (Rockland Psychiatric Center and Letchworth Village) or for mainstreaming the former residents of these huge facilities (RPC would house 9,000 patients, Letchworth 5,500) would take place in Rockland? Who would have believed that Kathy Lukens of Tappan and I would establish the first voluntary agency-operated community residence in New York State specifically designed and built for formerly state-institutionalized mentally retarded adults?

My lawd, the place turned out to be a hot-bed of revolution. The American Revolution, the Civil Rights Revolution, the Environmental Revolution, the Equal Rights Revolution and my own Human Rights Revolution for the Mentally Disabled. It's no wonder I never got to my lawn.

John Murphy

The Day a County Cried

March 24, 1972: Five teen-age boys were killed and 44 children injured when a school bus bound for Nyack High School from Valley Cottage was demolished by an 84-car Penn Central freight train at a Congers road crossing. Two girls lost legs, and others were seriously hurt. The driver of the bus, Joseph Larkin, was convicted of criminally negligent homicide a year later, and 49 civil suits were settled out of court. Reporters and photographers who covered the story still wince at the memories.

The Journal-News, 7/15/82

Midair Collision

December 4, 1976: Five persons were killed when two light-engine planes collided just south of the Tappan Zee Bridge, the wreckage narrowly missing residents on the Rockland shoreline. The crash killed three Maryland residents in one plane and a New Jersey flight instructor and a New York City student pilot in the other. Nine months later, a federal report blamed the crash on pilot error.

The Journal-News, 7/15/82

The Long Clove Railroad Tunnel Accident

Since colonial times, the communities known as Congers and Haverstraw were connected by the Kings Highway which ran through the South Mountain or Verdrietege Hook by way of a mountain pass called the Long Clove. A railroad tunnel through the Clove was completed in 1882, and then enlarged in 1988 to accommodate double-stack freight cars.

The tunnel required constant attention, and railroad men patrolled it twice an hour, twenty-four hours a day, to inspect for debris, fallen rock and ice. Despite the precautions, accidents did happen. The worst occurred in 1974 when a 52-car freight train derailed as its three diesel engines were emerging from the tunnel's south portal. Thirty-eight automobile carriers and others carrying washing machines, chemicals and other products, were wrecked, strewing autos and debris throughout the tunnel. A conflagration engulfed the length of the interior, causing hundreds of tons of stone to fall from the ceilings, and it was feared that the entire tunnel would collapse.

Over 500 firemen and policemen pumped water from as far away as three miles in an attempt to quell the blaze. Local residents were evacuated and Route 9W was closed. The following day, bulldozers began removing the still-smoldering wreckage. Despite millions of dollars of damage, the debris was cleared, new tracks were put down and the tunnel reopened only a week later.

John Scott

Suffern Bicentennial

Suffern's 200 years, from 1773-1973, were commemorated with this special envelope depicting the home of John Suffern.

Note that the rate for first class postage was only eight cents.

Envelope courtesy of Scott Webber.

World War I Veterans: The Last Man's Club, 1925-1971

They were from Rockland and Orange Counties and went into the army in 1917. They became members of Company M, 310th infantry, 78th division, and went to war in France in the war to end all wars. They called it the Great World War. They came home in 1919, and in 1925 held their first reunion in Newark when 184 members showed up to form what they called "The Last Man's Club," a group that promised to meet every year until there were only four left, at which time they would break open the champagne bottle dating from 1925 and drink a final toast to Company M.

However, the club didn't meet again until 1935, but from then they carried on until the final seven came together in 1971 at the Green Room in Suffern. By then, most of them had to be chauffeured to the luncheons, their hearing aids were turned up high and they leaned heavily on the arms of their children/grandchildren and a cane. The old company commander, Lieutenant Gus Wallace, would come from Middletown with his son, who did the driving. They came from Suffern and Haverstraw. Their leader and organizer was John D. Cook (former Mayor of Haverstraw and Rockland County Sheriff) who made all the arrangements and sent out the notice every spring.

I was invited (I'm a Korean War vet), since I was John's driver starting in the mid 1960s. The 1971 gathering was the thirty-ninth reunion. For the first twenty reunions they met in the Eureka House and then moved to the Lafayette Hotel and its Green Room. By the time I got involved, they skipped elections of officers; who cared anyway as long as John kept going?

When they tried to pinpoint dates of events in their lives, which had spanned 80 years, they had a hard time. The only sure dates were 1918 when the war ended, and when they retired from working.

"Who the hell cares when it was!" was the refrain heard that afternoon.

With a sense of mortality closing in on them they

decided to pop the bottle open that afternoon after a motion was made and they all decided, "What the hell, we're getting too old to keep coming back every year, let's get it over with now!"

The cork was found to be rotted and the contents had turned to sour vinegar. For years the bottle had been cared for by various members, including Mark L. Stewart of Tallman and Harry Sinell of Suffern. Now it was found to be no good. The restaurant manager came to the rescue with a new bottle of champagne. Glasses were raised in remembrance of those who were buried in Flanders Field and who never came home, as well as those that did, and now lie in cemeteries all over the area. Goodbye, Tipperary.

The bottle and the cup, carefully preserved over many years, were given to the Historical Society of Rockland County. In the late, warm afternoon sun they got back into their cars and drove off. They never came back again. A few weeks later John Cook died and was buried in St. Peter's Cemetery, Haverstraw.

Scott Webber

The Last Man's Club original champagne bottle (left) and the bottle provided by the manager of the restaurant at their last meeting.

Photo by Scott Webber.

John Zehner
and the Formation of the Historical Society of Rockland County

John Zehner was born February 8, 1905 in Brooklyn. He graduated from Cornell University as a civil engineer in 1926 and was employed by Turner Construction. In 1937 he married Margaret Chapin Bolles of Bellows Falls, Vermont. Except for a period from 1933 to 1940, when he worked for Montgomery Ward and Company, he remained with Turner until his retirement in 1971.

A family story holds that, in 1941, Mr. Zehner boarded a Rockland bus in New York and viewed the countryside along the way until the last stop in Nyack. Walking about the Nyacks, he decided, fortunately for Rockland County, that this was where he would like to

settle with Margaret and their young son, Robert. They built a house at 11 Central Avenue in Nyack.

While fully employed and commuting to New York City, Mr. Zehner took an active role in a number of community and county projects. He also had a deep knowledge and enduring interest in local and American history which led him to the most important and long-standing volunteer commitment of his life.

For almost a century, well-intentioned citizens and historians had on several occasions attempted to establish an historical organization to preserve and celebrate the rich history of Rockland County. For a variety of reasons, their initial enthusiasm waned, primarily because of the inability to acquire their own permanent museum building and history center.

In the 1950s the extension of the New York State Thruway and construction of the Tappan Zee Bridge marked the end of the relative isolation of Rockland County. In 1954, an aroused group of people met in an attempt to save from destruction the historic Salisbury House near the bridge in South Nyack. They organized themselves as the Tappan Zee Historical Society and elected John Zehner president. Although they failed to save the building, they held numerous meetings and lectures on local history that had an impact on the public. By 1958, they had achieved a membership of over 500.

An eighteenth-century sandstone building in Orangeburg, offered by Irving Maidman rent-free, served as the society's temporary headquarters and museum from 1958 to 1974. Mr. Zehner continued to serve as president of the Tappan Zee Historical Society until its merger with the Rockland Historical Society in 1965, when he became founding president of the new organization, the Historical Society of Rockland County.

President Zehner, kindly but insistent, inspired the support of trustees and numerous volunteers eager to assist in a variety of fund-raising events and exhibitions. He was determined to build the society into a visible force in historic preservation throughout the county and ideas poured out of him day and night. Through correspondence and by telephone he kept in contact with many county business organizations, corporations, labor groups, councilmen and legislators, seeking and achieving their cooperation in the society's growth. He became known as "Mr. Historical Society," a well-deserved title.

A major goal for Mr. Zehner was acquiring a permanent large building for the historical society's headquarters and museum exhibits. A special committee was formed for that purpose, and, in 1970, the society negotiated the purchase of a 4-acre site with an 1832 brick homestead and outbuildings in New City. Building then commenced on a fireproof museum.

In 1977, the new museum was dedicated. With spacious grounds and a museum, the society could attract large crowds for such events as the Doll House Festival and Homelands Day. Under Mr. Zehner's leadership, the membership soared to more than 1,850, making the Historical Society of Rockland County one of the most successful in the rural tri-state area.

Mr. Zehner retired as president of the society in 1978 after 24 years of continuous service. However, he retained in close association as a trustee and as a member of various committees and of the advisory council. One of the many legacies of his work is *South of the Mountains,* the quarterly journal of the society, which is now in its 40th year of publication.

John Zehner's example and spirit will guide the society he created and sustain us as we continue to keep history alive in Rockland County.

John Scott, *South of the Mountains*,
July/September 1996

Previous page: John Zehner in 1981, and an aerial view of the grounds of the Historical Society of Rockland County during Homelands Day. Such events throughout the 1980s often drew crowds in excess of 3,000 people.

Left: A family gets a lesson on preparing wool for spinning during the Autumn Harvest held at the Society on October 18, 1987.

Photos courtesy of John Scott.

Countess Tolstoy and the Tolstoy Foundation

Rockland County is the home of an agency that aids refugees from countries where people have few rights, private property simply doesn't exist, and if you criticize the government you're likely to be declared insane and placed in an asylum. Since America seems to be the politically naive and idealistic country it so often is, willing to try anything once, the day may well come when those who are eager to implement such a government here may see it happen.

It is a thought that chills the bones of Countess Alexandra Tolstoy of Valley Cottage. The daughter of Leo Tolstoy, author of *War and Peace*, who turned 88 yesterday, is president of the Tolstoy Foundation Center in Valley Cottage. At age 33, she saw one of the greatest countries in the world undergo a violent civil war in which Communist forces overthrew the Russian government. As a result, Miss Tolstoy lost all her property and was put into prison as punishment, presumably for having owned too much of it.

"I expected a worse fate," Miss Tolstoy recalled, "but Trotsky came to my defense."

After being released from prison, Miss Tolstoy was allowed to return to her family's former estate, Yasnaya Polyana, and she was also allowed to continue the school she had founded. It turned out to be one of the few schools in Russia where Lenin permitted prayer and religious instruction.

However, when Lenin died in 1924 and Stalin took over, he forbade the Tolstoy school from holding any further prayers or classes in religion. When only three of the 60 teachers at the school had the courage to back Tolstoy's protest of Stalin's policy, she decided it was time to leave Russia.

Once she reached America, she immediately set about aiding refugees from her native land. At the same time she attempted in a small way to bring world opinion to bear against the Stalin government to allow religious freedom. In 1939 her efforts were aided considerably when the Tolstoy Foundation was formed to continue her work, and a few years later the land in Rockland was purchased for the center. Since then more than 20,000 refugees have passed through the center on their way to assimilation into the life of this country and others in this hemisphere.

At one point, the Soviet government offered to give Tolstoy money to return to Russia. Her eyes reddened as she described the scene. "I showed them where they could catch the elevator," she asserted. "I will not let them use me. Never!" she declared.

Yet, Alexandra Tolstoy thinks about home all the time. True, she has her own quarters and garden at the center in Valley Cottage. A little brook running by her building is humorously referred to as the Volga. There is even a church at the center, St. Sergius, built in the old Russian style. The center is a little bit of Holy Mother Russia as it might have been 60 years ago. But it is not Yasnaya Polyana.

Miss Tolstoy frequently writes to the Brezhnev-Kosygin government in Moscow imploring leaders to correct injustices. The letters are never acknowledged, but she writes anyway. Her most recent letter urged the leaders to release from asylums those writers, poets and scientists who are being confined.

Previous page: Countess Tolstoy speaking in Valley Cottage (photo by Scott Webber). Right: St. Sergius Church (photo by John Scott).

"Release them!" Her letter demanded. "Open the doors, give freedom to those outstanding innocent people whose only fault is wanting to think and speak freely!"

John Dalmas, *The Journal-News*, 7/2/72

Peace Through Violence?

In the early 1970s, journalist Scott Webber covered a debate that was being held at the auditorium of Orange & Rockland in Spring Valley. The well-intentioned debate over the Vietnam War quickly degenerated into an argument, and a shouting match ensued, each side screaming that they loved peace the most.

Anti-war protestors, in a seriously misguided attempt to prove their point, began using their protest signs covered with peace symbols as weapons, hitting their opponents over the head with them.

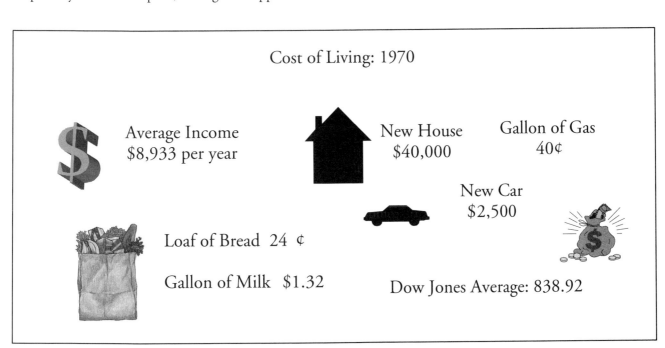

Cost of Living: 1970

Average Income
$8,933 per year

New House
$40,000

Gallon of Gas
40¢

New Car
$2,500

Loaf of Bread 24 ¢

Gallon of Milk $1.32

Dow Jones Average: 838.92

...In 1972 the Watergate scandal erupts, leading to the resignation of President Nixon in 1974...

Pearl River Firsts

Although many are hidden in obscurity, Pearl River claims many "firsts" in the fields of science, education, recreation and construction.

Pearl River has always maintained its founder, Julius Braunsdorf, was the true inventor of the electric light bulb, not Thomas Edison, and points with pride to books and a plaque in the Braunsdorf Memorial Park attesting to this achievement. His invention came about 10 years before Edison's patent, according to Orangetown historian and Pearl River resident Ralph Braden, one of Braunsdorf's champions.

Pearl Riverite Fred J. Schmidt was the inventor of the automatic pin spotter for bowling alleys. An employee at the Dexter Folder Company, he was a tinkerer, inventing first the collapsible shipping container and the "perfect carton opener" before patenting the pin spotter in 1944 which replaced the traditional pin boys at the back of the alleys.

Douglass College in New Jersey, the state's female counterpart of all-male Rutgers, was named for a Pearl River woman, Mabel Douglass. She had been in the first graduating class of Barnard College in New York City, and felt New Jersey deserved a similar institution.

A list of other firsts claimed for Pearl River includes:

- First Boy Scout Troop in Rockland, Troop 1, now Troop 36, which began in 1911 and was the 11th troop formed in the United States.
- First chartered volunteer ambulance corps in New York State (1936).
- First pre-fabricated housing development (Reld Park in 1946) in the United States.
- First large-scale post-war housing project in the county (Brunard Village).
- First supermarket in Rockland (Safeway in 1950 at Central Avenue and Middletown Road).
- First shopping center in the metropolitan area when the Food Fair center opened on Middletown Road in 1956.
- First "garden" style apartment house in Rockland (Pearl River Apartments, Middletown Road at Braunsdorf Road, 1939).
- Oldest railroad station in Rockland (1872).
- Oldest wooden building in Rockland County (Conques House, 1730).
- First Baptist Church in Rockland (1797).
- Only Rockland community to star in a television series (*Norby*, 1955-56).
- Home of Rockland's largest industry and world's largest drug firm (Lederle Laboratories with 4,000 employees).
- Home of the Rockland County Soap Box Derby since its inception in 1949.

The Journal-News, 8/1/74

Memories: Born and Raised in Rockland

I was born at Good Samaritan Hospital in Suffern on March 17, 1959. One of the nurses, an Irish Catholic nun named Sister Joseph Rita, took a liking to me and insisted that I be named Patty, since I was born on St. Patrick's Day. My parents had already picked out the name Linda, so they politely declined the Sister's suggestion. However, Sister Joseph Rita was not to be deterred, and for the remainder of her life she sent me birthday cards addressed to Patty Zimmermann.

I was the sixth and final member of the Zimmermann family to occupy our modest Cape Cod home on East Lewis Avenue in Pearl River. My father, Walter, was born and raised in Nyack, my mother, Ruth, had moved from Boston to Nyack in the 1940s, and siblings Walter, Nancy and Jim had all preceded me during the 1950s. As I look at the house and yard today, I can't imagine how six of us managed in that small space, but everything seemed so much larger when I was a kid.

My earliest recollections are of Christmas, when the family would pile into the station wagon (an essential

Heavy snows in the early 1960s made for great childhood memories. This circa 1963 photo was taken by my father, Walter, in our backyard in Pearl River. I am the little Eskimo in the front, and behind me are (left to right) my sister Nancy, brother Jim, mother Ruth and brother Walter.

for 1960s suburbia) and search for the perfect tree at Schultz's on Middletown Road across from Lederle. The Fourth of July also made a big impression, as the family station wagon was called into action to bring us to the school field in Nanuet to watch the spectacular fireworks display. The station wagon also served as the ideal vehicle for the drive-in movies, one of my favorite pastimes.

Since stores were closed at night and on Sundays, it was a big deal when Miller's dairy installed milk vending machines on Middletown Road across from the Masonic temple. I always begged to have the honor of putting in the quarter so that the quart of milk would slide out. Before Korvettes and Grant's were built in Nanuet, we would have to drive to Hackensack, N.J., to Sears for a "real" department store.

One of Miller's Milk Automat machines which made milk accessible 24-hours a day.
Photo courtesy of Orange & Rockland.

Just about every weekend in the summer, we would go to Hook Mountain to go fishing. Of course, we had to throw back everything that we caught because of the pollution. All of the talk of polluted water and air certainly made me think that everything would be ruined by the time I became an adult. We also spent a lot of time at Lake DeForest, and I have many happy memories of long summer evenings there.

Pearl River schools were safe and tranquil. I can't recall a single incident of any kind of trouble, which created a wonderful opportunity to actually learn. I did notice that around the fourth or fifth grade there were a lot of new faces, New York City accents, and fathers who were cops or firemen. One classmate could not get over the fact that most Pearl River streets did not have sidewalks.

When I was in high school in the 1970s, the bowling alley was built, and we joked that civilization was finally coming to Pearl River. Apart from the two movie theaters, there was nothing else to do. The real hangout was the Nanuet Mall, and I remember one teacher asking what we could possibly do there all day. I haven't a clue now, but at the time it seemed like fun.

For financial reasons I was limited to going to college locally. At first I resented not being able to go away to school like all of my friends, but that feeling quickly changed. St. Thomas Aquinas College was small, friendly, and had a wonderful staff of teachers. (In fact, it was one of their English teachers, Patricia Rock, who first insisted that I become a writer.) While my friends were lonely and miserable with their noisy dorm roommates and lousy school food, I was having the time of my life.

The late 1970s and early 1980s was the time of gas shortages and disco dancing. While I had no choice but to endure the former, I was successfully able to avoid the latter.

The gas crisis forced rationing, with cars only allowed to be filled on odd or even days, depending upon your license plate numbers. Residents often waited for hours to buy a few gallons of precious gas, sometimes even getting on line the night before and sleeping in their cars until the gas station opened.

This 1979 photo by John Scott shows a line of cars stretching south down Route 303 beyond the Route 59 overpass in West Nyack waiting to buy gas at the Texaco station.

In 1979, I got a job at Fisher Diagnostics on Route 303 in Orangeburg, just a couple of minutes away from STAC. I was going to school full time doing a dual major in English and chemistry, working full time in the lab at Fisher, and somehow still found time for my boyfriend and me to enjoy all that Rockland had to offer. It was a hectic time, but it seemed as if everything that I would ever need was within the confines of our little county.

I moved to Nanuet in 1978, where I was to remain for the next twenty years. While not as quiet as Pearl River, it was easy to get used to the convenience of being able to walk to the 24-hour Pathmark, the Nanuet Mall, the movies, or just about anything else I needed. As each year passed, however, the traffic congestion grew, woods disappeared and condos sprang up, and it seemed that the Rockland I knew and loved would be lost forever.

By the late 1990s, I was looking for a larger house on a couple of acres of property. Unfortunately, soaring real estate prices and high taxes forced me to look beyond Rockland's borders. I hated to leave the area where I had lived all of my life, but you could not argue the economics.

Like the people who moved from New York City to Rockland in the last few decades, I have now become part of the new exodus northward to Orange and other counties. The conveniences are gone, but it is also easy to get used to the peace and quiet, and the open spaces reminiscent of the Rockland of my childhood.

In December of 2000, my mother died, and a few months later the house in Pearl River was sold. It was tough to see the place pass into the hands of "strangers," people who couldn't possibly understand that each nick on the wall was connected with a childhood memory, or that every coat of paint represented an era of family history.

But such is life, and the gutting and renovation of that little Cape Cod house will allow the creation of a new family's memories—although hopefully they will leave the slab of concrete in the backyard in which all the Zimmermanns placed their handprints one summer's day in the 1960s. After all, now it's old enough to qualify as local history!

Rockland will always be my home, and I am perhaps one of the few who are optimistic about the county's future. Despite the enormous changes that have taken place in the last few decades, Rockland still retains all of the wonderful aspects that make it an ideal place to live and work.

Linda Zimmermann

The Changing Night Life

As the decades rolled on throughout the twentieth century, the jazz era passed on to swing, through the big bands and on to rock 'n' roll. As the hard rock-hippy-LSD culture of the 1960s and early 1970s began to fade, the disco-polyester-cocaine era burst upon the national scene. Rocklanders had their own bout of "Saturday Night Fever" as dancing made a huge comeback in local bars and clubs. Even those well into their middle ages tried to look like John Travolta as they did the "Hustle."

However, the counter-culture was still alive and kicking in the form of Punk Rock, with its admirers' spiked, multicolored hair and safety pins in their flesh creating a unique polarization amongst Rockland's youth. You loved disco, or you hated it, and rarely did dating cross those lines.

One of the most popular night spots in the county during the 1970s was Maximus in New City at 200 South Main Street. Formerly called The Marshmallow, it was *the* place to catch the latest trends.

However, as the decade passed, both the days of the glitter balls of disco and the spikes of the Punks were numbered. Although rock would stay and continue to change, rap music was right around the corner.

Linda Zimmermann

At the Movies
1970: *Patton.*1972: *The Godfather, Cabaret.* 1973: *The Sting, American Graffiti, The Exorcist.* 1975: *Jaws.* 1976: *Rocky.* 1977: *Annie Hall, Star Wars, Close Encounters of the Third Kind, Saturday Night Fever.* 1978: *Superman, The Deer Hunter, Animal House.* 1979: *Alien, 10.*

NIGHT SPOTS

If you like music and you like to dance, then check out Spots in Rockland. Sounds range from Country and Wes. The listings below are just a sampling of what's available:

DANNY BOY'S
27 River Road
Grassy Point
Stony Point, N.Y.

A Hudson River wate
live country and west
box offering the san
The dance floor has
there is a limited food
is mixed but generally

GAME ROOM
Route 303
Blauvelt, N.Y.

THE GREEN ROOM
122 Orange Avenue
Suffern, N.Y.

MAXIMUS
200 S. Main Street
New City, N.Y.

634-0550

ADDIE'S
Congers Rd. & Route 304
New City, N.Y.

An ad in the 1976-77 *Rockland County Almanac* listed the county's night spots and described Maximus with the following: Open seven nights a week from 8 p.m. to 4 a.m. The Maximus record selection is one of the best; liquor is served and hot dogs. The age group is 18 to 25 and double ID is required.

Courtesy of Paul Suchanyc.

Haiti on Hudson

Between 1957 and 1984, some 900,000 Haitians, or 15 percent of the population, felt compelled to leave Haiti for either political or economic reasons. During this period, the Haitian community was one of Rockland's fasting growing segments, and by the turn of the century the population was estimated to be as high as 25,000.

The first Haitian pioneer of Rockland County was Dr. Edgar Milford, Sr., a resident of Nanuet. Born in Haiti in 1895, Milford held degrees from the Schools of Law and Medicine in Port-au-Prince. After receiving special training in bacteriology and parasitology in the medical corps of the American Army of Occupation in Haiti, he became laboratory chief of the General Hospital in Port-au-Prince.

He emigrated to the United States in 1922, where he attended City College of New York. Milford was one of the first blacks to become a member of the medical staff of Cornell University Medical School, in 1927. In 1929, he and his supervisor, Dr. A.F. Coca, were lured to Rockland County by an offer from Lederle Laboratories to establish an allergenic department. Milford soon became a leading expert in the field and supervised pioneering work in the development of the first human immune globulin, as well as methods of purifying and concentrating biologics. After his retirement, he worked tirelessly for over thirty years on behalf of the Nanuet public library and was a member of its Board of Trustees for more than twenty years. The community room in the library's new wing was named for him and dedicated in 1990.

After Milford's arrival in the late 1920s, there was no record of any Haitians settling permanently in Rockland County until 1948 and the arrival of Bochard Jean-Jacques. While studying painting in Port-au-Prince, Jean-Jacques happened to meet with the Kennedys, a Piermont family, who invited him to come work for them and sponsored his immigration. Bochard studied English and continued to take painting classes at the Rockland Foundation and decided to stay on permanently.

Jean-Jacques was soon joined by another group of Haitians, some of whom had been his friends in Port-au-Prince. While some of these earlier arrivals moved away or went back to Haiti, many stayed, inspiring still more people to come to Rockland. Today the Jean-Jacques, Mondésir, and Sorel families represent the original nucleus of the present Haitian community.

One of the important early employers of Haitians, and a company indirectly responsible for the growth of the community, is Chromalloy Research and Technology. Originally located in West Nyack and now in Orangeburg, Chromalloy manufactures and repairs airplane engine parts. It grew rapidly during the late 1960s and the Vietnam War era. Haitians began working there around this time and became known for their reliable and steady work, especially their skills in the finishing stages of manufacture. Some of the Haitians who commuted from New York City settled in Rockland County to be near their work. Today, half of Chromalloy's 1,050 workers are minority people.

In the mid 1960s, a few Haitian families, including some from the city of Jacmel in southern Haiti, moved to Spring Valley. Earlier in the century, Spring Valley had been a Jewish summer resort with a large year-round Jewish population. As its population moved to outlying hamlets, much of its housing became available to newly arrived immigrants, especially Haitians. The early nucleus of families from Jacmel was joined by new arrivals from other cities in Haiti as well as by workers from New York City.

The appointment of "Baby Doc" Duvalier as president for life in 1971 increased the flow of migration from Haiti, and with Rockland County being a known destination for Haitians leaving the country, its Haitian population increased tremendously. Spring Valley was overtaking Nyack as the Haitian center of Rockland and was, in fact, on its way to becoming a predominantly Haitian village. Haitian-owned businesses began to appear along North Main Street in the mid to late 1970s. Among the oldest in continuous operation is Nick's Tropical Foods, established in 1978 by Antoine Nicholas. It carries a number of Haitian imports not available in local markets. North Main Street is also shared by some Jamaican- and Hispanic-owned stores.

Even more recently, Haitians have begun moving in large numbers to the Haverstraw area. They're following both the availability of affordable housing and pressures of gentrification. The village of Haverstraw itself is heavily Hispanic, having been settled by Puerto Rican agricultural workers after World War II. More recently, it has received many Dominicans and other immigrants from Central and South America. While some Haitian families live in the village itself, most have settled in the area surrounding the village, especially in Garnerville and West Haverstraw.

Perhaps most interesting aspect of immigrants in Haverstraw is that Haitians and Dominicans find themselves neighbors, just as they are in the Caribbean. While relations between the two Caribbean countries are often strained, few of these tensions are visible in Rockland County. Haitians and Dominicans often share the same work places, and before Haitian food stores opened in Nyack and Spring Valley, early Haitian residents of Rockland would go to Haverstraw to buy tropical produce from Hispanic merchants.

From the start, it was work opportunities that brought Haitians to Rockland County. Although the county has its share of Haitian professionals, intellectuals, and artists, its Haitian community is mostly working-class, although this term, like the notion of "suburban," can be deceptive. Rockland County's suburban nature is somewhat more complicated than what is usually conveyed by that word. In the case of the Haitians, at least, it does not generally mean that people have succeeded in the cities and moved to the suburbs. While many Haitians own single-family homes, some live in crowded conditions. And as with other recent immigrants, it is not uncommon to find Haitians with professional degrees working in factory jobs until they can receive certification in this country. Even some Haitian professionals may continue to work part-time in high paying factory jobs, in companies such as Chromalloy.

Many Haitians in Rockland County work two jobs, sometimes commuting between them using one of the many Haitian-owned car services. Other large employers of Haitians include Lederle Laboratories and Avon products, as well as many smaller manufacturers. The healthcare field in Rockland is dominated by Haitians. State facilities have many Haitian employees, and Haitians often work in nursing homes and care for the elderly.

The establishment of a cohesive Haitian community in Rockland County has been due in good part to the Catholic Church. A turning point for Rockland Haitians was the establishment of French and Creole masses, first at St. Ann's Church in Nyack and then at St. Joseph's Church in Spring Valley.

There are also a large number of Protestant denominations in Rockland County. Protestant churches, especially those of the Pentecostal and evangelical variety, have been winning many converts in Haiti. People are joining Protestant churches as a complete renunciation of *vodun* (Haiti's folk religion, a synthesis of the Dahomean, Yoruba, and Kongo belief systems, with an infusion of Roman Catholic elements).

As the century turns, Haitian arts are thriving. Many individuals and groups are expressing their heritage through painting, music and dance. On the other hand, like other immigrants groups, Haitians in Rockland County are faced with the simultaneous process of integrating into American society, while maintaining their unique culture and their ties to their country of origin. Such a process obviously has difficulties, and among the problems that have arisen are the American-style street gangs some young Haitians have formed in reaction to non-acceptance by other teenagers. But Rockland Haitians are also using culture as a way to solve social problems—as Haitians have so often done in the past.

It is probable that with improved conditions in Haiti, some of the Haitians living in Rockland County and struggling to get by will return, along with professionals who want to contribute their skills to the new Haiti that is emerging. However, the Haitian communities in Rockland seem to be there to stay, continuing to grow and to contribute to the economic and cultural life of the county.

Morton Marks, excerpted and condensed from
Haiti on the Hudson

The Jewish Community
1970-1979

The Congregation Sons of Israel of Spring Valley continued to serve as an Orthodox shul until it was destroyed by fire in the early 1970s. The congregation now meets on Williams Avenue, in Hillcrest, and has been expanded and renovated to meet the needs of the community.

Meeting in private homes, a handful of families organized the Reform Temple of Suffern in the fall of 1971. The small congregation expanded rapidly, and soon began holding religious school and services at the Suffern Presbyterian Church and at Temple Beth El in Spring Valley. In the spring of 1975, the Reform Temple purchased a private home on Haverstraw Road that was converted into classrooms, offices and a sanctuary.

The Solomon Schecter School, now the Reuben Gittleman Hebrew Day School, began in 1971 at the Jewish Community Center in Spring Valley and now serves pre-kindergarten through eighth grade.

Serving the Dexter Park area of South Spring Valley, Ramat Shalom ushered in its first Jewish New Year in 1972 without a rabbi. The congregation was organized because its members felt that their children were discouraged by the rigidity of institutional religion. They refused to label themselves as Orthodox, Conservative or Reform. A converted high ranch on Lomond Avenue serves as their synagogue. Today, Ramat Shalom belongs to the Reconstructionists movement.

During the Yom Kippur War in 1973, the youth of the Center conceived a "Walk for Israel," which later became known as the UJA Walk-A-Thon.

Harold L. Laroff

Plymouth Rock(land)?

In 1972 students of Gladys Webber's class at Lakewood School in Congers get in the Thanksgiving spirit by dressing as pilgrims.   Photo by Scott Webber.

Food Prices in 1972

(per pound, unless otherwise noted)

Ground Beef	.69
Sirloin	1.06
Chicken	.29
Eggs, one dozen	.39
Cheese	.39
Pork Chops	.69
Flounder	.89

Fishing the Hudson

Commercial fishing in the Hudson River once sustained generations of Rockland families. Using everything from small boats to 100-foot barges, fisherman could be seen year-round bringing in their catch of the day: striped bass, eels, crabs, shad, sturgeon or herring.

However, by the 1970s, the fishing industry's days were numbered as pollution began to take its toll on the river. In 1976, it was announced that a ban was being imposed on striped bass due to high concentrations of cancer-causing PCBs in the fish. While many companies had been dumping toxic waste into the Hudson for decades, the General Electric plants in Hudson Falls and Fort Edward in particular were cited as major polluters. (It is estimated that General Electric discharged over a million pounds of PCBs into the river over a span of thirty years.)

By the end of the twentieth century, only a dozen part-time fisherman still worked the 150-miles of river south of Troy, and their catch was limited to shad and crabs. As pollution levels gradually drop, hopes are being revived for the fishing industry, as well as for swimmers who have gazed longingly at the cool river waters on a hot summer's day.

If environmentalists' efforts continue, the Hudson River may again be something more to Rocklanders than an obstacle to cross over on the Tappan Zee Bridge.

Linda Zimmermann

The widest point of the 315-mile Hudson River is at Haverstraw. The deepest point is World's End near West Point, which is 216 feet deep.   JSC

...In 1976 fluorocarbons from aerosol cans are found to be destroying the ozone layer...In 1978 families leave Love Canal, N.Y., due to chemical contamination causing severe birth defects...

253

Natural Beauty Preserved

In 1974, Iona Island Marsh was designated a Natural Landmark (below left, JSC). Once the site of an ammunition depot, the area is now a bird sanctuary. Its tranquil, scenic beauty is also a sanctuary for Rocklanders looking to escape the more hectic places in the county.

This old marker (right) stands along the railroad tracks by the original depot buildings. A summer's day on the marsh (below) in 2001 seems to be a million miles away from the hustle and bustle of modern Rockland.

Photos by Linda Zimmermann.

Rockland County Sports Hall of Fame
1970-1979

Joe Alleva (Suffern) Outstanding quarterback who held almost every major passing record in Rockland when he graduated.

Jim Brechbiel (North Rockland) One of the finest running backs in Rockland scholastic history. During his junior year he set a county record of 1,109 rushing yards. Went on to play for the University of Maryland and the Canadian Football League.

Darryl Brown (Nanuet) Considered to be Nanuet's best basketball player ever. Held three-year varsity record of 1,188 points. Was MVP for Fordham and played pro basketball in Sweden.

George Dalzell—New City resident named All-America in college, toured the world with U.S. All-Star basketball team, and with the Metropolitan Basketball League he averaged 48 points per game.

Kathy Miller Dapolito (Ramapo) One of the top female athletes in Rockland history. Excelled in basketball, softball, tennis and bowling. Earned basketball scholarship to Niagara University team placed third in NAIA nationals.

Mike Deane (North Rockland) Was All-County in basketball, and went on to highly successful college coaching career. Was named NABC District II Coach of the Year in 1988.

Don Driscoll (Tappan Zee) Without peer as a competitive swimming coach in Rockland, named Coach of the Year nine times. Began swim program in 1970, and by the time he retired in 1995 he had amassed a dual meet record of 313 wins and only 10 losses.

Joe Goldsmith (Ramapo) One of Rockland's all-time great wrestlers, won two state championships. High school career record of 69-1-1, and went on to championship collegiate career.

Mike Hagon (Suffern) One of the most dominant runners in Rockland track history. State mile champion in 1974. Attended William and Mary on full track scholarship.

Pete Haubner (SpringValley) Earned varsity letters in football, basketball and track. Named All-Region in

basketball at RCC. Also awarded two purple hearts and two Crosses of Gallantry as a Marine in Vietnam.

Kevin Kane (Nyack) All-County in four sports, county scholastic tennis champ, and All-State in lacrosse. Went on to record-setting career as soccer goalie for University of North Carolina.

Dale Lydecker (Nyack) Talented tennis, baseball and football player who was drafted by the Chicago White Sox, played one year of minor league baseball with the Mets organization, and had tryouts as a punter with two NFL teams.

Bob Mathias (Clarkstown) One of Rockland's greatest basketball players. From his first game as a seventh grader to his final game as a senior, his teams never lost to a Rockland opponent. Earned full basketball scholarship to the University of South Carolina.

Sylvester "Molly" McGee (Haverstraw/North Rockland) Excelled in football and baseball. Went on to five-year pro football career with the Atlanta Falcons and the CFL, where he was the leading receiver 1978.

Denise McGuire (Pearl River) Regarded by some as the finest female basketball player in Rockland scholastic history. First girl to score 1,000 points. Earned scholarship to Stanford where she earned Phi Beta Kappa honors, then worked for Mother Teresa in Calcutta.

Howie McNiff (Albertus Magnus) One of Rockland's finest distance runners ever, first in N.Y.S. history to win state individual titles in all three seasons of one school year. Earned 12 varsity letters at Fordham.

Patty Dillon Solliday (Clarkstown South) U.S national champion in the three-mile swim in 1972. Over 12-year career she competed in 700 events, winning 487 awards, including 200 gold medals, 85 silver and 147 bronze.

Steve Wanamaker (Nyack) Excellent baseball player, but was also called the best linebacker to ever play in Rockland. Went to Penn State on a scholarship and played in the Sugar Bowl in 1976.

Dick Yerg—Native Nyacker who spent four years covering Rockland sports for the Bergen County *Record*, and 32 years for the *Journal News*.

The Requas: Three Centuries of History

When the Requa family held its first national family reunion in 1978, three centuries of notable history in America were proudly on display. The Requas, a fixture in Rockland for more than 150 years, have produced inventors, military officers, movie stars, architects, politicians, judges, doctors and businessmen.

From left: Don, Shirley, Glode M., Ann and Robert Requa at the Tricentennial Reunion at Requa Lake in Monsey in 1978.   Courtesy of Ann Requa.

The Tricentennial Reunion drew more than 200 family members from across the country and even garnered national TV coverage, says Ann Requa of Monsey. It was 300 years after Claude Equier, a French Huguenot, fled religious persecution in France and settled in New Rochelle. When Equier moved to the Tarrytown area in the 1720s, he changed his name to Glode Requa so the Dutch settlers there could pronounce his name more easily.

While some Requas made a name for themselves nationally, the Requas of Rockland were busy staking a claim to local fame. The Rockland Requas are descended from James H. Requa, a grandson of Captain Glode, who settled in Piermont in the early nineteenth century. The family genealogy notes that James Requa organized the Orangetown Guards, a military guard reserve unit and the first uniformed company in Rockland County.

One of James Requa's sons, another Glode Requa, was described by his descendants as one of the youngest men in the country to handle a steam injection locomotive when, at age 17, he was an engineer for the New York and Erie Railroad. He later founded the Glode Requa Coal and Lumber Co. of Monsey, which supplied "the wood for numerous Rockland homes" from its opening in 1857 until 1960, when the property was sold to a cement block company.

And thousands of Rocklanders associate the name "Requa" with invigorating waters, family picnics and other fun-filled summer outings at Requa Lake, a popular, private club for swimming and recreation in Monsey that operated from 1931 to 1986. The Requas also ran an apple and peach orchard from 1942 to 1953.

Jamie Kempton, *The Journal News*

Garry   Onderdonk, Doing the Job

If the fortunes of life had been different, Garry Onderdonk might have been the Baron of Rockland, for his family once was a vast landholder of county properties, including parcels from Piermont to the Nyacks along the Hudson. There is even the famous Onderdonk house in Piermont, where George Washington met Sir Guy Carleton in 1783, after the new American nation received the first official gun salute from the British.

But Onderdonk, born in 1896, instead found himself in Spring Valley and with his own connection to the United States. For generations, this great-great-grandson of original Onderdonk's was Draft Board chairman. It was a job he did not like, and when he was required to retire at the age of 75 in 1971, he gladly did so. But in all those seasons, from 1943 to 1971, Onderdonk always said that whether it was World War II, Korea or Vietnam, "I never liked the idea of sending someone off to fight in the war. But unpleasant jobs have to be done."

And do them, Garry Onderdonk did. As a 17-year-old sailor, then Marine in World War I, he fought the central powers, and also "did what I had to do." After the war he became a longtime stockbroker and just before World War II he organized Rockland's office of civil defense, as well as the American Legion brigade, which gave basic training to more than 2,500 young men, training that they later used to much good advantage when they were called or volunteered in the war.

Onderdonk also organized Moscarella Post 1199, American Legion. In 1943, County Judge John A. McKenna "stuck" him with the Draft Board job, and he was actually involved with three boards that were later consolidated into one county-wide board, located in Spring Valley and called Local Board 13. Many a Rockland youngster reported there for the trip to Whitehall Street in the bowels of lower Manhattan, where a physical was given to determine fitness for duty. For all his efforts, Onderdonk, who never minced words and told you off if he felt like it (and he often did), was the personal target of protests.

In the Vietnam War, antiwar groups called him all manner of names. While the Draft Board chief personally believed that the Vietnam War was a delaying action that caused the loss of so many American lives, he felt that he had to serve as his country asked him to. For that he could win few friends.

When Onderdonk retired, he often wrote to the *Journal News* to protest big government, or taxes, or people who were so caught up in themselves that they forgot the sacrifices made by others. Truly, Garry Onderdonk was a "defining moment" in Rockland during this century because he "did the job" no one else wanted, but which had to be done.

Arthur H. Gunther, *The Journal News,* 11/10/99

That Star-Spangled Banner Still Waved

The "generation gap" was perhaps never more evident as it was during the Vietnam War. Young anti-war protestors not only demonstrated and clashed with authorities in the streets, but in their homes, as well. Many of those protestors who openly despised the military were children of World War II and Korean War veterans.

Rockland households experienced the turmoil of the conflict between a generation who had sacrificed everything in defense of the country, with a generation who believed that peace was the only hope for the future.

However, even as the word "patriot" began to be portrayed in a negative way, veterans still faithfully remembered their fallen comrades each year at Memorial Day parades and services. In this 1970 photo, veterans (from left to right) Charles Newcomb, Robert G. Strong and Bob Kraft marched in the Memorial Day parade in Congers.

It would not be until the Gulf War twenty years later that the United States military would begin to regain respect, and after the terrorist attacks on September 11, 2001, the men and women of the armed forces were finally once again seen as heroes.

Linda Zimmermann
Photo courtesy of Robert and Diane Strong.

Bicentennial Fever

The celebration of the nation's 200th birthday in 1976 involved countless events across the country. As early as 1968, bicentennial plans were underway in Rockland and both local town and county commissions were soon formed to bury time capsules, dedicate plaques and memorials, conduct tours and events, and hold parades.

The ensuing commercialism was nothing short of overwhelming—just about any product you can imagine suddenly had an American flag and the word "Bicentennial" on it. The bumper sticker below (courtesy of Rachel Kaufmann) was one of the many items that local residents used to adorn their cars, homes and themselves.   Linda Zimmermann

Items in the News

Who Wants to be a Millionaire?

A surprised Ness Martinez, co-manager of Motel on the Mountain, had expected a money order from a Suffern bank for $1,000, but instead received one for $1,000,115. Martinez will inform the bank Monday of its mistake "because obviously the check is not cashable," according to Richard Silvan, another co-manager. But at least for the weekend Martinez can dream how he would spend the money if only it was his. *The Journal-News, 8/25/73*

Mrs. Cornell Heads Democratic Party

Rockland County Democrats beat the national organization to it this summer by naming their first woman chairman in history, Mrs. Harriet Donow Cornell. A county resident since 1958, Mrs. Cornell has long been active in Clarkstown and county Democratic politics, heading up fund-raising musicals and promotions, and serving on the county executive committee. *Clarkstown Courier, 1973*

...In 1979 the Russians invade Afghanistan...

Hillcrest Hospital Closes

Community Hospital locked its doors Friday night after closing its emergency room and transferring 35 patients to other facilities or sending them home.

The 100-bed hospital locked its doors barely 24 hours after a Bankruptcy Court hearing in White Plains found federal Internal Revenue Service officials unwilling to lift liens on $100,000 owed by the hospital, even after warnings that the money was needed to keep the facility open. In all, Community owes $500,000 in back taxes.

Over 200 employees will be out of work as result of the closing. Patients who used the facility praised the nursing staff and worried how the hospital closing would effect the local residents, especially in times of emergencies.

Kathryn Kahler, *The Journal-News, 12/29/79*

Medical Examiner

In 1974, Rockland County created the position of Medical Examiner, and the job went to Dr. Frederick Zugibe, an expert forensic pathologist.

Dinosaurs in Blauvelt

Over 200 million years ago, Rockland was a hot, tropical jungle. The Triassic-period dinosaurs that roamed the area left their distinctive footprints in the muddy soil. In 1972, students Paul Olsen and Robert Salvia found some of those fossilized tracks in Blauvelt.

The site, between Route 303 and Greenbush Road, held the first dinosaur tracks to be discovered in New York and they were removed and brought to the State Museum in Albany. Originally misidentified as *Coelophysis*, they are now believed to have been made by a small herbivore dinosaur known as *Atreipus*.

However, *Atreipus* was not alone in Rockland. Other dinosaur tracks were later found in Grand View, Upper Nyack and Haverstraw, all of which went into the hands of private collectors. By the year 2000, Paul Olsen (who went on to become a professor of earth and environmental sciences at Lamont-Doherty Earth Observatory) was concerned that the paleontology record of these dinosaurs would be lost due to private fossil hunters and the building boom.

For example, the original Blauvelt site, which no doubt contains many more tracks, became the target of a developer who wanted to build a car dealership, thereby obliterating any fossil records. Olsen and others hope that such development will not be allowed to take place on such scientifically important sites.

As suburban sprawl continues to place profit over preservation, let's hope that education and scientific research do not go the way of the dinosaurs.

Linda Zimmermann

1980-1989

Real Estate Rises
More Farms Fall

In 1970 the average price of a house was $40,000. By 1980, the price had more than doubled to $86,000. The economic pressure to sell land to developers was great, and by the end of the century only a handful of farms still operated in Rockland. However, unlike the modest single-family home developments of the decades immediately following the building of the Tappan Zee Bridge, condos, luxury townhouses, and large, upscale houses began to fill every scrap of available land.

There were some shocking crimes in Rockland in the 1980s that made national headlines. There were still many trouble spots around the world, potentially threatening our security. Social reforms had overlooked many, and poverty and prejudice were still alive and kicking.

However, despite these problems, there was a general feeling of optimism in the country. A section of the middle-class was growing in affluence, and those people wanted a bigger and better piece of the suburban American dream. They wanted a condo, a luxury townhouse or a large, upscale house in Rockland, built upon land that had been previously farmed for generations.

Plowing the Smith farm in New City in May of 1983.
Photo by Warren Inglese.

Photographing the photographer: Warren Inglese, *Journal-News* photographer, at West Point in 1987. Inglese's photographs of Rockland are among the finest ever taken. The scenes he captured of the rural locations in the county will preserve the memory of a vanished era.   Photo by Scott Webber.

The Coachlight Dinner Theatre in Nanuet was a popular nightspot. It was located in the domed building to the west of the Nanuet Mall on Route 59.   Postcard courtesy of Scott Webber.

Janet Hogan's Diner on Route 59 in West Nyack. Any time of the day or night, Hogan's Diner was the place for locals of all ages to meet and greet, and of course, eat. It was demolished in the 1990s to make way for the Palisades Center.

Photo courtesy of Scott Webber.

Cost of Living: 1980

 Average Income
$9,916 per year

 New House
$86,159

Gallon of Gas
$1.03

New Car
$5,413

 Loaf of Bread 48¢

Gallon of Milk $1.60

Dow Jones Average: 963.99

Shaking Up Rockland

Early Saturday morning, on October 19, 1985, things started to rock and roll in Rockland. An earthquake, measuring 4.0 on the Richter scale, and centered on a fault line in Ardsley, woke up many local residents and sent them running to their telephones to report the unsettling tremor. The quake lasted about a minute, and caused no injuries or damage, other than to shake the nerves of those who experienced it.

Linda Zimmermann

Drought struck the county in 1981 as this photo of the Lake DeForest reservoir shows. Former roads that had long been submerged were exposed as the lake dried up.

Photo by John Scott.

261

Keeping your front door unlocked and your keys in the car were not uncommon practices in Rockland throughout much of the twentieth century. By the 1980s, however, the increase in population brought an increase in crime. Along with the popular smoke detectors, sales of home burglar alarms and auto security systems were brisk. Yet even with this new fear and awareness, no one expected that the county would be thrust into national headlines from an event that occurred on what appeared to be a typical autumn day in 1981.

The Brinks Robbery

On Tuesday, October 20, 1981, a Brinks armored truck pulled up to an entrance to the Nanuet Mall in the rear parking lot. Joseph Trombino and Peter Paige, who had been partners for 14 years, sat in the back of the truck surrounded by bags of money; just a typical day on the job. The two men knew this was their last day working together, but they thought it was because Paige was transferring to a different route. They had no idea that one of them would be dead in a matter of minutes.

Their last pickup of the day was at the Nanuet National Bank, where they collected $839,000. Returning to the truck at approximately 3:50 p.m., they began to load the heavy sacks of money. Suddenly, a red Chevy van screeched to a halt next to the Brinks truck. Three men jumped out. Another man, who had been sitting on a bench on the sidewalk, also jumped to his feet. All four men were carrying guns and immediately opened fire.

Peter Paige was killed by two shots to his chest. Trombino was severely wounded in his left arm as he desperately tried to close the door. The driver, Jim Kelly, was wounded when the intense gunfire shattered the bullet-resistant glass. What seemed like an eternity was over in minutes, and the assailants sped away with bags of cash, wet from their victims' blood.

Local authorities immediately began a county-wide manhunt, which would lead to wild car chases, another gun battle and more casualties.

Reports came over the police radios that the armed robbers and their cash had been transferred to a U-Haul truck that was headed east on Route 59. Alert Nyack police officer Brian Lennon stopped a U-Haul truck on Mountainview Avenue just as it was trying to turn onto the New York State Thruway. Detective Arthur Keenan, Sergeant Edward O'Grady and Officer Waverly "Chipper" Brown quickly joined Lennon.

As the officers questioned the man and woman in the cab of the truck, the rear door opened and six men poured out, guns blazing. Keenan began returning fire, but was struck twice. Chipper Brown was killed instantly by a hail of bullets to his chest. O'Grady emptied his revolver before he was hit by a fatal volley from the assailants' automatic weapons. Lennon grabbed a shotgun from the car, emptied it, and then began firing his revolver.

When the shooting finally stopped, the chase began again. Rockland streets have rarely been witness to such dangerous and tragic events. Fortunately, by 4:15 p.m., several of the gunmen had been captured and $800,000 recovered (a total $1.6 million had been taken in the heist). While investigations and arrests were to continue for years, involving the FBI and numerous law enforcement agencies throughout the country, the focus for local officials inevitably turned to the prosecution of the Brinks robbery defendants.

The court case was to draw national interest, as the defendants were not just a bunch of small-time crooks. They consisted of former members of the terrorist organization the Weather Underground, as well as the Black Liberation Army. Controversial and high-profile attorneys took up the defendants' cases, and they began to employ unscrupulous tactics to delay and disrupt the pre-trial proceedings. Rockland County District Attorney Kenneth Gribetz soon found himself knee-deep in a court battle that often took on the appearance of an absurd circus, rather than a serious murder and robbery trial.

The members of the Black Liberation Army claimed that they were not citizens of the United States. They claimed to be citizens of a new country composed of six former slave-owning Southern states known as the Republic of New Afrika. Defendants like Nathaniel Burns, who insisted on being referred to by his New Afrikan name of Sekou Odinga, claimed not to be criminals under arrest, but actually prisoners of war—a revolutionary war for independence.

Another defendant, David Gilbert, claimed, "We're neither terrorists nor criminals. It is precisely because of our love of life, because we revel in the human spirit, that we became freedom fighters against the racist and deadly imperialist system." The fact that they murdered three men, one of whom was black (Officer Chipper Brown), didn't seem to matter to this reveler in the human spirit.

Every day, both terrorist-supporters and local residents lined the sidewalks outside the courthouse in New City. Supporters chanted such things as, "The BLA is alive and well; the FBI can go to hell." Residents responded by shouting, "The USA is here to stay; if you don't like it, go away." In the midst of these crowds of angry people were hordes of reporters from the across the country, eagerly covering every detail of the bizarre proceedings.

Sanity and justice eventually prevailed. The actual trials were held in Orange and Westchester Counties, and although there were plenty of legal fireworks to come, the final verdicts were all guilty.

The robbery and subsequent trials took their emotional and physical toll on all involved. In addition, the taxpayers of Rockland had to foot the bill for all of the legal proceedings—a whopping $5.4 million. Of course, the real cost was the lives of three innocent men just trying to do their duty.

Linda Zimmermann

Thousands of people a day drive by this pointed stone on Mountainview Avenue, just before the Thruway entrance, but few realize its significance.

This is a memorial to two of the three victims of the Brinks robbery, the two Nyack police officers who were gunned down near this spot.

Photo by John Scott.

The Sohn Murders

In 1968, Arnold and Elaine Sohn left their neighborhood in the Bronx. They moved to Jill Lane in Spring Valley so that their children would have a safe place in which to grow up. In December of 1980, Mr. and Mrs. Sohn were found brutally murdered in their own home, victims of their daughter's twisted plans.

On the morning of Sunday, December 28, a neighbor entered the home and discovered the horrible scene—Arnold Sohn was on the floor of the bedroom, his face unrecognizable from the vicious beating he had received. His wife's lifeless body was in the bathroom; she had been drowned in the tub. Crimes like this were not supposed to happen in quiet Rockland County neighborhoods.

While the Sohns' son, Mark, had moved to Florida, their daughter Sheryl was still living at home. However, when investigators arrived at the house, they found a note from Sheryl to her parents from the night before saying that she would be staying at a friend's house. Initially, the detectives were relieved that the daughter had not been home at the time of the murders and was thereby saved from a similar fate. But veteran detectives Cliff Tallman and Eddie O'Neill knew that Sheryl had a history of drugs and soon became suspicious that she had somehow been involved.

Sheryl Sohn eventually confessed, and the gruesome details of the horrible crime became known. She had met ex-convict Belton "Panama" Brims at the Camelot bar in Spring Valley, and arranged for him to break into her house and rob her own parents. He could keep everything he could get; all she wanted was the diamond ring on her mother's finger. Brims brought James Sheffield with him to the Sohns' house that night, where the robbery turned violent and deadly. James Sheffield had used a handgun to bludgeon Arnold Sohn to death. Brims had dragged Elaine into the bathroom and held her head under water until she drowned.

Brims was arrested, but managed to escape from the Rockland County Jail in June. Seven weeks later, he was apprehended in Selma, Alabama and finally brought to justice. Brims was sentenced to twenty-five-years-to-life on each count of murder. James Sheffield was a fugitive until July of 1982, but he was also arrested and eventually convicted of the crimes.

Sheryl Sohn, who maintained that she never meant for the men to actually harm her parents during the robbery, was found guilty of felony murder. While the case eventually faded from the front page, it did not fade from the memories of local residents whose illusions of a quiet and safe county had been shattered by the terrible events.

Linda Zimmermann

Judge "Tries" 80s Values

John Skahen likes to talk about the "old fashioned" values of respect for people and property. If there was more of that, says the surrogate court judge, everyone would be better off. Skahen knows about the problems caused by not following the Golden Rule. He's also been a county court judge, a family court judge, and a Rockland district attorney.

He's seen the county grow from a smattering of quiet farms and factory towns, where everyone knew everyone else, to the anonymity of a suburban, bedroom community. Skahen's proud to say he grew up in Garnerville, decades before the exodus from the city.

"It was a textile town," he says. "Almost everyone worked in the factories. The companies owned the houses, the streets, everything. The names of the streets, like Calico Hill, reflected the factory."

He recalled the days of the Great Depression. "Everyone helped one another. The men got together, cut down big trees and split them with wedges for firewood. Most of the people then had coal stoves, but coal was just too expensive." It was also the time of the Saturday Night Bath. "We didn't have running hot water," he explains, "and the big, galvanized tub in the kitchen was the ritual of the day."

For the most part, his neighbors were descendants of people who had lived there for generations. "Everyone on my street was my father," he says with a laugh. "I didn't get away with anything. We had then what I guess you could call community standards, something that I think was lost as the population grew. You can't disgrace your father if no one knows who you are."

After graduating from high school, Skahen took a business course for a year, and then went to work in 1934 in a Haverstraw taxi office. The pay was $8 a week. He then took equivalency tests to show he had a grasp of college level subjects. "I got my two years of college by taking examinations at New York University," he said. "If you passed, they gave you a penny postcard saying you had two years of college behind you."

With postcard in hand, Skahen got a job clerking for attorney George Raymond. He worked in the office for seven and a half years, and was admitted to the state bar after Navy service in World War II.

He practiced law in Haverstraw, and then in 1950, Gov. Thomas Dewey appointed him county district attorney. He served through 1959.

Staff Photo – Al Witt
Surrogate Court Judge John Skahen
...talks about the 'old-fashion values.'

"There were no assistants in the office for the first three and a half years," he recalls. "They told me it was supposed to be a part-time job, but as it worked out, it was really full-time. I remember the police called you up about everything. A guy could break into a garage and steal peanuts, and you'd have to go down and interrogate him all night."

Nowadays, the district attorney has assistants to handle things like that. There are 15 attorneys in the office, along with 10 investigators and 8 secretaries.

"There were a handful of murders," Skahen recalls, "some gambling raids, a few drug raids—guys from the city bringing in heroin. Then there were the burglaries and some armed robberies here and there. For the most part though, we were dealing with crimes less violent than you have today."

From 1962 through 1968, he served as county family court judge and has been surrogate court judge since 1969. In 1978, an elderly New York City dowager threatened to kill Skahen after he granted the woman's husband a divorce. The woman was later acquitted of plotting the murder with an undercover police officer. Skahen says he wasn't worried. He said he merely followed the law in deciding the case. "It really didn't bother me," he says of the murder threat. "I wasn't concerned. Besides," he adds with a laugh, "I'm well insured."

Skahen checks the time. He's due back court in a few minutes. A visitor quickly asks him about a speech he gave at a community gathering in which he called for people to re-establish a sense of personal responsibility.

"Sometimes people think that they're owed something, that everything should be done for them by the government. It's a something-for-nothing age. Sometimes I think that we parents who went from the Depression to the post war affluence, and had the idea of giving our children much more than we ever had, are to blame for it."

Outside his office, a suspect in the Brinks robbery, which left two police officers dead, is being led into the county jail. Upstairs in the courthouse, a murder trial is in progress.

It's 1982 in Rockland County, a time far from the simple days Skahen so fondly remembers.

James Walsh, *The Journal-News,* 3/16/82

Helen Hayes and Pretty Penny

Actress Helen Hayes of Nyack, often called "The First Lady of the American Theater," has her own reminiscences about the many decades she's lived in Rockland. One of them is how she and her husband, playwright Charles MacArthur, acquired their Nyack home, Pretty Penny (below, JSC), after another house deal fell through.

"On a sparkling autumn Sunday when the changing maples along Broadway gave Nyack a golden glow, we drove out for a last good-bye to our dream. I carried Hobe Irwin's blueprints for our reconstruction (of the house in the failed deal), to throw into the Hudson. Charlie thought we should set fire to the house with them, but I fancied myself at the water's edge flinging them dramatically upon the tide.

"On the way back, I was crying, so I missed the 'For Sale' sign, but Charlie did not. He stopped the car with a jerk; we stumbled out and stood by a graceful white frame house with a cupola, a front porch with Corinthian columns and dark green shutters and that blessed sign stuck in the front lawn—'For Sale.'

"We were silent after that as we went up and looked into the front windows. In the dim light we could see glittering crystal chandeliers, front and back parlors, huge gilt mirrors over marble mantlepieces, intricate plaster-work on the ceilings—a little palace.

"We went around to the back. There was the sweeping view down to the Hudson, in all its glory. The Sunday sailing regatta was on, filling the river with what looked like white butterflies. A huge tanker happened to be sailing downstream toward Manhattan.

"Charlie, looking on it all, nodded. 'It works,' he said."

Miss Hayes recalls that later, "Charlie and I were giving a bridesmaids' dinner for the daughter of beloved friends. It was a warm June night and some time quite late the wedding party donned the bathing togs we kept for guests and plunged, whooping and laughing, into the pool. The lady to the north phoned the stationhouse and reported an orgy in progress.

"When the officers arrived at the poolside, they were greeted by the bride-to-be, Bobby Boll, and the bridegroom-to-be, Lew Herndon, and the wedding party, made up mostly of Nyack's old families. Red-faced, the police retired with the admonition, 'Keep it down, Bobby.'"

Miss Hayes once told a London newspaper reporter that she felt sorry the police officer had not witnessed the times when Kate Hepburn used to come swimming there, and Norma Shearer and John Barrymore. One morning, Barrymore said the pool wasn't cool enough, so Charlie ordered two truckloads of ice, and they floated around in it looking like flies in a highball."

Helen Hayes (right) with her husband, Charles MacArthur, and their daughter, Mary, in this wonderful informal photo taken in the garden of Pretty Penny in 1946 by Fred Crum.

But, Miss Hayes once recalled, "There was a brief interval when I almost let slip the silken cord that has held me in Nyack all these years. It was right after Charlie's death. I was living alone. I didn't think I could cope alone, and decided to sell Pretty Penny.

"I auctioned off the accumulated memorabilia of Charlie's career and mine, emptied the house of its past, and agreed to sell it to two friends who had fallen in love with it, Nora Kaye and Herbert Ross. I desperately hated to leave, but thought it was God's will.

"It turned out I was wrong. When the hour came to execute the final papers, Nora Kaye was too frightened to sign. 'I've never lived in anything larger than a trunk,' she said. 'I can't face all that space.'

"The deal fell through and I decided to stay. I sold off the waterfront property to the William Hopes.

"When Charlie was wooing me he promised, 'You may never be contented, but you will never be bored.' Bringing me to Nyack was the first step in keeping that promise. I have known contentment here, and fury, too, and frustration, but never boredom."

Nancy Cacioppo, *The Journal-News*, 5/21/89

Rockland Attracts the Famous

Rockland has been endowed with people who are nationally known in music, theater and the arts—personalities, past and present, who live here now or at one time had "live-in" connections with Rockland, for a few months or many years. The following list was composed by Nancy Cacioppo, *The Journal-News*, 5/21/89:

Helen Hayes, actress
Charles MacArthur, playwright (and the late husband of Miss Hayes)
James MacArthur, actor (and the son of Miss Hayes and MacArthur)
Ben Hecht, playwright
John Houseman, actor and producer
Maxwell Anderson, playwright
Bill Mauldin, cartoonist
Milton Caniff, cartoonist
Guthrie McClintic, director
Madeleine Carroll, actress
Norman Corwin, comedian
Maurice Evans, actor
Noel Coward, playwright and actor
William Sloane, publisher
Mary Mowbray-Clarke, artist
Ina Claire, actress
Margalo Gilmore, actress
John Van Druten, director
John Dos Passos, writer
John Steinbeck, writer
Ellen Burstyn, actress
Bill Murray, actor-comedian
Al Pacino, actor
Mikhail Baryshnikov, dancer and actor
Valerie Harper, actress
Jon Voight, actor
Chiz Schultz, producer
Isley Brothers, singers
Elaine Stritch, actress
Arlene Dahl, actress
Chita Rivera, actress
Toni Morrison, writer
Thomas Berger, writer
Skitch Henderson, conductor
Carson McCullers, writer
Myron Cohen, comedian
Freddie Roman, comedian
Morty Gunty, comedian
Dick Lord, comedian
Sandy Baron, comedian
Vic Arnell, comedian
Andre Watts, pianist
Tom Chapin, singer
Harry Streep, dancer
Harry Nillson, singer
Jimmy Webb, composer
Mick Jagger, singer

Bill Boggs, TV host
Zita Johann, actress
Lotte Lenya, actress
Kurt Weill, composer
Rollo Peters, actor
Mike Kellin, actor
Harry Bellaver, actor
Kim Stanley, actress
Fred Gwynne, actor
Richard Kiley, actor
Pat Hingle, actor
Casper Roos, actor
Burgess Meredith, actor
Mitch Miller, conductor
Mike Wallace, TV newsman
Morley Safer, TV newsman
Katharine Cornell, actress
Thomas Meehan, playwright
Big Chief Moore, musician
Eddie Sauter, musician
Edward Hopper, artist
John Costigan, artist
Millia Davenport, scenic and costume designer
Hermann Rosse, set designer
Charles Ellis, actor-artist
Elmer Stanley Hader, illustrator, writer, painter
Berta Hader, illustrator, writer
Marion Hargrove, writer
Hazard Reeves, Cinerama entrepreneur
Henry Varnum Poor, artist
Gilbert Rose, artist
Martha Ryther, artist
Hugo Robus, artist
John Flannagan, artist
Arnie Zane and Bill T. Jones, dancers
Ruth Reeves, artist
Rebekkah Harkness, arts patroness
Henry LeTang, choreographer
Betty Friedan, writer
Richard Daly, Tyne Daly, Tim Daly, actors
Connie Selleca, actress
Audrey and Judy Landers, actresses
Margot Kidder, actress
Ruppert Holmes, composer
Christine Andreas, actress
Tito Puente, musician
William Hurt, actor
Ellen Simon, playwright
John Johnson, TV newsman

Other Famous Faces

Sculptor Ted Ludwiczak displays his carved stone faces on the porch of his home in Haverstraw.

...In 1980 the nation erupts in celebration when the U.S. Olympic Hockey Team wins the gold medal at Lake Placid...Mount St. Helens volcano in Washington state erupts, killing 8 and devastating the area...The United States, West Germany and Japan boycott the summer Olympics in Moscow in protest of the Soviet invasion of Afghanistan...Ronald Reagan is elected president...Former Beatle John Lennon is shot to death in Manhattan—he was 40...

Historic Treasures in County Archives

Since 1987, County Archivist Peter Scheibner has kept track of everything from census records (1855-1925), naturalization papers (1812-1991), marriage registers (1908-1935), tax and assessment rolls, and map collections to deeds from Orange and Rockland counties, mortgages and court records dating back to 1703. The archives also include a 1786 speech by George Washington and an 1891 atlas of the Hudson Valley.

The task of managing 26,000 to 30,000 cubic feet of written records from 50 county agencies—5 to 10 percent of which is historic—is now less daunting for several reasons. One reason is the new 17,000-square-foot, state-of-the-art County Records Center and Archives, a part of the County Clerk's Office, located in Building S at the Dr. Robert L. Yeager Health Center in Ramapo. Opened in 1998 during Rockland's Bicentennial, the building has 12,000 square feet for storage of county documents alone. There is also space for historic archives, a research room and microfilm equipment. People can request court records and, for a fee, can have them copied and certified.

Scheibner also credits the help he receives from members of the Retired Senior Volunteer Program and the Rockland County Genealogical Society for the improved records management. George Fee of Nyack,

president of the genealogical society, is one of more than a dozen volunteers who contribute about 3,000 hours a year helping Scheibner and his six-member staff to inventory, microfilm and preserve the county's historic and court records.

"The idea behind genealogy is to look to the past to find one's ancestors," said Fee. In the same way, "We're trying to help the county preserve its genealogy and history."

Among the items Scheibner hopes to see preserved and microfilmed are the 10,000 items in the Sherwood Map Collection. The collection, which belonged to Spring Valley real estate attorney Harold T. Sherwood, runs the gamut from maps of early patents and farms, to aerial photos of Rockland from the 1930s and maps of the New York State Thruway, the Palisades Interstate Parkway, Shanks Village and more recent subdivisions.

Last year, the Finkelstein Memorial Library donated its collection of photographs, books, albums, scrapbooks, diaries, newsletters and documents reflecting life in Spring Valley and Sparkill from the mid-nineteenth century to the mid-twentieth century to the County Archives. "This is a collection that needs to be better preserved, micro-filmed and made available to the public," Scheibner said.

Nancy Cacioppo, *The Journal News*, 4/2001

Grant Jobson, *Journal-News* Editorial Page Editor, Retires

Grant Jobson wouldn't be where he is today if it wasn't for the Garnerville Indians.

For those of you not in the know, the Indians were a neighborhood football team in the 1930s. Where Jobson came in was that he had a grandfather who wrote for the *Rockland County Times* in Haverstraw, and it seemed logical to the players that Jobson could get an article written about the squad.

"The kids asked me if my grandfather, that was John Henry Smith, would put something in the paper, and he said OK, but I'd have to write it," recalled Jobson. "So I wrote a couple of sentences and they put it under the smallest headline they had. After a while I got a little bolder and worked my way up from three sentences to three paragraphs."

What ensued was a career spanning a half-century in which Jobson wrote hundreds of stories and edited thousands of others, first for the *Rockland County Times* and then for this newspaper.

He was born to Charles and Frances Jobson on Bridge Street in Garnerville on June 30, 1921. His father was a shipping clerk for Kay-Fries. Jobson attended the Garnerville Grammar School, and was graduated from Haverstraw High School. Jobson's initial lesson in journalism—that you don't go into it for the money—came from his maternal grandfather who wrote without the incentive of a paycheck.

"He just had his heart in it," Jobson said with a smile. "He wrote about all the local boards and everything else...His pay was a free Christmas basket with the biggest turkey you'd ever see, plus fresh vegetables from the editor's garden during the summer."

Jobson reported the ups and downs of the Garnerville Indians for three years. Then in 1937, when he was 16, he got a job as a high school sports correspondent for the *Rockland County Times*. "The first year it was $10 pay and a free pass to the toboggan run at Mount Hoevenberg in Lake Placid," Jobson recalled with a laugh. "I never did make it to Mount Hovenberg."

By 1938 the Garnerville Indians were also playing in a baseball league, and they relied on Jobson to call in the box scores and a brief account of their home games to The *Journal-News*. Not long afterwards, Norman R. Baker, then sports editor of this newspaper, asked Jobson to be the Haverstraw sports correspondent.

"I was writing for both papers, and I always wrote two different stories," said Jobson. "I had to use different leads, different approaches. It was the best training I got...The *Journal-News*, incidentally, paid me a nickel an inch, I think the most I ever made in a month was $24."

In 1941, Jobson replaced Michael Prendergast, who would become the state Democratic Committee chairman, as a general assignment reporter at the *Rockland County Times*.

"I wrote weddings, I wrote showers, I wrote obituaries, I wrote the general news story. I wrote the whole damn thing," Jobson said. "And I had to sweep the front office floor every Saturday morning. On a country paper you work all the time. Days, nights, weekends. That's what a country newspaper is all about. I like country papers."

He remembers that he also liked to throw in what he calls "big words," but more often than not, they were scratched out by the editor, William J. McCabe, who managed the operation with six employees.

"Bill McCabe was a guy well-suited to puncture egos...I remember he strolled out one day and said to me: 'You know, you're not a genius.' So that kind of set the top on the pickle barrel right there."

In 1942, Jobson was offered the sports editing job at The *Journal-News*. "I was all gung ho for it," Jobson said, "but then I found out I'd have to deliver newspapers. That was one of the things the sports editor did in those days...It was one of the quaint ways of operating a newspaper. Well, it just wasn't my bag, so I stayed in Haverstraw."

It wasn't until 18 years later, in 1960, that Jobson joined this newspaper's copy desk for $35 a week more than he was making in Haverstraw. In 1963, Jobson became city editor, and then news editor a year later. He was named editorial page editor in 1973.

For nine years, Jobson wrote a column, "One Man's Rockland," that took a tongue-in-cheek look at issues ranging from sandlot baseball to gasoline shortages, and from false fire alarms to dowsing for water.

Jobson characteristically dismisses many of the columns as efforts slapped together between his other duties, and says that his glory days were spent as a copy editor. "It's not glamorous. It's like working in a boiler room," he said, "but I think copy editing was the best thing I ever did."

James Walsh, *The Journal News*, 1/4/87

Chief Ronald "Redbone" Van Dunk (1933-2001) was born in Hillburn and became the spiritual and political leader of the Ramapough Mountain Indians. Chief Redbone tried for many years to obtain official status for the 3,000-member tribe, a struggle which often stirred up considerable controversy. Due to the strict requirements of an uninterrupted bloodline (the Ramapoughs had intermingled with both white and free black settlers), the requests for official recognition have so far been denied.

Isabelle Savell

A voice of Rockland's history died yesterday (October 27, 1988) with Isabelle Savell. Mrs. Savell, a retired journalist and tireless researcher of local history, died of cancer at her Grand View home. She was 83.

While undergoing treatment at Nyack Hospital Tuesday, Mrs. Savell was told of her final project's success: the state agreed to designate Rockland's Tappan Zee shore a "scenic area." A letter announcing the decision arrived yesterday and was being read to Mrs. Savell when she died, according to S. Hazard Gillespie, a Piermont resident who worked with her for the designation.

Mrs. Savell had lived in Rockland 62 years. She was a former editor of the Nyack *Evening Journal*, the forerunner of the *Journal-News*. She also held the posts of assistant press secretary and administrative assistant for Gov. Nelson Rockefeller.

As senior historian for the Historical Society of Rockland County, Mrs. Savell worked devotedly to answer public requests for information.

"She would exhaustively research something that anyone else would give up on," said John Scott, senior historian of the society. "She was certainly one of the most energetic historians the society ever had, and a prolific writer."

Virginia Parkhurst, Nyack Village historian, recalled her as "spunky, energetic and very, very bright. She seemed to write effortlessly. The miracle is the way she worked when she was getting frailer and frailer. She just worked her head off."

Among the books written by Mrs. Savell and published by the Historical Society are *Wine and Bitters*, an account of Revolutionary War negotiations held at Tappan; *Ladies' Lib*, about the woman's suffrage movement in Rockland; and *The Tonetti Years at Snedens Landing*, which showcased the history of a wealthy Palisades family.

"They are the most important books we ever published," Scott said. "Mrs. Savell also wrote articles on Rockland history for the society's quarterly journal, *South of the Mountains*, and a history of the executive mansion in Albany for the state office of general services.

Mrs. Savell, the former Isabelle Keating, was born in Pueblo, Colorado, and attended the University of Colorado. She came to Rockland in 1926 to accept a job as reporter for the *Evening Journal*, then an eight-page paper with an office on South Broadway in Nyack. The paper had three employees, including the editor and Linotype operator who doubled as a sports writer. When the editor left soon after Mrs. Savell arrived, she took his place.

She left to become a reporter for the *Brooklyn Eagle*, and soon after, she married Morton Savell, the paper's Sunday editor. Later, she worked for the Associated Press and *New York Herald Tribune*, and taught journalism at Sarah Lawrence College. In the 1940s and 1950s, she was staff director for the state Joint Legislative Committee on Interstate Cooperation, and later as assistant to state Rep. Harold Ostertag. Mrs. Savell joined Rockefeller's campaign in 1958 and served as his assistant press secretary until 1961. Rockefeller appointed her to the Workmen's Compensation board in 1961, and she served on it until 1971.

"She was a lovely, brilliant, beautiful lady," said Gene Setzer of South Nyack. "She was one of the stalwarts, and one of the finest history researchers we've ever had around here—a beautiful writer so useful to the community."

Tim Henderson, *The Journal-News*, 10/28/88

Future Governor in Stony Point

Assemblyman (and future New York State Governor) George Pataki was the guest speaker at the Stony Point Town Hall on Memorial Day in 1988.

Photo courtesy of Ann O'Sullivan.

Dr. Robert L. Yeager Health Center

Robert Lee Yeager never wanted his son to be a doctor. Robert L. Yeager, Jr., born in Texas in 1907, never planned to be a pulmonary specialist or to work in New York. Yet, he led the effort to create Rockland County's centralized health facility in Ramapo.

Yeager began working at Summit Park Hospital, which then served tuberculosis patients, in 1942. He lived on the hospital's grounds until his death in 1988, occupying a white house that today serves as the Sheriff's Department offices. Once quick treatments for tuberculosis were found in the early 1950s, the hospital and its 110-acre campus began to seem superfluous. However, Yeager, who was active in local medical circles as one of the county's few pulmonary specialists, saw a unique opportunity as Rockland's population burgeoned.

He explained his thinking in an interview a few months before his death. "As the county grew, it was quite evident that we needed better services for medical care, particularly for the chronically long-term illness cases, of which there were a great many," Yeager said. He also wanted to centralize the county's health services because it was all fragmented.

Dr. Robert L. Yeager Center in 2001. Photo Scott Webber.

Initial plans were completed in 1965, and construction of the center at Summit Park began in 1975. In 1987, the center was named after Yeager, despite his reluctance to take sole credit for the campus. Today, the Dr. Robert L. Yeager Center in Ramapo has few parallels elsewhere.

Yeager will also be remembered for his intelligence, compassion and humanitarian efforts. "His mind was always working for the residents of Rockland County, and he always gave priority to patients," said Dr. Nancy Pablo, Yeager's assistant medical director.

Matthew Milliken, *The Journal News*, 5/22/01

Dr. "Bobby" Martha MacGuffie

Although she would hate the description, Dr. Martha MacGuffie is indeed a renaissance woman.

The 65-year-old New City resident, known to colleagues and friends as "Bobby," is, in alphabetical order: animal lover and animal rights activist, burn treatment specialist, environmentalist, inventor, Lady of High Tor manor, mother of eight, philanthropist, plastic and reconstructive surgeon, project director and last, but certainty not least, unicorn lover.

To know Bobby MacGuffie is, to most people, to love her. To keep up with Bobby MacGuffie is, for most people, impossible.

Asked what makes her work so hard, run so fast and so far, and generally put in 18-hour days, the ebullient doctor said, "Energy and the physical and mental desire to get something done. I can't identify it specifically, I keep looking. I guess I'm trying to find solutions to

Dr. Martha MacGuffie.

multiple things at once."

High Tor is home to many fund-raising activities during the year. Politicians, animal rights groups and theatrical organizations are among those with whom MacGuffie shares her home and 30 acres. She is soft-hearted, a soft touch.

After a trip to Africa where she saw the terrible poverty and horrific conditions in many hospitals, she contacted the UN ambassador from Kenya. They talked, found their ideas were identical and Dr. MacGuffie suggested the formation of SHARE, the Society for Hospital and Resource Exchange.

"SHARE has been founded to get materials to Kenya, especially to the sister hospital at Homa Bay on Lake Victoria," Dr. MacGuffie said. "Everything we throw away in this country can most likely save a life in Kenya. You, me, anyone can save a life with a dollar and a sheet. For every dollar we get, 10 cents will go for a toy for a child, the rest for medicine, equipment and bedding."

And when all is said and done, is there some particular thing Dr. MacGuffie would like to be remembered for?

"I don't think in terms of being remembered. I hope it would be for something I haven't yet accomplished."
Richard Gutwillig, *The Journal-News*, 7/31- 8/1/89

A Legacy of Ship Building

More than 200 years ago boats known as market sloops began stopping there to pick up produce for New York City. During the Revolution a British ship put ashore a foraging party only to have it soundly chased by a handful of armed farmers in the area.

By the 1820s they were building boats on the beach, and in 1834 they laid down the first marine railway in Rockland County. The 1880s saw the launching of bigger and bigger boats, including a 155-foot sternwheeler christened the *Wilbur A. Heisley*. A few decades later it was the *Arrow*, hailed as the "fastest yacht in the world."

Then in World War I they built submarine chasers, and in World War II both sub chasers and air-sea rescue boats for the U.S. Air Force. Shipbuilding halted in 1948, and now it is used mainly for storing boats and making repairs. But it still boasts the only covered storage remaining on the river, with space for 190 boats.

The place? Petersen's Boat Yard in Upper Nyack, whose origins as "Upper Nyack Landing" go back well before the Revolution, and whose name, Petersen's, surprisingly is only little more than 50 years old.

"The landing has a long history as a boat yard, but someday someone is going to come along and build 20 Cape Cod houses on it," predicted T. Craig Carle, the gruff, 78-year-old owner of the yard, whose pessimistic

view, he said, was prompted by a failure several years ago to persuade Albany to designate the yard a state landmark.

When that happened, Carle said, he lost heart and got rid of a lot of "old things" around the yard, including an elaborate 19th-century capstan used for hauling boats out of the water. The capstan had a reduction gear of 600-to-one, and until it was converted to steam sometime after 1900, was turned by a team of horses pulling a 25-foot pole around a circle.

"I hated to do it, but it was an economic necessity," explained Carle, who said there "was no money in a yard like Petersen's anymore. "I don't take anything out of the business, you know. There's very little net. But the yard gets into your system. You want to keep going."

A former insurance executive who bought the yard with three other men in 1948 from the estate of the late Julius Petersen (he is the only surviving partner), Carle likes to talk about the history of the landing. He mentions a few names—Eddie Wenzel, Bill Knudson, Karl Schreiber—men in their sixties and seventies whose average length of employment at Petersen's is at least 40 years and who began working at the yard under the former owner.

"Petersen was a Danish shipbuilder who came to this country around the turn of the century," Carle said. "He

A late 1800s view of a Nyack shipyard.
JSC

271

had a boat yard in Tarrytown before he came over here. His first yard was in Nyack, but then he got a contract to build a big boat for the owner of the Simmons Mattress Company. That's why he bought this place, so he had the room. It was a good-sized yacht, 110 feet. Petersen was known by the boats he built. Some are still in existence, in fact. We had one come in here a few years ago."

He pointed to a photograph on the wall of his office. "That's one of the last ever built by Petersen, for Cyrus McCormick."

When he sought landmark status for Petersen's, Carle had hoped somehow the yard might become something on the order of Old Mystic Seaport in Connecticut, a bit of history preserved for all to see. While those hopes weren't realized, Carle firmly believes that, "there is a lot to preserve" at Rockland's historic boat yard.

John Dalmas, *The Journal-News*, 8/26/80

Night Falls on the Day Line

Day Line cruises on the Hudson River between New York City and Poughkeepsie with stops at Bear Mountain and West Point may be a thing of the past after this summer due to declining business.

Six-day-a-week cruises began in 1807 with Robert Fulton's side-wheeler, *North River Steamboat*, running between New York and Albany. *The Dayliner*, a four-deck, $3.5 million boat that measures 308 feet by 65 feet, was put into service in 1972, the 14th ship to be operated by the Day Line on the river. It replaced the

Alexander Hamilton, a 338-by-77-foot vessel, that was first put into operation in 1924 and carried 3,250 passengers. It was the last of the side-wheeler vessels to operate on the river. (Photo below by Warren Inglese.)

Sunday service was added in 1918 after consultation with various clergymen. To allow for religious observances, church services were conducted aboard ship.

Scott Webber, *Rockland Review II*, 7/21/88

...In 1981 the 52 people held hostage in Iran for 444 days are released...President Reagan and Pope John Paul II are both shot but survive assassination attempts...Egyptian leader Anwar Sadat is assassinated... The space shuttle *Columbia* is launched and completes the first orbital shuttle flight..Prince Charles and Lady Diana are wed...Polish Solidarity leader Lech Walesa is arrested...

The lighthouse at the Nyack marina.
Photo by Warren Inglese.

Tom Lake (center) and a group of hungry participants gathered at Nyack Memorial Park in 1988 for the annual shad bake.　　　　　Photo by John Scott.

Keeping the Past Buried

Usually, it is the job of the writer and historian to keep the past from being buried. However, for Nanuet resident Peter Krell, preserving burials became something of a quest.

Considering all of the development Rockland has seen in the past few decades, it is not surprising that local cemeteries have also fallen under the bulldozer. Realizing that many small or abandoned cemeteries were threatened by this shameful fate, Krell decided to research and record the names and details on more than 7,000 graves.

His efforts resulted in the 435-page book *So That All May Be Remembered*, published in 1989 by the Clarkstown Bicentennial Commission. The book is a wonderful reference for people trying to research their ancestry, and it is also an essential tool for raising awareness to the fact that even cemeteries are fair game to developers.

Linda Zimmermann

Thiells United Methodist Church

Members of the Methodist Church officially began their third century of worship on Rosman Road in Thiells in services held this past Sunday morning. Chartered by John Wesley in London in 1784, the Thiells church was started as an Indian missionary work and was served by circuit rider preachers from New York City and Westchester County until 1855.

When the Minisceongo Indians started leaving the county in the 1820s, the parishioners decided to continue the church. They put up a chapel on Rosman Road in the 1830s. This was the church that was destroyed by fire on November 18, 1973. Immediately after the fire, the 120-member congregation voted to build a new church on the site of the old. The new sanctuary was formally dedicated on April 27, 1975.

Church records show that the cost of heating the church with firewood from April 1861 to January 1862 was $2.47. The church paid $3,000 for land and a parsonage in 1872. The furnishings came to $73.45.

Scott Webber, *The Rockland Review*, 5/9/84

Popular Pastor Steps Down After 40 Years

This Sunday morning, the Reverend Leslie B. Flynn will preach his final sermon as pastor of the Grace Conservative Baptist Church in Nanuet after 40 years of ministry in this community.

When Flynn and his wife, Bernice, arrived in 1949, all there was to the church was the wooden auditorium built in 1860. The church budget was $8,000 a year. Now, the church needs that amount each week to meet the budget of $450,000 a year. Since then a new education wing and a whole new sanctuary were added at a cost of half a million dollars. There were 70 members in those days compared with 500 on the role now.

Moving to Rockland meant that Flynn had to learn to drive a car. This made possible his more than 1,000 hospital and home visits he made each year. He was also a part-time teacher at Nyack College in the areas of journalism and pastoral methods, had a radio program on WRKL and wrote over 30 books.

Flynn has been noted for his sense of humor. He calls himself "Father O'Flynn of Girlstown," referring to living in a house full of women (he and Bernice had seven daughters). Several of his books are about humor in the ministry and his sermons are sprinkled with humor.

The verse from the Bible from Psalm 37, "Delight yourself in the Lord and He will give you the desires of the heart," has come true for Leslie and Bernice Flynn. He recommends this verse to all who would like to have a happy and rewarding life of their own, particularly the youth today. "It works," he explains.

Scott Webber, *Rockland Review*, 2/16/89
Photo courtesy of Rev. Flynn.

From One-room Schools to Declining Enrollment:
The Development of Rockland Education

Lucien Conklin still remembers what happened to students who cursed in the old red schoolhouse on Route 210 in Stony Point.

"The teacher had a ruler and she said, 'You took the Lord's name in vain, give me your hands,'" Conklin, now 68 and the supervisor of Stony Point, recalled, "And then she'd give you three or four raps with the ruler."

That was in the 1930s, when students from the first to eighth grades (in Stony Point's case to the sixth grade) were all taught in one room and, as native Rocklanders like Conklin remember, the walk to school could be miles. Conklin graduated from Stony Point High School in 1939 with a class of eleven students.

The schoolhouse in Stony Point, closed years ago, and others like it dotting the region's countryside, are perhaps the single, most obvious reminders of Rockland County's rich and colorful educational history. In the past 50 years, education in Rockland has experienced tremendous changes, both in size and concept. It has developed from a county of small, country schoolhouses stressing only the basics (at the time, not many students went on to high school, usually because they were needed at home or on the farm), to a system of eight highly sophisticated, centralized school districts offering a myriad of educational programs.

By the early 1930s, former Clarkstown schools Superintendent Felix Festa, 75, recently recalled, some 40 to 50 school districts existed in the county. Each district had its own Board of Education, budget and taxes. In some cases, such as at Street School in New City, the districts were so small that the board consisted of one trustee. When he started teaching at Congers High School (now the elementary school), enrollment was about 80 or 90.

Those districts that did not have high schools sent their students to other districts on a tuition basis. How students got to school, though, was another matter. Students lucky enough to be near a railroad would take the train to school; others, however, had to walk.

It was also during the 30s that a vocational training program was conceived. The schools under the county's Vocational Education and Extension Board each provided one or two vocational classes, and students throughout the county would go to the school for the particular course they wanted. The board also hired part-time teachers who would go from school to school to teach music and art.

Then the state began urging districts to centralize. That concept ultimately proved to be one of the biggest factors in changing Rockland County education. But the concept was not readily welcomed in Rockland, and to this day opinions about centralization still run deep.

Supporters of centralization argued that by creating one umbrella district, the outer districts would have a voice in the education of secondary school students. Before centralization, those school boards that sent their students outside the district to high school were not allowed any input into secondary education. In addition, supporters said, centralization would also create a larger pool of students, and therefore allow for more programs beyond the basics.

The opponents, however, viewed centralization as an erosion of their local power. They also feared that with a centralized school system, community schools would be closed and students would have to travel long distances to get to school So, time and again when educators put centralization on the ballot, residents voted it down.

Finally, the supporters won. But the state apparently played a big part in the process because it introduced special incentives for centralized districts, including additional aids that would help hold down local taxes. In 1941, Suffern (now Ramapo Central) became the first to join a centralized district. Combined in the district were the Sloatsburg, Bear Mountain, Johnsontown, Suffern, Hillburn, Airmont, Tallman and Viola schools. With 1,400 students, the district became the largest in the county and remained so until the Clarkstown and Ramapo Central No. 2 (now East Ramapo) districts were created.

In the next 15 years, all the schools in the county would centralize or consolidate, forming the eight districts that exist today: Ramapo Central, East Ramapo, Clarkstown, Nyack, Pearl River, Nanuet, North Rockland and South Orangetown. North Rockland turned out to be the staunchest opponents of centralization, partly because both Haverstraw and Stony Point had their own high schools. But in 1956, the two towns centralized, creating the last central school district in the county.

Also created during this period was the Board of Cooperative and Educational Services, established in 1951, recalled Dr. John Hopf, the former Rockland County schools superintendent. The school, which Hopf helped develop and then ran until 1979, was created to provide occupational instruction. Later, it expanded to include special education, instructional services programs, administrative services and transportation.

By the late 1950s, Rockland County's educational systems started to experience a series of rapid and dramatic changes. The construction of the Tappan Zee Bridge in 1955 opened Rockland to thousands of urban dwellers seeking moderate housing and good schools. The rapid increase in population caused by the bridge, paired with the 1950s baby boom, put increasing demands on the school systems throughout the 1960s and early 1970s. When Clarkstown centralized in 1949, for instance, the yearly budget was $375,000 and there were 1,100 students, Festa recalled. When he left in 1977, the district had 13,000 students and a $36 million budget.

The 1960s saw school construction taking place all over the county to accommodate students. In 1970, East Ramapo broke the enrollment record with 16,627 students. As a result, many districts, such as East Ramapo and North Rockland, were holding split sessions until new schools were opened. Half the students would go to school from 7:30 a.m. to 12:30 p.m. and the other half would attend from 12:30 to 5:15 p.m. "They had them (students) hanging from the ceilings, there were so many," recalled Priscilla Gannon, who was a teacher in North Rockland from 1931 to 1978.

Millions of dollars were raised through bond issues to pay for school construction. By 1966, for example, East Ramapo had raised $30 million, Clarkstown had a $19 million debt and South Orangetown had $12 million to pay back. Many of the bond issues, which were to be repaid over a period of years, are still being paid for today.

Then, in the mid-1970s, enrollment started to drop off. The baby boom generation was finishing school, young couples started having fewer children and the days of inexpensive housing ended. Meanwhile, inflation and the cost of educating students soared. So, schools began to close. By June of 1982, 17 schools had been closed in Rockland, and more closings are expected. The controversy sparked by school closings, may in the historical view far surpass the battles caused by centralization.

Now, school districts across the county are battling to maintain the innovative and often expensive programs introduced in the 1960s while having fewer students to fill the classes. Some districts are repeating history by sharing special services. And there are on the horizon thoughts to further consolidate; by regionalizing, though the controversial concept has never gone beyond the philosophical stage.

Pat Winters, *The Journal-News*, 7/15/82

...On October 19, 1987 the Dow Jones industrial average plunged 508 points, $500 billion lost...

Walt Weiss, Rookie of the Year

Every kid who picks up a bat dreams of one day making it to the major leagues. For one Suffern boy, that dream became a reality.

At the age of nine, Walt Weiss played baseball for the Suffern Little League Yankees. Through four years with the Suffern High School team he batted .449 and stole 41 of 42 bases in his senior year.

Turning down an offer from the Baltimore Orioles, he went to the University of North Carolina. In 1985, he was the first-round draft pick of the Oakland A's. In 1988, as the A's shortstop, he earned the coveted title of American League Rookie of the Year. He was also a member of Oakland's 1989 World Championship club.

Weiss was traded to the Florida Marlins in 1992, granted free agency in 1993 and signed with the Colorado Rockies and then with the Atlanta Braves in 1997. Though injuries and time have taken their toll, Walt Weiss will always be a symbol to the children of Rockland that no goal is out of reach.

Linda Zimmermann

Mary McPhillips and Walt Weiss listen to Senator Eugene Levy at the "Walt Weiss Day" celebration in Suffern, January 15, 1989. Photo by Scott Webber.

Rockland County Sports Hall of Fame
1980-1989

Jim Cann (Clarkstown South) One of the greatest running backs in Rockland Scholastic football history. Chosen by the *Journal-News* as the best male athlete in school in 1988. Also excelled in baseball.

Rich Conklin (Nanuet) Rockland's all-time winningest coach for wrestling dual meets, and second winningest coach for football. Among the highlights was the outstanding 1989 season, when Nanuet's Golden Knights football team had ten straight shutouts in ten games.

Tod Giles (Ramapo High School) Outstanding twenty-year career in wrestling, narrowly missing two opportunities to compete in the Olympics. Place-winner in many National and World Championships.

Debbie Grant (Ramapo High School) Local track star who not only went on to shine at Villanova University, but also earned international acclaim. She missed a spot on the Olympic team in 1988 by only four one-hundreths of a second in the 800-meter.

Kevin Houston (Pearl River) Outstanding basketball player with "one of the sweetest shooting touches Rockland County has ever seen." Went on to

successful career at West Point and continued to play semipro after graduating.

John Mercurio (Tappan Zee H.S.) Founder of the Rockland County Sports Hall of Records in 1980 and wrote a 300-plus-page book on county sports from 1990-81. Also played professional softball.

Dawn Royster (Nyack) One of the county's premier female athletes, dominating the basketball court and the track. She earned a basketball scholarship to the University of North Carolina and went on to play professionally in Europe.

Bill White (Suffern) A championship high school wrestler in the 1950s, White returned to Suffern to enjoy an 18-year reign as head wrestling coach (1970-1988), leading the Mounties to dozens of team and individual titles. White's record 179 wins was not surpassed until the year 2000.

Blaise Winter (Tappan Zee H.S.) Outstanding T.Z.H.S. football player (he graduated in 1980) who went on to an 11-year NFL career with the Colts, Chargers and Green Bay Packers as a defensive lineman.

...In 1986 the N.Y. Mets are World Champs, beating the Red Sox in a heart-stopping series...

From Spring Valley to the Stars

In the 1950s, Bronx High School of Science student Al Nagler chose an interesting project for shop class—a 300-pound telescope. In order to carry the massive scope to observing sites, he bought a used Checker cab and was once stopped by a cop who mistook the telescope for a coffin!

It was not surprising, then, when Nagler chose a career in optics. While working for Farand Optical Company he designed the original eyepieces for the U.S. Army's first night-vision goggles. In the 1960s, he designed the optics for the visual simulators used to train NASA astronauts in the Gemini and Apollo projects.

Al Nagler in 1999 with one of his telescopes.   Photo by David Nagler.

In 1977, he founded Tele Vue Optics in Spring Valley, and began designing and marketing high-performance eyepieces (and later telescopes, as well) for amateur astronomers. The business took off and suddenly in the 1980s everybody wanted a "Nagler" in their telescope.

One of the original members of the Rockland Astronomy Club, Al Nagler loves sharing his views of the universe at local events. His philosophy is simple, "The more people who enjoy and understand our place in the universe, the better our own planet will be."

Linda Zimmermann

The County Executive

On January 1, 1986, John Grant became the first County Executive of Rockland County. Grant, who began his political career in 1960 by ringing doorbells for the election of John F. Kennedy for president, called upon the people of Rockland to join him in a "partnership between government and the people...built on trust and understanding."

He understood the historical importance of the day, noting that six times the voters had rejected propositions establishing his new office, believing that the Board of Supervisors and then the County Legislature forms of government were adequate to deal with the problems of running Rockland County.

"But things change," he added, "and the problems began to appear larger in scope than the ability of the government to solve them."

Scott Webber, *Rockland Review*, 1/8/86
Photo of Grant's inauguration (below)
courtesy of Scott Webber.

The Jewish Community
1980-1989

In September 1988, ground was broken at the Pomona Jewish Center for an expansion project that would add classrooms, a new sanctuary and catering facilities for the 300 families that are members. Also in 1988, the Reform Temple of Suffern completed its expansion program, which gave them an enlarged sanctuary.

The Chabad Lubavich sect of Hasidic Judaism arrived in New City in 1983. New City was deliberately searched for and selected as a site away from the other Hasidic sects in the county. The Hasidim are considered by many as the most Orthodox Jews and are often called ultra-Orthodox. Five years later, on Chanukah, ground was broken for an educational center near the corner of North Main Street and Phillips Hill Road. The initial project, on three acres of land, has an 8,500 square-foot building housing classrooms and a sanctuary.

"Chanukah commemorates the rededication of the first temple in Jerusalem," said Rabbi Auremel Kotlarsky, director of the center. He said he hoped the new building will "bring light and warmth to the lives of many."

New City was chosen because it's a growing community and it's the county seat. "That's symbolic," Rabbi Kotlarsky said. The goal of the educational center was not to create a Lubavich enclave in New City as other Hasidic groups have done elsewhere. Most Hasidic groups form tight communities often cut off from the secular society. The Lubavich sect, named for the White Russian community where it was founded, is an exception. "We try to reach out to the entire Jewish Community in Rockland. We consider every Jew a member regardless of affiliation." The movement has become known for its mitzvah-mobiles driven around by members encouraging Jews to observe holidays and religious laws.

"Our programs focus on the non-observant Jewish Community and are designed to bolster Jewish pride and identity. We try to make everyone fully comfortable and welcome," the rabbi said.

Incorporation did not come easy to residents in a small area straddling Route 306 in Monsey. Citizens overwhelmingly approved the formation of Kaser, Ramapo's 11th village on January 4, 1990. Kaser, composed predominantly of the Visnitz sect of Hasidic Jews, is a 1.2-square-mile village, roughly bordered by northwestern Spring Valley, New Hempstead and Viola. It became embroiled in boundary disputes with two other proposed villages, Monsey and Viola Heights.

Community leaders proposed the new village in 1985 to relax the town's zoning code. A leader of the incorporation movement said the community has many young people in their late teens that will soon be getting married. Hasidim live close to their families and religious institutions. Under Ramapo zoning laws multiple family homes needed by these people could not be built. Less than six months after incorporation, Kaser introduced a high density housing plan that would allow one to five family homes on 10,000 square foot lots not permitted under the town's code.

Kaser is now the worldwide headquarters of the Visnitz sect of Hasidic Jews. They were driven out of the Soviet Ukraine and initially settled in Brooklyn. They were one of the first Hasidic groups to relocate and settle in Monsey.

Harold L. Laroff

Rockland Center for Holocaust Studies

First Public Program
The Rockland County Commission on the Holocaust held its first public program on April 13, 1980. The "Remembrance Program" was dedicated to the victims of the Holocaust and featured County Court Judge William Zeck, a key prosecutor at the Nuremburg War Crimes Tribunal.

Choosing to go to Nuremburg as a war crimes prosecutor after his military service in WWII, Zeck has written and lectured extensively on the Nuremburg trials.

"I had a part in trying to develop a formula to prevent this genocide from recurring, and in fixing individual criminal responsibility of the leaders of state who initiate wars of aggression," he said.

The Rockland Center for Holocaust Studies in 2002.
Photo by Linda Zimmermann

According to Harry Reiss, administrative director of the 14-member commission and adjunct professor of the Holocaust at RCC, the commission was established to set up a suitable memorial and commemorative events on the Holocaust.

Nancy Cacioppo, *The Journal News*, 4/80

Work Begins

For Georgine Hyde, the cold, overcast sky above the Finkelstein Library Annex Sunday afternoon was symbolic of the long, hard winters concentration camp prisoners endured before and during World War II. Endured, that is, if they lived.

"I remember," she said to about 50 people bundled up in their winter overcoats at the groundbreaking ceremony for the new Rockland Holocaust Center, "when I stood in weather this cold without the trappings of shoes and coats. I don't know how I did it."

Mrs. Hyde is a survivor of Auschwitz, the Polish "death camp" where more than three million Jewish men, women and children were murdered in the Holocaust, the systematic destruction of better than six million Jews before and during World War II.

And while it's more than 37 years since the end of the war, many people like Mrs. Hyde and the others who are involved with the building of the Holocaust Center will never forget the atrocities.

Sunday afternoon members of the Rockland Center for Holocaust Studies, concentration camp survivors and concerned residents gathered at the Finkelstein Library Annex in Spring Valley for the groundbreaking ceremony for the new center, which organizers say will be a "living memorial" to those who perished in the Holocaust.

A new wing will be constructed adjacent to the annex and both buildings will be used for the center.

Holocaust officials say that the center will cost $250,000 and will be completely funded by private contributions. More than half of the money has been raised, and construction is expected to begin this spring, according to center Executive Director Harry Reiss. The center should be completed in November.

Reiss said the center's aims are threefold: to encourage the "dissemination" of educational material dealing with the Holocaust, including the teaching of Holocaust studies in the public and private schools in the county; to have annual commemoration ceremonies and exhibits honoring the memory of those who perished in the Holocaust; and to house a museum, library, resource center, audio-visual material and exhibits for use by students, educators and the public, free of charge.

"It's one of the greatest days of my life," said Rubin Josephs, a center fundraiser and a camp survivor. "It brings back memories of the past, which are painful. But it ensures that people will see what could happen if they are not on guard."

Mrs. Hyde, vice president of the Rockland Center for Holocaust Studies and a member of the Ramapo School Board, was 18 when she was taken from her home in Prague, Czechoslovakia and thrown into Auschwitz. She said the center will be a place where people can learn about the "terrible lesson of the Holocaust."

"I couldn't talk about my experiences for many years," she said. "A few years ago an organization asked me to speak to them about my experience and I found it very difficult. But I realized then that I owe it to the memory of those who did not survive to tell the world what happened to them."

Mitchell Weiss, *The Journal News*, 1/17/83

New City Library
220 North Main Street

The first New City Library was opened in 1933 in a small room of an elementary school located on Old Schoolhouse Road. The year 1953 marked the construction of a building on Maple and Demarest Avenues, and in 1967, the library moved to a renovated garage on South Main Street. The Board of Trustees purchased three acres of land at North Main Street and Squadron Blvd. in 1977, resulting in the present building's construction in 1980. A new wing and renovations were completed in 1989, with separate children's, adult, and check-out areas. Its Rockland Room holds more than 2,000 volumes of local, county, and state history.

1990-1999

In With the New

From the perspective of the time when this book was first published in 2002, the 1990s were hardly considered to be history. Yet, a little reflection shows just how much the average home and lifestyle changed in the last decade of the twentieth century—courtesy of technology.

Throughout the 1900s, Americans often defined themselves with technology—a car in every garage, a portable transistor radio, a color television, a food processor. "Gadget Appeal" was responsible for many of the items we felt we could not live without, but as history has so often proved, yesterday's novelty is today's necessity. As the 1990s began, few homes had personal computers, access to the Internet, fax machines, pagers or cell phones. By the end of the decade, America was wired and wireless, with a typical teenager carrying more electronic and computing power than the Apollo astronauts.

As local businesses raced to go high-tech and catch the dot.com wave, many of the "old-time" Rockland businesses closed forever under the relentless pressure of modern consumerism that constantly demanded bigger, faster and more, more, more. This trend was epitomized with the highly controversial, yet highly successful, Palisades Center shopping mall in West Nyack, which was the final nail in the coffin of many struggling local businesses.

Preservation was also on the mind of concerned Rocklanders. The county's bicentennial in 1998 helped raise awareness that if we didn't save our landmarks and open spaces now, they would be lost forever. Part of the challenge for the 1990s (and the decades to come) was to foster an understanding and appreciation of the county's history in the waves of new residents. It is a difficult challenge, but as future generations make their own history, hopefully they will have the insight and wisdom to preserve it.

One of the "tall ships" that took part in Rockland's bicentennial events, anchored in Haverstraw in 1998.   Photo by John Scott.

Future leaders of Rockland? Nina Johnson's first grade class at Stony Point Elementary enjoys the Halloween parade as 101 dalmations.   Photo by Scott Webber.

The Challenge of the Future

A probe has just returned rock samples to the space shuttle's lab and the crew begins its analysis. Suddenly, there's a malfunction in one of the shuttle's crucial systems. Mission Control has also detected the malfunction and their specialists work quickly and efficiently with crew members to correct the problem. Thanks to training, education and above all, teamwork, this shuttle mission will be a success, and all of the fifth graders involved can congratulate themselves on a job well done.

This is not the scenario for a science fiction movie; this is a twice-daily occurrence at the Challenger Learning Center in Airmont. Every morning and afternoon, fifth and sixth graders from across Rockland take their seats at the various computer stations of Mission Control, or don their "flight suits" and enter the shuttle's laboratories through a dramatic, black-lighted hallway and "airlock." The Challenger Center is a fabulous educational tool that will encourage and inspire thousands of local children to become involved with the technology of the twenty-first century.

This is not all just some clever simulation; *everything* has been designed by NASA and is so accurate that you could actually train real astronauts there. The BOCES-operated center's programs are also state approved, so students are technically still in school even while controlling robotic sampling arms or punching new coordinates into the navigational computers.

The Challenger Center officially opened its doors in November of 1999. The center's director, Richard Borakove, not only brings his expertise in technology and education to the center and its programs, but his substantial enthusiasm as well. As one of only 36 such centers around the world, Borakove explained how lucky Rockland is to have such a facility. While the three R's of "reading, 'riting and 'rithmetic" are still the basics of education, the computer age has necessitated

strong programs in "MST": math, science and technology. Not only does the Challenger Center provide an exhilarating learning environment for all three, it fosters a skill that is arguably the most important of all, teamwork.

There is a special gleam in Richard Borakove's eyes as he explains another feature of the center, Electronic Field Trips. These "trips" are actually live, interactive hookups with the real Mission Control in Houston, as well as with shuttle astronauts in space! Even if students aren't attending this deep space classroom, the center is affiliated with the Goddard Space Flight Center in Maryland, which is always available for technical assistance and questions.

It should come as no surprise that soon after opening its doors, the Challenger Center was already booked solid for the next year. However, this apparent "overnight success" was over six years in the making. Thanks to people like Ramapo School student Christine Rodriguez and teacher Phil Tisi's fund-raising and the lobbying efforts, this center was able to become a reality. One can only wonder if when the Rockland histories of the twenty-first century are written, how many future educators, scientists and astronauts will point to the Challenger Space Science Center in Airmont and say that was where their journeys began.

Linda Zimmermann

The Challenger Space Science Center in Suffern.
Photo by Linda Zimmermann.

Tribute to Daniel deNoyelles

Daniel deNoyelles, noted Rockland historian and official historian for the village of Haverstraw, died on May 28, 1991 at age 86. It is ironic that Dan, whose ancestors played such an important role in Haverstraw's, then Orange and Rockland Counties', history in the eighteenth century and beyond, was born in New York City on August 31, 1904. At the age of three, he moved to Haverstraw and graduated from Haverstraw High School in 1921 and from Colgate University in 1925. He was a member of Theta Chi Fraternity and remained an active officer of his class throughout his life.

After his graduation from college, he began his association with the family brick enterprise. He served as assistant manager until 1927, when after his father's death, he became president and chairman of the board of directors. He retained these positions until 1939 when the company was sold. From 1939 until his retirement in 1963, he worked for the New York Trap Rock Corporation. During this time he volunteered to serve in the United States Naval Seabees from 1943 until 1945.

Beyond his professional career, the focus of his life was the history of Rockland County. He was the unparalleled expert on the brick industry in North Rockland. He wrote six books on this county's history and contributed more than 30 articles to *South of the Mountains*.

He also served as historian of both the Town and Village of Haverstraw, trustee and senior historian of the historical society and at his death, he was a member of the Advisory Council.

Daniel deNoyelles was not just a chronologist of history, he was an active advocate of it. He, along with his wife Helen, shared their knowledge of local history through countless presentations of his historical slide show to organizations and particularly to school children. He relished the presentations to the students, and they always responded with interest and enthusiasm. In addition, Helen and Dan served as guides, first at the Orangeburg Museum and then at the Jacob Blauvelt House in New City.

Daniel deNoyelles was a warm, friendly and very modest man. He always downplayed his contributions, but those who knew him appreciated his knowledge and more importantly, his kindness.

Seneca once said, "Nothing is less worthy of honor than a man who has no other evidence of having lived long except his age." Daniel deNoyelles was the complete reverse of that statement. The eight decades and more of his life have proved that a lifelong commitment to preserving the best of our past is a most honorable legacy.

Thomas F.X. Casey
SOM, July/Sept. 1991

Saving Lost Towns' Memories

The voices of children seem to echo still from the meadow where the Sandyfields school used to stand.

"There are ghosts in the old towns in the park," says Jack Focht, director of the Trailside Museums and Zoo at Bear Mountain. "When you walk through one of the old towns, you can smell the bread baking, you can hear the kitchen door squeak and the sound of wood being chopped in the back yard. You can sense the life."

At the turn of the century, hundreds of people lived in what is now Bear Mountain and Harriman state parks in the villages of Sandyfields, Doodletown, Queensboro, Johnsontown, Baileyville and Pine Meadows. But between then and the mid-1960s, the Palisades Interstate Park Commission bought up the land, and the people moved out, most to nearby Stony Point and Fort Montgomery. For years, Focht

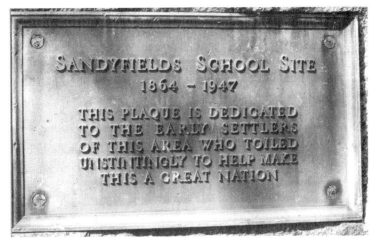

Plaque dedicated to the Sandyfields school.　　JSC.

283

wanted to record the memories and the old place names, but people were wary of him.

"I'm an outsider," Focht says. "I'm from the Park, and the Park took their homes. Sometimes they'll give you wrong answers just to see if you can figure it out. It's not malicious; they just don't trust me."

Then last fall Andy Smith—who has "park" in his veins—became a forest ranger at Bear Mountain State Park. His grandparents and parents were born and lived most of their lives in Sandyfields, which now lies under Lake Welch. His great-grandfather is buried in a tiny cemetery shaded by pine trees and within earshot of Lake Welch Beach.

So with Smith aboard, Focht had what he needed, and the two have started The People's Park Project. "What better project is there for the Trailside Museums than to trace the history of the park's people?" Focht says. The project will record the histories and memories of the former residents, and much of the material will be gathered at the "Lost Towns" reunions.

While former park residents yearn for the past, they know that if the park hadn't taken over the land, it would be "covered by development."

"Condos and strip malls and half-million-dollar houses on half-acre lots," Smith says.

Looking at the park's woodlands today, it's difficult to imagine what the land looked like at the turn of the century.

"There was a timber industry in much of the park," Focht says. "The brick industry needed wood for its kilns and the iron foundries needed charcoal for smelting. It was a mess. The park took land that had been shot out, burned out, dug out, and trapped out, and the animals came back.

"We have a treasure here. We have wilderness in the middle of development. But we have to acknowledge the people who sacrificed to allow us this. They left the homes they had known for generations, and they left behind a trail of tears."

Where crops once grew, tall pines stand. Many of the backyards where children once played are inundated by Lake Welch and other lakes that were created by damming streams. The new lakes provide places to swim, boat and fish, but they drowned the memories of generations.

Many of the park residents are aging now. And some—with names like Herbert and Scandell, Gannon and Odell, Bulson and Livingston, Bailey and Conklin—have died, taking their stories with them to the grave. Smith and Focht want to record everything before it's too late.

"I want the original names on record," Smith says. "I want the stories of the people on record. I don't want this history lost."

Leslie Boyd, *Rockland Journal-News*, 3/7/93

The "Wildman" of the Parks

While fast food long ago replaced foraging as Rocklanders' meals of choice, there are still those who look at the green landscape and think dinner.

Naturalist and author Steve Brill, a.k.a. "Wildman," conducts lectures and walking tours to teach residents about the nutritional and medicinal value of those plants most regard as simply weeds. His hunting and gathering of local plants has led to such culinary adventures as knotweed ziti, sarsaparilla tonic and ginkgo tea.

One thing he doesn't recommend, however, is the skunk cabbage. Even after dehydrating the plant for more than a week to remove its poisonous properties, it still tastes terrible. "The day you find skunk cabbage is the night you go out to dinner," Brill warned tongue in cheek.

With Rockland's natural spaces dwindling, it's good to know that its parkland and backyards still hold some of Mother Nature's gifts. However, it's best to check with the Wildman before you serve up a meal of things better left in the ground.

Linda Zimmermann

Too Little Too Late?

Less than a month after Piermont halted a construction project because the developer had cleared too many trees, a builder in Clarkstown is under scrutiny from town officials for the same reason.

Earlier this month, Piermont issued a Clausland Mountain developer a stop-work order when he cleared about 75 percent of the trees he was supposed to leave standing. Both incidents come as municipalities are clamping down on clear-cutting.

Last month, Clarkstown adopted strict regulations on removing trees from properties, and Orangetown enacted similar legislation earlier this year.

Environmental and governmental officials at the village, town and state levels agree that trees are needed to prevent erosion and to improve the aesthetics of a community.

John Barry, *The Journal News*, 11/30/99

284

The Indian Rock Controversy

If you ever tried to plant a garden in Rockland, you have no doubts as to how the county earned its name, so it may be surprising to learn how upset some people were when a developer wanted to remove a large rock from a building site on Route 59 in Montebello. However, when that rock happened to be part of local history, the concern is understandable.

The controversy over Indian Rock, as it is called, began in the mid-1990s after the developer requested approval to build on the site, with the understanding that the rock remain intact. While there was no definitive archaeological evidence that the rock was the site of an Indian settlement, or that the rock was sacred, it was fairly certain that this huge hunk of stone was a landmark on the old Indian trail. The trail came from upstate, passed Spook Rock, to Indian Rock and on to the tribal meeting place in Mahwah, New Jersey. It was also a local landmark for generations of recent Rocklanders who grew up in the area.

However, despite his previous agreement, once the developer began clearing the land, he quickly came to the opinion that it was only a useless piece of rock that was getting in the way. He decided that rather then work around it, he was going to have Indian Rock pulverized and carted away. Upon hearing this, historian Craig Long spearheaded a campaign to save the rock. It would not be an easy task, as the planning board did not seem sympathetic to the cause of preserving history over that of "progress."

The night for the board's vote arrived, and so did Craig—along with over 100 people prepared to speak in favor of saving Indian Rock. No doubt quickly realizing that unhappy voters were not an asset on Election Day, the board agreed that the developer must stick to his earlier promise and keep Indian Rock intact. Construction did then proceed, although all of the stores slated to be built pulled out of the deal, except for the McDonalds. It wasn't until several years later that the new "Indian Rock Shopping Center" expanded to include many stores and restaurants.

Linda Zimmermann

Indian Rock in 1985 (above left), as it had appeared for centuries surrounded by trees (JSC), and how it looked in 2001 surrounded by stores (photo by Robert A. Strong).

The Story of the Decade

The Palisades Center—To Be, or Not To Be...

Not since the days of the planning and construction of the Tappan Zee Bridge had Rockland residents witnessed such a storm of controversy. What began in the 1980s as a reasonable idea to give the growing county an alternative to the Nanuet Mall, grew into a legal wrestling match that seemed to embody the classic American struggle of the evil big business against the good local citizenry. The argument against the building of the Palisades Center was based upon two extremely sensitive issues in Rockland in the latter half of the century—quality of life and environmental impact.

As the years passed into the mid-1990s, the force behind the Palisades Center, the Pyramid Company, wielded its power and money (and many, many lawyers) like an unconquerable army. Conservation groups, local residents and some politicians valiantly fought back in the legal courts, and the court of public opinion, and at times they seemed to have actually slain the Goliath Pyramid Company.

John Scott's photo of the clearing of the land for the Palisades Center, looking west. The white spots on the hill are the gravestones of the Mont Moor cemetery, which is now surrounded by parking lots and the parking garage on the Route 59 side of the Center.

In one instance on Friday, April 8, 1994, the *Journal-News* ran the following story: "We have made a decision to halt construction on the Palisades Center Project," the Pyramid company stated in a brief press release. Due to the eight years of controversy, escalating costs and ongoing struggles with local officials and residents, 80 workers were pulled from their jobs at the $200 million project. Silent equipment scattered the bulldozed landscape, but some people believed that Pyramid was only bluffing, trying to bring pressure on the planning board to agree to its requests.

Of course, the project did continue, and considerable effort in the site preparation involved the removal of the hazardous contents of a landfill. However, despite the removal of this environmentally dangerous material, the opposition was still firmly against the entire project. The battle raged on year after year, but slowly the massive shopping mall took shape.

Although not yet complete, the Palisades Center opened its doors in March of 1998. As the bands played

and the celebrations took place, however, there seemed to be a general uneasy feeling in those early days—after so much controversy, would people actually come?

That question was soon answered as almost day by day it seemed harder and harder to find a parking space. As more restaurants and stores opened, more people thronged to the Palisades Center from across the region.

Of course, with such a history of bad feelings, there were those who swore to never step foot in the Center. There were also alarmist reports that cracks in the floors indicated that the entire structure was in danger of collapse, and was sinking into the former swampland. Nyack resident and popular talk show host Rosie O'Donnell had almost daily reports on the allegedly imminent demise of the new shopping center.

The center did not collapse or sink, but that still did not end the controversy. The Dal Pos Architect, P.C., design of "an industrial theme with utilitarian finishes," left most people wondering for months when the builders would get around to finishing the interior—for instance, covering the long expanses of exposed pipes. When it was finally understood that the interior *was* finished, critics jumped all over the seemingly crude design plan, as well as remarking on the stunningly incongruous exterior.

While opponents will no doubt carry their animosity to the grave, it is difficult to argue with the popularity and success of the Palisades Center. Billed as "3.5 million square feet of shopping excitement...Offering unsurpassed access and combining traditional tenants with power anchors, food, entertainment and theaters, and providing a single destination for all customer needs," the Palisades Center has ultimately let the people decide its fate. And if you have ever tried to find a parking space on a Saturday afternoon, it is clear what the majority of people have decided.

Linda Zimmermann

An aerial view of the construction of the Palisades Center (top), looking east. Route 303 is in the upper left portion of the photo (courtesy of the Palisades Center). The completed Center (above), looking north. The New York State Thruway is on the far side of the Center, Route 59 is in the foreground. Photo by Bob Vergara, All Photographic Services, courtesy of the Palisades Center.

The Palisades Center: The Legal Battles

In 1997, Clarkstown Supervisor Charles Holbrook told the zoning board, "Since Pyramid approached the town in 1985, that company repeatedly changed and expanded its plans. Because of those almost constant changes, the approval process for the Palisades Center has taken over 10 years."

When the Clarkstown Town Board finally considered the application to build in October of 1996, Pyramid was told that the permit was for 1.85 million square feet and no more than that. The board said they wanted to wait several years to see how the shopping center blended in with the community, and if all went well, they would put any expansion plans before the voters in a referendum.

On December 6, 1996, Building Inspector Adolph Millich issued a building permit allowing extra square feet for a third and fourth story that brought the total area up to about 3 million square feet, all without town approval. The application process was marked by uproars of fury from local residents, as well as from Nanuet Mall officials and tenants. At one point it was even reported that Millich had obtained a $1 million loan from Pyramid's bank, increasing the cries of foul play.

Also, the Town Board's action in October had violated the law in that the town transferred to Pyramid two streets that were town property, and should have required voter approval to sell them to the developer. Not willing to face the angry voters, Pyramid got the town board to pass a non-referendum resolution transferring the roads to them.

Then State Supreme Court Justice Howard Miller ruled that the roads were still town property and could not be part of the mall. The two streets were Virginia Avenue and Basco Street in West Nyack. Miller said that the Planning Board exceeded its authority in overriding zoning laws to approve the mall application.

On September 27, 1997, the Clarkstown Zoning Board of Appeals revoked the building permit. Then on October 9, the *Journal-News* reported that the Planning Board backed the Building Inspector's decision to increase the size of the mall by a 5-1 vote, contending that it "would not adversely affect the environment significantly," an opinion that was applauded by Thomas Valenti, a Pyramid partner, who ironically declared, "You can't bully the law."

Planning Board Chairman Rudolph Yacyshyn argued that the County Planning Board had no authority in the matter to require an environmental study. Acting on Yacyshyn's ruling, the Board approved what had been done. The lone No vote came from Board Member Richard Paris. Following the tumultuous meeting, Supervisor Holbrook told the press that the Planning Board action "showed a shameful disregard for the environmental impact."

Holbrook promised that when the Town Board met on October 14 they would vote to challenge the massive project in court. When Holbrook came to make his motion, he could not get a second to his motion, which meant the motion failed. Sitting there in silence and saying nothing were the other four Town Board members: Ralph Mandia, John Maloney, Ann Marie Smith and Louis Profenna.

This entire long, drawn-out process drew a lot of commentary in the press, much of which was scathing. In an editorial entitled, "Clarkstown's Secret Shame," on April 16, 1997, the *Clarkstown Courier* wrote: "What we don't understand is why the people of the Town of Clarkstown continue to allow themselves to be slapped in the face by the Pyramid matter. By now we think they would be sick enough of council people who allow Pyramid's attorneys to write their resolutions for them, a town highway superintendent who allows his opinion letters to be drafted by Pyramid's attorneys, a Planning Board Chairman who throws out the First Amendment and the Open Meetings Law to make sure Pyramid gets back into court with a clean slate (they asked Miller for another hearing to "correct" parts of the application), and a building inspector who can't tell when his own building permits have been violated."

Among the opposition to the Palisades Center, whose concerns ultimately went unheard, were the West Branch Conservation Association, and a large number of residents of West Nyack, the Town of Clarkstown, and the entire county, as well.

Scott Webber

...In 1990 Germany begins the process of reunification...The Hubble Space Telescope is launched...Iraq invades Kuwait prompting the 1991 Gulf War...In 1991 the Soviet Union comes to an end...Princess Diana and Prince Charles split up...Mt. Pinatubo in the Philippines erupts and its ash disturbs weather patterns across the globe...In 1992 Bill Clinton is elected president...There are riots in Los Angeles over the Rodney King verdict...Hurricane Andrew devastates south Florida...16-year-old Amy Fisher pleads guilty to shooting her lover Joey's wife, Mary Jo Buttafuoco...Boxer Mike Tyson is convicted of rape...A fire ravages Windsor Castle in England...

Steve Wendell and Cable Television

Rockland County has seen a media revolution over the years, especially with how people receive television programs in their homes. In parts of the county, television signals broadcast from New York City were hard to receive clearly. Often the TV signals continued to be snowy and fuzzy even after constantly readjusting rooftop antennas to try to get a better signal. Similar situations existed all over the United States.

And then someone in Pennsylvania came up with a great idea to get crisp and clear TV signals into the home—cable. The idea called for putting a big antenna on top of the highest mountain to get the best TV signal and then sending the signal to homes via cable lines strung on telephone poles. Soon, cable systems were popping up all over the country, including Rockland.

Cable television started in the county during the late 1960s. Each town and some of the villages signed separate cable franchise agreements for set periods of time, usually between five and ten years.

Clarkstown signed agreements with Good-Vue CATV, TKR (Telecommunications, Inc., and Knight Ridder, Inc.) and TCI (Telecommunications, Inc.). Haverstraw residents were served by Rockland Cablevision, Action CATV, American Cablesystem Corp.-Continental, Media One and AT&T. Orangetown awarded franchises to Orangetown Cablevision, TKR and TCI. Ramapo residents received the services of Good-Vue, Continental, Comcast, Twin State Cablevision Corp., Group W Cable (Teleprompter Corp./Westinghouse Broadcasting), TKR and TCI. And, Stony Point was served by American Cablesystem Corp.-Continental, US West, Media One and AT&T.

Then in 1999, Cablevision purchased TCI and took over the franchises for Clarkstown, Orangetown and Ramapo. In 2000, Cablevision swapped some of its franchises in the Boston area for Media One/AT&T's franchises in the New York City metropolitan area. At that time, Cablevision took over the franchises for Haverstraw and Stony Point.

Local-oriented news programming has been an important part of cable in Rockland, especially in Clarkstown, Orangetown and Ramapo.

Over the years, I've been the host and producer of numerous talk shows featuring interviews with local and state political leaders and community organizations. In 1988, while working with the local radio station WRKL, I was the host of the cable-TV program "In Session," interviewing former New York State Senator Eugene Levy. Later the program name was changed to "County Forum," giving me the opportunity to interview a variety of individuals. The show later was transformed into "Meet the Leaders," seen all over the Hudson Valley.

As news director from 1992-1999, I anchored and managed news programming on local cable that included a weekday newscast, feature reports and the popular yearly November election night coverage. The nightly weekday six-minute "TKR Local Headline News" began in 1992 as part of the local insert for the CNN Headline News network. It was the first time Rockland residents could watch a newscast that featured local news and information.

Then in 1993, because of the popularity of local news in Rockland, the newscast expanded to 30 minutes and was aired weeknights at 7 p.m., 10 p.m. and 11 p.m. The newscast was repeated weekday mornings from 5 a.m. to 9 a.m.. The program's name was changed to "News Source 8" and later was cancelled in 1999 due to programming changes made when Cablevision took over TCI.

Steve Wendell—the familiar face of Rockland news.

New programs focusing on politics, community issues, lifestyle and entertainment are now being produced locally in Rockland County. In addition, hundreds of residents are involved in producing local public, government and education access programming seen by thousands of people.

And what's the future of television for Rockland and the world? Future trends will mesh television, computers and telephones into one electronic unit, and will include:

- digital cable–with 500 plus channels
- wireless cable–where TV signals are sent over the air just like radio and TV stations to a home antenna
- HDTV—high definition television, providing unbelievable picture quality
- Satellite TV—providing direct television to home satellite dishes

- Streaming Video on the Internet—allowing an unlimited number of niche programs to be received on your home computer
- Satellite Internet—hooking up home computers with a satellite dish that allows uploading and downloading of video and other information

Steve Wendell
Producer/Political Affairs Programming
and former News Director, Cablevision

WRKL Radio: The Voice of Rockland

Al Spiro had a dream. In 1964, seemingly going against all common sense, he began a radio station in a Pomona swamp. Mortgaging his home to finance the endeavor, he began with two small house trailers and a shack. On July 4, WRKL hit the airwaves, providing generations of Rocklanders with local news and programming. Whether for headlines, sports scores, or those all-important school closing announcements on wintry days, few radios in the county didn't have a button preset for WRKL.

One of their most popular programs was the call-in show "Hotline." Over the years Hotline was a powerful force in the county to aid charities and fight injustices. It also stirred up controversy. After a Hotline discussion in July of 1967 on racial tensions, the station received threats—threats which came to pass in the form of a firebombing that burned down the station.

Spiro was not a man to give up, however, and only four days later WRKL was back on the air—broadcasting from a tiny trailer with guests perched two-high on kitchen stepstools. The station was eventually rebuilt, and after Al's death, his wife Betty Ramey continued the tradition of providing a voice for the people of Rockland.

In 1985, Betty sold WRKL to Rockland Communications. The station continued to change hands in the 1990s, until the local news and information gave way to a Polish language station. While other radio stations broadcast in and around Rockland, they will need about 40 years of colorful history and award-winning programming to compete with WRKL.

Linda Zimmermann

Helen Hayes Performing Arts Center

On December 4, 1995, the Helen Hayes Performing Arts Center opened in the heart of Nyack. Plans to renovate and use the old Tappan Zee Playhouse, which closed in 1975, proved too costly, so the Arts Center chose the former 700-seat Cinema East. In addition to bringing live performances back to Nyack, the center will also be a boost to the economy. It is estimated that for every dollar spent in the theater, nine dollars will go to the community, for example, at one of Nyack's many restaurants.

The Egyptian House

In 1992, Deborah and Steven Preston of Wesley Hills were winners of the Historical Society of Rockland County preservation merit award for their outstanding preservation/restoration efforts to preserve the badly deteriorated Egyptian House. This house, also known as the Temple of Luxor, was built in 1915 as a summer residence for millionaire Joseph M. Goldberg. Suffering from tuberculosis, Mr. Goldberg had spent much time in Egypt and was considerably influenced by archeologists and their work there. His interest in Egyptology resulted in this magnificent and rare example of Egyptian

290

Revival architecture.

Designed by the architectural firm of Wilder and White, the concrete Egyptian temple and its accessory structures were built at the apex of a hill on a 600-acre estate. The site insured unobstructed views of Rockland County, the Ramapo Mountains, New York City and Westchester County, as well as provided a view of the temple-like house against the sky. Even today, the ascension to the site is a processional experience, culminating at the monumental stair and columnar portico.

The architect of the house, Walter Robb Wilder, lived in Pomona and maintained his architectural office in New York City. He worked in the office of the eminent architectural firm of McKim, Mead and White before forming his own firm in 1906. However, his partner was not the famous Stanford White, but rather Harry Keith White. Wilder and White specialized in designing country houses, and unquestionably the Egyptian house is an outstanding example of this firm's work.

After Goldberg's death, the Egyptian House passed through several owners, became a multifamily residence, and lost its acreage to subdivision. Finally in 1984, the deteriorated house and its overgrown grounds of a few acres were purchased by Deborah and Steven Preston. The Prestons recognized the architectural importance of the house and asked experts from Columbia University, the Brooklyn Museum, the American Institute of Architects, and the Historical Society of Rockland County to evaluate the structure and its history. Sensing an obligation, the Prestons embarked on a preservation program under the direction of architect R. Todd Campbell to rescue the house from neglect.

Exterior concrete finishes were repaired and resurfaced where needed, overgrown and obliterated historical paths were excavated, and damaging foundation plantings were removed. The Prestons are currently undertaking interior rehabilitation. Their long-term goal is to restore the exterior polychromed painted decorations, which are documented by early photographs. The Prestons are also pursuing a National Register of Historic Places designation.

South of the Mountains, July/September 1992
Photos courtesy of John Scott.

112-year-old Bar Changes Hands

The shelves that held bottles of liquor are bare. The steel refrigerators and stoves are turned off. And the walls have been stripped of pictures of family and old-time customers at the Dunnigan's Bar and Grill. An era ends today as family members close the sale of this 112-year-old establishment in West Haverstraw. Yesterday, as members of the family walked around for one last look, melancholy was etched in their eyes.

Dunnigan's Bar began as a Mom-and-Pop business in 1884, established by Frank and Maggie Dunnigan. They ran a brickyard and a variety store and also did a little bit of "bar business" by selling liquor to their customers.

As the business grew, the Dunnigans bought a tavern on Railroad Avenue in 1903 that later became the full-grown Dunnigan's

Bar and Grill, a meeting place for politicians and area workers, including employees of the O&R and Bowline plants. The place was frequented by Tappan Zee Bridge workers in the 1950s. The bar also bloomed with West Shore Line train riders until the line was closed in the 1960s.

While the price of the sale was not disclosed, Jack Dunnigan somberly stated, "It's hard to explain. Something like this is more than what it appears to be. From an emotional value, I'd say it's worth a million dollars." Diana Pena, *Rockland Journal-News*, 6/7/96
Photo courtesy of Jack Dunnigan.

Death of an Ice Rink

Dads and moms took their sons and daughters there for their first wobbly strides on skates, and their first knee-jolting sprawls on unforgiving ice. When the kids grew older and mastered the crossover step, they went there on Friday nights to tease and tame the opposite skating sex. And when the kids grew older they still took their own kids there to begin the cycle all over.

Those days are gone.

After 35 years, Low Tor Ice Center in Garnerville has closed. Day by day and piece by piece it is being torn down and hauled off, to make way for condominiums. Soon nothing of it will remain except remembered visions of ice-bruised knees, of hands held in mittens, and visions of blades as sharp as knives across ice as smooth as the wind.

Rockland Journal-News, 9/25/90

Goldband's Army-Navy Store

Though economic prosperity has long since passed Haverstraw village, Leo Goldband has successfully peddled his wares here for thirty-eight years.

Next month he's closing up shop.

Leo's Army-Navy store at 18 Broadway is a throwback to earlier times in this once bustling waterfront community. During its heyday, which he said dates back 15 to 20 years, celebrities such as actor Burgess Meredith and musical director Mitch Miller shopped at his Haverstraw store.

While other shops have gone out of business or were relocated to more prosperous commercial districts in the county, Goldband has stayed put and thrived, he said, because his business easily adapted to the downward economic climate of the 1970s.

"This is the kind of store that appeals to people because the products are cheap, but good quality," he said. Goldband sells jeans, workboots, sweaters and pants. His aisles and shelves have thinned because he hasn't ordered accessories for the past year. He has 1,500 items remaining. Whatever is left when he closes February 28 will be donated to charity.

His secret to business longevity: "I give good service. That's the most important thing in business. I take the time for my customers. I know them and I can appreciate them. Can't buy good service."

"It's time to retire. I'm sad, because I love this village. Oh, yes, we have our bums like everyone else, but the people who live in the village are honest, church-going

people," said Goldband yesterday, during a break from customers.

"Frankly, he'll miss it, but I won't because I'm looking forward to him finally retiring," said his wife, Ruth, cracking a smile. She does the bookkeeping.

The Goldbands said they treat their business like a family and through the years, that has been reciprocated.

Mayor Thomas Watson and the Goldbands know each other very well. Leo Goldband hired Watson when he was 15.

"I was the first black person to work as a clerk in a village store," Watson, 54, recalled yesterday. "I was 15 and I worked after school every day until I graduated and went off to the Air Force."

Goldband said he's proud of Watson's achievements. "He didn't have much money. I encouraged him to go to school and work hard. Look at him today."

Goldband's roots go back to Brooklyn, where he grew up in a working-class family of eight. His father designed women's hats. He served in the Army in World War II and when he returned, he worked for Modell's in New York City, which he said was the largest Army-Navy retailer in the country. He saved up the $6,500 and got a $1,000 loan to open his store in 1951.

"I started with almost nothing and I made it because I worked hard—I worked hard for my customers," said Goldband, looking away, his eyes welling up. "I'll miss them."

Henry Frederick, *Rockland Journal-News*, 1/17/90

...In 1993 Muslim fundamentalists bomb the World Trade Center...The Branch Davidian compound in Waco, Texas burns during a government siege, killing many cult members...The North American Free Trade Agreement is ratified...In 1994 South African blacks get the vote...The Whitewater scandal begins to be investigated...Comet Shoemaker-Levy strikes the planet Jupiter...

100 Years of Chocolate

Nick Loucas remembers when walking into his family's candy shop and ice cream parlor was like walking into a land of sugarplums. With the rich aroma of sweet chocolate filling the air, Lucas Home Made Candies, founded in 1896, was the epitome of the old-fashioned Greek confectioner's store once popular in the Hudson River Valley.

Loucas, now a 6th-grade science and reading teacher at James Farley Middle School in Stony Point (his name is spelled differently than that of the store, which was named after a relative with an Americanized name), said Lucas Candies is celebrating its 100th anniversary as a village institution.

The flowered terrazzo floors and ornate tile logo of the original proprietor, G.L. Tsoukatos & Co., remain, as do the tin ceilings, ceiling fans, red mahogany showcases and Italian black marble trim. But 30 years ago, Loucas said, there were also mirrored walls, black onyx tables and ice cream counters, Louis XV-style pillars and decorative trim, and Tiffany stained-glass windows that spelled out "Ice Cream Soda," "Chocolates" and "Bon Bons." In the late 1960s when the business took a downturn, the family sold many of the ornate fixtures to the Agora boutique in Manhattan.

One day, Loucas came home from college to find his great-great-uncle Constantine—for whom the store is named—trying single-handedly, at age 89, to make the Easter candy.

"Work was his life," said Loucas, who immediately pitched in. The two managed to turn out the holiday candy that year, working 10-hour days. As with many family businesses, creation of a product was a family art that passed from one generation to the next.

Lucas had come to America in 1908, at the bidding of his friend George L. Tsoukatos, who wanted him to join the business. He took over the business in 1941. Around the same time, Constantine Lucas' nephew Anargyros Loucas came to America. He and his wife, Penelope, raised their son, Nick, and Penelope managed the store while her husband was at sea with the Merchant Marines.

Nick and Gail Loucas, who married and took over the business in 1968, raised their own three children in the shop. Although the demands of the business have meant long, hard hours, Gail Loucas said the shared work has been a unifying force for the family. After a hard day at work, she said, "We'll all go out to dinner. It keeps us close."

As Lucas Candies launches its second hundred years, Gail and Nick Loucas look to the future. Nick hopes to retire from teaching in a few years and go back into the candy shop full-time. And their sons have plans to expand the business.

Nancy Cacioppo, *Rockland Journal-News*, 3/13/96

The Strawtown Market

Many things have changed during the past 66 years, but the Strawtown Market in West Nyack has intentionally stayed the same.

The humble 2,400-square-foot grocery store located off Strawtown Road is a throwback to an era before cavernous supermarkets were built in nearly every community. Although the Strawtown Market has but a fraction of the inventory available at nearby supermarkets, the conversation here is as important as food to its clientele. On most weekday mornings, customers gather around the newspaper stacks to sip 60-cent cups of coffee as they discuss topics ranging from George Bush to the nearby proposed Palisades Center.

"This is an old fashioned market," said Nancy White, who said she's been coming here to the Strawtown market for the last twenty years. "We come here to find out what's going on as much as we come here to buy food."

Preserving the tradition of the Strawtown Market for nearly seven decades has been the responsibility of three generations of the Wolanski family. Today, 69-year-old Ted Wolanski and his 34-year-old son, John, are usually to be found behind the counter in the back of the store. The Wolanskis said that building customer loyalty through convenience and service is the key to the longevity of their business, especially now when many established stores are closing their doors.

The first generation of the Wolanski family immigrated from Poland to the United States in the 1920s. Ted's parents, Frank and Julia, worked in several grocery stores before buying the Strawtown Market in 1926. Tragedy struck the family two years later when Frank died. Ted, then only four years old, was pressed into service of the store. After school and on weekends, he would help out his mother by stocking shelves and sweeping floors.

"My mom worked very hard to keep this place going," Ted recalled. "I did whatever I could. When I came back from the Army after World War II, the first thing I did was grab a broom and start sweeping."

John began working in the store as a teenager, after school and during holidays. He joined his father full-time when he graduated from Albertus Magnus High School in Bardonia. "I've never considered doing anything else," said John, who lives with his wife and young children in an apartment in the back of the store.

The children, Robert, 12, and Kristina, 9, may be candidates for the fourth generation of storeowners
Stephen Britton, *Rockland Journal-News*, 1/2/92

Rudy

At the time this photo was taken in 1994, no one would have predicted that in 2001 New York City Mayor Rudolph Giuliani would be called the "Mayor of the World," or would be named Man of the Year by *Time* magazine. In fact, many people in Rockland disliked him so much that they protested when he visited the county as during this trip to a senior housing facility in West Haverstraw.

There would be no protests, however, in the months following the 9/11 attacks in 2001, when Rudy Giuliani came to Rockland to attend funerals of the victims.
Linda Zimmermann
Photo by Scott Webber.

Dragon of West Nyack

If there was a snowstorm during the 1990s, chances were that some strange, colorful creatures like this dragon would soon emerge from the white powder.

The wizard behind these amazing snow sculptures was Mike Conklin of West Nyack. People who drove by unaware of the massive creations would be shocked to see one or more of these brightly colored (Mike would dye the snow with food coloring) figures resting on the lawn.

Those who knew about Mike's interesting hobby would return each season, after the first significant snowfall, to see what else this innovative artist had created.
Linda Zimmermann
Photo by John Scott.

District Attorney Gribetz Convicted

Rockland has seen scandals in its time, but the conviction of District Attorney Kenneth Gribetz on federal tax evasion and misusing public money charges kept his name public in the county for years. Gribetz won fame for his work as a prosecutor during 20 years of high-profile court cases and had his eye on state office before it all came tumbling down.

In 1994, federal investigators began looking into Gribetz and some members of his staff on rumors they evaded taxes and betrayed the public trust. Investigators

found Gribetz evaded income taxes and misused county funds by using his office's investigators and aides as chauffeurs and for personal purposes. In 1995, Gribetz resigned, pleaded guilty to the charges and eventually was sentenced to probation, community service work and restitution. He was disbarred, and his law license was suspended in 1995. After leaving office, he became president of a New City title insurance company.
The Journal News, 1/2000

Deregulation Sparks Change in Electric and Gas Industry

As New York's electric and natural gas industries open for competition through deregulation, Orange & Rockland Utilities faces sweeping changes.

The O&R, which marks its 100th birthday next year, will bear little resemblance to the electric and natural gas utility you have come to depend on for the past century. O&R will still warm the community's homes and businesses, its factories and stores; and light hospitals and houses of worship, but that's where the resemblance ends.

O&R will deliver electricity to its customers, maintain the lines and poles, read the meters, send the bills and restore service in the event of emergency interruptions.

But, the company will no longer generate that electricity. The principal power plants in Stony Point and Haverstraw, as well as the gas turbines in Middletown and Hillburn, and the hydroelectric facilities in Sullivan County will be sold at auction.

Once the plant sales are complete, O&R will purchase electricity as a regulated delivery company for resale to its electric customers who do not select an alternate supplier of generation services.

Hudson Valley Business Journal, 3/30/98

General William Ward

William F. Ward was born in Everett, Mass., and graduated from West Point in 1950. A few weeks later he was leading a tank battalion near the Yalu River in Korea, where he was wounded by Chinese Communist troops.

After the war he remained in the Army Reserve while enjoying a successful career as a publishing executive, and he moved to Suffern in 1960. In 1986, he was called back into the army on a full-time basis, becoming Chief of the U.S. Army Reserve in the Pentagon. As Chief, he was responsible for calling up 90,000 reserve troops to active duty to take part in the Persian Gulf War.

Scott Webber

General Ward testifies before a Congressional Committee on Capitol Hill about the $3.4 billion budget for the Army Reserve in 1989.   Photo courtesy of William F. Ward

 Persian Gulf War
In Memoriam

DEES, TATIANA   FONTAINE, GILBERT

...In 1994 O.J. Simpson is arrested for the murder of his wife, Nicole, and her friend Ron Goldman—the entire country is later captivated by Simpson's trial as he is acquitted...Jackie Kennedy Onassis dies...In 1995 168 people are killed when a federal building in Oklahoma City is bombed—Timothy McVeigh and Terry Nichols are convicted for the bombing... Ebola kills 244 in Africa...In 1996 the Unabomber is arrested...Olympic Park in Atlanta is bombed...

Spring Valley Memorial Park

Judging by the thousands of persons, especially children of all ages, who attended the re-dedication of Spring Valley's Memorial Park on June 10, 1990, the event was a huge success.

As proclaimed by Mayor Joel R. Rosenthal, this celebration marked the 40th anniversary of the opening of the Memorial Park, both as a memorial to veterans of past wars and a facility for all residents.

As the Spring Valley weekly, *Rockland Leader,* noted in 1950, the Memorial Park is "a combination of playground, parking area, and war memorial. The tales of the transformation of a smelly, mucky swamp into a thing of beauty will live beyond this present generation."

For years the big swamp directly off the main business center had been used as a dump. In addition to the horrendous smell, the dump drew myriads of mosquitoes. A favorite sport there was shooting rats. Periodically the dump would catch fire. Thick smoke would hang over the village for days.

Credit for eliminating the dump and creating the park is given to former Mayor Anthony S. Milewski. In 1945, Milewski and his running mates, Frank Haera and William Stetner, ran on the platform "Eliminate the Swamp and Dump Now."

In the 1940s, it took great effort to drain the swamp, level the land and create the lake and fields. Generations of residents have fond memories of the park and with this new million-dollar renovation, hopefully many more generations will enjoy its facilities.

Peter Krell

Memories of Spring Valley

I am one of the relatively few Rockland residents who still resides in the house where I was born—that was in 1927. My parents met at romantic Rockland Lake and they married in 1907; their marriage contract still hangs on a wall in my home.

My memories of growing up are tied to "neighborhood kids"—playing hide and seek, baseball with the boys and dressing in my sisters' discarded dresses. This is what we did in the 1930s. We weren't too alert or too bright, but just happy kids enjoying each other and family radio.

World War II during my high school years resulted in graduates and some teachers being drafted or volunteering. Half-time sessions were held to conserve fuel. In my family there were two brothers in the Army in Europe's battles, a mother who cried every day (either when she received a V-mail or when there was none), and a father who secured donations to build the Spring Valley Honor Roll of village servicemen.

A secretarial internship at a local bank, Ramapo Trust Co., in 1945, resulted in a summer job that lasted 44 years, through three bank mergers, until retirement from the Bank of New York in 1988. A real stick-in-the-mud career, but one which now allows me to maintain this home, and to be very active and comfortable in the later years.

Here are a few of the more interesting stories I recall in the past years:

-My sister was a private secretary for the patent attorney at RCA, and through him, arranged to get us the first, small screen, black and white TV set to arrive in the neighborhood. It was a gift from the family to my mother and father on their 50th wedding anniversary. What excitement! We watched Fred Allen, George and Gracie Burns and especially Snookie Landon on the Saturday Night Hit Parade!

-There was quite a local "to do" when the idea to centralize local schools was presented in the early 50s. The talk became very heated for at least a year before a vote was finally scheduled. I helped count and recount ballots long into the night and when they were tallied, centralization was approved. The dire consequences that this would bring to the children were of great concern to many people—much like our anticipation of Y2K today (1999)!

-In the early days of banking, one customer who struggled financially to continue his efforts to record Rockland history was Saxby V. Penfold. He was a customer of the Ramapo Trust Co. and would bring the bank president, Louis M. Drew, a dozen fresh eggs each Saturday morning to compensate for his past-due loan payments.

-One of the county's big scandals of the day was the scam to divert Rockland Coaches Bus Company deposits to other accounts. Unfortunately, an officer of the bank, Delbert Dennis (too nice a guy) became involved, confessed and eventually committed suicide.

-When the three banks merged to form Rockland National Bank about 1960, checks were still being posted to accounts based on the reading of signatures. When departments were merged and clerks couldn't read signatures on checks from other banks, it turned into a real disaster for many, many months. Eventually, there were conversions to tabulating equipment and thousands of 80-column cards, a whole room of machines and cards in the basement of what is now the Bank of New York building in Suffern. Then came a new building in New City, with a computer room with special air-conditioning. As Rockland boomed, banks were frantically opening branches on not-so-busy corners anticipating the growth of families, housing and cars. Many of these branches were very quiet and unprofitable for years, but I see them now and realize the marketing predictions were very accurate!

-In 1995, we had our 50th high school reunion. Several of us have remained close all these years. As I listened to Tom Brokaw being interviewed about his new book and his meeting with neighborhoods of Americans, it reminded me of my friends—our close association, our work ethic, faith and patriotism. My hope is that all is not lost for the current generation, and the Rockland County children of today will have the same feelings after 50 years, even if gathered by the computer and TVs to come.

Gloria Wiedmiller

The Davies

One of the few remaining farms in Rockland County is that now owned by Niles Davies of Congers. The Davies family is not the oldest in Rockland, but it has farmed land in Clarkstown for more than 100 years.

"I sleep in the same bed I was born in," Davies, 66, said.

According to family histories, Davies can trace his ancestors back to Meriwether Lewis, who helped explore the West with William Clark. His great-grandparents, Niles and Lide Meriwether, lived in Memphis, Tenn., where Niles Meriwether was the city engineer and his great-grandmother was a suffragette, who helped Susan B. Anthony and Lucy Stone get the 19th Amendment (the one granting women the vote) ratified by enough states to become law.

Niles and Lide Meriwether had three daughters: Lucy Virginia, May and Mattie.

"My grandmother (Lucy) came to New York City and studied medicine under the Blackwell sisters," Davies said. Elizabeth Blackwell was the first woman physician in this country, and Lucy Meriwether followed in her footsteps in a time when women doctors were spat on in the streets.

Doctoring and the county were among Lucy's passions. Her parents purchased a working farm of about 35 acres in Congers in 1891 for her, and when she married artist Arthur B. Davies in 1892, the two set up housekeeping in Congers. Their home, built in 1836, is still the main house on the Davies farm (photo above right, JSC).

Arthur Davies was a well-known artist and art collector, president of the American Artists and Sculptors, a group that put on the Armory Show in 1913 that introduced the modernist painters—Picasso and Van Gogh, among others—to the American public. After an abortive attempt at farming, he spent his time in New York City and touring the world, leaving the farm to his wife and children. Of their four children,

two died in infancy and two survived: Niles Meriwether Davies and Arthur David Davies.

Both became full-time farmers, graduating from Cornell University in 1916 and 1917, respectively, and returning to the land. Arthur "farmed on 80 acres on the other side of the road where there's a golf course now," Davies said. Niles farmed on the main property in Congers.

The main farm at that time was dairy, but when the price of milk dropped to below 3 cents a gallon in the late 1920s, the profits fell and the family farm gave up on cows. The cash crops since the 1930s have been fruits and vegetables, most of the crop in the early years being sold to greengrocers in Nyack, Haverstraw and Stony Point. Some of the produce was sold through the A&P markets and a wagon of farm goods went to the AT&T building in New York City.

"I remember Dinty Moore. He used to come here with a special car, and I remember as a kid dumping vegetables in the open car. It was probably a Packard."

297

At its height, the Davies farm stretched to about 120 acres. Today, the farm does mostly a retail business through its market, with a wholesale fruits and vegetables business serving the Orthodox Jewish market in nearby communities. A pick-your-own apple business keeps the farm in the black. A once-thriving pumpkin patch had to be discontinued because the deer ate the pumpkins. Deer continue to nibble the profits off the apple business, but so far the farmers have won.

Farming hasn't stood still, of course, even if the same families till the land.

"Plowing used to be done with horses, and now I plow and 'disc' and spray in air-conditioned splendor, and I'm able to listen to the stock market reports every half hour" on the radio, he said with a smile. "It's a terrific difference" from the way his grandparents' farm was run.

But Rockland has changed, even in Davies' memory.

"As recently as 45 years ago, Rockland was an agrarian society. Then the Tappan Zee bridge opened.... .

"In 1952, there were around 600 farms in Rockland County,

primarily in Ramapo and Clarkstown. The Orangetown farms were absorbed by Camp Shanks" in the early 1940s, Davies said. Now there are three large working farms remaining—Concklin, Cropsey and Davies. His farm was featured photographically in the April 1998 edition of *Life* magazine.

Of his three children, none has shown an overwhelming interest today in carrying on the family farm, although his two sons both have studied agriculture.

"The farm will be here for them if we're still alive," Davies said. "Even though we sold some of it for development, the bulk of the farm will still be farmed as long as my wife Janet and I can afford to do it."

Randi Weiner, *Rockland Journal-News*, 3/31/98

Davies farm, c. 1943. Back row, from left to right: Evan Anderson, George Andrews, Sylvia Diehl, Ann Davies, Barbara Boll, Stanley Boll, Dick English. In the driver's seat: Niles Davies, Jr. Foreground: Mary MacArthur.

JSC

Felix V. Festa

Felix V. Festa of Congers, the man for whom the middle school in Clarkstown is named, died Friday, Aug. 8, 1997, at Nyack Hospital. He was 90.

Mr. Festa was a well-known educator and community advocate. He taught math and science at Congers High School and, in 1932, he was appointed supervising principal of the Congers schools. In 1934, he married Mildred Andres. The couple met at Congers High School, where she taught business classes.

Mr. Festa was instrumental in centralization and became the first superintendent of the new Clarkstown Central School District in 1949, a position he held for 28 years until his retirement in 1977.

Under Mr. Festa's leadership, two high schools, a junior high school and 13 elementary schools were built to serve the needs of the growing student population. His administrative and management skills and his love of children created a school district that grew in reputation and was recognized as one that provided academic excellence. In honor of his retirement, the junior high school—now the middle school—was named after him.

Mr. Festa was an accomplished violinist who established and directed the first Congers High School orchestra. He was a treasurer of the Boy Scouts of America. He was past president and a charter member of the New City Rotary, and was designated as a Paul Harris Fellow for tangible and significant assistance with chapter projects. He was on the board of directors at the Home Aides of Rockland County, Jawanio, BOCES,

Rockland Community College, the Red Cross and the United Service Organizations.

Rockland Journal-News, 8/9/97

The Jewish Community
1990-1999

Rabbi Paul Schuchalter of the Congregation Sons of Israel retired in 1991 after serving the Conservative shul for 35 years. In October 1995 they initiated plans to construct a new synagogue on 11 acres of woodland on Montebello Road. The land also includes a lovely large house previously owned by Dr. Joseph Licata.

Prior to constructing the new building the congregation sold its large 6,000 square-foot recreation hall to the village of Suffern, which will use it as a community and recreation center. The synagogue portion was sold to a Moslem organization. The new building was dedicated on July 1, 1999.

In the summer of 1998, Paul Adler, chairperson of the Jewish Community Relations Council, expressed concern over the fate of a sacred religious article contained in B'nai Israel, the closed chapel on the grounds of Letchworth Village. The chapel opened in 1965 and closed in 1984. According to Adler, the Safer Torahs found a new home at the Congregation Sons of Jacob in Haverstraw.

Over the past few decades, zoning has been the key issue in the formulation of separate political units, such as the villages of Wesley Hills (1982), New Hempstead (1983), Chestnut Ridge and Montebello (1986).

Several incorporation movements became highly controversial issues in the 1980s and early 1990s. Opponents to incorporate both Wesley Hills and New Hempstead stated the reasons for incorporation were to gerrymander village boundaries to keep Orthodox Jewish communities from building and expanding into them. Incorporation would allow villages to enact zoning codes stronger than the town of Ramapo's.

The first of several lawsuits by the Jewish community were filed prior to Airmont residents voting by a 3-1 margin to form the village in 1989. After the election, there were additional lawsuits that contended the village of Airmont was created to enact and enforce strict zoning, which would have made it nearly impossible to establish home synagogues. The case was in the courts for many years with the U.S. Federal Appeals Court finding the village of Airmont was founded on the grounds of religious discrimination against Orthodox Jews. The October 1995 ruling overturned an earlier lower court's decision that the village founders had not

been discriminatory. The court ruling made way for the construction of the first free-standing synagogue in October of 1998.

In September 1991, the United Jewish Appeal (UJA) and Federation of Rockland launched their own newspaper, *The Jewish Herald.* The paper was initiated in response to a "long manifested need and a service to the growing local Jewish population." Federation Executive Director Michael Bierman said the *Herald* will provide a forum for communication about Israel and world Jewry while maintaining a constant focus of local concerns. The paper joins *The Jewish Tribune,* which has been published for several years, and *The Advocate/Monsey Voice* that began publication in 1974.

After many years in rented quarters at various locations in the county, the United Jewish Appeal and Federation of Rockland County began the construction of the Rockland Jewish Community Campus on Route 45 north of Spring Valley, in New Hempstead. The renovation of an existing 23,000 square-foot building began in May 1997. At that time, UJA-Federation president Bob Silverman said, "This project will definitely change the landscape of the Jewish Community of Rockland County—not just for our time but for future generations."

When finally completed in September all of the organizations were housed at the Campus. This includes the UJA-Federation, the YM-YWHA, which houses a the new Fitness Center, Jewish Family Service, the Center for Jewish Educational Resources, *The Rockland Reporter,* Hadassah and Young Judaea.

In 1994, Rabbi Louis Frishman retired as Senior Rabbi of Temple Beth El in Spring Valley, after 43 years in the pulpit, but not before being installed as president of the New York Board of Rabbis.

By mid-decade, the Nanuet Hebrew Center was ready for a change. A new center was constructed on Little Tor Road just north of the Palisades Parkway overpass. In September of that year, the congregants marched the Torahs from the old building two miles to the new edifice. The original has been torn down and a modern supermarket is on its old site.

Harold L. Laroff

...In 1997 Princess Diana dies in a car crash and millions around the world watch her funeral...

Rockland County Bicentennial
1798-1998

The events commemorating the county's 200th birthday (when it separated from Orange County) were officially launched on February 22, 1998 with "A Spectacular Star Studded Celebration" at the Lafayette Theater in Suffern. The event was also simulcast on WRKL radio.

Throughout the year bicentennial celebrations were held across the county and were as diverse as an international dance festival and a salute to 200 years of the United States military. Schools and libraries also participated with exhibits and lectures. The Tall Ships came up the Hudson and docked

at Rockland ports on Memorial Day weekend. And, of course, bicentennial souvenirs and T-shirts were in abundance.

Thousands of residents enjoyed the parades, concerts and ceremonies marking 200 years of fascinating people and events in the county. When the tricentennial rolls around in 2098, much of the customs and habits of twentieth-century Rockland will be a mystery to our descendants, but by looking back to the year 1998, they will at least understand that we knew how to celebrate.

Linda Zimmermann

Lamont-Doherty Earth Observatory

As the twentieth century comes to a close, we often take for granted the technology that surrounds us. It is hard to imagine what homes, businesses and schools would be like without all of our sophisticated electronics and computers. We often forget that such technology does not grow on store shelves. It is often developed by dedicated people in basements and garages on a budget no bigger than the few dollars they have in their pockets. Great discoveries and innovations are also made out in the field, in remote and inhospitable locations, from the searing heat of deserts, to the icy depths of the ocean floor.

Lamont-Doherty Earth Observatory in Palisades has been one of the pioneers in the research and development of groundbreaking technology and scientific theory. From the poles to the equator, from mountaintops to the bottom of the sea, Lamont-Doherty's geologists, physicists, chemists, engineers and biologists have literally rewritten the science of our planet. However, this facility did not begin with state-of-the-art laboratories and a simple set of instructions. As one of the original scientists, J. Lamar Worzel, said, "We were physicists and engineers, using our wits and flying by the seat of our pants to bring these sciences to bear on the study of the Earth, working out the methods as we went along."

In 1937, Worzel was a student of Lamont-Doherty's founder, Maurice Ewing, a professor of geology at Columbia University and an intensely driven scientist who considered sleep to be a great inconvenience and

tried to avoid it. Ewing did not agree with the contemporary belief that the ocean floor was barren and static and of no scientific value. Due to this pervasive attitude and a lack of funding because of the Depression, Ewing and his students were forced to improvise, creating sound and seismic testing equipment from "fruit salad cans, drinking glasses from diners, pocket watches and electric motors from toy trains."

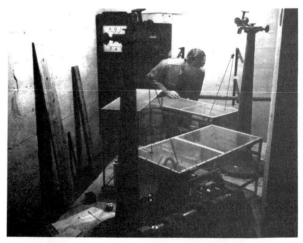

Maurice Ewing and an early seismograph.

With the onset of World War II, however, the funding picture changed dramatically. Suddenly, the Navy was very interested in research on the oceans and especially how sound was transmitted through them. Ewing's research finally had a firm footing on which to grow. Unfortunately, the actual ground at the campus at Columbia was not as firm as he would have liked, as the rumble of passing subways was not exactly ideal for delicate seismic experiments.

Fortunately, in December of 1948, Florence Lamont (a Columbia alumna) donated her estate, on the solid, rocky heights of Palisades, to Columbia University. The property was originally owned by John Torrey, a famous nineteenth century botanist who discovered a wealth of plant life along the cliffs. Torrey built a summer home there and over the years collected and cataloged thousands of specimens that he presented to Columbia University in 1860. In 1928, the financier Thomas W. Lamont purchased Torrey Cliff and adjacent parcels of land to create an estate of more than 100 acres. Upon his death in 1948, his widow Florence personally presented the deed of the property to Columbia's president, Dwight D. Eisenhower. Professor Ewing then formally founded Lamont Geological Observatory on the estate in 1949. While it underwent several name changes, the work and level of dedication has remained the same.

In the following decades, scientists from many fields of study came together at the Observatory to create one of the leading institutions of its kind in the world. One of their most startling discoveries was the globe-encircling mid-ocean ridges, where magma erupts from the mantle and creates new seafloor. By analyzing the magnetic data of this region, they realized that the seafloor was actually spreading out, creating new ocean basins and splitting apart continents. As unbelievable as this data was at first glance, it ultimately confirmed the theory of plate tectonics.

Lamont scientists have also conducted extensive and innovative research with core samples, the circulation of the oceans, the ebb and flow of ice ages and the growing problem of environmental pollution. They were also the first to create computer models to predict El Niño, a climatic phenomenon of which some Rocklanders are painfully aware. From its humble beginnings of a few dedicated scientists with tin cans and toy motors, Lamont-Doherty Earth Observatory has grown to a state-of-the-art facility with a staff of almost five hundred. Today, Lamont-Doherty scientists literally explore every corner of the globe and continue to make valuable contributions to our knowledge of our planet.

The Lamont-Doherty research ship *Vema* docks at the Piermont pier during the 1950s.

In a book dedicated to Lamont-Doherty's 50th anniversary in 1999, editor Laurence Lippsett summed up this extraordinary facility in the following way: "Lamont has always been a unique, close-knit village of energetic, insatiably curious people who combine the cleverness of detectives and the dedication of soldiers—along with the vision that can encompass the entire planet throughout time, and all the possibilities therein."

Linda Zimmermann
Photos courtesy of
Lamont-Doherty Earth Observatory.

Visitors examine a core sample display (left) and the marine biology lab (below) at the Observatory's open house in 1999. The annual events attract large numbers of adults and children.

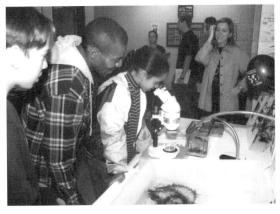

Rockland County Sports Hall of Fame
1990-1999

Joe Casarella (North Rockland) The most successful football coach in the annals of Rockland, dominating county football during the 1990s. He led North Rockland's High School football team to a record of 160-22-1, the highest winningest percentage in the state (.879). As an athletic director, Red Raider teams have won 119 league titles, 43 sectional crowns and countless top-10 state rankings.

Seth Joyner (Spring Valley) One of the finest professional football players to come out of Rockland. While playing outside linebacker for the Philadelphia Eagles in 1991, Joyner was named NFL Player of the Year by *Sports •Illustrated* magazine. He went to the Superbowl twice, a loss while playing for the Packers and then a win with Denver.

Sarah Will (Nyack) An outstanding athlete who sustained a spinal cord injury while skiing in 1988, yet went on to win eight gold medals in the Paralympics (the Olympics for people with disabilities) and over twenty other medals and titles. Considered the finest female mono-skier, she not only competes but is an instructor, and was the co-founder of a mono-skiing camp for disabled skiers.

Rockland Golf Courses

By the end of the twentieth century, Rockland still possessed long stretches of green—in the form of fairways on its nine golf courses. Although the cost of membership was often beyond the range of most residents, public courses were also available.

Blue Hill
Broadacres
Dellwood Country Club
Minisceongo Golf Club
Phillip J. Rotella
Rockland Country Club
Rockland Lake
Rockland Lake Par 3
Spook Rock

Floyd Floods

By the time Hurricane Floyd reached Rockland on Thursday, September 16, 1999, it had been downgraded to a tropical storm—but that didn't mean it wasn't still dangerous. In some of the heaviest downpours residents had ever experienced, Floyd dumped between 10 to 15 inches of rain on Rockland, causing devastating flooding. One person was killed, hundreds were forced to abandon their cars and flee their homes, 40,000 O&R customers lost power, and falling trees wreaked havoc across the county. Mud slides and erosion also added to the problems as many local roads and bridges sustained significant damage, or were swept away entirely. Storm damage estimates in Rockland exceeded $60 million.

In many cases, it was months before downed trees were cleared, roadways were repaired and homes were back to normal. Unfortunately, the loss of personal items, such as photo albums and family heirlooms, can never be recovered. Linda Zimmermann

The Virus

A deadly strain of virus that had never before been seen in North America suddenly begins claiming victims. Birds, especially crows, literally drop from the skies. Then people are stricken, some never to recover. The carrier appears to be mosquitoes, and in an effort to stop the virus, entire communities are sprayed with pesticides while frightened residents remain indoors.

Was this the plot of a Stephen King novel? No, this was reality for New York and New Jersey residents in 1999. The West Nile virus, which causes potentially fatal encephalitis, was responsible for several deaths in southern New York State. Many residents of Rockland and the surrounding areas were in a panic and demanded that officials take action. Countywide pesticide spraying was ordered, and while there was not supposed to be any side effects to humans, people were urged to remain in their homes with their windows closed while the spraying was going on.

Subsequently, Rockland legislators approved the spending of $265,000 for a staff of six mosquito-control personnel. This money was in addition to a previous $118,000 for three staff vehicles, as well as the actual costs of the spraying itself. Residents were instructed to remove any standing water that could be breeding grounds for the virus-carrying mosquitoes, wear long sleeves, avoid swampy areas and remain indoors during the hours that mosquitoes were the thickest.

The medieval, plague-like fear brought on by this virus was a startling reminder that for all of our modern technology, Mother Nature is still a force to be reckoned with.

Linda Zimmermann

Millennium Madness

It will be difficult for future generations to comprehend both the hype and hysteria that swept the globe during of the year 1999. On the one hand, it was a marketing dream. Baseball caps had clocks above the brim that counted down the seconds until the year 2000. *Cheerios* cereal added pieces shaped like a "2" to their usual "0" shapes and became *Millenios*. From fine Waterford crystal to cheap plastic tableware, everything and everyone succumbed to the millennium hype. Couples even tried to time pregnancies so that their child might be the very first of the twenty-first century.

On the other hand, it was a nightmare of paranoia and hysteria. There were those who believed in an apocalyptic doomsday—that the world would come to some horrible, fiery end at the stroke of midnight on New Year's Eve. Fanning those flames were the fears of the Y2K (Year Two Thousand) computer problem. The problem stemmed from the early days of computer development when systems were designed for only two-digit dates, thereby causing the year "00" to be misinterpreted as 1900 instead of 2000. Despite the fact that companies and government agencies spent millions of dollars to correct the Y2K bugs, many people were firmly convinced that the moment the new century began the entire infrastructure of our civilized world would collapse into chaos as computer systems crashed like a house of cards. Terrorists would strike at our moment of weakness, and roving bands of desperate people would riot in the streets.

In Rockland, the sale of gas-powered generators skyrocketed as people feared massive power failures. Stores could not keep bottled water on the shelves. ATMs were drained of cash. Canned foods were stockpiled in basements and gun sales rose as normally rational homeowners prepared to defend their families and their hordes of food, water and cash. Of course, not everybody created survival bunkers, but the majority of people made plans to be at home on midnight on New Year's Eve, just in case.

In the months leading up to the end of the millennium (which technically was not until 2001, but that's an entirely different story!), Rockland officials hosted a series of ten public meetings. The purpose of these meetings was to update everyone on the county's Y2K preparedness and to make assurances that all police, fire and essential services would be at the ready. However, despite such assurances, the media continued to warn that there was a good chance that Y2K computer problems would lead to failures of power, water, telephone and banking systems. Even those who did not believe the doomsday scenarios put a little extra cash in their pockets and gassed up the car.

Tensions were running high on the night of December 31, 1999. In Albany, an emergency services command center staffed by 150 employees braced for impact. In Rockland, a year's worth of preparation was about to be tested. However, in the midst of all the paranoia, Sheriff James Kralik stated with confidence, "We're all prepared for the worst possible scenarios and have plans in place." He then added, "I don't believe any law enforcement agency here expects any of those catastrophes hyped in the media, and we've been assured that computers will not break down, so we won't have any Y2K-caused problems."

The brightly lit crystal ball in Times Square began to descend in the final few seconds of the year 1999. At the instant the ball went dark to signal the new millennium, people wondered whether their homes and neighborhoods would also go dark. Would the telephone systems fail? Would they be without heat, without water? Would their life savings be lost in a series of irreparable computer glitches? Would criminals and terrorists swoop out of the darkness and threaten their very lives?

The crystal ball reached the bottom of its pole, its lights went dark, and the new century began. Many people cheered, but many held their breath. Anxious seconds ticked away, but the power did not fail and lights remained on. The telephones still worked. Hot and cold water still flowed through the faucets. There was no sound of gunfire, no bombs exploding in the streets. The hand of God did not shower fire and brimstone down upon creation. In fact, as the seconds turned to minutes and the minutes to hours early on the morning of January 1, 2000, it became clear that it was just another Saturday morning.

The prophets of doom, who had made a lot of money spreading their fearful predictions, were quick to say that the real problems would actually begin on Monday morning when businesses opened. Monday morning came and went. Life went on as usual. As the week progressed, politicians began patting themselves on the back for their preventative actions, while people wondered just what the heck they were going to do with all those gallons of water and cans of corn. Millennium pencil holders, T-shirts, and beer mugs were packed away in hopes that someday they would become valuable collectibles.

Across Rockland there was a collective sigh, partly in relief that there had been no problems, but mostly in gratitude that we would not have to hear anymore millennium nonsense for another thousand years.

Linda Zimmermann

...In 1997 scientists clone Dolly the sheep...In 1998 John Glenn returns to space...President Clinton admits to Lewinsky affair...In 1999 two students go on a shooting rampage at Columbine High School in Colorado, killing 12 students and a teacher before killing themselves...The Panama Canal is given back to Panama...Young Cuban refugee Elian Gonzales is forcibly removed at gunpoint from a relative's home in Florida and sent back to Cuba...

THE NEW CENTURY

Living a Century

When Florence Kiernan (1901-2001) of Bardonia reached the age of 100, she was asked what was the secret to her longevity. While she didn't have any particular suggestions, she did offer jokingly, "I suppose it doesn't hurt to take a drink every now and again."

From the 1900s to the 2000s

So this is 2000!

I wonder what my grandfather, Arthur Henry, Sr., would have thought about that. If he were with us today, he would be nearing 101 and would have lived in three centuries, having been born in 1899. His old house at 14 Ternure Avenue, in Spring Valley, still stands, itself almost a home of three centuries.

It was built just as the twentieth century began by the Haera family next door, and, when Arthur, Sr., came to it in the 1930s, it still seemed new. It wasn't until the 1950s that my grandfather "modernized" the house, updating the very limited 30-ampere electrical service (just two circuits) and re-doing the bathroom.

His hand-fired coal furnace was converted to burn natural gas, which meant he no longer had to get up at five in the morning to take the hot embers that had been "banked" the night before and use those to start a new fire. The kitchen coal stove was replaced in the early 1940s.

His sanitary system was a hand-built cesspool, not a septic tank or village sewer, which was so well-engineered it never required cleaning. The kitchen sink was originally a large, indestructible cast iron outfit, open underneath and with a drain board built in and a heavily chromed faucet with soap dish in its back splash. Not only did that sink serve for cooking and washing dishes, but for laundering, and baths for young people like myself.

My grandfather did his lawn by hand, not easy since the rather expansive property included another building lot. He had the blades sharpened in a waterwheel-driven shop off Route 59, near the big glacial rock that kids always played on. The sound of the ball bearings in that mower, and my grandfather's methodical, non-hurried push across the lawn on a lazy Sunday afternoon still play in my head as the soothing music of a quieter time. In the 1950s, he turned the mower in for a motorized reel outfit that seemed to amaze him, as it quickly drove itself across the lawn.

So, some 50 years ago, in the middle of a century now ended, life seemed easier for my grandparents, both born before automobiles and in homes with gas lamps. They walked miles to school, worked from early ages, saw relatives and friends die young from a worldwide influenza pandemic, survived two world wars and the Great Depression and then entered the Eisenhower Fifties, when we were still rebuilding Europe, and American progress was impossible to defeat.

They, like many Rocklanders, cashed in a bit on that progress, enjoying the modernization of their lovely home, originally lit with the first electrical lamps available in this century in Rockland. In time, "progress" would actually cause them to leave Spring Valley, for rising taxes and no pension despite forty years of working in the smoking pipe industry meant a move to cheaper Florida.

My grandfather lived just a few years down South before succumbing to leukemia, but my grandmother was there until she passed away in 1988. To the end, both missed Spring Valley and the North, and the good years of twentieth century in Rockland.

That their old home, even more modernized by a succession of new owners, still stands and will do so in the twenty-first century is testimony to improvements of an even more modern age, but also the endurance of what and who have gone before.

Arthur H. Gunther, *The Journal-News*, 1/4/2000

The Revitalization of the Downtown

Slowly, but surely, businesses and customers are returning to Rockland's villages.

That's what a panel of five experts told two dozen county government and business leaders attending "The Future of Downtown Rockland County." The forum, sponsored by Democratic Assemblymen Alex Gromack of Congers and Sam Colman of Monsey, was the fourth of its kind organized by the pair in the past two years.

At the forum, held at Rockland Community College, the speakers singled out Spring Valley and Haverstraw as two of the county's best examples of downtown revitalization.

"We're seeing new faces; we're seeing new interest. People are excited," said Jeanne Struck, marketing coordinator for the villages of Spring Valley and Haverstraw. Success has come in both large and small packages for both villages, Struck said, with the most recent example being Spring Valley's Street Fair, in which more than 3,000 people and 80 vendors took part. Struck also said the arrival of Union State Bank in the village and a new ferry in Haverstraw represent partnerships that have given the municipalities a new identity. In fact, she said, there isn't any retail space available in Haverstraw village these days.

"Consumers are looking for safety, variety and choice," Struck said. "A downtown can do that."

William Mooney, executive vice president of Union State Bank, which invested a million dollars in its Spring Valley building, attributed part of the growth to Rockland's buzzing economy.

In the past three years, the number of private sector jobs in Rockland has increased by 14,000, or 17 percent, to a total of 93,000. The biggest boom areas have come in construction and healthcare sectors. At the same time, public sector growth, which includes government and civil service jobs, has maintained itself.

The growth rate in the county is double the growth rate of the state. The fact is, Mooney said, Rockland has the seventh-largest job growth rate in the nation.

"These are big numbers," he said. But Mooney cautioned that people shouldn't lose sight of the "burden of prosperity," which, in Rockland, manifests itself as increasing housing costs (the average home is $310,000), traffic congestion and changing quality of life.

County Legislator Chris St. Lawrence, D-Wesley Hills, who also chairs the Legislature's visioning committee, said downtowns must grow at their own pace and make changes from within. "It has to work from the ground up," St. Lawrence said. "You cannot impose any structure from the outside and expect it to have any sustainability."

Near the end of the two-hour seminar, Al Samuels, of the Rockland Business Association, gently reminded his fellow panelists not to lose sight of the big picture.

"The revitalization of downtowns is tied to the success of Rockland County as a whole," Samuels said.

Khurram Saeed, *The Journal News*, 9/22/00

Jeanne and Hamish McIntosh in front of their Haverstraw shop, Ironhorse Antiques and Restoration.
Photo by Scott Webber.

Main Street in Spring Valley in 2002.
Photo by Linda Zimmermann

... In the year 2000 a Piermont resident reported that she now paid more in taxes on her property than she originally paid for the house in the 1940s...A Spring Valley resident claimed that Rockland had changed too much since he moved up from the South, and said that it was just a "one-horse county" when he arrived—in 1993!...When asked about their general impressions of Rockland County, most residents replied that taxes were too high and it was too crowded...

Another View:
Competition Brings the Curtain Down

The 11-screen United Artists Theater in the Spring Valley Marketplace on Route 59 opened in 1988, giving Rockland its largest and most modern movie theater. After only 12 years in operation, it was forced to close, due to competition from the new 21-screen Lowes Palisades Center Theatre. (The Nanuet and Pearl River theaters also closed their doors around the same time.)

The UA Theater's demise followed the close a year earlier of another Marketplace anchor store, Pergament, as well as many of the smaller retail stores and restaurants. Competition from the Palisades Center, as well as safety concerns about area crime, left the once thriving shopping center with large stretches of vacant storefronts.

In 1999, Route 59 in Nanuet saw the loss of Caldor, A&P, Service Merchandise, Rockbottom, Ground Round and the Hess gas station. The Nanuet Mall also had several of its stores and restaurants close.

Businesses in Nyack reported dramatic decreases in sales, particularly during the crucial holiday season, since the opening of the Palisades Center. While some locations have been filled by new tenants, others have not.

The last two generations have seen "Mom & Pop" businesses in downtown areas disappear as big retailers move in, but this may be the beginning of a new trend, when even national chains are feeling the pinch. There is clearly a suburban saturation point, a point where the population can support only a finite number of retailers and restaurants, and developers should take heed.

If such business closings are taking place during the booming economy we have experienced in recent years, what will happen to Rockland retailers when times are lean? The curtain may fall on more than just the theater.

Linda Zimmermann

Signs of the times: "BUILDING FOR RENT" is the only thing on the marquee at the defunct Pearl River Theater on Central Avenue in 2001. On the other hand, the housing market in Pearl River was so hot that year that prospective buyers carried special beepers so that realtors could alert them the instant new properties came on the market. It was not uncommon for a house to sell in one day.

Photo by Linda Zimmermann

LAST Chance for Lafayette Theater

The Lafayette Theater, Rockland's last link to the golden age of movie palaces, has escaped the developers plan to carve up the beaux-arts structure into a 7-screen multiplex. Robert Benmosche of Wesley Hills, chairman of MetLife, Inc., has offered to buy the theater and preserve the historic building. Benmosche's son, Ari, made the announcement on March 1, 2000 at a meeting of the County Legislature that was called by legislator Christopher St. Lawrence, D-Wesley Hills, who chairs the county's downtown revitalization committee.

About twenty members of LAST Chance—the Lafayette Association to Save the Theater—who attended the meeting reacted with riotous applause, squeals of joy and tears of happiness at the news of the pending purchase.

"This wasn't about business or making a profit," Ari Benmosche said of his father's decision. "Just the theater's history and knowing it will be safe for now was important to him. It was purity of action from the heart."

The 1,150-seat Lafayette Theater, the last of Rockland's single-screen movie houses, was built in 1924 at the height of the silent film era. It has been described by the state Office of Parks, Recreation and Historic Preservation as a "highly intact example of early twentieth-century movie palace architecture," and a structure that is eligible for the state and national Registers of Historic Places.

"I'm absolutely thrilled," said association member Sarah Mondale of Suffern, an independent filmmaker who makes historical documentaries for the Public Broadcasting System. "It's been a total roller coaster ride and a real cliff-hanger for the past two weeks. This sends a positive message of what people can do when they make a team effort."

"I'm ecstatic," added Ramapo town historian Craig Long. "It's a preservationist's dream come true. To have a movie palace angel come in and rescue such a conspicuous landmark from sure desecration is literally saving a piece of Americana. It's a great victory for Suffern that will enhance the village's restoration and downtown revitalization."

Nancy Cacioppo, *The Journal News*, 3/2/00

The golden age of movie theaters is well represented by both the theater of the Lafayette (above left) and in the lobby (above right), in these 1977 photos.
John Scott Collection

914 to 845

In the early days of telephone service, only three or four numbers were needed to make a local call. In the 1960s, a three-digit town or village prefix was added. For the remainder of the century, Rockland shared a 914 area code with the rest of the region.

However, in the year 2000, high demand for telephone numbers generated by cellular phones, beepers and Internet accounts necessitated a change. Only Westchester was allowed to keep the 914 area code, while Rockland and other former 914'ers were switched to 845. Apart from the inconvenience and expense of changing stationery and business forms, the switch should not have been a big deal.

Some residents didn't see it that way. It was viewed by many to be just another blow to the county's identity, with preference once again going to our more affluent neighbors across the river. People had been born and raised under 914, and some argued against the change as if an area code was some kind of birthright.

Rocklanders slowly and grudgingly accepted 845, but it would be best if they did not become too fond of their new three digits. Telephone company officials predict that steadily increasing demand will necessitate yet another area code change within the next six or seven years.

Linda Zimmermann

Are You a Boomer?

As boomer (post-WWII baby boom) author Michael Gross points out, a generation defines itself not by what the Census Bureau says, but by shared experiences, beliefs and cultural references. In his book *My Generation*, he suggests defining boomers as people born between Pearl Harbor Day and the assassination of JFK. Are you a boomer? Answer yes if you:

- Owned a copy of *Jonathan Livingston Seagull*.
- Remember when the Dodgers were still in Brooklyn.
- Stayed up to watch the first moon landing.
- Know exactly where you were when President Kennedy and Martin Luther King, Jr., were shot.
- Read a book or took a seminar on TM.
- Watched newscasts that ended in "And that's the way it is" and "Goodnight, David," "Goodnight, Chet."

- Had original Elvis records.
- Remember the introduction of Polaroid instant cameras.
- Thought microwave cooking was just a fad.
- Were surprised to see someone your age elected to the White House.

The Baltimore Sun
(Reprinted in *The Journal News* 4/9/2001)

Rockland County boomers might also share these memories and experiences:

- Almost all the kids in your class were born in Rockland and you knew everyone who lived within a few blocks of you.
- There was no Tappan Zee Bridge, Palisades Interstate Parkway or NYS Thruway.
- If you wanted to go to a "real" department store, you traveled to New York City, or to Sears in Hackensack, N.J., because there was no Nanuet Mall.
- Traffic consisted of more than one car in front of you.
- You could see the Milky Way from your backyard at night.
- Most stores were closed on Sundays and holidays.
- You only had to dial four numbers to call someone in your town.
- Job listings in the newspaper were separated into categories of "Help Wanted: Men," where the high-paying executive positions were listed, and "Help Wanted: Women," which generally contained secretarial and low-wage jobs.
- Apart from an occasional fight, no one even thought about school violence.
- Almost every kid carried a metal lunchbox to school.
- You frequently find yourself saying, "That used to be woods when I was a kid," or "I remember when that was being built."
- Your children are attending the "old school" that was brand new when you were enrolled there.
- Families lived in the same house for generations.
- It was a big deal when the first family on your block got a color television, a VCR or cable.
- Kids didn't have cell phones, pagers and credit cards.

Linda Zimmermann

...The 2000 presidential election results between Al Gore and George W. Bush remained in limbo for several weeks as ballots in Florida were checked for "hanging chads" and partially punched holes. While Al Gore had the majority of the votes in the country, Florida and the election went to Bush...

Rockland's Royalty

Princess Vera Constantinovna of Russia, great-granddaughter of Czar Nicholas I and a member of the Romanoff family, has died at age 94.

Constantinovna died yesterday of natural causes in her private apartment at the Tolstoy Foundation in Valley Cottage. She had worked for charitable organizations in New York since 1951, and was a devoted member of the Russian Orthodox Church in Exile.

In theory, Constantinovna was the legitimate heir to the Russian throne.

The Associated Press, 1/13/01

Nuclear Power Plant Shutdown

The Indian Point nuclear power plant may be in Buchanan, in Westchester County, but it is actually separated from Rockland by only a short span of the Hudson River, putting local residents in grave danger should an accident ever occur. On Feb. 15, 2000, the Indian Point 2 nuclear power plant did undergo its first shutdown in its 26-year history after a small amount of radiation escaped.

Residents of Stony Point, Tomkins Cove and Jones Point were upset that no emergency sirens were sounded, but spokesmen for Consolidated Edison said no notification was necessary because the amount of leakage was insignificant. Strong public and political pressure came to bear, and Con Ed finally agreed to replace the old steam generators that had caused the radioactive leak.

While plant officials continue to assure Rocklanders that there is no cause for alarm, the site of the nuclear power facility looming across the river (on a geological fault!) is a constant reminder to those living in the northern part of the county that accidents can happen.

Linda Zimmermann

Indian Point nuclear power plant, as seen across the Hudson River from Route 9W in Rockland County.
Photo by Dominick Morelli

Helen Hayes Hospital Celebrates its Centennial

Elwood Ennis remembers, as a 5-year-old in 1941, sitting in a chair, coloring, and suddenly not being able to pick up a crayon. Another image sticks in his mind—looking at the troubled faces of his parents outside the glass hospital cubicle where he was placed in isolation.

Ennis, a retired graphic artist who grew up in Central Nyack and now lives in Bardonia, was one of approximately 21,000 people who were found annually to have poliomyelitis before the Salk and Sabin vaccines were created in the 1950s. Like Ennis, hundreds of those with polio were treated at Helen Hayes Hospital.

The hospital, which is celebrating its centennial this year, has helped thousands of people with debilitating conditions in its history, from bone tuberculosis and rheumatic fever to cerebral palsy and spina bifida. The effects of the crippling disease polio, which was also known as infantile paralysis, ranged from mild to severe. For some stricken with the virus, like Ennis, survival and rehabilitation meant months, and often years, of operations and physical therapy.

For others, like Mary MacArthur, daughter of Nyack actress Helen Hayes and her husband, playwright Charles MacArthur, the outcome was tragic. Mary MacArthur died from polio in 1949 at the age of 19, shortly before she was to have performed in a Broadway play with her mother.

Ironically, Helen Hayes had been appointed in 1944 by Gov. Thomas E. Dewey to the board of visitors of

Helen Hayes Hospital in 2001.
Photo by Linda Zimmermann.

renovate the circa-1860 Lilburn estate and 48.5 acres in West Haverstraw. The hospital moved there in 1905.

In 1923, the hospital changed its name to the New York State Orthopedic Hospital for Children. In 1929, it was renamed the New York State Reconstruction Home and established a physical therapy department. The state Health Department took over full operation of the facility in 1931. A severe polio epidemic increased the number of patients from 274 in 1934 to 418 in 1935.

the New York State Reconstruction Home—today's Helen Hayes Hospital—which treated hundreds of people stricken during the polio epidemic of the 1930s.

By 1974, Gov. Malcolm Wilson signed legislation that changed the name of what was then known as the New York State Rehabilitation and Research Hospital to Helen Hayes Hospital. Hayes, who continued to serve on its board until her death in 1993, often remarked that she and the hospital were the same age. With a board of managers appointed by Gov. Theodore Roosevelt, the facility first opened its doors in Tarrytown in 1900—the year Helen Hayes was born—as the New York State Hospital for the Care of Crippled and Deformed Children.

The hospital was the brainchild of Dr. Newton M. Shaffer, a New York City orthopedic surgeon, who first thought of establishing a rural hospital for indigent city children suffering from bone and joint tuberculosis.

In 1903, with an increased demand for beds, the state Legislature appropriated $50,000 to purchase and

In 1941, the hospital established a children's cardiac unit for youngsters convalescing from rheumatic fever and rheumatic heart disease. In 1944, it started accepting adult amputee veterans from World War II. The facility was renamed the New York State Rehabilitation Hospital in 1948.

As the polio epidemic subsided in the 1950s, the hospital admitted cerebral palsy patients and launched a pilot study in the treatment of muscular dystrophy. By the mid-1960s, half of the patients were adults who had suffered stroke, spinal cord injuries, amputation, multiple sclerosis or arthritis. The majority of child patients were being treated for cerebral palsy or congenital conditions such as spina bifida.

Today, Helen Hayes Hospital is a teaching and research facility associated with Columbia University's College of Physicians and Surgeons. The average length of stay for patients, which was once one to three years, is less than three weeks.

Nancy Cacioppo, *The Journal News*, 4/9/00

Fighting to Preserve the Land: Zippy Fleisher

It's only fitting that there isn't a single square inch of space open on Zipporah Fleisher's dining room table. Like most furniture in the 83-year-old's home, the wooden surface is covered with piles of legal briefs, flyers and newspaper clippings that reflected three decades of fighting for land preservation in Rockland. From her resistance to a sewer project she said would have destroyed a wildlife habitat, to her work to save one of the county's highest mountains, the woman both friends and foes call "Zippy," has been a tireless advocate for the environment.

Fleisher, who was honored on April 15, 2000, by the Rockland County Conservation Association as part of its 70th anniversary celebration, spent her youth surrounded by the concrete and steel of Manhattan. An art major in college, she toured the museums and went to galleries to study her craft. But as long as she could remember, the time she spent in more rural environments was where she felt most at home.

"All the advantages of the city, sure, they were great, but they never really attracted me like watching wild animals," Fleisher said as she peered out of a large window in search of the deer that graze on the property. "I think that the dirtiest word to call anyone is city folk."

Until she was 12, Fleisher's parents owned a weekend house in southern Dutchess County, where she played cards by candlelight and searched for peeper frogs in a nearby stream. Her current residence, in relatively more developed central Rockland, remains little changed since her late husband, Walter, built the pine-and-cypress structure on his family's 27-acre estate in the early 1950s. As testament to Walter Fleisher's commitment to the belief nature is for everyone to enjoy, the couple donated their land to the town of Clarkstown for the creation of the Charles B. Davenport Preserve. And it is a crusade Zippy Fleisher, now living with her seven Kerry blue terriers as the tenants on the wooded property along Buena Vista and Sawmill Roads, has continued since her husband's death nearly a decade ago.

"They put their money where their mouth was. He gave their capital interest away for the cause," said Martus Granirer, president of the West Branch Conservation Association, which Walter Fleisher founded in 1970 and where Zippy still serves on the Board of Directors. Shortly after Granirer moved to Rockland in the late 1960s, he said he discovered that county officials wanted to hook up homes in outlying New City to the sewer system. Granirer and other residents worried about the effects on their well water.

"Everybody said I had to call Zippy, and I found out why," added Granirer, who now practices environmental law from his South Mountain Road home. "You might find her tough and cranky sometimes, but she gets things done."

Largely as a result of Fleisher's activism, Granirer is still defiantly served by a septic tank. And on Clarkstown's official road map, South Mountain is still designated as rural.

Even those who have butted heads with Fleisher on a variety of preservation issues over the years limit their criticism to her views on development, acknowledging she is a tireless and formidable opponent. Anne-Marie Smith, a longtime Clarkstown councilwoman and former planning board member, said she vividly recalled the prolonged battle Fleisher helped mount against the Palisades Center on Route 303 in West Nyack.

"You'd think environmentalists would have been for it, because it did away with toxic landfills and cleaned up the site," Smith said. "But Zippy wasn't one of those who came out and just didn't listen to what the other side had to say... She has all her research done."

Zippy Fleisher blazed a trail as a member of only the second class at the experimental Bennington College in

Vermont in 1933. Today, as she sits amid the clutter of her book-lined rooms, she recounts her greatest victories. Like the time she helped save one of Rockland's tallest mountains from development. A lawsuit brought by the West Branch Conservation Association in 1991 ultimately led to the preservation of the South Mountain section of Palisades Interstate Park. At the time, 20 luxury homes had been planned for a 53-acre tract below the summit of High Tor. She also put pressure on local utilities to conserve natural resources. A United Water spokesman, Rich Henning, called Fleisher's crusade in early 1990s to enforce low flow showerheads for all Rockland families a prime example of her idealism.

These days, she's slowed down a bit, though her health remains mostly good. But just when she was trying to retire from environmental causes, they're pulling her back in. The most pressing issue for Rockland in the next few years, Fleisher said, is the prospect of up to four new power plants in the northern and western reaches of the county. Her biggest fear, she explained, is that the projects will drain water she said is already scarce.

"I'm not against all new development at all—it depends on the contribution," Fleisher said with a wry grin. "If they're willing to come here and help keep the land the way it should be, that's one thing. But if they're just here for cheap land, let them go to New Jersey."

Pamela Weber-Leaf, *The Journal News*, 4/2000

The view from Perkin's Peak of the beautiful, rolling green hills of Rockland County—a landscape worth preserving.
Photo by Linda Zimmermann

The Changing Face of Rockland

The aging of America, coupled with a remarkable change in its ethnic mix witnessed by a rapid growth of Hispanic and Asian Americans, poses serious ethical, legal and social challenges to a hitherto Euro-centric nation. However, it also creates new possibilities and opportunities in an increasingly diverse nation. The nation's challenge is to integrate these "new" immigrants into "main stream" America without stripping them of their unique cultural identities, and the newcomers' obligation is to facilitate the process. The extent to which we are able to manage and achieve this integration will determine the social, and political well-being of this nation.

In this changing ethnic mix, Asians are relatively newcomers. Until the liberalization of the U.S. immigration laws in 1965 their numbers remained small. Since then the number of Asian Americans has increased dramatically, from about 1.5 million in 1970 to about 7.3 million in 1990, and possibly exceeding an estimated 13 million in 2000. Heavily concentrated in such large metropolitan areas as New York, Los Angeles and Chicago, these newcomers are vibrant parts of the cultural mosaic in these places and contribute significantly to the economic well-being of their adopted communities.

Rockland County has not escaped this change, but it has managed to take the change in its stride without either creating undue burdens on the host community or relegating the "newcomers" to "ghetto" enclaves. The county's Asian population has increased from 10,753, or about 4% of the total population in 1990, to more than 15,770, or 5.5% of Rockland's population of 286,475 as of the 2000 census count. This increase of almost 50% is second only to the increase in Rockland's Hispanic population that surged by more than 64% from 17,711 in 1990 to 29,182 in 2000.

Many Americans erroneously assume that Asian Americans are a homogeneous group. Nothing could be further from the truth. In contrast to Hispanic Americans, who at least share a common language and religion (Catholicism), Asian Americans are physically and culturally a diverse group of people. They speak different languages, have different customs and culinary tastes, and belong to different religions encompassing almost the entire world spectrum of religions. Their religious diversity is most marked among Indian-Americans whose religious practices span from Hinduism, Sikhism, Buddhism and Jainism with roots in the subcontinent, to Islam and Christianity, which originated in the Middle East.

This diversity among the Asian Americans has spawned a variety of cultural, religious and linguistic organizations that cater to their needs. For example,

Classical Indian dancer Sona Aggarwal. Classical dance expresses devotion to the gods and was traditionally performed within places of worship and in the courts. One major nationally celebrated event is the Festival of Nine Nights in honor of the god Ram. As in India, this festival is a major event in Rockland, with festivities and dancing that take place over an entire weekend.

Photo and information by Hemu Aggarwal.

Indian-Americans in New York alone have tens if not hundreds of such local and regional organizations that have become the focal points of cultural and religious life for these new immigrants. Rockland County is well served by numerous such cultural/linguistic organizations. The Indian Cultural Society of Rockland County, the Rockland Chinese American Cultural Association, the Filipino Association of Rockland and

314

the Hudson Valley Malyalee Association are the ones that serve the three largest Asian groups (Indian, Chinese and Filipino) in Rockland. It is only natural that new immigrants gravitate towards such ethnic organizations to find comfort and cultural affinity in an otherwise "strange" land.

These ethnic organizations hold a vast potential to serve as conduits for institutional outreach programs, by government as well as non-government entities alike, aimed at educating the new immigrants as to their rights and responsibilities as new Americans, sensitizing them to the social and cultural sensitivities of host communities in which they reside and have made their homes, and eventually facilitating their integration into mainstream America. Except for sporadic efforts and isolated instances of success, unfortunately this potential remains largely unexploited in any systematic way or in a concerted manner.

In Rockland, however, such umbrella organizations as Asian Americans of Rockland (AMOR) and the Asian Women's Alliance for Kinship and Equality (AWAKE) have ventured beyond serving only the cultural and "ethnic affiliation" needs of the Asian Americans. They have sought to build bridges between the host and immigrant communities and help sensitize elected and government officials to the needs of Asian Rocklanders while facilitating the integration of the "newcomers"

into the mainstream. In this regard, AWAKE, founded by Hemu Aggarwal in 1993, has played a significant role in bringing the diverse customs, religious practices and other cultural traits of Asian Americans to "mainstream" Rocklanders, while attempting to bridge the inevitable socio-cultural gap between the young Asian Americans born here and their parents who came from abroad.

Despite the cultural, religious and linguistic diversity, there are common interests and experiences that bind Asian Americans and could prove to be a uniting factor for political strength. Most Asian Americans are driven by an unrelenting quest to better themselves economically and to see that their children receive a good education, for which they are willing to work hard and drive their children "crazy" by insisting on good grades above everything else. Hard work and persistence are reflected in the perceived economic "success" of Asian Americans and the disproportionately large number of Asian American students enrolled at leading U.S. universities and colleges, although such gains and successes are not uniform throughout the Asian American ethnic spectrum. For example, Asian Americans of Vietnamese and Cambodian origin have had much greater difficulties and harder times than their counterparts of Indian or Filipino origin.

Despite their growing numbers and economic success, Asian Americans have yet to make significant inroads politically, not withstanding such remarkable instances of success such as the recent election of Gary Locke, a Chinese American, to the governorship of the state of Washington. Barring such isolated instances however, Asian Americans have yet to be appointed in significant numbers to high government positions or run successfully for the United States Congress.

Rockland, however, has had more than its share of Asian Americans aspiring to get elected to local and national political office. Dr. Vijay Pradhan, an Indian-American, was elected to the Rockland County Legislature in 1997. Cherian Kuruvilla, another Indian-American, ran unsuccessfully twice for Orangetown's receiver of taxes, and the writer, after winning the Democratic party's primary election, unsuccessfully ran in 1996 for the U.S. House of Representatives for New York's 20th Congressional District comprising Rockland and surrounding counties. Still, it is only a matter of time that Asian Americans will find their due share of political representation in this vast land of opportunities.

Yash Aggarwal

This display represents a traditional Hindu marriage ceremony. Because marriage is one of the most significant events in the lives of individuals and their families, it is the focus of a tremendous amount of traditional activity.

Photo and information by Hemu Aggarwal.

315

Hindu Temple

After years of tireless work and fundraising, families from India yesterday (February 25, 2001) held a prayer service in a new Hindu temple set among suburban trees.

"This has been in the planning stages for so many years," said Vimala Rajaji, whose husband is treasurer for the temple's Board of Trustees. Her family has been involved in the effort to bring the temple to Pomona since 1987.

That was the year when Dr. Venkat Kanumalla, a physicist working in the radiation oncology department at Good Samaritan Hospital in Suffern, got together a group of Hindu families in the area who wanted to build a temple.

They bought land in Pomona and submitted their plans for the site to the village board in 1991. But some local residents fought to block the building of the temple, saying it would change the residential character of the area. The dispute went to federal court, in the form of a discrimination lawsuit by the temple members, before the temple plans were finally approved and construction began in 1997. Yesterday, temple members praised Kanumalla for his tireless dedication in turning their dream of the temple into reality. Kanumalla, who is not only a physicist but also priest, blushed at the praise.

"Because of the God, the temple is here," said Kanumalla, who was dressed yesterday in the traditional clothes of the Hindu priest, consisting of a long garment, similar to a sarong, worn with bare chest, a basil-wood rosary and ritual paint markings on his face, neck and body. "I am just a servant."

He said that a dozen families had dug deeply into their assets to help build temple. "There are 10 or 12 devotees who have taken second mortgages on their homes, or taken out loans from their retirement accounts," he said. "We raised $1.2 million."

Temple members are still busy raising funds to pay off construction loans, but the temple's treasurer, Raj Rajaji, said he's confident that Hindus throughout the United States will pitch in to help.

Blair Craddock, *The Journal News*, 2/26/01

Historic Clarkstown Church

Travelers along the New York State Thruway often notice a storybook church near the busy interstate highway. Surrounded by sugar maples, with its tall spire piercing the skyline, it is often referred to as "the church by the Thruway."

The Historic Clarkstown Reformed Church on Strawtown Road, the third oldest church in Rockland County and the first church in the town of Clarkstown, is celebrating its 250th anniversary this year. The congregation formed in 1750 when travel over rough roads to the Tappan Reformed Church proved too arduous for distant parishioners.

In 1871, the present church was built on 18-acre parcel on Strawtown Road. It was constructed in the old Swiss style of architecture, with a sanctuary that resembled the inverted hull of a ship.

The church, which added the word "historic" to its name about three years ago, is a testament to the area's past, said William Vines, a former county legislator, town supervisor and judge, and current church elder and vice-president of the church consistory. "Americans do not preserve history. We keep tearing down."

Nancy Cacioppo, *The Journal News*, 7/16/00

The Historic Clarkstown Reformed Church in 2002.
Photo by Linda Zimmermann.

September 22, 2000 marked the 200th anniversary of Catholic schools in New York. Celebrations were held in Rockland's eleven Catholic elementary schools, which have a total enrollment of almost 2,900 students. The county also has one Catholic high school, Albertus Magnus in Bardonia. St. Peter's school in Haverstraw was the first to open its doors in Rockland in 1863.

Marycrest

More than 120 people and four generations gathered yesterday (July 16, 2000) to celebrate the 50th reunion of the homeowner's association that bonded families together while defying the odds. Jack Dermody, one of three surviving founders of the Marycrest Association in Pearl River, described how 12 families, who came out of World War II wanting to have a Catholic community based on teachings of goodness and charity, were determined to make their vision reality despite numerous obstacles.

The plan was for members of the association to do all of the building of the private homes themselves. Since none of the members had professional training, the path of finding funding was a difficult one. They eventually bought 56 acres for $7,500 in what was then the boondocks, but now is prime real estate. And given the lack of training, "The fact that no one was killed building these homes is a miracle," Frank Rubino declared.

While the neighbors lived a stone's throw away then, they are now dispersed. That didn't stop many from coming to the reunion yesterday. Liv Willock, the daughter of founder Ed Willock, came from Denmark for the reunion. Maryanne Henderson came from Miami to see her old friends and neighbors. She said that Marycrest was a fun place to live as a child.

The Marycrest Association was the epitome of community, according to Dot Heider, who came from Alabama to see some friends she had not seen for dozens of years. She described how there were 84 children among the 17 families. The 71-year-old said she misses the days when children could walk and play freely. "There was no fear then."

Alan Zeitlin, *The Journal New*, 7/17/00

Lawyers Spent Lives in Service

Two of the county's most esteemed attorneys received the Rockland Bar Association's Liberty Bell award posthumously at the Law Day ceremony on May 1, 2000. The late Anne Glickman, who was the first director of the county's legal aid society, and the late Robert Kassel, local champion of civil rights who chaired the Rockland Civil Liberties Union, were honored for decades of work.

"Both of them gave of themselves for the law and the profession," said Suffern attorney Rubin Ortenberg, who presented the award to relatives of Glickman and Kassel. "They sacrificed more than most lawyers do."

The Liberty Bell award is a national award presented each year through local bar associations. Ortenberg said it was created to recognize lawyers and nonlawyers alike who have made contributions to law.

Glickman earned her law degree from New York University Law School in 1959. She was one of only three women in her graduating class. After moving to Rockland in the early 1960s, Glickman soon became the first director of Rockland's newly created Legal Aid Society. She became a crusader fighting substandard housing in the county. "She just as easily could have gone into private practice and made a lot more money," Ortenberg said.

In 1996, Kassel was recognized for his dedication to those who couldn't always afford to hire an attorney. He received the Rockland Bar Association's first Pro Bono award. Kassel maintained a law practice in Nyack, specializing in civil rights employment law, domestic relations and real property and personal torts. Kassel received his bachelor's degree in 1951 from Upsala College and his law degree in 1954 from Brooklyn Law School.

Laura Fasbach, *The Journal News*, 5/2000

The Grass Can Be Greener on Your Side

For 35 years, Suffern resident Ralph Snodsmith has dispensed his gardening advice to radio listeners across the country in his program "Garden Hotline." In addition to talking about plants, he also writes about them. His book, *The Tri-State Gardener's Guide*, specifically addresses plants and techniques best suited for this area's unique conditions.

As Rockland shifted from farmland to

suburbia in the last few decades of the century, individual lawns and gardens became an important feature of our landscape. Generations of successful gardeners in the county have acquired valuable information every Saturday morning from Snodsmith, who has never missed a broadcast, and never missed an opportunity to make life a little greener.

Linda Zimmermann

2,000 in 2000

It began in the 1950s with three senior citizens in a tailor shop on Main Street in New City. In the year 2000, there were over 2,000 members in Clarkstown's Senior Citizen Program. Sponsored by the town of Clarkstown Parks Board and Recreation Commission, the numerous programs include arts and crafts, education, exercise and travel.

Frank DiMaria, the program's director, explained that for the grand total of one dollar per year, any Clarkstown resident over 60 years of age can join one of twelve clubs. In addition to the clubs, all members are eligible to attend an annual picnic. Another annual event is the musical theater or variety show that allows them to strut their stuff on the stage of Clarkstown High School. Whether it is the Caribbean-themed picnic of 1998, or the show to salute 100 years of music in 1999, every event requires an enormous amount of talent and dedication. As anyone who has ever seen or participated in any of these programs can tell you, there is certainly no lack of either quality among the 2,000 members.

Several times a year, trips are organized to all parts of the world, from Alaska to Hawaii to Europe. A particularly poignant excursion was to the beaches of Normandy, where many veterans of the invasion recalled not only the terrible battle, but the friends they left behind. Realizing how many veterans filled the ranks of the Senior Citizen Program, Frank DiMaria invited members to bring in World War II photos and memorabilia for a temporary display in the administration building on Zukor Road.

The response was overwhelming, and it soon became evident that something more permanent was needed to honor all of the veterans. The idea evolved into the Hall of Heroes, a lasting tribute to the brave men and women who served in all branches of the armed forces.

Transforming the hallway of the old Street School into a small museum was no easy task. However, by relying upon the same talent and dedication devoted to other events, the seniors created attractive displays, stained glass windows and special lighting to highlight the exhibits. More than a tribute, the Hall of Heroes provides an educational opportunity for Rockland students to learn about and appreciate the sacrifices made by the generations that came before them.

Linda Zimmermann

A Twenty-First Century Library

The long-awaited opening of the Suffern Free Library was celebrated on Sunday, April 16, 2000, with balloons, cappuccino and cookies, and hearty words of congratulation from local officials. More than 1,000 people attended the inauguration of the 37,000-square-foot building on Route 59 next to the Tagaste Monastery.

"Tomorrow we'll be open for business. Today it's just a party," Library Director Ruth Bolin told the happy crowd.

It had long been recognized that Suffern needed a larger children's library, and Craig Long, president of the library's Board of Trustees, told the assembled visitors that the children's section of the library is as big as the adult space. Long also congratulated the principal architect, Todd Harvey, for designing a building in harmony with its natural surroundings. "We wanted to have a building that would mingle with, rather than intrude, on the landscape. So we used similar natural elements," he said. "Native stone is incorporated into the design, and wide windows allow views of the trees.

At the dedication, the prior of the Tagaste Monastery (which previously owned the land where the library was built), the Rev. John A. Gruben, prayed, "May this library always be a place where one can encounter truth."

The library, which cost approximately $7.3 million, has five times as much space as the old building on

The Suffern library in 2001. LZ

Maple Avenue. The new building has smooth wooden floors, wide windows, a dozen Internet-ready computers and long worktables that can accommodate laptops. A stained glass window from a Civil War-era mansion is placed above the entrance to the local history room. The downstairs children's section has several large rooms that can be used for community activities. And after a hard day of studying, you can relax with a cup of cappuccino and a croissant in the café.

A visiting official from neighboring Westchester admitted that the library made him jealous.

Colleen Roach, *The Journal News*, 4/2000

Landmark Businesses Receive Honors

As difficult as it is to start a business, perhaps the greatest challenge is to make that enterprise last. On February 27, 2000 the Historical Society of Rockland County honored eight local businesses that were not only successes, but have lasted so long they are now recognized as landmarks.

Annie's Snack Shack: In 1952, 17-year-old Annie Ciabattoni and her father opened the Snack Shack on Route 9W in Stony Point. Beginning with a tiny hot dog stand, the restaurant grew and became a regular part of the lives of generations of people in the community. Considering the almost total domination of fast food chains, it is a credit to Annie and her customers that the Snack Shack has not only survived, but thrived for over 50 years.

Customers flock to Annie's on a summer afternoon in 2001.   Photo by Linda Zimmermann.

Lydecker Agency, Inc., Nyack: There have been Lydeckers in New York long before there even was a New York. First arriving in America in 1653, generations of the family have witnessed the growth of both the country and the county. Homer Lydecker founded the Lydecker Real Estate and Insurance Agency in Nyack in 1930. Despite being in the midst of the Depression, Lydecker was able to make his business a success. His first sale was a home that went for $2,000, from which he received a commission of $100. Lydecker probably never imagined where real estate prices would be at the turn of the century, and he probably also could not have dreamed that his business would still be in operation 70 years later.

Vanderbilt Lumber, New City: In the nineteenth and early twentieth centuries, the general store was the hub of the community. It was not only the place to purchase all of your essentials from bacon to sewing needles to horse feed, it was also the place to get the latest news and gossip. Jacob E. Vanderbilt began his general store in New City in 1869. The business continued with his daughter, Sarah, and her husband, William Debevoise. Despite the growth of the massive home center chains, the Vanderbilt business is still being run by Jacob's descendants, marking over 130 years of operation.

Orange and Rockland Utilities, Inc., Pearl River: Like Rockland's communities, O&R is the result of the melding of many different entities. With its earliest origins dating back to 1859, the company has had the monumental task of bringing electricity and gas to every corner of the county. From your grandparents' streetlights, to your mother's stove, to your computer system, O&R has been a part of every family in Rockland during the twentieth century.

Provident Bank, Montebello: First opening its doors in 1888, Provident Bank has survived a century of economic ups and downs. Growing to 13 branches, Provident not only provides the county with basic banking services, it also gives back to the community in the form of educational programs and scholarships.

Safe Harbour Group Ltd., New City: The result of the merging of numerous insurance agencies, Safe Harbour can trace its beginnings in Rockland back to the 1890s when it was the Bedford Insurance Agency in Spring Valley. It has grown considerably in the last century and now not only serves Rockland County, but tri-state, national and international markets as well.

Tilcon New York, Inc., West Nyack: From the time of the first Dutch settlers, the rocks in Rockland have been essential construction materials. It is not surprising then, that one of the oldest industries in the county is the quarrying of stone. New York Trap Rock began its operations in West Nyack in 1912 and continues today under the name Tilcon. Tilcon supplies the southern New York and northern New Jersey area with all types of materials for construction of homes, businesses and roadways.

Wyeth-Ayerst Pharmaceuticals, Pearl River: In 1906, Dr. Ernest Lederle began his laboratories on Middletown Road in Pearl River to produce an improved diphtheria antitoxin. Over the decades, Lederle Laboratories became a leader in vaccines and pharmaceuticals, gaining international attention in 1962 with the first successful polio vaccine. The company was purchased by American Cyanamid in 1930, and again in 1994 by American Home Products. Lederle's legacy has not only provided a century of health benefits to people around the world, but has also been a major source of employment for generations of Rockland residents.

A Century of Sports

Call it an embarrassment of riches. The tiny triangle of turf in southeastern New York known as Rockland produced an impact on twentieth-century sports far exceeding its Lilliputian size.

Olympic athletes? We have had five reach that holy grail of amateur athletics. Pro football players? No less than eleven locals have plied their gridiron prowess in the National Football League. Seven Rocklanders have graced major league baseball diamonds. While none have yet broken through in professional basketball or hockey, many have gained distinction in those sports on the college and semipro levels.

And that's not even mentioning the national championships local sportsmen and women have procured in a variety of athletic pursuits such as auto racing, trapshooting, handball, billiards, bowling, racewalking, swimming and tennis, to name a few.

The list of Rockland's dominant athletic teams of the century must include such scholastic boys' dynasties as the Congers soccer squads of 1931-55; Nyack tennis, 1939-56; Tappan Zee golf, 1941-56; Suffern wrestling, 1951-65; Tappan Zee swimming, 1971-95; Suffern ice hockey of the 1980s to the mid-1990s; and North Rockland football from the mid-1980s to the mid-1990s.

The girls' honor roll includes dreadnoughts like the Pearl River cross country team from 1979 to the present; North Rockland volleyball and soccer in the 1990s; and Suffern lacrosse in the 1980s and 1990s.

Jamie Kempton

While politics and scandal often go hand in hand, the following two incidents in the early years of the twenty-first century brought national notoriety to the county.

Mentor and Protégé: Winikow and Adler

Back when Linda Winikow represented Rockland and a sliver of Westchester in the state Senate, she went nowhere without an entourage. There were always two or three people making the rounds with her, but sometimes the group was closer to a half-dozen strong.

The one person who was always by her side back then was Paul Adler. He was just a pup. He was smart and hardworking, to be sure, but he was just a pup. He had volunteered to work for Winikow when he was 17, and he was learning the political ropes from a master. He learned so well that he became her chief of staff.

He worked hard at his craft, rising through the party ranks to become county Democratic chairman. But in September of 2000, after the announcement of charges of fraud, extortion and both giving and receiving bribes, Adler said he would not seek re-election to the party post. The events bring to mind the parallels between mentor and protégé.

Throughout her time in office, Winikow was a champion of the little guy. Particularly when it came to utilities, Winikow was always ready to fight for a lower rate, better response to customer service needs, a better response during emergencies, like Hurricane David.

Long before consumerism was the vogue, that was her thrust. It was what got her elected in Ramapo and what won her higher office. Everyone knew Winikow, and Winikow let everyone know she knew them. And knew about them. People believed in her and believed she cared about them, that she was fighting for their best interests.

And then came the betrayal. Sensing she had gone as far as a Democrat could go in the Republican-controlled Senate, she looked at other opportunities. A run for Congress, trying to unseat Rep. Benjamin Gilman was out of the question. She considered running for the newly created post of County Executive.

Haverstraw Democrat John Grant had the inside track and the support of then party chairman Vincent Monte. Winikow's strategy was to undermine support for Monte, who would say later, "She's a real political operative. Let's put it this way. I've never had any other political official try to take me out." Monte kept his job, Grant got the nomination and became Rockland's first County Executive.

By then Winikow had shocked voters and political observers when she accepted a job as a vice president of Orange & Rockland Utilities in 1984.

She had hopped the fence, fashioning herself as fighting from the inside. But worse than just changing sides, in the eyes of many, she was now the apologist for the enemy she had fought so long and so hard. The confidence and arrogance she showed in political office followed her into the corporate suite. She still had an entourage, she still kept people waiting. Things would happen, not only the way she wanted, but on her schedule.

It's hard sometimes to tell whether arrogance breeds power, or power breeds arrogance. But usually they go hand-in-hand with greed.

Winikow still tried to wield power, and again it brought her to a dead end. Eventually, in 1993, she was charged with influence peddling and misuse of O&R corporate funds. Guilty pleas brought just months in jail.

From 1996, when he became chairman, until September of 2000, it was Adler who had been the leader of the entourage, guiding the likes of Hillary Rodham Clinton around his county. In August, he was at the center of the action during the Democratic National Convention. Just a month later, he faced as much as 20 years in prison and a $250,000 fine for trying to clear the way for the controversial Smith Farm housing development in New City and for failure to divulge on ethics forms some money he earned while working behind the scenes for the Pyramid Co., developers of the Palisades Center mall, who were not accused of any wrongdoing.

You have to wonder whether the mentor taught too much, and the protégé learned too well.

Bob Baird, *The Journal News*, 9/14/00

New Square: The Clinton Pardons

Back in the mid-1970s, I had an exchange with a leader of the New Square community regarding the outcome of the latest town election. Of the votes cast in the village, one of the candidates for supervisor had gotten about 690 votes to only four votes for his opponent.

Joking, I asked, "How did four votes get away?"

"It's all right," he said with a chuckle, "We know who they are."

It was one of the first times we at the newspaper noticed New Square's bloc voting pattern, which is attracting attention because of the suggestion that 1,400 votes for Senator Hillary Rodham Clinton may have been traded for presidential clemency for four men with ties to New Square. In the final hours of his presidency, Bill Clinton reduced the sentences of the men, who are in prison for stealing tens of millions of dollars from federal programs.

The New Square leader may have been smiling back then, but somehow I always thought he had really meant it—that those four residents asked for and gotten dispensation to break with the community's voting bloc.

Back then, just as it is now, one of the most contentious issues in town was enforcement of zoning and building codes, particularly on the fringes of New Square and in the Monsey area.

New Square's bloc vote would usually go to those candidates who seemed most sympathetic on that and other issues. In the decades since, we've seen the bloc vote in general and primary elections at all levels.

Sometimes, it has appeared easy to draw a line from a candidate getting backing to some form of post-election payback. What's been impossible, and likely will remain so this time, is nailing that there was a deal up front.

But what everyone has believed—and what several Rockland politicians confirmed to reporter Steve Lieberman late last week—is that in the words of former County Executive John Grant, "No pre-election meeting with the rabbi came without a deal associated with it."

The parade of politicians to visit New Square over the years has included names like Gore, Lazio, Pataki, D'Amato, Schumer and Cuomo—both Mario and son Andrew. Of course, not all got the endorsement or the bloc of votes. But Hillary Clinton did, getting 1,400 votes to 12 for her U.S. Senate opponent, Rick Lazio, who had the support of the rest of the Orthodox and Hasidic community. Clinton met with New Square leadership in August, but says there was no discussion then of clemency for Kalmen Stern, Jacob Elbaum and Benjamin Berger, all of New Square, and David Goldstein of Brooklyn. That didn't come up until December 22, when Grand Rabbi David Twersky visited the White House to meet with the president and first lady. According to a spokesman for Hillary Clinton, she listened, but made no recommendation to her husband.

But even if no deal was cut in August, it would have been naive of Hillary Clinton to think the grand rabbi wouldn't come calling. In other cases, in other races, the result might have been a break on the zoning code, a little more money from a grant program or help with a state or federal agency.

This time, cashing in the chips took a trip to the White House. This time, the cause and the participants were high profile. They may have thought no one would care, but they had to know someone would notice.

New Square's spin has always been that the men were stealing for their community, not themselves. But some of the money involved fraudulent tuition aid paid to supposed New Square students taking Judaic study courses at Rockland Community College. The college had to make restitution to the tune of more than $5.2 million. That came out of the pockets of Rockland and New York taxpayers.

The four men, who will be out of jail next year, are expected to make restitution, too. Assuming each makes $60,000 per year, at the rate set by the government, it would take more than 200 years to pay back the $5.2 million.

I guess that's why we all get to help.

Bob Baird, *The Journal News*, 2/01

A New War

On September 11, 2001, the world watched in horror as terrorists hijacked four commercial airliners. One crashed in Pennsylvania, one struck the Pentagon, and the others were flown into the two towers of the World Trade Center. It was the beginning of a new kind of war--a war against terrorism.

Of the estimated 3,000 people killed that day, 67 were from Rockland County. Below are the names of these first innocent victims of this new war. (Names obtained from local and national databases as of 2/02.)

Albert, Jon L.	McGowan, Stacey (Sennas)
Alonso, Janet	McCarthy, Robert
Anaya, Calixto, Jr.	McHugh, Dennis
Aryee, Japhet	McIntyre, Donald
Bosco, Richard	McPadden, Robert
Chiang, Alex	Monohan, John
Coughlin, John	Nee, Luke
Crowther, Welles	Nevins, Gerry
D'Allara, John	Nimbly, Paul
Favuzza, Bernard	Novotny, Brian
Fegan, Sean Bernard	O'Connor, Dennis, Jr.
Fiore, Mike	O'Leary, Gerald
Flickinger, Carl M.	Ortiz, David
Foley, Thomas	Princiotta, Vincent
Fredericks, Andrew	Reilly, Kevin
Furman, Steven	Roberto, Joseph
Gabler, Fredric	Roberts, Michael
Ginley, John	Ryan, John
Graifman, David	Scheffold, Fred
Gschaar, Robert	Schoales, Tom
Hannon, Dana	Scudder, Christopher
Ill, Fred, Jr.	Shajahan, Mohammed
Jain, Yudh	Sikorsky, Gregory
Jeudy, Farah	Simon, Arthur
Joseph, Robert	Smith, Cathy
Lehrfeld, Eric A.	Spear, Robert
Longing, Laura(Petitus)	Vernon, Richard
Ludvigsen, Mark	Vero, Loretta
Lum, William, Jr.	Walker, Benjamin
Magazine, Jay	Wang, Wei Bin
Marchbanks, Joseph	Weinberg, Steven
Marshall, John Daniel	Wholey, Michael
McAneney, Patricia	Woods, James
	Wooley, David

OUR HOME TOWNS

Rockland's Growing Population: 1800-2000

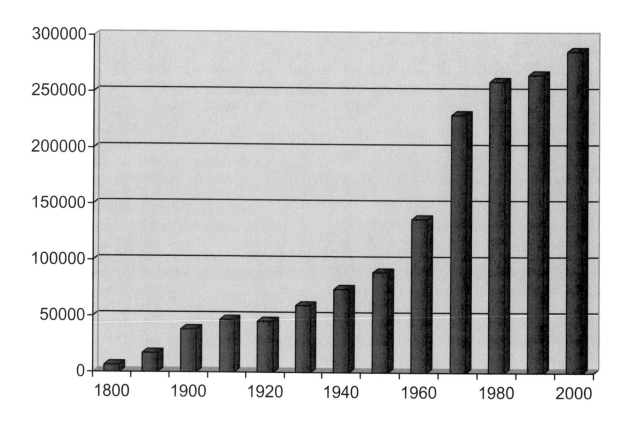

Year	Clarkstown	Haverstraw	Orangetown	Ramapo	Stony Point	Total
1800	1806	1229	1337	1981	**	6353
1850	3530	5612	4623	3197	**	16,962
1900	6305	9874	10,450	7502	4167	38,298
1910	7980	9335	14,370	11,537	3651	46,873
1920	7317	9027	14,284	11,709	3211	45,548*
1930	10,188	11,603	18,029	16,321	3458	59,599
1940	12,251	12,443	26,662	18,007	4898	74,261
1950	15,674	12,979	34,554	20,584	5485	89,276
1960	33,196	16,632	43,172	35,064	8739	136,803
1970	61,653	25,311	53,533	76,702	12,704	229,903
1980	77,901	31,929	48,612	89,060	12,838	259,530
1990	79,346	32,712	46,742	93,861	12,814	265,475
2000	82,082	33,811	47,711	108,905	14,244	286,753

*Loss of population because of flu epidemic.
** Formed from Town of Haverstraw in 1865.

Data from Frank Smith Schnell

Editor's Note: The following chapter contains a look at the communities that made up Rockland in the twentieth century. This section contains a mix of brief descriptions and more in-depth histories. There are several excerpts from the 1927 *Rockland County Red Book,* which may not provide the most current information on a town, but does give the unique perspective of the past. As many of the larger communities are covered more extensively in the decade chapters of this book, more text and photos have been allotted here to some of the less publicized areas. The goal was to provide something for everyone.

Airmont

Rockland's newest village, incorporated in 1991, was a consolidation of the hamlets of Tallman, Airmont, and South Monsey. The earliest settlement began during the mid-eighteenth century. One of its oldest roadways is Cherry Lane, a name that appears on maps of the Revolutionary War era. Before the construction of the Nyack Turnpike (a forerunner of Route 59), what was called the old south road to Nyack passed through the village.

Farming was the principal occupation of Airmont residents from its eighteenth-century beginnings into the 1950s. In later years Airmont farms supplied the New York City cut flower market. Similar to other farming communities in the area, another cash crop was strawberries, which were shipped by special trains to the marketplace.

According to Cole's *History of Rockland County,* published in 1884, Tallman was named for Tunis Tallman, who opened a store there in 1836. Tunis was a direct descendant of Rockland's oldest family. While the Nyack Turnpike and Erie Railroad made transport of local products to market easier, the hamlet experienced little growth until the 1860s. During that decade, storekeeper Henry Tallman was appointed postmaster, becoming station agent at the new railroad depot and opening a hotel. A small commercial district grew up between the railroad, the Nyack Turnpike and Cherry Lane. Henry became Ramapo Town supervisor and might be considered Tallman's founding father. The Airmont section south of Tallman was part of a larger area called by the native American name Masonicus.

The state boundary during the nineteenth century was inconsequential as the hamlet straddled the border. On Church Road was Cornelius Wanamaker's tavern and general store. Most of the nineteenth-century farms along South Airmont Road in this section were once part of the Wanamaker estate.

A general store was opened by William Forshay in 1891. A blacksmith shop stood alongside. When it was thought a post office might be established in the general store in the 1890s, the wife of the local cleric suggested Airmont as a possible place name. The post office never materialized, but during the next decade Airmont was gradually adopted by the citizenry.

South Monsey's main street was the Saddle River Road, another early thoroughfare and onetime Indian trail. At the junction of the Nyack Turnpike and Saddle River Road was the general store of Mr. Jersey. Numerous other small business enterprises stretched from the Turnpike to the New Jersey boundary. Commerce was brisk and the Saddle River was utilized by grist, saw and cider mills.

One of the most important buildings in the farming community was the Grange Hall on Spook Rock Road where every important function took place. The rapid growth in the area during the 1960s and 70s, the inability of the older villages to expand and the gradual decline of the small farm led to construction on large tracts of land. Despite the close proximity of the town, residents became concerned that decisions about their backyards were being made at town hall beyond their control.

The shortcomings in the efforts of town planners in regards to the Route 59 corridor increased the anxieties of residents as well. The idea of a new village, where residents might exercise tighter control over their future landscape, was suggested in the 1980s by the Airmont Civic Association. Although incorporation was finally realized in 1991, with the citizens of Airmont having voted 3 to 1 in favor of the plan, accusations of discrimination and religious intolerance had delayed the village's creation.

Despite its difficult beginnings, the village of Airmont has begun to deal with the complex problems that brought it into existence. Where the many mills once stood are today private residences and summer camps and recreation areas. As Airmont

Postcard, circa early 1900s, reading "State Road leading to Suffern, Tallmans, N.Y." The large house on the right later became the Spook Rock Inn, which was destroyed by fire. Today the road is Route 59.

Courtesy of Craig Long.

journeys into the twenty-first century, a sense of village pride and independence is evident among its residents. At Village Hall, there are displays of the villages past landmarks and a sense of anticipation for the next chapter in Airmont's history.

Kenneth Kral

The intersection of Route 59 and Airmont Road (looking toward Suffern) in January of 2002 bears no resemblance to the early 1900s postcard. The once quiet area is now one of Rockland's busiest intersections. This photo was taken early on a Saturday morning—before the lines of traffic back up in all directions.

Photo by Linda Zimmermann.

The Tallman post office occupies the corner unit of this strip mall of stores. While the building is modern, the concept of locating a post office next to a store is as old as Rockland. (Note that SUVs and minivans have eclipsed cars as the suburban vehicle of choice.)

Photo by Linda Zimmermann.

Bardonia

This hamlet is about a mile northeast of Nanuet and about one-third mile west of where the old Reformed Church of Clarkstown on Germonds Road once stood. It was a farming community consisting of thirty-three families until the New City Branch of the New Jersey and New York Railroad passed through in 1875.

In 1849, three Bardon brothers, John and twins Phillip and Conrad, immigrated to America from Bavaria and settled in Clarkstown. Phillip built his home on the south side of present Parrott Road in West Nyack, where the Board of Cooperative Education Services is now located. Phillip had a shop in which he produced iron products. He was the father of eight children. Conrad built his farmhouse on West Nyack Road, Nanuet in the 1850s. He was a farmer and hotel proprietor. John settled in this hamlet and became a businessman.

In 1903, Bardonia had a big league baseball player in its midst: Leon DeMontreville, who played with the St. Louis Cardinals.

In 1904, the Siegmund family built a house on Bardonia Road and farmed the surrounding 20 acres. In 1933, the house became a German restaurant, and then changed hands several times until in 1975 it became the popular Lock, Stock and Barrel.

In 1902, Arthur Tompkins predicted that "As the neighborhood is only a short distance from the turnpike to Nyack, it is likely to become a place of importance in the near future." However, Bardonia defied predictions and remained a small and quiet hamlet.

John Scott

Bardonia Road & Station - Bardonia N. Y.

Brown's Hotel, Bardonia, N. Y.

Clockwise from top: Bardonia Road and station, c.1915; Bardonia school, c.1915; Monterey Pool, c. 1940; and Brown's Hotel c. 1910.   Photos courtesy of John Scott.

MONTEREY POOL   BARDONIA, N. Y.

327

Blauvelt

The area of the Orangetown, or Tappan, Patent north of Orangeburg was called Greenbush. Two of the earliest settlers here were the sons of Gerrit Hendricksen, who as a young boy sailed on the *Kalmer Nyckel*. In early records he is referred to as Gerrit de blau boer (blue farmer/bluefield farmer). In 1682 these two sons were among 16 farmers who purchased land from the Tappan Indians on the west bank of the Hudson River. Around this time, the family name was changed to Blauvelt (bluefield).

The earliest settlers here built numerous so-called Dutch colonial sandstone farmhouses. These handsome dwellings are unique to this southern part of Rockland and North Bergen Counties, mostly contained in the Hackensack Valley. They are considered to be America's first original architectural contribution. The native sandstone used in construction was often obtained from outcroppings on the farmer's land on which it was built.

Many of the houses have been removed but a number still remain along Western Highway.

The road in this area was called the Greenbush Road, a part of the colonial road that had great significance. The well-preserved sandstone homes along this route afford a rare view of early America. Several of these houses now have historical markers erected by the Historical Society of Rockland County.

In the hills west of Blauvelt was the World War I Camp Bluefields. After the armistice it was used as an ROTC camp and then in 1926 it became a fresh air camp for boys.

The farming community of Blauvelt vanished with the construction of Route 303 and the Lake Tappan Reservoir. After World War II, the remaining farms gave way to housing developments. Today, Blauvelt is a mixture of residential and business districts.

John Scott

Clockwise from top: Circa 1910 view of Blauvelt looking east from Erie Street, Blauvelt's first firehouse, view north on Greenbush Road, c. 1905-10.

Photos courtesy of John Scott.

Central Nyack

This small community drapes over and around the strategic pass in the mountains, half facing Nyack to the east and half facing West Nyack. Only a few scattered farmhouses occupied the region that appeared in mid-nineteenth century maps as West Nyack.

Among the early settlers in the pass was W.S.H. Waldron, a large landowner and farmer. Others included Lyon, Trumper, Lydecker, Towt, VanHouten and Baker families who managed to produce excellent fruit, berries and poultry on the rough terrain that was not adaptable to large scale farming.

The upper levels of the hamlet gradually developed and numerous houses were built along Waldron and Mountainview Avenues and West Broadway. In 1886, Angelo Sidoli bought the Baker premises and constructed a large greenhouse business on the site. The Nyack Rural Cemetery was incorporated in the 1880s and a Congregational Church organized in 1901. Several grocery stores and a meat market opened and in 1910 a schoolhouse was built.

Late in the nineteenth century, powerful interests of the New York Central Railroad west of the swamp, desired a Nyack name as a scheduled stop for their new station. This was conveniently arranged to suit them. The pass in the mountain region was changed to Central Nyack and the West Shore railroad station at Mont Moor and Clarkstown now became West Nyack.

The first tollhouse for the Nyack Turnpike was located near present-day West Broadway. By 1900, there were more than 100 families living within the Central Nyack limits. In 1932, the Clarkstown Country Club Sports Center Stadium was constructed, an impressive project for the time, and the first outdoor stadium in New York to have night lighting. The sports field area is now part of Waldron Terrace Apartments.

The most notorious event of Central Nyack's history was the Brink's Robbery of October 20, 1981, in which two police officers died.

John Scott

The ice house (above) and ice pond skaters (right), c. 1905-10, in Central Nyack, which became the site of the West Gate Motor Lodge and the Thruway entrance. JSC

Chestnut Ridge

Formerly known as South Spring Valley, Chestnut Ridge was incorporated as a village in 1986. Residents, concerned over what they perceived to be a lack of zoning enforcement, incorporated as a way to have a greater voice in government.

During the 1920s, a community of Scotsmen settled in the area of the present Green Meadow School and established a store, public house and post office which they called Scotland (hence the name, Scotland Hill Road).

The derivation of Hungry Hollow Road has several possibilities. When the Munsee Indians lived in the area, there were many beaver dams, and their word for beaver was "haungi." Another theory is that hungry runaway slaves sought food and refuge in this area. Reputedly, there was a farm on Hungry Hollow Road that was a stop on the Underground Railroad.

Today Chestnut Ridge has modern residential houses, as well as historic homes dating back to the Revolutionary War. The community also has commercial and retail businesses to help support its tax base. With the help of donations from local businesses, a family picnic day is held each year for residents to help foster the sense of community.

Congers

Congers was named for Abraham B. Conger who moved to the area from New York City around 1840, calling his new home Waldberg (meaning "forest city" in German). The local church, school and later the community took on this name. However in 1883, Waldberg became known as Congers when Abraham Conger donated land for the new West Shore Railroad station.

Speculators believed that the railroad was sure to bring development, and in 1889, John McGinnis and Will Van Guilder purchased 2,400 acres. They divided the land into 10,000 lots, some as small as only 25 by 80 feet, which made them the smallest parcels in the county. This scheme was the beginning of the Boston Improvement Company and their efforts at promoting Congers as a summer resort area, coupled with the local ice and quarry industries, attracted large groups of Irish, Bohemian and Italian Catholics.

The first Catholic Church in Clarkstown, St. Paul's, was built on land donated by McGinnis and held its first mass on Easter Sunday in 1894. The church burned down in September of 1967 and was rebuilt on the same site. The Boston Improvement Company also donated the land for the First Presbyterian Church of Congers in 1891.

Due to the Depression of 1893 and some shady business dealings (it had apparently sold the same lots to several different buyers), the Boston Improvement Company hastily left Congers. This created years of confusion in obtaining clear titles to the company's former holdings.

By the turn of the century, Congers had a broom factory, six stores, four hotels (the Globe, Mayo's, the Central, and one other), two livery stables, and the Methodist, Catholic and Presbyterian churches.

With the building of Route 9W in the late 1920s, Route 303 in 1930 and the bridges across the Hudson, Congers underwent greater development. However, unlike some communities, Congers resisted numerous building projects, both residential and commercial, including a facility for Reynolds Aluminum. While the plant would have brought many jobs, fear of pollution was of greater concern. As the twentieth century came to a close, Congers remained as one of the few communities in the county to retain much of its small town roots.

Information and excerpts from: Thom Olsen, *Centennial History of Congers, 1883-1983*

Postcard, early 1900s, reading: Birds' Eye View of Congers, N.Y. Courtesy of John Scott.

Durant

Durant was one mile south of New City; it was a small settlement of private residences. In the early 1900s a shed-type railroad station was built here to accommodate the New York City commuters. This was the third stop on the New City Branch of the New Jersey and New York Railroad.

The station was named after Thomas C. Durant, who lived in this hamlet. He was the organizer and builder of the Union Pacific Railroad, the first transcontinental railroad in the United States, which was completed in 1869. His daughter, Heloise Durant Rose, lived on Maple Avenue, New City, and later moved to Durant (present day Laurel Road area). She was the founder of the Rockland County Welfare Society and of the Dante League of America.

Information from the 1927 *Rockland County Red Book*.

Garnerville
An Industrial Heritage

"I know, it looks like a bit of Dickens," said Bill Decker while talking about the buildings of the Garnerville Holding Company which he manages. And it's no wonder because some of the buildings on the 45-acre site situated on the shores of the Minisceongo Creek date back to before that Victorian author published his first book.

Bricked up windows, narrow alleyways and a general atmosphere reminiscent of England's industrial midlands permeate the surroundings, courtyards and paths that distinguish this Industrial Terminal. Can anything so old be functional today? To judge, it's necessary only to watch the trucks that often completely block the winding streets, loading and unloading merchandise from the 28-odd manufacturers and businesses that rent space.

In the late 1700s, a grist mill was powered by the creek. In 1828, that was replaced by a calico printing factory. Thomas and James Garner purchased the property in 1838. Later, another brother, Henry Garner, bought a share.

These owners seemed to have a magic touch because after the addition of several buildings, the factory soon became a major industrial success. In 1853, the company was incorporated as the Rockland Print Works with a capital of $100,000, "for the purpose of manufacturing, printing and dying woolen, cotton or linen goods."

Dan deNoyelles, a Rockland historian, noted the factory was enlarged from time to time and in 1884 produced a gross product of one million dollars. When William T. Garner, sole heir to the estate, died in 1876, the company was reputed to be one of the largest in the country. Trustees ran the company for Garner's three daughters until it was sold in 1909 to Deering, Milliken & Company.

The Rockland Print Works was innovative in labor relations. They gave Christmas bonuses, built a YMCA (complete with bowling alley, gymnasium and reading room) and constructed and managed tenements and boarding houses for their employees. The print works also built the S. W. Johnson Fire Company in 1876 and this proved to be a stroke of luck because the next year a fire destroyed most of the factory buildings. A larger and more modern plant was soon built on the site.

In 1905, Harmony percales were introduced by the Rockland Print Works when they exclusively adopted

Looking east toward the factory buildings in Garnerville. Photo by Linda Zimmermann.

some new vat colors discovered in that year. By 1915, the *Rockland County Times* stated, "The Village of Garnerville is owned by the Print Works and the company maintains the streets, lights them from its own power plant, and polices them."

But later advances in industrialization and the Depression took their toll. The mighty print works abandoned the buildings and moved south where labor was cheaper.

The men and women who had looked to the Print Works for their livelihood (over 900) were starting to move out of the area in 1934 when Thomas Larson, a local entrepreneur, together with 91 other businessmen secured a Rural Finance Corporation loan and formed the Garnerville Holding Company. They started to rent out space to small businesses for manufacturing and storage.

Though technology marches on, many Rockland businesses still build their futures on the obviously firm foundation of the past.

Today, according to a spokesman for the Garnerville Holding Company, the buildings house such diverse businesses as manufacturers of artists paints, barber, beauty and industrial chemical supplies, dye works, a coat factory, chemical manufacturers, educational toy makers, a sauna bath factory, T-shirt mills, producers of medical and non-medical products, modern furniture,

Brick archways in the factory complex do resemble nineteenth-century England.

Photo by Linda Zimmermann.

knitting mills and paper mills, aside from renting storage space to many larger companies.

Behind these old brick facades, modern machinery enables one worker to produce what ten workers produced 100 years ago, and Rocklanders are employed by companies whose combined gross product reaches into the millions.

Anne Golar, *The Journal-News,* 7/28/80

Grand View

A large portion of the almost two-mile Hudson waterfront between present Piermont and the Nyacks, known in colonial times as the northern part of Tappan, had been almost inaccessible because of the cliffs of brownstone that extended in places to the shoreline. A rough Indian footpath became widened for horseback and later for two-wheeled farm carts as quarrying began in the late eighteenth century. In 1790, what had previously been a private lane between Nyack and the Slote was recognized as a public road.

By 1859, the Northern Railroad of New Jersey had extended its tracks from Jersey City to Sparkill where it joined the main line of the Erie that ran from Piermont pier west to Buffalo. Passengers to and from Sparkill, the still unnamed Grand View area and the Nyacks, were then transported by horse drawn carriages on the unpaved dirt roads that became quagmires in inclement weather.

In 1869 Boss Tweed, heading powerful Erie R.R. interests that had taken over the Northern R.R., prepared to extend the line from Sparkill to Nyack with tracks to run along the riverfront. Their surveys were made and plans drawn but strenuous organized opposition from the local residents resulted in a compromise of having the tracks placed further up the

Postcard entitled: Tappan Zee Yacht Club and Lyall's Hotel, Grand View, N.Y., dated 1907. JSC

hillside which then divided the community into upper and lower sections.

The new extension opened in 1870 and soon 20 to 30 trains a day were rushing passengers, freight and mail between Nyack and Jersey City, a service that continued for almost a century. Upon completion of the railroad a group of Erie officials came to inspect and name the new station perched next to the tracks on a steep hillside overlooking the Tappan Zee. One of them, enchanted with the view, exclaimed, "What a grand view!" All those gathered agreed it was the perfect name and it was adopted for the station and hamlet. A new road, "Station Lane," made trains available to River Road commuters below.

The fast train service available to commuters and vacationers caused a boom period in the entire Tappan Zee communities that became popular summer resort areas with the reputation of being healthy places to live. New homes were constructed along the riverfront and slopes of Grand View, and several hotels opened to accommodate the visitors and guests of the new boat club.

On September 15, 1900 the Village of Grand View was incorporated, making it one of the smallest villages in New York State. The people above the tracks along Route 9W soon complained of the increasing taxes with fewer benefits received than those living below, and in 1917 decided to disincorporate themselves from the village. On May 29, 1918 lower Grand View was incorporated as Grand View on Hudson and Upper Grand View remains as a hamlet of Orangetown.

Perhaps the residents above were also unhappy with the many village ordinances and by-laws which somewhat restrained their previous freedoms.

Some of the fifty laws included these provisions:
1. No person, horseback or mule, shall proceed at greater speed than 8 miles per hour—bicycles no greater speed than 8 m.p.h. $25 for violation.
14. Horses, cows or oxen may not be hitched to trees or hydrants. $3 fine.
15. No ball playing, discharge of fire-arms, bon fires or other explosions permitted in village streets or sidewalks—except on July 4th.
17. No beating of drums or noise making with any instrument without written permission of the President of the village. $5 fine for each offense.
21. No "Strays" allowed: cattle, horses, sheep, swine, or geese may not run at large or be pastured; $3 fine.
29. No bone-boiling or fat-rendering in village. $15 fine.
33. No gaming house, house of assignation, brothel or house of debauchery shall operate. $25 fine and $10 after notice is given by President or Clerk of village
34. No instrument or device for gaming permitted. $25 fine.
35. Places selling intoxicating liquors to be closed Sundays. $25 fine.
36. No congregation of crowds on street corners. Fine $25.
37. Intoxicated or noisy persons defacing any property or inciting dog fights or defying order of village. $10 fine for each offense.
38. No Sunday disturbing of the peace with ball playing. $10 fine.
50. No nude bathing in river from 7 A.M. to 8 P.M. Fine $2.

John Scott

Grand View cyclers, c. 1910, in front of the Carlton Gilson Homestead at 81 River Road. JSC

333

Grassy Point
and Proudfoot's Landing

Grassy Point, a plateau on the river front containing groves of chestnut and oak trees, was part of the huge Allison farm at the time of the Revolution. It became the country estate of William Denning, Sr., circa 1798. A deepwater dock was built there by Dr. Lawrence Proudfoot in 1830, enabling river steamers to land and making it an important shipping and passenger point used by the famed vessels *Chrystenah* and *Emeline* into the twentieth century.

Dr. Proudfoot petitioned to maintain a ferry from his dock to a convenient place in Westchester County on the east bank of the Hudson, stating that the only other ferry service in the county at that time was from the point at Dunderberg to Peekskill six miles to the north. The new ferry was authorized in 1833.

The community of handsome dwellings soon gave way to the brick industry that had been extending northerly as far as Stony Point. David Munn arrived in Grassy Point in 1834 and bought into and invigorated the small local brick business there. The area was soon producing more than 3.5 million bricks a year.

An outstanding event of the nineteenth century was the visit of Martin Van Buren (president 1837-41) who landed at the new Proudfoot dock and was welcomed by residents from miles around.

Jim Farley, born in Grassy Point in 1888, became the small community's most noted native son. He worked in the brickyards to help support his widowed mother and four brothers. His political career began as town clerk of Stony Point (1912-19). He steadily climbed the political ladder until, in the 1930s, he became chairman of the National Democratic Committee and Postmaster General of the United States.

John Scott

St. Joseph's Church in
Grassy Point in 1969. JSC

Jim Farley's boyhood home in Grassy Point. JSC

Haverstraw

Haverstraw was founded by Dutch settlers in 1666 (although a village historian asserted that the name was on Dutch maps as early as 1616). The name was originally Haverstroo, meaning oat straw, deriving from the oats that once grew in the area.

Haverstraw's setting is one of the most dramatic in Rockland, with the Hudson River stretching to its widest point to the east, and the 832-foot High Tor Mountain rising to the west. While the scenery is spectacular, it was what couldn't be seen that led to the town's rapid development—the vast clay deposits that provided the material for the brick industry. Fortunes were made, fine houses were built and immigrants from many countries came to work in the brickyards.

However, the brick industry declined in the early part of the twentieth century. By the end of World War II, the closed brickyards signaled a period of economic decline. The post-war decades also saw a shift in the make-up of the population.

According to the 1980 census, the median family income in Haverstraw was $17,900, compared to $28,240 for Rockland County and $20,180 statewide. The census also reported that sixteen percent of village residents lived below the poverty level. Forty-eight percent of the population was Hispanic and eleven percent was African-American.

In the 1990s, revitalization became the keyword for Haverstraw. New businesses came to the downtown area and ambitious plans for waterfront development were being discussed.

Linda Zimmermann

View of Haverstraw from the Short Clove. Note the brickyards on the river. JSC

Main Street, Haverstraw, 1875. JSC

Central Presbyterian Church, in 1994. JSC

335

Hillburn

From the 1927 *Rockland County Red Book*:

One mile west of Suffern, Hillburn is a beautiful residential village which includes several pretentious estates, formerly a part of the estate of John Suffern. Because a sawmill formerly operated there, it was called Woodburn, but, when the post office was opened in 1881, the name was changed to Hillburn, to avoid confusion with another post office in the state.

While the village and the local industries date from 1795, when John Suffern built a sawmill on a small stream tributary to the Ramapo, its real industrial beginnings date from 1852 when James Suffern obtained power to operate a charcoal forge by throwing a dam across the Ramapo and installed a rolling mill for the making of car axles and other railroad materials.

In the early 1870s, officers of the Ramapo Foundry and Wheel Co., attracted by the beauty and the advantages of the locality, purchased acreage on the present site of Hillburn from James Suffern, laid out a village and encouraged their employees to buy lots and to build homes, marking the beginning of residential Hillburn which, its residents claim, is the most beautiful village in the county.

Top: Postcard of the Majors Bridge, Hillburn, c. 1910s. Right: Hillburn park.   Courtesy of Chuck Stead.

Hillcrest

The busy intersection of Route 45 and Eckerson Road in Hillcrest.   Photo by Linda Zimmermann.

From the 1927 *Rockland County Red Book*:

One and one-half miles north of Spring Valley, Hillcrest is also called Moleston from William Moles, who, in 1910, started development there which was arrested by the depression period of 1915. During the last few years, a progressive community of homes has developed itself there, largely, thanks, to the efforts of the Hillcrest Fire Company around which the civic activities of the community center.

Johnsontown, St. John's and Sandyfield
(The Lost Home Towns)

Johnsontown, Sandyfield and St. John's were thriving communities lying in the mountainous western region of the town of Haverstraw before the Palisades Interstate Park Commission turned the area into parkland. Johnsontown stretched along what is now Lake Sebago and Lake Kanawauke. Lake Welch partially submerged Sandyfield when the park commission dammed the swampy Beaver Pond to form the lake. Nearby, the forty acres encompassing St. John's-in-the-Wilderness is the only private land within Harriman State Park. It stands as a testimony to the once thriving St. John's mission, established in 1880.

Marianne Leese

Jones Point

From the 1927 *Rockland County Red Book*: Jones Point—population 200: Three miles north of Tomkins Cove. From Joshua Cholwill who first settled there in 1791 the original settlement was name Cholwills, later corrupted to Coldwells, and finally Caldwell's Landing. The name Jones Point dates from the opening of the Post Office in 1885, in honor of the Jones family, prominently active in the region.

For a time Caldwell's Landing promised great development; it was an emporium for the provisioning of sailing vessels trading in the Hudson. That and the persistent legend that Captain Kidd's treasure was sunk nearby—near the bend of Dunderberg—induced the laying out of a town that was to be named Gibraltar. The advent of the steamboat and railroad and the failure of treasure seekers deprived Jones Point of the promised prosperity.

Ladentown

Ladentown is in the center of the triangle between Haverstraw, Spring Valley and Suffern, two miles west of the Mt. Ivy station. It owed its origin to Michel Laden, a nail cutter in the Ramapo works, who opened a trading store and tavern in 1816. However, long before his time a number of Quaker families had established themselves in the region. In 1927 the population was 300.

1927 *RCRB*

Main Street of Ladentown, showing the residence, store and garage of Pincus Margulies, Justice of the Peace and leading merchant—a pioneer in the development of the locality.   1927 *RCRB*

The interior of Margulies store. JSC

Monsey

From the 1927 *Rockland County Red Book*: Monsey—population 500: One and one-third miles west of Spring Valley. The village stands on land bought by Eleazar Lord, founder of the Erie R.R., who, in 1842, had a platform built where the station now stands which was named Kakiat, a name which, because improperly applied there, was soon afterwards changed to Minsey (the name of a sub-tribe of the Delawares) and later to Monsey. The first store was opened at the station in 1843.

Monsey is a village of homes and the center of considerable benevolent activities which include St. Zita's Villa, the Herriman Farm School, and St. Zita's Home for Friendless Women, founded in 1890 by Ellen O'Keefe.

Lacking industries and business activities, Monsey is often characterized as the slowest village in the county, an injustice which is documented by its residents' voting $100,000 for a new school house.

The Brewer Fire Engine Co., has a new fire house and hall designed in a chalet style, erected on the site of the old Grove Street Church, and one of the two nicest in the county.

Bokar Lake, the beginning of a small settlement, three and a half miles north of Monsey, on Willow Tree Road, was begun by C. Bockar, who transformed a swampy pond into a picturesque little lake by building a dam, and provided swimming, boating and fishing facilities.

Postcard of the "Old R.R. Station and Vicinity, Monsey, N.Y.", c. 1910s. Courtesy of Ken Kral.

Maple Avenue, Monsey, after a snowstorm c.1900. JSC

The public school in Monsey, c. 1910. JSC

Montebello

Montebello's streams once provided power for numerous mills. Large country estates were built here by wealthy New York City residents. While modern highways bypassed the community, it was nonetheless incorporated as a village in 1986 in response to the growing demand to control development in the area.

338

Mount Ivy

From the 1927 *Rockland County Red Book*: Mount Ivy is in the northern part of a region extending south to Spring Valley unsurpassed for the loveliness of its scenery and its healthfulness, producing much fruit, vegetables, dairy products and honey, dotted with pretentious residences and modest cottages of employees in state and county institutions in the vicinity or engaged in road making.

The region was until recent years the habitat of people who were gradually driven to the higher hills further west and south by modern progress, especially road traffic which destroyed their privacy, and also by school and health authorities in the enforcement of sanitary and school laws. The name Mount Ivy is said to have been given to the locality because of its elevation and the ivy swamp, now partly reclaimed.

Until a generation ago, Mt. Ivy was the center of an important Quaker settlement. The Camp Hill School is maintained jointly by the townships of Ramapo and Haverstraw. Where the old Camp Hill School House now stands is the place where the Marquis de Lafayette's troops rested one night in July of 1778.

The largest single industry is sand and gravel shipped by Dalrymple & Gurnee. Much cordwood for brick kilns is cut and shipped from Mt. Ivy. Hudson Manor, one of the most up-to-date roadhouses in the county, has accommodations for swimming, fishing and various sports.

THE OLD DADDY LINKLETTER HOME. MT. IVY, N. Y.
BUILT DURING THE REVOLUTIONARY WAR.

JSC

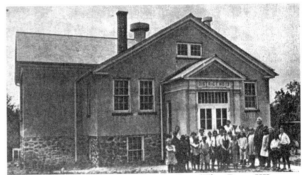

Camp Hill School, Mt. Ivy. The Rev. Wm. Briscoe, with teachers and pupils. 1927 *RCRB*

Nanuet

Hutton's store, Nanuet, c. 1870-75.
The Erie R.R. crossing is in the background. JSC

This small hamlet of less than a dozen dwellings and isolated farms was home to Dutch, English and Scottish settlers. Some of their red sandstone houses can still be found along Middletown and Pascack Roads.

The area had been known as Nanawitt's Meadow, named after a Kakiat Indian who lived in the area. Later, there were a series of names, including Middletown and Clarkstown. The name Clarkstown remained until 1856 when James DeClark suggested Nanuet.

Nanuet remained a small hamlet until the Erie Railroad came through, circa 1841, when more houses were built as well as grocery stores, a foundry, a wheelwright shop, and a saw mill to name a few. Dr. M.C. Hasbrouck built a brick store that became the Hutton Lumber Yard; later the Huttons introduced a department store for agricultural implements. The Hutton-Johnson Co., Inc., stood for many years at 135 South Middletown Road.

A fire company was organized in 1860. Around 1845, there was a Nanuet Debating Society formed by several prominent men—Blauvelts, DeBaun, Hopper, Demarest and Bogert. They met to socialize and discuss the important issues of the day. The first post office was established here in 1846 in the home of David DeClark which was built in 1841; this house also served as an early railroad station or waiting room.

St. Agatha's Home and School at 135 Convent Road was founded in 1884 "for the care, education and maintenance of orphans and dependent children, for the

An aerial view of Middletown Road at Nanuet's old railroad crossing, c. 1950s. JSC

instruction of such children in some useful trade or business." It was supervised by the Sisters of Charity of St. Vincent DePaul of Mont Saint Vincent-on-the-Hudson. Most of the children came from the New York City area.

During its first 23 years (1936 to 1959), the Clarkstown Police Department operated in Nanuet out of three make-shift locations: one of which was a house at the intersection of West Nyack Road and Route 304.

Henry Earle Insley, pioneer photographer, purchased a 35-acre farm on Middletown Road in 1860. His second oldest child, Albert Babb Insley (1842-1937) became an artist in the Hudson River School tradition. Albert lived in Nanuet from about 1866, and purchased a home on Orchard Street in the 1920s. In the late 1800s, many of Albert's paintings were of country scenes in and around Nanuet, Spring Valley and West Nyack.

With the construction of the Tappan Zee Bridge, the New York State Thruway and the Palisades Interstate Parkway, life in Clarkstown changed. The old Nyack Turnpike is now Route 59 and has become the major commercial artery. One of the first shopping centers, Korvettes, opened its doors in 1962 and closed by 1980. The Nanuet Mall became Rockland's shopping capital for almost three decades. With the construction of the Palisades Center in West Nyack in the late 1990s and the subsequent widening of Route 59, many old buildings in Nanuet—homes and businesses—have been destroyed.

It could easily be argued that Nanuet has undergone the most dramatic changes during the twentieth century.

John Scott

Nanuet's Four Corners, looking east, c. 1900-05. What looks like a little dirt path is now Route 59. JSC

Nanuet's Four Corners (intersection of Route 59 and Middletown Road, looking southwest toward the Nanuet Mall) in 2002. The house of Ellen Ferretti stands alone against the area's commercial development. Photo by Linda Zimmermann.

340

Nauraushaun

Nauraushaun is on the Hackensack River and derives its name from a creek tributary, which was also known as Nauraushank. For many years the area was called Orangeville, and was the location of one of the oldest cotton mills in the county, the Atlantic Cotton Works, which were dismantled in the early twentieth century. In the late 1800s, the Naruraushaun school was the only one available to the children of Pearl River. In the 1920s, it was the location of The Cat and Dog Hospital.
                                                                          Information from the 1927 *Rockland County Red Book.*

New City

From the 1927 *Rockland County Red Book:* New City is four and a half miles southeast of Haverstraw on an elevated plateau, in the northern part of the fertile Clarkstown plain, in the center of an intensive farming and attractive residential district.

Tappan was the county seat until 1774, but the increase in population in the northern part of the county demanded a more central location for the transaction of official county affairs, and the site of New City was selected in the hope that its central geographical position would lead to the growth of a large city there. The failure of any railroad to construct its main line through the locality caused the prediction to fail and, after regular service between Nyack and other points to New York City began, and especially after the advent of railroads, almost every village had better means of communication with the outside world than the county seat. In our era of private cars, taxis and buses, and of good roads, the difficulties of access to the county seat have been removed, and it is only now, after a century, that the county at large begins to benefit by its central location.

The second courthouse and jail in New City, postcard c. 1912. JSC

Postcard of "Upper Main Street, New City, N.Y." c. 1905-10. JSC

New City school, c. 1910. JSC

341

New Hempstead

In 1983 the village of New Hempstead was created for the purpose of controlling its own zoning and planning. It was carved out of an area within the town of Ramapo that had been settled in the early 1700s by families from Hempstead, Long Island. The new village set up its offices in the vacant English Church Schoolhouse (built 1867, enlarged 1896), which provided the space it needed. However, the property, located at 108 Old Schoolhouse Road, was one block to the east of village boundaries. The New York State Legislature passed a bill to allow the village legally to set up its offices in the school until it could annex the less-than-an-acre property.

Marianne Leese

New Hempstead Road looking east to New City, c. 1910. The old courthouse is in the background on the right. The present day County Clerk's office and highway department are now located in the farm field on the right. JSC

Another c. 1910 view of New Hempstead Road. County roads were very dusty in dry weather and morasses of mud in rainy weather and during the spring thaw. JSC

342

New Square and Kaser

New Square was incorporated in 1961 and Kaser in 1990. Both communities were formed by members of orthodox Jewish groups, whose faiths are the basis of all aspects of their daily lives.

Nyack

Postcard with view of Nyack from the Hudson River, 1905. JSC

From the 1927 *Rockland County Red Book:* On the majestic Hudson, facing the Tappan Zee, with attractive homes on the riverfront and on the sloping land, Nyack, the Gem of the Hudson, with its sister villages South and Upper Nyack, presents a charming picture. To the north Hook Mountain, a miniature Gibraltar, rises abruptly from the water, the end of a semi-circle which embraces the hills surrounding these villages and terminates at the northern point of the New Jersey Palisades. From these wooded heights, but a brief climb from the towns, magnificent views in all directions are an ample reward for the pedestrian. Thus, sheltered from the northern winds, the Nyacks escape some of their bitterness in winter, while in the heat of summer days the river breezes give solace and relief.

This region was settled by Hollanders, whose vast land-grants are the basis of all present realty titles, and the first record of the name Nyack was in 1707. It belonged to a tribe of Indians, the original denizens of this section, and in the early records was variously spelled as Nayeck, Naieck or Nijack. This name was not, however, their exclusive possession, as the name means a corner or point of land.

Before the days of railroads, the convenient location of this bay at the end of the Palisades caused the building up of a busy trading and supply post for the back country. When the steel rails came, contact was gradually established with the big city below and in time this section was settled by those who found attraction in the scenery and the water.

Postcard of Main Street, Nyack, at the intersection of Broadway, c .1905-10. JSC

Orangeburg

Orangeburg lies north of Tappan and south of Blauvelt in what was known as the Orangetown or Tappan Patent. This patent was purchased from the Tappan Indians in 1686 and was also known as the Nawasunk lands as late as 1769. The early Dutch farmers built one-and-one-half story homes out of the native sandstone, stone outcroppings, and hand-hewn logs. There were approximately 150 sandstone houses in the county with about 125 in existence today.

The Dutch language and Dutch influences predominated in the communities that made up Orangetown into the late 1700s. Early church records and services were conducted in Dutch and later, when the English came in the seventeenth century, services were in Dutch and English on alternate Sundays for many years.

When the Erie Railroad came through, a country railway station and post office were built and the area was called Orangeburg Station. James Haring built a small chapel for a Sunday school and church service.

Bel-ans Building on Greenbush Road was a pharmaceutical company (1897-1971) founded by John Lanphere Dodge (1865-1940). During the last 30 years of his life, Mr. Dodge bred, trained and raced trotters on the property.

The Rockland County Agricultural and Horticultural Association was organized in 1848 and incorporated in 1897. In 1907 it began leasing the racetrack and grounds from John L.

Orangeburg railroad station, c. 1905. JSC

Dodge (present site of Volkswagen of America, 39 Greenbush Road). The agricultural fairs were held on Labor Day until 1920. Horse shows and horse racing were the favorite entertainment until the advent of the automobile.

S.R. Bradley, an investor in Nyack Utilities, was instrumental in bringing electricity to Orangeburg. He built a power generating plant near the intersection of the Erie and West Shore Railroads in Orangeburg that supplied electricity to Nyack. In the 1920s he built a plant on the east side of Greenbush Road. Bradley believed the heat from the exhaust steam could be used to dry the fibre tubing manufactured at the Orangeburg Pipe Manufacturing Company, later known as Flintkote. The plant closed in 1972. Worldwide, companies still refer to fibre conduit as Orangeburg pipe.

In the 1930s, Rockland State Hospital was built to care for the mentally ill. In 1982 a renovation project was begun and completed in 1992 and the name changed to Rockland Psychiatric Center.

In the summer of 1942, the U.S. Army seized 1,300 acres of tomato farms and cornfields in Orangeburg and converted it to the largest Port of Embarkation on the east coast—Camp Shanks. Over 1.3 million men and women passed through here on their way to the European theater of war. In 1945/46, the camp processed and held German and Italian prisoners of war until they could be returned to their homelands at the end of WWII.

Postcard of "section of Maple Avenue Looking West, Orangeburg, N.Y." in 1917. JSC

From 1946 to 1957 the camp became Shanks Village—housing for the returning veterans, and their families, while the husbands pursued their education at nearby colleges and universities. Many of Rockland's prominent judges, lawyers and politicians are "alumni" of Camp Shanks.

When the students moved out in 1952, the Public Housing Administration took over for another four years. By the end of 1957 Shanks Village was demolished, New York State sold some of the land to the Palisades Interstate Park Commission for the parkway, and private builders purchased land for housing developments.   John Scott

344

Palisades and Snedens Landing

1900-1920

The Census of 1905 documents 458 residents in the hamlet of Palisades, with houses mainly clustered in two areas: along the road leading down to the Hudson River and in the center of the village, near the post office and general store. Most travel was by horse and carriage, but if you wanted to go as far as Nyack or New York City you took the train from the station at Tappan or Sparkill. The ferry started in the eighteenth century by Robert Sneden was still running from the Landing, across the river to the train at Dobbs Ferry. The Palisades Presbyterian Church, the Palisades Library, and the two-room Palisades School were the most important local institutions.

The Lawrences, Gilmans and Agnews were all well-to-do New York City residents who had settled here towards the end of the previous century and had a great influence on the community. Local businesses included Dumkin's Blacksmith Shop, and Brown and Jordan's greenhouse, both near the center of the village. Sam Brown also owned the Palisades Cemetery, which had started in the eighteenth century as the Lawrence Burying Ground. James Post owned the main store and also ran a livery stable and an ice business, cutting the ice at Post's Pond. The Post Office was sometimes located next to the Post store, but when the administration in Washington changed, it moved across Oak Tree Road to Mr. Wahrenberger's house.

1920-1945

Gradually things began to change. Water and electricity came to Palisades in 1920. Route 9W was put through in the late 1920s, and as a result the few families who still lived in the hilly southern section called Skunk Hollow abandoned the area. The first cars and telephone had appeared around 1910, but they were so rare that in 1929, when Henry Kennell started a gas station on 9W, there were only four cars in town. Kennell's Palisades gas station survived for nearly 60 years.

Mary Lawrence Tonetti, Lydia Lawrence's daughter, owned 16 houses near the river in the section of Palisades known as Snedens Landing and began to rebuild them and to rent them to artist friends in the summers during the 1920s. When Wine Hill, who had run the ferry for 24 years, retired in 1927, Mrs. Tonetti created the Snedens Landing Association to continue the ferry service. Many well-known artists, writers, musicians and theater people lived briefly in the Landing during this period: the list includes Orson Welles, Burgess Meredith, Noel Coward, Lawrence Olivier, Lynn Fontaine, and Aaron Copland. Katharine

Circa 1900s views of Palisades. JSC

345

Cornell, after staying in various Tonetti properties, finally built her own house here.

The Palisades Post Office moved for several years to the house next to the old Methodist Church. A few new houses appeared on the side roads, but the year-round population of the village was still only 522 in 1925.

Between 1928 and 1932, the very successful Blacksmith Tea Shop occupied the old Dumkin smithy. A new brick school was built across the street from the old school in 1930. Tippy O'Neill started an auction house, Yonderhill, in the old Methodist church in 1935. In 1939 the Abels and MacIvers, who taught at Columbia University, and several friends bought 24 acres off Oak Tree Road. They put in a new road, called Heyhoe Woods, and built houses on the land. The 9W Golf Driving Range, which has become the longest continuously surviving business in Palisades, started operation in 1939 and continues today, in a considerably expanded form. Mary Tonetti died in 1945, ending an era: her extensive property holdings were divided among her four children, who gradually began to sell them off. The ferry stopped running after the last boat sank during the hurricane of 1944.

The Palisades Parkway cut through the southwestern corner of the hamlet in 1955, necessitating the destruction of several houses. In 1956 a group of former Camp Shanks residents bought 16 acres cooperatively west of Closter Road and built contemporary houses; the small development was called Indian Hill. During the next three years a larger commercial development of 75 houses was built south of Oak Tree Road, near Route 340. Advertised as Palisades Gardens, these houses sold quickly.

Nellie Knudson was instrumental in starting the Palisades Swim Club on vacant land just south of the village in 1965. Another small development, Century Road, appeared off Closter Road in the mid-1960s. Three changes during this mid-century period had the effect of reducing local autonomy, in spite of the benefits they brought to the community. In 1957 the South Orangetown School District was created. In 1962 four local libraries joined together to become part of the Orangetown Library District and the next year all four became part of the Ramapo-Catskill Library System. In 1967 Palisades was included in a new Historic Zoning district, joining Tappan, which had created a historic district the year before.

Before these changes, Palisades residents had argued the pros and cons of school issues on their own school board, run their library as they wished to, and built any kind of house they wanted to. Residents had enjoyed a kind of participatory democracy that brought them together and increased their knowledge of the community. With the various kinds of centralization, much of this disappeared.

Early 1900s view of Snedens Landing. JSC

1945-1970

At the beginning of this period, Palisades was still a small community where most people knew their neighbors. However, the twenty-five years after World War II brought major changes to the community. In 1949 the Thomas Lamont estate at the top of the hill was given to Columbia University as a site for the Lamont Geological observatory. John Collins bought a large piece of property north of the village in 1950 and established Birchwood Day Camp. The Palisades Cemetery was sold in 1950 to Karl Kirchner, a realtor, who resold it in 1960 to a group of investors in New York City.

1970-2000

It was this same desire for autonomy, as well as perceived threats to the community, that led a group of residents to make two attempts, one during the 1970s and again in the 1980s, to incorporate Palisades as an independent village. Both times the motion was narrowly defeated in a community-wide vote. Those who wanted incorporation were reacting, among other things, to the closing of the Palisades School in 1976. From then on our children were bussed to school, first to Tappan and then to Sparkill.

In 1970 Palisades Gardens, a residence for senior citizens, opened on the north side of Oak Tree Road. Not counting these residents, the population of the hamlet reached 1,200 in 1971.

In 1977 a small group of women started a community newsletter, called *10964* after the Palisades zip code, and it is now published four times a year with a volunteer staff.

Another threat to the community appeared when the family which owned the empty triangle of land near the post office decided to sell it to a commercial enterprise. Led by Reg Thayer, Palisades residents donated enough money to buy the land in 1979 and to give it to the Town of Orangetown, which promised to protect it.

Several small developments were built during the mid-1980s. Post Lane and Fern Road led off of Closter Road; Red Oak and White Oak were south of Oak Tree Road, just west of Route 340. In 1984 residents created the Palisades Civic Association in order to deal with further problems. Led by Eileen Larkin, the Association successfully fought for a ban on large trucks on Oak Tree Road, and in 1987 defeated a proposal to put 70 houses on the corner of Oak Tree and Route 340. The land was finally developed in 1992 as Lauren Road with only twelve houses.

The IBM Conference Center on Route 9W opened in 1989 on the site of the former Birchwood Day Camp. In 1994 the John W. Cumming home for a small group of developmentally disabled adults began operation on Oak Tree Road across from Palisades Gardens.

Although auctions at Yonderhill stopped in 1989, the building continued to function as an antique shop. In 1999 it briefly closed its doors but reopened in 2000 with new owners. Henry Kennell died in 1993. His son kept the gas station open for a few more years but closed it for good in 1998.

Palisades continues to grow; according to the Palisades Post Office, it now consists of 640 households. Many new houses have been built in the last 20 years, and they seem to be getting larger and larger. It is hard to keep up with the names of the new neighbors, who come and go at a dizzying speed. For a number of them, oriented towards New York City, Palisades is only a weekend pied-à-tèrre. Signs of conspicuous consumption abound, especially in Snedens Landing; few impecunious artists can afford to live there any more. In spite of these concerns, Palisades remains a small, attractive community, largely composed of one-family homes, with undeveloped woodlands to the north and south of a good portion of the village. The population is more diverse ethnically, if not economically, than in the past. The library, the church and the post office are still centers of community participation; the village newsletter, *10964*, keeps us all in touch.

Alice Gerard

Pearl River

Pearl River includes six separate communities of the seventeenth and eighteenth centuries which were a part of the Kakiat Patent: Nauraushaun, Sickletown, Orangeville, Middletown, Pascack and Muddy Brook/Creek. The boundaries were undefined. The one fixed boundary of Pearl River ran southeast to northwest along the New York-New Jersey state line.

Middletown was the name given to a section midway between the Kakiat and Tappan Patents—the current intersection of Old Middletown and Orangeburg Roads. All that remains from the very early times is the old Middletown Burying Ground (the cemetery of the Middletown Baptist Church, c. 1797) and the Salyer/Leach/Conque house, which was built c. 1730.

Muddy Brook or Muddy Creek was the section around present Central Avenue and Main Street where the running brook can still be seen. During the 1870s when the railroad came through, the name was changed to Pearl

The home of Julius Braunsdorf on Middletown Road in Pearl River. In the mid-twentieth century the house became the popular Silver Pheasant restaurant. After changing hands several times, at the end of the century, it was Keane's restaurant.   JSC

River. It is said that pearls were found in the mussels of Muddy Brook.

Julius E. Braunsdorf is credited as being the "Father of Pearl River." Among his other credits, he was a city planner—he laid out the wide street through the center of town (Central Avenue), a parallel street (Franklin Avenue),

347

Postcard of Main Street and Central Avenue, c. 1905-10. Courtesy of the Orangetown Museum.

and connecting streets that he named for his sons William, John and Henry. He built a large factory complex in town in 1872 for his Aetna sewing machine business. The buildings were later used by the Dexter Folder Company. Braunsdorf made the first electric light bulb, which he unveiled in 1873 to a group of local and New York City friends. Another of his factories was a three-story structure on Railroad Avenue, which is now an American Legion Post.

Religion played an important role for the residents. The first Baptist Church in the county was founded here in 1797 by Edward Salyer, Sr., and James Blauvelt.

The first public school classes in Pearl River proper were held above Burdef's blacksmith shop. A two-room school was built in 1894. After many additions this building was razed and a new school erected in the 1920s. Prior to this, children attended the Nauraushaun school, private schools or other public schools that could be reached by train.

Although the twentieth century saw the building and expansion of Lederle Laboratories and the Blue Hill office complex, Pearl River still remains one of the quieter communities in the county. However, that does all change during the annual St. Patrick's Day parade—the second largest in the country.

John Scott

Piermont

From the 1927 *Rockland County Red Book:* Piermont—Population 1,539: Three and one-half miles south of Nyack. Formerly called Tappan Landing or the Slote, a mile from the northern end of the Palisades and near the beginning of Tappan Bay. The name Piermont was given because of the mile long pier which extends into the Hudson and the mountains in the background.

Piermont has had a more dramatic history of the peaceful kind than any other village in the county. It is near its shore that Hendrick Hudson anchored the Half Moon. It is there that, nearly a century earlier, Verrazano landed. There was located the first port of entry in the region between Manhattan and Fort Orange (Albany). It is there that, no doubt, the first canal was built in America out of public funds—the cutting of curves in Tappan Slote. In more recent times, Piermont was the terminal of the Erie Railroad and the outlet for a wide range of territory; it enjoyed great prosperity until in 1852, the Erie car works were removed to the new terminal at Pavonia, New Jersey. A further decline was experienced when Piermont ceased to be the passenger terminus of the line.

This may not look like a scene from 1983, but thanks to a little Hollywood magic, downtown Piermont was transformed for Woody Allen's movie *The Purple Rose of Cairo.*   Photo by John Scott.

348

After trying times, from an economic standpoint, Piermont is now looking forward to renewed prosperity through her industries, but possibilities of large extension are limited because of lack of land for development, the area of Piermont being only a narrow strip of territory between the river and the hillsides. The village was incorporated in 1850.

The local industries include the Robert Gair Co., paper mill and box factory, employing an average of 450 hands. There is a branch of the Meisch Ribbon Works.

Circa 1900 view of Bogartown and the pier in Piermont. Note the large sailing vessel in the river. JSC

Pomona

Pomona was a sparsely populated area which began to be developed in the 1920s, being promoted as "The Switzerland of America" (a significant exaggeration with an altitude of only 650 feet). During the latter half of the century, fruit orchards and dairy farms were gradually replaced with housing developments.

This circa 1900 farm in Pomona enjoyed beautiful views of the mountains,
even if they didn't resemble the Swiss Alps.   JSC

Quaspeck
A Lost Town

Quaspeck was a growing business, residential and recreational (Quaspeck Park) area at the foot of Hook Mountain at the southern end of Rockland Lake. The original Quaspeck Patent is dated 1694 and included 5,000 acres. Twentieth-century residents had hopes of incorporating a village, but the creation of the Rockland Lake State Park ended the community.

Rockland Lake
A Lost Town

From the 1927 *Rockland County Red Book:* Rockland Lake—population 500—Rockland Lake is on the east side of Rockland Lake, a miniature valley between the mountains, giving access to the Hudson, 4 1/2 miles northwest of Nyack.

Until 1835 the village was known as Slaughter's Landing because an Englishman, John Slaughter, purchased the site in 1711. According to another account, the British, during the Wars of Independence, slaughtered there the cattle obtained by raids throughout the region before they shipped the meat to their vessels in the Hudson. This occurrence is probably a coincidence. The present name was given on opening the post office in 1842.

The store of J.W. Lappe in Rockland Lake, c. late 1930s. JSC

The beauty and healthfulness of the region of Rockland Lake, its fine water supply, and its healthfulness, have often aroused dreams of a great residential city on the shores of the lake, with elegant villas and modest cottages nestling in the foliage of the hillsides, church spires dotting the landscape and their chimes echoing over the still blue waters of the lake. If Stony Point has what is required to become a great art center, it would seem that the region of Congers in the west, Rockland Lake Village in the east, and Quaspeck and Valley Cottage in the south, offers an opportunity for a community center second to none in present opportunities and future prospects.

For nearly three generations the great industry of the village was ice cutting and storing. It began in 1831 with a modest capital of $2,000. From this grew the business of the Knickerbocker Ice Co., which now has assets of over a hundred million dollars. In recent years, ice cutting was discontinued, the huge ice storing houses dismantled and the land sold to a resort syndicate.

(The town came to an end as a result of the formation of Rockland Lake State Park.)

Circa 1900 view of Rockland Lake homes and buildings involving the ice industry. JSC

350

Sloatsburg

The area originally known by the Indian name Pothat (part of the hunting grounds of the Lenape Indians) became a significant industrial center during the 1800s and was renamed after its founding family, the Sloats. Sloatsburg was part of a strategic area for the colonial army as the Ramapo Pass served as a key defense point on the route from the Hudson River to battles in New Jersey.

The Colonial Era lasted from 1724 to 1799. The Industrial Era began in 1800 with the iron business. There were forges on the banks of the Ramapo, a grist mill and a saw mill on Stony Brook. Jacob Sloat had a smithy and a machine shop where heavy mill screws were made. He manufactured cotton cloth in addition to stocks and dies to compete with the Piersons of Ramapo who were also manufacturing steel goods. Later, cotton

The historic Sloat house.
Photo by Linda Zimmermann.

twine was produced. Manufacturing continued until the Civil War. The railroad was one of the greatest factors that contributed to the growth and success of industry and manufacturing in Sloatsburg.

During the early 1900s, Sloatsburg businesses continued to provide employment for hundreds of its residents and, in 1929, became an incorporated village to form its own governing body and to establish local municipal services for its 1,500-plus residents.

As the population of Sloatsburg increased, various local businesses appeared: a bakery, a clothing store, three general stores, a butcher shop, a barbershop and a blacksmith shop. Throughout the life of the village, farming provided a livelihood for many village families. Every family had a large garden to supply vegetables for the table, for canning and preserving for winter use. The farmers found ready markets for their produce in New York City, Paterson, New Jersey, and later, Newburgh, New York.

Changes came to Sloatsburg in the twentieth century when it experienced a flood in 1903. After the village dried out, the Erie Railroad rebuilt its roadbed, but the flood had dealt a deathblow to Sloatsburg as an industrial center. That same year the first automobile appeared in the village.

As the new century progressed, a church was built in the heart of the village, and a three-story building in the business district. Unions developed—the masons, painters and carpenters. In 1916,

Postcard of the Henry Inn in Sloatsburg, c. 1920s.   JSC

electricity came to Sloatsburg. A polio epidemic broke out in this year and civil restrictions on children were enforced—children under sixteen years of age were prohibited from attending any public functions.

In 1917 the United States declared war; considering the size of Sloatsburg's population, an inordinately large number of men entered the service. Industries were geared for defense work, nearby iron mines reopened and employment was readily available. After the Armistice was signed, Sloatsburg offered little in the field of employment;

351

men and women commuted to work in Suffern, New York City, and Paterson; the Erie Railroad provided easy access and cars had become commonplace.

The Roaring Twenties again brought a period of prosperity to the village with high employment, good wages and people spending their money. In 1929, the prime industry was a fabric-printing mill; electricity replaced waterpower. Small businesses operating at the time were a blacksmith shop, an ice cream and confectionery store, a laundry, a shoemaker shop and a meat market. Expansion was a slow process because of the Depression in the 1930s. With the outbreak of World War II the nation and even this community felt its far-reaching effects. One precautionary measure was to distribute sand throughout the village to be used in the event of incendiary bombing. Family life was disrupted when many of the working force were called to war.

Construction of the New York State Thruway through Sloatsburg in the 1950s changed Sloatsburg's suburban atmosphere and also relieved some of the traffic congestion that had existed prior to that time. During the late 1940s and 1950s the population climbed steadily; and a master plan for the village was introduced as a guideline for future growth, but commercial development was slow.

In 1973 the village attracted its first industry since the closing of the mill when Tuscan Dairy Farms located here. Significant cultural development came in 1975 when Rockland Community College located a satellite campus in Sloatsburg. Since the 1970s, Sloatsburg continued to be primarily a small, scenic, semi-rural home for residents who commuted to work locations in other areas. Local industry and business locations continued a slightly declining trend both before and since 1976. Consequently, shopping within the village was limited. The general trends of the 1990s—smaller and later families, a depressed housing market, and loss of small businesses to supermarkets and discount stores in centralized shopping locations are not unique to Sloatsburg.

Most residents enjoy the natural environment of wooded hillsides and wildlife, and they find Sloatsburg to be a satisfying and friendly community for family life. Pride in the village seems to be extremely high. This pride also relates –partially cause and partially effect—to the high quality of community services in the village.

Information taken from *Historic Sloatsburg 1738-1998. The Way it Was and Can Be,* published by the Sloatsburg Historical Society, compiled by Eugene L. Kuykendall, Village Historian.

View of Sloatsburg's homes and industry, c. 1920s-30s. JSC

Sparkill

From the 1927 *Rockland County Red Book:* Sparkill—population 1,000—One mile west of Piermont. First called Blanch's Crossing, then Upper Piermont until, in 1870, the growth of the village made residents dissatisfied with a name indicating dependence upon a less prosperous neighbor, and they selected Sparkill, the name of the creek which passes through the village.

It is about Sparkill that much of the history not only of Rockland, but of the State of New York north of Manhattan begins. It is thereabouts that Hudson traded with the Tappan Indians (the first transaction between whites and Indians in that part of the continent).

St. Agnes' Convent and School, of the order of St. Dominic, is an extension of the work of Sisters of that order in Blauvelt. Rockland Cemetery includes 200 acres facing the Hudson; it was founded by Eleazar Lord in 1847. For a time its operations were almost at a standstill, but they were revived and the property much improved in 1880 under the presidency of William H. Whiton. Wayanda Lodge, F. & A. M., has bought land in Sparkill for a monumental Masonic Temple.

This 1887 photo shows a train passing the hill of dirt in Sparkill that was used as fill for the Piermont pier swamp area. Town square buildings would be built on this site.   JSC

The bank (right) in Depot Square in Sparkill in the early 1900s.
OTM

A view of Sparkill's Depot Square, the former site of the hill of dirt, circa 1920. JSC

Spring Valley

From the 1927 *Rockland County Red Book:* Spring Valley—population 3,779—Greater Spring Valley, 6,000. Located between the picturesque Ramapo Mountains and the Palisades, in the center of a fertile region producing much fruit and dotted with many beautiful homes and large estates of business men and wealthy New Yorkers. The healthfulness of the district of which Spring Valley is the hub is documented by the number of people with respiratory troubles who have come here for rest and have been entirely restored to health.

Immediately east of the village are the limpid waters of small but unusually picturesque Hyenga Lake which, besides supplying water power as yet unused, could, at comparatively very small cost, be transformed into a park and playground in the summer and skating ground in the winter that would attract visitors from everywhere.

Before the opening of the Erie Railroad there was not even a house on the site of Spring Valley, whose beginnings date from the opening of a store in the station, in 1842, by Henry Iserman. A hamlet quickly grew around it and six years later a post office was opened which was named at the suggestion of Samuel Springsteen.

In industry, Spring Valley has become one of the two important, and in population, the second village of the county. Its progress has been steady and along substantial lines. It enjoys two house-to-house mail deliveries, a complete sewer system, an abundant water system, and a new railroad station, in attractive Rockland County style, is about to be erected at the cost of $30,000, half of which sum is provided by the citizens of Spring Valley.

Postcard of "Camp Hyenga 1953." Courtesy of Ken Kral.

Postcard Reading : "What Spring Valley is Proud Of," circa 1905. This was Ivy Barnes' "White House" diner. Pictured are proprietors Demarest Youmans and Charles Westlake.   JSC

Decoration Day (Memorial Day) on Main Street in Spring Valley in 1907. JSC

Intersection of Central and Main Avenues in Spring Valley, circa 1905. JSC

Sterlington

One mile east of Sloatsburg, Sterlington was at the junction of the Sterling Mountain Railway, which was built to transport ore to the furnaces at Sterling. Originally known as Sterling Junction or Pierson's Depot, the name Sterlington was adopted when the post office opened in 1882. When the mines, furnaces and railway ceased operating, there were no longer any businesses operating in Sterlington.

Stony Point

PENNY BRIDGE AND COUNTY ROAD, Stony Point, N. Y.

Postcard of the Penny Bridge (so-called as it cost a penny to cross) in Stony Point, c. 1900. JSC

Stony Point was originally part of the precinct of Haverstraw and was set off as a township extending north to the Orange County border on March 20, 1865. The hamlet of Stony Point, the small community south of the peninsula, was earlier known as Antioch, Knights Corner, North Haverstraw and Flora Falls.

Prior to the Revolution, the hamlet and peninsula area consisted of small farms. During the Revolution, the King's Ferry played a key role in transporting troops and supplies. On July 16, 1779, General "Mad Anthony" Wayne's men captured the British fort at Stony Point and this important battlefield is now a State Historic Site.

MAIN STREET, Stony Point, N. Y.

Early 1900s postcard of Main Street in Stony Point.   JSC

355

South Nyack

Until the middle of the nineteenth century, the community of South Nyack was considered a suburb of the Nyack area with its large commercial center. Following the completion of the Northern Railroad (later the Erie) to Nyack in 1870 there was a gradual influx of families who wished to enjoy the rural amenities of South Nyack with the convenience of fast train service and connections to New York City.

Nyack, which then included South Nyack, was incorporated as a village in 1872. In 1876 South Nyack, wishing to extricate itself from the larger growth problems and tax burdens of Nyack, successfully negotiated a legal separation from the larger community enabling it in 1878 to incorporate itself as the village of South Nyack.

The lower part of the new village remained largely residential, though shipbuilding on the Hudson shore continued for many years, together

South Nyack Town Hall and police car in 1983.
Photo by John Scott.

with commercial fishing and some shipping from docks and piers. Felter's Nyack Ice Company on Clinton Avenue enlarged under new owners to include coal and fuel oil. The Missionary Training Institute (now Nyack College) and the Clarkstown Country Club (closed in the 1950s) covered large acreage areas on the heights above.

In earlier scattered locations there was a small pipe organ factory, a large brick shoe factory (Jackman's) which was converted to Wilcox & Gibbs Sewing Machines adjacent to the railroad station (in South Nyack), and the Prospect House Hotel, none of which existed when as the New York State Thruway arrived.

South Nyack suffered more destruction than any other county community when that huge highway project cut through the heart of the village and built a large traffic circle at the approach to the Tappan Zee Bridge. The nucleus of the small commercial center was obliterated, including the railroad station, police station, village hall, two restaurants, grocery stores, garages and an antique shop. Altogether more than 100 buildings were destroyed or relocated.

John Scott

Suffern

The earliest settlers of the village of Suffern, incorporated in 1896, were German Palatines who settled there about 1740. A handful of families were in residence at the time the Revolutionary War began, and among these was Irishman John Suffern, whose inn and general store were located at the junction of three roadways. Because of the military importance of this site, John Suffern's tavern was frequently utilized as a military post during the war. General Washington's headquarters were here in July of 1777 and close to 4,000 French soldiers en route to Yorktown encamped here in the summer of 1781.

Following the revolution, Mr. Suffern was appointed the county's first postmaster with the office located in his New Antrim Store. Despite the opening of the Nyack Turnpike in the 1800s, Suffern remained a farm crossroads of little importance until the opening of two railroad lines in the 1840s. The establishment of Suffern as a railroad junction was the most important event in its history and ensured its future growth. The community officially became Suffern when a post office was re-established in 1850 bearing that name probably in honor of Judge Edward Suffern, the hamlet's most prominent citizen.

Postcard of Washington Avenue in Suffern, c. 1910. JSC

During the 1860s George W. Suffern divided his inheritance into building lots, opened streets, provided land for new businesses, a schoolhouse and local churches. The majority of the village's early citizens in this era were the mostly Irish employees of the Erie Railroad. Because of the quick access between New York City and the Ramapo Valley provided by the railroad, Suffern became a popular summer resort and during the next 60 years attracted both wealthy New Yorkers, who constructed summer cottages, and the middle class people, who stayed in the numerous hotels and boarding houses.

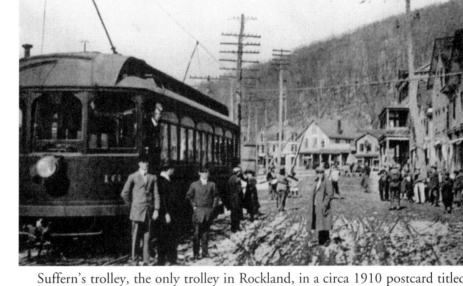

Suffern's trolley, the only trolley in Rockland, in a circa 1910 postcard titled "Cervieri's Corner, Suffern, N.Y."   Courtesy of Craig Long.

Among these was David H. McConnell, who soon after his arrival, brought his California Perfume Company (later renamed Avon Products), which became then, as now, the village's principal industry.

At the dawn of the twentieth century, Suffern's population reflected America's own growing diversity due to the influx of immigrants. Between 1900 and 1910 the village experienced the greatest growth in its history and began an era of expansion that lasted through the 1920s. Woods and farms gave way to housing developments.

Its location on the main line of the Erie Railroad also placed Suffern on the campaign trail of state politicians. Officeseekers, beginning with Teddy Roosevelt, who visited on three occasions, and William Jennings Bryan, came mostly by rail to bring their messages to the people of Suffern through the 1930s.

Lafayette Avenue in Suffern, c. 1919. JSC

357

As Suffern progressed so did its commercial district that had begun on Orange Avenue and extended up Wayne and Lafayette Avenues. Rockland County's only trolley line connected Suffern's shopping district with northern New Jersey towns. In the 1930s a new era of modernization began and many of the village's nineteenth-century landmarks became a memory.

Suffern's unemployment rate during the Great Depression was relatively slight compared to some communities. In 1939 Suffern had a stable population with less than 6% of residents in homes there under ten years.

Following World War II, the era's technological advances brought new industry and individuals along with the New York State Thruway. The Thruway, like the railroad of a hundred years earlier, was a key factor in creating the second largest growth period in village history. Once again the demand for houses exceeded the supply. During the 1950s the Fox estate was annexed and by the 1960s the Bon Aire and Stonegate neighborhoods were added to Suffern neighborhoods. In 15 years the population increased by more than 50%.

Some enterprising Suffern boys are open for business in this 1930s photo.
Courtesy of Kenneth Kral.

Several destructive fires in the downtown area during the 1960s and the growth of shopping centers along Route 59 helped create a decline in the village's aging business district. Large developments in neighboring communities where land was more abundant resulted in a shift of Ramapo's greater population away from the older villages. Between 1985 and 1990, about half of Suffern's population changed residences. Many of these were longtime residents who were relocating to warmer climates.

While Suffern's growth had slowed by this time, the 1980s and 1990s brought a new chapter in village history. Young families seeking the comfort and security of village life claimed older houses and revitalized neighborhoods. A partnership between municipal government and business leaders provided the commercial district with a facelift. The establishment of a village historical museum and the commemoration of the village centennial led to a rediscovery of the community's backyard heritage and provided a sense of place for newcomers. The railroad continued to play an important role for the modern commuter.

A time capsule of the village's earlier heyday is its landmark business district; from the northern entrance and the distinctive Comesky Block, to the Lafayette Theatre, opposite the site of John Suffern's tavern and the last of the county's grand movie houses: a reflection of what was and what will be in the twenty-first century.

Kenneth Kral

Tappan

From the 1927 *Rockland County Red Book:* Tappan—population 900—The name of the village is derived from the Tappan Indians (that spelling is found on maps as early as 1675), which occupied a territory south of the Ramapaughs, extending west as far as Monsey, and south as far as Staten Island. On the site of the present village were the crossroads of travel of Indian tribes of the region, to and from Staten Island which appears to have been a neutral trading ground, and east-west, for such traffic that used the Hudson River.

Tappan was the center of general staff activities of the Continental armies during the War of Independence because it was the village farthest south to which the American forces dared to come, between the Lower Ferry at Sneden's Landing (the present Palisades) and the Upper Ferry (King's Ferry) at Tomkins Cove.

Tappan was the first village to be organized in the whole region between the present New Jersey line and Albany; indeed it was the center of the first region settled by whites in New York State outside of Manhattan, and for many years the site of the first and only school in Orange County which then included the present Rockland. It was the county seat until it was moved to New City in 1774.

An historical reminiscence is the '76 House, where Major André was held prisoner until he was executed and buried a one-quarter mile west. The Tappan Reformed Church is the oldest organization in the county, dating from 1694.

Tappan's age is showing in this illustration in an 1887 issue of *Harper's Bazaar.*   JSC

Postcard of Washington Avenue, Tappan, c. 1905.
JSC

The funeral procession of the former chief of the fire department, Robert Jones, c. 1900, passing the 76 House (right).   Photo donated by Tommy Quinn to the OTM.

Thiells

From the 1927 *Rockland County Red Book:* One mile west of Haverstraw. The origin of the village dates from the Methodist meetings held by a circuit rider at the house of a farmer named Thiells. The first store was opened and the first church edifice erected in 1835.

Tomkins Cove

From the 1927 *Rockland County Red Book:* Tomkins Cove—population 1,300—Five miles north of Haverstraw. The beginnings of the village and of its main industry dates from 1838 when Calvin Tomkins and his brother Daniel purchased about 20 acres of land underlaid with rock suitable for burning along the river shore for the purpose of making lime. A village grew up around the works and when the post office was opened it was naturally called both by the name of the founder of the village, and its location, in a cove north of Stony Point promontory.

At the southern limits of the village was the old King's Ferry, called the Upper Ferry during the War of Independence, which played a very great role in maintaining communication between the north and south armies.

Dan Tomkins and the Tomkins house in 1988. Photo by John Scott.

Circa 1900 postcard of the Tomkins Cove quarry.

JSC

Upper Nyack

At the time of the Revolution, there were only six farms in the Upper Nyack hamlet. After the war, Major John and Captain Aurie Smith opened a quarry that produced much of the sandstone used in Rockland's Dutch-style homes. Shipbuilding also became a major industry.

In 1872, the village of Upper Nyack was incorporated to avoid being a small part of the large community of Nyack, also intending incorporation.

During the 1920s, the now called Julius Peterson shipyard built custom yachts for wealthy patrons and during WWII built crash boats similar to P.T. boats.

From the Hook to Nyack, a distance of about one mile, North Broadway contains an unusual architectural diversity of elegant homes and sumptuous estates as well as more modest dwellings of varied and interesting styles, some of early nineteenth-century vintage. The lands extending to the waterfront became especially appealing to yachtsmen during the era of the gilded age.

Early 1900s postcard of Hook Mountain. JSC

The late nineteenth century and first few decades of the twentieth century brought on an affluent period of a surging economy, especially in the mercantile class of nouveaux riches with a desire for spacious mansion-style homes. There was no income tax, except for a short interval during World War I. Low-cost labor for construction and maintenance was in plentiful supply, as was domestic help of cooks, maids, nurses, chauffeurs, etc., necessary to service the large estates.

Numerous examples of these show-place houses were scattered throughout Rockland, with an unusual concentration of them on both sides of North Broadway in Upper Nyack, where there was a dramatic transition from the old family farms to the new arrivals.

John Scott

360

Valley Cottage

The Valley Cottage. Photo by John Scott.

From the 1927 *Rockland County Red Book:* Valley Cottage—population 800—Valley Cottage is 27 miles from New York City on the West Shore Railroad; a community of commuters, professional men, artists and writers. The first known resident of the locality was a John Ryder, who had a large farm comprising all or most of the area of the present school district. The name of the village dates from a meeting held just before the opening of the West Shore railway station, in 1887. The residents assembled in the school room, unable to agree upon another name, decided that it should be that of the house nearest the station, "that cottage in the valley," and as it did not have any name of its own, the conclusion was that the station should be called Valley Cottage.

Another version has it that the origin of the Cottage part of the village name was given because of a famous trotting horse, Cottage Maid, owned by Ed Green, who then lived in the brown sandstone house and owned the land where the station, the Marcus store and other buildings stand. The post office at first opened in the station, in 1892, but was shortly afterwards transferred to the store.

1892: Kearney's Meat Market (of Congers) wagon at the Valley Cottage general store and post office. The two small children at the far left are Arthur and Lillie Hickey. JSC

Viola

An oft-repeated story is that Viola was named after a baby girl born at the nearby county almshouse (now the site of Rockland Community College). Irma Dempster (1895-1991), who grew up in Viola and was related to the Young family living there, claimed that Viola was actually named for the daughter of her great-uncle Charles Young. The notion of Viola being named after some obscure child rather than a member of a prominent local family was to her preposterous. She very likely was right, but which story captured the imagination and remained in people's memories?

Marianne B. Leese

Wesley Hills

The village of Wesley Hills was incorporated in 1982. The population at the end of the twentieth century resembled that of the larger county in regard to the length of residency of its citizens. Most oldtimers of the village trace their arrival to the 1960s and 1970s. More than 80% of the homes were constructed after 1960.

The newness of the village institutions and housing developments disguises one of the older sections of Rockland County. A journey along the village's old country roads takes the traveler past unadorned landmarks, memorials to village pioneers.

The village was named after the Wesley Chapel district and the Ramapo hills. The Wesley Chapel was constructed in 1829 by one of the oldest Methodist congregations in Rockland County. The church was built largely through the efforts of Rev. James Sherwood. The Sherwood family also operated one of the earliest industries in the area, a cotton batting factory. Other mills and factories populated the village, many utilizing the waterpower of the Mahwah River.

The tiny crossroads hamlets of the nineteenth century often reflected the name of the miller. Sherwoodville near the Wesley Chapel was named after Rev. James Sherwood and his descendants. Furmanville was where Furman had a sawmill near the junction of Lime Kiln Road and the Haverstraw Road. At the opposite end of Lime Kiln Road at its junction with Route 306 was a limekiln. Generations of the Forshay family produced an enormous quantity of cigars on Forshay Road.

The discovery of Rockland County as a tourist mecca in the late nineteenth and early twentieth centuries provided Wesley Hills with its share of summer residents. The village, however, was a little harder to reach than some villages in Ramapo. Visitors had to take a train to Suffern or Monsey or travel by boat to Haverstraw and then journey overland to Wesley Hills.

Some boarding houses existed, but most people who came to stay annually built their own permanent residences. Many of these manufacturing executives and professionals were sportsmen lured by the Ramapo hills and concept of the gentleman farmer. The locations of some of these estates is evidenced by the remaining stone pillars along the Haverstraw Road.

Wesley Hills changed little during the first half of the twentieth century. Residents generally made weekly shopping trips into Suffern to pick up needed supplies unavailable in the neighborhood. One unique feature of the community was the small Kakiat Airstrip that existed on Haverstraw Road during the 1920s and 1930s.

The idea of creating their own village government was conceived as a way to rein in what many felt was uncontrolled development of their neighborhoods.

Kenneth Kral

West Haverstraw

West Haverstraw was incorporated as a village in 1883 and includes the hamlet of Garnerville. The first president was Adam Lilburn and the population was 1,602. In the year 2001, the approximate population of West Haverstraw was 9,183, including 3,281 families. Unique to the village is the existence of two post offices, Garnerville and West Haverstraw.

West Nyack

From the 1927 *Rockland County Red Book:* West Nyack—population 700—Three miles west of Nyack Village; one-half mile west of Central Nyack.

West Nyack is really two hamlets; Clarksville and Mont Moor, the former being the older, formerly called Oblenis, from a Dutch yeoman who acquired land on part of which the West Shore station now stands. At the time of the opening of the Nyack Turnpike, in 1828, the name Oblenis Corners was given to the whole locality, including Mount Moor, but it was changed to Nyack Turnpike and later to West Nyack, at the opening of the post office. The crossroads, which for a time gave the name Oblenis Corners to the village, are now called the Four Corners.

A historical reminiscence of the region is the last trial of a

A nineteenth-century view of the Clarksville Inn. JSC

362

witch in New York State, and probably in the United States, which took place little more than a century ago. West of the old Clarkstown church stood the cabin of widow Naut Kanif who had some knowledge of the medicinal value of herbs, and quite a good deal of understanding of human nature, and had effected some cures. That, with the fact that she had a son of a somewhat eccentric nature and a black cat, was sufficient to justify suspicion by her neighbors. Prominent citizens, men and women, in a secret meeting in a mill which stood at the corner of the road to Bardonia decided that the widow Kanif should be put to a test. She was to be thrown into the mill pond, tied hand and foot, and if she floated, she was unquestionably a witch; if she drowned, her innocence would be proclaimed. It was only when threatened with the law that her persecutors desisted and she was allowed to return to her cabin. The wheel and part of the wheel house of the mill where the trial took place are still standing adjoining the house of Louis Richard, just before the turning of the roads toward Germonds in the west, and the Belmont-Gurnee crusher in the east.

The Dutch Reformed Church of West Nyack is the Old Clarkstown Church, the third oldest in the county.

Circa 1900 postcard of the Four Corners in West Nyack. JSC

Special Thanks

Contributors of $250 or more:

John E. Bauer

Janet E. Brown

Frances H. Casey

Thomas F. X. Casey and Nancy Casey

Fred J. Cifuni, Sr.

Vincent J. Collins, M.D.

Kenneth W. & Johanna C. Conklin in memory of William Conklin

F. Gordon & Gail A. Coyle

Patricia and James W. Cropsey

Mrs. Frances Daly

Jan & Niles M. Davies

Catherine Dodge

Grant, Smith & Dassler, Inc.

Mr. Gregory Fisher, Precast Concrete Sales Co.

Cordelia Hamilton

Mr. & Mrs. F. J. Hoyer, Sr.

Jeffrey Keahon

Lois Katz

Albon Man, in memory of Harry J. Carman

Corinne McGeorge

Paul & Betty Melone, in memory of Charlotte Talman
and all her good works and her love of Wilfred.

Robert G. Requa

Dorothy Forni-Rusch

John Scott

Mr. & Mrs. Ray Stout, Jr.

Erskine Blauvelt van Houten, Jr.

Strasser and Associates, Inc.

Leonard Merril Kurz

Tappantown Historical Society

Generous grants were received from:

Library Association of Rockland County

Orange & Rockland Utilities, Inc.

New York State Senator Thomas P. Morahan

New York State Assemblyman Sam Colman

New York State Assemblyman Alexander Gromack

Index

Contributors of articles are not listed in the index unless their articles are autobiographical.
Names that appear in all capital letters are of Rocklanders killed in action in wars in the twentieth century.

Abel family, 346
ABLONDI, BRUNO, 169, 189
Ablondi's Bar, 98
Abraham, Lawrence, 84
ABRAMS, ROBERT L., 156
Ackerly, Everett, 9
Ackerson,Donald, 154
Adler, Paul, 299, 320, 321
Adler's saloon, 67
Adolph H. Schreiber Hebrew
    Academy, 195
Aetna Sewing Machine Company,
    99, 348
Aggarwal, Hemu, 315
Aggarwal, Sona, 314
AHLMEYER, HEINZ (JR), 218
Airmont, 231, 275, 282, 299, 325
Albany, N.Y., 52, 179, 180, 183,
    184, 258, 269, 271, 272, 303,
    348, 359
Albert, Jon L., 322
Albertus Magnus High School, 203,
    232, 294
Alden, Rabbi, 44
Aleno, Chuck, 169
Alexander Hamilton, 272
ALLEN, EDWARD, 156
Allendale, N.J., 59
Alleva, Joe, 255
Allison family, 92
Allison farm, 334
ALLISON, WALTER H., 156
Alms House, 198
Alonso, Janet, 322
Alpine, N.J., 52
American Aniline Products, 20
American Brake Shoe and Foundry
    Co., 59, 104
American Institute of Operatic Art,
    116
American Red Cross, 68
AMORY, EDWARD, 112, 156
Anaya, Calixto, Jr., 322
Anderson family, 92
Anderson, Elizabeth Knapp, 77
Anderson, Emily, 77
Anderson, Evan, 298
Anderson, Maxwell, 95, 97, 121,
    160, 166, 266
Anderson, Stephen, 86
André, Major John, 98, 359
Andreas, Christine, 266
ANDREW, WALTER E. (JR), 218
Andrews, George, 298
ANDREWS, JOHN R., 156
Annie's Snack Shack, 319

Anthony, Caroline, 142
Appel, Stanley, 139
Arden Farms, 127
Arietta, Wil, 169
Arnell, Vic, 266
Arnold, Benedict, 98
ARRANCE, EDWIN S., 156
Artopee, Henry, 93
Arts Council of Rockland, 210
Aryee, Japhet, 322
Ashcroft, Jim, 232
Asian community, 314, 315
Atkins, Willie, 27
ATTENA, LOUIS F., 156
Atterbury, Harold, 113
Atwood, Harry, 50-52
Auerbach, Percy, 195
AUGENBLICK, IRA, 189
Austin, Warren, 109
Averbach, Max, 61
Avery, Gilbert, 162
AVERY, WILLIAM H., 156
Avon Products Inc., 5, 59, 104, 127,
    357
Babcock family, 82
Babcock, Caroline Lexow, 69-71,
    242
Babcock, Harry, 203
Babcock, Moses, 10, 11
Babcock, Philip, 6, 71
Bacall, Lauren, 233
Bacheller, Bob, 93, 112
Bacheller, Elaine, 112
BACKELIN WALTER, 156
Bacon, Charles, 73
Bader, Louis, 61
Bailey family, 284
Bailey, Pearl, 149
Bailey-Graff, Debbi, 223
Baileytown, 126
Baileyville, 283
Baird, William, 241
Bais Medrish Elyon, 162
Baker family, 329
Baker, Bertram, 226
Baker, Dick, 173
Baker, Norman, 128, 129, 173
BAKER, PHILIP T., 189
Ball, Edward, James & Thomas, 192
BALLAR, CHARLES, 156
Bamberger's, 207
Bang, Elsie, 118
Baracks, Clarence, 119
Bardin Hotel, 119
Bardon, John, Phillip & Conrad, 327

Bardonia, 121, 139, 294, 306, 311,
    327, 363
Barker farm, 49
Barker School, 210
Barnard College, 70
Barnes, Ivy, 354
BARNES, JOHN W., 156
Barney's Restaurant, 175
Baron, Sandy, 266
BARRETT, CHARLES W., 156
Barrymore, John, 265
Bartine, G. Wilson, 128
Baryshnikov, Mikhail, 266
Bates, Don L., 92
BATES, ROBERT M., 218
BATES, ROBERT T., 156
BAUER, ROBERT E., 218
Baugh, Barbara, 230
Baum Brothers, 73, 118
Baum family, 44
BAUMAN, EUGENE, 66
BAUMEISTER, RAYMOND, 156
Bayard Lane, 130, 131, 132
Bear Mountain, 31, 49, 101, 113,
    116, 118, 127, 137, 166-168,
    183, 195, 272, 275, 283, 284
Bear Mountain Bridge, 49, 50, 113,
    179
Bear Mountain Inn, 31, 167, 191,
    221
Beard, Dan, 83
Beard, Mr., 115
Beaver Pond Creek, 49
Beaver Pond, 126
Becraft, Ron, 169
Bedle, Alonzo, 3
BEEDON, JOHN W., 156
Begbie, George, 128
Bel-ans, 5, 36, 344
Bell & Co., 36
Bellaver, Harry, 266
Benmosche, Ari, 308
Benmosche, Robert, 308
Benny, Jack, 149, 211, 212
Benson, Charles, 73
Benson, Jane, 14
Benson, Ned, 238
Benson, William, 3, 11
Bergen County, N.J., 39, 149, 191,
    194, 328
Berger, Benjamin, 321
Berger, Thomas, 266
Bergman, Ray, 136
Bernard, Dr. Pierre, 25, 110, 111,
    118
BERNTSEN, ROBERT, 218

Beth Am Temple, 220
Betsy Rose Estates, 186
Beveridge Island, 127
Beveridge, Dr., 127
Bialkin, Dr. George, 119-121
Bialkin, Essie, 119
Bierman, Michael, 299
Biograph Company, 83
Birchwood Day Camp, 347
Birchwoods, 221
Bitzer, Billy, 83
Blacker, Lena, 127
Blacker, Meyer, 127
Blackout of 1965, 213
Blauvelt, 10, 13, 18, 21, 35, 61, 62,
    70, 81, 113, 142, 186, 208, 230,
    258, 328, 343, 353
Blauvelt, Judge Cornelius, 35
Blauvelt family, 61, 174, 340
Blauvelt Free Library, 35
Blauvelt Rifle Range, 61
BLAUVELT, CHARLES R., 66, 76
Blauvelt, James, 348
Blauvelt, Martha, Ettie & Alice,
    14
BLAUVELT, RAYMOND 66
Blizzard of 1888, 18
Blizzard of 1947, 167
Blue Hill Golf Club, 113
Blue Hill Plaza, 237, 238
BOCES, 282, 299, 327
Bockar, C., 338
Bogartown, 349
Bogert family, 340
Boggs, Bill, 266
Bogle, Wes, 112
Bohnel, Jay, 203
Bokar Lake, 338
Bolack, Josh, 169
BOLFORD, CHARLES, 156
Bolin, Ruth, 318
Boll, Barbara, 298
Boll, Bobby, 265
Boll, Stanley, 298
BOLLINGER, J. NEWTON, 156
Bonniwell, Fred, 238
Bonomolo, Dominick, 99
Bonomolo, Jerry, 203
BOORMAN, STANLEY H., 156
Borakove, Richard, 282
Borsodi, Myrtle Mae Simpson, 130
Borsodi, Ralph, 130-132
Bosco, Richard, 322
Bosio, Fr. August, 196
Bott, John, 129
Boulderberg Manor, 175
Bouton, Ed, 99, 209
BOWLES, FRED L, 66
Boy Scouts, 113, 248, 298
BOYAJY, HENRY, 156
Braden, Ralph, 87, 248

Bradley, Stephen R., Sr., 8, 32, 344
Bradley, Stephen, Jr., 32
BRADNER, VINCENT J., 156
Brady, William, 76
Branche, Marvin, 203
Bratton, Jack, 112
Brattleboro, Vermont, 32
Braunsdorf family, 347
Braunsdorf, Julius, 33, 99, 248, 347
Brechbiel, Jim, 255
Bremer, Fred, 172
BREMS, JAMES F., 156
BRENTNALL, LAWRENCE, 156
Brewer Fire Engine Co, 338
Briarcraft Inc., 5
brick industry, 4, 7, 41, 105, 126,
    132, 165, 334
Brien, Albert, 118
Brill, Steve "Wildman", 284
Brims, Belton, 263
Brinks robbery, 262, 264, 329
Britnell, W.H., 190
Broadway Theater, 211
BRONICO, ANTHONY J., 156
Brook School, 161, 162
Brooklyn, 44, 88, 115, 119, 162,
    167, 174, 220, 226, 236, 244
Brooklyn Bridge, 49
Brooklyn Dodgers, 168
BROOKS, ANDRE M., 218
Brooks, Napoleon, 3
Brookside Ice Cream Parlor, 76
Brophy, Mrs. James A., 139
BROPHY, RICHARD, 66
BROQUIST, STEPHEN A., 218
Brown, Abraham, 15
Brown, Darryl, 255
BROWN, JAMES, 156
Brown, James J., 59
Brown, Jim, 203
BROWN, RICHARD C., 218
BROWN, ROBERT A., 189
Brown, Roger, 232
Brown, Sam, 345
BROWN, SYLVESTER O., (JR),
    156
Brown, Waverly "Chipper", 262
Brown's Diner, 167
Brown's Hotel, 327
Brucker, Dan, 197
Bruckner, William, 133
Brundage, Lew, 203
Brush, Brad, 113
BRUSH, RICHARD B., 218
Bryan, William Jennings, 357
Buck, Walton, 213
Budke, George, 35
Buffalo, N.Y., 183, 184, 332
Bulson family, 284
Bulsontown, 126
BUNTING, WILLMAR C., 156

Burda, Helen & Stanley, 220
Burghardt, Robert, 158
BURLEIGH, PHILIP T., 156
BURLEIGH, RICHARD C., (JR),
    156
Burns, David, 10
Burns, Johnny, 93
Burns, Nathaniel, 262
BURRIS, FREDERICK, 218
Burstyn, Ellen, 266
Butler, Naomi, 215
Butz, Siegfried W., 87
Byard, Babe, 115
BYRNE, JOHN B., 156
Byrnes, Hildegarde, 112
Cable television, 289
Cadig, Bill, 231
Caldwell, Charles, 208
Caldwell's Landing, 175, 337
California Perfume Company, 5, 59,
    104, 357
Call Hollow, 141
CAMERON, ALEXANDER, 156
Camp Bluefields 61, 62, 328
Camp Gen. Louis Blenker, 120
Camp Hill, 141, 233, 339
Camp Kilmer, 148
Camp Shanks, 62, 123, 146, 148,
    151, 152, 154, 167, 172, 173,
    195, 298, 344, 346
Camp Upton, 64
Camp Venture, 13, 219
Camp Wadsworth, S.C., 63
Campbell, Bill, 9
Campbell, Clarence, 27
CAMPBELL, FLORENCE WILDA,
    66
Campbell, Hilda Smith, 27
Campbell, John, 10
Campbell, R. Todd, 291
Campbell, W.N. & H., 86
Canada, 27, 43, 44, 133
Caniff, Milton, 97, 114, 266
Cann, Jim, 276
Canty, Tom, 232
CAPUTO, LOUIS, 189
CARDILLO, JOSEPH P., 156
Carle, T. Craig, 271, 272
Carnegie, Betty & Jerry, 119
Carnera, Primo, 112
CARNOCHAN, GOVERNEUR,
    156
CARNOCHAN, GOVERNEUR,
    (JR), 156
Carpenter, Dr. Cameron, 100
Carr Pond Mountain, 126
Carroll, Charles, 104
Carroll, Madeleine, 266
Casarella, Joe, 302
Celery farm, 92
Centenary, 28

Central Nyack, 89, 199, 227, 311, 329, 362
CERVENE, SAM J., 189
Challenger Learning Center, 282
Chapin, Tom, 266
Chapman, Augusta, 74
Chappaqua, N.Y., 29
Chestnut Ridge, 94, 299, 329
Chiang, Alex, 322
Cholwill, Joshua, 337
Christian Herald Children's Home, 11, 12
Christian, Buddy, 160
CHRISTIAN, CLAUDE, 156
Christie family, 126
Christie, Bill, 114
Christie, Dave, 104
Christie, James, 114
Christie, John D., 11
Christie, John, 114
Christie, William, 114
Christie's Airport, 114, 154
Chromalloy Research and Technology, 251
Chrystenah, 11, 27, 334
Church, Alice Huested, 142
Church, B.W., 51
Ciabattoni, Annie, 319
Cienfuegos, Cuba, 3
Civil Defense, 114
Civil War, 3, 7, 15, 35, 36, 38, 69, 133, 242, 318, 351
Claire, Ina, 266
Clancy, Don, 232
CLARK, GEORGE W., 66, 156
CLARK, JOHN H., 156
Clark, Robert, 92
Clarke, Bothwell, 96
Clarke, Mary Mowbray, 94, 96, 138, 180, 266
Clarkstown, 4, 11, 86, 93, 97, 163, 172, 173, 179, 181, 192, 198, 201, 203, 208, 215, 231, 232, 241, 255, 274-276, 284, 288, 289, 297, 298, 313, 316, 318, 324, 327, 329, 330, 339, 340, 341, 363
Clarkstown Country Club, 25, 103, 110, 111, 118, 329, 356
Clarkstown High School, 318
Clarkstown Parks Board and Recreation Commission, 318
Clarkstown Reformed Church, 14, 316, 363
Clarksville Inn, 28, 362
Clarksville, 362
Clausen, Elton, 231
Clausland Mountain, 284
Clearwater, 240
Cleary, Anna, 56
Cleary, William V., 56, 57, 147

Cleveland, Grover, 17
Clinton, Bill, 321
Clinton, Hillary, 321
Clune, Maureen, 193
Coachlight Dinner Theatre, 260
Coan, C. Arthur, 70
Coatti, Aldino & Jean, 164
Cobb, Rev. Eben, 35
Cobbett, Leon, 128
Coca, Dr. A.F., 251
COE, ROBERT W., 156
Cohen, Myron, 266
Cold Spring, N.Y., 50
Cole, Rev. David, 35
COLLINS, JOHN H., 156
COLLINS, RICHARD R., 156
Collins, Tom, 232
Collins, Tony, 115
Colman, Sam, 306
Colsey, Francis, 118
Colton, Dr. Merrill, 208, 209
Columbia University, 70, 133, 136, 150, 151, 197, 236, 301, 312, 346
Columbian Engine Company #1, 19, 59, 164
Columbian Exposition, 17, 18
Comesky Block Fire, 59, 60
Comesky, Frank, 59, 60, 118
Comesky, Fred, 56
Conace, Emma Burnett, 128
Conace, Mary, 128
Concklin farm, 298
Concklin, Irving, 141
Concklin, Isabelle, 141
Conger, Abraham, 330
Conger, Abram B., 92
Congers, 13, 43, 44, 49, 68, 70, 92, 93, 109, 112, 120, 125, 141, 154, 169, 173, 242, 243, 253, 257, 274, 297, 298, 306, 320, 330, 350
Congers High School, 298
Congregation B'nai Israel, 15
Congregation Shaarey Tifloh, 220
Congregation Sons of Israel, 15, 91, 220, 252, 299
Congregation Sons of Jacob, 15, 44, 299
CONKLIN, BERNARD, 218
Conklin family, 82, 284
Conklin, Jean & Raymond, 165
CONKLIN, JOSEPH P., 218
Conklin, Lucien, 274
Conklin, Mike, 294
Conklin, Mrs., 70
Conklin, Norman, 127
Conklin, Ramsey, 126
Conklin, Rich, 276
CONKLIN, ROBERT C., 156
CONLIN, PETER E., 218

CONLON, WILLIAM H., 156
Connolly, Regina, 154
Consiglio, Ralph, 169
Consolidated Edison, 18, 213, 311
Constantinovna, Vera, 310
CONWAY, MICHAEL, 66
COOK, ADOLPHUS, 66
COOK, HENRY M. (JR), 189
Cook, John D., 244
Cook, John E., 159
Cooke, Leonard, 226
COOPER, HIDLEY T., 66
Cooper, Jackie, 112
Copeland, Royal S., 143
Copland, Aaron, 345
Cordisco, Ralph, 109
Cornell University, 124, 142, 244, 251
Cornell, Harriet, 258
Cornell, Katharine, 96, 180, 266, 346
Cornish, Richard, 235
Corrado, Joe, 126
Corwin, Norman, 266
Coryat, Thomas, 215
Cosentino, Frank, 203
Costigan, John, 266
Costino, Joe & Tony, 128
Coughlin, John, 322
COVATI, JOSEPH F., 156
Coward, Noel, 345
COX, HOWARD L. (JR), 156
Cox, Monsignor James, 225
Coyle, John, 198
COYNE, WILLIAM M., 156
CRANDALL, WILLIAM C., 156
CRAVEN, JOSEPH A., 66
CRAWFORD, CONRAD, 66
Crawford, Dorothy Hand, 105
Crawford, Gilbert H., 36
Crawford, Morris, 70
Cropsey family, 174
Cropsey farm, 174, 298
Cropsey, James, 172
Cropsey, Pat Deacon, 174
Croton, N.Y., 54, 113
Crowther, Welles, 322
Crum, Fred, 134, 135
Crumbie's Glen, 30
Cucchiara, Dominick, 99
Cucchiara, John, 98
Cucchiara, Mary, 99
Cucchiara, Pete Spooner, 99
Cullen's, 191
Cumming, John W., 347
Cunningham, Arthur, 227
Cunningham, Rachel, 227
Cuomo, Matilda, 219
Curtiss, Elmer H., 133
Cutler, Henry, 115
Cutler, Otis, 59

Cyler, Henny, 173
Czechoslovakia, 140
D'Auria, Jerry, 109, 192
D'Auria, Joe, 203
D'Auria, Pat, 109
D'Auria, Pete, 109
Dahl, Arlene, 159, 266
Dahl, Walter, 118
D'Allara, John, 322
Daly, James, 211
Daly, Richard, Tyne, Tim, 266
Dalzell, George, 255
Danbury Fair, 89
DANIEL, ANDREW J., 218
Daniel, Rev. Wilbur, 220, 225
DANIELS, JOSEPH D., 156
Danko, Steve, 128
Dapolito, Kathy Miller, 255
Darby, Rev. Thomas, 219
Darsche, Henry, 87
Dater, George W., 10
Davenport, Millia, 266
David B. Roche Volunteer Fire
    Company, 19
Davidson, Mary, 70
Davies, Arthur B., 30, 297
Davies, Arthur D., 297
Davies, Erica, 31
Davies family, 297, 298
Davies farm, 297
Davies Lake, 173
Davies, Dr. Lucy, 30, 31, 140
Davies, Niles, 31, 297, 298
Davies, Niles, Jr., 31, 215
Davies, Sylvia, 31
Davies, W.D., 50
Dawson, Frank, 203
Day, Mr. & Mrs. Kevin, 231
Dayliner, 272
DE BEVOISE, WILLIAM, 156
DE FREESE, SAMUEL W., 189
DE GROAT, ROLAND, 189
DE LONGIS, VINCENT, 156
Deane, Mike, 255
DeBaun family, 340
DEBAUN, HENRY, 66
DeBaun, Mrs. Denton, 68
Debevoise, Sarah & William, 319
DeBevoise's Corner, 10
DEC, ALEXANDER, 156
Dechelfin, Harold, 109
DeChelfin, Samuel, 118
Decker, Bill, 331
DeClark, Daniel, 340
DeClark, James, 339, 340
DEDERER, ELLSWORTH H, 66
Deed, Marion, 128
Deed, Robert, 128
DEES, TATIANA, 295
DEGRAW, JOHN HENRY, 66
DeGroat, Ron, 202

DEL REGNO, VICTOR R., 156
DELLORO, JOSEPH A., 156
Dellwood Country Club, 84
Demarest family, 340
Demarest, J. Orville, 118
Demarest, Dr. Sylvester, 38
Dembnicki, Harry, 169
DEMEOLA, RAYMOND W., 218
Deming, McDonald, 112
DeMontreville, Leon, 327
Denning, William, Sr., 334
deNoyelles, Dan, 25, 69, 105, 283,
    331
deNoyelles, Helen, 283
deNoyelles, Pauline, 120
DePatto, Frank, 169
DEPATTO, LOUIS A., 156
DePew, C.M., 18
Dermody, Jack, 317
DeVoe, William, 235
Dewey, Gov. Thomas, 143, 158,
    183, 264, 311
Dexter Folder Company, 5, 87, 99,
    248, 348
Dexter Press, 109
Dexter, Talbot, 5
DICK, FREDERICK W., 156
Dickey, George, 69
Dickey, Judge, 8
DIEDERICH, HAROLD M., 189
Diehl, Sylvia, 298
Dillon, Irvin, 181
Dillon, Kevin, 231
DiMaria, Frank, 318
DINGMAN, BENNY L., 156
Dingman, Dr. James A.., 215
Dingman, Dr. John C., 214
dinosaurs, 258
Dixson, T/Sgt., 152
D'LOUGHY, CHARLES, 66
DOANE, PAUL, 156
Dobbs Ferry, N.Y., 52, 53, 179, 345
Dobbs, William, 52
Dodge, John Lanphere, 36, 344
Doellner, Viola, 119
Dolan, William, 154
Doller, Ethel, 169
Dominican Congregation of Our
    Lady of the Rosary, 12
Dominican Republic, 137
Dominican Sisters, 197
Dominicans, 251
Donaldson, Michael A., 65, 118
Donaldson, Thomas, 118
Donnellan, Jerry, 217
Doodletown, 126, 127, 136, 195,
    283
Dorcas Society, 14
Dormann, Edward, 158, 159
DORNBURGH, EDMUND, 156
DORSEY, WILLIAM T., 218

Dos Passos, John, 266
Douglass,Mabel, 248
DOWD, ROBERT J., 156
Dowling, Mother Dominic, 12
Downs, Hugh, 233
DOYLE, ABRAM, 66
Doyle, Joseph, 60
Doyle, William, 64
DOYLE, WILLIAM, 66
DRAB, ALEXANDER, 156
DRAKE, JAMES E., 156
Drescher, Bill, 169
Dress Barn, 5
Drew, Louis, 296
Driscoll, Don, 255
Drive-in movie theaters, 114, 178,
    192
Drummond, Steve, 232
DUCEY, JOHN J., 156
Duchess County, 73
DUGAN, THOMAS, 66
Duggan, Thomas, 64
DUHAIME, LOUIS S., 189
Dumkin's Blacksmith Shop, 80, 345
Dunderberg, 17, 18, 137, 175, 334,
    337
Dunlop Silk Mills, 4, 5
Dunlop, John, 4
DUNN, HERBERT B., 156
Dunnigan, Frank & Maggie, 291
Dunnigan, Jack, 292
Dunnigan's Bar and Grill, 291
Durant Station, 173
Durant, 331
Durant, Thomas, 331
Durante, Jimmy, 149
Duryea's farm, 94, 223
Dutch Garden, 138
Dutch Reformed Church, 327, 363
Dutcher, Arthur, 73
DUVALL, HAROLD L., 66
Dykstra, Allen, 210
E.J. Korvettes, 127, 249, 340
Eagle Confectionary, 171
EAKINS, ARCHIE, 156
EARL, WILLIAM S., 156
East Ramapo, 275
Easter, Hezekiah, 227
EASTON, JOHN J., 156
Eberlin, Captain B., 64, 65
Eberling family, 119
Eberson, Major Drew, 148
Eckerson brickyard, 41
Eckerson's Field, 85
Eckoff, Dr. William, 39
Edwards, Bessie, 64, 65
EDWARDS, DONALD, 156
Edwards, Ron, 232
EDWARDS, WALTER, 156
Egyptian House, 290
EICKOFF, RAYMOND, 66

Eisenhower, Dwight D., 151, 301, 306
Elbaum, Jacob, 321
Eldenbaum, David, 44
ELENEL, AMSY, 156
Ellington, Emory, 227
Ellis, Charles, 266
ELLIS, MELVIN T., 156
ELMENDORF, FRED, 156
Elms Hotel, 119
Elson, George, 43, 44
Emeline, 54, 334
Emerson, Fred, 208
Emerson, Maryann, 166
Empire Engine Company, 2
Empire Hose Company #1, 19
ENGLE, ARCHIBALD J., 66
English, Dick, 298
Ennis, Elwood, 311
Eppie's Grove, 139
Erickson, Gene, 203
Erickson, Jane, 221
Erickson, Nick, 3
Erie Canal, 183
Erie Railroad, 9, 15, 28, 29, 37, 59, 60, 99, 148, 158, 171, 174, 183, 185, 193, 325, 332, 337, 339, 344, 348, 351, 354, 357
Etna Sewing Machine Company, 99
Eureka House, 244
Evans Park Elementary School, 210
Ewing, Maurice, 300, 301
Excelsior brickyard, 41
FAIRBAIRN, SETON H., 156
Faist, William P., 125
Fajen, Henry & John, 119
FALDERMEYER, HAROLD, 218
Fales, Charlie, 119
Falkenberg, Charles, 15
Falkenberg's, 61
Farley, Elizabeth Finnegan, 107
Farley, James A., 106-108, 147, 179, 221, 334
Farley, Thomas, 81
Fassler, Frank M., 110, 111
Faulk, Captain James, 13, 109
Favuzza, Bernard, 322
Fee, George, 267
Feeney family, 68
Feeney, James, 169
Fegan, Sean Bernard, 322
Felter Ice Company, 6, 27, 356
Felter, Dr. Robert, 100
FERGUSON, HAROLD, 66
Ferguson, Pat, 167
Fernekes, Henry, 87
FERRACANE, ANTHONY, 156
Ferrel, Jeffrey, 231
Ferretti, Ellen, 340
Ferris, Katherine, 70
Festa, Felix, 274, 275, 298

Festa, Mildred Andres, 298
Fibre Conduit Company, 32, 33
Figueroa, Ronaldo L., 137
Filleggi Dominick, 81
Finegan, Bill, 136
Finegan, Jim, 55
Fink, Mrs., 70
Finkelstein Memorial Library, 162, 170, 267, 279
Fiore, Mike, 322
Fioriti, Marjorie Anderson, 86
Fire Training Center, 20
First Presbyterian Church of Congers, 330
Fish, Rev. A.H., 70
Fisher Diagnostics, 249
Fishkin, Joseph, 209
Fitton, Margaret, 241
Fitzpatrick, Dr. Margaret, 197
Flagg, Ernest, 130
Flannagan, John, 266
Flannery, Walt, 108
Fleisher, Walter, 313
Fleisher, Zippy, 312
FLETCHER, LEE CHASE, 66
Flickinger, Carl M., 322
Flintkote Company, 33
FLOTARD, RAYMOND, 189
Flower, Governor R.P., 10
Floyd Bennett Air Field, 115
Flushing, 54
Flynn, Bernice, 274
Flynn, Rev. Leslie, 274
Flynn, William, 73
Focht, Jack, 283, 284
Foley, Thomas, 322
FONTAINE, GILBERT, 295
Fontaine, Lynn, 345
Ford, "Kig", 73
Ford, John, 84
Ford, Michael, 56, 118
FORMATO, CARMINE, 66
Forshay Cigar Factory, 5, 134
Forshay family, 362
Forshay, William, 134, 325
Fort Comfort, 47, 100
Fort Lee, N.J., 83
Fort Montgomery, 283
Fortmann, Dan, 109
Fortmeyer, Fred, 118
Foster, Mr., 19
FOURNIER, RICHARD E., 156
Fowler, Denton, 35
France, 63-65
Fredericks, Andrew, 322
Freilich, Robert, 236
French, Carroll, 96
Freyfogel, Ed, 73
FREYTAG, PETER D., 189
Friedan, Betty, 229, 242, 266
Friedan, Carl, 229

Friedman, Seymour, 225
Frishman, Rabbi Louis, 195, 299
Frohling family, 172
FROHLING, FREDERICK W, 66
FROMM, JOHN PAUL, 66
FROST, GERARD W., 156
Frost, Leroy, 51
Fuchida, Mitsuo, 235
Fujitsu Communications, 5
Furman, Steven, 322
Gabler, Fredric, 322
Gagan, Thomas, 41, 56, 57, 70, 234
GALGANO, JOHN J., 156
GALOWSKI, EDWARD J. (JR), 156
Gamboli, Dominic, 203
Gamboli, Nick, 109
Gamboli, Tony, Jr., 203
Gannon family, 284
Gannon, Priscilla, 275
Garden Hotel, 162, 164
Gardner, Helen, 84
GARDNER, WILLIAM HENRY, 66
Garland, Judy, 149
Garner, Thomas & James, 331
Garner, William, 19, 331
Garnerville, 4, 13, 19, 28, 35, 49, 69, 82, 137, 138, 141, 154, 208, 219, 221, 232, 251, 264, 268, 292, 331, 332, 362
Garnerville Holding Company, 4
Garrabrant, Mr., 19
Garrecht, George, 169
Garrison, Judge Samuel, 120
GARRISON, WILLIAM L., 218
GASSNER, HUGH J. (JR), 156
Gate Hill, 10, 78
GDULA, ANDREW, 156
Gebnor family, 99
Geddes, Barbara Bell, 211
Gehrig, Lou, 107
Geiger, Augustus, 87
Geist, J. Fred, 128, 129
Gemma, Tony, 203
Gen. Warren Emergency Company #2, 19
General Electric, 253
George Washington Bridge, 49, 54, 91, 118, 173, 179, 183
GERE, EDWIN E., 156
German Masonic Home, 118
German-American Bund, 120
Germany, 104, 112, 119, 125, 136, 147, 154
Germonds, 10, 121
Gettysburg, PA, 3
Gilbert, David, 262
Gilbert, Fidelia Forshay Coe, 134
Gilbert, Robert, 213
Giles, Tod, 276

Gillespie, S. Hazard, 269
Gillies brickyard, 41
GILLIES, JAMES F., 218
Gilman family, 345
Gilman, Rep. Benjamin, 320
Gilman, Charlotte, 70
Gilman, Winthrop, 35
Gilmore, Margalo, 266
Gindroz, Charles, 175
Ginley, John, 322
Giovannini, Fr. Ernest, 196
Giuliani, Rudolph, 294
Glassing, George, 118
Glickman, Anne, 317
Goddard Space Flight Center, 282
Goddard, Paulette, 141
GOEHRING, VALENTINE J. (JR), 156
Goetschius' ice pond, 28
Goetschius, Francis A., 83
Goetschius, Henry D., 11
Goldband, Leo, 292
Goldband's Army-Navy Store, 292
Goldberg, Joseph M., 290
Goldfinger, Murray, 139
Goldsmith family, 15
Goldsmith, Joe, 255
Goldstein, Alvin, 226
Goldstein, David, 321
Golf courses, 302
Good Samaritan Hospital, 36-40, 60, 194, 214, 248, 316
Gordon, Dr. Edmund, 216
Gordon, Grace, 236
GORDON, JOHN G., 66
GOSWICK, JESSE O., 156
GOTCHER, HAROLD C., 156
Gould, Edwin, 12, 118
Gould, Elliot, 211
Governor's Island, 52
Grable, Betty, 149
Grace Conservative Baptist Church, 235, 274
Graifman, David, 322
Grand View, 20, 27, 85, 95, 104, 125, 180, 181, 184, 242, 258, 269, 332, 333
Granirer, Martus, 313
Grant, Debbie, 276
Grant, John, 277, 320, 321
Grant, U.S., 2
GRANT, WALLACE E., 156
Grassy Point, 4, 11, 27, 28, 106-108, 291, 334
Gray, Joel, 211
Graziano, Dr. Fred, 215
Great Depression, 4, 7, 101, 103-106, 111, 116, 118, 119, 120, 127, 130-133, 137-139, 141, 218, 264, 300, 306, 319, 330, 332, 358

Great Suffern Fire, 59, 60
Greco, John, 115
Green Meadow Waldorf School, 94
GREEN, DAVID, 66
Green, Ed, 361
Green, Elizabeth, 52
Green, Frank, 35
GREEN, RALPH, 156
Greene, Ed, 108
Greene, Frank, 115
GREENE, FRANK A. (JR), 156
Greenwood Lake, 134
Gribetz, Kenneth, 262, 294
GRIFFIN, DANIEL, 156
Griffith, Aline, 153
Griffith, D.W., 83
Gromack, Alex, 306
Grossman, Bob, 232
GROSULAK, PETER, 156
Gruben, Rev. John, 318
Gruin, Fred, 131
Gschaar, Robert, 322
Guccione, Guy, 232
Guelich, Mr., 112
Gugliuzzo, Biagio, 138
Gunther, Arthur, 306
Gunther, Arthur Henry, Sr., 306
Gunty, Morty, 266
Gurnee family, 92
Gurnee, Harry, 10
Gwynne, Fred, 266
Gypsies, 88- 90
Hackensack & New York Extension Railroad, 9
Hackensack River, 27, 28, 122
Hadar, Elmer S., 180
Hadar, Mrs. Elmer, 180
HADDEN, HAROLD B., 156
Haddock, Roger, 76
Hadeler family, 99
Hadeler's Hardware, 99
Hader, Berta, 266
Hader, Elmer, 266
Haera family, 306
Haera, Frank, 296
Haerle, Dorothy, 55
Haerle family, 83
Haeselbarth, William, 35
HAGAN, ROBERT, 218
Hagon, Mike, 255
HAGUE, RAYMOND F.X., 156
Hahn, Fred, 169
Haig, General Sir Douglas, 63
Haines, Charlie, 9
Haitian community, 251, 252
Halbone, Walt, 108
Half Moon, 113
HALGREN, ALEX J., 156
Hall of Heroes, 318
Hall, Radcliffe, 125
Hall, Washington, 55

Hamilton, Dan, 64
HAMILTON, JAMES, 66
Hamilton, Walter, 73
Hand family, 105
Hand, William, 76, 148
HANDELMAN, IRWIN, 156
Handley, Sam, 113
Hannigan, Daniel J., 63, 64
HANNIGAN, DANIEL J., 66
Hannigan, William, 63
Hannon, Dana, 322
Hans, Father Nicholas, 91
Harding, Warren G., 87
Hargrove, Marion, 96, 97, 266
HARING, BERNARD F., 156
Haring, James, 344
Haring, William, 104
Harkness, Rebekkah, 266
Harniman, Ken, 231
Harper, Valerie, 266
HARRIGAN, GERARD J., 156
Harriman, Averell, 158, 182
Harriman, Edward, 31
Harriman Park, 31, 126, 183
Harriman, Mrs. Mary, 31
Harrimans, 242
Harrison, President Benjamin, 17
Harrison, Ray, 57
HART, MAURICE, 66
Hartel, Fred, 230
Hartman, Johanna, 6
Hartman, William, 6
Hartwell, Eddie, 115
HARTY, WILLARD, 156
HARTZ, JOSEPH E., 218
Harvey, Todd, 318
Hasbrouck, Dr. M.C., 340
Haskett, Margaret, 95
Hassett, Bryan, 232
Hastings-on-Hudson, 179
Hatzolah, 125
Haubner, Pete, 255
Havermale's, 211
Haverstraw, 4, 7-11, 15, 19, 20, 23, 25, 28, 35, 41, 43, 44, 48, 49, 54-56, 59, 63, 65-70, 72- 74, 77, 78, 81, 83-85, 89, 90, 92, 105-107, 109, 112, 118, 125, 126, 132, 133, 137-139, 141, 147, 159, 165, 167, 169, 172-174, 195, 197, 203, 204, 208, 221, 226, 227, 232, 234, 243, 244, 251, 252, 255, 258, 264, 268, 275, 281, 283, 289, 292, 295, 297, 299, 306, 307, 320, 324, 334, 335, 337, 339, 341, 355, 359, 362
Haverstraw Fire Department, 72
Haverstraw landslide, 41
Haverstraw Presbyterian Church, 335

Hayes, Helen, 96, 112, 125, 141, 150, 166, 171, 180, 182, 211, 265, 266, 290, 311, 312
Hearst, William Randolph, 114
Heaton, Maurice, 166
Hebrew Institute of Rockland County, 195
Hecht, Ben, 96, 112, 266
HECHT, FREDERICK, 156
HECK, CHARLES, 156
Hedges, Catherine M., 92
Hedges, Ira, 3
Hedges, Irene, 70
Hedges, Katherine Gibbons, 81
Hedges, Phineas, 11
Hegner, Bill, 9
Heider, Dot, 317
Heim, Raymond, 213
Heitman, Charles, 192
Hekker, Terry Martin, 168
Helen Gardner Picture Players, 84
Helen Hayes Hospital, 311, 312
Helen Hayes Performing Arts Center, 290
Helmke Meat Market, 119
Helmle, George, 51
Henderson, Elmer, 211
Henderson, Maryanne, 317
Henderson, Skitch, 266
Hendricksen, Gerrit, 328
Hendricksen, Miss, 69
HENION, WILLIAM H., 66
Henning, Rich, 313
Hepburn, Katherine, 265
Herbert family, 284
Herbert farm, 23
HERDMAN, WALTER L., 156
Herman, Dave, 231
Herndon, Lew, 265
Herrick, Christine Terhune, 24
Herriman Farm, 220
Herriman Farm School, 158
HERRING, WILLIAM, 189
Herzog, Harry, 91
Hess, H., 19
Hick family, 86
Hickes, A., 19
Hickey, Arthur & Lillie, 361
Hickory Hill, 151
High Tor, 68, 78, 96, 136, 137, 142, 270, 313, 334
Highland Hose Fire Company, 171
HIGINSON, VAUGHN L.D., 156
Hill, Frank, 95
Hillburn, 9, 28, 39, 40, 59, 60, 67, 70, 81, 108, 109, 161, 162, 183, 184, 195, 202, 275, 336
Hillcrest Community Hospital, 258
Hillcrest Fire Company, 336
Hillcrest, 184, 208, 252, 336
HINCHELWOOD, JAMES, 66

Hingle, Pat, 231, 266
HIRSCH, DAVID J., 156
HIRSCHBERGER, ALEX, 189
Hispanic community, 314
Historic Clarkstown Church, 316
Historical Hikers, 194, 195
Historical Society of Rockland County, 4, 111, 200, 201, 244-246, 290, 291, 328
Hoehn, Bill, 128
Hoey, Francis, 213
Hoey, Robert, 154
Hoffman, Dr., 100
Hoffman, Franklin, 155, 163
HOFFMAN, JOHN R., 156
Hoffman, Milton, 163
Hoffman, Rev. Walter, 159
Hogan, Billy, 93
Hogan, Dennis, 133
HOGAN, DENNIS (JR), 156
Hogan's Diner, 93, 260
Hoke, William, 118
HOKE, WILLIAM B., 156
Holbrook, Charles, 232, 288
Hollahan, Jerry, 93
Holland, Joe, 45
Hollings-Smith Co., 36
Hollister, Gloria, 115
Holmes, Ruppert, 266
HOLT, HAROLD B., 66
Honig, George, 61
Hook and Ladder Fire Company, 57
Hook Mountain, 8, 31, 50, 51, 101, 113, 118, 124, 128, 139, 171, 249, 343, 350, 360
Hoover, Herbert, 78, 80, 143
Hopf, Dr. John, 275
Hopf, John, Jr., 216
Hopper family, 340
Hopper, Art, 93, 231
Hopper, Edward, 234, 266
Hopper, Marion, 234
Horan, Frank, 203
HORN, CHARLES, 189
Horn, Fred, 179
HORN, ROBERT, 156
Hornick's, 137
HORTON, JOHN M. (JR), 218
Hostetter, Doug, 217
Hotel Elms, 119
Hotel Rockland, 59, 60
Hotel St. George, 52
Houseman, John, 97, 266
Houston, Kevin, 276
Houston, TX, 282
Howe, Louis, 107
Hoyt, Louis, 25, 48
Hubbard, Leonidas, 43, 44
Hubbard, Mina Benson, 43, 44
Hudson River, 6, 7, 11, 17, 27, 29, 30, 31, 34, 49, 50, 52, 54, 78, 83,

85, 91, 93, 110, 113, 116, 118, 119, 129, 137, 139-141, 148, 166, 168, 173, 175, 176, 179, 180, 183, 184, 193, 211, 214, 217, 253, 265, 267, 272, 311, 328, 330, 332-334, 337, 340, 343, 345, 348, 350, 351, 353, 356, 358
Hudson River Valley School, 340
Hudson Yacht and Boat Company, 51
Hudson, Josephine, 6
Hughes, Gov. Charles, 31, 36
Hughes, William, 44
Hull, Cordell, 147
Hunderfund, Horace, 230, 231
Hungry Hollow, 94
HUOTT, WILLIAM D., 156
HURD, DONALD W., 156
Hurricane Floyd, 302
Hurt, William, 266
Hutton Lumber Yard, 340
Hyde, Georgine, 279
Hyenga Lake, 163, 165, 354
HYMEN, SAMUEL, 66
IBM, 347
Ill, Fred, Jr., 322
Imwolde, Herman, 104
Indian Point, 311
Indian Rock, 285
Industrial Fair, 25
INGALLS, JOHN, 66
Inglese, Warren, 260
INGRAM, EDWARD L., 156
Insley, Albert Babb, 340
Insley, Henry Earle, 340
Iona Island, 3, 127, 254
Ireland, 63, 119, 242
Iserman, Henry, 354
Isley Brothers, 266
Israel, 242
Italy, 242
JACARUSO, FRANK, 218
JACARUSO, JOHN J., 66
Jackson Hose Company #3, 19
Jackson, Harry, 109
Jacobs, Martin, 169
Jagger, Mick, 266
Jain, Yudh, 322
Jakowenko, George, 232
James, Dr. Charles, 226
James, James E., 213
Jansky family, 141
Jansky, Edward, 141, 155
Japan, 147-149, 155, 215, 235
JASINSKI, VINCENT, 156
JAUSS, RAYMOND BOYD, 66
Jawanio, 299
Jean-Jacques, Bouchard, 251
Jenison, John, 232
Jenkins, William, 73

Jersey City, N.J., 9, 10, 29, 332
Jersey, George and Peter, 95
Jeudy, Farah, 322
Jewett family, 2
Jewett, Rev. A.D.L., 11
Jewett, Major E.D., 11
Jewett, Marion, 112
Jewish Community Center of Spring
   Valley, 91, 252
Jewish Society, 15
Jobson, Arthur, 198
Jobson, Grant, 85, 268
Joe Fisher's Livery Stable, 57
Johann, Zita, 16, 266
Johnson, Annie, Elizabeth & Ida, 24
Johnson, Arthur, 144
JOHNSON, CLAYTON L., 156
Johnson, Mrs. Erastus, 24
Johnson, Howard, 169
Johnson, John, 266
JOHNSON, KENNETH E., 156
JOHNSON, KENNETH R., 156
Johnson, Nina, 281
Johnson, Samuel W., 19
Johnsontown, 126, 275, 283, 337
Johnston, Virginia, 166
Jones Point, 126, 127, 175, 311, 337
Jones, Bill T., 266
Jones, Captain Ed, 96
Jones, Gloria Callen, 169
JONES, JAMES, 156
JONES, LOUIS E., 156
Jones, Muzz, 126
Jones, Robert McKean, 118
Jones, Dr. Willard, 216
JORDAN, EDWARD H., 156
Joseph, Robert, 322
Joyce, Jack, 128
Joyner, Seth, 302
June, Clarence,Jr., 126
Kadushen family, 172
Kakiat Field, 115
Kakiat, 337, 339, 347, 362
Kalmer Nyckel, 328
Kane, Jim, 169
Kane, Kevin, 255
Kanif, Naut, 363
Kanumalla, Dr. Venkat, 316
Kaplan family, 15
Kaplan, Ruth, 241
Kapusinsky, Gerald, 232
Kapusinsky, Hank, 203
Kaser, 278, 343
Kassel, Robert, 317
Katamah, 52
KAUFMAN, HAROLD J., 218
Kaye, Danny, 168
Kaye, Nora, 265
KEARSING, DONALD R., 156
Keenan, Arthur, 262
KEENAN, GREGORY, 189

KEENAN, RICHARD J., 156
Keesler's Market, 18
Kehilath Israel, 91
KEITH, KENNETH A., 218
KELEHER, CLARENCE, 156
KELLEY, JOHN J., 156
KELLEY, LEO E., 157
Kellin, Mike, 266
KELLY, EDWARD L., 157
Kelly, Jim, *262*
Kennedy, Anthony, 115
Kennedy, Fred, 100
Kennedy, Irving, 159
Kennedy, Jackie, 206
Kennedy, John F., 206, 217, 277,
   310
Kennedy, Robert., 224
Kennell, Henry, 345
Kent, S.R., 84
KERCHMAN, THEODORE, 157
KERNAN, MICHAEL R., 218
KERR, ALBERT W., 66
Kidder, Margot, 266
Kiefer, Dr. Raymond, 39
Kiernan, Florence, 306
KILE, JOHN T., 218
Kiley, Richard, 266
KING, LOUIS W., 66
King's Daughters Public Library, 35
Kings Highway, 86, 89, 136, 243
KINSMAN, WILLIAM P., 157
Kirchner, Karl, 346
Klee, John and Philip, 81
KLEIBER, ALFRED G., 157
KLEIN, JOHN R., 157
Klein, Phil, 152
Kliewe, Lou, 203
KLINE, HARRY L, 66
Klopchin, Joe, 169
Klopsch, Louis, 11
Knapp, Martin, 213
Knapp's Corner, 11
Knickerbocker Fire Engine Company
   #1, 19, 140
Knickerbocker Ice Company, 4, 6,
   19, 97
KNIGHT, HOWARD M., 157
Knight's Corner, 11
Knights of Columbus, 196, 226
Knights of Pythias, 166
Knudson, Nellie, 346
Koblick, Henry, 139
Koch, Henry, 51
Kolb, Hugo, 112, 199
Kolter, Roy, 9
Konagewski, Sandra, 230
Korea, 188, 189
Korn family, 138, 139
Kornbekke, Barbara & Janet, 221
Koster, John, 45
Kotlarsky, Rabbi Auremel, 278

Kovalsky, Vincent, 203
Kraft, Bob, 257
Kralik, James, 303
KRASHES, HAROLD D., 218
Krebs, CHARLES W., 66
Krell, Peter, 273
Ku Klux Klan, 16, 88, 120, 127
Kulhan, Jean, 230
Kulle, Henry, 191, 192
Kuruvilla, Cherian, 315
KWIECINSKI, JOHN W., 157
LA FRANCE, T.R. (JR), 157
LA POLLA, MARK O., 157
Labrador, 43, 44
LaCombe, Brother Andrew, 196
Laden, Michael, 337
Ladentown, 141, 337
Ladentown Methodist Episcopal
   Church, 141
LADERS, LEO B., 66
Lafayette Hotel, 244
Lafayette Theater, 300, 308, 309
LAGOIS, FRED G., 157
Laird Pharmacy, 73
Laird, Dr. Eugene, 28, 77
Lake Antrim, 184
Lake DeForest, 249, 261
Lake Welch Beach, 284
LAKE, ALPHEUS GEORGE, 66
Lakewood School, 253
Lamont, Florence, 301
Lamont, Thomas W., 180, 301, 346
Lamont-Doherty Earth Observatory,
   258, 300, 301, 346
Landa, Jack, 220
Landers, Audrey & Judy, 266
Lane, William, 73
LANG, JAMES W., 157
Langer, Blackie, 112
LANGER, PETER, 157
Lake, Tom, 273
Lappe, J.W., 350
Lappin, Peter, 196
Larkin, Eileen, 347
Larkin, Joseph, 242
Larson, Thomas, 332
Laskey, Harold, 198
Last Man's Club, 243
LAWLESS, VINCENT G., 157
Lawrence family, 345
LAWRENCE, GEORGE H., 157
Lawrence, Lydia, 201
LAYDON, ROBERT, 189
Lazio, Rick, 321
LE CLAIR, ALFRED J., 157
Leber, Mrs., 70
Leber, Robert, 70
Lee, Lt.Clyde, 152
Lederer, Charles, 112

Lederle Laboratories, 5, 86, 98, 99, 135, 155, 165, 172, 199, 208, 248, 251, 252, 319
Lederle, Dr. Ernest, 5, 98, 319
Lederman, Harold, 232
LEE, FRANCIS X.J., 157
LEE, IVAN R., 157
Lee, James, 11
Lee, Mrs., 70
Lee, Thomas, 70
LEGGETT, PAUL, 66
Lehman, Gov. Herbert, 118, 158, 180
Lehrfeld, Eric A., 322
Leiper, Rev. J.M., 70
Lemond, Mr., 108
Lenhart, Phil, 112, 128
Lennon, Brian, 262
Lent, Clarence, Jr., 213
LENTZ, ROBERT J., 157
Lenya, Lotte, 96, 97, 166, 266
Lepori, Lester, 109
Lespinasse, Peter, 15
LeTang, Henry, 266
Letchworth Village, 127, 164, 208, 219, 242, 299
Levine, Ervan, 109
Levison's Hill, 89
Levy family, 15, 164
Levy, Eugene, 199, 208, 219, 276, 289
Levy, Walter "Red", 203
LEWIS, CHARLES R., 157
Lewis, Orville, 112
Lexow, Clarence, 70
Liberty Street School, 20, 82, 170
Licata, Dr. Joseph, 299
LICHENSTEIN, GEORGE J, 66
Lieberman, Steve, 321
LIFRIERI, PAUL J., 218
Lilburn, Adam, 362
Lindbergh, Charles, 80, 114, 115
Lindsay, Mayor, 238
Linguanti, Anthony, 164
Linguanti, Charles, 164
Linguanti, Vincent, 164
LINGUANTI, VINCENT S., 157
Link, George, Jr., 179
LIPMAN, WALTER, 157
Lippsett, Laurence, 301
Livingston family, 284
Lock, Edward, 86
Lodico, John, 226
Loeb, Harold, 96
LOGATTO, BENJAMIN, 66
Logue, John, 51
Lomagno, Fr. John, 196
Lombardi, Vince, 168
Long Clove Railroad Tunnel, 243
Long Island, 28, 64, 93, 95, 115, 168, 208, 212, 238, 342

Long, Craig, 285, 309, 318
Longing, Laura (Petitus), 322
Lord, Dick, 266
Lord, Eleazar, 337
Loucas family, 293
Loucas, Gail & Nick, 293
Loucas, Nick, 293
Love in the Hills, 83
Lovett, Ed, 74
Lovett, John, 231, 237
LOVETT, WENDELL H., 157
Low Tor Ice Center, 292
Lowes Palisades Center Theatre, 307
Loy, Myrna, 149
Lucas Home Made Candies, 293
LUCAS, WILLIAM H., 189
Ludvigsen, Mark, 322
Ludwiczak, Ted, 267
Lukens, David, 218
Lukens, Kathleen, 218, 219, 242
Lum, William, Jr., 322
Lupino, Ida, 152
Lyall's Hotel, 332
Lyceum, 211
Lydecker Agency Inc., 171, 319
Lydecker family, 329
Lydecker, Dale, 255
Lydecker, Homer, 319
Lyman, Richard, 131
LYNCH, THOMAS F, 66
Lynn, Conrad, 226, 242
Lyon Family, 329
Lyon, John, 53, 54
MacArthur, Charles, 96, 112, 265, 311
MacArthur, James, 266
MacArthur, Mary, 171, 265, 298, 311
MacGuffie, Dr. Martha, 228, 270, 271
MacIver family, 346
Mack Paving Company, 8
MacKellar, Archibald, 70
Mackey, Jo Jo, 232
MACKEY, JOHN R., 189
MACKEY, JOSEPH F. (JR), 157
Mackey, Lee, 73
MacMurray, Rev. James, 70
Macy's, 207
Magai, Martin, 128
Magazine, Jay, 322
MAGRO, JAMES A., 218
Mahwah River, 28
Mahwah, New Jersey, 285
Maidman, Irving, 245
Maine, 27
Maines, Emmet, 187
MALONE, CHARLES M., 157
Maloney, John, 288
Maltbie/Messimer mansion, 38
Manchester, Mrs., 70

Mandia, Ralph, 288
MANGHU, DWIGHT, 157
Manion, Frank, 159
Manley, Frank, 197
Mann, Willie, 39
Mansfield, L. Delos, 69
Mansfield, Mrs., 69
Marano, Rocco, 169
Marchand, Bolivar, 137
Marchbanks, Joseph, 322
MARESCA, GEORGE M., 157
Margulies, Pincus, 141, 337
Marian Shrine, 196
Markham, L.O., 55, 68
Marshall, John Daniel, 322
Marshall, Kenneth, 128
Marshall, Thurgood, 161
MARSICO, ANTHONY T., 157
Martin, John, 167, 191
Martinez, Ness, 258
Martio's pizza, 191
Martire, Vince, 128
Marycrest Association, 317
Mason, Florence, 166
Masonicus, 325
Mastick, Seabury C., 179
Mathias, Bob, 255
Maudlin, Bill, 97, 266
Maurello, Carmen, 115
Maurer, Belle, 128
Maurer, Edward, 93, 128
Maxfield, William, 115
Maximus, 250
Maxwell, Estelle, 104
MAXWELL, WILLIAM H., 66
Mayo, Charles, 16
Maze, Montgomery, 37, 237
Mazeppa Fire Engine Co., 19, 59
McAneney, Patricia, 322
McCabe, Anne, 72, 178
McCabe, Bill, 67
McCabe, Brose, 67
McCabe, Joan & Rosie, 178
McCabe, Margaret, 68
McCabe, Michael, 57, 72
McCabe, William J., 268
McCabe, William, 72
McCANDLESS, GEORGE (JR), 154, 157
McCandless, Mary, 187
McCandless, Russell, 154, 171, 187
McCarthy, Robert, 322
McClintic, Guthrie, 96, 266
McCloskey, Cardinal John, 12
McConnell, David H., 5, 59, 357
McCoy, Dr. John C., 38, 39
McCullers, Carson, 266
McCULLOUGH, JACK R., 157
McDADE, WILLIAM, 189
McDERMOTT, W.R. (JR), 157
McDermott's, 192, 199

McDonalds's, 285
McDowell, Joe, 203
MCELREE, REUBEN, 66
McElroy, Judy, 221
McGee, Sylvester, 255
McGinnis, John, 330
McGOVERN, MICHAEL E., 218
McGowan, Stacey (Sennas), 322
McGrath, Ed, 203
McGRATH, EDMUND, 189
McGuire, Denise, 255
McGUIRE, MICHAEL J., 66
McGUIRE, RUSSELL E., 157
McHugh, Dennis, 322
McHUGH, RUSSELL, 157
McIntosh, Hamish & Jeanne, 307
McIntyre, Donald, 322
McKenna, John, 161, 256
McKinney, Rev. Petty, 227
McNelis, Dr. Donald, 197
McNiff, Howie, 255
McPadden, Robert, 322
McPhillips, Mary, 276
McQuaide, James P., 8
MEAD, GEORGE J., 157
Mead, Margaret, 151
Mechanicstown, 361
Mechanicsville, 198
Meehan, Thomas, 266
Meislin Bungalow Colony, 195
Mel's Army and Navy Store, 99
MELNICK, JOHN, 157
Melvin, George, 73
Mendelson, Jacob, 15
Mendelson's Lake, 15
Mendlowitz, Rabbi Sharga, 162
Mendolia, Angelina and Angelo, 99
Mercurio, John, 276
Meredith, Burgess, 96, 114, 141,
    142, 233, 266, 292, 345
Meredith, Kaja & Tala, 233
Merman, Ethel, 149
MERRICK, WILLIAM E., 157
Merrill, Mrs., 69
Meyer, Bill, 90, 132
Meyer, Leland, 208
MEYER, WILLIAM A., 157
Meyer, William H., Sr., 132
Michalak, Joseph & Diane, 186, 187
Middletown Hospital, 38
Milewski, Anthony, 296
Milford, Dr. Edgar, Jr., 251
MILKS, DONALD, 157
Miller, Adolph, 87
Miller, Alfred, 73
Miller, Charles, 188
MILLER, CLARENCE I., 153, 157
Miller, F.R., 128
Miller, Gus, 165
Miller, Howard, 288
Miller, Irene, 153

Miller, Mitch, 231, 266, 292
MILLER, ROBERT S., 157
Miller, Rudy, 129
Miller, Winnie, 188
Miller's airport, 114
Miller's dairy, 249
Millich, Adolph, 288
Minelli, Liza, 211
Minisceongo Creek, 331
Minisceongo Yacht Club, 165
MISCH, ANTHONY, 157
Missionary Training Institute, 356
Mississippi, 16
Mitchell, Harold, 227
MITCHELL, HERBERT, 157
Moffat, Mrs., 70
Mohawk River, 27
Moles, William, 336
Mondésir family, 251
Monks, Mabel, 142
Monohan, John, 322
Monroe, N.Y., 9
Monsey, 10, 15, 29, 61, 80, 89, 115,
    135, 158, 162, 164, 165, 192,
    195, 220, 226, 256, 278, 306,
    325, 337, 338, 358, 361, 362
Monsey Jewish Center, 220
Mont Lawn, 11,12
Mont Moor, 114, 286, 329, 362
Monte, Vincent, 320
Montebello, 38-40, 285, 299, 319,
    338
Monterey Pool, 327
Montvale, N.J., 199
Mooney, William, 307
Moore, Big Chief, 266
Moore, Dinty, 297
Moore, James B., 87
MORAN, JAMES T., 157
Morgan, Edward, 161
Morgan, James, 17
Morgan, J.P., 242
MORGAN, NORMAN R., 157
MORINA, ANTHONY J., 218
MORRIS, CHARLES B., 157
Morrison, Toni, 266
Morschauser, Judge, 56
MOSCARELLA, ANTHONY, 66
MOSER, DAVID, 66
Moses, Dr. Max, 194
Moses, Robert, 167
Motel on the Mountain, 202, 258
Mott, Valentine, 118
Motta, Mr., 115
Mottola, Nick, 169
Mounkhall, Tom, 232
Mountain View Farm, 84, 134
Mt. Ivy, 10, 164, 337, 339
Mt. Repose Cemetery, 44
Muddy Creek, 122
Mueller, George, 128

Muise, Bill, 128
MULLER, CHARLES G., 157
Mulligan, Jim, 115
MULRAIN, HARRY, 157
Mumford, Henry, 17
Mumford, Thomas, 17
Munkelt, Donald, 235
Munn, David, 334
Munson, Dr. Albert, 238
Munson, Jeffrey, 169
MUNTZ, GIRAUD D., 218
Murphy, John, 219, 242
Murphy, Ken, 222
Murphy, Nick, 73
Murray, Bill, 266
MURRAY, JOHN L., 66
Murray, Lawrence, Jr., 158
Mushel, Rabbi Nachum, 195
Myers, William Henry, 16
N.Y. Mets, 206
N.Y. Yankees, 80, 85, 107, 169, 232
Nadler family, 15
NAGLE, EUGENE J., 157
Nagler, Al, 277
Nanuet, 9, 10, 12, 29, 91, 154, 163,
    172, 173, 186, 191, 192, 203,
    207, 215, 217, 231, 232, 235,
    249- 251, 255, 260, 262, 274-
    276, 307, 308, 310, 327, 339,
    340
Nanuet Fire Engine Company, 19
Nanuet Hebrew Center, 299
Nanuet Hotel, 187
Nanuet Mall, 163, 187, 207, 250,
    262, 286, 288, 308, 340
Nanuet Public Library, 235
Nanuet Theater Go Round, 217
NAPPO, ANTHONY J., 157
Nash family, 92
NATALE, PATRICK H., 218
Naurashaun, 85, 341, 347, 348
Naurashaun Presbyterian Church,
    225
Navin, William, 19
Nazi, 103, 138, 144, 154, 219, 241
Nealy, Hubert, 203
Nee, Luke, 322
Nelke, Edmond, 100
Nelson family, 92
Nelson, Benjamin, 44
Nelson, Bob, 112
Nelson, Frank, 203
Nelson, Harry, 44
Nemeroff, Bernard, 114
Nemeth, Dan, 128
Nevins, Gerry, 322
New City, 9, 10, 25, 45, 70, 81, 83,
    84, 95, 97, 112, 114, 119-121,
    124, 125, 132, 138, 172-174,
    180, 198, 200, 202, 215, 226,
    229, 241, 245, 250, 255, 260,

262, 270, 274, 278, 294, 297, 299, 313, 318, 319, 327, 331, 341, 359

New City Fire Engine Co. , 120, 173

New City Garden Club, 138

New City Hotel, 119

New City Library, 215

New City Park Lake, 173

New Hempstead, 278, 299, 342

N.J. and N.Y. Railroad., 49, 331

New Square, 208, 219, 220, 321, 343

New York Central Railroad, 63, 77, 148

New York City, 4, 6, 11, 15, 17, 27, 32, 36, 37, 43, 52, 56, 61-63, 73, 77, 81, 83, 85, 86, 88, 94, 95, 98, 99, 107, 121, 124, 130, 131, 133, 137, 139, 141, 149, 158, 161-163, 167, 173, 174, 208, 213, 219, 224, 228, 229, 238, 241-243, 244, 248, 249, 250, 251, 264, 271, 272, 283, 289, 291, 292, 294, 297, 310, 312, 325, 330, 331, 338, 340, 341, 345-348, 351, 352, 356, 357, 361

New York Jets, 231

New York State Thruway, 113, 162, 164, 168, 171, 173, 178, 179, 181, 183-185, 193, 223, 245, 262, 267, 287, 310, 316, 340, 352, 356, 358

New York Stock Exchange, 38, 238

New York Trap Rock Company, 4, 8, 96, 283

Newburgh, N.Y., 51, 54, 73, 83, 86

Newcomb, Charles, 257

NEWELL, ROGER V., 157

Newman family, 15

NEWMAN, CHARLES J., 157

Newman, Eugene M., 56

Nicholas, Antoine, 251

Niero, Joe, 52

Nikola, Mr., 112

Nillson, Harry, 266

Nimbly, Paul, 322

North Carolina, 27

North Ferry River Company, 54

North River Steamboat, 272

North Rockland, 275, 320

NORTH, NORMAN P., 189

Novartis, 5

Novotny, Brian, 322

Noyes, Clarence, 198

Nugent, Sgt. Robert, 153

Nyack, 4, 6, 11, 15, 16, 18-20, 23, 27-30, 32, 34, 37, 44, 50-54, 59, 64, 65, 67, 69, 70, 74, 75, 81, 82, 84, 87-91, 93, 103, 104, 106, 107, 109-13, 118, 124, 125, 128, 129, 136, 141, 151, 154, 158,

163, 166, 168-172, 179, 180, 181, 184, 190-193, 197, 200, 203, 204, 208, 211, 212, 217, 220, 223-228, 232, 234, 236, 244, 248, 251, 252, 255, 262, 265, 267, 269, 271- 276, 286, 290, 297, 302, 308, 311, 317, 319, 320, 325, 327, 329, 332, 341, 343, 345, 348, 350, 356, 360, 362

Nyack Beach, 171

Nyack College, 111

Nyack Electric Light and Power Company, 8, 32

Nyack Female Institute, 69

Nyack Field Club., 112

Nyack High School, 129, 242

Nyack Hospital, 30, 36, 38, 89, 113, 119, 170, 214, 223, 228, 269, 298

Nyack Ice and Coal Company., 171

Nyack Missionary College, 20, 208

Nyack Presbyterian Church, 128

Nyack Public Library, 32, 34, 111

Nyack Sea Scouts, 113

Nyack Tennis Club, 51

Nyack Turnpike, 10, 15, 28, 89, 91, 191, 325, 329, 340, 356, 362

Nyack-Tarrytown Ferry, 179

O'Connor, John Cardinal, 196, 219

O'Donnell, Rosie, 286

O'Grady, Edward, 262

O'Neill, Eddie, 263

Oak Hill Cemetery, 113, 124, 234

O'Connor, Dennis, Jr., 322

Odd Fellows Hall, 57

Odell family, 284

O'DOWD, DENNIS H., 66

Ofeldt, Frank & George, 2

O'Keefe, Ellen, 338

Olderman, Murray, 169

OLDFIELD, JOHN CASHMAN, 66

O'Leary, Gerald, 322

Olivier, Lawrence, 345

OLOFSON, GUSTAV, 157

Olsen, Ellyn, 202

Olsen, Paul, 258

OLSON, ERIC T., 157

Onderdonk, Garry, 256

O'Neill, Tippy, 346

Oppenhimer, Moses, 15

Orange & Rockland Utilities, Inc., 8, 9, 175, 190, 193, 197, 207, 208, 213, 247, 292, 295, 302, 319, 320

Orange County, 8-10, 29, 39, 73, 134, 136, 159, 180, 183, 243, 250,263, 267, 283, 300

Orangeburg, 8, 10, 25, 32, 33, 36, 70, 81, 93, 112, 148, 149, 151,

152, 185, 186, 189, 192, 195, 203, 208, 232, 234, 237, 238, 245, 249, 251, 328, 343, 344

Orangeburg Fair, 25, 26, 118

Orangeburg Fibre Conduit Company, 8, 344

Orangeburg Library, 234

Orangetown, 4, 11, 16, 19, 87, 125, 129, 134, 151, 167, 179, 181, 195, 198, 207, 208, 226, 231, 234, 237, 238, 242, 249, 289, 298, 315, 324, 328, 333, 343, 344, 346, 347

Orangetown Fire Engine Co., 19, 59

Orangetown Guards, 256

Orangetown Police Department, 100

Orangetown Resolutions, 42

Orchards of Concklin, 133

Orlando, Art, 203

Orlando, John, 232

Orner's Hotel, 164

Ortenberg, Rubin, 317

Ortiz, David, 322

ORTIZ, ROBERT I., 157

Osborn, Dr., 213

Osborn, Dr. Richard, 213

Osborne, Frances, 38

OSBORNE, JAMES, 157

OSBORNE, JAMES, 189

Osborne, Jared, 71

Osborne, Mr., 115

Ostrom, Walter, 203

OWEN, ARTHUR J., 157

Pablo, Dr. Nancy, 270

Pabst, John, 133

Pacino, Al, 266

Paddleford, Clementine, 12

Paddock, Jeanette, 232

Paddock, Peter, 228

Pagett, Dr. Frank E., 39

Paige, Peter, 262

Palisades, 35, 80, 88, 118, 135, 179, 180, 183, 211, 269, 300, 301, 345

Palisades Amusement Park., 231

Palisades Center, 28, 110, 114, 207, 223, 240, 260, 281, 286-288, 293, 307, 308, 313, 321, 340

Palisades Interstate Park Commission, 62, 92, 100, 116, 124, 126, 141, 183, 283, 313, 337, 344

Palisades Interstate Parkway, 164, 168, 173, 178, 183, 185, 242, 267, 299, 310, 340, 346

Palisades Library, 35, 201, 345

Palisades Presbyterian Church, 345

Palmer, Fred, 208

Panteleom, Johnny, 99

Paone, Cy & Terry, 193

PAQUIN, PAUL E. (JR), 218

Pardington, Dr., 47
Paris, Richard, 288
PARKER, JAMES E., 218
Parkhurst, Virginia, 128, 129, 269
Partridge, Ray, 112
Pascack Brook, 122
Pascack River, 28
Pataki, George, 269, 321
Paterson, N.J., 98
Patterson, Brit, 109
PAUL, HENRY C. (JR), 157
Peace Corps, 215
Pearl Harbor, 146-148, 152, 167,
   170, 235, 310
Pearl River, 5, 9, 32, 33, 36, 45, 57,
   58, 71, 81, 85-87, 93, 98, 99,107,
   109, 112, 114, 122-125, 153,
   154, 163, 169, 172-175, 188,
   199, 203, 204, 208-210, 214,
   220, 225, 230-232, 237, 238,
   248-250, 255, 275, 276, 307,
   317, 319, 320, 341, 347, 348
Pearl River Alumni Ambulance Corp,
   124, 125
Pearl River Hook and Ladder, 100
Pearl River Library, 234
Pearl River Soap Box Derby, 93
Pearl River Tennis Club, 112
Peck, Elisha, 222
Peckman, Charlotte, 57
Peckman, Herbert, 57
Peckman, Otto, 57
Peekskill, 27, 334
Peerless Finishing Company, 51
Pelligrini, Roger & Maureen, 76
Penfold, Saxby V., 296
Penny, Fred, 92
Perkin's Peak, 313
Perruna's, 191
Perry, Bill, 109
PERRY, JOHN MARDER, 66
Perry, Win, 111
Personeus, Gordon, 115
Perth Amboy, N.J., 54
Peters, Rollo, 95, 266
Petersen, Julius, 271, 360
Petersen's Shipyard, 51, 271
Pettis, Miss, 69
Phelps, Carl, 231
Phelps, George, 231
Philadelphia, PA, 92
Phillips, Helen, 128
Phillipsburgh Manor, 52
Picarello, Joseph, 204
PICARIELLO, R.P. (JR), 157
Piermont, 9, 10, 15, 27, 34, 47, 81,
   84, 93, 100, 118, 125, 133, 134,
   148, 149, 163, 180, 181, 208,
   227, 242, 251, 256, 269, 284,
   301, 332, 348, 349, 353
Piermont Public Library, 34

Pierson Ironworks, 4
Pierson, Howie, 204
Pierson's Cranberry Pond, 28
Pigeon, Walter, 211
Pigknoll School, 47
PILGRIM, HOWARD D., 157
Pilgrim, Kenny, 99
Pine Meadow, 126, 283
PINTO, GEORGE J., 157
Pitt, Maggie & Gilbert, 105
Pitt Town, 126, 127
Pitts, Melvin, 230, 231
Pittsboro, 126
Poland, 15, 125, 138, 293
Polhemus, Mrs., 70
POLHEMUS, WILLIS, 157
Pomona, 20, 47, 133, 142, 164, 208,
   216, 233, 242, 290, 291, 316, 349
Pomona Jewish Center, 220, 278
Poor, Henry Varnum, 97, 166, 266
Pope Pius X, 39
Popolopen Bridge, 49
Popolopen Creek, 49
Popp's Corner, 10
Port Jervis, N.Y., 193
Post family, 68
Post, James, 345
Poughkeepsie, N.Y., 73
Pozsar, Dennis, 232
Pradhan, Dr. Vijay, 315
Prall, Nona, 104
PRATO, LEO J., 157
Pratt family, 228, 229
Pratt, Frances, 228, 229
Prendergast, Michael, 268
Prentice-Hall, 5
Pressler, David, 73
Preston, Deborah &Steven, 290
Prezioso, Victor, 99
Princiotta, Vincent, 322
Profenna, Louis, 288
Prohibition, 80, 81, 86, 87, 103,
   119, 135
Proudfit, David, 17
Proudfoot, Dr. Lawrence, 334
Proudfoot's Landing, 334
Provident Bank, 5, 319
Provitch, Wolf, 44
Puente, Tito, 266
Puerto Rico, 137
Purdy, Herman, 67
Purdy, Lavinia Meyers, 118
Pyramid Company, 286, 288, 321
PYTLIK, KARLO P., 157
Quaspeck, 350
Queen Elizabeth, 149
Queen Mary, 149
Queensboro, 126, 283
Quiros, Anita, 230
Raab, Anne, 21
Rabinoff, Max, 116

Rackow, Simon, 15
Rae, John, 39
Rajaji, Raj, 316
Rajaji, Vimala, 316
RAKENTINE, KENNETH C., 218
Ramapo, 10, 11, 28, 29, 69, 105,
   125, 129, 183, 185, 194, 197,
   204, 208, 232, 236, 255, 267,
   270, 275, 276, 278, 279, 282,
   289, 296, 298, 320, 324, 325,
   336, 337, 339, 351, 357, 358,
   362
Ramapo Airport, 114
Ramapo Foundry and Wheel Co., 4,
   336
Ramapo Iron Works, 60
Ramapo Mountains, 38, 78, 119,
   137, 194, 195, 291, 342, 354
Ramapo Polo Club, 103
Ramapo River, 28, 336
Ramapo Torne, 195
Ramapo Trust Co., 296
Ramapough Mountain Indians, 268
Ramsey Fire department, 59
Ramsey, N.J., 39, 59, 183
Rand farm, 16
Rapinsky, R.H., 15
Raymond, George, 264
Reece, Barbara, 219
Reeves, Hazard, 266
Reeves, Ruth, 97, 266
Reibstein, Paul, 220
Reilly, Kevin, 322
Reiner, Walter, 209
Reiss, Harry, 279
Reissmann, Ernest, 118
Requa family, 256
Requa Lake, 165, 256
Rescue Hook and Ladder Company
   #1,, 19
Reserve Fleet, 175, 176
Retz, George, 99
RETZ, GEORGE J., 157
Reuben Gittleman Hebrew Day
   School, 252
Rhodes, LuRoy, 172
Rice, John, 53
Richard, Louis, 363
Ridgewood, N.J., 59
Ridlon, Jim, 204
Riis, Jacob, 11
RITCHINGO, JAMES W., 157
Rittershausen, A.W., 129
River Vale, N.J., 238
Rivera, Chita, 266
Rizzo, Pete, 99
Rizzo, Sam, Sr., 100
ROACH, BILLY JOE, 157
ROBBINS, HARRY E. (JR), 157
Robbins, Nathan, 195
Robert Gair Company, 133, 349

Roberto, Joseph, 322
Roberts, Michael, 322
Robus, Hugo, 97, 266
Rock, Patricia, 249
Rockefeller family, 242
Rockefeller, John D., Jr., 118
Rockefeller, John D., 135
Rockefeller, Gov. Nelson, 219, 226, 241, 269
Rockland, 53, 54
Rockland Astronomy Club, 277
Rockland Center for Holocaust Studies, 210, 278
Rockland Center for the Arts, 166
Rockland Community College, 20, 197, 241, 279, 299, 306, 321, 352
Rockland Country Club, 124
Rockland County Bar Association, 124
Rockland County Bicentennial, 267, 300
Rockland County Fair, 25, 36
Rockland County Hebrew Day School, 220
Rockland County Sports Hall of Fame, 45, 74, 93, 109, 169, 203, 204, 232, 255, 276, 302
Rockland Finishing Company, 4
Rockland Jewish Community Campus, 299
Rockland Lake, 4, 6, 19, 30, 31, 92, 97, 126, 139-141, 296, 302, 350
Rockland Lake State Park, 141
Rockland Light and Power Company, 8, 9, 32, 96, 133, 185
Rockland Psychiatric Center, 123, 124, 149, 242, 344
Rockland Sports, 320
Rockland Spring Works, 11
Rockland State Hospital, 123, 149, 225, 237, 344
Rockland theater, 211
Rockwell, Fred, 131
Rodriguez, Christine, 282
Rogan, Janice, 241
Rogers, Will, 85
Rolls, David, 212
Roman, Freddie, 266
Romero, Caesar, 211, 212
Rooney, Mickey, 149
Roos, Casper, 266
Roosevelt Field, 115
Roosevelt, Eleanor, 130
Roosevelt, Franklin D., 99, 106, 107, 143, 147, 148, 168
Roosevelt Military Academy, 80
Roosevelt, Theodore, 16, 18, 124, 242, 312, 357
Roper, Edna, 174
Rosary Academy, 13

Rose family, 82
Rose Memorial Library, 170
Rose, Ezekiel, 170
ROSE, GEORGE E., 157
Rose, Gilbert, 266
Rose, Heloise Durant, 331
Rose, Henry, 86
Rose, Ken, 119
ROSE, LAWRENCE O., 218
Rose, Sadie, 86
Rosen, Marc, 159
Rosenthal, Joel, 296
Rosner Auerbach Hotel, 164
Rosner, Murray, 61
ROSS, CHARLES (SR), 157
ROSS, DEANE L., 157
Ross, Herbert, 265
Rosse, Hermann, 266
ROTC, 62
Roth, Frederick, 193
ROTUNDO, LOUIS J., 157
Rounds, Dr. Lester, 197
Route 202, 35, 130, 141, 222
Route 303, 25, 114, 148, 173, 192, 202, 223, 237, 249, 258, 287, 313, 328, 330
Route 304, 172, 173, 340
Route 45, 94, 172, 219, 220, 299
Route 59, 15, 27, 28, 61, 114, 158, 170, 172, 173, 186, 192, 260, 262, 285-287, 306-308, 318, 325, 326, 340, 358
Route 9W, 25, 44, 49, 98, 139, 148, 163, 168, 171, 174, 175, 180, 191, 201, 211, 220, 221, 234, 243, 319, 330, 333, 345, 347
ROWAN, OGDEN W., 157
Royster, Dawn, 276
Rubino, Frank, 317
RUPPEL, ADAM A., 66
Rushmore, Dr. E.C., 39
RUSSO, WILLIAM, 157
Ruth, Babe, 80, 84, 85, 107
Ryan, John, 322
Ryan, Maj. Gen. John, 63
Ryan, Joseph J., 59
Ryan, Mrs. Thomas Fortune, 37-39, 60
Ryan, Thomas Fortune, 38, 39, 59
RYDER, DONALD J., 157
Ryder, John, 361
Ryder, Nick, 232
Rye Cliff, 54
Ryther, Martha, 97, 266
S. W. Johnson Fire Company, 19, 331
Sacred Heart Chapel, 13
Safe Harbour Group Ltd, 319
Safer, Morley, 266
Salisbury House, 200
Salisbury Point apartments, 200

Salk, Jonas, 199
Salla, Louise, 128
Salmon, Richard, 52
Salomon, Julian, 105
Salvia, Robert, 258
Salyer, Edward, Sr., 348
Saminson family, 122
SAMSON, HARRY, 157
Samsondale, 222
Samuels, Al, 307
Sandt, Dr. Frank R., 39
Sandyfields, 126, 283, 284, 337
Sanford, Dr. M.J., 39
Sauberman, Louis, 61
Sauter, Eddie, 136, 160, 266
Sauter, Mildred Bailey, 136
Savell, Isabelle, 269
Sayres, Milton, 118
Sayres' market, 51
Scandell family, 284
Scarpulla, Chuck, 204
SCHAPER, HENRY M., 66
Scharpf, Bob, 128
Schassler, Robert, 204
Scheffold, Fred, 322
Scheibner, Peter, 267
SCHETTIG, ROBERT S., 218
SCHEU, PHILIP, 66
Schmeling, Max, 112
Schmidt, Don, 230, 231
Schmidt, Fred, 248
Schmidt's/Blumaneur, 171
Schnaars, Al, 112
Schnaars, Jimmie, 109, 112
SCHNELL, HAROLD, 157
Schoales, Tom, 322
School of Living, 130-132
Schools, 1960s construction, 208
Schreeder, Foster, 73
SCHREIBER, LUDWIG T., 66
Schroeder, Dr. Fred, Sr., 100
SCHROEDER, GOODSON S., 66
Schuchalter, Rabbi Paul, 299
Schuck, Mrs. Joseph, 173
Schultz, Chiz, 266
Schuster, Abe, 169
SCHWARTZ, ISRAEL, 157
Schwarz, Gary, 174
SCOLARO, PETER F., 157
Scotland, 114, 329
Scott, Bill, 226
Scott, John, 65, 158
Scott, Julia, 158
Scozzafava, Theresa, 175
Scudder, Christopher, 322
Seaman, Ed, 10
Sears, 207, 249, 310
SECOR, JOHN, 66
Secor, Louise Butz, 87
Sedgemore, Joseph, 39
Seifried, Dean B., 215

Selleca, Connie, 266
Selman family, 15
Sengstacken family, 210
Serven, Mrs. William, 71
Setzer, Gene, 269
SEYLLER, GUY L., 157
SEYMOUR, HARRY P., 66
Shaffer, Dr. Newton, 312
Shajahan, Mohammed, 322
Shankey family, 166
Shankey Pill Company, 81
SHANKEY, JOSEPH I., 157
Shankey, Richard "Gus", 74, 81
Shankey, Vicki & Sondra, 221
Shankey, Victor, 45, 81, 197, 226
Shanks Village, 148, 150-152, 154,
    187, 235, 236, 267, 344
Shanks, Gen. David, 148
Shapiro family, 15
SHARE, 270
Sharkey, Jack, 112
SHEA, MORTIMER G., 157
Shearer, Norma, 265
Sheehan, Joseph, Jr., 115
Sheffield, James, 263
SHELLITO, WALTER C., 218
Sheridan, Cynthia, 65
SHERIDAN, OWEN, 66
Sherwood, Donald "Pop", 74
Sherwood, Harold, 267
Sherwood, John W., 70
Sherwood, Rev. James, 362
Shirley Hollow, 126
SHUART, PERCY W., 157
SHUREMAN, OLIVE, 66
Shuttleworth, Ira, 93
Sibley, George, 213
Sickels, Berne, 28
Sickels, John, 16, 70
Sickles, Walt, 109
Sidoli, Angelo, 329
Sidoti, Patricia, 186
Siegel, Benjamin, 208
Siegel, Brook, 209
Siegel, Irving, 195
Siegmund family, 327
Sikorsky, Gregory, 322
Silberman, Morton, 230
SILBERSTEIN, HENRY, 157
Silver Pheasant, 238
Silverman, Bob, 299
Silverman, Mr. & Mrs. Abraham, 44
SIMENOVSKY, SOL, 157
Simon, Arthur, 322
Simon, Ellen, 266
Simonds, Al, 204
Sinatra, Frank, 149, 217
Sinell, Harry, 244
Sing Sing Prison, 31, 121
Singer, Louis, 61
Sister Anna de Sales, 39

Sister Joseph Rita, 248
Sister Margaret Josephine, 39
Sister Mary Basil, 39
Sister Melita, 39
Sister Miriam, 194
Sister Thomas Gargan, 13
Sitler, Grace, 70
Skahen, John, 194, 264
SKERRY, WILLIAM H., 157
Skunk Hollow, 345
SLATER, CLIFFORD F., 157
Sloane, William, 266
Sloat family, 351
Sloat, Jacob, 351
Sloatsburg, 10, 28, 69, 70, 81, 104,
    118, 125, 183, 184, 202, 225,
    227, 236, 275, 337, 351, 352,
    355
Sloatsburg Public Library, 202
Slocum, Robert P., 221
Smith & Sons farm, 173
Smith family, 15
Smith farm, 260
Smith, Adeline, 14
Smith, Gov. Al, 56
SMITH, ALEXANDER, 157
Smith, Andy, 284
Smith, Ann Marie, 288, 313
Smith, Captain Aurie, 360
Smith, Bill "Showboat", 160
Smith, Cathy, 322
Smith, Charles & Ben, 76
Smith, Clarence, 73
Smith, Edwin, 27
Smith, Gordon Dean & Doris, 166
SMITH, HALLIDAY SPENCER, 66
SMITH, HILTON H., 66
SMITH, JAMES N., 189
Smith, Jimmy, 25
Smith, Major John, 360
Smith, John Henry, 268
Smith, Joshua Hett, 98
SMITH, MARVIN, 157
Smith, Parke, 112
Smith, Roscoe W., 9
Snapps, Mr., 19
Snedeker family, 92
SNEDEN, ARTHUR P., 157
Sneden, Robert, 345
Snedens Landing, 52, 269, 345, 359
Snodsmith, Ralph, 317
Soap Box Derby, 230, 248
Sohn, Arnold & Elaine, 263
Sohn, Mark, 263
Sohn, Sheryl, 263
Solliday, Patty Dillon, 255
Sorel family, 251
South Mountain Road, 95-97, 121,
    180, 313
South Nyack, 19, 61, 69-71, 92, 105,
    118, 148, 160, 169-171, 181,

184, 193, 212, 242, 245, 269,
    343, 356
South Orangetown, 275
Sovak, Mike, 108
Spain, 153, 175
Spanish influenza, 47, 65, 77
Sparkill Creek, 49
Sparkill, 12, 13, 49, 81, 109, 159,
    197, 219, 332, 345, 346, 353
Spear, Robert, 322
Spiro, Al, 290
Spiro, Betty Ramey, 290
Spook Rock, 285, 302
SPORDONE, G., 157
Spring Hill, 125
Spring Valley, 4, 5, 8-10, 15, 19, 23-
    25, 29, 48, 59-61, 65, 70, 74, 81,
    87, 89, 91, 94, 105, 107, 109,
    112, 118, 119, 134, 158, 162-
    165, 169, 170, 172, 184, 191,
    192, 203, 204, 208, 209, 214,
    220, 226-228, 232, 247, 251,
    252, 256, 263, 267, 277, 278,
    279, 296, 299, 302, 306, 307,
    319, 329, 336, 337, 339, 340,
    354
Spring Valley Hook and Ladder, 59
Spring Valley Marketplace, 114, 307
Spring Valley Memorial Park, 296
Springstead, Marty, 232
Springsteen, E.C., 48
Springsteen, Margaret, 55
Springsteen, Samuel, 354
SPRUILL, JAMES P., 218
St. Agatha's Home, 340
St. Agnes School & Home, 12, 13,
    109, 353
St. Ann's Church, 252
St. Anthony's Church, 13, 91
St. Catharine's, 13
St. Dominic's Convent, 13
St. Gregory's, 13, 219
St. John's, 337
St. Joseph's, 108, 252, 334
St. Joseph's Hospital in Paterson,
    N.J., 38
St. Lawrence, Chris, 307, 308
St. Lawrence, Joe, 169
St. Margaret's, 122
St. Mary's, 7
St. Paul's, 13, 70, 330
St. Peter's Cemetery, 64, 107, 244
St. Peter's, 219
St. Philips A.M.E. Zion, 227
St. Thomas Aquinas College, 13,
    197, 208, 249
St. Vincent's Hospital, 39
STAGEN, CHARLOTTE S., 66
Staggs Corner, 10
Stall, M.E., 59
Stalter, Richard, 118

Stamos, Jim, 204
Standard Oil, 135
Stanley, Kim, 266
Stanton, Mrs. Cady, 69
Staten Island, 29
STAUBITZ, PHILIP, 66
Stead family, 108
Stead, John, 81
Stebbins, Edward, 133
STECZ, JOSEPH M., 157
Steel, Bob, 108
Stegmeyer, Mrs., 172
Steinbeck, John, 266
STEINER, EMANUEL F., 157
STEINER, JOSEPH, 157
Steinhoff, Walt, 174
Steinkraus, Bill, 233
Sterling Junction, 10
Sterlington, 355
Stern, Abe, 129
Stern, Kalmen, 321
Stetner, William, 296
STEVENS, TIMOTHY D., 157
Stewart, Mark L., 244
Stillman, Chauncey D., 130, 132
Stockmeyer, Lewis, 128, 129
STONEHOUSE, ALFRED L., 218
Stony Point, 7, 9, 11, 49, 63, 64, 70,
    81, 86, 106, 107, 108, 116, 118,
    121, 125, 147, 170, 198, 210,
    213, 221, 231, 274, 275, 281,
    283, 289, 293, 295, 297, 311,
    319, 324, 334, 339, 350, 355,
    359
Stony Point Battlefield, 7, 224
Stony Point Elementary School, 281
Storms, Edwin, 179
Storms, Thomas B., 27
STOUGHTON, HOMER R., 157
Strack, Bob, 204
Strawtown Market, 293
Streep, Harry, 266
Streisand, Barbra, 212
Stritch, Elaine, 266
Strong, Robert G., 257
Struck, Jeanne, 306
Suchanyc, Paul, 189
Suffern, 5, 8, 10, 13, 23, 28, 38, 39,
    40, 59-61, 65, 81, 83, 88, 91 104,
    107, 109, 112, 115, 118, 130,
    131, 144, 183-185, 193-195, 197,
    212, 227, 232, 243, 244, 248,
    252, 255, 275, 276, 278, 282,
    285, 295, 297, 299, 300, 309,
    316-318, 320, 325, 326, 336,
    337, 352, 356-358, 362
Suffern, Judge Edward, 356
Suffern, Elsie, 70
Suffern Fire Department, 59
Suffern Free Library, 170, 318
Suffern, George W., 357

Suffern High School, 194
Suffern, James, 336
Suffern, John, 336, 356
Sugarman, Dr. Alan, 208, 209
Sullivan County, 8, 43
Sullivan, Dr. Matthew, 73
Sullivan, John F., 225
Summit Park Hospital, 270
Summit Park, 48, 208
Sunrise Bungalow Colony, 163
Sutherland, Bill, 165, 166
Sutherland, George, 39
SUTHERLAND, THOMAS A.,
    157
Sutter, David, 162
Sweet, Blanche, 83
Sweet, William "Gibby", 232
SWINTEK, WALTER J., 157
Switzerland, 139, 140
Taft, William H., 57
Tagaste Monastery, 318
Talaska, Max, 169
Tallamy, Bertram, 181, 182, 184
Tallman, 10, 59, 70, 103, 124, 135,
    236, 244, 275, 325, 326
Tallman, Charlotte, 209
Tallman, Cliff, 263
Tallman, Henry, 325
Tallman, Tunis, 325
Talman, Howard, 74
Tappan, 10, 84, 98, 118, 148, 151,
    155, 213, 216, 235, 242, 269,
    328, 332, 341, 343, 345, 346,
    348, 358, 359
Tappan Library, 235
Tappan Reformed Church, 316, 359
Tappan Zee, 53
Tappan Zee, 49, 51, 53, 54, 133,
    169, 179, 181, 203, 204, 269,
    320, 332, 343
Tappan Zee Bridge, 5, 17, 49, 54,
    86, 125, 129, 162, 164, 168, 173,
    178, 179, 181, 186, 187, 193,
    242, 243, 245, 253, 275, 286,
    292, 310, 340, 356
Tappan Zee High School, 13, 186,
    203
Tappan Zee Historical Society, 245
Tappan Zee Playhouse, 163, 211,
    290
Tarrytown, N.Y., 20, 52-54, 113,
    163, 171, 175, 179, 180, 231,
    272
TASMAN, DONALD R., 157
Taylor, Cecile, 115
Taylor, Elizabeth, 223
TAYLOR, FRED M. (JR), 157
Taylor, Snowden, 216
Tellefsen, Ron, 204
Temple Beth El, 61, 162, 195, 227,
    252, 299

Temple Beth Torah, 220
Temple, Shirley, 149
Tenney Company, 8
Thayer, Reg, 347
The Marshmallow, 250
The Principal, 208, 209
Thiell's Corners, 77
Thiells Fire Department, 19
Thiells Methodist Church, 273
Thiells, 35, 164, 227, 273, 337, 359,
    362
Thiesen, George, 128
THOMPSON, GEORGE C., 157
Thorpe, Alice M., 12, 13
Threefold Community, 94
Tierney family, 92
Tierney, Bob, 109
TIFFANY, JAMES GOELET
    DUBOIS, 66
Tilcon New York Inc, 4, 319
Timoner, J. Victor, 139
Tisi, Phil, 282
Tolstoy Foundation Center, 246,
    310
Tolstoy, Countess Alexandra, 246,
    247
Tomkins Cove, 4, 11, 17, 64, 107,
    118, 167, 175, 191, 201, 225,
    311, 337, 359, 360
Tomkins Cove Public Library, 201
Tomkins Cove Lime Company, 201
Tomkins, Calvin, 201, 359
Tomkins, Daniel, 4, 359, 360
TOMOVCIK, MICHAEL J., 66
Tompkins, Judge Arthur, 8, 179,
    180, 327
Tonetti family, 346
Tonetti, Mary, 345, 346
TOPPING, HUGH, 66
Torrey, John, 301
Toscano, Paul, 232
Towt family, 329
Trailside Museums and Zoo, 283
Travis Monument, 171
TRAVITZ, HARRY, 157
Treason House, 98
Trezini, Carl, 13
TROINA, CALOGERO, 66
TROJAHN, DARRELL C., 218
Trombino, Joseph, 262
Troup, Lenore, 68
Troy, N.Y., 13, 253
Truman, Harry S., 158
Trumper family, 329
TUCKER, ARTHUR B., 157
Tucker, Arthur C., 8
TURNER, WILLIAM R. (JR), 218
Tuxedo, N.Y., 59, 125, 337
Twersky, Grand Rabbi David, 321
TYRELL, STANLEY, 189
Tyrus, Horace, 109

Ulster County, 73
Union Electric Company, 8
United Artists Theater, 307
United Methodist Church, 170
Upper Nyack, 2, 8, 11, 12, 30, 33, 49-52, 88, 91, 124, 128, 180, 211, 258, 271, 343, 360
Urban, Paul, 169
Uris Corporation, 207, 237, 238
USO, 149, 155
Valenti, Thomas, 288
Valley Cottage, 19, 30, 48, 70, 86, 112, 125, 190, 197, 202, 242, 246, 247, 310, 350, 361
Valley Cottage Library, 202, 236
Van Buren, Martin, 334
VAN COTT, PETER, 157
Van Cura, Andrew, 97
Van Decker, Harry, 133
Van den Hende, Jan, 233
Van der Weyde, Dr., 214
Van Druten, John, 266
Van Dunk, Chief Redbone, 268
VAN DUNK, JOHN, 66
VAN DUNK, WILLIAM, 189
VAN DUNK, WILLIAM H., 66
Van Duyn, Dr. Robert, 215
Van Guilder, Will, 330
Van Houten family, 14, 28, 329
Van Houten farm, 85
Van Houten Fields, 131, 132
Van Houten Tavern, 77
VAN HOUTEN, HOMER H., 157
Van Houten, James, 209
Van Houten, Jim, 28
Van Houten, Mabel, 28
Van Houten, Morris, 85
Van Ingen, Mrs., 70
Van Ness, Margaret, 215
Van Orden, Elmer, 96
Vandenburgh, E.P., 73
VANDERBEEK, GEORGE R., 66
Vanderbilt Lumber, 319
Vanderbilt, Cornelius, 111
Vanderbilt, Jacob E., 319
Vanderbilts, 242
Vanderhoef, C. Scott, 5
Varker place, 8
Vassilakos, Leo, 112
VELIE, JACK W., 157
Verdin, Florent, 9
Vernon, Richard, 322
Vero, Loretta, 322
Verplanck, 17
Vietnam, 206, 217, 218
Vilord, Joe, 59
Vines, William, 231, 316
Viola, 5, 134, 144, 195, 198, 208, 275, 361
Virginia, 16, 27
VITALE, SALVATORE, 66

Voight, Jon, 266
von Hemilnijck, Chris, 231
VOORHIS, MILTON, 66
VORONIESK, ALEXIS, 157
VRANISKY, JOSEPH P., 157
Wahrenberger, Mr., 345
Waldberg, 330
Waldron, W.S.H., 329
Walker, Benjamin, 322
Wallace, Dillon, 43, 44
Wallace, Edwin, 197
Wallace, Gus, 244
Wallace, Mike, 266
Wamsley, Robert, 182
Wanamaker, Cornelius, 325
Wanamaker, Gertrude, 104
WANAMAKER, HARRY S., 66
Wanamaker, Jacob, 39
Wanamaker, Steve, 255
Wang, Wei Bin, 322
Ward, Gen. William, 295
WARNER, CHARLES H., 157
Warren Gas Light Company, 8
Washington, D.C., 33, 38, 71, 104, 209, 229
Watari, Countess, 97
Watson, Thomas, 292
Watts, Andre, 266
Watts, Gardner, 112, 194
Watts, Josephine, 194
WAVES, 154
Wayne, Anthony, 339, 355
Wayside Inn, 221
Webb, Jimmy, 266
Webber, Bobby, 216
Webber, Gladys, 240, 253
Webber, Scott, 221, 238, 247
Webber, Stephen & Nancy, 206
Weehawken, N.J., 27
WEIGAND, ROBERT, 157
Weill, Kurt, 96, 97, 160, 166, 266
Weinberg, Steven, 322
Weiss, Walt, 276
Weleda Apothecary, 94
Well-Bred Loaf, 5
Welles, Orsen, 345
Wendell, Steve, 289, 290
WENZEL, CHAR.LES W., 157
Wesley Chapel, 362
Wesley Hills, 134, 278, 290, 299, 307, 308, 362
West Clarkstown Jewish Center, 163
West Haverstraw, 11, 107, 180, 196, 222, 251, 291, 294, 312, 362
West Nile virus, 303
West Nyack, 27, 28, 45, 47, 59, 76, 83, 88, 114, 122, 131, 166, 172, 184, 192, 193, 212, 213, 223, 229, 231, 240, 251, 260, 281, 288, 293, 313, 316, 319, 327, 329, 340, 362, 363

West Nyack Free Library, 201
West Point, 98, 127, 166, 168, 171, 197, 272, 276
West Shore Railroad, 17, 54, 68, 92, 329, 330, 361
West, Garner, 49
Westchester County, 17, 149, 168, 179-181, 184, 186, 263, 291, 309, 311, 320, 334
Westlake, Charles, 354
Westwood, N.J., 87
Whalen, William, 115
WHEELER, CRAWFORD (JR), 157
WHELEN, WILLIAM, 66
Whipfall family, 171
White House on the Lake, 164
White Plains, N.Y., 29
White, Bill, 276
White, Justin DuPratt, 124
Whiton, William H., 353
Wholey, Michael, 322
Widmann's Bakery Co., 171, 192
WIEBICKE, HUGO P., 157
Wiedmiller, Gloria, 297
Wilder, Walter Robb, 291
WILDING, GEORGE H. (II), 157
Wilfred, Thomas, 131
Will, Sarah, 302
Williams, Harold, 181
WILLIAMS, ROBERT E. (JR), 157
Williams, Walter, 128
Willis, Emil, 109
Willock, Ed & Liv, 317
Willow Grove Road School, 11, 81
Wilson, Charlie, 128
Wilson, "Doc", 119
Wilson, Mrs. Grenville D., 61
Wilson, Gus, 112
Wilson, Gov. Malcolm, 312
WILSON, RUSSELL A., 157
Wilson, Woodrow, 63, 146, 175
Winter, Mr., 108
Winikow, Linda, 320, 321
Winter, Blaise, 276
WISNER, EMANUEL, 157
Wittman, Mickey, 232
WITZEL, ROBERT C., 218
Wolanski family, 293
Wolanski, Ted & John, 293
Wolansky, Olegh, 219
Wolff, Bob, 169
Wolfson, Herbert, 237, 238
Women's Army Corps, 148
Women's Liberation Movement, 241
WONZEL, CHARLES W., 157
WOOD, ANDREW, 157
Wood, James, 4, 7
WOODRUM, JOHN J., 218
Woods, James, 322
Woodward, Charlotte, 71

Wooley, David, 322
Woolsy, D.C., 54
World Trade Center, 189, 322
World Wide Volkswagen Corp., 25
Worzel, J. Lamar, 300
Wright Brothers, 50
Wright, Brooks, 31
Wright, Fred, 213
WRKL, 274, 289, 290, 300
Wurtsboro, N.Y., 43
Wyeth-Ayerst Pharmaceuticals, 319
WYSOCKI, JOSEPH B., 157
Y2K, 303
Yacyshyn, Rudolph, 288
Yeager Health Center, 267, 270
Yeager, Robert L. Jr., 270

Yerg, Dick, 255
YMCA, 85, 90, 111, 211, 331
Yonkers, N.Y., 52, 53
Youmans, Demarest, 354
Young, John, 40
Young, Natalie, 71
Yuda, Bill, 109
YWCA, 62
Zane, Arnie, 266
Zeck, Judge William, 278
Zehner, John, 244, 245
Zehner, Margaret, 244
Zelanka's Hotel, 164
ZELENKA, WILLIAM G., 66
ZELLER, ROBERT F., 157
Zenovic, Joe, Jr., 231

Zenovic, Joe, Sr., 230
Zenovic, Tom, 231
Zilko, Alex, 109
Zimmermann, Jim, 213, 248
Zimmermann, Linda, 192, 210, 216, 248
Zimmermann, Nancy, 248
Zimmermann, Ruth, 210, 248
Zimmermann, Walter, 90, 154, 248
Zimmermann, Walter, Jr., 248
ZOMEROWITZ, LOUIS, 157
Zorn, John, 73
Zugibe, Dr. Frederick, 258
Zukor, Adolph, 76, 83, 84, 114